Morality Tales

Political Scandals
and Journalism
in Britain and Spain
in the 1990s

Political Communication
David L. Paletz, Editor

Morality Tales

Political Scandals and Journalism in Britain and Spain in the 1990s

María José Canel
Universidad Complutense de Madrid
Spain

Karen Sanders
University of Sheffield
United Kingdom

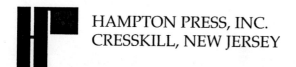
HAMPTON PRESS, INC.
CRESSKILL, NEW JERSEY

Printed in the United States of America

Canel, Mariá José.
    Morality tales: political scandals and journalism in Britain and Spain in the 1990s / Mariá José Canel, Karen Sanders.
        p. cm. -- (Hampton Press communication series. Political communication)
    Includes bibliographic references and index.
    ISBN 1-57273-564-3 (hardcover) -- ISBN 1-57273-565-1 (paperbound)
    1. Communication in politics--Cross-cultural studies. 2. Communication in politics--Great Britain. 3. Communication in politics--Spain. 4. Scandals--Press coverage--Spain. 7. Press and politics--Cross-cultural studies. 8. Press and politics--Great Britain. 9. Press and politics--Spain. I. Sanders, Karen, 1961-   . II. Title. III. Series.

JA85.C36 2005
941.085'9-dc22

                                                                    2005052509

Cover photo of Westminster courtesy of Francesco Guidicini

Hampton Press, Inc.
23 Broadway
Cresskill, NJ 07626

For Carlos, Carmen, Susana, Rafa, Luis, Gabi y Sonsoles Canel

For John and Linda Sanders

Contents

Contents

LIST OF TABLES

Foreword

We understand cultures in part by their stories. In ancient times the storytellers were the bards, the priests, and the poets. Aesop's tales provide an example of one kind of story, the morality tale: dramatizations intended to inculcate a moral lesson through the characterization of abstract qualities. In more recent times the storytellers have been joined by the journalists. Journalists not only inform they also—if they are good journalists—create interest in the subject they cover. They tell stories.

This is the starting point of our study. In this book we explore the press coverage of political scandal during the 1990s in Britain and Spain. We examine the construction of scandal stories, their plots, characters, and moral drama, the principal frames governing the different scandal narratives, as well as the stories told by the storytellers themselves about how and why their work was done. This study points us to the conclusion that in many important respects media scandal narratives are contemporary morality tales.

The journalists' work is examined in Britain and Spain, two countries with many similarities and also great differences: both are parliamentary democracies with constitutional monarchies; they are member states of the major Western economic, political, and military alliances with prosperous, enterprising societies comprised of diverse national groups; both are countries with rapidly changing media landscapes; in the 1990s both had governments,—conservative in the British case and socialist in the Spanish one,—that were dominated by the political scandals that came to define the era. There are also many differences. Spain is a newcomer to parliamentary democracy compared to Britain (Franco only died in 1975). Most of its institutional and constitutional traditions are Napoleonic in origin; Britain's, or more correctly England's, arrangements are the pragmatic, higgedly-piggedly outcome of centuries of history dating back to early medieval times. The culture of Spain—its art, values, literature—are permeated by its Christian Catholic heritage, Britain's by a Protestant tradition that over the centuries has brought it into conflict with continental neighbors, not least Spain.

Examining political scandal coverage in these two sharply delineated yet related cultural contexts is one of the main interests of this book. It allows us to explore the significance of political culture as a factor and the context for the impact and nature of political scandal. Political culture consists of "widely shared, fundamental beliefs that have political consequences" (Paletz & Lipinski, 1994, p. 1). It sets the context for politics. It places ideas and history at the center of the frame for understanding the way politics works at a national or subnational level.

In this book we explore how the British and Spanish political scandals of the 1990s, their narration by the press, and their ensuing outcomes constitute and are constituted by the political cultural context in which they occurred. Press power is seen to be in part a function of this larger context. One of the book's ambitions is to ascertain how the framing of political scandals in the British and Spanish press can provide insights into specific cultural contexts that themselves are key to shaping the precise features of political scandals in the different times and places.

The work that follows is very much a team effort, born out of shared intellectual interests and a determination to pursue the difficult but rewarding path of comparative research in countries each of us knows well. This would not have been possible without the help of a great number of individuals and institutions.

We want to thank especially Timothy Bale, Wolfgang Donsbach, Maxwell McCombs, Stephen Reese, and Holli Semetko for their invaluable comments and suggestions. We owe a particular debt of gratitude to David Paletz for his encouragement and support in publishing this book.

Our thanks to those who assisted with pilot coding. In particular, we would like to thank John Sanders for his many trips to Colindale Newspaper Library, Teresa Sádaba for her exemplary efficiency, and Margaret Vaudrey for her thorough and professional work in compiling the index. We are also grateful to Nazareth Echart for her work on the interviews in Spain. We are indebted to the editors at Hampton Press for their patience and for the excellent work of Barbara Bernstein in editing the book.

We are grateful to the Department of Journalism Studies of the University of Sheffield (Britain) and the Department of Public Communication of the University of Navarra (Spain) for their support, and to the latter's PIUNA grant scheme for awarding research funds to the project.

Finally, we would not have been able to complete this research without the generous help of the professional community, journalists, editors, press chiefs, spokesmen and women, who so readily allowed themselves to be the objects of this study. Everyone we approached not only agreed to be interviewed but also subsequently offered further invaluable information.

1

Introduction

RESEARCH AIMS

The linkages between politics and the media are a staple of communication research and their analysis forms the broad field of study known as political communication (Del Rey, 1989; Gauthier, Gosselin, & Mouchon, 1998; Monzón, 1996; Nimmo & Sanders, 1981; Nimmo & Swanson, 1990; Paletz, 1997). Research has focused on a number of subjects. Several studies have centered on the *mediation of the political message*, examining areas such as the sociology of newsrooms, journalists-politicians' relationships, and legal requirements for access to governmental information. Another area of research has examined *communication actions*, that is to say the different ways in which messages have been communicated in, for example, debates, political advertising, press conferences or talk shows. *Media effects* constitutes a very extensive research field and includes audience studies, the influence of interpersonal communication on political judgments and behavior and the contribution of the media

1

to political socialization. Disciplines such as rhetoric and linguistics have also contributed to work on the *analysis of political messages*. As far as *political processes* are concerned, political communication research has centered primarily on election campaigns, examining areas such as the creation of party and candidate images, the management and organization of campaigns, the communication of electoral messages, voters' reception of electoral messages and the influence of campaigns on voting intention.

This book takes a different tack in exploring the connections between politics and the media. It examines the coverage of political scandal during the 1990s in Britain and Spain. Our main interests are first, to understand how and why journalists constructed the scandal stories they did and second, to analyze what kinds of scandal narratives were created by the press. This prompts a third question, more difficult to answer, about the impact of political scandal and what, if anything, this tells us about the putative power of the press.

Exploring these themes, we find evidence to support the view that the British and Spanish political scandals of the 1990s constituted part of and were constituted by the political cultural context in which they occurred. In particular, we emphasize the role of the press as arbitrators of themes from the cultural repertoire, fixers of symbolic content and framers of narratives about political scandals. Using a variety of methodologies, we believe it is possible to produce a richly textured account of narrations of political scandal which also provides insights into political culture. Within this framework, our research examines:

First, the attitudes and values of journalists and spin doctors towards the coverage of political scandals.

Second, the press coverage of political scandals and the characteristics of political scandal narratives in news frames.

Third, the differences and similarities in scandal outcomes in both countries.

THEORETICAL RATIONALE

Comparative Research

The underlying theoretical effort concerns the challenge of conducting comparative research. Comparative work is difficult (Blumler & Gurevitch, 1995), which is perhaps why comparative media research is relatively thin on the ground (Blumler, McLeod, & Rosengren, 1992; Hallin & Mancini, 2004). It requires deep knowledge of the worlds being examined as well as methods that allow meaningful equivalences to be established that, at the same time, do not neglect the wealth of different meanings that exist in diverse cultural contexts. Indeed, although comparative research has gained in frequency and scope in recent years, it is still an extendable frontier (see Blumler, McLeod, & Rosengren, 1992).

In particular, "little attention has been paid to framing in a cross-nationally comparative fashion" (De Vreese, Peter, & Semetko, 2001, p. 108). The analysis of news frames provides one of the focuses of this study. Of course, the frames themselves are not here directly comparable. The scandals were different in each country and thus their framing cannot be compared as one would the cross-national coverage of a single international event such as the September 11, 2001, attack on New York's World Trade Center. Scandal frames are examined in this study in the political, historical, cultural, and production context in which they were created. In other words, this study provides deep description and analysis of political scandal coverage in two Western liberal democracies. Hallin and Mancini's excellent study of comparative media systems calls for 'more case studies of the interaction of the media with other social actors in the coverage of particular kinds of events or issues' and gives scandals as an example among others of possible areas of study. They argue, and we agree, that this kind of study is useful "for exploring issues of power that . . . are very much underexplored given their significance to many of the normative questions that communication researchers often return to in the end" (Hallin & Mancini, 2004, p. 304). Esser and Pfetsch (2004) advance the comparative cause and Tumber and Waisbord's (2004) edited volume takes forward the scandal and media research agenda. Our study is a further contribution to this body of work.

The comparativeness of the project lies in the analytical methods used and the research sites identified, rather than in the conclusions that can be reached about the comparability of the scandal cases themselves, which are clearly incommensurable. However, in placing side by side a study of the two countries we can test the limits of some of the more general claims made about the media and political scandal. It is in this context, too, that we will examine whether the notion of political culture has anything to contribute to an understanding of political scandal and to its media coverage and impact.

THE POLITICAL CULTURE PERSPECTIVE

What about the notion of political culture itself? In the work of earlier political scholars it was a term assimilated to nebulous and impressionistic concepts such as "national character", with little explanatory power or theoretical purchase. Later, political scientists, influenced by an objectivist paradigm that sought to assimilate the social sciences to the methods of natural science, aimed to develop a science of the political process where political culture was defined as the "pattern of individual attitudes and orientations towards politics among the individuals of a political system. It is the subjective realm which underlies and gives meaning to political actions" (Almond & Bingham Powell, 1966, p. 50). In their classic work *The Civic Culture*, Almond and Verba (1963 and 1989) developed a typology of political culture to understand why democracy exists in some countries and not in others. Political culture was posited as a distinct variable or set of variables that could be successfully isolated from, for example, demographic variables. Using survey research methodology, political scientists sought to identify with precision the subjective basis of democratic politics. Cross-national comparative research of political culture has usually been carried out with a view to providing a register of political cultural factors that allow distinct cultural profiles to be established (see Almond & Verba, 1963).

This approach undoubtedly focuses attention on the importance of the study of political attitudes and values for the understanding of political systems and institutions. However, this scientist paradigm of political culture has been criticized (Taylor, 1971; Welch, 1993). Welch takes the pessimistic view that "to see political culture as a separable factor in comparative explanation while beginning with an account of cultural difference is doomed" (p. 71). How do you limit the concept to one part of the context to account for national differences? How do you decide which measures constitute "political culture"? And, as Charles Taylor points out, how can we be sure that we are not simply interpreting other societies with the categories of our own (1971, p. 34)?

In our view, a more fruitful avenue for exploring political culture in a cross-national context can be found in the Geertzian tradition, which understands culture not simply as "as a system of attitudes, values and knowledge" (Inglehart, 1990, p. 18) but as webs of significance we ourselves have spun (see Geertz, 1973, p. 5). This interpretivist paradigm examines political culture in terms of establishing meaning based on criteria of plausibility rather than empiricist standards of verification. The aim is to establish the meaning that determined social actions have for the actors and to enunciate what that knowledge shows about the society to which it refers. It requires a deep knowledge of the universe that politicians and journalists inhabit. It means researchers must have been immersed in the culture, understand the language, and know the history of the environments they are studying. This kind of analysis allows us to conjecture meaning, evaluate the conjectures, and arrive at explanatory conclusions on the basis of our best guesses (see Geertz, 1973, p. 25). In other words, political culture is not treated as an isolatable phenomenon but as a context for interpretation. Political culture in this view is that web of significance continually being constituted and reconstituted by language, history, tradition, and institutions in relation to a society's political aspects.

Our approach is interpretivist and based on case studies; for, although we recognize and identify broad systemic differences and similarities, we are more concerned with teasing out from the detailed understandings of the actors we interviewed and the specificity of the political scandals analyzed, an understanding of the weft and warp of political culture (see Welch, 1993).

Scandal and Political Culture

In March 1999 the entire European Union Commission was forced to resign after allegations of corruption against some of its members. In British newspapers some journalists chose to see the events as evidence of the cultural divide between Southern and Northern Europe. *The Times'* journalist, Roger Boyes, spoke of the "Protestant North . . . celebrating a moral (though probably pyhrric) victory over the Catholic South" in an article entitled "Sober North Vies with Siesta South" (March 17, 1999, p. 6). His colleague, Simon Jenkins, writing of the allegations of corruption, back-handers and nepotism, compared the Commission to the "pre-Reformation episcopacy" and claimed, "In these matters, Paris, Madrid, Lisbon, and Rome inhabit a separate moral realm" (March 17, 1999, p. 20).

These events and media coverage of them underlined how political scandal may be considered a useful entry point in to the exploration of political cultural differences and similarities (see Esser & Hartung, 2004). Of course, as we mentioned earlier, there is no doubting the difficulty of this endeavor. In examining the framing of political scandals across cultures a great number of factors need to be taken into account, including the media and political system and the historical context. Cross-national comparisons are themselves fraught with danger and, as no one can be in any doubt about the difficulties surrounding the concept of *nation* (Sanders, 1997), it is legitimate to question whether national comparisons have any validity. Indeed, one of the main complaints against the term "political culture" is its use to differentiate between national contexts in an enterprise that woefully neglects the subnational (Welch, 1993).

However, as Blumler and Gurevitch have pointed out, cross-national comparisons have the advantage of displacing ethnocentric perspectives and rendering the invisible visible (1995, pp. 75-76). They can show

how social, political, and cultural reality often defies our often simplistic attempts to find general patterns that apply to all social and political arrangements. This was the conclusion of a ten country cross-national study that found that "the nature of the political impact the media may have is strongly shaped by the interaction among a number of macro- and micro-level variables, and this interaction can take different forms in different countries" (Gunther & Mughan, 2000, p. 402). Their study showed that among the most important "macro-level national (and often subnational) characteristics are political culture, the structure of society, the media and government institutions, the norms governing the relationship between journalists and politics, regulatory practices, and the level of technological development of the communications industry" (p. 402). They concluded that research into the relationship between the media and politics should seek not "universal generalizations, but . . . more middle-level and contingent theoretical propositions" (p. 404).

We would agree. The exploration of the coverage of political scandal in Britain and Spain will, we hope, enable us to understand more fully the relationship between politics and journalism. But at the same time, the subject of political scandal is, we believe, one that particularly lends itself to illuminating the contingencies of that relationship and it is one of our main reasons for choosing it. As we shall see, political scandals, their coverage and impact, are not givens. They arise out of specific sets of events, circumstances, and cultures. In this sense, their study in differing national contexts is a valuable antidote to the predominance of anglocentric models of the relationship between politics and journalism.

METHODS

The Principle of "Triangulation"

In this study we adopt the methodological principle of triangulation. Triangulation in communication research has been understood in different although compatible ways. For Laitin (1995) the methodological principle of triangulation consists in the analysis of historical context with the use of quantitative methods (p. 172). Nimmo and Swanson (1990) consider it to be an approach that relates analytical descriptions of messages with theorizing about the production of the message, its consumption, and responses to it (p. 19). Del Río (1996) interprets triangulation as the structured observation of the producers of the message, the media transmitting the message, and of those who receive it (p. 368).

We use the principle of triangulation in the sense of making use of various streams of evidence and methods to corroborate (or not) conjectures or "best guesses" taken from any one specific domain of evidence. We analyze media scandals following the lead of studies that relate media content with the processes of news production (De Vreese, Peter, & Semetko, 2001; Semetko et al., 1991), using this evidence in the context of documentary material and in relation to systemic and cultural factors that may influence or be reflected in news.

Adopting the principle of triangulation, the research methodology uses three approaches. First, the examination of media content using quantitative and qualitative content analysis. Second, the analysis of news production through interviews with the journalists involved in the discovery and reporting of scandal stories as well as with those attempting to manage this news, the government and party officials involved in media operations relating to the scandals.

Finally, documentary evidence is used: reports, memoirs, year books, parliamentary proceedings, as well as surveys of public perceptions of politicians and political institutions. We have also carried out a careful review of literature published about the media and political context of the political scandals being studied as well as about the scandal cases themselves.

Qualitative and quantitative methods are used, a strategy that makes for a rich body of evidence (Deacon et al., 1999; Denzin & Lincoln, 1998; Miles, 1984; Wimmer & Dominick, 2000). The data gathered from the qualitative research (both from qualitative content analysis and from interviews) acted as a control of the content analysis data, providing information about the attempts by the politicians and party officials to control damaging stories and the attempts by the journalists to pursue alternative source strategies.

SELECTION OF SCANDALS AND NEWSPAPERS

Seven scandal stories were analyzed in both countries in a total of seven newspapers.

A time line was produced for each country detailing the evolution of a selection of major scandal stories. In Spain these included the corruption story concerning Mariano Rubio, governor of the Bank of Spain; the murders of two alleged members (José Antonio Lasa and José Ignacio Zabala) of the Basque terrorist group, ETA, by State-sponsored death squads (GAL), and the associated theft of secret service (CESID) papers; and finally, the story of the corruption of the head of police, Luis Roldán, and the links uncovered to GAL.[1] These cases were selected as being representative of the different types of scandal story in Spain.

They also shared a similar time line from their discovery, development, and final court proceedings that allowed study of their press coverage to be followed with relative ease. This was not the case with the Filesa scandal which, though representative of a specific type of political scandal (illegal party funding), had an uneven development in time. It was therefore not included in the study.

In Britain the cases chosen were the Cash for Questions case, in which government Members of Parliament (MPs) were accused of being paid to ask questions in Parliament; the Arms to Iraq story, in which Conservative government ministers were alleged to have conspired to mislead Parliament about the illegal export of equipment to Iraq and permit the possible conviction of innocent businessmen; and, finally, three separate sexual scandals involving the Conservative ministers David Mellor and Tim Yeo, as well as the Conservative parliamentary candidate, Piers Merchant. They were selected as representative of the three major types of British political scandal (scandals about power, money, and sex). The Arms to Iraq and Cash for Questions scandals had extended coverage over a long period of time. The sex scandals did not, and yet—because of their profusion—were a major ingredient of British political scandal reporting in the 1990s. For this reason, the first of the major sex scandals (Mellor's infidelity in 1992), a sex scandal detonated at the midpoint of the research period (Yeo's infidelity in 1994), and one at the end of the Conservative government's period of power (Merchant's infidelity in 1997) have been selected as a representative sample of sexual scandal coverage of the era.

For ease of reference, in the rest of the book the Spanish scandal stories will be referred to as *Roldán, Rubio, Gal-Cesid,* and *Gal-Lasa and Zabala*; the British scandal stories will be referred to as *Cash for Questions, Arms to Iraq,* and *Sexual Misdemeanors.* Table 1.1 provides the main details of each of the scandals.

Content analysis was carried out of *El Mundo, El País,* and *ABC* for Spain and *The Guardian, The Independent, The Sun,* and *The Sunday Times* for the United Kingdom. These newspapers were selected as providing a representative sample of styles, readership, and the spectrum of political beliefs in both countries. They also included the newspapers that had taken the leading role in breaking political scandals.

All articles were coded for the day in which a major incident was reported and the subsequent day's newspaper, yielding a total of 3,760 (1,781 British articles and 1,979 Spanish articles) from articles covering news stories, features, cartoons, editorial, comments, and diary pieces.

The events covered spanned a period beginning in April 1990 and ending in April 2000. The analysis covers a total of 256 days for the United Kingdom and 338 for Spain.

TABLE 1.1 Scandals Analyzed

NAME OF THE SCANDAL	DATE	CONTENT OF THE SCANDAL
Sp Roldán	1993	Corruption of the head of the police, Luis Roldán.
Rubio	1994	Insider share dealing and falsification of documents by the head of the Bank of Spain, Mariano Rubio.
Gal-Cesid	1995	Theft of secret service papers referring to the state- sponsored terrorist group, GAL.
Gal-Lasa and Zabala	1995	Murder of alleged ETA members (Lasa and Zabala) by GAL death squads.
U.K. Cash for Questions	1994	MPs accused of being paid to ask parliamentary questions.
Arms to Iraq	1992	Ministers alleged to have misled Parliament about the illegal sale of dual use equipment to Iraq and permitted the possible conviction of innocent businessmen.
Sexual Misdemeanors	1992	Three sexual scandals involving Conservatives: David Mellor, Tim Yeo, and Piers Merchant.
	1994	
	1997	

Quantitative Content Analysis

For the quantitative content analysis a code book (see Appendix 1) was produced during several meetings by the authors. The coding of the data in this research was undertaken by experienced coders working with the Spanish author and one working with the British author. The coders were required to master all aspects of the coding frame, and training sessions were designed to familiarize the coders with the details of the coding schedule and to ensure that they understood the definitions of the different variables and coding categories. Pretests were carried out and intercoder consistency was checked by the authors. Checks were made by monitoring judgments made about content categories, both during training and during coding. Coder reliability on these variables was above 90 percent. An intercoder reliability test was also performed between the two principal coders, which achieved a satisfactory level of agreement. A similar coding frame was used in each country, with minor adjustments made to take account of linguistic and style differences.

The unit of analysis is an article, that is to say a written piece that is separated from others with a graphic device. The code consists of fifteen variables. Several variables code basic information such as the newspaper's title, date, and page number. Other variables code characteristics of coverage such as the section it appears in, its genre, the length of the article, number of photographs, the use of original documents, and graphics. All mentions of media organizations were coded.

We wished to examine, too, the occurrence of certain words in referring to scandals. A number of terms were established as key words in political scandal coverage after a review of newspaper coverage in both countries to establish any patterns of prominent word use in articles and graphics. Therefore, news articles were coded for mentions of these key words and their cognate forms. These words were "scandal" and "corruption" and their equivalents in Spanish. In addition, British coverage was coded for the mention of the word "sleaze," a term found not to have an equivalent in Spanish.

Finally, the three first sources used were coded for each news story. The source type was coded, including, for example, prime minister, leader of the opposition, member of the government, member of the civil service, and so forth. This variable was recoded into binary variables with source categories defined as government/opposition, official/nonofficial and media/nonmedia. An official source was defined as a source speaking on behalf of a socially recognized institution.

Qualitative Content Analysis

The authors also carried out joint qualitative analysis of newspaper editorials and the bar straps used for special sections devoted exclusively to scandal coverage.

A representative sample of editorials in terms of scandal cases and newspaper titles was selected for each country. A total of 135 editorials (78 for the United Kingdom and 57 for Spain) was analyzed. Editorials in both country act as the voice of the newspaper. They are supposed to be opinionated and for that reason we believed they would be a useful site to explore the way in which the press framed the responsibility and consequences of scandal.

Entman's (1991) identification of three framing characteristics of news narratives was a helpful starting point for our analysis. He identifies the assignation of agency as well as the assessments used and the generalizations generated as being key areas in which framing takes place. *Agency* refers to *how* responsibility is assigned—is the act considered to be an outcome of incompetence, fate, criminality, arrogance, or greed? *Who*, if anyone, or *what* is considered *responsible*? What is considered to be the causal force that brought about the action or incident? All attributions of cause and agency were noted down, as well as the *characters* to whom responsibility was attributed (including all named individuals and institutions). All *assessments* of people and institutions involved in the scandals were noted down in full (for instance, terms such as "foolish", "out of touch", "hypocrite", and "grossly presumptuous"). Under *generalizations* statements about the more general problems implied by an event were noted down in order to identify the kind of debates generated by scandal coverage. Finally, shorthand expressions for the scandals were also noted.

Special section bar-straps and their accompanying graphics pointed to the evolving story line for each scandal case. Bar straps are a useful index of the newspaper's interpretative framework for a story. Coverage in the United States and Britain, for example, of the aftermath to September 11 as "War against Terrorism" evokes a very specific interpretative framework for readers. A great deal of scandal coverage (20.7% for British press and 22.4% for the Spanish press) appeared in special sections with bar-strap and graphic. The title of each bar-strap was noted down (100 for Spain and 74 for Britain) for all the special scandal sections published in both countries.

Interviews with Journalists

Semi-structured interviews were conducted with nineteen (seven Spanish and twelve British journalists) reporters and editors involved in the investigation or in the coverage of the cases analyzed in this book (see Appendix 2 for the list of people interviewed). The interview schedule was refined and modified to take into account new, related questions as the research progressed.

The interview schedule covered three areas. The first refers to the journalist's background (including his/her career background, education, position in the paper both at the moment of the scandal and of the interview, awards received), the organizational environment in which he or she worked (organization of the newspaper's investigative team, relationships with other members of the newsroom, involvement of political correspondents in the scandal coverage). The second block of questions refers to the specific scandal and partly follows the phases that Protess et al. (1991) suggest in relation to the investigative process: initiation of the story, conceptualization of it, and development of the evidence (pp. 205-230). Hence, our questions refer first to how the story was initiated, approaches by sources, mechanisms used to establish credibility of the source, evaluation of the credibility of the information, discussion with the newspaper's editor about the feasibility of the story, and so forth. Secondly, questions refer to how the story was conceptualized: what was the story thought to be about? We wanted to know how the journalists established the dramatic potential of a story; why was it regarded as compelling; and what was considered to be wrong. Thirdly, and referring to the development of the evidence, we asked about how the story was constructed: the kinds of sources used, the assessment of the usefulness of official sources, the role of leaks and of experts and the use of documentary sources.

We wished to examine this information in the context of the perceptions journalists themselves have of their own roles and of the role the media have in relation to other institutions and to society. Therefore, the final block of questions asks about the role of investigative journalism, the impact of media scandals, and professional attitudes. Questions such as the following were posed: Do you think facts speak for themselves? In general? In scandal stories? Is there a moral imperative in what journalists do? What do you see as investigative journalism's role in uncovering scandal in relation to parliamentary and legal investigations? To what extent do market considerations come into play in deciding whether scandal stories should be pursued? What ethical debates occurred? Finally, we asked them for their view of scandals' outcomes for the paper, for politics, for the public, and for the standing of journalism.

All the journalists interviewed were extremely helpful and happy to provide additional information and answer follow-up questions. In part, this probably reflects the professional satisfaction journalists in both countries felt for having played a significant role in some of the major political stories of the 1990s. An additional incentive for them to tell their story is the dearth of detailed studies of investigative journalism, particularly in Spain.

Interviews with Politicians

Using the same semi-structured questionnaire for both countries, in-depth interviews were also conducted with a selection of key officials (politicians and senior party officials) employed in the media operations of the two prime ministers. Nine (five Spanish and four British officials) interviews were conducted. Those interviewed had been involved either in the government or in the political party in decisions about how to manage news about scandals.

We wished to obtain a detailed account of the workings and organization of the prime minister's and president's[2] media operations in general and in relation to scandal news in particular. The interview schedule had four parts. The first examined the structure of the government's media operations: those involved, distribution of roles, decision-making procedures, relationship to other ministries. The second part dealt with the relationship to the media: the ordinary (and not so ordinary) channels of communication and assessments of the media's performance. Questions in part three explored the relationship to the political party. The final block of questions asked about the specific actions taken in relation to scandal news.

Despite the sensitivity of the interview subjects (some of the cases had not yet been resolved), the interviewees were very helpful, although several preferred some of their comments to be "off the record" and these have been used as background. Only one person approached refused to be interviewed.

These interviews were conducted in both countries after there had been a change of government and political party. This was certainly a factor in explaining why many of those involved were willing to speak to us. All interviews were conducted by the authors of this book and carried out on the days indicated in Appendix 2.

All interviews were tape recorded and subsequently transcribed. In several cases follow-up interviews were conducted.

PLAN OF THE BOOK

The book is divided into three parts: the first (Chapters 2 and 3) provides the conceptual background that underpins the empirical analysis; Part Two (Chapters 4, 5, 6, and 7) sets out the research findings; Part Three (Chapters 8 and 9) provides discussion and concluding thoughts about the nature of press power in political scandal coverage and the relationship of scandal coverage to political culture.

The following two chapters, then, examine the notions of "political scandal" and "media scandal." Chapter 2 sets out the political and media context to the scandals and provides a classification of the major political scandals in both countries during the 1990s. The chapter deals with the characteristics of political scandal, providing a conceptual and historical analysis of the notions of scandal, sleaze, and corruption, reviewing the relevant literature on political scandals. In Chapter 3 we look at the role of the media in converting wrongdoing by public figures into political scandal. We review the literature on the construction of news frames and news icons and examine the application of these models to the creation of scandal narratives. Examining media scandals from a news narrative perspective requires us to focus on the story tellers and on the characters and plots of the stories they tell. This is what we do in the second part of the book.

Part Two begins with an analysis of the tellers of scandal stories. Chapter 4 deals with who they were, the assumptions they brought to their task, the methods they employed to obtain their stories and their relationship to sources. We draw on evidence from interviews, memoirs, and content analysis to provide an account of the relationship between journalists and their sources in covering political scandal stories. In Chapter 5 we look at the "other side" of the story: we examine the strategies of those who attempted to manage scandal stories, looking at the work of spin doctors and press officers. More specifically, Major and González's offices are analyzed on the basis of interviews with politicians, journalists, party officials, and the memoirs of some of those involved.

Chapters 6 and 7 examine the stories told, the specific frames that are created in news narratives. In Chapter 6 we base our analysis on, first, a cautious reading of frame prominence and second, on frame dimensions suggested by Entman; namely, agency, identification of characters, categorizations, and generalizations. Once actors and agency are identified, journalists, in seeking to create a compelling tale, look for language and images to characterize the actors' behavior, and thus frame the wrongdoing. Therefore, having identified the characters and agency of those present in British and Spanish news scandal narratives, in Chapter 7 we examine the kind of morality tales—moralizing frames—constructed by the press, looking at two specific dimensions of frames, "categorizations" and "generalizations." We look at the sort of moral assessments, the debates that are implicit or explicit in the generalizations made about the political system, at the identity associations established, and, finally we examine a specific type of frame, the news icon, which, because of its symbolic strength, is pertinent to scandal news narratives.

In the final part of the book we examine what these scandal narratives can tell us about the power of the media. In Chapter 8 we examine the outcomes of political scandals, reviewing theories about media scandals, and looking at the specific outcomes of the scandals analyzed in this book. The evidence from this analysis is used to assess the extent to which the notion of a powerful press holds true for Britain and Spain. Finally, Chapter 9 examines what evidence is provided by the cross-national study for debates about how the values, traditions, and practices of particular political and media cultures configure both the enabling and constraining communication and political environment within which politicians, spin doctors, and journalists operate.

NOTES

1. GAL is the acronym for *Grupos Antiterroristas de Liberación* or "Anti-terrorist Freedom Groups"; ETA refers to *Euzkadi ta Azkatasuna*. CESID is the *Centro Superior de Información de la Defensa*, the Spanish state's security office.
2. In Spain the Prime Minister is usually referred to as the "President" and the Prime Minister's Office is the "Presidency." Both terms will be used in this study.

2

Political Scandals

POLITICAL DISORDER IN THE 1990s

As memories of the 1990s begin to fade, it is hard to imagine the hope with which the decade began. It was thought that the collapse of the Berlin Wall in 1989 would inaugurate a new international world order. The dangerous Cold War had finished. Globalization, symbolized by the emerging World Wide Web, seemed to herald the beginning of a new dispensation that would spread prosperity across the planet.

Some of this promise was fulfilled. A new political and economic order, however, failed to materialize. The final decade of the twentieth century was instead characterized by war in Europe and the Middle East and political scandal in the Western democracies. The abiding images of the 1990s include war in Bosnia and Monica Lewinsky.

Political scandals seemed to come in all shapes and sizes: arcane land deals in Whitewater; government death squads in Spain; squalid sex scandals in Britain; illegal party funding in Germany and more con-

17

ventional venality in Italy. A veritable library of books about political scandal was produced (Della Porta & Mény, 1997; Heywood, 1997; Jímenez, 1995; Laporta & Alvarez, 1997; Levi & Nelken, 1996; Little & Posada-Carbó, 1996; Ridley & Doig 1995; Tortosa, 1995). This chapter will provide the historical and conceptual background to the more sharply focused empirical study of political scandals in Britain and Spain in later chapters. It begins first by setting out the main features of British and Spanish political and media landscapes of the 1990s.

BRITISH AND SPANISH POLITICAL LANDSCAPES

The political landscapes of Britain and Spain have rarely been in party political harmony. The 1979 British general elections ushered in a long period of Conservative dominance only brought to an end in 1997 when Tony Blair's New Labour defeated John Major's Tory government. In Spain, Felipe González's Socialist party (PSOE—*Partido Socialista Obrero Español*) was the dominant political force from the 1982 elections until its defeat by José María Aznar's conservative Popular Party (PP—*Partido Popular*) in 1996. Britain's New Labour was re-elected in 2001 and the Socialist Party was voted into government in Spain in 2004. The economic boom of the 1980s, crowned by Spain's entry into the European Community in 1986, prompted, in Heywood's words (1995b), "a spectacular economic takeoff" (p. 179). Here we will examine more permanent features of the political landscape of both countries.

Parliamentary Democracies

Britain and Spain share much. Both are parliamentary democracies with constitutional monarchies that have played an important stabilizing and unifying role in their respective country's history. They are member states of the major Western economic, political, and military alliances including the European Union and NATO. They are prosperous, enterprising societies, heirs to great cultural riches enshrined in art, literature, and architecture and to the legacies of empire.

These similarities, however, cannot disguise significant cultural and systemic differences. Let us take first the history and stability of political institutions in both countries. Spain's current political settlement came into being only with the death of General Francisco Franco in 1975. The first democratic elections since the 1930s were held in 1977. For much of the nineteenth and twentieth centuries Spain was in political turmoil: foreign invasion, dynastic strife, republicanism, civil war, and dictatorship chart the history of those troubled years. The monarchy was only reinstated in 1975, and the written Constitution dates from 1978. The latter establishes a decentralized territorial regime: Spain is an autonomic state (*Estado Autonómico*); that is, it is a national state in which autonomy for the nationalities and regions is recognized. The process of devolution was initiated by the Constitution and enacted by the Autonomy Statute Laws (*Estatutos de Autonomía*) between 1979 and 1984 (Canel, 1994). Every Autonomous Community has its own legislative, executive, and judiciary infrastructure. Having said this, a Madrid-focused centralism is a notorious feature of Spanish political life and a constant source of tension with the vigorous political communities of Catalonia and the Basque Country (Canel, 1994).

Contrast this to Britain. There is no codified constitution, but rather an assemblage of statute and common law, treaties, and conventions, some of which date from the beginnings of the English state in the tenth century. The "constitution" is untidy, eminently pragmatic, and most Britons know little about it and probably care even less.[1] Even Queen Elizabeth II is alleged to have remarked that "the British Constitution has always been puzzling and always will be" (cited in Hennessy, 1995, p. 33). The monarchy and parliamentary government in Britain have also enjoyed remarkable continuity and stability. Apart from the hiatus of the civil war and the rule of Oliver Cromwell in the seventeenth century, there have been no breaks in the existence of the monarchy since the tenth century and some form of parliamentary governance since the thirteenth century.

Despite its erosion by Brussels and the debates about Britain's executive turning into an elective dictatorship (especially during the prime-ministerships of Margaret Thatcher and Tony Blair), the doctrine of parliamentary sovereignty remains one of the central pillars of Britain's constitutional arrangements. This contrasts with the deliberately weak parliament created by Spain's 1978 Constitution in anticipation of the formation of coalition governments. In practice, the Spanish executive has been stronger than anticipated, and the country's parliament has been unable to act as an effective check upon it. Other measures of control of the executive have taken time to develop. Parliamentary questions to the president, for example, were only introduced in September 1994. Previously the president could decide which questions he would respond to, but in fact the convention had fallen into disuse (Guerrero, 2000, p. 183). Parliamentary Committees of Investigation were also intended as a control mechanism of the executive, but in reality their limited resources blunted their effectiveness. Parliamentary Study Committees are an even weaker instrument of executive control. Their decisions and recommendations have no binding power on the government. They were constituted to investigate several of the major political scandals of the González era to little effect.

Some institutions are still "under construction" (see Paniagua-Soto, 1997). The Senate, for example, has still some way to go before it can claim to be the chamber of territorial representation that it was originally designed to be.

PRIME MINISTERIAL POWER

How do the United Kingdom and Spain compare in terms of prime ministerial (PM) power? We can begin by looking at differences in terms of the accountability of the prime minister to Parliament (Budge, Newton et al., 1997). First, there is a different tradition of PM appearances before Parliament. The U.K. parliament has a regular weekly (and in Major's time, twice-weekly) slot for questions to the prime minister. Unless they are planted by their own side, PMs have no prior knowledge of such questions, although they and their advisers spend anxious hours beforehand trying to second-guess them.

In Spain, there is no such strongly established tradition of calling the chief executive regularly to account. Indeed, for most of the time since 1977 the opposite was the case, González being famed for his dismissive attitude toward (and the rarity of his appearances in) the Spanish Parliament, the *Cortes*. Things changed towards the end of his time in office when a weekly question time was introduced in 1994, but this change could be seen as something forced upon him by his government's minority status following its narrow victory in 1993. A second difference is that until 1993 there was little opportunity for Spanish parliamentarians to conduct the sort of sustained, detailed, and public investigations into pressing issues that the British Committee system can encourage. Indeed, as we will see, Spanish deputies made the point during the examination of one of the country's major political scandals that the media had done as much as the official Committee of Investigation to reveal what had gone on. The debate about the role of Committees of Investigation arose again in the context of an inquiry into the March 11, 2004 Madrid bombings.

There are, however, more similarities between the parliamentary systems of each country than at first appear. For example, the ability of the prime minister and his/her government to control Parliament's (and its committees') agenda, timetable, and outcomes is significant in both countries but easy to overstate. To take the British example, the convention by which the government majority extends to committees as well as the plenary session gives it a great advantage, which the government's business managers are willing to use if at all possible. The reality, however, can be more complicated. An example from the Major years is instructive here. Labour made a huge amount of fuss at the beginning of the 1997 general election campaign about the government supposedly using its majority on a parliamentary committee to block publication of a report into one of the major scandals of Major's government.[2] In fact, as we suggest in Chapter 5, there were many involved with the Conservative campaign who argued strongly that the prime minister should try to ensure publication of a report that could have been positively spun as clearing a large majority of those MPs under suspicion. The report was not published, however, because the committee's Conservative chairman felt that it would be improper to rush it through (Lewington, 1999).[3] It may be that Prime Minister Major was honor bound to support such a decision; but the point is that even had he disagreed, he would have had no power to enforce his line on a properly constituted committee of the House of Commons. Here we see how a polity's institutional rules and conventions can indirectly determine—if not delimit—the power of the chief executive in the field of publicity and media relations.

To take a second area for comparison, in both Spain and the United Kingdom political practicalities as much as constitutional guidelines (Gallagher, Laver, & Mair, 1995) are a source of PM power. Yet in both cases the very same things that can be sources of strength can simultaneously prove to be liabilities rather than assets. Take, for example, the prime minister's position as party leader: this normally provides him/her with a good deal of power; on the other hand, this close association with the party can prove to be extremely problematic for a prime minister. However little s/he has to do with the misdemeanors of more or less significant members of his/her party, s/he is arguably seen as responsible for their continuance or eradication.

In Britain especially, however, such things may in fact be out of the control of the PM and of the whips or party managers who report to the Prime Minister. Government control of both the main parties in the United Kingdom, because it relies ultimately on little more than moral suasion and peer pressure, and because it can often only be exercised within the legislature rather than, say, the electoral district or constituency, is much overrated. As John Major (2000) commented about his approach to local party support for the candidature of one his errant ministers, Neil Hamilton. "I wanted him to withdraw, but under the traditional structure of local Conservative associations this would not have worked. I could have disowned his entire constituency party, but he would have remained a candidate, backed by a rebel association. This made me look powerless—and indeed, in this case, I was" (p. 712).

The situation in Spain stands in marked contrast. The Spanish leader's influence over the electoral list—and the crucial rank order on that list—constitutes both an inducement to loyalty and a sanction of last resort. On the other hand, his/her control is far from total. Often carefully contrived ideological, regional, and personality balances need preserving.

Another political reality that adds to the power of a prime minister is his/her de facto role as the representative embodiment of not just the government but the nation. Again, however, this can prove as much an asset as a liability, as the Spanish-British, González-Major comparison clearly demonstrates. Where there is general consensus about the direction of the nation in respect to its world or continental role, the fact that the head of government is seen to represent that nation may put him/her—at least temporarily—above serious criticism. Where there is no consensus, their international role may in fact be the occasion (perhaps even the source) of such criticism. In John Major's case, his role as the face of the United Kingdom when dealing with the outside world, and particularly Europe, damaged rather than reinforced the regard in which he was held by the media and the public, partly because certain powerful press proprietors and a large number of citizens were ideologically hostile to his compromises, and partly because the issue symbolized to those same people his supposed inability to "get a grip" on his increasingly fissiparous government and party.

In the Spanish case, the European issue operated in almost exactly the opposite way. Spanish enthusiasm for the European Union as an economic future as well as a symbolic legitimator for the "New Spain" encouraged a kind of unofficial close season on attacks on Felipe González when his government took its turn to assume the six-month rotating presidency of the European Council in 1995.

Likewise, the other main factors cited as a source of so-called "prime ministerial power"—their role as the hirer and firer of ministerial colleagues or as the all-seeing, agenda-setting spider in the web of government—have the capacity to work to their disadvantage as well as in their favor. We may be aware that such metaphorical descriptions of a prime minister's position vis-à-vis colleagues and administration are actually highly misleading. Nevertheless, these metaphors continue to inform the media presentation and the public perception of what the head of government can and should do.

MEDIA LANDSCAPES

The media environment—its institutions, structure and culture—contributes (or not) to the constitution of the public sphere(s). At the same time it is itself constituted and constrained by the economic, legal, and political environment in which it functions. Here we will examine the media landscapes of Spain and Britain, looking at the chief characteristics of the newspaper market and broadcast media as well as norms and conventions surrounding the practice of journalism and, in particular, political journalism.

The Newspaper Market

The U.K. newspaper market is highly competitive: at the high point of British sleaze in 1995, around 40 percent of adults read one or more national dailies every day, one of the highest figures in Europe; the percentage was even higher for those who bought a national newspaper on a weekly basis (Tunstall, 1996, p. 223). British readers have a choice of ten national dailies and nine Sunday newspapers whose combined circulation figures averaged above 22 million throughout the 1990s (Audit Bureau of Circulation). This compares to a total of seven national newspapers in Spain with an average total circulation of just over 1 million in the 1990s (Oficina de Justificación de la Difusión).[4]

In Britain the relatively high number of national press titles, declining circulation from the high levels of the 1960s, as well as the strong tabloid sector and Sunday market made for a fiercely competitive newspaper market in the 1990s. From 1993 newspaper price wars drove down editorial standards and stretched the boundaries of what was considered permissible for publication (Chippindale & Horrie, 1999). Lurid stories were splashed by the Sunday tabloids and followed up by broadsheets and broadcast media. Debates about the need for a privacy law and the threat of the introduction of a statutory body to regulate the unruly British press dominated the decade. In the event, the Conservative government decided against legal control of the press and in favor of stronger self-regulation to be championed by the print industry's Press Complaints Commission (Shannon, 2001).

Partisan press coverage was and is the norm in both countries. In Spain during the 1990s, *El País* maintained its support for the Socialist government, *ABC* its conservative and monarchical preferences, and *El Mundo* followed a more liberal line. Up until the 1992 election the British press was largely Conservative. However, withdrawal from the European Exchange Rate mechanism in 1992 saw an ebbing away of press support for the Major government (see Major, 2000, pp. 334-335). Some newspapers returned to the fold in time for the 1997 election, but by this time old allegiances had been broken and even *The Sun* deserted the Conservative camp.

Shifts in broadsheet political journalism, driven in part by television's increasing role as a political news provider since it began televising Parliament in 1989, also produced a more personality-driven form of political journalism: reporting of parliamentary debate all but disappeared and was replaced by parliamentary sketch-writing and more background and speculative pieces (Tunstall, 1996). Political scandal or stories emphasizing division provided the staple political news fare of the 1990s. There is no equivalent in Spain to Britain's tabloid press nor to its Sunday newspapers and their coverage of sexual morality as a fitting subject for scandal. Circulation figures show that the British public enjoys reading about such matters, but the poll figures indicate they don't altogether approve of those who report them (see Sanders, 2003).

Spain's smaller press came to have a highly significant role in breaking corruption stories in the 1990s. The national daily *Diario 16*, which folded in 2001, began to publish articles in 1986 about the possible involvement of the Socialist government in the murders of alleged Basque militants by a shadowy paramilitary group. Its editor was sacked in 1989 and he went on to found *El Mundo* that year, which quickly became the standard bearer of investigative journalism in Spain. *El Mundo*'s sales figures showed that its high-profile scandal coverage attracted increased readership.[5] The Spanish public took these matters very seriously: a survey showed that 75 percent of Spaniards considered the scandals to be the most significant events in terms of their social and political consequences; they were considered more important than the results of the Andalusian and European elections, the economic and employment situation, the reform of the labor market, and the government agreements with other political parties (Fundación Encuentro, 1995, p. 21).

Broadcast Media

The broadcast media presented a more varied picture. The British broadcast media are constrained to impartiality by statutory regulations covering fair and balanced political coverage. The BBC, in particular, has a special duty to provide adequate and fair political coverage and, despite complaints from Conservative spindoctors about its "pro Labour agenda", was considered to have done a reasonable job in the 1990s and continued to be trusted as an impartial news provider by the public.

This, perhaps, provides the biggest contrast with the Spanish media landscape. In the late 1980s, Spanish television moved from being a public monopoly, with only two state channels, to a competitive multichannel system. Although the special duty to provide balanced and fair political coverage also applies to the Spanish public service, TVE1 and TVE2, the public service channels are closely identified with the governing political party (both with PSOE and with PP) and often accused of pro-government bias (Canel & Innerarity 2000; Díez Nicolás & Semetko, 1995; Rospir, 1996; Semetko & Canel, 1997). Between 1982 and the 1996 election, they were perceived by the public to be a mouthpiece for the Socialist government (Rospir, 1996),[6] whereas its main competitor, the private channel *Antena 3*, was perceived to be anti-government (or pro-opposition).

On the whole, the Spanish prefer to watch television: 90.4 percent for TV compared to 36.8 percent for the press, 54 percent for the magazines, and 55.4 percent for radio (Central Media, 1996). In Heywood's (1995a) words, "Whereas newspaper readership has always been low in Spain, with a diffusion rate lower than any other European Union country except Portugal, television has always commanded massive audiences" (p. 130). Television news has also enjoyed high audience figures in part because, as Barnhurst (2000) points out, viewing television news at lunchtime and in the evening is an important ritual of family life.

In the 1990s broadcast outlets expanded in Britain and Spain and this was matched by an increase in the kinds of political news programs politicians could be invited to appear on: breakfast shows, phone-in programs, and, most dangerous of all, Sunday sofa shows in which unwary guests, lulled into a false sense of security, would provide the "gaffe" or "spat" headline so popular with the next day's newspapers. In Britain these kinds of programs began to rival BBC Radio 4's *Today* program as the agenda setter for the elite political debate.

In Spain an important agenda setter is the radio chat-show (from early morning until two p.m.—the Spanish lunch-hour—and at night between ten and midnight). Politicians are often invited to participate by the programs' star presenters, who are opinion leaders in their own right and often the major listener attraction for the radio channel. The "radio and TV breakfasts," in which politicians always participate, set the agenda for other media during the rest of the day.

Journalism Practice

Spanish journalists were rated highly in polls measuring the trustworthiness of different professions. As a comparative study shows, the Spanish media enjoyed the highest scores for credibility of any media in the European Union after Germany (cited in *Anuario El Mundo*, 1998). It seems likely that the more sensational, sex-orientated political reporting in the British press accounted in part for the extremely low scores registered in MORI's "veracity" and "respectability" polls recorded for journalists (Mortimore, 1995). However, polls in Britain continued to show both that the public strongly supported proper investigative journalism of matters of real public interest and that tolerance of the invasion of privacy of every single group included in MORI's survey rose between November 1989 and August 1992, but was highest in the case of politicians (Mortimore, 1995).

As we saw earlier, parliamentary mechanisms of executive control were comparatively weak in the Spanish *Cortes*. In addition, cut and thrust adversarial democratic politics were also less marked than in the British Parliament, where Her Majesty's Opposition enjoys constitutional status. In the latter part of the González era, the opposition role appeared to have been assumed by a section of the press. All the political scandals were revealed by newspapers founded in the democratic era whose journalists were very much seen as the real brake on executive power.

Survey evidence bears this out. It suggests that there is a first generation of Spanish journalists, composed of those who trained and worked during the Franco era, who see the media's role in democracy as contributing to the development and consolidation of the democratic system and its institutions such as the Crown and the executive. They tend to play the part more of advocates than impartial commentators; their work is more interpretive than factual and tends to be more supportive than critical of institutions. A second generation of journalists consists of those who have only worked and trained in the democratic era and whose work is more impartial, factual, and critical than their older colleagues. The survey research suggests that Spanish journalists are moving from a partisan-ideological paradigm towards a more adversarial-apolitical one (Canel & Piqué, 1998, pp. 317-318).

Differences between Spain and Britain are clearly apparent in the traditions and rules surrounding journalists' access to politicians. The peculiar British system of the "lobby," the collective of around 250 officially accredited political journalists with privileged access to Parliament and permission to attend briefings by the prime minister's press secretary provided they abide by "lobby terms" (all the information provided is unattributable), continued its arcane existence into the 1990s, augmented by large numbers of radio and television journalists.[7] The lobby system works on the basis of semiformalized rules governing the relations between journalists and politicians, chief of which is the distinction between on- and off-the-record briefings (Manning, 2001, pp. 120-123). The latter permit reporters to receive a great deal of unattributable information, much of it not much better than gossip and rumor (Cockerell, 1984).

In the 1990s civil servant press secretaries were often no match for the combined expertise and experience of the lobby, and as the decade progressed, it became clear that there were often too many journalists chasing too few stories (Tunstall, 1996, pp. 276-280, and personal interviews). The development of Millbank—studio facilities for the major television companies just opposite Westminster—also fed the need for ever more political stories: the combination of large numbers of lobby journalists and ever-increasing media outlets produced a perfect environment for the work of opposition spindoctors, disgruntled MPs, and former ministers.

In Spain there are around 3,000 journalists accredited to Parliament; the main political correspondents have offices based in the Parliament building and about 100 are in regular attendance. Little research has been done on the development of the reporting of Parliament (Innerarity & Canel, 2000). However, it can be said that the political journalists who cover the *Cortes* have not developed the ritual and strong sense of identity of the British lobby.

In sum, analysis of the media landscape in both countries shows a variegated pattern of some similarities—an increasingly competitive media market, marked partisanship—but distinct and significant differences in, for example, journalistic cultures.

Sleazy Britain

> The corruption across the Channel is of a different order altogether, involving millions, murder, paedophile rings, and includes presidents and prime ministers.

> (Letter to *The Spectator*, 5 February 2000)

In early 1994 a prominent member of the British Conservative government made a highly publicized speech contrasting British "purity" with foreign "corruption" (Adonis, 1997, p. 103). Six years later in a speech to world leaders at Davos, the former American secretary of state, Madeline Albright, stated that corrupt politicians were one of the main threats to democracy. She singled out Italy, Japan, and Britain for special criticism (see Farrell, 2000, p. 10). Britain's reputation for probity was not what it was.

Of course, political scandal is not a new phenomenon in Britain; the sleazy sex scandal exemplified by the Profumo scandal in the early 1960s has never gone out of fashion (Baston, 2000; Parris, 1996). Political corruption was endemic in the country up until the mid-1800s. However, in the Victorian period, a combination of constitutional reform and political changes eliminated most forms of political corruption (Adonis, 1997, p. 112). Events during John Major's years in office from 1990 to 1997 appeared to undermine this Victorian legacy, harkening back to an earlier Hogarthian world of venal, corrupt politics. There were more ministerial resignations than in any other parliament of the last century (Butler & Kavanagh, 1997, p. 16). Three kinds of political scandal characterized Britain during this period (Smith, 1995, p. 6): sexual misdemeanors, misuse of public position for private gain, and abuse of power.

Sexual Misdemeanors. A total of ten Conservative ministers, MPs, and parliamentary candidates were "exposed" in lurid tabloid style for infidelity or other "irregular" sexual practices.[8] The most notorious cases concerned the ministers David Mellor and Tim Yeo and the Conservative parliamentary candidate, Piers Merchant.

David Mellor's infidelity with an actress in July 1992 was the first big political scandal of the newly elected Major government. The minister with responsibility for the media, Mellor famously described his office as the Ministry of Fun. He resigned as minister in September 1992 after further revelations concerning favors received from Palestinian friends made his position untenable.

John Major's "Back to Basics" speech at the Conservative Party Conference in October 1993, despite later protestations that it had nothing to do with private moral values, provided the press with a useful stick to beat errant Conservatives.[9] The first victim was Tim Yeo, Agriculture Minister, who resigned in January 1994 after revelations of infidelity and two illegitimate children. Photographs of a married Piers Merchant, Conservative candidate in the 1997 general election, cavorting with a young girl reinforced the public perception of a louche, hypocritical Conservative Party and allowed the subject of sleaze to dominate the first part of the election campaign (Butler & Kavanagh, 1997, p. 95).

Misuse of Public Position for Private Gain. This was at the root of the two major political corruption scandals, the so-called *Cash for Questions* and Aitken affairs. *Cash for Questions* revealed that a system that depended largely on trust and honor to maintain standards in public life was no match for the temptations proffered by a newly emerging, unregulated American-style lobby industry. A number of Conservative ministers and members of Parliament were found to have broken parliamentary rules by accepting cash to ask parliamentary questions.

The story was first broken in July 1994 by a *Sunday Times* "sting" operation that entrapped two Conservative MPs. *The Guardian*, relying mainly on the revelations of the embittered Harrods owner, Mohammed al Fayed, published in October 1994 more serious allegations concerning the activities of two ministers, Tim Smith and Neil Hamilton (Leigh & Vulliamy, 1997). Both men resigned their office and in 1997 were censured by the Parliamentary Commissioner for Standards, Sir Gordon Downey, on conclusion of his investigation into the matter. Hamilton, however, pursued a libel action with the lobbyist Ian Greer against *The Guardian* newspaper. The action collapsed in October 1996 (Boyd Hunt, 1998; Greer, 1997). Hamilton, continuing to protest his innocence, initiated a second libel action against Mohammed al Fayed, which he lost in December 1999.[10]

The Aitken affair was perhaps the most dramatic of all. Jonathan Aitken, government minister and spoken of as a possible future leader of his Party, ended his career in 1998 serving a jail sentence for perjury. His libel action against *The Guardian's* allegations of corruption collapsed when it was shown that he had lied on oath and had asked his daughter to do so too.

These and other cases led to the establishment of the Nolan Inquiry into Standards in Public Life. Its recommendations resulted in the appointment of an independent Parliamentary Commissioner for Standards, the reform of the Select Committee structure, and the establishment of a permanent independent committee to consider standards of conduct of all holders of public office.

Abuse of Power. This was at the heart of the *Arms to Iraq* scandal. It was a complex tale involving espionage, the Ministry of Defence, illegal equipment sales to Iraq, and allegations concerning the misleading of Parliament, civil service obfuscation and secrecy, and a willingness to see innocent men go to jail rather than expose government deceit about arms sales to Iraq.[11]

Allegations of illegal equipment supply to Iraq surfaced in April 1990 after Customs officials impounded material thought to be destined for the construction of an Iraqi "Supergun." This was against a background of heightened tension between Iraq and Britain after the arrest and summary execution in March 1990 of the Iranian freelance journalist, Farzad Bazoft, working in Bagdad for the *Observer* newspaper on an arms story. Iraq's invasion of Kuwait in the summer of 1990 and Britain's involvement in the operation to remove Saddam Hussein's army from Kuwait in January 1991 gave the Arms to Iraq story added piquancy. The allegation that British companies (Sheffield Forgemasters, Matrix Churchill, Ordtec, BSA Tools) had been illegally supplying equipment to Iraq with the complicity of government departments now had potentially devastating political implications.

The collapse of the prosecution against the engineering company, Matrix Churchill, on 9 November 1992 precipitated the establishment of the Scott Inquiry into U.K. equipment exports to Iraq (Henderson, 1993; Leigh, 1993; Norton-Taylor & Lloyd, 1995; Norton-Taylor, Lloyd, & Cook, 1996). The publication of the Inquiry's report in February 1996 prompted a far-reaching debate about the power of the executive and the culture of secrecy in British government (Scott, 1996; Tomkins, 1998). It did not, however, lead to any Conservative resignations.

After eighteen years of Conservative rule, Major and his government went down to a crushing defeat on 1 May 1997, the worst Conservative result since 1832 when the Duke of Wellington won only 185 seats. Tony Blair and New Labour won 418 seats with a majority of 179 (43.2 percent of the vote). One hundred and sixty five Conservatives (30.7 percent of the vote) were returned to Parliament. Neil Hamilton's defeat by an independent, anticorruption candidate in the fifth safest Conservative seat in the country was the surest indication that political scandal had taken a heavy toll on Major's government.

But what did these political scandals mean? Had the economic and political changes introduced by successive Conservative governments led to the undermining of the underlying ethical consensus concerning the duties of public life? Did this situation represent the wider difficulties of the public sector where the promotion of a business culture had neglected a concern for the promotion of an ethical one (Doig, 1996)? Or did the scandals point to systemic changes in the media where increased competition fuelled a demand for ever more sensationalist stories?

We will return to these questions later. Certainly, events in Britain seemed to give the lie to the view that in Europe there is a divide between more corrupt southern states and their upright northern neighbors (Della Porta & Mény, 1997, p. 2; Heywood, 1997, p. 11).

Corruption in Spain

On 3 March 1996, Spain's charismatic Socialist president, Felipe González, lost the general elections. He had been in power since 1982 and had overseen the development of a vibrant economy and the country's entry into NATO and the European Union. However, he also presided over a government increasingly tainted by a stream of political scandals that undermined the people's confidence in politics and politicians themselves (CIRES, 1997, p. 755; Jiménez, 2004).[12]

The stories began with allegations in 1988 of extravagant spending on expenses by the flamboyant director general of Spanish Public Television (*Radio Televisión Española*) Pilar Miró, followed in 1990 by the more serious charges against Juan Guerra, the brother of the Deputy Prime Minister, Alfonso Guerra, of misuse of party offices for private

gain and of corrupt practices in party finances. He was eventually found guilty in 1992 of tax fraud, fined, and given a suspended one-year jail sentence.

These cases and those that followed became emblematic of a get-rich-quick mentality, the so-called *cultura del pelotazo*, which curiously paralleled British perceptions of the greedy Thatcherite 1980s and sleazy 1990s of the Major years. *Hola!* magazine chronicled the activities of the so-called beautiful people who populated the Socialist world (Heras, 1990; Rivasés, 1991). The scandals that subsequently emerged in Spain were of three kinds: illegal party funding, illicit enrichment, and State terrorism.

Illegal Party Funding. The *Filesa* case centered on the existence of a network of front companies, including the eponymous Filesa, run by two elected representatives of PSOE. The money raised by charging businesses for fictitious consultancy work between 1989 and 1991 was used to finance the Spanish Socialist Party. The case was revealed by a disgruntled former accountant of the company, Carlos van Schouwen, who told his story to *El Mundo* and *El Periódico de Catalunya,* which published it on 29 May, 1991. An official investigation was launched by the high court judge, Marino Barbero. Verdicts were not handed down until 1997 by the Supreme Court and 2001 by the Constitutional Court. Several Socialist Party members received prison sentences.

Illicit Enrichment. Two of the most venerable institutions of Spain, the Civil Guard and the Bank of Spain, were brought into disrepute by the corrupt activities of their respective heads, both appointees of the Socialist government. The governor of the Bank of Spain, Mariano Rubio, was accused of illicit enrichment through illegal insider dealing and misuse of privileged information. Rumors about Rubio had circulated in the press since 1992, after the discovery in the so-called *Ibercorp* case that a number of people had engaged in insider share dealing, falsification of documents and influence peddling in connection with the Bank of Spain and the Economics Minister. In April 1994 *El Mundo* published what proved to be conclusive proof of Rubio's corruption, and of his implication in the *Ibercorp* case, for which he was later sentenced to prison. In January 1997 further charges were brought against Rubio, but his death in October 1999 effectively brought the case to an end.

Luis Roldán was appointed by the Socialist government as the first civilian director-general of the Civil Guard in 1986. His case, brought to light by *Diario 16* on 23 November 1993, became the center point of the many scandals uncovered in Spain in the 1990s (Irujo & Mendoza, 1994). He was accused in 1994 of siphoning off cash from various sources, including the Civil Guard's orphanage and funds reserved for payments to state security agents, to the value of millions of dollars (19,592,994 euros).

His escape from the country to Laos on 27 April 1994 took on a farcical character as he continued to make declarations to *El Mundo*, implicating a number of senior officials and ministers in corrupt activities and, more seriously, accusing them of involvement in state terrorism. He fled to Laos and was eventually arrested in Bangkok. *El Mundo* showed that there were even irregularities in the government's actions in bringing Roldán to justice. He was eventually charged in 1997 and sentenced in 1998 to 31 years of prison for fraud, embezzlement, perversion of the course of justice, falsifying documents, and tax evasion.[13]

There were also charges concerning illegal payments from reserved ministry state funds to two former interior ministers and to a significant number of other ministry officials in October 2004. The Supreme Court ratified the lower court's decision to absolve the two former ministers and to sentence a number of other officials to between four and seven years in prison.

State Terrorism. In 1987 *Diario 16* published information showing a possible link between the terrorist group GAL and the Socialist government. GAL had been acting against ETA since December 1983 and, by the end of its existence, had committed a number of kidnappings, bomb attacks, and 27 murders. Statements by two former policemen and Roldán's revelations in 1994 revealed GAL's links with the Civil Guard and the Interior Ministry. In 1995 a disgruntled official of the Spanish secret service, the *CESID*, leaked papers to the press (giving rise to the *CESID* papers scandal), documenting GAL's activities, including its so-called "founding document", providing evidence of GAL's links to the government.

The GAL is a complex case that includes the kidnapping of Segundo Marey—a businessman with no terrorist connections kidnapped by mistake—(for which the former Interior Minister, José Barrionuevo, and Secretary of State, Rafael Vera, were sentenced to prison in 1998), as well as cases of alleged murder, torture, and kidnapping (Miralles & Arquéz, 1998; Rubio & Cerdán, 1997).

The *Lasa and Zabala* case, which we examine in this book, is also part of the GAL saga. It was one of the most disturbing crimes committed by GAL. In 1995 the remains of José Antonio Lasa and José Ignacio Zabala, suspected members of ETA, were discovered. They had been tortured and horribly murdered by GAL in 1983. In 2001 several policemen were given jail sentences of 73 years and the former civil governor of Vizcaya, Julen Elgorriaga, was sentenced to 75 years for the illegal detention and murder of the two men.

Between 1990 and 1996 two deputy prime ministers (Alfonso Guerra and Narcís Serra) and five ministers resigned or were dismissed. Two other former ministers resigned. Two officials (the director-general of the Civil Guard and the governor of the Bank of Spain) also resigned and were given jail sentences.

In 1996 the Socialist Party lost the elections after fourteen years in government. The conservative victory was, however, a close-run thing, despite all the scandals, the Socialists actually gained 349,460 votes compared to their previous result. However, they won only 141 seats as against their previous 159 with just over one percent less of the vote than the Popular Party, which won 156 seats.

Political scandal became the leitmotif of the Major and González administrations, as it was for a number of other Western governments. And yet if we examine the range of events outlined above, we might legitimately ask what it is that allows us to describe them as political scandal. The *GAL* case and Mellor's infidelity are hardly in the same league. We will discuss this question next.

PUBLIC VICE

Events in Spain and Britain revolved around what one might term the revelation of public vice. As we have seen, this ranged from the misuse of public office for criminal activity, to private actions considered either hypocritical or immoral carried out by public office holders.

Here we will examine the notion of public vice as expressed by the terms "corruption", "sleaze", and "scandal." None of these denote fixed realities. Thinkers from Arendt (1958) to Giddens in his 1999 BBC Reith lectures have alerted us to how the very texture of the world and our understanding of it shift with economic, political, and technological change. More particularly, Giddens underlines why, in a globalized world, the boundaries of what counts as corruption in politics have shifted. In the following section we will examine the explanations developed by scholars of the vocabulary of public vice.

Political Corruption

There is a vast literature on political corruption examining its nature, causes, content, and history (see Garzón Valdés, 1997; Heidenheimer et al., 1997). It has been argued that it is "impossible to develop one generalizable and uncontested definition of political corruption" (Heywood, 1997, p. 6). In part this is because it depends on what one means by politics: to speak of corruption in politics is to have a sense of what "uncorrupt" politics might mean.

Notwithstanding these definitional difficulties, much of the literature has followed Heidenheimer et al. (1997) in differentiating three models for understanding corruption. *Public office*–centered definitions understand corruption as the use of public office for private gain. A second model centers on the theory of the *market,* where corruption is understood as a market mechanism by which individuals or groups seek to maximize their income in circumstances where the norms governing public office are not clear. *Public interest*–centered definitions take the "public interest" to be the key normative reference and understand corruption to be behavior where a power holder charged with doing certain things "is by monetary or other rewards . . . induced to take actions which favor whoever provides the reward and thereby damages the group or organization to which the functionary belongs" (Friedrich, cited in Heidenheimer et al., 1997, p. 15).

At the root of each of these approaches is a question about norms. Of the three categories into which the *Oxford English Dictionary* (1999) groups notions of corruption—as (a) physical or (b) moral corruption or (c) a perversion from an original state of purity—political corruption falls into the second category. Moral standards are at the heart of the matter. But how are they to be defined? Some have claimed that formal legality should be the test. However, definitions based on legal norms are faced with the difficulty that the law varies and fails to capture some of the more subtle aspects of corruption (Heywood, 1996, p. 118).

Another approach to political corruption is to argue that it is socially defined, that a political action is corrupt when public opinion determines it to be. Perception is important but, as Heywood (1977) has shown, this approach has too many difficulties. How do we determine what public opinion is? What happens where there are conflicting views?

Alatas (1990) has produced a typology of political corruption based on a parsimonious definition of corruption as "the abuse of trust in the interest of private gain" (p. 1). He distinguishes between "extortive" corruption, entailing some form of coercion, and "transactive" corruption, where mutually beneficial arrangements between donors and recipients are made that offend accepted notions of trust and public morality. However, it is clear that private gain has not always been at the heart of what has been considered "corrupt" behavior. The *Filesa* case was about party political gain and *Arms to Iraq* and *GAL* concerned the abuse of power. Alatas' definition also assumes that it is possible to distinguish clearly between public and private roles. In some cultures this kind of sharp distinction is not so clear (Rose-Ackerman, 1999). Heywood seems closer to the mark in viewing corruption as an abuse of trust and an attempt to control the political arena through an unaccountable use of power and influence (1996, p. 119).

Many scholars have raised the question as to whether some countries are more prone to corruption than others. Are there cultural or institutional explanations? Cultural explanations have often been advanced in terms of "national character." Institutional explanations have been given greater importance by political scientists. As Heywood (1997) puts it, "Institutional settings breed certain types of relationship and social practice" (p. 11). Institutional change, privatization, party funding, and globalization have all been adduced as factors affecting "opportunity structures" for corruption (Doig, 1996; Heywood, 1996; Nieto, 1997).

Explanations for the apparent prevalence of corruption in parts of Europe have ranged around "disturbances in social equilibria"; new wealth; the arrogance of those with newly acquired power; the rise of social forces, such as the media, creating a virtuous circle involving press, public opinion, the judiciary and the political class; the increased financial needs of political parties; the development of investigative journalism and determined action by the judiciary (Della Porta & Mény, 1997, pp. 3-4; Nieto, 1997). Clearly, each of these factors requires detailed assessment before a definitive answer can be given.

Analyses of political corruption chart one area of public vice. They leave untouched other types of political scandal that were so vividly documented by the media in Britain and Spain. In Britain the whole panorama of public vice in the 1990s was encapsulated by the word "sleaze", a term for which there is no equivalent in Spanish.

Sleaze

Associated with gangster movies and places of ill repute, "sleaze" is defined by the *Oxford English Dictionary* (1999) as a slang term describing something as sordid, squalid, "of inferior quality or low moral standards" or "a person of low moral standards." Its first recorded use was in 1967.

The term was practically unused in Britain until the late 1980s when it came to be used by the British press to describe all manner of wrongful acts on the part of public office holders. As Heywood (1995b) put it, it is an "amorphous concept with inescapably normative connotations" (p. 178).

Different sectors of the British press gravitated towards different types of political scandal story. As we saw earlier, the pattern was for the sexual irregularities to be first covered by the more populist "tabloids" and later picked up by television and the elite market "broadsheets." The weightier corruption stories were championed by the broadsheets. The term "sleaze" itself became a crucial word formula that conveniently brought together a number of discrete acts under one umbrella term; between 1994 and 1995 it was used by the press more frequently than in the previous nine years put together (Dunleavy & Weir, 1995, p. 58).

"Sleaze" became emblematic of the Major era. It was used not only in newspaper articles and headlines but also as a graphic and cartoon feature. As the 1997 election campaign began, Major was shown in the *Times* attempting to escape with fellow ministers from a labyrinth drawn to form the word "sleaze"; during the campaign the *Sun* newspaper featured a Conservative rosette with the ironic words "Vote Sleaze" emblazoned across it. "Sleaze" usefully expressed the idea of a moral shadow land inhabited not by evil men and women but by weak individuals on the make.

UNDERSTANDING SCANDAL

Sleazy and corrupt behavior does not make a political scandal. Political scandals require something extra.

Scandals have an ancient pedigree as indicated by the antiquity of the term "scandal", which can be traced back to Greek, Latin, and early Judaeo-Christian thought (Soukup, 1997). The original Greek terms, the noun *skandalon* and the verb *skandalizein*, referred to a spring-trap for prey, recalling its Indo-Germanic root—*skand* to spring or leap. It was used in a figurative way by the Greek-speaking translators of the *Septuagint*, the Old Testament, to describe a trap, an obstacle, or a cause of moral stumbling.

In this religious context, scandal came to mean a stumbling block placed in someone's path and, by extension, things that lead others astray or make them lose their faith. Scandal was to cause someone to stumble as Christ's words of reprobation make clear: "Whoever causes one of these little ones who believe in me to stumble, it would be better for him. . . ." (Mark 9, 42). St Paul speaks of Christ crucified being "a stumbling block to the Jews and folly to the Gentiles" (I Corinthians 1, 23). In the thirteenth century St. Thomas Aquinas distinguished between active scandal—that given—and passive scandal—that received. He argued that both should be avoided (1964-1973 vol. 35, 2a2ae, 34-46). The *Oxford English Dictionary* (1999) defines scandal in six senses:

1. In a religious context, something that is an occasion of unbelief or a stumbling block to faith or which brings discredit on religion because of the conduct of a religious person.

2. Damage to reputation or rumor injurious to reputation.
3. A person whose conduct is grossly disgraceful or an event or circumstance which is.
4. An offense to moral feeling or sense of decency.
5. Talk concerned with disreputable behavior or imputations of such conduct.
6. In legal terms, an injurious report published about another that may be the foundation of legal action.

More recently, "scandal" has been defined as "the symbolic representation of acts deemed morally reprehensible" (Lull & Hinerman, 1997, p. 2). This seems to draw the net too widely. A court case might be considered symbolically to represent acts deemed morally reprehensible. Scandals do indeed provide part of the symbolic terrain on which social values are rehearsed and teased out and the terms and boundaries of public morality are explored. The medieval morality play has its equivalent in the headlines of the tabloid press. However, it is possible to be more precise than this definition would allow.

Focusing more particularly on political scandal, Markovits and Silverstein have described it as, "The presence of any activity that seeks to increase political power at the expense of process and procedure" (1988, p. 6). This refines the area of discussion. However, it leaves out too much. It is hard to consider the Lewinsky affair as anything other than a *political* scandal and yet it was not about increasing political power. Political scandal implies, too, as Jímenez Sánchez points out, an indignant response to what is perceived as the violation of social norms governing the conduct of those who hold public office (1997, p. 293).

We can think of scandal in two senses. First, an action that violates social norms is a scandal or is scandalous. In this sense, scandal is similar to corruption understood in a broad sense. Second, it refers to the public reaction of indignation, a dimension not included in the term "corruption." Jímenez Sánchez defines political scandal as the "reaction of public opinion to a political agent who is considered responsible for conduct which is perceived as an abuse of power or a violation of social trust upon which the agent's actual or potential position of authority is based" (1997, p. 298). This is a useful starting point for understanding scandal.

Political power's basis in social trust is key to understanding political scandal. In a representative democracy, power is ceded on the basis of trust and accountability and it is precisely these areas that scandal affects. In addition, for scandal to be possible there must be mechanisms that allow its expression. There must be means for public opinion to be formed and expressed. In twentieth century democracies this has been the mass media.

Expressing political scandal through the mass media begins a battle to stigmatize an individual in order to confer an inferior moral status on them (Sherman, 1978). The Durkheimian functional model of scandal argues that scandal reinforces the primacy of certain shared norms and values (Arroyo, 1997, p. 356; Markovits & Silverstein, 1988, p. 2). However, as we shall see in later chapters, scandals are not always functional in this sense. Once battle commences, outcomes are unpredictable. Furthermore, as Jímenez Sánchez points out, many scandals arise in areas of uncertainty about norms (1997, p. 313). Political scandals are best understood, then, as open processes with unpredictable consequences that can only be understood by taking fully into account the cultural, institutional, and temporal contexts in which they occur. They generally consist of a number of elements including the transgression, the phases of revelation, publication, defense, dramatization, prosecution, and labeling, and finally, the consequences for the political system (see Jímenez Sánchez, 1997; Sherman, 1978).

The British sociologist John B. Thompson also takes a nonfunctionalist view of scandal, pointing out that scandals are often messy affairs because they are about norms or values that may be open to debate. For Thompson, "scandals" are "actions, events or circumstances" characterized by five features (1997, pp. 37-48).

First, an initial transgression of social norms and values that typically leads to "second order transgressions," actions taken to conceal the first involving lying, obstruction, and deception. These second order transgressions can come to assume more importance than the original transgression. The paradigmatic case is Watergate[14] and more recent examples include the former British Conservative minister, Jonathan Aitken, imprisoned for perjury. In Spain, the government's alleged payment of 200 million pesetas from security funds to buy the silence of GAL members, Amedo and Domínguez, would be a second order transgression of lesser importance than the original crimes.

Second, nonparticipant knowledge of the transgression, hence the important role of the media.

Third, disapproval of the action. Shock is a rare phenomenon. Most people are either too cynical or more accustomed to the kinds of behavior that, in other times, may have been an occasion for shock. Indeed, the transgressions can sometimes appear to be of token values and norms that people usually consider to play a marginal role in their own lives. When this is so, the transgression can take on a farcical character. This was the case in some of the British sex scandals. In this respect, it is possible to argue that there has been a parting of the ways between political scandals and scandals in their original sense as being not only wrongful acts but also causes of spiritual and moral harm to others.

Fourth, the expression of disapproval. As Thompson puts it, "No responses, no scandal" (1997, p. 44). The response is constitutive of the scandal and takes the form of "opprobrious discourse", language implying that the action is shameful or disgraceful (p. 45), which is articulated in public. Thompson maintains that for a scandal to rise from the level of gossip or rumor, it must transcend private communication between friends and neighbors. However, this is not entirely convincing. We would argue that for scandal to occur, it seems more important that the "opprobrious discourse" reach a certain threshold in terms of numbers and consensus. Certainly the media act as loud-speakers for scandal, and "publicity" is its necessary condition, but this can be achieved just as well by the whole village discussing the adultery of the local vicar as by its appearance on the front page of the daily newspaper. For this reason, we would argue that scandals can exist without the media and thus, that it is not the case that scandal can *only* be understood as a media phenomenon (Arroyo, 1997, p. 355).

Finally, Thompson points out a key feature of scandals that is missing from other accounts; namely, the potential harm to the reputation of a person that the allegation of scandalous behavior can cause. The issue of reputation allows one to understand why scandal or the threat of scandal is of such importance in politics. Reputation is a kind of resource, a symbolic capital, allowing politicians to build up legitimacy, to develop trust among several publics including fellow politicians, the electorate, and media professionals. Politicians must constantly use "symbolic power" to persuade, confront, and influence actions and beliefs (Thompson, 1995, pp. 12-18).

Scandal is so important because it can destroy this resource, which is why scandals are often characterized by struggles for one's name (the Hamilton case), denials (Aitken, various Spanish politicians), appeal to higher values (the GAL case), open confession, or downplaying the importance of the scandal (Clinton's approach on the Lewinsky case). We will explore this aspect of scandals in the next chapter, exploring why the media matter in understanding how political scandals are shaped and their impact upon society.

NOTES

1. There was, however, a notable upsurge of scholarly, political and journalistic interest in the subject during the 1990s in part spurred by Britain's difficult relations with the European Union and the feeling that Britain's constitutional arrangements were in need of modernization (Bognador, 1997; Hennessy, 1995; Marr, 1996). The debate was given added zest by the constitutional

reforms introduced by the Labour Party on its election to government in 1997.

2. The report by Sir Gordon Downey, Parliamentary commissioner, examined allegations that various Members of Parliament had accepted cash for asking questions in Parliament, the *Cash for Questions* affair. The report was subsequently leaked in March 1997 to *The Guardian* newspaper and eventually published in full the following July.

3. John Major was adamant (2000): "I had no involvement in the timing of the report. . . . But the row erupted in the media. We were made to appear evasive and guilty of sharp practice, which we were not. It was a dispiriting little spat, and politics at its worst" (p. 710).

4. The seven newspapers referred to are *El País, El Mundo, ABC, La Razón, Diario 16, El Correo,* and *La Vanguardia.* However, it should be noted that there is a strong regional press market with a circulation of 2.7m (*OJD,* 1997) and that the national figure excludes sports newspapers' readership, which in Spain is extremely high: *Marca* is the best-selling Spanish newspaper, selling nearly 500,000 copies. Spain also has the so-called "prensa del corazon," which deals with the social activities of the rich and famous, and sales amount to 2.2 million (*Anuario El País,* 1998).

5. *El Mundo's* exclusive stories on the Ibercorp and Filesa scandals, its interview with Roldán, when he was a fugitive, the story of his capture, as well as its exclusive on the Cesid papers produced peaks in newspaper sales.

6. Part of the reason of this governmentalization of the public channel is its structural organization. The chief RTVE post of director general (DG) is appointed by the government for a four-your mandate, which expires with the election of a new government. Hiring policy is very linked to the DG, who appoints the four key personnel for the news programs and the heads of various news desks (national, economic, culture, for example). Thus, a change in the government can mean changes in the key posts in the newsroom. This is what happened when the Socialists came to power in 1982 and replaced all those in key positions at TVE. It happened again when the conservative party, *Partido Popular,* came to power in 1996 and again in 2004.

7. Prime Minister Tony Blair's former press secretary, Alastair Campbell, introduced significant changes to the lobby's arrangements. In November 1997 he agreed that briefings could be attributable to the press secretary. He later agreed to the audio taping of the lobby briefings to foreign and specialist correspondents and to have televised American-style press conferences with government ministers.

8. These included the Heritage Minister, who resigned on 22 September 1992; a junior minister, who resigned office on 7 January 1994; another junior minister, who resigned on 11 January 1994 following his wife's suicide allegedly linked to her husband's infidelity. There were further revelations concerning a crop of Conservative Members of Parliament from 1994 to 1996, as well as Conservative parliamentary candidates during the 1997 election campaign.

9. The fuse was provided by this extract from John Major's speech at the October 1993 Conservative party conference: "We must go back to basics.

We want our children to be taught the best; our public service to give the best; our British industry to be the best. And the Conservative Party will lead the country back to these basics right across the board: sound money; free trade; traditional teaching; respect for the family and the law." The detonator came from Tim Collins, Conservative Party press officer at the time, who confirmed a journalist's query that this included going back to moral basics (Major, 2000, pp. 554-555). The "Back to Basics" controversy blew up again in October 2002 with the publication of a former Conservative minister's diaries. Mrs Edwina Currie's revelation that she had had an affair with John Major cast a very different light on his reactions to colleagues' misdemeanors.

10. There was a final bizarre footnote to the Hamiltons' story in the summer of 2001 when they were both the subject of allegations of sexual assault. The police found insufficient evidence to support an investigation and the alleged "victim" was convicted in May 2003 of wasting police time.

11. For critical accounts of the background to the *Arms to Iraq* case see Cowley (1992) and Friedman (1993). The case for the defense is forcefully put by Ian Lang (2002), one of the ministers criticized in the case, in his memoirs.

12. Approval ratings for the government and political parties rose until 1993, fell in 1994 and 1995, and rose marginally in 1996.

13. Roldán was also implicated in *Urralburu* case, which involved the former president of the government of Navarra and secretary of the Navarra Socialists, Gabriel Urralburu, in illegal land estate deals. Urralburu was also later sentenced to prison.

14. "Watergate" was the term given to the series of crimes and misdemeanors that the *Washington Post* helped to bring to light and that contributed to the bringing down of the American President, Richard Nixon, in 1974. See Schudson's (1992) illuminating account of the role of Watergate in the mythology of American journalism.

3

Media Scandals

Communication technologies allow information to be diffused over large areas. This has led scholars to assert that "scandal is always shaped and given force by the technological means through which information is transmitted to the public as news" (Lull & Hinerman, 1997, p. 7). Other authors have also pointed out how technological development has contributed to the phenomenon of media scandals (Castells, 1998; Garment, 1991; Jiménez, 1995; Lang & Lang, 1983; Laporta, 1997; Protess et al., 1991; Sabato, 1993).

Exploring the nature of media scandals requires an examination that goes beyond this basic assumption, looking at the nature of the media, the characteristics of those communicating through the media, and the sort of social relationships that mass media generate.

WHAT IS A MEDIA SCANDAL?

In the previous chapter we discussed the specific criteria that actions or events must meet in order to be regarded as scandalous.

Of the ten criteria proposed by Lull and Hinerman (1997), three deserve a more detailed consideration here. These authors state that for scandal to occur the revelations must be *"widely circulated via communications media* where they are *effectively narrativized into a story* which *inspires widespread interest and discussion"* (p. 13; italics in original).

Thompson (1997) refers to similar criteria when he proposes as a characteristic of scandals that "they [actions or events] are known or strongly believed to occur or exist by individuals other than those directly involved" (p. 39) (he refers to these people as "non-participants"). Scandals imply (a) a degree of public knowledge of the actions or events; (b) a public of nonparticipants who know about them; and (c) a process of making public or making visible through which the actions or events become known by others (p. 43). It is for this reason that "communication media play a crucial role in many scandals" (p. 43).

Thus, scandals first imply *wide and public knowledge* of certain actions or events; and second, this public knowledge is made possible by *processes of communication*. What is the specific element that the media add to political scandals and why do the media have such a powerful role in scandals?

Thompson (1997) suggests three reasons. First, media organizations want to increase their audiences. Put simply, "scandal sells" (p. 49). Scandals provide the sort of stories that have all the needed ingredients to attract audiences. They are vivid and racy, they have drama, they are compelling. Lull and Hinerman (1997) argue in similar terms: "Scandals are entertaining, and as such they are marketable to a much wider audience" (p. 6). Bird's study of the reception of scandal stories by the public offers a similar argument: "Scandal sells newspapers and tabloids, keeps people in front of their televisions, and provides endless opportunities for conversation" (Bird, 1997, p. 99).

Protess et al. (1991) attribute the development of the investigative tradition in American media after Watergate to market considerations, fuelling the drive for Watergate-like scoops, and intensifying the search for news about scandal (pp. 51-52).

But the market, Thompson (1997) says, is not the only factor to account for the affinity between scandal and the media. He suggests two other factors. One is that the rise of mediated scandals is, to some extent, a product of the transformations wrought by the developments in communication media. "Scandals," he says, "are symptoms of a profound set of transformations which extend well beyond the sphere of scandals as such" (p. 49). He speaks of a new form of visibility and publicness in the modern world, something for which the media have created new opportunities, as well as new problems and risks for political leaders.

The second factor is the capacity that the media have to fix symbolic content. Thompson argues that "by using technical media of communication—paper, photographic film, electromagnetic tape, digital storage systems, etc.— the contents of symbolic exchange can be fixed or preserved in a relatively durable fashion" (p. 52).

New forms of visibility and the fixing of symbolic content are two elements made possible by the media. Thompson suggests they merit further study in order to understand more clearly the close relationship between scandals and the media. This will be our task in this chapter.

THE VISIBILITY OF POLITICAL LEADERS

The notion of visibility of a political leader has to do with the relationship that any leader needs to establish with his/her followers in order to gain support from them. This support is mainly based on credibility. If leaders want to be followed, they need to be trusted. Reputation becomes thus a kind of resource. Being a leader requires one to look after one's own reputation, for which it is important to be known, heard, and viewed by those from whom one seeks support. The role of the leader's visibility has become the focus of attention of studies that examine how power emerges in the relationship between leaders and the led.

Richard Neustadt (1960) was one of the first scholars to explore presidential power in terms of the personal characteristics of the political leader. He understood presidential power as the personal capability that the president has to influence, understanding this power to be distinct from charm or reasoned argument. Presidential power is the power to persuade; it is the ability that the president has to bargain with his/her counterparts (pp. 101-125). Neustadt's thinking offered not so much a structural as a more personal and dynamic approach to explain presidential leadership. But in his time television communication was just beginning, and leaders were less visible (Smith & Smith, 1994, p. 3). The targets of presidential persuasion that Neustadt had in mind were restricted publics such as congressmen and women, judges, party officials, and other members of Washington's elite.

A large number of scholars have subsequently focused the study of presidential power on the persuasive abilities of the leader (Campbell & Jamieson, 1990; Denton & Hahn, 1986; Edwards, 1983; Lowi, 1985; Smith, 1983; Smith & Smith, 1985; Tulis, 1987). These studies move away from Neustadt in the sense that they look at the leader's followers in terms of mass publics that have resulted from the development of televisual communication. They center on the tools that the president has to look after his/her reputation. Lowi (1985), for instance, argues that presidents are elected on the basis of personal popularity, and concentrates on rhetoric as a political tool.

An important set of studies has approached the relationship between the political leader and mass publics going beyond a rhetorical perspective and focusing on broader communication issues such as politicians' relationships with journalists, image construction, and the opening up of the sites from which political leaders communicate to their constituencies (Blumenthal, 1980; Cockerell, 1988; Cook, 1998; Denton & Holloway, 1996; Grossman & Kumar, 1981; Kernell, 1986/1993; Kurtz, 1998; Roncarolo, 1994; Seymor-Ure, 1982; Smith & Smith, 1994).

Kernell's (1986/1993) approach to the visibility of political leaders is a necessary reference point, for he is one of the first scholars to identify the negative consequences that political visibility can have. He argues that American politics has evolved from an institutional pluralism to an individualized pluralism, that protocoalitions (coalitions mainly between congress groups) have weakened and diversified, and the main target whose support must be enlisted is the mass public. In this forum, the president is the one who can best attract supporters, and it is with the mass public (and not restricted publics like Congress) that he/she needs to establish his/her popularity. Therefore, in Kernell's well-known phrase, "presidents go public." Going public is a strategy whereby presidents promote themselves and their policies by appealing directly to the public.

The need of the leader of the country to look for public support has led to what Blumenthal (1980) has called "the permanent campaign", a phenomenon that has turned governing into perpetual campaigning. "The permanent campaign is the political ideology of our age," combining "image-making with strategic calculation"; it refashions "government into an instrument designed to sustain an elected official's public popularity" (p. 7). This permanent campaign has brought political consultants into the very core of the political system and has made the parties weaker in contrast with a stronger media.

Much has been written about the impact of a "public president" engaged in a "permanent campaign" on the political system. Iyengar and Reeves (1997) argue that election campaigns have been extended to the whole governing period, encouraging the candidate (the president, once the election has been run) to acquire media skills. Media strategies work; elected officials who enjoy a high level of public approval are more powerful. As a consequence, political leadership has become a leadership of media-based strategies (p. 320). This effect is described in similar terms by Kernell (1997) when he argues that as a consequence of the public president, the bargaining environment has been undermined and the ability to generate popular support has become the key for leadership: "Going public renders the president's future influence ever more dependent upon his ability to generate popular support for himself and his policies. The degree to which a president draws upon public opinion determines the kind of leader he will be" (p. 326).

The parameters for the relationships between political leaders and those who are led had changed by the end of the twentieth century. The evolution from restricted to mass publics has created a new notion of leadership in which the struggle for name and reputation among followers operates in a different way, introducing a new form of visibility.

NEW MEDIATED VISIBILITY
AND POLITICAL PERSONALITIES

A number of scholars have discussed how the communication media have transformed the spatial and temporal organization of social life (Castells, 1998; Giddens, 1991; Thompson, 1995). In contemporary Western society most individuals derive their knowledge of major events not from direct personal experience (or from the personal experience of others), but from the products of the media industries such as books, newspapers, films and television programs. There is a distance between the producer and the recipient of this information. When we read the newspaper or watch a television program we do not share a locale nor usually the time frame with those producing the message. Consumption of media products, Thompson (1995) states, presupposes "a kind of space-time interpolation which involves imaginary as well as real space-time, and . . . viewers are continuously and routinely engaged in negotiating the boundaries between them" (p. 95).

Thompson (1995) has described this relationship between producers and their recipients as one of "mediated quasi-interaction" (pp. 82-87), differing from face-to-face communication, where there is copresence of participants and a genuine dialogical relationship; one person says something and another can immediately react. In this sort of communication reflexivity and reciprocity are instantaneous. Also, in face-to-face interaction symbolic cues are shared in order to interpret messages transmitted by others. When I am talking to somebody I accompany my words with movements of hands or of eyebrows, which help my interlocutor to understand what I am saying.

Mediated quasi-interaction creates new kinds of bonds between people, which Thompson describes in the following terms:

> Individuals are linked together in a process of communication and symbolic exchange. It is a structured situation in which some individuals are engaged primarily in producing symbolic forms for others who are not physically present, while others are involved primarily in receiving symbolic forms produced by others to whom they cannot respond, but with whom they can form bonds of friendship, affection or loyalty. (1995, pp. 84-85)

Mediated quasi-interaction is characterized, then, by an "extended availability of information and symbolic content in space and/or time"; by "a certain narrowing of the range of symbolic cues by comparison with face-to-face interaction"; by "symbolic forms (that) are produced for an indefinite range of potential recipients"; and by a "monological character" (the flow of communication of mass media is predominantly one way) (Thompson, 1995, p. 84).

Writing on the cusp of change, Thompson's characterization of the *monological* nature of this kind of communication is somewhat dated. Nevertheless, despite the ability of the Internet and other digital technology to allow interactivity, Thompson's description of this as "quasi-interaction" still holds true.

What are the components of this interaction? Thompson (1995) speaks of producers, recipients, the production context, and reception.

First, the producers. As producers of communication content, politicians can be seen and heard, but usually they can neither see nor hear the recipients. They are personalities with whom recipients can sympathize or empathize; they can be liked or disliked, detested or revered (Thompson, 1995, p. 99). Political leaders are producers when they give speeches, perform at public ceremonies, appear in press conferences, participate in the group photograph at a summit of world leaders. They try to put their message across through the media in order to get closer to those from whom they need support. But they don't know the context and conditions in which their message is being received. They cannot even have precise and accurate feedback about whether and how much they are liked. The political leader as producer of communication media content is, to a great extent, uncertain about the effects of his/her communication.

Second, the recipients. Recipients can see and hear producers without usually being seen or heard by them. They are anonymous and invisible spectators (they can be pleased or persuaded, entertained or informed) of a performance to which they cannot contribute directly. But without them that performance would not exist (Thompson, 1995, p.

99). In this sense, recipients of political leaders' messages have a certain power: they are the target of the leader's attention and can scrutinize the leader's activities. The people can thus see the leader of the nation practicing sport, crying at a catastrophe, making gaffes in a public ceremony, or hesitating at unexpected and aggressive questions.

Third, the context of production will significantly mold the nature of this interaction. For example, undercover camera work provides a very different interpretive context from the transmission of media events. Media events are defined by Dayan and Katz (1994), who first analyzed the notion, as reverently staged, exceptional, preplanned occasions, which are broadcast live to massive audiences and which celebrate reconciliation, not conflict. Papal visits, royal weddings, Olympic games, or State funerals are media events. Occasionally during media scandals, events can occur that have the symbolic strength of media events. The address of a president after a process of impeachment has started, a televised trial in which a high official is involved, or the performance of a prime minister at Question Time reacting to an exposé are events of high symbolic meaning which can become turning points in the development of a scandal. The media are agents of legitimization or, *pace* Dayan and Katz (1994) who argue that media events always "*integrate* societies in a collective heartbreak and evoke a *renewal of loyalty* to the society and its legitimate authority" (italics in the original, p. 9), the contrary can occur. It can be argued that Princess Diana's funeral in 1997 was one such occasion (Sanders & Harrison, 2001).

Finally, Thompson refers to the context of reception and responsive action in distant contexts. In receiving media messages, individuals routinely orient themselves towards space-time coordinates that differ from those characteristic of their contexts of reception, and interpolate mediated space-time coordinates into the spatial-temporal framework of their lives (Thompson, 1995, p. 93). When I read the newspaper I am having access to something that has happened at least several hours before. Through media content I can also have access to countries I have never been to. Recipients, through media content, become travellers of extended space-time coordinates (pp. 91-92).

As a consequence, individuals, both producers and recipients, are linked together in a process of communication and symbolic exchange. If it is true, as we saw, that mediated quasi-interaction narrows the range of symbolic cues, it is also true that mediated quasi-interaction is richer in symbolic terms: the media use flashbacks, voice-over, or archival material that can refer to and evoke absent meanings. Flags, official uniforms, emblems, standards, and so on play a very important role in the interpolation of the time-space coordinates of the recipients and of the producers.

NEW VISIBILITY, POWER AND MEDIA SCANDALS

However—and this is a conclusion offered by several scholars—mediated visibility is a double-edged sword (Canel, 1999; Cornwell, 1966; Denton & Hahn, 1986; Denton & Holloway, 1996; Smith, 1996; Smith & Smith, 1994; Thompson, 1995). It has advantages and disadvantages. Political leaders have in the media the platform to reach more extended publics than in the past. But at the same time the mediated arena of modern public life is more open and subject to public scrutiny. It becomes a source of new risks:

> The visibility created by the media may become the source of a new and distinctive kind of fragility. However much political leaders may seek to manage their visibility, they cannot completely control it; the phenomenon of visibility may slip from their grasp and, on occasion, work against them. (Thompson, 1995, p. 141)

The exercise of political power today takes place in an arena that is increasingly open to public view. The "public president" who is engaged in a "permanent campaign" has become a continuous presence, literally constantly in the public eye.

In this atmosphere the reputation of the leader becomes vulnerable. Here lies the scope for scandal. Instead of generating bonds of friendship and loyalty, scandals cause politicians to lose their reputation and, consequently, relationships between political leaders and the people are pervaded with distrust. It is this potential for damage to the reputation of the leader that makes the media so powerful in scandals. This is why management of visibility has become the main aim of the communication strategies of political institutions. Strategies move from disclosure of information to secret keeping.

We can conclude that the relationships between political leaders and the people now operate in an intensified mediated field of interaction, and this is one of the reasons the media have such power to create scandal.

MEDIA SCANDAL NARRATIVES

Once a scandal begins to emerge, a whole process of mediated communication unfolds. This process, which consists of a set of subsequent revelations, reactions, accusations, and defenses, has a very specific characteristic: facts and events *are told* by journalists. Thus *stories are created* and reported following narrative codes.

Narrative "is the organization of material in a chronologically sequential order and the focusing of the content into a single coherent story, albeit with subplots" (Stone, 1979, p. 3). In explaining narratives most scholars tend to underline the idea that narratives involve organizing actions and happenings into a coherent whole with an inner logic that gives meaning to and explains each of its elements (Abbott, 1990; Bird & Dardenne, 1988; Griffin, 1992, 1993; McCullagh, 1978; Stone, 1979; White, 1984). As Griffin puts it, "Narratives are made up of the raw materials of sequences of social action, but are defined and orchestrated by the narrator to include a particular series of actions in a particular temporal order for a particular purpose" (1993, p. 1097).

Is journalism narrative? To grant journalism the status of narrative is not uncontroversial; it might more easily be considered as chronicle. However, there is a solid corpus of literature that shows that news writing follows common narrative codes (Cook, 1996; Fairclough, 1995; Roeh, 1989; Schudson, 1995a; Zelizer, 1992).

Roeh (1989) understands journalists' work within the context of human expression and suggests that news writing is, in essence, storytelling. He supports other scholars' assumptions that "journalists' stories of the real are constructions of meanings, and they seek, as all narratives do, to establish meaningful closure of moral significance. At the same time they also obey most of the same laws and codes of story telling" (p. 165). News writing, Roeh asserts, is pegged to old conventions of storytelling (p. 167).

It is this understanding of journalists as storytellers that leads Cook (1996) to put limits on the "indexing theory", which claims that "mass media news professionals, from the boardroom to the beat" tend to "index" the range of viewpoints represented in news and editorials according to the range of views expressed in mainstream government debate about a specific issue (Bennett, 1990, p. 106). Journalists, Cook explains, "assemble *stories* and focus their attention on fashioning a quality story from the material they receive" (p. 473). He extends the notion of news narratives beyond daily narratives, because stories are visualized by journalists as part of a broader story line, which allows them to move the plot along from one episode to the next. Therefore, Cook concludes, to index the political elite opinion is just one news value that competes with other values such as production values or storytelling codes. As a result, "the storytelling imperative may then push the news in directions that may not be so easily controlled from on high" (p. 478).

To look at the journalist as a storyteller, embedded in a cultural tradition of storytelling, with a number of core assumptions or tacit platforms of understanding about the world means taking what Schudson

(2000) has called a cultural approach to the sociology of news production. As he puts it, "The 'routines' of journalists are seen not only as being social (emerging out of interactions among officials, reporters, and editors) but literary, emerging out of interactions of writers with literary traditions" (p. 193). In an earlier piece Schudson (1995a) discusses what looking at news as a form of culture means. It implies, he says, looking at how journalists' work draws on and depends on particular cultural traditions, which brings into the analysis shared values among journalists. "News as a form of culture incorporates assumptions about what matters, what makes sense, what time and place we live in, what range of considerations we should take seriously" (p. 85).

Zelizer (1992) argues that the sense of community among journalists is not based on formal professional codes but on journalistic practice, and that journalism is an "interpretive community" that uses narratives and collective memories to keep itself together. In Zelizer's words:

> Through narrative, the role of the individual, the organization/institution, and the structure of the profession become key factors in delineating the hows and whys of journalistic practice. Through shared narrative lore, reporters are able to espouse collective values and notions that help them maintain themselves as an authoritative interpretive community. (p. 9)

Understanding media coverage as a form of narrative opens up a broader approach in which the dynamics of media scandals are better grasped.

COMPONENTS OF MEDIA SCANDAL NARRATIVES

Scandals provide compelling stories that serve as a hook for media audiences.

The dynamics of the creation of a scandal story have been well described by Protess et al. (1991). The first phase is for "the convergence of several factors . . . necessary to drive a nascent story forward. Allegations of wrongdoing tend to rise in salience when they appear to be credible, potentially provable, in sync with competitive realities, and to maximize the possibilities for personal, professional, and societal gain. Others may flounder or fall off the investigative agenda" (p. 210). Once the story is on the agenda, ". . . journalists begin a search for meaning: What is this story really about? This implies conceptualizing the story, thinking about the story line: who is implied, what is the cause for action, who is responsible for what and so on" (p. 211).

To narrate the story, journalists try to create a coherent whole, ordering facts and events within a cogent logic of space and time. But that logic has to be adjusted to the rhythms of media production. Events are thus framed in the media. As Thompson (1997) explains, "as events which are shaped by and played out in the media, scandals take on the character of stories. They follow the rhythms of newspapers' publications or televised hearings; new hypotheses suddenly emerge" (p. 53). Media scandals gradually tend to cohere into a story as they develop, so that after a while, the public recognizes the central narrative associated with the specific scandal.

The process of reporting scandal can be long and complex. Reporters might find that their information cannot be confirmed, and the story might lose salience; a story might need to be reconceptualized as new information is received. Journalists move under the pressure of searching for evidence and keeping alive the audience's interest in the story. As Bird (1997) explains, what results is more "a news story" than "news reporting."

In media scandal stories characters are created and qualities attributed. Stories have plots with turning points; they receive a specific temporal order to construct a coherent whole. "In their coverage of events and individuals, journalists can provide narrative accounts which uncover the 'who' of action, expose the agent in the public sphere, confer a coherence deserving to be recounted and assure the immortality of reputation" (Sanders & Harrison, 1998, p. 1). In order to understand how the media frame scandals, we will look at the components of media scandal stories.

First, the *characters*. News stories are often personalized. This is even truer for scandal stories. "With media narrative, the story which frames the scandal, populates it with characters, gives it a structure and longevity" (Lull & Hinerman, 1997, p. 3). Protess et al. (1991) suggest that in order to create compelling stories and to give them a coherent meaning characters are identified in terms of villains (investigative targets) and victims (accusers or expert witnesses) (p. 10).

The following cast of characters of a political scandal story is typical: (a) elected officials who may be held accountable according to the legal requirements of their office and the moral principles of public service; (b) political office seekers whose public and private integrity may be challenged; (c) government bureaucrats expected to administer programs properly and enforce regulations in their domains; (d) business executives whose commitment to corporate responsibility may be tested; and (e) an array of victims, including taxpayers, voters, and consumers, who expect their public and private services to be delivered with honesty, efficiency, and fairness.

Second, the *plot*. "By identifying who is protagonist and who is antagonist, journalists then have a storyline to follow, and off they go, until the storyline is resolved, or stalls or is interrupted by these actors shifting their activities to a newer story" (Cook, 1996, p. 477). Scandal stories are even more complex, because they may have no closure.

The plot is related, thirdly, to *drama*. In preparing an investigative story the journalist needs to allow the audience to make clear inferences about who is to be blamed for what. As Protess et al. (1991) argue, there is little room for ambiguity in painting pictures of villainy and victimization. The task is to present as many examples of pure venality as time or space will allow. Loaded language is used to characterize the wrongdoing for viewers or readers, even before its manifestations are presented. Scandal narratives are full of terms such as "corrupt", "wasteful", "greedy", "lazy", and "scandalous."

The drama, in media scandal stories, is, fourthly, *moral drama*. "The scandal story, above all, interrogates morality" (Bird, 1997, p. 107) Media scandal stories establish patterns of what is acceptable and what is not; correct or illicit behavior is identified. "Scandalous celebrities . . . become even more the property of the public. People feel free to speculate about the most personal aspects of their lives, using them as props to work out their own moral codes" (Bird, 1997, p. 116).

As a result media scandal stories become the center of public attention and news scandal stories become morality tales. Wrongdoers are stigmatized; the standard of what is correct and what is not is delineated. As Bird (1997) explains:

> Scandal stories, like other tales, bring changing mores into sharp focus through media narratives and the popular discussion that takes off from those narratives. Media scandals help set the agenda for discussion, but they do not exist as some definable text separate from the wider cultural conversation. Thus the biggest media scandals are open texts: they draw some lines about morality, but they do not answer all the questions. (p. 114)

FRAMING IN MEDIA NARRATIVES

A story has its characters, its plot, its drama. The question now becomes how do all these elements take on "a form" in the media, how are they shaped in the media, or, as communication research would have it, how are they framed by the media?

Research into the notion of framing is diffuse and has attracted the attention of scholars from a number of different disciplines. Reese argues that it attracts so much interest because "it is a helpful analytical approach which opens a field of analysis of how issues are constructed, discourse structured, and meanings developed" (Reese, 2001, p. 7).

In short, framing is concerned with the way the world is understood. Referring to the media, the notion has been used to express how journalists understand events and issues and explain them to their audiences.

The notion of frame was first used in sociology, in the field of research into social movements. The sociologist Erving Goffman (1974) is regarded as the first to introduce it, together with the anthropologist-psychologist Gregory Bateson (1972) (Reese 2001, p. 7). Referring to the way messages are received, Bateson used the concept of frame to refer to the context of interpretation: when processing reality, people pay attention to some aspects whereas others are ignored (Bateson, 1972). Goffman (1986) uses Bateson's idea of frame to explain how reality is mentally organized: "I assume that definitions of a situation are built up in accordance with principles of organization which govern events—at least social ones—and our subjective involvement in them; frame is the word I use to refer to such of these basic elements as I am able to identify" (p. 10). What Goffman was trying to do was to describe what a person does when he or she asks the question "What's going on?"

From a sociological perspective, theorists of social movements took Goffman's notion of framing and suggested that social movements contribute to frame collective demands (Gitlin, 1980; Tarrow, 1997; Zald, 1999). As a consequence, interest in framing moved from a focus on individual experiences to an examination of collective frames. Within this context media frames began to be looked at from the perspective of their effects on audiences. The media were here seen as powerful agents in the processes of framing social discourse (Tarrow, 1997). Analysis proceeded along the lines of an exploration of which frame predominated in the "battle" among different frames in the media.

Framing and frames have been applied to communication research in many very different ways. Without trying to offer an exhaustive map of research, we will explain the main areas to which the idea of framing refers. What is common to them is that framing research explores how the media frame an issue or a problem and how this affects people's understandings of that issue.

Definitions of framing and frame refer, first, to *the idea of selection*. Framing is a result of inclusion and exclusion of contents. "To frame, Entman (1993) explains, "is to select some aspects of a perceived reality and make them more salient in communicating a text, in such a way as to promote a particular problem definition, causal interpretation, moral evaluation, and/or treatment recommendation for the item described" (p. 52). Tankard et al. (1991) say that a frame "suggests what the issue is through the use of selection, exclusion, and elaboration" (p. 5). For Entman (1993) frames "call attention to some aspects of reality while obscuring other elements, which might lead audiences to have different reactions" (p. 55).

Second, most definitions have to do with *the way things are understood* or, more precisely, mentally organized. A frame has thus been associated with the notion of schemata: "The schemata of interpretation which are labeled frames enable individuals to locate, perceive, identify, and label" (Goffman, 1974/1986, p. 21). Within this perspective the role of reality organization is attributed to the frame: A frame is a "central organizing idea or story line that provides meaning" (Gamson & Modigliani, 1987, p. 143). In a later piece, Gamson and Modigliani (1989) refer to frame as an interpretive package. They claim that every policy issue has a culture where the discourse evolves and changes over time and provides interpretive packages: "A package has an internal structure. At its core is a central organizing idea, or frame, for making sense of relevant events, suggesting what is at issue" (p. 3).

Third, the idea of the *context of an issue* has also been related to the notion of frame. According to Meyer:

> A frame refers to both the constitutive elements of an issue around which details are built, and the borders of discourse of the issue. Frames define which elements of an issue are relevant in public discourse, which problems are amenable to political action, which solutions are viable, and which actors are credible or potentially efficacious. (1995, p. 175)

Or as Rachlin more straightforwardly puts it, "fundamental assumptions will be identified that serve to provide the 'frames' or contexts within which the events are presented" (Rachlin, 1988, p. 3).

Fourth, applied to newsmaking, the frame is seen as the *story line*, an angle, or news judgment. The essence of news judgment, according to Tiffen (1989), are story frames or angles. A story angle or story line "which transforms an occurrence into a new event, and that, in turn, into a news report, is a frame" (Mendelson, 1993, p. 150). Tankard et al. (1991) describe a frame as "a central organizing idea for news content that supplies a context and suggests what the issue is through the use of selection, exclusion, and elaboration" (p. 5). As a consequence of news judgments, news frames "describe attributes of the news itself. . . . News frames are constructed from and embodied in the keywords, metaphor, concepts, symbols and visual images emphasized in a news narrative" (Entman, 1991, p. 7).

Gitlin (1980) links the concept directly to the production of news discourse by saying that frames "enable journalists to process large amounts of information quickly and routinely [and to] package the information for efficient relay to their audiences. . . . Media frames are persistent patterns of cognition, interpretation, and presentation, of selection, emphasis and exclusion, by which symbol-handlers routinely organize discourse" (p. 7).

Definitions refer, in general, to how things are understood by an individual and to how journalists recount them to others. Both cognitive and societal elements need to be taken into account. But studies have tended to concentrate either on the psychological perspective or on the sociological one. This difference has been mapped by Pan and Kosicki (1993). Sociological studies are likely to analyze qualitatively the news content and infer its effects on the audience members or some interest groups (Takeshita, 1997, p. 24). In this group Gitlin (1980), Gamson (1989), Goffman (1974/1986), and Gamson and Modigliani (1987) are included. The second area of research is based on a psychological perspective and focuses on the effects of message framing on the audience members. According to Pan and Kosicki (1993):

> This is a constructionist conception of framing that makes strong assumptions about individual cognitive processes-structuredness of cognitive representations and theory guidedness of information processing. These are the same assumptions that are shared or investigated by cognitive psychologists or other cognitively oriented researchers using similar terms. Within the same psychological approach, framing is viewed as placing information in a unique context so that certain elements of the issue get a greater allocation of an individual's cognitive resources. An important consequence of this is that the selected elements become important in influencing individuals' judgements or inference making. (pp. 56-57)

Kahneman and Tversky (1984) and Tversky and Kahneman (1990) have worked in this tradition (Amadeo, 1999; Takeshita, 1997).

Pan and Kosicki (1993) have tried to integrate both these perspectives. They view news texts as "a system of organized signifying elements that both indicate the advocacy of certain ideas and provide devices to encourage certain kinds of audience processing of the texts" (pp. 55-56). They understand the domain in which the news discourse operates as consisting of shared beliefs about society:

> These beliefs, despite the elusive nature of their content, are known to and accepted by a majority of the society as common sense or con-

ventional wisdom. . . . They are pervasive and are often taken for granted. They set the parameters of a broad framework within which news discourse is constructed, transmitted, and developed. (1993, p. 57)

They stipulate a much wider framework for news discourse that involves not only the cognitive activities of the players in the process but also the social and cultural contexts in which these players operate.

TOWARDS A DEFINITION OF FRAMING
FOR A CULTURAL ANALYSIS

Reese's definition of a frame is a useful step forward in the task of integrating both the psychological and the sociological perspectives of framing. He tries to bridge the critical, qualitative, and ideological perspectives and the behavioral, content, audience, and effects tradition. From a normative and ideological standpoint, he regards framing as an exercise in power, and concentrates particularly on how it affects our understanding of political issues. He defines frames as *"organizing principles* that are socially *shared* and *persistent* over time, that work *symbolically* to meaningfully *structure* the social world" (2001, p. 11; italics in original).

Reese's definition could be summarized as follows:

Organizing: Frames make the world coherent; they structure meaning.

Principles: Below the surface there is a generating principle that produces one way of framing a story; a frame is an abstract "schemata" of interpretation that works through media texts.

Socially shared: Frames are embraced because they are idiosyncratic or culturally and deeply accepted.

Persistent over time: Frames continue to be used, because they provide a structure that satisfies some important need.

Work symbolically: Frames operate through symbolic devices.

Meaningfully structure the social world: To frame is more than just an act of inclusion or exclusion; it is structuring of meaning. Frames impose a pattern on the social world.

This definition is extremely useful. First, it combats the view of framing as a mere process of selection. It goes beyond the idea of agenda-setting that understands the definition of reality as a matter of competition among issues, inherited from the notion of gate-keeping. Even what has been called the "second level of agenda-setting" (where the focus is shifted to the "attributes" of issues) (McCombs & Evatt, 1995)[1] is a perspective that depends on an analysis of frames (attributes) selected versus those that are not.

However, the essence of framing is not only about selection but also inclusion and exclusion. In our view Reese is right to argue that the way reality is understood and explained to others refers to something that goes beyond what is said as against what is left unsaid. When understood in this way, certain ways of attributing meanings are missed. An absent content is not salient but can be evoked by manifest content and thus can be more effective than what is presented to us. For example, the coverage of candidates' standing in the polls can evoke the idea of a battle or competition. Thus, the most important frame may not be the most frequent (and the most selected). As Reese says: "The positive, behavioral measures of frames based on manifest content, don't capture the tensions among expressed elements of meanings, or between what is said and what is left unsaid" (2001, p. 8).

Second, Reese's definition provides an understanding of framing that integrates the psychological perspective with the sociological one. "Principles that are socially shared that work symbolically" refer to the cultural dimension by which some individual's perception of a reality can be embraced by others. Frames can use resonant cultural codes such as historical or identity associations. As we shall see, when looked at cross-nationally, frames of media scandal narratives speak to us of different cultures.

Our difficulty with Reese's definition refers to the statement that "[frames] meaningfully structure the social world." In a certain sense this is true. However, we do not share the constructivist view of reality that is here implied.

What frames do, in using symbolic devices (such as metaphors, examples, catch phrases, depiction, visual images), is something that is very close to what a metaphor does. A metaphor is a figure of speech in which a word or phrase is applied to something to which it is not literally applicable. It is a thing regarded as symbolic of something else. A metaphor describes something in terms of another concept. What frames do, then, is not organize, but resume, condense, or represent wider (and absent) meanings. In doing so, a frame implies judgment of something, which at the same time makes sense of it.

Therefore, we propose a definition of frame, which will be applied in the empirical analysis of chapters 6 and 7, as *manifest content (including symbolic devices) that can evoke absent content and that, by making use of resonant cultural codes, implies judgment of something to make sense of the social world.*

NOTES

1. For discussion of the second dimension of agenda-setting and framing, see McCombs and Ghanem (2001). They argue that "frames are attributes that characterize the dominant traits of an object and are the central theme of a particular message" (p. 79) and thus there is a conceptual convergence between the second level of agenda-setting and framing. Maher (2001), on the other hand, considers this to be a narrow view of framing, and that "agenda-setting theorists are borrowing a limited subset from the overall concept of framing" (p. 90).

4

The Storytellers

Journalists and their Sources

The principal tellers of political scandal stories in both Britain and Spain were newspaper men. In analyzing the dynamics of press coverage of political scandals, it is important not to lose sight of their role. In this chapter we will examine who they were, the assumptions they brought to their task, the methods they employed to obtain their stories, and their relationship to sources. We draw on evidence from interviews, memoirs, and content analysis—what Schleslinger and Tumber have described as "internalist" evidence (1994, p. 26)—to provide an account of the relationship between journalists and their sources in covering political scandal stories. In chapter 5, we will consider source strategies—"externalist" evidence—in the reporting of scandal.

THE STORYTELLERS

Reporters and Editors

Despite the displacement of much investigative journalism to television (De Burgh, 2000, p. 51), all the major political scandal stories in Britain and Spain were first broken by newspapers. Each scandal story was identified with a particular publication, either because the story was first published there or because the newspaper paid special attention to its coverage. In Britain *The Guardian* was the paper of *Cash for Questions* (even though it was *The Sunday Times* that broke the original *Cash for Questions* story on 10 July 1994) and, with *The Independent*, devoted most attention to the *Arms To Iraq* story (although the Sunday newspapers— *The Sunday Times* and *The Sunday Telegraph*—provided key parts of the story). Sex scandals were the speciality of the tabloids: the Mellor and Piers Merchant stories were broken by *The Sunday People* and Yeo's indiscretions were chronicled first in *The News of the World*.

In Spain all the scandal stories were broken in *Diario 16* and *El Mundo*. *Diario 16* was the first to report on the *Roldán* and *GAL* scandals. Journalists working on *GAL* then moved to *El Mundo*, where they and others proceeded to investigate the remaining cases examined in this book: *Lasa and Zabala*, the *CESID Papers* and the *Rubio* case. *Diario 16*, together with *El Mundo* for some parts of the story, investigated the *Roldán* case, breaking exclusive stories such as the announcement of his unaccounted-for wealth, the interview with the former head of the Civil Guard when he escaped from Spain, and the inconsistencies in the Spanish government's account of his capture in Laos.

Political scandal stories tend to be high profile and high risk. The legal, political, and ethical complexities surrounding them mean that the newspaper editor will be the key decision maker on whether to go with a story. In Britain at least, the trend has been towards a more dominant pattern of editorship (Tunstall, 1996, pp. 116-135). One of the key points about scandal coverage was the existence or nonexistence of editorial support. Time and again British and Spanish journalists pointed out in interviews that at moments of crisis it was the editor's support that made the difference. As one journalist said about Pedro J. Ramírez, editor first of *Diario 16* and then of *El Mundo*, "I don't believe a journalist could have a better editor. . . ; he's extremely demanding, a pain in the neck. He's continually pressurizing you. He follows the big stories in great detail. He gets involved. He commits himself. But he's a bloke who never abandons you" (Miralles, personal interview, 2001). And when Preston (Preston, personal interview, 2000) was asked what was key to building his trust in a story he immediately replied, "Confidence in the reporters." Editors matter and they matter a great deal in scandal stories.

Let us take the two newspapers acknowledged by their peers to have been the leading papers in exposing political scandal in the 1990s, *El Mundo* of Spain and *The Guardian* in Britain.[1] The editor of *El Mundo*, Pedro J. Ramírez, was twenty-eight when he first became editor of the newspaper, *Diario 16*, saving it from closure and turning it into one of Spain's major national newspapers. In 1989 he founded *El Mundo*, bringing together a young team and introducing an innovative design, using color for the first time on a national daily. Within a year the paper had a circulation of 131,626 copies and it went on to become one of Spain's best-selling newspapers. Ramírez is considered one of the country's most influential journalists,[2] and a number of the journalists interviewed mentioned his crucial role in backing their investigative work (Miralles, personal interview, 2001; Rubio, personal interview, 1998).

His counterpart at *The Guardian*, Peter Preston, is a less flamboyant figure, in manner more university don than entrepreneur. However, there are parallels between the two men. Both were ideologically out of step with the governments of the day and both were influenced by the United States. Ramírez had imbibed the crusading tradition of the *Washington Post* after an internship there in 1973; Preston had watched the growth of the American lobbying industry and observed with concern its development in Britain (Preston, personal interview, 2000). Both men were university educated (Preston at Oxford and Ramírez at Navarra) and had followed the conventional paths into mainstream journalism in their respective countries (Preston served his apprenticeship on a local newspaper, Ramírez on a national one). Preston, the clever grammar school boy, was from a provincial English town; Ramírez from Logroño, provincial capital of the wine-producing region of La Rioja. Each felt a sense of moral outrage when the initial allegations of wrongdoing were put to them. As Preston put it (Preston, personal interview, 2000), "When Fayed told me about the money passing hands, I just thought it stank, I felt extremely cross. If this is true, it needs to be stopped."

Ramírez's defense of investigative journalism, and his decision to publish revelations about the close links between GAL and González's government, led to his removal from the editorship of *Diario 16* in 1989 and the foundation of *El Mundo* six months later with a group of journalists who followed him from *Diario 16*.[3] In the words of columnist Franciso Umbral, "For Pedro running a paper has never been just a job but a way of being in the world. To this radical sense of calling, in the foundational years there was the added spark of a new kind of journalism, unprecedented in Spain, investigative journalism, which came into being not as a new literary genre but as a response to what was happening in Spain" (cited in Esteban, 1995, p. 16). *El Mundo* became Spain's most important investigative newspaper. As Ramírez himself explained:

> From the moment we founded El Mundo in 1989 we were clear that our mission was to serve the citizens' right to know and reject any attempt to gag us such as had brought about my removal from the editorship of Diario 16 and the resignation in solidarity with me of a great number of my colleagues. The Constitution's protection of freedom of expression is not just to allow reporting of chaotic press conferences or Sunday football matches but also to make sure that those significant matters that the powerful would like to remain hidden see the light of day. And in the Spain of the 90s there was no greater taboo or forbidden territory than the GAL crimes. (2000, p. 45)

Reporters matter, too. In common with 75 percent of British journalists at the time, all the scandal story tellers in the United Kingdom were men (Henningham & Delano, 1998, p. 147-148). This was also true in Spain despite the greater proportion of women journalists, who make up 34 percent of the workforce (Canel, Rodríguez Andrés, & Sánchez Aranda, 2000, p. 12). In Britain the broadsheet journalists were on the whole graduates who had followed the regional press route onto a national paper and become specialists in a given area. *The Guardian's* Richard Norton-Taylor specialized in Whitehall and the security services, for example, whereas Mark Skipworth at *The Sunday Times* was an expert in consumer affairs. The tabloid journalists were less likely to be graduates but had followed a similar career path to their broadsheet colleagues. They were more likely to be generalist newshounds, good at cultivating a wide and varied network of sources and contacts.

All the Spanish journalists had a degree in journalism.[4] Some had also studied a second degree in law or politics and taken postgraduate courses. Several had previously worked on news magazines such as *Cambio 16* or generalist magazines such as *Tiempo* and *Interviú*, specializing in various areas of political reporting. José María Irujo, who revealed the *Roldán* case and worked on the *GAL* case with the reporter who first discovered it, Ricardo Arqués, began his working life on the regional newspaper, *Diario de Navarra*, where he specialized in the activities of the Basque terrorist group, ETA. Antonio Rubio, who covered the *Roldán* and *GAL* cases, began on a Catalonian newspaper. Like several of their British counterparts, all of them have subsequently published accounts of the cases of political corruption they covered.[5]

The following table (Table 4.1) sets out data showing a number of the principal scandals and the editors and reporters associated with them.

TABLE 4.1 Scandals and Reporters

NEWSPAPER	EDITOR	SCANDAL	MAIN REPORTER(S)
The Guardian	Peter Preston (1976-1995)	Cash for Questions	David Hencke
	Alan Rusbridger (1995-)		John Mullin
The Guardian	Peter Preston (1976-1995) Alan Rusbridger (1995-)	Arms to Iraq	Richard Norton-Taylor
The Independent	Ian Hargreaves (1995-1996) Charles Wilson (1996- 1997)	Arms to Iraq	Jonathan Foster Anthony Bevins David Connett Chris Blackhurst
The Sunday Times	Andrew Neil (1983-1994) John Witherow (1994-)	Cash for Questions	Mark Skipworth Maurice Chittenden
The News of the World	Patricia Chapman (1991-1994)	Tim Yeo	Staff reporters
The Sunday People	Bill Hagerty (1992-1993)	David Mellor	Phil Hall
The Sunday People	Bridget Rowe (1996-1998)	Piers Merchant	Staff reporters
Diario 16	Pedro J. Ramírez (1980-1989)	Beginnings of GAL	Melchor Miralles Ricardo Arqués
El Mundo	Pedro J. Ramírez (1989-)	Rubio	Jesús Cacho Casimiro García Abadillo
Diario 16	José Luís Gutiérrez (1992-1996)	Roldán	José María Irujo Jesús Mendoza
El Mundo	Pedro J. Ramírez (1989-)	Roldán (interview during his flight and farcical details about capture)	Antonio Rubio Manuel Cerdán
El Mundo	Pedro J. Ramírez (1989-)	Gal-Lasa and Zabala	Fernando Garea Fernando Lázaro (José Luis Lobo)
El Mundo	Pedro J. Ramírez (1989-)	Gal-Cesid	Manuel Cerdán Antonio Rubio

Investigating Scandal

By definition scandal stories tell us things those reported on would prefer us not to know. Unlike other more reactive forms of journalism, reporting scandal often, although not always, requires more probing than the more run-of-the-mill story. Some journalists would argue that "all journalism worthy of the name carries with it a duty to ask questions, check facts, investigate" (Foot, 1999, p. 81). This is true. But "investigative" journalism, as it has become known, requires an investment in time and resources that sets it apart from other kinds of reporting. It is the "journalism of outrage", which seeks to reveal wrongdoing and bring about change (Protess et al., 1991).

British and Spanish reporters and editors saw themselves as part of a tradition of investigative journalism that in its classical version "provides the first rough draft of legislation" (De Burgh, 2000, p. 3); the example of Watergate stands as the crowning achievement.

In Britain investigative journalism is as old as newspapers. It became respectable with W. T. Stead's exposures of child prostitution in Victorian England. The 1960s and 1970s have often been regarded as a kind of golden age of investigative journalism. In those years many national papers had dedicated investigative personnel, the most famous of which was the team known as *Insight* at *The Sunday Times*, first established on 17 February 1963 (De Burgh, 2000, pp. 286-287) and which achieved its greatest renown under the editorship of Harry Evans (1994). It is often claimed that since then, investigative journalism has been in decline in Britain. The campaigning journalist working in the United Kingdom, John Pilger, stated in an interview in 1999: "If the Kosovo bombing had happened in the 1960s journalists would have investigated how it came about and whose interests it serves; today the British press is degraded by its ludicrous drum beating and rhetorical jingoism" (cited in De Burgh, 2000, p. 314). However, the 1990s certainly bears comparison to any previous decade in terms of the number of major investigations carried out by national newspapers.

The Sunday Times' Insight four-man team brought to light the scandal *Cash for Questions*. According to one of them, their modus operandi was "to go for big hits and that meant on average between four and six big stories a year" (Skipworth, personal interview, 1999). *The Guardian* operated differently. It would use journalists on an ad hoc basis who could be detailed to an issue for weeks at a time and then return to normal reporting duties. When asked why he had decided on this option, Preston explained, (Preston, personal interview, 2000): "I always think on a daily paper the difficulty with investigative units is that they signal to the rest of the staff that they're not expected to be greatly engaged when a story worth investigating comes along."

Instead *The Guardian* had roving reporters with "a very sharp eye for a story," specialists in their chosen areas. David Hencke, Westminster correspondent, was expected to "hang loose and speak to all those people you don't have time to speak to if you're following a lobby agenda" (Preston, personal interview, 2000). Speaking of *The Guardian*'s loose, flat structure, Norton-Taylor (Norton-Taylor, personal interview, 2000) said:

> Just as you should have joined-up government, you have to have joined-up journalism. Otherwise it helps the government too much. If you have a coterie of diplomatic editors close to the Foreign Office or of defense editors close to the Defense Office, you might develop too close and unhealthy a relationship. . . . there has been too cosy a relationship. And because people are seeing each other everyday, they say 'we can't embarrass the Ministry of Defense'. They become a cartel. The Westminster lobby is similar to that. Hencke [*Guardian* reporter] does non-diary stories but gets around looking at the undergrowth.

The Sunday People had had an investigative unit, but by the early 1990s it had been disbanded because of budgetary constraints. However, *The People* had an outstanding news editor, Phil Hall, who was a "very good news man. His skill was in doing those kind of Sunday stories, those digging stories. His contacts were brilliant. He picked people very well . . . and he had a wonderful network of freelancers" (Hagerty, personal interview, 2000).

Investigative journalism in Spain is relatively recent. After the death of Franco in 1975 and the transition period leading to democratic elections in 1977, *Grupo 16* publications such as the magazine *Cambio 16* and, from 1976, *Diario 16* begin to develop this kind of journalism. In 1977 they reported on the Boeing scandal of illegal payments by Iberia, the national airline.

Journalism in Spain has been greatly influenced by the Anglo-American tradition. A number of the journalists interviewed spoke about the influence of Watergate. "Every first-rate Spanish journalist," said one, "hopes to be the one who uncovers a case like Watergate" (Garea, personal interview, 1998). The pioneers, and more particularly those who worked for *Grupo 16*, learned their trade in Britain and the United States (Gutiérrez, 1996, p. 63).

The creation of *El Mundo* began a new era of Spanish investigative journalism. As one of the founding journalists, Ferndando Garea, explained, "The initial idea at *El Mundo* was that we would all do investigative journalism from our own sections" (1998). If an idea took off, the reporter would be released from other duties and freed up to work exclusively on the story. It was not until 1993 that the newspaper took on two reporters—Manuel Cerdán and Antonio Rubio—to work exclusively on stories such as the CESID Tapes, where it was found that the Spanish security services were carrying out illegal taping of a number of individuals, including King Juan Carlos. They would normally report directly to the editor and were given considerable independence to develop stories (Garea, personal interview, 1998). They became in effect one of the first investigative teams in Spanish journalism.

Crafting the Story

Scandal stories are carefully crafted narratives. They typically take weeks or months to research, but they almost all begin with a tip. As *The People* editor put it: "Having gone on and on about the wonders of investigative journalism, many of the stories, most of them, come these days from someone talking" (Hagerty, personal interview, 2000). Garea (personal interview, 1998) makes the same point:

> In the final years of the PSOE government, the great majority of stories came from calls, anonymous and sometimes not, to the newspaper from people prepared to talk to us. That's why I think the myths about investigative journalism should be exploded because it's really much more simple. It's true that you then have to verify the information but some of the most talked about stories have come from anonymous letters.

The Mellor story was initiated by a so-called friend of Mellor's actress girlfriend going to the papers to tell them about their relationship. The *Roldán* case began with a casual conversation in a Saragossa street between a journalist and an acquaintance (Irujo, personal interview, 2001). An embittered businessman, Mohammed al Fayed, ignited *Cash for Questions* as he hawked his stories of betrayal and corruption first to *The Sunday Times* and then *The Guardian*. GAL came from anonymous tips and *Rubio* from an "internal" source who was unhappy about how he or she had been treated and, after a fruitless attempt at negotiation, had decided to go to the press and reveal the existence of the governor of the Bank of Spain's secret account (García Abadillo, personal interview, 2002).[6]

Arms to Iraq worked on a slower fuse. It involved more disparate elements—the Iraqi execution of *Observer* freelance journalist Farzad

Bazoft, Supergun, nuclear triggers, the Gulf War, the prosecution against the engineering company Matrix Churchill, the Scott Inquiry and Report—which journalists struggled to build into a coherent narrative. That's not to say that the story didn't also involve some hard digging. *The Independent*'s correspondent, Jonathan Foster used some old-fashioned journalistic skulduggery to track down one of the main characters in the Supergun story (Foster, personal interview, 2002).[7] Its complexity, however, made it "a colder, more distant story" and it never came to grip the public imagination as other scandal stories had (Norton-Taylor, personal interview, 2000).

Tips were frequently a starting point. They also often acted to confirm reporters' suspicions about a subject. The story of *Cash for Questions* is a good example of this. Hencke had seen for himself the growth of the lobbying industry in Britain and had serious concerns, fuelled by a number of Labour MPs, about the activities of some of these companies. In particular, Ian Greer Associates (IGA) provoked much critical comment even from rival lobbyists. His six-weeks' long investigation of IGA with John Mullins provided a great deal of background material from former employees to show, as Hencke (Hencke, personal interview, 2001), put it, that something "fishy" was going on. This provided some of the corroborating evidence for the claims made by the principal sources about Conservative MPs.

The *Roldán* case is an example of laborious, painstaking investigative work using a variety of sources including archives and property and commercial registers. Two hundred people were interviewed including friends, builders, architects, neighbors, civil guards, police, business people, and spies (Gutierrez, 1996, p. 67; Irujo & Mendoza, 1994, 1996). The crucial information about the extent of Roldán's properties came from Irujo's thorough checking of first the commercial and then the property register (Irujo, personal interview, 2001). These revelations then brought a flood of calls and anonymous tips from people willing to provide more information about Roldán's illegal activities. Many could not be corroborated; those that could be, confirmed Irujo's suspicions of extensive corruption.

In the *Lasa and Zabala* case the reporters received an anonymous tip about where the two men had been detained and how they had died. They communicated with the source through an ad published in the paper, which signalled that they wanted him to call them.

> After months of work, Lázaro, Lobo and I succeeded in identifying the source as a policeman working in the Civil Government of San Sebastián. We persuaded him to testify before Judge Bueren, with whom we also had contact. This policeman eventually became the

main witness against General Galindo and other civil guards.
(Garea, personal interview, 1998)

In Spain there was a great debate about the legitimacy of investigative journalism that relied on leaks for much of its information. The information about Filesa, for example, came from a disgruntled employee. The source approached two newspapers that first decided not to publish the information. Eventually, *El Periódico de Catalunya* and the newly established *El Mundo* decided to publish it. A number of journalists claimed that much of *El Mundo's* reporting had been paid for by the anti-Socialist banker Mario Conde. As shown by Miralles' reporting of the *GAL* case or Hencke's of *Cash for Questions*, investigative journalism often involves information received from sources with their own agenda. This seems to be true of journalism in any country. As former *News of the World* editor Patricia Chapman said in evidence to Britain's Press Complaints Commission (PCC):

> While the possible/probable motive of those who supply information is always a factor in considering whether a story be published, it is not, in itself, decisive as to whether journalistic enquiries should be made. If the nature of the information deserves proper scrutiny then it is legitimate for the Press to ask questions regardless of the source's motives. The day that ceases to be the case will be the day investigative journalism dies. (1991, p. 10)

In Britain it was the techniques used by some journalists that sparked controversy. *The Sunday Times*, for example, mounted a "sting" operation, creating a false company that approached MPs from both parties to ask them to ask questions in Parliament in return for cash. Just two took the bait.

The story arose out of the reporters' picking up developments that had yet to be clearly identified. As *The Sunday Times'* reporter, Mark Skipworth explained (Skipworth, personal interview, 1999):

> What we picked up on before anybody else . . . was that a U.S. style lobbying system had developed and no-one had really noticed. And if people had noticed, they hadn't really got a handle on it even journalistically. So they hadn't really worked out a way of getting to the story, getting a story which epitomised or encapsulated that move. What we did with our sting is to put that into focus in a way no-one had done before.

The sting was also borne out of their frustration that their "businessman" source refused to go on the record, "so we only had half a story. What we did is we re-grouped. There was an obvious story here. We were all agreed and I suggested to Maurice [Chittenden] "why don't we just do a sting? Here's how we do it." It seemed very simple. Just see what happens. The story caused huge anger in Parliament, and *The Sunday Times'* editor and reporters were called to give evidence before a Parliamentary Select Committee, and accused of being *agents provocateurs*. Skipworth (Skipworth, personal interview, 1999) saw matters very differently: "We went through the Code of Practice [of the industry watchdog, the Press Complaints Commission]. It was greatly in the public interest so there was no problem on that level."

The Sunday People also found itself under attack from Parliament and fellow journalists for using telephone conversations secretly taped by a source who sold the information to the newspaper. The concern of the editor, Bill Hagerty (Hagerty, personal interview, 2000), was first to verify the information: "We went to an audio-tape screener to establish it was Mellor's voice and not an impersonator. It was definitely Mellor." However, he also recognized the moral qualms such methods might cause:

> Now there's a big debate there, isn't there? A big ethical debate of whether or not a newspaper should take a tip from someone who's quite plainly as awful as the person he was taping. Antonia de Sancha [Mellor's girlfriend] wasn't awful, she was just used. The other answer is would you suppress it then? If you find out there's something bad happening but the information's been obtained by not the most legitimate means, would you suppress the information? Of course that's nonsense. How would the police ever function? Practically every major police arrest is made because somebody "finks" on somebody else.

For Hagerty the final imprimatur for the methods used was to have stayed within the PCC Code and to have received public support.

Source credibility was built up in every case by corroboratory evidence from documentary or other sources. Ultimately reporters were dealing with stories that made serious allegations against prominent people. As we shall see next, the main sources were not the usual government press officers; they were "flaky" businessmen, disaffected or opposition politicians, and anonymous policemen. More than ever, journalists had to make the call on the story. As Skipworth (Skipworth, personal interview, 1999) said about al Fayed, "There are certain things he gets wrong and there are certain things he gets right. It's really up to us to use our judgement. That's what we're paid for, to decide when he's got it right and when he's got it wrong."

JOURNALISTS AND SOURCES

There is a rich tradition of research into the relationship between journalists and sources (Anderson, 1997; Deacon & Golding, 1994; Ericson, Baranek, a Chan 1989; Manning, 2001; Palmer, 2000; Schlesinger & Tumber, 1994; Sigal, 1973). We will see now how examining this relationship in the coverage of scandal can add texture and depth to our understanding of it.

Primary Definition

Much sociological research into news sources has been inspired by the notion of "primary definition" proposed by British academic, Stuart Hall (Hall et al., 1978). He argues that those who enjoy special status by virtue of their institutional power are given privileged access to the media. The media are held to be structurally biased towards powerful sources, who achieve the status of being "primary definers" from both a temporal and an ideological perspective. The organization of journalistic practice is here seen as promoting the views and interests of authoritative sources.

Many studies have provided evidence supporting the existence of "authoritative primary definers" (Deacon & Golding, 1994; Gandy, 1982; Gans, 1979; Goldenberg, 1975; Sigal, 1973; Tunstall, 1971); this view of journalists' relationship to news sources has found classic expression in Hermann and Chomsky's *Manufacturing Consent* (1988). The American academic Herbert Gans put it simply:

> While in theory sources can come from anywhere, in practice, their recruitment and their access to journalists reflect the hierarchies of nation and society. The President of the United States has instantaneous access to all news media; the powerless must resort to civil disturbances to obtain it. (1979, p. 119)

Economic and political power bestow source power. However, more recent research has shown that source-journalist relationships are imbued with complexities that are not fully accounted for by the notion of "primary definition" (Bale & Sanders, 2001; Ericson et al., 1989; Negrine, 1996b, pp. 23-51). Schlesinger and Tumber (1994) argue that the notion lacks explanatory strength because it "resolves the question of source power on the basis of structuralist assumptions, closing off any engagement with the dynamic processes of contestation in a given field of discourse" (p. 21).

Analysis of journalistic practices and source strategies shows that power is not the only determinant as to who gets access to the news, and that therefore explanations that go beyond the notion of primary definition are necessary. Official and nonofficial sources can struggle for media access, and it is the latter who sometimes win. Official sources lose credibility and trust (political scandal coverage would seem to be a particularly good example of this) and journalists can attempt to regain what they consider a loss of control by signalling official sources' attempts at news management—what Blumler and Gurevitch have referred to as journalists' "disdaining" the news (1995, p. 93). Pressure groups and nonofficial sources are becoming more expert at using professional public relations to gain access to the media (Anderson, 1997; Davis, 2000, 2002). As Manning puts it: "The evidence . . . suggests that it *is* possible in certain circumstances to counter or resist definitions offered by the powerful and to exert power in a counter direction (2001, p. 17). All this suggests the need for a more nuanced account of journalists' use of news sources.

Political Reporting

The relationship between political institutional sources and journalists has been one of the most thoroughly explored in production research in both Britain and the United States (Schlesinger & Tumber, 1994, p. 22). In Britain, Jeremy Tunstall (1971, 1996) has provided a substantial body of work on the sociology of specialist political reporting. A number of academics and journalists have examined the professionalization of political communication and its associated impact on reporters (Franklin, 1997, 2004; Ingham, 2003; Jones, 1995, 1997, 2001; Scammell, 1995; Seymour-Ure, 1974, 1996). Scholars and journalists have also examined political sources (Cockerell, 1988; Harris, 1990; Negrine, 1996a) and their routinized relationships with reporters (Barnett & Gaber, 2001; Blumler & Gurevitch, 1995; Kuhn & Neveu, 2002; Negrine, 1996b).

In Spain, work has been done on the sociology and development of political journalism as a specialist area (Canel, Rodríguez Andrés & Sánchez Aranda, 2000; Dader, 1992; Diezhandino, Coca & Bezunartea, 1994; Ortega & Humanes, 2000); on the professional attitudes of journalists (Bezunartea, 1995; Canel & Sánchez Aranda, 1999); on the coverage of political events and institutions (Benavides & Palacio, 1994; Huertas, 1994; Innerarity & Canel, 2000) and on the coverage of election campaigns (Arceo, 1982; Canel, 1998; Cotarelo, 1996; Muñoz-Alonso & Rospir 1995).

Less has been done, however, to examine the journalist-source relationship at times of crisis (Murphy, 1991; Tiffen, 1989). The complexity in journalistic use of news sources is especially apparent where conflict and misunderstanding in the relationship between the journalist and the politician arise. This can occur because of a lack of official regulation governing the forms of relationships between journalists and their political sources; a lack of standardized access to places in which political information is produced; or because of an overlap between political and journalistic figures (Mancini, 1993, pp. 41-42). When suspicion dominates the relation between journalists and official sources, when journalists know or suspect that behind-the-scenes forces are corrupting the democratic process, other normative pressures may shape the reporting of a political story (Bennett, 1996). These are cases in which traditional patterns of coverage may be substantially modified. As a consequence, specific noneconomic and nonpolitical considerations such as trust and confidentiality come into the equation; the coverage of political scandal provides us with one of those moments when these extrapolitical economy factors come sharply into focus and where obtaining justified true belief becomes a complex practice of the operation of journalistic judgment. As Ettema and Glasser put it, '"journalists are often able to avoid responsibility for justifying their claims . . . especially when they report on government officials and bureaucracies . . . daily reporters often don't have to *decide* what they believe to be true in the same way that investigative journalists have to decide" (1998, p. 159; italics in original).

Telling the Story. Sources of Scandal

According to Melchor Miralles, one of the journalists who investigated *GAL*, investigative journalists rely on the three Ps for their stories— "periodistas, putas, y policías [journalists, prostitutes, and police]." Examining evidence from interviews and content analysis the picture is more complex.

Content analysis of the most used first source showed that for British scandal stories journalists most commonly used governmental sources, whereas in Spain legal sources were the most frequently used first sources (see Table 4.2).[8]

The analysis of first source use in scandal stories showed that in both countries political scandal news showed considerable reliance on official or governmental sources. However, reliance on official sources was significantly greater in Spain than in the United Kingdom (see Table 4.3). As we've just seen, government sources were more frequently used in the U.K. scandal coverage, however stories there used a greater range of sources—including less reliance on official sources—than the scandal stories reported in Spanish newspapers, where there was a notable lack of nonofficial sources used.

Why might be this be? The nature of the political scandals would certainly have some impact on the types of sources used. For example, British sex scandals would lend themselves to the use of lovers and family as sources. However, nonofficial sources were also found to have been more commonly used across the more conventional kinds of British scandal story. Thus, it might be conjectured that the style and character of the press in each country might have an impact on source use. Put most simply, a more populist, broad-based press would seem to reflect a more populist source agenda.

TABLE 4.2 Most Used First Sources

UNITED KINGDOM		SPAIN	
SOURCE	PERCENTAGE (N)	SOURCE	PERCENTAGE (N)
Member of government party/not of government	17.8 (161)	Member of judiciary	28.3 (320)
Member of government	13.3 (120)	Member of government	10.4 (117)
Published documents	12.7 (115)	Member of opposition	9.6 (108)
Prime Minister	7.6 (69)	Member of Civil Service	9.4 (106)
Member of an opposition party	7.4 (67)	Member of Security Forces	9.4 (106)
Business people	5.1 (46)	Published documents	9.2 (91)
Total Number	902	Total Number	1,129

TABLE 4.3 Officialdom in Source Use

	PERCENTAGES	
	Nonofficial	Official
U.K.	45.1	54.9
Spain	14.5	85.5

However, it would be wrong to conclude from this finding either that the Spanish press is a conduit for "official" news or that, given the predominance of government/official sources in both countries, both countries confirm the "primary definition" hypothesis. To take the Spanish case, our analysis shows that members of the legal profession and the civil service were much more prevalent as sources than in the United Kingdom, and government as a source was less represented than in Britain. Given the important role of judges and lawyers in Spain in prosecuting scandal cases, the significant presence of legal sources in coverage there would suggest that Spanish newspapers were pursuing a contentious, polemical agenda, inimical to government interests, rather than the opposite. It is clear from interviews that journalists often actively assisted judges in their investigations. Speaking of his relationship with the judge who investigated GAL, Baltasár Garzón, Miralles (Miralles, personal interview, 2001) said:

> I've contributed a great many things to this investigation. And on many lines of investigation that were fed to us, I've gone to Garzón's court and said, I've got this information. I can't do anything with it. I can't publish it, I can't carry on investigating it. But you're a judge and you'll be able to. I've given him this information and later seen it published in other media.

Indeed one of the striking features of Spanish scandals was the extent to which journalists' work later became the basis for criminal prosecutions. As Miralles (Miralles, personal interview, 2001) said:

> Legal investigations have always lagged behind journalistic ones. That's the plain and simple truth of the matter. The law has only acted when the media have placed the evidence on the table. . . . Without journalistic investigation there would not have been legal investigation.

There was a widespread belief, shared by some journalists, that Spanish newspapers had supplanted the functions of other institutions. According to one: "In recent years . . . we became a kind of prosecuting judge. I don't think that was our job but perhaps we did it because other people didn't. That is to say, politicians didn't do what they should do and prosecutors didn't do what they had to do" (Rubio & Cerdán, personal interview, 1998).[9]

The reliance on legal sources in Spain is also borne out by an analysis of sources divided into those representing executive, legislative, and judicial powers. In the British coverage we find a relatively high reliance on executive (20.9%) and legislative (28.5%) sources as compared to legal ones (16.9%). In Spain, the figures are 12.7 percent for the executive; for the legislature, 16.7 percent; and for legal sources, 36.4 percent.

Contrary to what journalists themselves sometimes say or believe, the data provided by content analysis shows that official sources are key to scandal stories. According to Rubio (Rubio, personal interview, 1998), for example, relationships to the official sources were nonexistent "except to confirm something which they will automatically deny." However, it is clear that once a scandal story is broken, its ensuing coverage—because it becomes a matter for the courts, for Parliament, or for the credibility of the executive—becomes bound up in the domain of officialdom. During the initial stages of a scandal it is different. Overwhelmingly, journalists attest that the sources who *initiated* a number of the scandal stories were not "official" sources. They were people with an axe to grind (*Cash for Questions*, Yeo, *Rubio*), a bad conscience (*GAL, CESID papers, Lasa-Zabala*), or out to make money (Mellor and Merchant). Only the *Roldán* case provided an example of a reporter-driven story, one that fitted the frame of the Watergate myth.

The apparent official closure of a scandal—a court decision, a resignation, a Committee report—usually provides the moment of journalistic closure except in cases where a person's notoriety may provide a new moment of journalistic tension and possibility. In Spain, for example, Roldán's continued possession of his ill-gotten gains continued to be subject to press probing in 2001; in Britain the Hamiltons continued to be in the news when they lost their libel case against al Fayed in 1999 and when they were accused of sexual assault in 2001.

Journalistic Authority and Autonomy

The ordinary authoritative sources become inoperative for the launching of scandal stories. Reporters must themselves authoritatively establish the credibility of the stories they publish. This gives journalists an opportunity for greater autonomy in story development. Examining source attribution to other media is an interesting indicator of the extent to which the media themselves were assigned importance in story generation and development.

As Table 4.4 shows, British coverage gave more prominence to media in scandal stories measured by mentions of media than Spanish coverage did. This cannot be attributed to the nature of the scandals. The role of the Spanish press was as significant in exposing scandal (it might be argued that it was more significant) than its British counterpart. It is possible that there was a reluctance for newspapers to source rivals. Of course, this is always the case, but it would be more likely to occur in the

TABLE 4.4 Media Mentions

UNITED KINGDOM		SPAIN	
Number	Percentage	Number	Percentage
614	35.8	438	22.5

fiercely competitive British newspaper market. However, in the Spanish case one newspaper, *El Mundo*, took a leading role in exposing scandal and, from interviews, it is known that there was considerable unease and even resentment about *El Mundo*'s role. This may have contributed to a reluctance on the part of other papers to buoy up their rival's success by mentioning their role in exposing scandal. Ramírez clearly thought so:

> I believe that when the press discovers something relevant the other newspapers and the rest of the media should not look away like a jealous prima donna who thinks that nothing is important unless she is singing it, or like in the fable of the fox and the grapes saying "given that someone else has published it, these grapes don't interest me or they're not ripe." This is a mistake that no-one in the media should make. I feel only scorn for the reaction of some competitors who behave that way every time *El Mundo* has a "scoop." We'll never take that attitude and the proof is how we tried to get in on the investigation of the Roldán case when we saw how big it was. (Ramírez, cited in AEPI, 1996, p. 46)

British journalists were more generous in their assessments of fellow journalists' performance. Speaking of *The Guardian, Sunday Times'* journalist Mark Skipworth, (Skipworth, personal interview, 1999) said: "I thought all their stories were sensational. There was an incredible week—Tim Smith, Hamilton and then Aitken. It was one of the most sensational weeks I can remember in journalism, fantastic." And of the editor's performance: "Peter Preston was superb. He judged it brilliantly." And writing of the *Cash for Questions* case, *The Independent* declared: "None of it would have come out without the angry anti-Conservative campaign of Mohammed al Fayed and some very fine journalistic digging, notably by *The Guardian*, whose courage and professionalism in all this we salute" (4 July 1997, p. 19).

However, as we shall see in the next chapter, those threatened by the stories attempted to undermine journalistic authority and autonomy. Journalists in Spain came under pressure from owners and government sources to drop stories. Government pressure on the owners of *Diario 16* to drop the investigation into *GAL* led to Ramírez's sacking and the departure of six other reporters (Miralles, personal interview, 2001). As editor of *El Mundo* Ramírez also came under direct pressure from the Spanish President, Felipe González, to take Miralles off the *GAL* case and to stop the paper's investigation. Government sources practically closed down for reporters working on scandal stories (Miralles, personal interview, 2001; Rubio, personal interview, 1998). Miralles himself was spied on, followed, and received anonymous threats (Miralles, personal interview, 2001).

British journalists also experienced hostility, but not just from the government. Skipworth (Skipworth, personal interview, 1999) spoke of his surprise at the reaction of the cross-party membership of the Parliamentary Privileges Committee to *The Sunday Times' Cash For Questions* story:

> I was expecting some of them to befriend us but we became pariahs. That's one of the reasons we were privately relieved when *The Guardian* came up with its stuff because the net effect of our story was that our Politics department was completely closed down even though they'd never been involved in the story. The government just sent them to Coventry. We had real problems speaking to MPs to try to take the story on anymore because we were pariahs. We had this bloody huge Privileges inquiry hanging over us as having behaved reprehensibly and the contrast between their reaction and the mood in the country was so marked at that time.

Regarding *The People*, Hagerty (Hagerty, personal interview, 2000) found that there was "no flak from the government. We were just pariahs to them and we were a Labour supporting paper." However, there was an interesting reaction from members of the opposition party:

> I went to a party, fairly shortly afterwards at Mandelson's flat, by then an MP for Hartlepool. He wrote a column for the *People*. I didn't get ostracised. I knew a lot of the shadow cabinet. But a couple of them really didn't want to talk to me. They were polite but icy. What we surmised was that, it wasn't that they disapproved of us kicking Mellor, but that there were skeletons rattling around in their, or more likely, colleagues' cupboards that if we could do it to Mellor, we could do it to them. And I think that's why there was this slight feeling of disapproval. Publicly they didn't go for him. They were very clever, and that was a lot to do with Mandelson.[10] They didn't go for Tories over sex, they went for Tories in the House on money.

Despite these pressures and some criticism from colleagues,[11] British journalists never saw their authority and autonomy undermined to the same extent as their Spanish counterparts. In Spain, attempts were even made to undermine the standing of the editor himself by the secret taping and release of a video in 1997 showing him with a prostitute. And to the great irritation of the reporters who had worked on the scandal cases (Rubio, personal interview, 1998), a number of commentators considered *El Mundo* simply to have been a pawn in wider ideological and economic battles (Castells, 1998, p. 373). This was not the view of Peter Preston, ideologically distant from Ramírez (Preston, personal interview, 2000):

> There's no doubt that Pedro—referring to Pedro J. Ramírez—was quite close to Aznar [head of the conservative People's Party] but I think if you wind the clock forward three or four years, the relationship between the two is nothing like it was and *El Mundo* is just the kind of paper it was: it's a turn over the stones, "kick shit" paper. The thought that it's a predictably Peoples Party paper rather than a Socialist paper is off the wall. It's just the kind of paper that does those things.

CUSTODIANS OF PUBLIC VIRTUE

Very few Spanish politicians of any party looked kindly on *El Mundo*'s revelations about GAL. According to Garea (Garea, personal interview, 1998), many were sympathetic to GAL's actions or at least looked the other way, and it is possible that the trial would never have taken place if *El Mundo* had not published what it did. Why did they? Miralles (Miralles, personal interview, 2001) took a principled view of his task. "Information isn't the journalist's property," he explained, "information belongs to the citizen. We are the intermediaries of a right which isn't ours . . . but which is the citizen's right to receive information." This understanding of the reporter's role means that: "Once a journalist has information he has to report it whatever the cost and it can often bring many upsets." Reflecting on his reporting of GAL, he considered "It would have been much simpler . . . to do nothing but we believe in this profession and I believe that that was our duty."

Peter Preston (Preston, personal interview, 2000) was equally forthright about the moral imperative underlying scandal coverage:

> I've always thought—and this is going to sound pious—you're not just there just to entertain and stimulate. You have a serious purpose in a democracy which you don't have to take seriously but which is

nevertheless serious. When you come across something about the working of public life in the broad which is simply not right, then you have a duty to do everything you can to get it into the open. And I thought that in this respect that if MPs could be bought this easily and on this scale, against a background of bland assumption that British politics was totally clean and wonderful, that we had a duty to do everything we could to get it into public print. It's one definition of what we're there for.

In their study of investigative journalism and public virtue, Ettema and Glasser (1998, p. 189) summarize investigative journalism's achievements as *publicity* (bringing wrongdoing into the public gaze), *accountability* (calling wrongdoers to account) and *solidarity* (creating bonds of compassion with those who have suffered). Certainly reporters in both countries considered that they had a duty to bring things out into the open. But this in itself was a task that required, in Ettema and Glasser's phrase, "moral craftwork." Even though journalists like to claim that facts speak for themselves, they often don't.[12]

Evaluating later their reporting of corruption stories, Rubio and Cerdán (Rubio and Cerdán, personal interview, 1998), two Spanish journalists believed they hadn't got it quite right: "We should have reflected much more that the money being taken by Rafael Vera, Luis Roldán, Filesa, the AVE train . . . is *our* money. That they were taking away from us a park-bench, a hospital-bed, a school-desk." Although people were clear about the GAL deaths—murder and torture were at least sharply focused moral facts, even though there was some ambiguity in some people's minds about possible justification—they were confused about the endless stories of corruption. Miralles (Miralles, personal interview, 2001) also reflected on the framing of scandal in Spain and the lack of impact he believed the reporting to have had. In particular, he spoke of foreign journalists' incredulity that the President, Felipe González, had survived and his view that instead of writing of the *GAL* case, reporters should have written of the *González* case because "finally this is all the *González* case."

Scandal storytelling necessarily embodies moral judgments that make the facts speak in a certain way. Journalists, despite their protestations, do "frame" stories. Part of the impact of *Cash for Questions* was the sense, expressed here by Hencke (Hencke, personal interview, 2001), that the holy of holies, the unsullied House of Commons, was being corrupted by a few rotten apples:

What I thought was fundamentally wrong was that a democratic institution of very high standing was being corrupted by its own members who were being aided and abetted by people outside. And I actually thought this was a corruption at the core of the health of democracy because if this took root basically you could only get something done if you bribed someone. It was never the kind of thing I expected to find in the UK. I'd known about it elsewhere but I never thought that anyone in the United Kingdom would behave like that.

By the very act of relating scandal, reporters hold wrongdoers to account, even if the final acts of the drama will probably occur in the law courts or parliament. Creating solidarity is a different matter. Solidarity requires clearly identified victims and where they are suspected ETA terrorists or arms-trading businessmen, scandal narratives become less clear cut or less acceptable to the public. Reporters themselves may seek to arouse outrage, as Spanish reporters did in providing graphic information about the torture and murder of Lasa and Zabala. But articulating public virtue may be an uphill task when the public itself is ambivalent. For Mark Skipworth (Skipworth, personal interview, 1999) this was part of the secret of *Cash For Questions*: "It's one of the few stories where you feel you've caught the mood—the timing was perfect." This "catching the mood" is, he explained, crucial. "It happens to investigative stories all the time. You see them in the papers and they're just not quite right. It's not that they haven't nailed their suspects. We just don't capture the mood." The stories of miscreant British Conservatives acting waywardly for sexual or financial motives struck a public chord and newspapers exploited it for all it was worth.

However, "capturing the mood" is also part of the craft and task of the storyteller. Sources are crucial; the public mood might be important, but ultimately compelling stories are told by good storytellers.

NOTES

1. The two newspapers were also business partners and their editors knew and respected each other (Preston, personal interview, 2000).
2. In July 1995 the magazine *Actualidad Económica* published the results of a readers' poll of those considered Spain's ten most influential figures. Pedro J. came fifth, after the politicians Pujol, González, Aznar, and the banker, Botín.
3. *El Mundo* was founded on 22 October 1989 by a team of seven journalists, most of whom came from *Diario 16* and some of whom are responsible for the scandal coverage examined in this book. They include Pedro J. Ramirez himself, Melchor Miralles, Fernando Garea, and Casimiro García Abadillo.
4. From the beginning of the 1970s Spanish universities have awarded licenciate degrees in Information Sciences (*Ciencias de la Información*),

roughly equivalent to a British journalism degree, in the areas of print or broadcast journalism and advertising and public relations.

4. Journalists involved in the scandals examined have published a number of books. Ricardo Arqués and José María Irujo published *ETA, la derrota de las armas* [*ETA. The Defeat of Arms*] (1993) about GAL. José María Irujo and Jesús Mendoza published *Roldán, un botín a la sombra del tricornio* [*Roldán. A Booty in the Shadow of the Civil Guard*] (1994) and *Comisión Ilegal* [*Illegal Payments*] (1996), both about the Roldán case. Casimiro García Abadillo published with Jesús Cacho *La estafa Ibercorp* [*The Ibercorp Swindle*] (1992). Antonio Rubio and Manuel Cerdán have published *El origen del GAL* [*The Origin of GAL*] (1997), and *El 'caso Interior'. GAL, Roldán y fondos reservados: el triángulo negro de un ministerio* [*The 'Interior Case'. GAL, Roldán and Reserved Funds: The Black Triangle of a Ministry*] (1995). Also about GAL, Melchor Miralles has published *Amedo. El Estado contra ETA* [*Amedo. The State Against ETA*] (1998).

5. In Britain David Leigh published *Betrayed* (1993) about the Matrix Churchill trial and with Ed Vulliamy *Sleaze. The Corruption of Parliament* (1997) about the *Cash for Questions* case. Richard Norton-Taylor published *Truth is a Difficult Concept* (1995) with Mark Lloyd and *Knee Deep in Dishonour* (1996) with Mark Lloyd and Stephen Cook about the *Arms to Iraq* scandal.

6. García Abadillo preferred not to disclose to us whether the "internal" source was a bank official or member of the Socialist Party.

7. Foster located the scientist working on the Supergun project by making a number of astute phone calls in which he failed to reveal his identity as a reporter.

8. See Chapter 1 for definitions of the different source categories.

9. The judges, of course, took a different view. The judge who investigated the *GAL* case, Baltasar Garzón, complained of the journalists' disclosure: "The report about Amedo and Domínguez in *El Mundo*, 'This is how they financed GAL', was terribly harmful to me because it revealed all my findings. Just when the legal proceedings should have been kept secret because I was trying to put all the pieces together, the publicity turned my investigation upside down. I remember that when I took Vera's evidence, he arrived already knowing everything, having found out from *El Mundo* what information I had" (Garzón, cited in Urbano, 2000, p. 205).

10. Peter Mandelson was Labour's head of communication in the 1980s and went on to become a minister in Tony Blair's government, resigning first as Northern Ireland Secretary after allegations about improper use of ministerial power three years previously and then as Trade Minister in 2001. He is widely regarded as one of the architects of New Labour and its spin-doctor supreme. Mandelson returned to front-line politics in 2004 when he became the European Union's Trade Commissioner.

11. *The Guardian* came under heavy attack from Conservative-supporting journalists such as Paul Johnson who accused it of unfairly hounding Neil Hamilton. The anti-*Guardian* thesis is set out in Jonathan Boyd Hunt's *Trial by Conspiracy* (1998).

12. Canel and Sádaba (1999) have explored this paradox in relation to journalistic practice, and various survey-based studies in Spain have shown how professional attitudes can influence news work (Martín, 1992; Canel & Sánchez-Aranda, 1999). For instance, surveyed journalists who fell into the category of "advocate" (a category constructed with a factor analysis of different variables related to the degree of agreement with statements about the journalist's role) consider that they edit the news to increase public interest. Those who fell into the "adversarial" category did not agree with the statement that they edit news to follow a certain political line.

5

Spin Doctors
and Press Officers[1]

Institutional sources lose credibility in the reporting of scandal. And yet often, where the scandal affects members of the governing party, the reputation of the government or chief executive (CE)[2] can be at stake. Here we will examine the strategies of those who attempted to manage scandal stories on behalf of the Major and González governments, on the basis of interviews with politicians, journalists, party officials, and the memoirs of some of those involved. We will see how the spin doctors and press officers sought to erect a firewall around their men with varying degrees of success.[3]

VISIBILITY AND CONCEALMENT
IN CHIEF EXECUTIVES' NEWS OPERATIONS

Most literature on news operations, as we saw in Chapter 3, has concentrated on the question of how the visibility of chief executives (CE) can be managed to establish a relationship with their followers and to gain support from them.

These news operations must work within the constraints that flow from the structural and contingent factors with which a CE must work. As we saw in Chapter 1, prime ministerial power in both Britain and Spain is often overrated, even though media coverage would often have us believe otherwise. This—as Kavanagh and Seldon (2000) have pointed out—can be an advantage when things go well, but very damaging when they do not. This is the case, too, for presidential power, often cited as the acme of "real" political power. But the judgment that a CE presides over much that is done by others and that the exercise of power is more limited than is often thought, "applies just as much to the US President" (Kavanagh & Seldon, 2000, p. 314). The President must negotiate with Congress to get legislation through and also depends on the Senate for the approval of some key appointments. It is Congress that ratifies certain acts. In a parliamentary system chief executives operate under different institutional constraints: in Britain the CE cannot ignore the party and is constitutionally compelled to act with the whole cabinet (Rhodes & Dunleavy, 1995); he/she is also submitted to the structural characteristics of the Civil Service. In Spain the CE cannot ignore the party either; the principle of collective responsibility also applies, albeit with less force than in Britain. On the other hand, the system of proportional representation favors a multiparty model in which absolute majorities are less common than in Britain, and the CE is required to negotiate with other parties.

The CE's job in a parliamentary and presidential system is a combination of an office, a building, a team, a constitution—written or uncodified —a role and a person (Neustadt, 1960; Smith, 1996). This complexity can be exploited by astute news operations to build public, parliamentary and party support. But the media, given the right circumstances, can just as easily exploit that same complexity to undermine the best efforts of spin doctors.

Managing a CE image means taking into account who s/he is and the nature of his/her job (Canel, 1999). A CE *is* his/her personal biographical details (age, education, social class, cultural level, religion, race, etc.), character (decisiveness, serenity, impulsiveness, sincerity, maturity, etc.), professional qualifications (curriculum, expertise, knowledge, bargaining ability, etc.), ideology (party, causes that have been pursued). Communication skills such as oratorical powers and debating skills are also important in shaping a leader's image.

The *nature* of a CE's job is a combination of formal (the CE is the head of government, of the military forces, etc.) and informal roles (the CE is also a moral leader, a public opinion leader); of institutional (the

CE represents something that is abstract and corporate) and personal roles (a prime minister is somebody with a personal story) (Seymour-Ure, 2000). The CE public image is managed through news operations that tend to modify the formal roles in relation to the informal, to personalize institutional roles, and to blur governing and nongoverning roles (Seymour-Ure, 1998). Chief executives are pictured doing sports, walking a dog, or on vacation: Tony Blair, for example, was heard on a radio program selecting his favorite music and José María Aznar appeared on television discussing his literary tastes. Communication strategies attempt to subsume governing roles into State ones by picturing the CE with nonparty symbols such as the national flag or photographs of the monarch. A leader must be portrayed as reliable (probity), qualified for the post (competency), and with a consistent message to coordinate the differing perspectives of different publics (Smith & Smith, 1994).

The analysis of visibility management should look at what we could call internal and the external dimensions of news operations. The internal dimension has to do with the structural conditions that shape news operations. The development of a 24-hour news cycle with its continuous coverage of political and governmental affairs, the increasing competition among institutions to get space in the mass media, and the development of company PR offices are factors, among others, that have led to the establishment of specific offices for communication, which have come closer to the core executive (Cook, 1998; Kavanagh & Seldon, 2000; Maltese, 1994). The kind of office that is established, the qualifications of the people who are hired for communication posts, and the relationship established between the CE and the principal communication officers are all fruitful areas for the analysis of news operations.

The external dimension is related to the news context in which spin doctoring operates and in which there is a constant clash between officials' and journalists' interests. As Cook (1998) says, "Government officials need to enlist the news media to help them accomplish their goals" (p. 123). But this is an assistance that "cannot come without some cost" (p. 123). Cook explains that through news operations, governments try to call attention to their preferred issues and position; but merely calling attention to an issue does not ensure that one's preferred choice will be pursued. And, although it is true that chief executives face the media with the advantage that what they do is attractive to journalists, not just anything they do is automatically newsworthy (Cook, 1998). The main problem is, as Seymor-Ure (1998) says, that "chief executives' news operations tend not to be in equilibrium with their media clientele" (p. 16), because the interests of chief executives and of journalists are not identical.

In the case of political scandals news operations can be particularly complex. When a CE is directly accused of wrongdoing or indirectly involved because of the misdemeanors of members of his/her government, party, or staff, choices can not be made without some cost. The CE can ignore criticism and avoid visibility in contexts in which s/he could be related to the scandal. Another approach is to respond to the allegation. Whichever alternative is chosen, the CE's reputation for probity or competence can be damaged.

In order to analyze the specific strategies that were followed to respond to scandal allegations during the Major and González governments, we will examine both the internal dimension—the structure and style of their communication offices—as well as the external dimension—the news context—of their news operations (see a summary of the prime ministers' styles and offices in Table 5.1).

PRIME MINISTERS COMMUNICATION OFFICES AND STYLES

Ten Downing Street: "Mr Nice Guy"

John Major's unexpected elevation to the Prime Ministership in November 1990 brought a wholly different media management style to 10 Downing St. His less aggressive approach contrasted with that of his predecessor, Margaret Thatcher, reinforcing an image of decency and plain dealing. Lobby journalists knew him well from his time as a government whip, and "related to him as a very likeable, clubbable human being who, unlike many politicians, did not play favorites" (Bale & Sanders, 2001, p. 95).

As one very experienced lobby journalist explained to us:

> When he came in, he was seen as the complete opposite of Thatcher. He made a virtue of being Mr Nice. His Press Secretary also made a virtue of being Mr Nice. They used to invite us to Downing Street parties. The PM would actually talk to the journalists on the plane. And there's no question about it that at the very beginning it did work extremely well for him. (Jones, personal interview, 1998)

He also cultivated an image of not being overly influenced or concerned by the media, deciding not to make use of the kind of slick, professionalized and overtly political spokesman that some urged on him as a necessary evil (Bale & Sanders, 2001, p. 95).

Second, Major strongly adhered to the constitutional tradition of strict separation between government and party political media managers. In the words of another political correspondent:

> The Number Ten press office wasn't so political, certainly not as political as it is now. . . . There was a very strict dividing line between the Number Ten Press Office and Conservative Central Office. The Tories always had this feeling that they had to play things by the book and the rules were that government information was done on an impartial, Civil Service basis and not on a party political basis. . . .There should be no blurring of the line. (Price, personal interview, 1998)

He appreciated the civil servants (Kavanagh & Seldon, 2000, p. 211) and had "sensitivity towards the manner and over-confident intellects of the grander members of the Civil Service *grand corps*" (Hennessy, 2000, p. 447). Throughout Major's time in office, the person in charge of his media relations was a career civil servant.

The three men who held the post were responsible for providing daily digests of press coverage (although various lobby journalists and officials pointed out that Major, unlike Margaret Thatcher, was an avid reader of the press himself), provided twice-daily briefings to the lobby about the business of the government (as well as a host of informal individual briefings and lunches), and chaired the weekly meeting of the government's most senior information officers to consider strategies for the presentation of government policy. The Prime Minister's Press Secretary also attended meetings of relevant committees in which governmental media relations were discussed. However, according to those interviewed, the Press Secretary would normally not participate or absent himself where discussion moved on to party political matters.

During the first phase of Major's incumbency a top official from the Treasury took charge of the Prime Minister's media relations. Control of overall strategy was placed in the hands of the Number 12 committee, which was first established in May 1991 and ran until 1995 (Hogg & Hill, 1995). In 1994, more or less at the midpoint of the political cycle, fresh faces were brought into the Major circle: a new Press Secretary, Party Chairman and Political Secretary were appointed. The party's media team was wound down.

Those who thought the changes might bring a fresh start to the government's media relations were, however, disappointed. According to those interviewed, the new operation could do little to re-establish control over the news agenda because it was so often driven by genuine and damaging events. It also had to combat a professionalized opposition media operation that fed stories to journalists already disillusioned with Major on Europe and his management of the economy and convinced that he couldn't win the next election.

After Major's re-election as leader in July 1995, the government's media operation was put on a new footing with the reorganization of EDCP[4] under the chairmanship of the recently appointed Deputy Prime Minister, Michael Heseltine. It was attended by party officials, civil servants, and ministers, and its purpose was to consider day-to-day media response and policy coordination in the short and long term. It was intended to create a strong central coordinating body with a chairman of sufficient authority to drive through government policy. It was attended by the prime minister's press secretary as well as the Conservative Party's director of communications. As we shall see, it had little success in effectively pulling together the government's media strategy and in retrospect many have seen Major's decision not to appoint a political chief press secretary—as indeed Tony Blair subsequently did—as either mistaken or naive.

However, quite apart from Major's own reluctance to change the rules (he was, after all, a Conservative), the political realities meant that any change would have been extremely difficult to push through against inevitable civil service disapproval and media outcries about the politicization of Whitehall. Furthermore, even though some political journalists considered an unwillingness to "put the boot in" as a central failing of the Conservatives' media strategy, the bully-boy Labour tactics, as one political journalist termed them, closely observed and admired by the Conservative spin doctors, would have been difficult to operate: the government's tiny majority, its low standing in the opinion polls and, in its final two years, its inability to control its members, seriously weakened its capacity to take the whip hand in media relations; attempts to do so went badly wrong.

MONCLOA: THE FELIPE FACTOR

Felipe González had become Prime Minister of Spain in 1982. Charismatic leader of the progressive Left who sought to democratize Franco's legacy, he was a natural and unrivaled communicator on the Spanish political scene, winning four successive election victories (1982-1993). Government media relations were the responsibility of the Prime Minister's Office (*Ministerio de la Presidencia*) headed by the Government Spokesperson, who had ministerial status, with overall responsibility for media relations. The Office was composed of two sections, one of which was responsible for relations with Parliament and the media covering Parliament and the other for relations with the foreign media. Both were headed by a civil servant.

The Government Spokesperson's function was to organize the Prime Minister's diary; brief the press every Friday; coordinate all ministerial press offices; gather information about what had been published both in the national and foreign media about the government and Spain (in the case of foreign media); and finally, prepare a daily press digest for Government ministers. While it governed as a minority from 1993 to 1996, González's government formalized relations with its coalition partners, a task also undertaken by the Prime Minister's Office. Daily morning meetings were attended by the government spokesman, and heads of sections. Discussion would concern the news prospects for the day, responses to the media, coordination of news releases from the various ministries, and news strategies for the weekend. However, the Prime Minister's Spokesman, Rubalcaba, and other officials regarded their work as one of simply collecting information and acting as a reactive body rather than having any remit to manage the message. In his words, "The Press Office worked as an Information Office, not as a Communication Office." The Prime Minister's Spokesman regarded his own appointment as a political rather than journalistic one. Indeed, he had never worked in the media nor had any of his predecessors.

Those interviewed considered the coordination between ministries to have been weak (see also López Agudín, 1996). Ministers sent their media spokesperson to attend the meetings organized by the Prime Minister's Spokesman at Moncloa rather than attending themselves. According to the head of one of the media sections, it was extremely difficult to centralize the organization of media relations for two reasons: first, ministers preferred to control their own media relations and second, the journalists who covered the Prime Minister's office were not the same as those who covered the various ministries. According to the Prime Minister's spokesman, his office only ever managed to coordinate ministerial appearances before parliamentary committees and receive notification of ministries' media activities. And, according to the Head of the Press Office of the Minister of the Interior, during the last year in government there were difficulties in co-ordinating the communication operations of the Prime Minister's Office with that of the ministry.

The Prime Minister's Spokesman believed that the weak central media office was a result of the party's lack of sensitivity towards political communication. González's government did not, for example, pay much attention to the news cycle: the Council of Ministers, for instance, would never end before 3:15 and as news programs were transmitted at 3:00 p.m., there was never time to get anything ready. As one official said, "I never had the time to get the press conference prepared. Many weekends were lost in terms of news management, since I could not say anything to the media until 3:30, when most news programs are over, and the press has already decided its agenda." This meant there was also no time for the government to react to other parties' statements about current issues. Rubalcaba often raised this problem with the prime minister, but according to him, González´s reply was, "It is more important to have the necessary time to make decisions, than to think of how to communicate them."

However, the personality of Felipe González himself was considered to make up to a certain extent for the lack of a strong communication structure. He was thought of as a popular, natural leader unlike the opposition leader, and a great communicator who needed little training. As his former spokesman put it, "He knew how to explain things to people. That is why I always trusted his decisions regarding relations with the media." Communication strategies were agreed upon by González and the Vice President, and communicated to the Spokesman, who simply gave general guidelines if coordination of ministries' press offices was required. At the same time this "communication bomb," as one official described González, could also cause problems: because he was the message, it was difficult for other ministers to be included, as later disagreements between Moncloa and the Ministry of the Interior showed.

According to party officials, lack of professionalization and reliance on González's ability to communicate characterized the party's press office. There was no fixed regular meeting between the party and the government. Party officials interviewed complained about the lack of coordination. The party's news operations were mainly agreed upon between González and his party chief, relying on informal communication between them. There were no formal meetings with the Head of the Press office.

MANAGING IN THE STYGIAN STABLES OF SLEAZE

Major's Sleaze Labyrinth

When the first critical media scandal after the 1992 election was broken by the Sunday tabloid, *The People*, Britain's had just calamitously withdrawn from the European Union's Exchange Rate Mechanism (ERM). The scandal concerned the extramarital relations of government Minister David Mellor. According to a party official, in standing firmly by his Minister, Major set an unfortunate precedent that would affect the behavior of those accused of misdemeanors in the future: "We had a succession of MPs misbehaving in one way or another and they all took their cue from the way things had been handled before. And they'd always argue: 'Why should we go when Mellor got away with it and Yeo got away with it?'" Of course both these MPs eventually resigned, but only after relentless pressure from the media. When party managers tried to persuade another misbehaving Tory to resign in March 1997 after *The Sun's* exposé of his adulterous dalliances, he refused on the grounds that others had not. Further accusations of sleaze surfaced after the collapse of the Matrix-Churchill trial in November 1992, and the Scott Committee, appointed by Major to investigate the affair, was to provide a further source of awkward stories for the government until its denouement in February 1996.

Journalists couldn't help notice and worry away at the gap between what they saw as the obvious politically expedient course of action (the dropping of a minister/the condemnation of an MP) and the combination of personal loyalty and adherence to official convention that characterized Major's handling of his colleagues' misdemeanors. Although there were more ministerial resignations than in any other parliament in the twentieth century, the overwhelming impression given was that these had been the result of public and media pressure rather than prime-ministerial action.

The year 1994 brought a deluge of sleaze stories, mostly broken by the tabloids and gleefully taken up by the lobby and the broadcast media. Major's "Back-to-Basics" conference speech in October 1993 provided welcome ammunition for an overheated tabloid market that, for the rest of Major's Premiership, sought to publish ever more lurid accounts of MPs' sexual misdemeanors. The final thread of the tangled web of sleaze stories was provided in 1994 by the revelation in July's *Sunday Times* that Tory MPs had taken cash for asking parliamentary questions. *The Guardian* followed this up in October with news that government ministers had received undeclared cash and hospitality. Two ministers resigned and another withdrew from the Cabinet. The reverberations from what became known as *Cash for Questions* rumbled on for the rest of Major's time as Prime Minister, providing a steady stream of difficult stories.

Media relations became almost an obsession. One strategy was to try to distance the Prime Minister from the hurly-burly of the scandal stories. However, Press Secretary Christopher Meyer's decision to reduce the informal contact between Major and the political editors and correspondents from 1994 onwards (Seldon, 1997, and personal interviews) meant that Number Ten sacrificed one of its greatest assets—Major's cordial personal relationships with those who reported politics and, of course, sleaze. At the same time it contributed to the increasingly thin-skinned Prime Minister's sense of isolation. In the words of one of Major's party officials (personal interview, 1998):

> John Major was often inconsolable because of the press coverage and there was some very vicious coverage. He could be too sensitive. A phone call would often be the solution to a bad story but by this time he was so battered and bruised that he didn't ring the press enough. He'd become very defensive.

This in turn fed his frustration with those journalists whose by-lines accompanied stories that were antipathetic to a government that he still considered was steering the nation in the right direction. His view of the media became increasingly negative; he remarked to one of the officials interviewed, "I sometimes think I've got a bad job but I wouldn't want yours."

After July 1995, reinvigorated by his leadership victory and con-scious of a fast approaching general election, Major reorganized media relations. Recruits were brought in from the ranks of political journalists to organize the Conservative Party's own media operations, and two heavy-weight ministers, Heseltine and Mawhinney, were charged with the coordination of party and government media strategy. A revamped EDCP was to be the vehicle for their efforts. Most of those interviewed agree, however, that the Committee was not very effective: it had little success in controlling the agenda and acted largely as a reactive force. In the words of one who served (personal interview, 1998) on it:

> Hezza [Heseltine] liked these Cecil B. de Mille creations. . . . [We] would conspire almost continually to change the EDCP structure, but it was the Deputy PM's baby created by him; it would have required the PM to take him on. The bigger the meeting the less can-did people are—that was the first problem. The second problem was that because it was a properly constituted cabinet committee, it couldn't talk politics. What you'd end up doing is having a half-hour formal discussion, which was a complete waste of time [and] by the time we'd finished the formal bit and got onto the political session, we'd started to look at our watches because there'd be another meeting. . . . So politics was always relegated. It was a night-mare. The structures were arcane. Major thought Hezza was getting a grip on it, but Hezza's answer to getting a grip on it was to create one of the most unwieldy management structures that we've ever known in British politics. . . . There were days when there might be a running sleaze story and . . . we wouldn't actually talk about it.

Even with Heseltine at the helm, Cabinet members could not be relied upon to carry out the Committee's directives; after eighteen years of government, ministers had built up powerful fiefdoms of their own and coteries of political advisers. One of the constant complaints of media officials concerned the unruly behavior of these political advisers and Major himself often despaired of the damaging leaks to the media. Party discipline was little better and, despite Major's confirmation as leader in the summer of 1995, contributed to the general impression of loss of prime-ministerial control.

In November 1995 the party's director of communication departed after a mere six months in the job. His successor was appointed by the new party chairman who considered trying to appoint a new spin doctor figure in the style of Labour's officials. In the end, *The Sunday Express* political editor was hired to undertake a more proactive media strategy, but without trespassing over the political/civil service divide. Although the new appointments undoubtedly gave a new shine to media relations, there was still no heavyweight figure who could provide an effective interface between government, party and the media. The public face of the government was considered competent, affable, but when difficult stories arose, utterly unable to dispel the impression of a weakened and weak executive. As former political journalist, Lance Price (Price, personal interview, 1998) said: "They really did play it very straight [on sleaze] . . . but . . . effectively it was stone-walling the whole time. It gave the impression . . . that Major was defending the indefensible."

The only bright spot for Major's media managers was the very effective media operation mounted by the government and the Conservative Party to counter the political fallout from the publication of the Scott Report in February 1996 (Norton-Taylor, personal interview, 2000). Even here it is questionable whether the objective (to prevent the forced resignation of ministers) was not gained at the expense of a further erosion in a belief in Major's ability to lead and act decisively (Negrine, 1996a).

This all came home to roost in the general election in 1997. The issue of sleaze dominated media coverage of the first two weeks of the election. It had been firmly placed there by clever opposition footwork, Major's "playing by the book" approach, the *Guardian's* missionary zeal, and "Events, dear boy, events." The Conservatives' inability to make the political weather could not have been more clearly evidenced than by their handling of the publication of the results of the parliamentary investigation (the Downey Report) into the *Cash for Questions* affair. It is difficult to prove that the government deliberately brought forward the dissolution of Parliament in order to avoid discussion of the Report. Evidence suggests that it was the government's distinctly nonpolitical approach to government that allowed them to be caught out by accusations that they had. As reported to us by Major's officials, the extraordinary fact is that before the issue was raised in Parliament, the political implications of the decision effectively to dissolve Parliament were not discussed. This left the government open to political ambush.

Major's last Prime Minister's Question Time on Thursday 20 March was spent defending his government against allegations of sleaze and the following day *The Guardian's* headline was: "Sleaze: The Evidence". A *Times'* leader accused Major of having failed Parliament and the country in not permitting the publication of the Report and once again the government was wrong-footed by a masterly opposition operation assisted by a compliant media. Ironically, however, it was Major's determined adherence to the conventions of the separation between party and government and a principled commitment to following parliamentary procedure[5] that landed his government in hot water. The media strategists would have preferred to get the Report out, believing they would have been able to mount a media operation on the back of Downey's exoneration of ten Conservative MPs.

One week later the opposition couldn't believe its good luck as another Tory MP was discovered *in flagrante* by the tabloid press. One party official recalls being tipped off by *The Sun's* political editor about another sex scandal on the way and Central Office's futile attempts to force the resignation of a Conservative candidate. A familiar and sorry series of events played their way out: a tabloid story, broadsheets, and broadcast media follow, a Prime Minister seen to be powerless in forcing the deselection of the Tory candidate. Events followed a similar pattern in the case of Neil Hamilton, the disgraced former Conservative minister who insisted on standing for re-election. The sense was that, try as he might, Major simply could not find his way out of the sleaze labyrinth.

In sum, the state of affairs at this time was cumulative: events and strategies interacted in a complex way so as, first, to make the reporting of those events even more damaging to the government than they may otherwise have been and, second, to give Major a reputation as personally honest but unacceptably politically weak.

Corruption in the Court of Felipe

Coverage of corruption stories in Spain reached its peak between 1990 and 1996. Those interviewed claimed that this did not result in the adoption of proactive media strategies by the government. However, it will be argued below that in fact several specific communication strategies were adopted. In this period, the government believed it had all but lost control of the news agenda. According to the Prime Minister's Spokesman, "Before we really managed to get into the news what we had made public. But from 1993 to 1996 we totally lost control of the news." In his view, credibility was completely lost and the corruption coverage generated a general climate of suspicion, that even affected normally supportive newspapers such as *El País*. The Secretary for Relations with Parliament considered that "the constant accusations of corruption against the government formed part of a strategy on the part of sections of the media to destroy the government's news agenda."

González's officials reported that every part of the media was treated in the same way and leaks were avoided, as they were considered damaging to the government in the long term. They also considered that no specific media strategies had been employed to counter the corruption stories. Nevertheless, it is possible to identify several strategies. First, from 1994 González's officials decided to organize press meetings on Mondays, traditionally a slack day for political news, to try to get something positive in the media on Tuesdays. From Wednesday on the government found it very difficult to get any good news across, as Wednesday was the day for parliamentary questions and Friday the day of the Council of Ministers' meeting. Press conferences after the Ministers' meeting became increasingly dominated by questions about corruption.

Secondly, after the flight of the Director of Police in April 1994, the loss of the European elections, and new allegations of corruption, González decided to adopt what was called the "New Political Style". This consisted in more appearances in Parliament and the media. *Antena 3*, for example, began a series entitled "Chats with the President". This new policy paid dividends: this period (September-October 1994) coincided with the only time that polls showed a rise in the Prime Minister's popularity. According to a government official, the policy of increased visibility was reversed when new corruption allegations emerged.

A third strategy was to keep *El Mundo* at arm's length from the government: although journalists from *El Mundo* had access to government press conferences, they were not given interviews with González. The government Spokesman put it this way: "It's obvious that we gave interviews with Felipe González to some sections of the media before others. *El País* was clearly favoured above *El Mundo*. The relationship with *El Mundo* was extremely tense. It was very difficult. . . . For Felipe González it would have meant giving an interview to a paper that was continually attacking us with falsehoods."

The government attitude to broadcast media was more subtle. The Prime Minister's Spokesman described their relationship as even-handed: "We tried to have daily telephone conversations with all the channels during corruption coverage, in order to explain things and to regain our credibility." However, this was not the perception at *Antena 3*.

Although there were some telephone calls to give advance notification
of legislation, say journalists at *Antena 3*, the relationship with Moncloa
was an uneasy one, in part because the private channel preferred it that
way. The relationship between *TVE1* and Moncloa was much warmer,
and the channel gave more coverage to government stories than was the
case on rival channels.[6]

The main specific strategy (never regarded as a "strategy" by those
interviewed) from 1993 to 1996 was to isolate González from those in the
party and the government implicated in corruption. In the Prime
Minister's Spokesman's words, "If you want González not to be linked
to certain matters, you have to avoid having him talking about them.
The opposition wanted González to take responsibility for whatever
happened in Spain. And we wanted to avoid that." In practice, this
meant, firstly, restrictions on parliamentary questions. During his last
two years in government, on various occasions González did not appear
for Parliamentary Question Time. It also meant efforts to generate news
about issues in which people were considered to be more interested,
such as the economy and employment. Finally, there was an attempt to
project an image of González as senior world statesman. Most of his
press conferences took place abroad with another international leader
and the Government Press Office was extremely efficient in distributing
information about these conferences to the national media. On these
occasions González usually responded to questions about corruption
back home by claiming that an international press conference was not
the place to deal with domestic matters.

There was just one press conference held by González about the
Roldán case, in which he made public his acceptance of the interior minister's resignation. His approach to the *Roldán* case was to claim ignorance. González's officials recognized the potential political and public
opinion cost of this approach, but at the same time considered it to be
the only way of establishing that González was not responsible for what
had occurred. The press conference held by the Interior Minister was,
however, considered to be a mistake. The following day *El Mundo* published an article showing that some of the information given by the
Ministry had not been true. According to the President's Spokesman,
"We should just have said that Roldán had been captured and kept the
whole operation a secret on the grounds of it being a state secret. This is
how many other countries such as the United States and France operate.
But this press conference was a decision of the Minster of the Interior
and I respected that."

The Spanish government's approach to communication about the
scandal cases was influenced by its conviction that the opposition and
the media continually sought to confound the different cases in the pub-

lic's mind with the aim of undermining trust in the government. This was the view expressed by Felipe González in an interview some years after losing the elections:

> I don't know what damaged the party most, whether it was the accusations about corruption or those they made against us about GAL. It's difficult to know because even when there was a ferocious campaign about GAL . . . it was never done without mentioning corruption. The two issues were and still are systematically confused, because they are matters which feed on one another, even though, from people's psychological point of view, corruption was considered more repugnant than the dirty war. All of this was and still is abused. The discourse was terrible. I had a bad time, a really bad time, all through that period, and it seemed to me, and it still seems to me, very unjust. . . . (González, cited in Prego, 2000, p. 289)

For the 1996 general elections the Socialist Party saw that the opposition was planning a "soft" campaign in which corruption would not be an important issue. They knew the opposition did not want to stir up political debate referring to the matter. González's officials considered that this helped the Socialist Party focus attention on other issues. This strategy was followed by *TVE1* (which did not bring the issue up in interviews with candidates the day before voting day) and by *El País*. It was not followed, however, by *El Mundo* and *Antena 3*, for whom "corruption" was a very important issue

In sum, González's media strategy involved the contrived absence of the Prime Minister—junior government colleagues responded to the corruption allegations—and his high visibility in carefully chosen international settings. Paradoxically, despite the fact that he headed a government which, as one party official pointed out, had "had fourteen senior officials prosecuted, suffered three devaluations of the peseta and seen the loss of 700,000 jobs," González still managed the notable feat of increasing his personal vote in the 1996 elections compared with those of 1993.

THE LIMITATIONS OF SPIN

Tables 5.1 and 2 provide a visual summary of how spin doctoring operated in British and Spanish scandals.

Both Major and González faced serious cases of political scandal during their administrations that severely damaged the standings of their respective governments and parties. But, in pleading ignorance

TABLE 5. 1 Chief Executives and their News Offices

UNITED KINGDOM—JOHN MAJOR	SPAIN-FELIPE GONZALEZ
Point of Departure	
Both Prime Ministers faced major political scandals that severely damaged the standings of their respective governments and parties.	
Personalities and Styles	
• Seen as likeable and "clubbable" human being.	• Charismatic.
• Human stoicism towards bad behavior of assorted colleagues.	• Popular and natural leader.
• Image of decency and plain dealing.	• Unrivaled communicator.
• Less thuggish style than his predecessor. Preference for cordial personal relations with the media.	• Seductive media style.
Communication Offices	
• Proactive rather than reactive office.	• Reactive rather than proactive office.
• Clear communication structure.	• Lack of strong communication structure resulted in a blurring of the boundaries between administrative and political media management.
• No blurring of the boundaries between government and party political media management.	• Coordination between party and government communication offices relied upon a personal basis, on González as head of the party.
• Constrained by institutional rules and conventions. Playing by the book style: government information should be done on an impartial, Civil Service basis, and not on political basis.	

and an incapacity to rid their governments of the sources of sleaze, both leaders effectively avoided being tarred by the sleaze brush and were not portrayed as the villains of the scandal stories.

In Major's case the response served to underline his personal probity—he always remained "Honest John"—but also reinforced his reputation as a weak and indecisive leader. It is, of course, a moot point as to whether, in the trade off between probity and weakness, the right choices were made. As veteran BBC political correspondent Nick Jones (Jones,

TABLE 5.2 Communication Strategies

VISIBILITY MANAGEMENT

United Kingdom	Spain
Unsuccessful management of visibility: inadequate balance between visibility and concealment.	Successful management of visibility: adequate balance between visibility and concealment.

- **Visibility:**

  Journalists abused the intimacy Major strove to create: what had been seen or heard was used to set him up for personal ridicule.

- **Concealment:**

  "Bunker mentality" in Downing Street: personal contact with the media was limited to Tory proprietors and editors. Reinforcement of Major's authority was attempted by keeping him distant from the media.

- **Visibility:**

  Deployment of media strategies that presented a strong and vigorous version of the leader.

  Successful attempt to manage the flow of information on slack days for political news.

  Successful management of visibility of the PM in international fora.

- **Concealment:**

  Avoidance of parliamentary question time, allowing González not to have to answer questions related to the scandals.

| Management of visibility was not helped by the absence of a compliant public service broadcaster plus a significant newspaper readership of a press which had become hostile. | A compliant public service broadcaster in a country with low newspaper readership helped management of visibility. |

PRESENTATION OF PM ROLES

United Kingdom	Spain

- Personal approach to media relations.

- No personalization of his institutional role: for instance, during the last few years, he hardly appeared in public with his wife.

- No blurring of boundaries: constitutional strict separation between government and party political media management; and between governmental and state role.

- Turning the PM's role into a world statesman's role.

- Major's international (particularly European) role was more a disintegrative than integrative force.

- González's governmental role was portrayed in international fora as a world statesman.

TABLE 5.2 Communication Strategies *(Continued)*

RESULTS: PRIME MINISTER'S MEDIA IMAGE

United Kingdom	Spain
• Nice: his personal probity was reinforced.	• Charismatic person.
• But weak and indecisive leader: doubts were cast about his capacity to "hire and fire", to handle incidents decisively.	• Though his position was weakened, his reputation for strong leadership was retained.
• In pleading ignorance, he was portrayed as a feeble leader. Distance between himself and the sleaze was achieved at the cost of his reputation for "decisiveness" and "knowing what's going on."	• In pleading ignorance, he managed to dissociate both his person and his premiership from the scandal accusations. Accusations involved lower ranks.

personal interview, 1998) put it: "Major wasn't tainted by the sleaze but part of the problem was that it did require a firm and strong leadership and a consistent message." González, on the other hand, although certainly finding his position weakened, was able to retain a reputation for strong leadership. How can we explain these different outcomes?

Structural and contingent differences in political and media arrangements in which values and traditions are also inscribed, as well as sharp contrasts in personality and style between the two prime ministers, help us to understand the similar yet dissimilar outcomes. González's ability to deploy media strategies which presented a strong and vigorous version of Felipe as world statesman, active in promoting peace in the Middle East, active in Europe, friend of Helmut Kohl, above the tumult of the domestic scene, succeeded in most of the media.

For a number of reasons, this option was simply not open to Major: first, he could not count on a compliant public service broadcaster; second, patterns of media use in Britain ensured that even if he could have counted on a helpful BBC, the importance of newspaper readership would have dissipated this effect; third, Major's international role, particularly on the European stage, usually functioned as a disintegrative rather than integrative force; and finally, Felipe's own charismatic personality made the "world statesman" version of González more credible than would have been possible for Major, so often cruelly lampooned as the man who tucked his shirt inside his underpants.

Media management techniques were clearly more professionalized in Britain than in Spain. In Spain, coordination of ministries and the link between party and government was not formalized and news management was not given high priority in the Government's thinking. This was not the case in Britain where numerous attempts were made to streamline and improve the government's media operation, partly to counter the sophisticated operation mounted by the Labour Party. However, even though more professional than its Spanish counterpart, the British government media machine was hamstrung by institutional and cultural complexities, which meant it was not as effective in managing its leader's image as the Spanish operation. John Major's "playing by the book" may have meant that sleaze damaged his government more than it might have done otherwise. However, it may also explain why he was able to salvage from the sleaze morass some sort of personal reputation among journalists and public alike.

This evidence leads us to a clear conclusion: talk of sound bites and spin doctors can understate the extent to which political actors operate in an institutionally and culturally delimited political space. Government media management—like prime ministerial power itself—is both subject to the course of the events it seeks to create and embedded in an environment constituted by norms, rules and personal preferences that at the very least constrain it. But this is not to say they must simply accommodate to that space, because (as New Labour has shown) they are over time helping to shape and constitute and change it.

Indeed, we would predict that in an increasingly fragmented and competitive media market in which informal networks and understandings are undermined, Spanish political parties will have little choice but to professionalize their media management strategies despite, as Major's case shows, their severe limitations. This chapter also points to a further conclusion; namely, that in order to understand media narratives and, in particular, the way in which the central characters are portrayed, it is important to understand the conditions and dynamics of news operations.

NOTES

1. This chapter is based on an article published in the *European Journal of Communication*, coauthored by Karen Sanders, Timothy Bale, and María José Canel, titled "Managing Sleaze. Prime Ministers and News Management in Conservative Great Britain and Socialist Spain" (*European Journal of Communication*, 1999, *14*(4), December, 461-486). A detailed analysis of the British case was published by Timothy Bale and Karen Sanders (2001). 'Playing by the Book': Success and Failure in John Major's Approach to Prime Ministerial Media Management,' in *Contemporary British History*, *15*(4), 93-110.
2. "Chief executive" is the term used by Colin Seymour-Ure, who directed a very useful workshop on government-media relations at the joint sessions of the European Consortium for Political Research in Warwick in 1998. The

authors would like to thank him and the other participants for their comments on an earlier version of this chapter.

3. The term "spin doctor" has, as McNair (2000) has pointed out, acquired a pejorative connotation referring to "an especially manipulative, sinister and threatening form of political public relations which goes far beyond the older, more respectable and accepted (by journalists) work of the press or publicity officer" (p. 126).

4. See Seldon (1997, pp. 601-602). The full name was "The Ministerial Committee on the Co-ordination and Presentation of Government Policy."

5. The leader of the House, as well as being a member of EDCP, was also chairman of the Standards and Privileges Committee and took his responsibilities very seriously. According to a party official, he did not consult with political strategists about the fate of the Downey Report and as a result the campaign machine was completely wrong-footed.

6. During the 1996 election campaign, there was a ratio of seven government stories (on TVE1) to three (on private channels) (Semetko & Canel, 1997).

6

Characters and Plots

In Chapter 3 we discussed the notion of the "framing" of news stories. Our purpose in this chapter and the next is to look at the specific frames created in the news narratives of the British and Spanish press in the reporting of scandal.

FRAMING AND FRAMES

Earlier we proposed a definition of a frame as "manifest content that can evoke absent content and, in making use of resonant cultural codes, implies judgments of something to make sense of the social world."

In order to identify specific frames, and based upon the assumption that meanings are expressed in present content, van Dijk (1998) has written of "surface structures" such as "concrete lexical items, clause and

sentence structure, syntactic categories, word order, discourse intona-
tion, graphical structures, and the organization of macrostructures in
canonical schemata, such as those of narration, argumentation or news
reporting" (p. 45).

Ghanem (1997) describes four dimensions of frames: the topic of a
news item, the presentation (size and placement), cognitive attributes
(details of what is included in the frame), and affective attributes (tone
of picture) (pp. 10-14). Focused specifically on how issues are presented,
Iyengar (1991) offers a general typology of frames: the episodic category
(issues are depicted predominantly as concrete instances or events) and
the thematic category (issues are depicted more generally either in terms
of collective outcomes, public policy debates, or historical trends) (p. 18).

The connection between absent and present content has been more
fully explored from a critical discourse analysis perspective (Pan &
Kosicki, 1993), an approach that looks for the functional relationships
that language use generates.[1] This connection between absent and present content has also been examined from a news narrative perspective.
Entman (1991) explains relations between present and absent content in
news narratives in the following terms:

> Frames reside in the specific properties of the news narrative. . . .
> News frames are constructed from and embodied in the keywords,
> metaphors, concepts, symbols, and visual images emphasized in a
> news narrative. Since the narrative finally consists of nothing more
> than words and pictures, frames can be detected by probing for par-
> ticular words and visual images that consistently appear in a narra-
> tive and convey thematically consonant meanings across media and
> time. By providing, repeating, and thereby reinforcing words and
> visual images that reference some ideas but not others, frames work
> to make some ideas more salient in the text, others less so—and oth-
> ers entirely invisible. . . . (p. 7)

Entman analyzes frames in terms of importance (amount of material
available and prominence with which it is displayed [p. 9]) and four
other frame dimensions; namely, agency, identification of characters,
categorizations, and generalizations. Taken together these characteristics
ensure that a frame will be established within a specific discursive
domain.

Entman's (1991) suggestion offers a useful perspective for examining scandal narratives and provides helpful tools with which to understand the discourse domain of media texts. He grants news stories the
status of narrative, and it is his model we largely draw upon to discuss
the frames of British and Spanish scandal stories.

However, his model does not provide a way of examining the plot of the story in terms of how relations between characters of media narratives are articulated. In this respect we have found van Dijk's and Protess et al.'s suggestions useful, as we will later explain in more detail.

In this chapter, then, we explore the characters and plots of scandal stories through a cautious examination of "importance" and a more thorough analysis of "characters" and "agency". In the following chapter we will turn to the kind of "moralizing frame" established for each scandal story in particular and for the overarching scandal frame in general.

De Vreese (1999) has established a useful distinction, later explored by De Vreese, Peter, and Semetko (2001), between issue-specific news frames and generic news frames that we will use here. Issue-specific frames "pertain to specific topics or news events, whereas generic frames are broadly applicable to a range of different news topics, some even over time and, potentially, in different cultural contexts" (p. 108). These authors regard Jasperson et al.'s (1998) study of national budget deficits and Entman's (1991) study of the reporting of two international airline incidents as examples of the first approach. Examples of studies of generic news frames can be found in Iyengar's (1991) work, which distinguishes between "episodic" and "thematic" frames, and Cappella and Jamieson's study (1996, 1997), which differentiates between a "strategy frame," a "conflict" frame, and an "issue-frame" in the coverage of politics. These frames "are examples of a more generic conceptualisation of a kind of news frame that has the capacity to transcend issue, time, and space limits" (De Vreese, Peter, & Semetko, 2001, p. 109).

Both approaches have advantages and disadvantages. An issue-specific approach can capture specific aspects of the details of selection and organization present in news coverage and pertaining specifically to a well-defined issue; but the high degree of detail makes it difficult "to generalize, compare, and use as a base for general hypothesis and theory building" the frames identified (De Vreese, Peter, & Semetko, 2001, pp. 108-109). Generic frames "offer less possibility for examining the framing of an event in fine detail, but they allow comparisons between frames, topics, and potentially framing practices in different countries."

Our analysis is not concerned with discrete events or specific issues, but scandal stories that extend over time. Furthermore, the scandal stories do not refer to one issue, but can link several at the same time. Coverage of scandal is linked to the coverage of politics in general. We will examine Entman's four frame dimensions in relation first to all the cases in each country and second in relation to each individual scandal case. This will allow us in Chapter 8 to see which generic frames predominated in the coverage of scandal in Britain and Spain.

First of all, some explanation is required of each of Entman's frame dimensions.

Importance

Scholars have suggested that "the essence of framing is sizing, the magnifying or shrinking of elements of depicted reality to make them more or less salient" (Entman, 1991, p. 9). Importance, in this sense, is seen in terms of salience or visibility of an issue or a person. It is measured in terms of the amount of material that is available and how prominently it is displayed. The problem here is what "prominently" means (Entman, 1991, p. 9). Ghanem (1997) looks at this idea in terms of emphasis given to topics in the media, such as placement and size, as well as other elements that influence the prominence of a news item such as photographs, pull quotes, and subheadings (pp. 11-12).

To measure importance or relevance of material in news narratives is a complex task. Certain patterns and variables have been recognized in calibrating importance such as even versus odd pages, degree of picture use, the relevance of people involved in the story, or the total number of published issues on a specific topic. These criteria are undoubtedly helpful and can provide indicators of importance. But they are more useful for analyzing discrete events such as, for instance, a murder or accident. Even then, different features of newspaper style complicate this exercise: font size, color use, tabloid or broadsheet genres all shape our perception of importance. Establishing importance as a frame dimension for scandal stories poses many difficulties. They can be complex narratives spread over time (*Arms to Iraq* and the *Gal-Cesid*, for example) or explosive short-term stories that lend themselves to vivid, tabloid presentation (the Piers Merchant sex scandal). Here we will present basic coverage details based on our sample, which includes variables such as article length, picture use, and page number, without claiming that some scandals were more important than others.

Identification of Characters

In general terms, agents of political news narratives are politicians, journalists, experts of various sorts (political analysts and academics, for example), employers, trade unionists, and ordinary people.

As we saw in Chapter 3, Protess et al. (1991) suggest that characters in scandal stories are framed as villains and victims. Cook (1996) talks of protagonists and antagonists. The relationship between characters is not as thoroughly explored in Entman's model. Entman (1991) states that characters can be framed with humanizing words, emphasizing the human nature of the victims and the guilt of the villains; alternatively, they can be portrayed through a technical discourse, making it difficult to establish empathy for the victims or assign guilt to the villains. Though this approach is helpful for analyzing agency, as we will see, it is not so useful for understanding the relationship of characters to each other.

Van Dijk (1998) examines relations established among characters in terms of the binary opposition of "Ourselves" (and our good actions) and "the Others" (and their bad actions):

> Good acts will usually be self attributed to Ourselves (or our allies) and bad acts other-attributed to the Others (or their allies), and in both cases these groups are assigned full control and responsibility for their acts. The converse is true for Our bad acts and Their good acts: Our bad acts will be de-emphasized and attributed to circumstances beyond our control and the same is true for Their good acts. (p. 43)

In news scandal stories, because the press is involved in the revelation of the scandal, it could be the case that the confrontation between "Ourselves" and "the Others" takes the form of a confrontation between the politicians, who are "the Others" (the wrongdoers), and the press ("Ourselves", who exercise a watchdog role). We will analyze whether this is the case for the British and Spanish news scandal narratives.

Agency

In news narratives acts are attributed to actors. This means evoking meanings for understanding the causes for action. As a consequence, agency is ascribed. In Entman's words (1991), "agency answers the question of exactly who did it" and what was the causal force that created the newsworthy act (p. 11).

In scandal stories "agency" is of special interest because the meanings evoked in narratives contribute to the allocation of responsibility and blame for the scandalous actions. The nature of the action is thus framed and particular species of moral disorder emerge. Protess et al. (1991) refer to this same idea when they explain how news scandal stories are conceptualized. Journalists, in attempting to visualize the story that might emerge from the raw facts, see the potential to tell a compelling tale. The first task is to identify the possible characters and the story line, which means asking who are the villains, the victims, and the causes that led villains to act (pp. 211-212). We will see in the empirical analysis different ways in which news narratives attribute agency of actions.

Categorizations

Having identified characters and agency, journalists need to find the appropriate language and images to place all the participants within a compelling story.

In scandal stories this means that wrongdoing is framed: moral assessments are made. "Journalists look for a picture frame around the early evidence of wrongdoing" (Protess et al., 1991, p. 212). There is a moralizing frame, "a discursive domain inhered in the choice of labels for the incidents, which tend to place them in categories that conventionally either elicit or omit moral evaluation" (Entman, 1991, p. 18).

Loaded and colorful language is used: "tragedy," "farce," "comedy," "humbug," "eccentric," "bizarre," "spectacle," "atrocity." As we shall see, the "picture frame," built out of moral assessments and the preferred evaluations for the events, often draws upon resonant and distinct cultural codes.

Generalizations

To frame the wrongdoing in a way that allows the story to remain alive implies that reporters look backward and forward in search of a fresh angle for the story. To do so, they look beyond the individual case and try to connect the specific characters and their agency to the problem that is at stake. Characters and plots take on a broader meaning that may be relevant to the existence and solution of more extensive social problems.

The "surface structures" in which this framing appears is through judgmental generalizations. The general realities that are referred to commonly have to do with the nature of the political system and reflect current debates in public opinion.

Entman (1991) argues that the degree of generalizations that appear in news narratives do or do not reinforce the moralizing frame (p. 20). The absence or presence of generalizations plays an important role: excessive generalization can help transfer the guilt from a specific actor to an abstract institution such as, for instance, the government. As a result, wrongdoing is framed not as a result of somebody's mistake but rather of the evil of a whole political system. Again, as we shall see, the sort of generalizations present in news narratives express the different debates that were generated by the scandal stories.

BASIC CHARACTERISTICS OF SCANDAL COVERAGE

United Kingdom

As Table 6.1 shows, a total number of 1,781 articles were coded on 256 different days.

Most coverage was in the form of news stories (52% of total sample, equivalent to 942 articles); 17.9 percent (318) are features, and 0.4 percent (8) interviews. Opinion articles are distributed as follows: 10.3 percent (183) are editorials, 6.7 percent (119) home columns, and 3.4 percent (60) guest columns.

If we examine the classical variables that imply importance or relevance, we find that 19.2 percent (339) of total articles are on the front page; 31.8 percent (567) are on an odd page; and more than one in three (34.7%, 597 articles) include one or more pictures. Distribution of articles by sections shows that one fourth of articles (369) were in a "special section", a section specially created by the newspaper for the particular scandal case.

If we look at data by cases, *Cash for Questions* was the most written about scandal case: 827 articles or 46.4 percent of the sample articles are about this scandal. *Arms to Iraq* receives considerably less coverage (28.6% or 510 articles) and 24.9 percent or 444 articles were produced about *Sexual Misdemeanors*. *Cash for Questions* is the scandal case with

TABLE 6.1 Basic Characteristics of Coverage

	UNITED KINGDOM										
	Number of Stories		Number of Days	Articles on Front Page		Articles on Odd Page		Number of Articles with Pictures		Articles in Special Section	
	N	% of Total	N	N	% Within Case	N	% Within Case	N	% Within Case	N	% Within Case
• Arms to Iraq	510	28.6	87	104	20.30	136	26.6	153	30.6	73	14.3
• Cash for Questions	827	46.4	120	149	18.01	294	35.5	289	35.9	248	29.3
• Sexual Misdemeanors	444	24.9	49	86	19.36	137	30.8	155	37.3	155	10.8
Total	1,781	100	256	339		567		597		369	

which most news events are associated, producing coverage on 120 days, as compared with 87 days for *Arms to Iraq* and 49 days for *Sexual Misdemeanors*. If we consider that *Sexual Misdemeanors* analyzes only a third of the total number of Tory sex scandals, it is clear that the amount of coverage dedicated to this issue was proportionately very great.

Figures for articles on front pages are quite similar for all the cases (20.3% in *Arms to Iraq*, 18.01% in *Cash for Questions*, and 19.36% in *Sexual misdemeanors*). If we look at articles on odd pages, there is a higher percentage for *Cash for Questions* (35.5%) over *Sexual Misdemeanors* (30.8%) and *Arms to Iraq* (26.6%). *Sexual Misdemeanors* is the scandal case that has a slightly higher number of pictures: whereas 37.3 percent of its articles have at least one picture, in *Cash for Questions* this figure is 35.9 percent and in *Arms to Iraq* is 30.6 percent. The most significant difference appears in the number of articles that go in a special section: whereas 29.3 percent of articles in *Cash for Questions* are in a special section, this figure is just 14.3 percent for *Arms to Iraq* and 10.8 percent for *Sexual Misdemeanors*.

Spain

As Table 6.2 shows, a total number of 1,979 articles was coded on 338 different days.

A majority of articles (67.9%, or 1,342 pieces) are news stories, 1.8 percent (36) are features, and 1.4 percent (27) are interviews. Opinion articles are distributed as follows: 5.8 percent (115) are editorials, 11.3 percent (224) home columns, and 1 percent (20) column by a guest.

If we examine position, 15.1 percent (300) are on the front page; 40.7 percent, (equivalent to 806) are on the odd page; and more than one in three (36%, 713 articles) include one or more pictures. Distribution of articles by sections shows that 22.8 percent of articles (444) were in a "special section".

Looking at data by cases, we see that of the four, *Roldán* is the scandal case about which most was published (46%, or 910 articles); 457 (23.1%) articles were written about the *Gal-Lasa Zabala* case; 372 (18.8%) about *Gal-Cesid*; and *Rubio* was the lowest with 240 (12.1%) articles. *Roldán* and *Gal-Lasa Zabala* were written about on 103 and 113 days respectively. The *Gal-Lasa Zabala* scandal had marginally more days' coverage but only half the number of stories of the *Roldán* case.

The *Gal-Cesid* case had most stories on the front page with 100 (26.8%), at least ten points more than the other cases. 46.2 percent of articles on *Rubio* were on an odd page, whereas for the *Roldán* case the figure was 42.6 percent, in the *Gal-Cesid* case 37.6 percent and in the *Gal-Lasa Zabala* case 36.5 percent.

TABLE 6.2 Basic Characteristics of Coverage

	SPAIN										
	Number of Stories		Number of Days	Articles on Front Page			Articles on Odd Page		Number of Articles with Pictures		Articles in Special Section
	N	% of Total	N	N	% Within Case		N	% Within Case	N	% Within Case	N	% Within Case
• Roldán	910	46.	103	91	10		388	42.6	321	35.2	287	31.5
• Gal-Cesid	372	18.8	67	100	26.8		140	37.6	117	31.4	48	12.9
• Rubio	240	12.1	55	38	15.8		111	46.2	107	44.6	29	12
• Gal-Lasa Zabala	457	23.1	113	71	15.5		167	36.5	168	36.8	80	17.5
Total	1, 979	100	338	300			806		713		444	

Again, as in the British coverage, the most significant difference appears in the number of articles published in the special section: whereas 31.5 percent of articles on the *Roldán* case are in a special section, this figure is just 12.9 percent for *Gal-Cesid*, 12 percent for *Rubio*, and 17.5 percent for *Gal-Lasa Zabala*.

These results show that there are no common patterns in terms of importance of coverage across cases. In other words, the scandal case about which most is published in terms of articles has fewer pictures than the others and fewer articles on an odd page.

What we can say from these results is that *Roldán* is the case with the greatest number of articles and the one for which more special sections were created by the newspapers. The whole affair made the story a high-profile "drama" with several acts. The elevated number of days for the *Gal-Lasa Zabala* case can be explained by the fact that the trial of this case was a news event that was spread out in time, with a few articles dedicated to it each day. *Rubio* was a case in which most articles (almost half) used a picture (of the accused person). And *Gal-Cesid* was the case with most articles on the front page, probably because many reproduced the original documents of the foundation of the GAL death squad.

FRAMING THROUGH CHARACTER

Qualitative analysis of editorial headlines and of the text allows us to identify references to actors in the terms suggested by van Dijk:

"Others" and "their bad actions" and an "Ourselves" and "our good actions".[2] On this basis we can draw up a cast list of main characters. In the British press there are three main participants: The others and their bad actions: the politicians; Ourselves and our good actions: the press. There are also references to a third participant, the People or sometimes, the Public. Relations among politicians and the press are portrayed in terms of confrontation and the public is presented as the victimized participant who suffers the effects of the politicians' bad actions. The public also "benefits" from the effects of the press' good actions.

In the Spanish case, the picture includes two participants. Confrontation here is not between politicians and the press, but has a more ideological dimension. The cleavage revolves around the assignation of guilt for corrupt acts. On the one hand are the Socialists, González and his government, who are criticized for corruption; on the other, are those who attack the Socialists and are stigmatized for their constant criticism of González. These characters vary with the newspapers: the "corrupt Socialists" are portrayed in *El Mundo* and *ABC* (both newspapers were ideologically hostile to the Socialist government), whereas "the enemies of the Socialists" appear in *El País* (a newspaper close to the Socialist government). In Spain there is an ideological battle among newspapers. No third character appears: there is almost no reference to the people, and no other participant could be identified in the analysis.

United Kingdom: Politicians, the Press, and the Public

As Table 6.3 shows, 51 references were found in editorials to "the Others and their bad actions"; 43 mentions were found referring to "Ourselves and our good actions"—"Ourselves" being the press; and finally, 38 mentions referred to the people as the ones affected by the actions of the first two participants.

Politicians: The Others and Their Bad Actions. Politicians as "the Other" are referred to in different ways: as a group—the Conservatives—or as a broader assembly—parliament or MPs in general: "They [the Conservatives] have let down not only their party but . . ." (*The Independent*, July 4, 1997); They [MPs] only want publicity when it suits them. Not when it suits the people who elect them" (*The Sun*, July 21, 1992).

The "Others" are the "politicians" who "pontificate" and are guilty of "rank hypocrisy" (*The Sunday Times*, July 26, 1992); "[Politicians] risk being routed by their own behaviour" (*The Sunday Times*, July 26, 1992); "They are uncritically beguiled by their traditions" (*The Guardian*, November 1, 1994).

Table 6.3 General Map of British Characters.

NUMBER OF MENTIONS		
Others (and Their Bad Actions): Politicians	Us (and Our Good Actions): The Press	The People (Those Affected)
51	43	38

They are linked with bad actions, regarded as being hypocritical ("What a two-faced bunch so many of them are" [*The Sun*, July 21, 1992], concerned only with their own interests ("It is their own dirty necks they are worried about" [*The Sun*, January 6, 1994].

The Press: Ourselves and Our Good Actions. Attribution of good actions comes, first, in the form of self-praise. For instance, *The Sunday Times* points out its role in disclosing scandal: "Had it not been for *The Sunday Times*, the practice of MPs accepting money for putting parliamentary questions would have remained secret" (April 4, 1995). Similarly, *The Guardian* points out the good job it has done in contributing to the creation of the Nolan Committee and in the publication of the Downey report: "Downey's work would have been impossible without the fruits of months of work by our reporters and without *The Guardian* spending tens of thousands of pounds in legal fees to assist him" (July 4, 1997).

As well as positive self-references, newspapers praise each other for their work. *The Guardian* writes that: "*The Sunday Times* did a public service by exposing the cash-for-questions culture . . ." (April 5, 1995). *The Guardian* receives from *The Independent* the following eulogy: "very fine journalistic digging" . . . "whose courage and professionalism we salute" (July 4, 1997). The editorials do not contain one single negative reference to another news organization.[3]

Finally, there are references to the press in general in order to applaud its role and to show journalists' work as something at the core of good politics: "Without them [journalists] there would have been no Nolan report, no Downey report, no rethinking of the Common's rules, and no unmasking of individuals. The greasy tenner culture would have spread further into government; the scandals would have been worse" (*The Independent*, July 4, 1997). Reporters and columnists are portrayed as having done indispensable work: ". . . the most damaging and useful probing of a governing party that had lost the old rule book came from reporters and columnists" (*The Independent*, July 4, 1997).

The way in which the relationship between politicians and the press is portrayed is that of confrontation. Politicians try to attack the press: "Tory MPs queued to tip manure over the Press" (*The Sun*, November 2, 1994). Editorials defend the press from the attacks of politicians: "What a nerve to accuse journalists of sinking to an all-time low when all we've been doing is investigate their rock-bottom standards" (*The Sun*, November 2, 1994); "They [MPs] don't want the Press's torch of freedom shone into the dark crannies of their own lives" (*The Sun*, July 21, 1992). Editorials criticize those politicians who are believed to feel contempt for the press: "[Major] has a disdain, verging on hatred, for papers like *The Sun*. Most of his Ministers do too" (*The Sun*, January 1, 1994). Politicians' cynicism is ironically pointed out by *The Guardian*: "What makes them [Tory MPs] really angry was not the activities of their colleagues but of the paper in exposing them" (April 5, 1995). It is made clear that wrongdoing is to be attributed to politicians and not to the press: "Now he [Mellor] must pay the price. It is not the tabloid press" (*The Sun*, September 25, 1992).

The People: Those Affected. Analysis of the editorials reveals that there is a third character, the people, who are portrayed as being the victim suffering from the bad behavior of politicians and benefiting from the press' good actions. The way in which "the people" character is portrayed articulates a villain-victim relationship between politicians and the people.

Politicians are the *villains*. They are arrogant towards the people: "A political elite that holds voters in such arrogant contempt that deliberate disinformation . . ." (*The Independent*, February 16, 1996) and "Politicians grown so complacent by their years in power that they regard the electorate as a hostile force . . ." (*The Independent*, February 16, 1996). And they are so far from the people that they are unaware of the negative consequences their actions have: "[MPs are] the last to realise the seriousness of the erosion of public confidence in politics . . ." (*The Guardian*, November 1, 1994).

The public is the sufferer, the *victim* of the villain politician who ". . . will do permanent damage to standards of behaviour in public life and public trust in the political process" (*The Independent*, February 17, 1996); "Public confidence in the Government has sunk so low . . ." (*The Sun*, October 22, 1994); ". . . destroy the last few scraps of trust the public has in the Government" (*The Sun*, October 21, 1994).

The way in which "the people" character is portrayed reveals a benefactor-benefited relationship between the press and the people, in the following terms.

Firstly, journalists are close to the people and working for them: "The Sun has worked behind the scenes for 10 weeks, fighting for the public's right to know" (*The Sun*, October 20, 1994). They are even closer to the people than politicians are: "They [politicians] think they know better than us what makes ordinary people tick. They forget that The Sun sells one third of the papers Britain reads each morning" (*The Sun*, January 1, 1994). Sometimes the press is portrayed as equivalent to the people: "The cost to us all if Waldegrave and Lyell survive" (*The Independent*, February 17, 1996); "We deserve better politicians than these" (*The Independent*, March 22, 1997).

Secondly, as they are closer to the people, journalists interpret better than politicians public demands and thoughts: "No wonder the public has a low opinion of politicians" (*The Sun*, November 2, 1994). The media are so close to the people that they get to know what people think and feel: "People feel betrayed" (*The Sun*, October 26, 1994). They can even become the people's representatives: "The Sun on behalf of its readers does expect standards" (*The Sun*, July 20, 1992).

Lastly, the press play a watchdog role for the benefit of the general public: "Part of a newspaper's role is to act almost like a moral policeman for people in public life" (*The Sun*, July 20, 1992); "Only one thing matters to The Sun: Our readers' right to know" (*The Sun*, November 2, 1994).

There appears to be a general consensus in the British press concerning politicians and with regard to the role of the press, a consensus that, as will be seen, is not found in the Spanish press.

If we look at specific cases, patterns of identification of characters and relationships among characters are quite similar, as Table 6.4 shows.

The confrontation between politicians and the press was more sharply focused in the *Cash for Questions* and *Sexual Misdemeanors* cases, both of which became part of larger debates. As we saw in Chapter 4, journalists involved in the *Cash for Questions* story were criticized by parliamentarians for the methods they had employed. The Mellor case came at a time when the press was under the microscope and threatened with statutory control by the government because of its frequent controversial invasions of privacy (Shannon, 2001). The exposés of sexual misdemeanors inevitably became a part of a larger debate about press behavior and the relationship between public and private morality. The *Arms to Iraq* case did not imply a specific debate about the role of the media.

TABLE 6.4 Map of British Characters by Case.

	NUMBER OF MENTIONS		
	Others (and Their Bad Actions): Politicians	Us (and Our Good Actions): The Press	The People (Those Affected)
Cash for Questions	24	23	19
Arms to Iraq	10	2	10
Sexual Misdemeanors	17	18	9

Spain: Political Polarization. The Left Versus the Right and the Absent Public

The three-character picture described for the British coverage does not apply to the Spanish case. Here, identification of characters is more complex, as are also the relations established among characters.

As a first step for analysis, three characteristics should be mentioned. First, there are almost no references to politicians as a whole class, as in the British case. Second, although there are some references to the media (for self-praise), there is not a single reference to praise for other news institutions. Cross-media references are negative, as if a battle were being sustained between the press. Third, very few references to the public are found.

As Table 6.5 shows, two categories of Spanish characters have been identified. As mentioned previously, what differentiates them is ideology: on the one hand, there are Socialist characters (and their bad actions); on the other, there are those who criticize people who try to blame González, his government, and the Socialists (and their bad actions). One hundred and thirty three mentions were found for the first category and 41 for the second. Most examples of the first group are found in *El Mundo* and in *ABC* (a few in *El País*) and almost all examples for the second group can be found in *El País*. Relationships are articulated in terms that show the difference in political orientation among the newspapers.

Socialist Characters and Their Bad Actions. Within this first category fall all references to what is considered the cause of the corrupt actions—the Socialist Party and González's government. There are negative references to the Socialist Party in general: "Socialist tribe" (*ABC*, April 30,

TABLE 6.5 General Map of Spanish Characters.

NUMBER OF MENTIONS	
Socialist People/Institutions and Their Bad Actions	Critics of Socialists and Their Bad Actions
133	41

1994); "Gang of little devils" (*ABC*, March 3, 1995); "Spanish Socialism will never renew itself" (*El Mundo*, April 27, 2000).

González is seen at the core of corrupt actions: "González has destroyed his own party, turning it into a despicable entourage" (*ABC*, May 2, 1994). In an earlier heavily sarcastic piece, the same newspaper writes:

> González . . . reveals his small, sectarian petty-mindedness, his slight moral stature . . . ; he can crush other institutions and powers of the State, filling them with his own place-men; he can entrust the highest financial and monetary organism to an alleged fraudster and the most venerable police body to an undesirable person; he can extort the Spanish business class to finance his party allegedly through Filesa; he can lie to and ignore Parliament . . . or deceive the electorate; all inspired by the patriotic and democratic aim of "not playing the right's game." (*ABC*, April 2, 1994)

"The Others" (the Socialists) are portrayed as those who commit fraud, who are corrupt. For example, there is the "Socialist Party's terror of the truth being disclosed" (*ABC*, April 19, 1997), and "the obscure action of Gonzalez's government" (*ABC*, April 19, 1997).

The identification of characters and the relationship between them is particularly complicated by the labyrinthine nature of accusations, suspicions and legal proceedings. Editorials have difficulty in pinning down precisely who is guilty of corruption and, after an ambiguous trial verdict, seek to level blame at specified individuals: "It is clear that when a reference is made to those 'implicated at a senior level,' the allusion is to the minister himself and to those above him" (*El Mundo*, March 23, 2000). Senior members of the government who once proclaimed their absolute faith in someone they now declare beyond the pale are considered specially suspect: "How shall we now believe those who call Rubio a traitor, when two years ago they would have sworn to his honorability?" (*El Mundo*, May 9, 1994).

In establishing guilt, the quality of evidence and the authority of witnesses become particularly important. Thus, those who obstruct investigations come to form part of the cast of "Socialists and their bad actions": "[A] Fierce Socialist campaign, which tried to suggest that a fragmented part of the documents would not be valid evidence" (*ABC*, April 19, 1997); "PSOE and its allies . . . abruptly broke off the work of the *Roldán* committee" (*ABC*, May 26, 1994).

With the aim of locating guilt in the senior ranks of the government, statements by someone accused of corruption and formerly a member of the Socialist party are contextualized in such a way as to give them credence among the readers. Commenting on Roldán's statements that effectively incriminate members of the Socialist government, *El Mundo* writes: "The Courts do not in any way scorn the confessions of criminals—specially of terrorists and drug traffickers—when they contribute to the clarification of crimes without attempting to exonerate themselves. And what Roldán said yesterday did nothing to benefit him: he admitted that he covered up the outrages he now denounces" (*El Mundo*, May 30, 1996).

Critics of the Socialists and their Bad Actions. The second category of characters includes those who are criticized for blaming members of the Socialist Party for corruption. For the most part they are conservatives and most of the criticism comes from *El País*.

The actions of these characters are interpreted as malicious. For instance, Federico Trillo (a conservative PP deputy) is considered frivolous in criticizing a Court's action in not pursuing a lawsuit against those alleged to be involved in corruption (*El País*, December 11, 1994).

Suspicion is cast on the reliability of statements made by those under investigation by the courts and that implicate the Socialist government. Thus, for example, Amedo and Dominguez, the policemen involved in GAL, are negatively assessed: they are "Doubtful people" (*El País*, March 22, 1995). Roldán is characterized as somebody who looks after himself. "Roldán Looks After Himself" is the headline of *El País*, May 15, 1996, where he is described as being "very talkative about the supposed or real responsibilities of others regarding GAL matters and the reserved funds, but he hasn't said a word about his own." In sum, in *El País* Roldán's contribution to justice is portrayed as suspicious: "There is now something quite clear: Roldán collaborates with the courts when it suits him and in the measure that it interests him. Everything else is hot air" (*El País*, May 15, 1996).

The Spanish legal system is negatively assessed as undemocratic. It allows criminals' statements to be considered as evidence and, according to *El País*, permits convicted criminals to abuse the system for their own ends: "It is inadmissable in a democratic society, subject to the principle of law and with instruments to resolve its conflicts and to demand responsibilities, that the mistakes and even the guilt of the Government can be used by alleged or confessed criminals to blackmail it in an attempt to change the rules of the game for their own advantage" (*El País*, September 22, 1995).

Judges are censured for their decisions. After the government ruled that it would not release the CESID papers, the judge decided to question members of the Congress' Committee on Official Secrets. According to *El País*, the judge had exceeded his powers:

> Above and beyond the specific incident, the decision shows once again the contradiction between the wish of some judges to take actions which go beyond their strict competences and their incapacity to do so according to a logic shared by the ordinary citizen. The consistent thing to do would simply be either to apply the law or to become an active agent in the resolution of conflicts because of a conviction that the law cannot deal with the complexity of real life situations. The worst outcome is this combination of supposedly moralistic judges who give political lessons to the Government—accusing it of putting obstacles in the way of justice or of giving undue importance to State security—with the logic of a legal curia which has nothing to do with real life. (*El País*, August 29, 1996)

In short, characters in Spanish editorials reflect a confrontation between members of the Socialist party accused of corruption and those criticized for accusing them. Examining them case by case, one finds appreciable differences in mentions of each cast of characters as can be seen in Table 6.6.

In the *Roldán* and *Rubio* cases there is more criticism of members of the Socialist party and significantly less, compared to other cases, of their accusers.

In the *Gal-Cesid* and *Gal-Lasa Zabala* cases the establishment of guilt is extremely complex legally and it thus becomes easier to criticize the accusers as well as the accused. The articulation of characters in Spain works along an axis of the accused and those who criticize the accusers, which, as we shall now see, reflects the battle of the press.

The Battle of the Press. The examples discussed so far show that there is a lack of consensus among those newspapers analyzed in evaluating corruption. The differences in assessments, reactions, and evaluations of characters are clear. The confrontation is established mainly between *ABC-El Mundo* and *El País*. All the examples of negative references to Socialist characters appear in *El Mundo* and *ABC*, whereas criticism towards those who blame Socialists comes from *El País*.

TABLE 6.6 Map of Spanish Characters by Case

	NUMBER OF MENTIONS	
	Socialist Characters and Their Bad Actions	Critics of Socialists and Their Bad Actions
Roldán	73	19
Gal-Cesid	17	8
Rubio	28	-
Gal-Lasa Zabala	15	14

This conflicting mindset is seen in reactions to court decisions. In December 1999 the trial against the police officers in the *Lasa and Zabala* case began. *El Mundo* and *ABC* both demanded that the issue of where guilt lay should be clarified. *El País*, however, reminded its readers that a fair judgment would take into account the climate of the times when the Lasa and Zabala murders were committed: "In the two months between the kidnapping of Lasa and Zabala and that of Marey, the first action claimed by GAL, ETA carried out twenty attacks intending to kill and murdered eleven people: one every eight days. Historians who analyze the dirty war against ETA must take into account the social climate created by these facts" (*El País*, December 14, 1999). The same editorial states that GAL predated the Socialist Government and had operated in a different guise under the previous government: "The continuity between both phases, through the same gunmen, is now a known fact" (*El País*, December 14, 1999).

On the day of the court sentence in the *Lasa and Zabala* case, in which the people found guilty were not members of the government, there was a clear difference in editorial reaction. *ABC* and *El Mundo* believed that guilt had not been sufficiently clarified. *El Mundo* claimed that the two guilty men, Galindo and Elorriaga, were guilty of the alleged crimes, but not on their own, and that there was still some uncertainty about the case: "The judgement . . . leaves numerous loose threads. . . . But even more frustrating is what it fails to clarify about the upper echelons of the plot" (*El Mundo*, April 27, 2000). *El País*, however, praised the sentence for being tough in punishing crime.

There are not, as there are in Britain, positive references to the role of the media as a whole. Some mentions are self-congratulatory references: "What *El Mundo* publishes today is a qualitative step forward in the investigation" (*El Mundo*, April 26, 1994); ". . . the pages of newspapers which perform the vital function for a healthy democracy. As *ABC* does today in reporting . . . " (*ABC*, May 26, 1994). Most references to the press are negative references to fellow papers. Many are statements in self-defense fending off attacks from other parts of the press.

There is also controversy among newspapers about the way other newspapers investigate. *El Mundo* refers with irony to the slowness of *El País* in investigating: Mariano Rubio favored his friends, "something that some media seem to have uncovered two years late" (*El Mundo*, April 26, 1994).

El Mundo accuses *El País* of being the media acolyte of the Socialist government. It also accuses it of having always been and continuing to be "in perfect agreement with those accused of the GAL crimes" (December 18, 1996). The court judgment in the *Lasa and Zabala* case is used by *El Mundo* to reply to *El País'* criticism. The judgment, *El Mundo* writes, is "indisputable backing for the investigative work carried out by *El Mundo* journalists, whose revelations were branded 'sensationalist', 'slanderous', and 'tabloid' by the politicians in power at the time and their media acolytes" . . . "the courts have confirmed our scoops" (*El Mundo*, April 27, 2000).

On 16 December 1996 *El Mundo* announced it would publish the CESID papers over several different days. The following day *El País* published all of them together. In its editorial, *El País* explained why it had decided to publish the documents all at once: "By publishing these papers in their entirety and all at once, *El País* above all wishes to stop any attempt to direct conveniently the political agenda through the rationed publication of compromising information and documents" (December 17, 1996). *El Mundo's* reply came the following day:

> *El País* unashamedly claims that *El Mundo* carried out no investigative journalism work to get hold of the *papers*. It maintains that it has been the mere "recipient of a leak". We maintain that we've struggled for over a year to get hold of them and they came from various sources. On the contrary, it is *El País* which has been the "recipient of a leak." . . . Someone has supplied them with the papers once *El Mundo* began to publish. This must be the case, otherwise one would have to assume that they had them and were hiding them. (December 18, 1996)

The conflict between the two papers is made clear: "*El País* . . . does everything possible to undermine the prestige of the judges who seek to throw light on those crimes and punish the guilty. Just as *El Mundo* has systematically done the opposite. It's as simple as that" (*El Mundo*, December 18, 1996).

The relationship between characters in the Spanish editorials shows that the consensus in the British media about government sleaze was not so clear in Spain where the trials of those accused of corruption were extremely complex. Criticism of members of the Socialist party was most frequent in the two newspapers more generally hostile to the Socialist government; the newspaper closest to the government contained most criticism of the government's accusers. This does not mean, however, that *El País* was entirely uncritical of the government. Its editorial of 13 January 1995 entitled "The End of an Era" reflected the public perception that the government's stock was on the wane: "There is what we think is a general impression that the model of Government led by González for the last 12 years has come to its end." After listing the corruption cases associated with the government, the piece affirms: "It would be infantile to try to deny that these events have severely weakened the Government's credibility and, more fundamentally, that of its President." However, at the same time, the piece refers to the links between journalists and judges and the possibility that they have had an adverse effect on investigations into corruption. The editorial concludes with an attack not on those who have been responsible for corruption and murder, but on those behind the accusations: "There are many dark motives harbored by those who have put in motion this process to unseat the Socialist Party at any price. . . ."

FRAMING THROUGH AGENCY

Agency answers the question of exactly who did something and what was the causal force for action.

Here we wish to see how agency is attributed in the editorials of both countries and whether the causal forces for the actions of the criticized characters are also identified.

We first examined headlines, because as Entman (1991) points out, "agency is an especially common attribute of headlines" (p. 11). We counted the number of headlines that attribute actions to specific, named people, or that give an idea of what the cause for action of the news event was. We further looked at the text of the editorials to see how agency is attributed.

The following tables (6.7 and 6.8) show attribution of agency in British and Spanish editorials.

If we look at the cases in the United Kingdom, identification of agency in headlines occurs in all three (51% for *Cash for Questions*, 55% for *Arms to Iraq*, and 47% for *Sexual Misdemeanors*). As for Spain, *Rubio* is the case with the highest identification of agency (though it should be taken into account that there are only five editorials analyzed for the *Rubio* case). Six headlines of editorials for *Roldán* (22% of editorials) identify agency, and all them refer to Roldán's wrongdoing. For *Gal-Cesid* and for *Gal-Lasa Zabala* identification of agency is very low and, as will be seen below, the reason for this has to do with complexity of the legal processes that characterize those two cases.

TABLE 6.7 Attribution of Agency in Headlines of British Editorials

NUMBER OF EDITORIALS WITH ATTRIBUTION OF AGENCY

	N	%Within Cases
Cash for Questions	21	51
Arms to Iraq	10	55
Sexual Misdemeanors	9	47
TOTAL	40	

TABLE 6.8 Attribution of Agency in Headlines of Spanish Editorials

NUMBER OF EDITORIALS WITH ATTRIBUTION OF AGENCY

	N	% Within Cases
Roldán	6	22
Rubio	2	40
Gal-Cesid	2	15
Gal-Lasa Zabala	1	8
TOTAL	11	

Britain: Pointing the Finger

Headlines of British editorials (40 headlines of a total of 78) show a direct attribution of agency, so that with just the headline the reader can learn that there is a wrongdoer. Headlines work to point the finger at the scandalous person or action.

Thus, specific named individuals appear in the headline: "The Young Dissembler. Yet Mr Willetts Will Not Accept He Was Wrong" (*The Guardian*, December 12, 1996); a front-page photograph of Neil Hamilton under the headline "A Liar and a Cheat" (*The Guardian*, October 1, 1996). There is no doubt that the named individual has done something wrong: "Silence from Number 10. Mr Major Knows Mr Hamilton Lied. Why so Quiet?" (*The Guardian*, October 3, 1996).

Even in those headlines in which the agent is an institution, agency is clearly attributed: "Misreading the Mood: Too Many Tories Voted with Their Wallets" (*The Guardian*, November 7, 1995); "A People Betrayed by Parliament" (*The Guardian*, March 21, 1997); "Commons Unite in Hypocrisy" (*The Independent*, July 14, 1994).

Some headlines are clear in identifying the causal forces for an event or action, pointing to motives such as greed, hypocrisy, deception, or negligence. For instance, *The Independent* argues that there is somebody who is "Either Negligent or Dishonest" in the *Arms to Iraq* case (April 19, 1990). Headlines such as "No more humbug" (*The Sun*, January 12, 1994) or "Stumbling in Secret" (*The Guardian*, March 25, 1994) point to hypocrisy, incompetence, and a culture of secrecy as being reasons for events.

Direct attribution of agency is also shown in the text of the editorials. It is expressed in sentences that have a clear structure of subject and predicate, with verbs and adjectives that refer to the action, categorizations of the action, or to the actor. For instance, referring to John Major, the editorial says: "We are in hands of people who appear to have little or no understanding of the issue involved" (*The Guardian*, October 7, 1996), who have a "rudimentary knowledge" (*The Guardian*, October 7, 1996); "John Major and his Government remained obdurate, wholly indifferent to the public's right to know" (*The Guardian*, March 21, 1997).

This sort of phrase structure helps to allocate responsibility ("Sir Richard is responsible for the delay" (*The Independent*, July 7, 1995) and clarification of actions (". . . denials given by ministers . . . were plain lies") (*The Guardian*, November 11, 1992).

Vivid and expressive language assigns responsibility: "Tacky business, the government is permanently stained with the brush of incompetence"; "[It is surprising] how hard Tories fight to keep their money hidden in their grubby mitts" (*The Sun*, November 7, 1995); "petty, foolish, grubby, dim and sleazy" (*The Independent*, July 4, 1997); "murky world of political lobbyists" (*The Sun*, October 22, 1994); "[they were caught] red-handed" (*The Guardian*, April 5, 1995); "The lobbyist's poison spread from the veins of the body politic into . . ." (*The Guardian*, October 7, 1996).

Agency is also expressed when the editorial takes the form of a "should-do" piece. In British editorials "should do" pieces are characterized by being direct and clear statements of what the wrongdoer must do: "Waldegrave should resign" (*The Independent*, February 16, 1996); "Mistakes should have been admitted, apologies given and steps taken to clean up the act" (*The Sunday Times*, April 9, 1995); "The Conservative Party should care" (*The Guardian*, March 22, 1997); "Merchant has to go" (*The Sun*, March 29, 1997).

British editorials point the finger at who is the guilty person and at the causes of their wrongdoing.

Spain: Lost in a Legal Labyrinth

The identification of agency in Spain is more diffuse. There are just eleven headlines out of 57, or 19 percent of editorials in which agency is clearly identified: "González or Indecency" (*ABC*, March 3, 1995); "Can Solchaga Remain in His Post for a Day?" (*El Mundo*, April 26, 1994).

There are headlines in which a named person is identified, but not as the agent: "What Cesid and Perote Should Do" (*El Mundo*, September 20, 1995); "What Roldán Is Saying Should Be Investigated" (*El Mundo*, May 30, 1996).

Most headlines of Spanish editorials (46 out of 57) denote no action (have no verbs), and refer to a thing, person, a case, or an institution: "Rubio and De la Concha" (*ABC*, May 20, 1994); "Roldán and González" (*ABC*, March 12, 1995), "The Hour of the Judges" (*ABC*, December 13, 1999); "Lasa and Zabala" (*El País*, December 14, 1999); "Severe Punishment" (*El País*, April 27, 2000). These headlines work as signposts, giving an idea of what the editorial is about, but not referring to any action.

If we examine the text of the editorial, attribution of agency is also diffuse. There are few examples of editorials in *El Mundo* and *ABC* referring to González in which there is a clear attribution of agency: "The only thing González has to do is to say good bye" (*El Mundo*, May 5, 1994); "There can be no doubt that for over ten years González has been deceiving all the Spanish; based on an imposture, maintained by the widest syndicate of interests" (*ABC*, March 3, 1995).

Instead of using vivid and expressive language, Spanish narratives are characterized by long explanations and legal and technical arguments: "[The Supreme Court] has correctly pointed out that the right place to present it [the decision] is in an ordinary court . . . it gives a judgment on the reported facts which, coming from the highest criminal legal body of the State, must be a reference point that the court, which in principle should deal with the legal action, should follow" (*El País*, December 11, 1994).

These explanations try to help the reader to interpret the nature and seriousness of the crime:

> There are overwhelming signs—as the justified action by the prose-cutor's office establishes—that Rubio has committed offences of tax evasion and co-operation in the falsification of documents and that he has enriched himself through speculative operations while exer-cising his position as governor. (*El Mundo*, May 9, 1994)

"Should do" pieces in Spain tend to be explanations of the technical and legal context in which newsworthy events (most of them related to actions taken by the legal power) should be understood. They are attempts to guide the reader in understanding where guilt lies. Editorials establish the map of those who are guilty and the actions of judges and institutions that are involved in the resolution of cases.

As we saw in the section about characters, there is a lack of consen-sus among the dailies about who is to be blamed; and there is a clear attempt on the part of *ABC* and of *El Mundo* to extend guilt to the higher ranks of the government and to implicate the Prime Minister.

"Perote should be punished. But he is not the main one or the only one involved in all this complex plot" (*El Mundo*, September 23, 1996); "What is reported today by El Mundo is a qualitative step forward in the Ibercorp affair, because it not only questions the head of the Bank of Spain's action but it also implicates the Government in the . . . murky business" (*El Mundo*, April 26, 1994); "Felipe González has an enormous political responsibility in all this affaire not only because he was Rubio's main backer but also because his attitude obstructed any serious investi-gation of Ibercorp" (*El Mundo*, May 9, 1994).

Some editorials try to help the reader to interpret a complex court judgment: "The judgment doesn't hide that it leaves numerous loose ends: it does not determine which civil guards . . . formed part of the *antiterrorism-terrorism* promoted by Galindo, nor who kidnapped Lasa and Zabala, nor who was most involved in the sinister operation which ended on an Alicante road. . . . But most frustrating is what is still left to be clarified about the upper tiers of the plot. We all know that Galindo and Elorriaga did it but they weren't alone. Whatever there is in the judgment pointing in that direction is scarcely developed, if not crude" (*El Mundo*, April 27, 2000).

The analysis of the first two frame dimensions—agency and identification of characters—allows us to conclude that the narratives of scandal stories encourage the recipient to develop particular understandings of events in which the guilty are identified together with those affected by their guilt. After examining two further frame dimensions—categorizations and generalizations—in the next chapter, in Chapter 8 we will offer conclusions about which generic frames characterized the scandal stories.

NOTES

1. The critical discourse analysis perspective "is a recognition that our social practice in general and our use of language in particular are bound up with causes and effects which we may not be at all aware of under normal conditions" (Bourdieu, 1977, quoted in Fairclough, 1995, p. 54); "a kind of linguistics directed towards understanding values which are thoroughly implicated in linguistic usage" (Fowler, 1991, p. 5). To look at discourse from a critical perspective "means an enquiry into the relations between signs, meanings and the social historical conditions which govern the semiotic structure of discourse, using a particular kind of linguistic analysis" (Fowler, 1991, p. 5).
2. For the details of the methodology used in this qualitative analysis, see Chapter 1.
3. This is not to say that there was no criticism of press behavior by fellow journalists. As we saw in Chapter 4, Paul Johnson of *The Daily Mail* and *The Spectator* was very critical of *The Guardian*'s work. The Mellor case also provoked some critical comment by broadsheets, nervous that *The People*'s action would result in the government realizing its threat to introduce a privacy law and a statutory body to regulate the British press (see Calcutt, 1993). *The Times*, for instance, wrote that *The People* had "done no favours to journalism" (21 July, 1992, p. 13).

7

Moral Drama

Journalists first identify actors and agency in a scandal story. They then seek to craft a compelling tale, selecting language and images to characterize the actors and their actions and in this way framing the wrongdoing they narrate.

This chapter will examine the kind of morality tales—moralizing frames—constructed by the press, looking at two specific dimensions of frame: "categorizations" and "generalizations". It will explore how the evaluations preferred for events, the critical terminology employed, and the generalizations stimulated or suppressed produced different kinds of morality tales for the various kinds of scandal stories.

Qualitative analysis allows us to argue that the British press, as compared to its Spanish counterpart, tends to "frame" scandal stories in such a way that moral judgments are made more explicit. We will examine the following: (a) the moral assessments made; (b) the debates that are implicit or explicit in the generalizations made about the political system; (c) identity associations; and, finally (d) we will look at a specific type of frame, news icons, which, because of its symbolic strength, is pertinent to British and Spanish scandal news narratives.

CATEGORIZATIONS

The choice of labels that journalists make for scandal incidents tends to place them in categories that conventionally either elicit or omit moral evaluation.

What are the categorizations used by editorialists in scandal stories in the British and Spanish press? To answer this, we established a typology based on four categories to which wrongdoing could be assigned, with the aim of elaborating a picture of the sort of evaluations that journalists preferred. Our final goal was to extricate the evaluating frame that dominated categorizations of scandal narratives. The four categories are the following (definitions are taken from the *Oxford English Dictionary*, 1999).

> **Mistake.** A mistake is "a thing which is not correct"; "an error of judgment, a faulty judgment."
>
> **Incompetence.** This derives from incompetent, which refers to "somebody who is not sufficiently skillful to do something successfully"; "who is not qualified to act in a particular capacity." As compared to "mistake", incompetence suggests a more generalized incapacity, whereas a mistake could be specific and forgivable. Although making an isolated mistake is not necessarily a resigning matter (although it can be), incompetence suggests unfitness for office.
>
> **Immorality.** This derives from immoral, which is "not conforming to accepted standards of morality." Morality refers to "the principles concerning the distinction between right and wrong, or between good and bad behaviour." A more general definition talks of a "system of values and moral principles."
>
> **Crime.** This is an "action which constitutes a serious offence against an individual or the state and is punishable by law."

All these categories imply a judgment or evaluation made referring to something. The labels chosen for the incidents imply a different discourse domain in which references to certain standards are made explicit or not.

The Legal/Moral Discourse Domain

Table 7.1 shows the different terms that were used in British and Spanish editorials to characterize wrongdoing.

TABLE 7.1 Terms Used for Categorizing Wrongdoing in Editorials

UNITED KINGDOM

MISTAKES	INCOMPETENCE	IMMORALITY	CRIME
mistaken defence, misjudgment	incompetence, inadequate response, totally powerless, unfit for office, weak, unaccountable, foolish, extraordinarily inefficient poppycock, rudimentary knowledge, pretty dumb politics, fail to protect the essential rights of the voter, dim, spineless handling of a case, incapable of understanding, narrow appreciation of his role, failed politicians, failure of self-regulation, lack of accountability, inertia, lack of action, rambling and incoherent, eccentric, bizarre, remiss, failed at their jobs, stupidity, futile, lack of judgement, protected fools, confusion, stew of uncertainty, stumbling confusion, merely mad, foolish defiance.	with no honor, to get moral values upside down, hypocrisy, misdemeanor, sleaze, cheat, shameless adulterer, pious propaganda, coward, reeks of hypocrisy, tainted source, absence of any sense of personal responsibility, riding roughshod over Britain's unwritten constitution, malpractice, lie, mendacity, falsehood, deceit, dupe, dishonesty, greed, smear, murky world, to spin a stupid yarn, to move from the darkness of lies to the twilight of half-truths, cynical world weariness, averse to clarity, cynical, dishonourable, dreadful display of contempt, without contrition, no acceptance of blame, manipulation, laxity, cover up, grubby cover up, masking expediency, connivance, arrogant almost beyond belief, travesty of the truth, deployed every trick, two-faced, secret machinations, unscrupulous.	bribery, cheating the Inland Revenue, high crimes.

TABLE 7.1 Terms Used for Categorizing Wrongdoing in Editorials
(Continued)

SPAIN

MISTAKES	INCOMPETENCE	IMMORALITY	CRIME
botch, continuous and grave mistakes.	a big joke, passivity, frivolous, fiasco, insane, incapacity to act following a logic shared with ordinary citizens, terrible state of the Judiciary, politically responsible, political guilt, lack of the sense of State, events are out of control, lack of agility, insufficient quickness, showing contempt for Parliament, chaos.	manichaeism, abuse, indignity, grotesque, dishonesty, sinister activities, laxness, threat, coercion, intolerable financial speculations, indecency, to break one's word, false, incompatible versions, farce, deception, lie to the country, lack of moral authority, outrage, grave excesses, government's irregular administration, murky business, corrupt, corrupted practices, giant farce of scheming people, cover up manoeuvres, of poor moral category, anti-paradigm of the virtues of the institution commanded, lying about one's curriculum.	grave transgressions of the law, criminal, against the law, to favor (illegally) someone's friends, tax evasion, contribution to falsification of documents, enrichment from illegal speculation on the Stock Exchange mishandling of public funds, obstructer of investigation, defender of a criminal, organizer of a complex network of black money and fiscal fraud, irregular fiscal practices, fiscal crime, dirty war, embezzlement of public funds, diversion of State funds, fraud, terrorist barbarism, accomplice, mismanagement of public funds, laundering of money, to cover up outrage, he obtained money which was not his own, to obtain money through illegal charges, murder, torture, protector of crime, illegal incompetence, kidnap, terrible State crime, blackmail.

Table 7.2 shows similarities and differences between the two countries.

In both countries incidents were scarcely referred to in terms of mistakes. Very few assessments (there are just two terms in both countries) fall into this category. The notion that scandals are the result of specific, forgivable actions did not dominate narratives in the British or Spanish press.

An assessment of incompetence is more common in both countries, although it should be noticed that it is more frequently used in Britain than in Spain, through categorizations in terms of "incompetence" (34 in Britain and 15 in Spain). Incompetence is referred to in terms of lack of knowledge (rudimentary knowledge, lack of judgment, confusion, stupidity) and with insufficient skills for the position (lack of control, spineless handling of the case, lack of agility, insufficient quickness).

Some categorizations of incompetence make reference to a third person, reflecting the accountability that political actors owe citizens: "to fail in protecting the essential rights of the voter," "showing contempt for Parliament," "incapacity to act following a logic shared with ordinary citizens." In the United Kingdom some assessments imply a general judgment that the politicians are so incompetent that they show a general "unfitness for office".

One clear difference between British and Spanish categorizations is that Spanish assessments are most often expressed in terms of criminal culpability (30, or 22.89% of total mentions), whereas this categorization is almost nonexistent in the British press (3, or 2.49% of total mentions). In Britain categorizations are expressed more in moral terms (44, or 36.52% of total mentions, compared with 29 in Spain or 22.04% of total mentions).

This difference is in keeping with the portrait of characters and agency discussed in the previous chapter. There we saw that through the use of the active voice, vivid language, and the names of individuals in headlines, direct attribution of agency was more common in the British press than the Spanish press, where the predominance of technical, complex language tended to diffuse agency.

TABLE 7.2 Categorizations in Editorials

	MISTAKE	INCOMPETENCE	IMMORALITY	CRIME	TOTAL
BRITAIN	2	34	44	3	83
SPAIN	2	15	29	30	76
TOTAL	4	49	73	33	159

British Moral Discourse

Over half of the total assessments (44 out of 83) in the United Kingdom fall under the categories of "immorality." Terms such as hypocrisy, malpractice, shameless adulterer, greed, smear, with no honor, are predominant in categorizing British actors.

Many of these kinds of moral assessments refer to lack of truth: lies, mendacity, falsehood, deceit, dupe, dishonesty, to move from the darkness of lies to the twilight of half-truths, false, cover up, deception.

As we will see below, part of the reason for this predominantly moral discourse has to do with the debates that British scandals generated. The fact that some of these scandals refer to sexual misdemeanors also accounts in part for why assessments are couched in moral terms.

If we look at specific British cases we can see that the predominant use of a moral discourse is clearer in the *Sexual Misdemeanors* cases (where terms referring to incompetence or crime are almost nonexistent) than in the other cases. Therefore, Yeo is accused of "hypocrisy" (*The Sun*, January 6, 1994), Merchant is a "liar and coward" and a "shameless adulterer" (*The Sun*, March 29, 1997), and there is Mellor's "damned cheek" (*The Sun*, September 9, 1992), and the accusation that he is an "ambitious, upwardly mobile minister (of limited financial means) who had come to believe that he could set his own terms and behave as he thought fit" (*The Guardian*, October 25, 1992). However, these moral expressions apply not only to those who were found guilty of sexual misdemeanors, but also to the government. Newspapers refer to the government's "cynicism" (*The Independent*, January 6, 1994), to politicians who "pontificate" and exhibit "rank hypocrisy" (*The Sunday Times* July 26, 1992), and to the general situation, which is a spectacle, a "blend of tragedy and farce" (*The Independent*, January 12, 1994).

The other two scandal cases, *Arms to Iraq* and *Cash for Questions*, show a similar pattern of assessments. Moral assessments are again frequently used, as well as terms referring to incompetence. We find actors who are "extraordinarily inefficient," with an "eccentric and bizarre view" (*The Independent*, February 16, 1996), who "completely failed to explain the affair," (*The Independent*, April 19, 1990), and who have a "narrow appreciation of [their] role" (*The Independent*, March 25, 1994).

Arms to Iraq is a case that prompted a debate about the way the government released information about the official investigation into the scandal. Thus, moral assessments refer frequently to governmental mendacity (dishonest, two-faced, deceit and secret machinations, and unscrupulous are terms used or applied to members of the government). In this case the government is depicted as an institution immersed in a culture of secrecy (expressions such as "travesty of the truth" or "honed official version" are common), which "deployed every trick in its prodigious defensive and diversionary repertoire to prevent the instant resignation of vulnerable ministers" (*The Guardian*, February 16, 1996). Moral assessments of the *Cash for Questions* affair are mainly orientated to show that corruption is a general evil of the decade, and that politicians and institutions are regarded as "discredited chums" (*The Sun*, October 21, 1994), "arrogant almost beyond belief" (*The Sun*, November 2, 1994), with problems of "public cynicism" (*The Guardian*, November 26, 1994).

Spanish Criminal Discourse

Criminal terms are used slightly more frequently than moral ones by the Spanish press (22.89% for the first case compared with 22.04% for the second). Terms are used to describe actions that are punishable by law: grave transgressions of the law, coercion, tax evasion, contribution to the falsification of documents, mishandling of public funds, the obstruction of legal investigations, irregular fiscal practices, fiscal crime, embezzlement of public money, diversion of State funds, fraud, mismanagement of public funds, laundering of money, extortion, murder, torture, protection of crime, kidnapping, State crime.

The use of criminal terms is clearest in the *Gal-Lasa and Zabala* case: the fact that the case consists of two murders and an illegal detention is sufficient explanation for this. Journalists write of "violation of human rights" (*ABC*, March 22, 1995), "terrorist barbarism" (*El País*, March 22, 1995), "murder" and "torture" (*El Mundo*, May 28, 1996), "dirty war" (*El País*, December 14, 1999), "terrible State crime" (*El Mundo*, March 31, 2000). In this case, references to incompetence and to immorality are almost nonexistent.

In the *Roldán* and *Rubio* cases criminal terms are also predominant and refer mainly to alleged fiscal crimes. Therefore we find references here to "tax evasion" (*El Mundo*, May 9, 1994), "black money" (*El Mundo*, March 10, 1994), or more extended judgments such as that "he [the Minister of Interior] has committed two crimes, embezzlement of public money and fiscal crime. There is no record of the money given by him; and this money has not been declared to the Treasury" (*El Mundo*, March 10, 1994).

In the *Roldán* case, apart from the great number of criminal assessments, there are more terms referring to immorality and to incompetence compared to the other cases. It is said that: "he laundered money" (*El Mundo*, July 10, 1995); "he lied about his curriculum"; [he is] "of poor moral category" (*El Mundo*, May 30, 1996); "he got money which was not his own" (*El Mundo*, June 5, 1997); "[he is the] anti-paradigm of the virtues of the Institution he commanded" (*ABC*, April 10, 1995).

Generalizations and Debates

Generalizations are another dimension of frames. They refer to the connections that journalists seek to make with bigger issues: journalists, in searching for a fresh angle to a story, look beyond the individual case and try to connect the specific characters and their agency to a more general problem. Generalizations are frequent both in British and Spanish editorials, and reflect the debates that dominated public opinion during the scandals.

There are several differences between British and Spanish generalizations. Firstly, in Spain the generalizations refer to how a democracy should function and what are its key features such as, for example, the role of the rule of law[1] and the separation of powers. In Britain the generalizations refer more to the need for reform of institutions and the specific role of Parliament.

In Spain there are frequent references to how a democratic system should or ought to function. "Democratic society has mechanisms—at times slow moving but eventually unstoppable—against power's claims to impunity" (*El País*, March 22, 1995); "It is inadmissable that in a democratic society, subject to the principle of legality and with the instruments necessary to settle its conflicts and demand accountability . . ."(*El País*, September 22, 1995); "For the democratic health of this country it is important that Roldán and his conspirators answer for his wrongdoing" (*El País*, May 15, 1996); "the newspapers, which fulfill the invaluable function of contributing to democratic health" (*ABC*, May 26, 1994).

Within this context, there are also generalizations that refer to the separation of powers as a requirement for a system to be democratic: "Felipism has gradually neutralized each and every one of the mechanisms that the Constitution foresaw to ensure that the Executive could not get out of hand and do as it wants" (*El Mundo*, May 5, 1994); "The division of powers appropriate in a democracy demands that political control be exercised here to force back the government" (*El Mundo*, July 20, 1995).

As might be expected in a discourse dominated by legal assessments, there are many generalizations in the Spanish press about the role of the judiciary ("justice judges facts not climates" [*El País*, December 14, 1999]; "The law cannot reflect the complexity of real situations" (*El País*, August 29, 1996). It also refers to the borderline between politics and justice: "The political crisis is not the responsibility of the Supreme Court" (*El Mundo*, July 20, 1995); "It is not acceptable that politicians transfer their own responsibilities to judges. Nor that they ask them to deal with extra-legal emergencies" (*El Mundo*, July 20, 1995).

Editorial comment is also made about the existence of the rule of law as established by the Constitution: "This trial is already in itself a huge triumph for the rule of law" (*El Mundo*, March 31, 2000); "It is undisputedly a triumph of the rule of law" (*El Mundo*, April 27, 2000).

British generalizations make claims about the need for wholesale systemic reforms: "The entire system needs to be reformed" (*The Independent*, February 16, 1996); This demands reforming Whitehall, which requires "both a Freedom of Information Act . . . and new statutory protection for civil servants blowing the whistle on ministerial misconduct" (*The Guardian*, February 17, 1996); "If trust in government is to be restored, then as a very first step the civil service machine must be able to stop ministerial fabrication" (*The Guardian*, February 17, 1996).

References are also frequently made to the image of Parliament. Parliament is portrayed as a sovereign and venerable institution which scandals put at risk: "The good name of Parliament was on trial yesterday. And it was found guilty of losing the trust of people" (*The Sun*, November 7, 1995); "We do not want to see one of the great political institutions damage itself in the defence of the indefensible" (*The Guardian*, March 22, 1997).

The specific role of the media receives more attention in Britain than in Spain. As we saw earlier, the Mellor scandal occurred at the time when press behavior was under close scrutiny and threatened with the introduction of a privacy law. The Mellor case prompted wider debates about the role of the press and its use of public interest arguments to justify intrusive reporting. Thus it was claimed that: "The Mellor scandal has freed newspapers from this debilitating posture (self-censorship in fear of privacy laws) and the cause of press freedom is now being more robustly defended" (*The Sunday Times*, July 26, 1992); "The Mellor Affair demonstrates why MPs of all parties clamour for a Privacy Bill to gag newspapers" (*The Sun*, July 21, 1992). The issue is treated ironically: "Fowler wins the Poppycock of the Year Award with the extraordinary view that the Press should keep its nose out if a minister wants to commit adultery" (*The Sun*, January 1, 1994), and the editorial defends the position of the press: "It is not the media's job to make life more comfortable for ministers—or even judicial inquiries" (*The Guardian*, June 7, 1995).

Sometimes, a cross-national comparative view is introduced in the debate: "France has a cowed and cribbed media culture in which investigative and campaigning journalism is almost entirely unknown . . . the idea that we should be kept in the dark about it all is self-serving nonsense from those who have most to gain from newspapers that are only half-free" (The *Sunday Times*, July 26, 1992).

Secondly, the generalizations and debates found in British scandal narratives examine the relationship between private and public morality. The reason for this is easy to find: sexual scandals favored this debate: "Public office and private imbecility" (*The Guardian*, July 24, 1992); "Where does privacy begin and end?" (*The Guardian*, October 25, 1992). The debate was further fuelled by the Conservative Party's "back to basics" policy, encouraging people to preserve moral standards and family values.

The press framed the debate in ironic terms ["pulpit politics" (*The Independent*, January 6, 1994)], contrasting the scandals of the Conservatives with Major's attempt to inject moral behaviour in his ranks: "The "back-to-basics" message, cynically devised . . . has boomeranged" (*The Independent*, January 12, 1994); "Mr Major, for all his lectures on moral standards in this country, cannot bring himself to utter so much as a batsqueak of disapproval" (*The Guardian*, October 3, 1996). In this context, the Prime Minister was portrayed as somebody who needed to change the line of discourse: "The only reason Mr Major wishes to deny the moralist logic of his own campaign is that he is trying to avoid saying that other morally frail Conservative MPs as well as Mr Yeo must live up to the rhetoric" (*The Guardian*, January 7, 1994). Therefore incoherence and moral ambivalence are frequently dealt with in British editorials: "Family values are supposed to be the solid bedrock of Tory philosophy" (*The Sun*, January 12, 1994). In a combative tone, the press defends itself from attacks of politicians: "[politicians are] more angry at journalists' ethics than at ethics of their parliamentary colleagues" (*The Independent*, July 14, 1994).

The press debated to what extent sexual misbehavior has an impact on public life: "By no reasonable standards can a marriage undermined by adultery be considered incompatible with public service" (*The Independent*, January 1, 1994); "To emphasise that there is a distinction between public and private morality is not to deny that the two can overlap. There are certain standards of private behaviour and sexual morality that cannot be flouted by those who hold public office without the risk of retribution" (*The Independent*, January 12, 1994). It asked whether the sexual misdemeanors of politicians are of public relevance as compared to other moral infractions: "The voters might forgive infidelity. They can't stomach lies and hypocrisy" (*The Sun*, January 12, 1994). And the emphasis placed on sexual scandal by some sectors of the press, by others was deemed to be "An inversion of morals. Why is sex more serious than corruption?" (*The Guardian*, March 28, 1997).

Debates of this kind did not exist in the Spanish press.

Thirdly, generalizations about the spread of scandal and corruption, and of its effects were made in Britain but not in Spain. In British editorials, and mostly in those discussing *Cash for Questions*, corruption was regarded as the climate of the time: "To say they are tainted is the understatement of the year" (*The Sun*, October 21, 1994). Corruption is a "present malaise" (*The Sun*, October 26, 1994). The late 1980s are "the beginnings of a significant culture of corruption at Westminster" (*The Guardian*, July 4, 1997), a "Greasy tenner culture" (*The Independent*, July 4, 1997), "the culture of a low, dishonest decade" (*The Guardian*, May 12, 1995).

The effects of this alleged general culture of corruption are clearly visible in the British press in reference to public trust in institutions: [Scandals] "destroy the last few scraps of trust the public has in the Government" (*The Sun*, October 21, 1994); "Public confidence in the Government has sunk so low you could slip it under a door" (*The Sun*, October 22, 1994); "Like a boil that must be lanced, sleaze has poisoned public life" (*The Sun*, October 26, 1994). There are attempts to show that the problem is not about distrust in politicians but in the system: "Healthy scepticism about politicians is natural and healthy. But cynicism about politics as a trade is a kind of poison" (*The Independent*, July 4, 1997). There are also frequent references to how this distrust can affect democracy: "There really is a cynical danger to democracy" (*The Guardian*, October 21, 1994); "Public trust is the cement which holds together a democratic society" (*The Guardian*, June 7, 1995). In sum, "Sleaze corrodes democracy" (*The Guardian*, October 21, 1994). "The culture is so deep-rooted that it is suffocating our democracy" (*The Independent*, February 16, 1996).

In Spain this sort of assessment was not common. More common in the Spanish press is editorializing about conspiracy theories advanced by those sympathetic to the government as possible explanations for the seemingly unending stream of scandals. Much press speculation concerned the alleged existence of plots to bring down the government through the concerted action of hostile journalists, judges and politicians. The allegations were in their turn the occasion for comment about attempts to polarize Spanish society and destabilize the political system, creating an "extremely tense debate" (*El País*, September 8, 1996). Press comment declared that "we are faced with a Government crisis not with a crisis of the system" (*El Mundo*, May 5, 1994). The discovery of the remains of Lasa and Zabala led *ABC* to declare that "It is not a question of competencies, revenge or party political manoeuvres" but "a matter of greatest importance for legal security in a State of Law" (*ABC*, March 22, 1995). The conspiracy theory is given short shrift by *El Mundo*. In its editorial "Conspiracy Against the State" (July 12, 1995), the paper concludes that it is difficult to "sustain the surrealist theory of conspiracy." *El País* takes the conspiracy theory more seriously and refers to the possibility of blackmail. "It is normal in a political regime based on the clash of ideas and projects that the opposition, including both individuals and the media, should conspire against the Government, always as long as it is done in a peaceful manner and respecting the democratic rules of play. However, blackmail of the Government or the State is another matter. It is a crime defined in terms of threats or coercion" (*El País*, September 22, 1995).

In summary, British generalizations and debates reflected more explicit references to moral standards, implying judgments about what is right and wrong, to what is accepted by the public and what is not, and to the erosion of public trust in politicians. They are also concerned with the line drawn between private and public life, and with the extent to which the private life of politicians should have public consequences. Scandal stories in Britain, above all, interrogate morality, establishing templates of what is acceptable and what is not. Spanish editorials, in which debates about ethics are almost absent, generalize more about the traits of the democratic system and related characteristics such as the rule of law and the separation of powers.

CULTURAL CODES AND IDENTITY ASSOCIATIONS

What resonant cultural codes and identity associations are present in the way British and Spanish press frame wrongdoing?

Both countries use popular cultural codes such as puns and popular sayings: "Roses can have painful thorns" (*The Sun*, February 16, 1996); "The apple's small spot of corruption will spread to the whole barrel" (*The Independent*, July 4, 1997); "Too much euphoria spoils the broth" (*The Guardian*, December 12, 1996); "The penal aspects of the case are the trees that obscure the wood" (*El Mundo*, May 9, 1994); "Vera, Roldán, Siemens: all roads lead to Genova" (*El Mundo*, July 10, 1995).[2]

Both countries use titles of films, television programs, and novels: "The minister's Alice-in-Wonderland position" (*The Guardian*, June 7, 1995); "The Magnificent Seven" (*The Sun*, October 20, 1994); "[The public thinks] politicians are a grubby bunch of Arthur Daleys" (*The Sun*, November 2, 1994); "Roldán is around, but who knows where? (*El Mundo*, April 29, 1994); "[Roldán] has become a new Wally with good reasons to be unfindable" (*El Mundo*, April 29, 1994).[3]

But there are interesting differences in the way British and Spanish editorials portray their own country's identity. British editorials make references to national history: MPs are seen as attached to the "traditions of the Victorian age" (*The Guardian*, November 1, 1994); "the Edwardian era" (*The Guardian*, May 12, 1995); "the Thatcherite era" (*The Guardian*, May 12, 1995). The only historical references in Spanish editorials are to mention the youth of the Spanish constitution: "Yesterday was 17 years since the first democratic elections" (*El País*, June 16, 1994); [the clean up of the Interior Ministry] "unresolved since the beginning of the Transition . . ." (*El País*, March 22, 1995).

There are also identity associations in British editorials that are absent in Spanish ones so that, for example, the *Arms to Iraq* scandal is described as "Britain's Iraqgate" (*The Guardian*, November 10, 1993).

Whereas in Britain political corruption is portrayed as something unusual and uncommon, there are words and expressions in Spanish editorials which connect this country's identity with the *picaresque*, a Spanish literary genre in which violations of social and legal norms are seen as clever and comical.

In British newspapers, scandal and sleaze are considered to be uncommon in the country's political tradition, an exception rather than the rule. Identity associations are made through comparisons with other countries: "British public life is among the least corrupt in the world" (*The Guardian*, July 4, 1997), because, "after all . . . the level of corruption in France-Belgium-Italy is so much worse" (*The Independent*, July 4, 1997); "For all the recent sleaze and scandal, Britain still has the most honest civil servants and politicians in the world . . . we can't say the same for our European partners, who deal with corruption by banning the press from reporting it" (*The Sun*, May 12, 1995).

Spanish editorials state that corruption would be more severely sanctioned in other countries; at the same time, they evoke the picaresque tradition in discussing corruption in Spain.

The picaresque, as Alborg (1966) explains, is a Spanish literary genre (the term comes from "pícaro", which means crafty, cunning), in which the central character "has an irregular life and is lacking in scruples" (p. 401). The *pícaro* is a rascal, shrewd and astute. His behavior often provokes the amused indulgence of others who half admire his cheekiness.

Roldán is often presented as a rogue who became director of the Civil Guard without having the qualifications he claimed to have and whose whole career was based on deceit: "It is not that he committed the occasional goof; he dedicated body and soul to it" (*El Mundo*, April 30, 1994). The whole case, the escape and the capture in curious and confusing conditions, was portrayed as a comedy: "a big joke" (*El País*, December 11, 1994), "a commotion" (*El País*, May 15, 1996), "a botched job" (*El Mundo*, March 2, 1995), "a comedy sketch" (*El Mundo*, March 3, 1995); "grotesque. A *happening* of those which represent a landmark" (italicized English word in the original) (*El Mundo*, April 30, 1994).[4] The Roldán case was a "tragedy of entanglement, mounted by greedy men" carried out by "a gang of scoundrels" (*ABC*, March 3, 1995).

FRAMING THROUGH NEWS ICONS

In Chapter 3 we discussed the concept of "frame". Here we will consider the nature of news icons in reference to frames. A news icon is an exceptional kind of frame that has a journalistic function. Recalling the definition given by Bennett and Lawrence (1995), "news icons occur when an entire story, narrative, or conflict becomes associated with and represented by a single event, which in turn is crystallized into a single image that dominates the original narrative and later shifts the framing of other news stories" (p. 46). A news icon is a condensational symbol (Dahl & Bennett, 1996, p. 46).

We will now examine British and the Spanish coverage to see whether there are incipient signs of emerging news icons and whether it was the case that those incipient signs allow us to talk about news icons "shifting the framing of other news stories."

In the first place, more explanation is required of what news icons are (Bennett & Lawrence, 1995; Dahl & Bennett, 1996):

First, a news icon is based upon a news event.

Second, a news icon is reporter-introduced and not pegged to sources.

Third, its initial appearance in a news story is as a vivid image or word picture.

Fourth, the "image" overwhelms the story and is reproduced throughout the mass media.

Fifth, a news icon is not specific to a single event but can link various events across time. This means that the icon is introduced in the narrative frame of other types of stories, breaking down narrative boundaries. Linkages between otherwise isolated events are thus made.

Sixth, not only are events linked, but thematic connections are also made through interpretive, less specific references. Thus, the image becomes suggestive of larger social issues or unresolved problems in society, prompting journalists to tell the story using the icon again and again, publicizing different points of view and disparate reactions. News icons are then used by journalists to evoke larger cultural themes, symbolizing values, contradictions, or changes that have begun to surface in society.

Finally, as a timeless reminder of enduring and unresolved problems, challenging news icons can be used to keep stories going when there are few breaking events. They can become surrogate events, providing the dramatic context for reports, press conferences, or technical information that may lack obvious news value.

In order to identify news icons we first examined signs of emerging news icons in the shape of word formulas, for which quantitative content analysis was carried out to establish the most frequent word mentions of certain terms in all articles coded. The words looked for were "scandal", "corruption", and, in the British case, "sleaze". Secondly, we looked for the most frequently used shorthand expressions referring to the scandal cases that appeared in the British and Spanish editorial pieces in order to see whether there were other frequently repeated words that could function as news icons. And finally, we looked at bar-straps of special sections, sections specially created by the newspaper for a particular scandal case. The use of the word formulas in the title of these sections (included in the bar-strap) would give an indication of the role these words played in the way journalists conceptualized the scandal stories.

Word Formulas for News Icons

After a first review of coverage, three words were identified as possible repeated word formulas: "corruption", "scandal", and "sleaze". The number of mentions in total articles was then codified with the following results (see Table 7.3).

These figures show that in both countries these words were frequently used in the coverage, though more in Britain than in Spain. Whereas in Britain 9.5 percent of articles mentioned the word "corruption" and 16.6 percent mentioned the word "scandal", in Spain only 7.8 percent mentioned "corruption" and 4.9 percent the word "scandal". As for "sleaze", 24.9 percent of British articles (that is to say, one in four) mentioned the term.

The word "sleaze" also merits comment. As we saw in Chapter 2, sleaze denotes disparate, unethical, and/or corrupt acts. Dunleavy and

TABLE 7.3 Repeated Word Formulas

	U.K.	SPAIN
Corruption	9.5 (164)	7.8 (152)
Scandal	16.6 (284)	4.9 (95)
Sleaze	24.9 (427)	-

Weir (1995) showed how this particular word label permitted "other-wise discrete problems to be connected in an innovative but easily understandable way" (p. 59).

The analysis of the most frequent shorthand expressions used in the editorials highlighted other words to be taken into account. In the United Kingdom, apart from "scandal," "corruption," and "sleaze," the other two words frequently used were "crisis" and "affair." In Spain, apart from the words "scandal" and "corruption", the words "crisis" and "plot"[5] were also frequently used. The word "case" was also frequently used, mentioned in 41 of the 100 bar-straps. The word is employed in popular usage to refer to a person as "a case [*un caso*]" or to an event as "a real case [*todo un caso*]." A newspaper founded in the 1950s called *El Caso*, which dealt with sensational crime cases, may have helped popularize the expression. The word "case" was frequently used in bar-straps: the *Caso Roldán, Caso GAL, Caso Lasa-Zabala, Caso Rubio*, the *casos Gal and Roldán*. The colloquial meaning of the word "case" was also used in editorials such as in "Roldán, a case" (*El País*, February 16, 1994).

The terms *scandal, sleaze, affair, case, crisis,* and *plot* were constantly used in coverage and were used in the titles of the bar-straps of special sections, thus functioning as general labels for stories related to a variety of topics.

Journalistic Origin of the Word Formulas

Were these word formulas source or reporter-introduced? Did journalists introduce them on their own authority or were they taken from politicians?

As far as the term "sleaze" is concerned, British prime minister John Major (2000) wrote: "Our critics chose the term shrewdly, and used it unscrupulously" (p. 550). According to journalist Mark Skipworth (Skipworth, personal interview, 1999), it was the then Labour opposition leader Tony Blair's use of the term in a conference that launched the term in the journalistic imagination. Its use by the British press slowly increased from 1982 up to 1993 and from then on shot up. In 1995 it was used forty times more frequently than ten years previously (Dunleavy and Weir, 1995, pp. 57-58).

The data suggests that journalists and commentators, through their opinion pieces, helped to establish "corruption," "scandal,", and "sleaze" as key words in the coverage of scandal. The words were repro-duced throughout the mass media, serving to label the coverage of a whole set of events and topics.

In both countries these terms were used more frequently in opinion pieces than in news. In Britain only 6.4 percent of news stories used the word "corruption" as compared to its use in 21.4 percent of opinion pieces. For the word "scandal" the trend is less strong: 15 percent of news articles used the word scandal as compared to 22.7 percent of opinion pieces. Finally, the word "sleaze" was mentioned in 22 percent of news articles and 35.9 percent of opinion pieces.

The same occurs in Spanish coverage. The identified words were more frequently used in opinion pieces than in news stories. The word "corruption" was only mentioned in 5.3 percent of news articles compared to 19.1 percent of opinion pieces. As for the word "scandal", it was used in 3.9 percent of news stories and up to 9.1 percent of opinion pieces.[6]

It cannot be conclusively shown who originated the terms to designate the various kinds of wrongdoing. Tony Blair may have picked up the expression "sleaze" from journalists. However, it is clear that the frequent journalistic use of the terms (and especially of the expression "sleaze") in contexts detached from the original usage allowed journalists and commentators to appropriate them as free-standing signifiers for disparate kinds of wrongdoing.

News Icons' Use for Thematic Connections

Did these terms serve to make connections among disparate events to generate a particular kind of reporter-driven narrative? To see this we looked at the way in which these terms were used for labelling the special sections in order to see whether links and connections among events and topics were made through these words, as well as less specific, interpretive, and euphemistic references to other social problems.

Spain: The "Case" of Generalized "Corruption." Firstly, these words were used to label, at the close of a set of events, a general situation. Thus the beginnings of an affair start with references to specific events (for instance, "Patrimony Under Suspicion" (*El País*, February 18, 1994) was the first piece of information that unleashed the whole *Roldán* affair. Once several events had occurred (for instance "The End of an Escape" (*El País*, February 28, 1995), "The Capture of Roldán" (*El Mundo*, March 1, 2, 8, 9 1995), the newspapers began to headline the special section with the word "caso": "Caso Roldán" (*El País*, March 3, 5; *ABC*, March 10, 11, 12, 15, 22, 23 and 30, 1995); and also the word "caso" was used to refer to a specific event (for instance "El caso Laos"; *ABC*, March 18, 1995). The word "case" is also used to introduce tension in the narratives, as if the coverage was a whole story with different chapters. For instance, in *El Mundo*, all the bar-straps of the trial of the *Lasa and Zabala* case take the formula "Caso Lasa Zabala" with variations according to the event of the day: Caso Lasa and Zabala / the witnesses; Caso Lasa and Zabala / the statement; Caso Lasa and Zabala / the defence; Caso Lasa and Zabala / the conclusions; Caso Lasa and Zabala / ready for sentencing; Caso Lasa and Zabala / the reactions; and finally, Caso Lasa and Zabala / the verdict. The term "case" was not specific to a single event, but linked various events across time.

Secondly, these words were used in the bar-straps to provide interpretation and commentary rather than to function simply as descriptive labels. During the month of May 1994 a number of events occurred: an interview with Roldán (while a fugitive from justice) was published in *El Mundo*, a parliamentary commission was established to investigate the *Rubio* affair, several officials resigned, and the Prime Minister went to Parliament to give an account of Roldán's escape. The bar-strap of special sections during this time denoted a general situation: "Institutional Crisis" (*El Mundo*, May 5, 1994) and "Political Crisis" (*El Mundo*, May 5, 8, 9, 10, 11, 12, 13, 14, 1994). Again the word "crisis" was used to describe the general situation after the arrest of Roldán led the Minister of the Interior to resign. The coverage of these days was characterized by the general formula "Political Crisis" (*El Mundo*, March 3, 12, 13, 14 and 15, 1995).

Thirdly, these words were used to make special links and connections between different topics and scandals. The beginnings of the *Roldán* case were heralded with bar-straps referring to different cases: the initial revelation related to the suspicions about Roldán's financial affairs ("Patrimony Under Suspicion" *El País*, February 16, 1994) as referred to above, revelations about the GAL affair ("The Gal Controversy", *El Mundo*, February 18, 1994), and about the misuse of state funds ("The Reserved Funds", *El Mundo*, March 12, 1994). All these were separate cases. From 22 April on, under the word formula '"corruption" ("Political Corruption" [*El Mundo*, April 22, 24, and 30 and May 2, 1994]); "The Status of Corruption" (*ABC*, April 20, 1994); and "Corruption Devours Government" (*ABC*, May 2, 3, and 4, 1994), coverage of these different cases came together. The word "corruption" seems to have become a shorthand expression to link the misuse of state funds (by Roldán) with the GAL case.

The use of these word formulas in the bar-strap helped to spin debate about whether state terrorism could be regarded as a kind of corruption. In linking the GAL affair with the *CESID* and *Roldán* affairs, coverage helped to show that state terrorism had been practiced along with irregular financial operations. *ABC* was in no doubt about the connection: "The GAL Case / The Roldán Case" and "The GAL and Roldán Cases" are the titles of bar-straps of special sections (March 23 and 30,

1995). *El Mundo,* makes a link between two cases in its bar-strap of September 22, 1995: "The GAL Plot/The CESID Scandal".

Graphics of bar-straps in which these word formulas were included helped to establish thematic connections and interpretive references. After publication of the information regarding the suspicions about Roldán's financial affairs, several bar-strap graphics depicted a specific event. In subsequent coverage more interpretive references were included. The first bar-straps with the term "State Reserved Funds" depicted somebody secretly handing over bank notes (*El Mundo*, March 12, 1994). Subsequent bar-straps ran the headline "Political Corruption" with a graphic showing a hand giving a bank note to someone else (*El Mundo*, April 24, 1994). These were followed with the even more interpretive and less specific headlines of "Institutional Crisis" and "Political Crisis" with a graphic showing a series of domino-style, falling briefcases, referring to the political resignations then taking place (*El Mundo*, May 5, 1994). Few icons represented the person at the center of the scandal: only Roldán's escape was shown in graphic form (*El Mundo*, May 3, 1994).

"Corruption", "case", and "crisis" were key words used in labelling special sections devoted to scandal coverage. They linked isolated events, overwhelming the original event and providing an overarching interpretive frame.

The "Sleaze" Umbrella. The use of word formulas in the bar-straps for special sections was also analyzed in British coverage. As was the case in Spain, word formulas were used as interpretive markers after having first described a specific event. For instance, in referring to sexual misdemeanor stories, the first bar-straps are very descriptive: "The Mellor Affair" (*The Sun*, July 22, 1992 and *The Sunday Times*, July 26, 1992); "The Mellor Crisis" (*The Sun*, September 24, 1992); "The Fall of David Mellor" (*The Guardian*, September 25, 1992); "Heave Ho for Yeo" (January 6, 1994); "Yeo Resignation" (January 6, 1994). Later bar-strap headlines contain more interpretive references: "Scandal of Tory MP's Mistress" (*The Sun*, March 29, 1997); "Tory Turmoil" (*The Sun*, January 11, 1994) and "Tories in Turmoil" (May 12, 1995). *The Sun's* bar-strap title, "Bonk to Basics with the Tories" (*The Sun*, January 10, 1994) manages to combine a crude reference to the Conservatives' "Back to Basics" policy and the sexual misdemeanors of its parliamentarians.[7]

The term "sleaze" was used in the same way. After descriptive labels such as "Cash for Questions" (*The Sunday Times*, July 17, 1994), "The Cash-for-Questions Affair" (*The Independent*, October 21, 22, 1994), "Cash for Questions Row" (*The Guardian*, October 21, 22, 25) or "The Cash for Questions Scandal" (*The Sun*, October 21, 22), some dailies used the word sleaze in the bar-strap to refer to broader issues: "The Attack on Sleaze" (*The Independent*, October 26, 27, 28, 29 and November, 1 and 3); "Welcome to the House of Sleaze" (*The Sunday Times*, October 23). In 1996 the *Sunday Times* used a series of bar-straps employing the metaphor of a tangled web to refer to a situation of chaos: "Hamilton's Tangled Web. Greer's Tangled Web" (October 2, 3); "The Tories Tangled Web" (October 7) and "The Tangled Web" (November 11). By 1997 titles of special sections were using the word "sleaze" to denote a general situation: "Sleaze. Corruption in the Commons" (March, 21, 22, 24, 27). This situation characterizes the election campaign: "Spotlight. Major's Troubled Campaign" (*The Sunday Times*, March 29, 1997).

Sleaze was frequently used in graphics of bar-straps and in cartoons, particularly in the final weeks of the 1997 elections. *The Guardian's* headline "Sleaze: The Evidence," summed up the paper's assessment of Major's attempt to defend his government against allegations of sleaze in the last prime minister's question time. As mentioned in Chapter 2, a cartoon published in *The Times* with the words "No escape from the maze" (March 27, 1997) showed the letters of the word "sleaze" forming a labyrinth from which Major found it impossible to escape. *The Sun's* front-page depiction of a Conservative rosette with a superimposed photograph of the disgraced Conservative candidate Piers Merchant ironically encouraged its readers to "Vote Sleaze" (*The Sun*, March 27 and 28, 1997). *The Guardian* used the term emblazoned across a photograph of Big Ben with the headline "Corruption in the Commons" (March 21, 1997).

"Sleaze" became the defining term of an entire political era, something John Major (2000) himself acknowledged:

> The word "sleaze" itself was a potent factor in the destructiveness of the issue. Its power lay in the fact that it was, at the same time, a very strong word and a very weak one. Strong in its ability to convey a generalised sense of decadence and wickedness. Strong in its catch-all ability to encompass everything from sexual sin to official malpractice. But weak in its capacity to identify with precision any actual misbehaviour. (p. 551)

Table 7.4 provides a summary of the dimensions of news frames used for scandal stories.

Underlying much of the debate about the media's role in political scandal are assumptions about media power. Our discussion in this chapter of the ways in which journalists frame political scandal gives some indications of where this power lies, a question which will be the subject of the next chapter.

TABLE 7.4 Dimensions of News Frames

	UNITED KINGDOM	SPAIN
CHARACTERS	Consensus among the press about who the wrongdoer is:	Lack of consensus among the press about who the wrongdoer is:
	• Politicians: them and their bad actions.	• Socialist characters and their bad actions.
	• The Press: us and our good actions.	• Critics of the Socialists and their bad actions.
	• The public: the affected.	
AGENCY	Direct attribution of action to specific individuals	Diffuse attribution of action
CATEGORIZATIONS	Moral evaluation is more explicit with predominantly moral assessments.	Moral evaluation is not as explicit, with predominantly legal assessments.
GENERALIZATIONS and DEBATES	High degree of moral discourse, generalizing about the principle of parliamentary sovereignty and consequences of malpractise for the political system and society.	High degree of technical and legal discourse with generalizations about the democratic system and the separation of powers
CULTURAL CODES	Historical references	Few historical references
	Identity associations with the traditional uncorrupted British culture	Reference to the picaresque tradition
NEWS ICONS	The word formula "sleaze" functioned as effective news icon.	Word formulas such as "case" and "crisis" were used for making thematic connections, though they did not function as effective news icons.

NOTES

1. The Spanish expression is *Estado de Derecho*.
2. Genova is the name of the street where the Popular Party's headquarters are in Madrid.
3. Arthur Daley was an unreliable character from a British television series. *Quien sabe dónde?* [Who knows where?] was the title of a Spanish television series.
4. In the original "comedy sketch" is "sainete," a one-act comedy sketch or farce typical of the Andalusian region of Spain. We have translated "esperpéntico" by the term "grotesque". The Spanish term comes from the term "esperpento" which was the theater of the grotesque created by the Spanish writer Valle Inclán.
5. The original Spanish term is "trama."
6. In Britain and Spain these figures were found to be statistically significant ($p = 0.00$).
7. "Bonk" was a British tabloid slang term to describe sexual intercourse. The doyen of "bonk journalism" in the late 1980s and early 1990s was the *News of the World*, followed by *The Sun* (Chippindale & Horrie, 1999, pp. 277-304).

8

Press Power

It is my belief that the level of sin in our political system holds fairly
steady. It is the media appetite for reporting it which goes in waves.

John Major, British Prime Minister 1990-1997

I believe that the worst corruption is the corruption of the political
debate, because it is precisely what fosters corruption. And what we
lived through here was a corruption of the political debate.

Felipe González, Spanish Prime Minister 1982-1996[1]

In his political memoirs the former British Prime Minister John Major
wryly comments: "There is a good chance that, when many of the
achievements of the last Conservative government this century [the

twentieth century] have been forgotten, people will still remember one word: 'sleaze'" (2000, p. 550). One month after having lost the Spanish elections, Felipe González spoke in a television interview about the impact of media coverage of corruption: "The media have had an absolutely key role. . . . And they have achieved a part of their objectives. Those who wanted me to lose the elections have achieved it" (cited in Prego, 2000, pp. 293-294).

Political scandals mattered to Major and González and to their governments. But *in what sense* did they matter? Apart from setting the mood music for the end-of-millennium governments of Britain and Spain, and aside from the impact on individual politicians, did political scandals really change anything? And what, if anything, can scandals show us about the power of the press in liberal democracies? In this chapter we will explore these two related questions—how do political scandals matter and what they can tell us about the power of the media—in different national contexts.[2]

DO POLITICAL SCANDALS MATTER?

The subject of political scandals and their consequences has been taken up by a number of scholars. Manuel Castells devotes a section of his monumental work to the issue, developing an analysis based on his notion of "informational politics" (1998, p. 342). He argues that because of the crisis of traditional political systems and the all-pervasiveness of the media, political communication has become trapped in the space of the media. In other words, the logic and structure of the media frame politics, and power cannot be obtained and exercised outside the confines it sets (p. 344). This is the rationale for the development of political marketing, where politics becomes spectacle and media event with an emphasis on personalization, negative advertising, and simplification of the message. It also explains the development of the "politics of scandal" (p. 366). According to this analysis, the explosion of scandal coverage is not due to an increase in corruption but to the fact that scandal politics has become the weapon of choice to compete in informational politics (p. 371).

Theories of Scandal Consequences

This analysis shares some points of view with the most thoroughgoing exploration of the issue to date, provided by John B. Thompson, whose work we have referred to in earlier chapters. In his *Political Scandals*

(2000) he develops themes examined in previous writing about the impact of media on social interaction. Following in part Thompson's own account, here we will consider six ways of thinking about scandals and their consequences (2000, pp. 234-245):

1. **The no-consequence theory**: This approach views political scandal as the ephemeral product of media culture. Scandals entertain, divert the populace, and cause inconvenience to public figures, but have no enduring consequences.

2. **The functionalist theory**: Here scandal is seen as a mechanism for reinforcing existing social norms and conventions. Scandal is essentially conservative in its impact, acting as a marker for the boundaries of acceptable public behavior, which, once crossed, are reaffirmed by the real and significant consequences of scandal. Following Durkheim's interpretative model, the quasi-religious ritual aspects of the unfolding of scandal are emphasized (see Alexander, 1988).

3. **The trivialization theory**: This approach considers the proliferation of scandal coverage as testimony to the decline of the public sphere. The Habermasian notion of the public sphere as the critical-rational domain of orientative public discourse is, in this view, undermined and impoverished by political scandals. Critics see three processes at work that combine to convert politics into a spectator sport for a cynical public, namely:

   Privatization of the public sphere: Distinctions are no longer drawn between what constitutes private affairs from public ones.

   Tabloidization of the media: Issue-based, analytical reporting is replaced by sensational journalism (Snow, 1997; Sparks & Tulloch, 2000).

   Personalization of politics: The decline of political parties and of the importance of ideology leads to an increasing emphasis on the personalities of public figures rather than the policies they advocate (Brants, 1998; see Stanyer & Wring, 2004).

4. **The carnival theory**: Here scandal acts to subvert the power and privilege of elites to the general merriment of the populace. The topsy-turvy world of carnival breaks into the political realm, increasing the general quota of scepticism with which the public views its political class.

As Thompson points out, each of these approaches has weaknesses. The trials, resignations, and procedural reform seen in Spain and the

United Kingdom provide sufficient evidence to show that the "no consequences" theory is untenable even on a very narrow view of "consequences". The three remaining theories all posit real consequences from
scandals but, in our view, provide an oversimplified account of these
consequences and of the role of the media in political scandals.

As we explained in Chapter 2, the functionalist approach simply
fails to take into account the way in which political scandal can underline moments of uncertainty and crisis regarding prevalent norms and
conventions. The *Cash for Questions* scandal is a good example of this.

The trivialization model provides a variant on the theme that liberal
democratic societies are suffering from "media malaise", as described by
Norris (2000). The argument here is that "common practices in political
communications by the news media and party campaigns hinder 'civic
engagement', meaning citizens learning about public affairs, trust in
government, and political activism" (p. 4). As Norris shows, on the
available evidence we should be wary about accepting this argument,
something we will return to later in this chapter. For the moment, we
note two contentious aspects of the trivialization theory: first, it appears
to underline a certain kind of "sleazy" sex scandal coverage—typical of
the Anglo-American world—failing to account for the more serious
kinds of scandal exemplified by the GAL death squads; second, it
hypothesizes a particular modality of media effect where trivialized
media coverage of politics causes political disengagement that, as we
shall see, has not been substantiated in the literature.

Turning to what we have called the "carnival theory", this provides
an attractive and, we would argue, partly convincing account of the consequences of a particular genre of scandal (for example, the
Clinton/Lewinsky affair, the Mellor story) or specific aspects of a scandal (for example, the Roldán escape). However, as an account based on a
model of popular culture that sets elite against mass culture and regards
laughter as essentially radical and subversive, it has serious deficiencies.
The tabloid, "popular" press can be as conservative as the "quality"
and—as one British tabloid editor once called it—"unpopular" press.
Equally, *El Mundo* and *The Guardian* demonstrate the latter's ability to be
radically subversive of elite power. Carnivalesque diversion can be simply that: a way of poking fun at figures of authority, overturning the
ordinary norms of deference and respect, and relativizing the importance of hierarchy and prestige.

Before examining Thompson's approach to the consequences of
scandal, we can add what might be considered the journalists' account
of the impact of political scandal derived from a view of journalism's
function as the Fourth Estate, the watchdog of the public interest, scruti-
neer of the powerful and righter of wrongs (see Schultz, 1998). We can

term this the Watergate theory after the archetypal political scandal of the late twentieth century.

5. **The Watergate theory**: Here political scandals act as mobilizing vectors, unleashing public indignation that in turn forces action by policy makers. Underlying this approach is the "mobilizing model" of journalism, according to which reporters dig out unsavory facts that powerful interests would prefer us not to know. Their crusade triggers public indignation, which leads to change (Protess et al., 1991). In this account, scandals form part of the journalism of outrage which is underpinned by the social responsibility model of the press.

We will return later to the issue of the nature of media effects, here posited as being particularly strong. The Watergate theory establishes political scandal and its consequences as a function of the media. First, this approach implies that "there can only be as much [media reporting of political scandal] as there are examples of sexual and financial deviance supplied by the politicians" (McNair, 2000, p. 56). Second, it argues that the media's exposure of wrongdoing, its laying bare of political scandal, is the trigger for policy action through the pressure of public outrage.

Both these assumptions are suspect. The first begs the question as to what is to be considered political scandal. Sexual and financial deviance are not givens (the absence of sexual scandal in Spain demonstrates this), nor are all clear-cut cases of them exposed by the media (as the nonreporting of John F. Kennedy's adultery and the homosexual promiscuity of a British Labour politician in the 1960s show). The second element of the argument has scant evidence to support it. Protess and his fellow researchers (1991) showed that even if the revelation of scandal did prompt public outrage—not always the case—public policy changes were more reliant on prepublication transactions between journalists and policymakers than on public response, leading the authors to speak of a "democracy without citizens."

6. **Social theory of scandal**: Thompson provides an analysis of political scandal and its consequences based on the premise that scandals are "struggles over symbolic power in which reputation and trust are at stake" (2000, p. 245). According to this view, the power of political scandals lies in their ability to damage reputation and undermine trust, both of which comprise the necessary symbolic capital of contemporary public figures.

The notion of "symbolic power" is crucial to Thompson's account of the impact of political scandal. Derived from Bourdieu (1991), it is one of four kinds of power (the others being political, coercive, and economic power) and Thompson defines it as the "capacity to intervene in the course of events, to influence the actions and beliefs of others and . . . to create events, by means of the production and transmission of symbolic forms" (2000, p. 98).

Political scandal strikes at the root of this power because, of the conditions of mediated visibility in which public figures must operate, as we saw in Chapter 3. This approach has considerable force: it posits the impact of scandal on an individual level (the loss of reputation of this or that politician) and, more significantly, on a systemic level. Survey data in liberal democracies indicate deepening public distrust of government and low esteem for politicians (Mortimore, 1995, pp. 38-39; Norris, 1999). Thompson takes this to provide "reasonable grounds for supposing that political scandals can have a corrosive impact on relations of trust" (p. 256). He also concludes that they can encourage assessments of public figures to be made on the basis of character rather than competence, lead to lame duck governments besieged by sleaze and, more seriously, the weakening of democracy through the effective withdrawal of disillusioned sections of society from participation in democratic politics. Although acknowledging the positive contribution that political scandals can make to the quality of public life, on balance Thompson thinks their impact is negative. In this he echoes views held across the Atlantic that consider that scandal coverage is "reducing voter turnout, distracting from important policy debates and discouraging the best politicians and journalists" (Sabato, Stencel, & Lichter, 2001, p.xvi). Thompson ends his analysis on a somber note, stating: "It is difficult to avoid the conclusion that the political culture of scandal is unlikely to make the task of creating a stronger and more inclusive form of democracy any easier" (p. 259).

SCANDAL AND TRUST

Thompson provides an extremely valuable analysis of the significance of political scandals. However, his conclusions about their consequences are perhaps overstated and certainly insufficiently supported by the evidence. Survey data is extremely limited: public opinion polling began in Britain in the 1930s and questions about standards in public life have only been included since the 1980s. In Spain the Center of Sociological Studies (CIS) only began to include questions about trust in and appraisal of the president and public institutions from 1988 onwards. Questions about standards in public life were not included. And, of course, the difficulty of establishing a causal connection between loss of public confidence and political scandals, as Thompson himself acknowledges, is considerable (2000, p. 256). It could well be argued that political scandals are symptoms of more deep-seated democratic malaises than the underlying causes of them.

Looking at the British political scandals of the 1990s, the Nolan Committee stated: "There is no precedent in this century for so many allegations of wrongdoing, on so many different subjects, in so short a period of time" (1995, p. 15). However, John Major suggests that "[t]he level of corruption in British politics, modest by world standards but still too high for my taste, remains fairly constant." He reverses scandal-distrust causality: "I suspect the national obsession with 'Tory sleaze' was as much a consequence as a cause of our fall from favour" (2000, p. 693). In other words, the Conservative government had already lost the people's trust and esteem for reasons unconnected to political scandal (splits over Europe; withdrawal from the European monetary system; perceived arrogance after eighteen years in power). In Britain, a strong case can be made for political scandals being the consequence and not the chief cause of public distrust.

In Spain the evidence is not so clear. Although the scandals undermined public trust in politicians, there was no widespread debate about standards in public life. The 1996 election results did not demonstrate a collapse of confidence in the Socialist party which, as was mentioned in Chapter 2, narrowly lost to the Popular Party but gained 300,000 votes on its previous election result. Conspiracy theorists had a field day in certain newspapers: as we saw in Chapter 6, it was conjectured that the scandals were the result of a plot between journalists and judges to discredit the Socialist government. The main scandal outcomes were those that resulted from the court proceedings that were completed some years after the height of public debate about scandal in Spain.

However, it is hard to dissent from the view expressed by philosopher Onora O'Neil (2002) that the creation of a culture of suspicion, generated by constant media allegations of wrongdoing against the political classes, is unlikely to contribute to the development of trust in politicians.

Scandal Outcomes

The preceding discussion shows that the consequences of political scandal are not easy to establish. Nevertheless, we will argue that scandals do have outcomes.

How can we calibrate scandal consequences? We tackle this question cautiously using two streams of evidence: first, records of events directly traceable to personal, executive, legislative, or judicial action linked to political scandal and second, measures related to trust and esteem of politicians and journalists collated from surveys, industry awards, and recorded views of legislative or investigating bodies.

The first kind of evidence is set out in Table 8.1. It is organized on the basis of an operational definition of scandal outcome that argues that an outcome must result from action; actions are undertaken by agents; thus, outcomes can be categorized according to the chief agent acting to bring about a consequence. Our summary of the most significant scandal consequences is divided into four categories:

1. Personal outcomes refer to consequences resulting from actions taken by individuals implicated in scandals; for example, resignation, libel action dropped.
2. Executive outcomes refer to consequences resulting from actions taken by the executive; for example, the establishment of a commission of inquiry.
3. Legislative consequences refer to outcomes resulting from actions taken by the legislature; for example, the approval of a new law, the decision of a parliamentary committee.
4. Judicial outcomes refer to consequences resulting from actions taken by the courts as a result of the revelation of the scandal; for example, trials, conviction, and imprisonment.

The findings summarized in Table 8.1 make it clear that political scandals in the 1990s did have consequences, as we will shortly discuss. A more difficult challenge, in our view, is to evaluate the second stream of evidence, which Thompson in part employs. Public opinion measures demonstrating levels of public trust and esteem of politicians and journalists appear to provide evidence about the consequences of political scandals but, as we saw earlier, must be used with caution.

Even if we cannot be sure that political scandals were the cause, survey figures show that public confidence in politicians in Britain plummeted during the sleaze years (Mortimore, 1995, p. 40). In Spain the picture is slightly different; although it is true that González and his government received their worst approval ratings between 1993 and 1996, the fall was not dramatic (CIS, Barómetros). Approval ratings for institutions such as the political parties and Congress did not suffer a significant fall (CIRES, 1997).

For British journalists, public opinion survey figures were no more encouraging than those for the country's politicians. As Professor Ivor Crewe explained in evidence to the Nolan Committee: "Whenever surveys have asked people to compare various occupations for honesty or trustworthiness or a moral example, Members of Parliament have been

TABLE 8.1 Scandals Outcomes

SCANDAL	PERSONAL	EXECUTIVE	LEGISLATIVE	JUDICIAL
Sexual Misdemeanors				
Mellor	Resignation of David Mellor as minister.	None	None	None
Yeo	Resignation of Yeo as minister.	None	None	None
Merchant	None	None	None	None
Cash for Questions	- Ministerial resignations of Tim Smith, Neil Hamilton, and David Willetts. - After he'd successfully lobbied for a change to the 1689 Bill of Rights to allow the action to go ahead, abandoned libel action by Hamilton, and lobbyist Ian Greer against *The Guardian*. - Failed Hamilton libel action against Mohammed al Fayed.	- John Major institutes investigation by senior civil servant, Robin Butler, of allegations against Hamilton and Smith. - Neil Hamilton asked to resign. - Establishment of the Nolan Committee on Standards in Public Life. - Adoption of recommendations of Nolan Committee (reform of Commons Committee overseeing standards; appointment of parliamentary commissioner for standards; ban on paid multiple client consultancies; MPs code of conduct).	- Privileges Committee suspends and fines two Conservative MPs. - Privileges Committee censures *The Sunday Times*. - Committee on Members' Interests investigates Ritz allegations against Hamilton and rules he was "imprudent." It recommends no action.	None

161

TABLE 8.1 Scandals Outcomes *(Continued)*

SCANDAL	PERSONAL	EXECUTIVE	LEGISLATIVE	JUDICIAL
Cash for Questions *(Continued)*			- Committee on Standards and Privileges censures Willetts and Hamilton. - Adoption of Downey report conclusions censuring Hamilton and Smith.	
Arms to Iraq	Exoneration of businessmen	- Establishment of Scott Inquiry. - Government response to Public Service Committee report .	- Trade and Industry Committee investigation of arms to Iraq. - Adoption of Scott's recommendations, after further investigation by Public Service Committee, requesting clarification of the doctrine of ministerial responsibility and of the constitutional position of the civil service. - A recommendation for stronger regulation of answers to parliamentary questions was taken up. - The subsequent Labour government adopted Scott's recommendation that a Freedom of Information Act be introduced.	- Prosecution and conviction of a number of businessmen. - Prosecution of Matrix Churchill businessmen and collapse of their trial.

TABLE 8.1 Scandals Outcomes *(Continued)*

SCANDAL	PERSONAL	EXECUTIVE	LEGISLATIVE	JUDICIAL
Arms to Iraq *(Continued)*			- Limited changes were made in response to Scott's suggestions for change in the use of legal instruments to ensure the secrecy of certain information.	
Rubio	- Resignation and imprisonment of the governor of the Bank of Spain, Mariano Rubio. - Resignation of Carlos Solchaga as PSOE spokesman for having supported Rubio in 1992. - Resignation of Agriculture - Minister, Vicente Albero, for illicit money invested in Ibercorp.	None	Establishment of a Committee of inquiry.	Rubio sentenced to prison. Guilty of: Insider share dealing Falsification of documents Fraud working for private company in 1980s. He died before the sentence could be carried out.
Roldán	- Resignation of Interior Minister Antonio Asunción. - Resignation of Luis Roldán. Director of the Civil Guard.	None	- Establishment of a Committee of Inquiry. - Congressional reform to allow more transparency in the reporting of the work of Committees of Inquiry in some cases.	- Prosecution and conviction of Roldán on charges of fraud and embezzlement, bribery and tax evasion. Sentenced to 31 years imprisonment. - Conviction and imprisonment of his wife and other associates on lesser charges.

TABLE 8.1 Scandals Outcomes *(Continued)*

SCANDAL	PERSONAL	EXECUTIVE	LEGISLATIVE	JUDICIAL
Gal-Lasa Zabala	None	None	None	The ex-civil governor of Guipúzcoa and 4 members of the Civil Guard are convicted of 2 murders and 2 illegal detentions, and given long jail sentences (average of 70 years).
Gal-CESID	None	Declassification of the CESID papers.	- Reform of the Official Secrets Act. - Law on CESID is put on hold.	Conviction and jail sentence for Juan Alberto Perote, CESID official. Judge uses papers for the GAL case.

at or near the bottom of the league, competing with estate agents and journalists to avoid the wooden spoon" (Nolan, 1995, p. 20). In fact, the U.K. survey evidence is slightly more subtle: it shows that television news readers come high up in the trust stakes whereas, journalists score below politicians and marginally below government ministers (see European Commission, 2001; MORI, 2000; and Mortimore, 1995, pp. 38-39).

The Spanish picture is different. As a comparative study shows, the Spanish media enjoyed the highest scores for credibility of any media in the European Union after Germany (SOFRES, cited in *Anuario El Mundo*, 1998). Surveys also showed that throughout the 1990s the media consistently received approval ratings higher than Parliament, the unions, business people, political parties, the Armed Forces, judges, and national, regional, and local government (CIRES, 1997).

There is a second set of related measures that provides useful, if limited, evidence of scandal consequences for the media. It is possible to consider outcomes for the media as measured by prizes and/or censure or praise for particular publications by an investigating or legislative bodies. Prizes are, of course, in most cases, measures of esteem bestowed by fellow journalists. The two most prestigious prize-giving bodies in the United Kingdom are "What the Papers Say," a television program reviewing newspapers, and the Press Awards, both of which are composed of editors and journalists.

The Guardian's role in revealing *Cash for Questions* received recognition in the 1997 Press Awards, and David Hencke's role was rewarded by the top journalist's prize from "What the Papers Say" in 1994. "What the Papers Say" also made *The Guardian* newspaper of the year in 1990, 1996, and 1997, and its editor, Alan Rusbridger, was singled out for recognition in 1995. *The Sunday Times'* Insight team won "Scoop of the Year" in the 1994 Press Awards and the investigations award from "What the Papers Say" that same year for their initial revelation of the case. No newspaper received an award for any part of the *Arms to Iraq* saga (even though there were some noteworthy journalistic coups, such as *The Sunday Telegraph*'s interview with minister Alan Clark). As we noted earlier, the tabloid press received no recognition even though it was their stories which contributed to the most senior loss of the Major government with the resignation of Cabinet minister, David Mellor.

In Spain there is no award-making body with the equivalent prestige and national industry recognition of their British counterparts. The PRISA group (to which *El País* belongs) awards the Ortega and Gasset prize for investigative journalism and the Press Association awards the Larra Prize. This award was made to José María Irujo and Jesús Mendoza in 1996 for their work on the *Roldán* case. Prizes are also given by the International Press Club, and the León Felipe prize is awarded for journalistic work in favor of human rights, and all the reporters interviewed as well as Ramírez received prizes from these and other bodies in recognition of their work on scandal stories.

In terms of censure and praise, both *The Guardian* and *The Sunday Times* received official rebukes from the House of Commons for the investigative techniques used by the former in the Aitken case (*The Guardian* editor used House of Commons' notepaper to forge a fax from Aitken to al Fayed) and the latter in the first stage of the *Cash for Questions* case where *The Sunday Times* was rebuked by the Commons Privileges Committee for using techniques verging on entrapment. However, the press was given cautious praise in its role as public watchdog in the Nolan Report on Standards in Public Life, even if this was hedged round with misgivings about the press' excessive "concentration on private sexual behaviour" (1995, p. 16).

A number of Spanish journalists were summoned before Parliament and their role in uncovering scandal was highlighted and praised by the opposition. In a debate about the *Roldán* case, a member of a Catalonian party declared: "Everything began with a headline, with the investigative work of three journalists from *Diario 16*, who published alone and to our incredulity, some surprising news: the Director General of the Civil Guard . . . appeared to have substantially enriched himself by abusing his position" (*Proceedings of the Congress of Deputies*, 1994, p. 4,236). In the same debate the contribution of journalists' work to the parliamentary investigation is highlighted: ". . . political consequences have been brought about through the work of the Committee and, to be fair to the truth, the work of the media" (*Proceedings of the Congress of Deputies*, 1994, p. 4,228).

Journalists' work also contributed significantly to legal processes: a judge's summary of evidence often included newspaper articles. A number of journalists appeared as witnesses in criminal investigations: Irujo and Mendoza in the trial of Roldán; Miralles and Arqués in the GAL case. The book published by Miralles and Arqués about GAL was used as part of the evidence in the criminal investigation (see Fig. 8.1).

The two streams of evidence—agent-based outcomes and measures related to trust and esteem—show an interesting pattern of consequences. British sex scandals had few outcomes beyond the impact on those immediately targeted by the allegations and even then the consequences were limited. Although David Mellor and Tim Yeo both resigned as ministers, they continued as Members of Parliament and Piers Merchant was elected to the Commons in 1997. There were no legal, executive, or criminal outcomes and the newspapers involved won no official plaudits from their peers. Indeed, as we were told by one of

Figure 8.1 Book published by journalists, Miralles and Arqués, shelved with GAL indictment papers at Court no. 5 of the Audiencia Nacional. (Melchor Miralles)

the tabloid editors involved and as press coverage showed, the reaction to the stories of some sectors of the media was negative (Hagerty, personal interview, 2000).[3]

Arms to Iraq and *Cash for Questions* produced prompt executive action from which specific legislative outcomes flowed. Personal outcomes were less significant and judicial consequences entirely absent. Journalists involved in the investigations received industry plaudits and from investigating bodies a mixture of praise for revealing wrongdoing and disapproval at some of their methods.

In Spain scandals very quickly became debates about crime, and personal consequences were extremely serious. On the other hand, there were limited executive and legislative outcomes. It is clear that the gravity of the Spanish scandals required legal action: many of them involved serious crime. However, the fact that the burden of inquiry fell on the courts rather than on Parliament meant that the pace of investigation was that much slower and that the implications of the scandals for the functioning of political institutions were never fully worked out.[4]

Two parliamentary committees of investigation were established, the Roldán Commission and the Rubio Commission. Although their investigations did have an impact on criminal proceedings (their reports were the starting point for the prosecutions of Luis Roldán and Mariano Rubio), they had no broader political consequences nor did they give rise to significant systemic or legislative reforms. The only change of note was the decision to increase the transparency of the proceedings of committees of investigation. However, the committees themselves had few resources at their disposal and relied heavily on evidence from journalists.

This analysis can leave us in no doubt that scandals have consequences. However, it does have two limitations. First, it records only those actions available to us on the public record; that is, as reported in the press or parliamentary proceedings, excluding actions that were carried out by quasi-institutional bodies or representatives but were not officially placed on the record. We know from other kinds of evidence (interviews, memoirs, biographies, "lobby rules" newspaper accounts) that such actions occurred. We know, for example, that the decision by the 1922 Committee (a Conservative MPs' committee) to withdraw its support for David Mellor was key to his resignation (Major, 2000, p. 553). In other words, we have to make sure that the "back regions" of politics are not forgotten in assessing political scandal outcomes (Goffman, 1969).

Second, it does not report tangential yet significant outcomes of scandal, such as the resignation by the anticorruption judge Garzón as a Socialist deputy because of his belief that González's government was soft on corruption.[5] There were also a number of outcomes that could certainly be said to be scandal consequences, but could not easily be attributable to any specific scandal. This was particularly the case in Spain where a number of important measures were taken, including, for example, modification of the Penal Code in relation to tax and social security offences, the establishment of a Prosecution Office for economic crimes linked to corruption, and a special unit of the State Legal Service to fight fraud and corruption.

THE POWER OF THE PRESS

We have explored at length different ways of thinking about the consequences of political scandal. We now turn our attention more specifically to the role of the press. In particular, we will examine—drawing on the Spanish and British case studies—ways of understanding press power in political scandals, returning to the findings of earlier chapters concerning source use, methods, and frames.

Mighty Media

There are two perspectives on the media's role in scandals, both of which adjudge it to be powerful. The first is characteristic of many journalists who see scandal disclosure as a subset of investigative journalism that, it is believed, acts as a powerful agent of change. This notion obtained widespread acceptance in post-Watergate United States and indeed elsewhere. *The Guardian*'s view that "[i]t was the work of the press and the press alone which led to the creation of Nolan [the Committee on Standards in Public Life] and the subsequent reforms" (July 4, 1997, p. 1) provides a good example of this perspective, one that is also shared by some media scholars. McNair, for instance, claims that, "The history of political journalism in the late twentieth century, both in Britain and the United States, showed that sleaze journalism can have serious effects on the exercise of political power, and on the political environment more generally" (2000, p. 59). He is, however, ambivalent about whether these effects are on balance positive or negative. What we might call the "journalists' view" is unequivocal: the press is carrying out its classic Fourth Estate role with positive consequences for liberal democracy.

The second perspective might be called the "politicians' view". Here the media's scandal coverage is seen as having a powerful but deleterious effect on public affairs. Theodore Roosevelt's warning to investigative reporters not to be "muckrakers", after John Bunyan's character in *The Pilgrim's Progress*, nicely expresses this perspective:

> The man with the Muck-Rake, the man who could look no way but downward with the muck-rake in his hands; who was offered a celestial crown for his muck-rake, but who could neither look up nor regard the crown he was offered, but continued to rake to himself the filth of the floor (cited in Protess et al., 1991, p. 6).

There is an important body of thought that considers "muck-raking" journalism to have increased and to reflect a change in the "dynamics of inter-communicator relationships" (Blumler, 1997, p. 397), which has shifted too far in the direction of the media. Blumler cites the case of former Labour Minister Peter Mandelson's first resignation over a house-purchase loan from a fellow minister as an example of this worrying power of the media. In his resignation letter of December 1998 Mandelson wrote:

I do not believe that I have done anything wrong or improper. . . .
But we came to power promising to uphold the highest standards in
public life. We have not just to do so, but we must be seen to do so.

In Blumler's view, whether politicians are perceived as upholding
the highest standards in public life is "predominantly media controlled—and at a time when the news media are becoming increasingly
competitive, aggressive and uninhibited in chasing scandalous stories"
(1999, p. 245). Once again we find the lineaments of the "media malaise"
argument—that the media contribute to the trends towards civic disengagement because of their concentration on relatively insubstantial
issues, of which scandal or "sleaze" is one. This view is echoed by the
politicians. John Major acknowledges that "[t]he media role . . . is a crucial part of our political scene," but he argues that "politics is treated as
soap opera, and the growth in political reporting is not matched by its
quality." More seriously, he claims that the public is being misled (2000,
p. 745). A more measured judgment of the press' role was given by the
Nolan Committee (1995, pp. 15-16):

> The newspapers may have run with or encouraged the "sleaze"
> issue, but they generally print what they believe to be the facts. . . . A
> free press using fair techniques of investigative journalism is an
> indispensable asset to our democracy. We would prefer more
> acknowledgement from the media that the overwhelming majority
> of public servants work hard and have high standards. We would
> prefer more recognition of the value of our democratic mechanisms
> and the dangers of undermining them. We would prefer less con-
> centration on private sexual behaviour. But we do not hold the
> media in any way to blame for exposing genuine wrongdoing. They
> have a duty to enquire—coupled with a duty to do so responsibly—
> and in that way can contribute to the preservation of standards in
> public life.

This assessment is more in keeping with what recent research tells
us about the media's role, as we shall now see.

Modest Media

As we saw earlier, Pippa Norris provides a useful counterblast to claims
about the media's power (and the tendency to blame the messenger) in
her exhaustive analysis of accounts of "media malaise." She shows, in
fact, that "[t]he survey evidence indicates that news exposure has not

been associated with civic disengagement at diffuse level in America and Europe" (2000, p. 17). Indeed, the contrary appears to be true. In both Europe and the United States, "[p]eople who watch more TV news, read more newspapers, surf the net and pay attention to campaigns are consistently more knowledgeable, trusting of government and participatory" (p. 17).

It would appear that "[t]he power of the news media to influence the public is . . . limited and counter-balanced by the growing power of media users to select their preferred information sources" (p. 252). She accepts that news media use may be one of many factors that explain the growth of citizens' cynicism (p. 253), but also that there is a "virtuous circle" at work, by which those already attentive to news will have their attention reinforced and galvanized. On the other hand, it appears that "the news media have far less power to reinforce the disengagement of the disengaged" (p. 19). Brants further points out that the "media malaise" argument is too rooted in "cross-cultural generalizations drawn from one country's data" (1999, p. 412).

Studies of the impact of investigative journalism on policy change tend to confirm Norris' findings rather than the "mobilizing model" proposed by many journalists. The research evidence for the mobilizing effect is slim (Lang & Lang, 1983; Protess et al., 1991). In particular, Lang and Lang's study of Watergate (1983) showed that although the media are crucial in highlighting a problem, public awareness or concern is not a sufficient condition for it to become a public issue. For this, it is necessary that the public can locate the concern on the political map, and it is here that the media's power lies. The press' ability to make linkages between the public and the political world is vital if a problem is to become a burning issue. Nixon, they argue, was not driven from office by the media or the public. Political insiders were the key. As a British writer put it, "It was the tapes, Congress and the courts that did for him, not the *Washington Post*" (Mount, 2001, p. 11). In other words, the media alone are insufficiently powerful to bring about change through triggering public outrage. Alliances are required; coalitions must be made in order for the press to matter.

An alternative perspective on limited media power is provided by Castells. He regards the media not as the fabled Fourth Estate but rather as the battleground upon which modern politics is fought. His analysis of the Spanish scandal cases places greater emphasis on the power of sources rather than the power of the media in scandal politics. He accepts that the fact of corruption and the development of investigative journalism provide the necessary background for the coverage of scandal. However, he then argues that the key to the coverage was the existence of a "coalition of interest groups", ranging from traditional conservative forces to internal factions of the Socialist Party itself, bent on end-ing the Socialist Party's domination of Spanish political life after its third consecutive election victory in 1989 (1998, p. 372). Their vehicle was *El Mundo*, which came into being "with its sights set on the destruction of the Socialist government" (p. 373). He is not clear about the reason for this, apart from alleging that its editor blamed the Socialist government for his removal from *Diario 16* and was pursuing a personal vendetta (p. 373).

Castells is right to underline source power in the development of Spanish scandal coverage. He is also surely right to argue that "scandal politics" is part of the development of media democracy and, in this sense, the media are at times pawns in an elaborate political chess game. However, he extends this analysis beyond the limits set by the evidence and, in our view, underestimates the extent to which journalism in Spain had developed its own sense of professional autonomy in the post-Franco years. As we saw in Chapter 4, recognition of this crossed nation-al boundaries. *The Guardian* editor, Peter Preston (Preston, personal interview, 2000), said of the editor of *El Mundo*: "We saw each other from time to time. I congratulated him and he congratulated me. I thought what he was doing was amazing."

To sum up, Norris shows the limitations of a version of media power that sees scandal coverage as a variant on the "media malaise" theme. The journalists' Fourth Estate version of press power must, in turn, be tempered by the acknowledgement of source power and the battlefield function of the media. Media power seems, then, not to be all that it is cracked up to be.

However, as we've seen, political scandals do have outcomes and the media have a role in bringing scandals to light. So what power does the press have in scandal coverage? Attempts to frame the argument solely in terms of media effects, a cause and effect relationship between media content, and effects on policy and/or public opinion indicators, seem doomed to failure. Indeed, we would argue that claims about scan-dal journalism's effects simply cannot be tested in these terms. Perhaps a more fruitful approach is to ask what journalists do in scandal coverage. We would argue that they do the following:

First, disclose information perceived as negative about an indi-vidual/ institution;

Second, give publicity to this information;

Third, place this information in a narrative frame.

It is in the power to disclose, publicize, and frame perceived misde-meanors that we can locate the power of the press.

Narrative Power

Press power in scandal coverage can only be examined with reference to journalistic cultures and traditions in different national contexts. Various studies have shown that there is no consensus among journalists about professional roles and ethical values (Weaver, 1998), nor indeed about the treatment of political scandals (Esser, 1999). However, as Preston's appreciation for *El Mundo* suggests (see p. 172), there are also points in common. One of these, we suggest, is the press' narrative power. In other words, one source of press power is its ability to construct compelling narratives that, as we saw in earlier chapters, frame incidents in memorable stories pointing to larger meanings. Thompson makes a similar point (2000, p. 82):

> In many scandals, the main activities of investigation are carried out by individuals other than journalists and by organizations other than the media (such as the police, the courts or official inquiries of various kinds), and the role played by the media is primarily that of selecting and relaying the information produced by others, turning it into engaging stories and providing frameworks of interpretation.

However, we would argue that this role is played by the press in every scandal it covers. As we have seen throughout this study, scandals are not just discovered by the media; they are not necessarily media-driven. Tips, leaks, and sources play as large a part as journalists' endeavor in their disclosure. Put rather extremely, "It is the court hearings and the proceedings of public bodies that do the crucial exposing, not the daredevil media" (Mount, 2001, p. 11). The interpretative frameworks, however, are to a greater extent in the media's hands.

Sleaze Journalism

The former British Prime Minister was very clear about the interpretative framework that did for his government: "The word 'sleaze' itself was a potent factor in the destructiveness of the issue . . . Under its broad branches gathered a huddle of tales: about 'cash for questions' . . . ; about 'arms-to-Iraq' . . . ; and about personal shortcomings" (Major, 2000, p. 551).

"Sleaze" became a journalistic shorthand to refer to the misdemeanors of the Conservative governments of the 1990s, and as McNair points out: "Sleaze journalism became a prominent sub-category of British political journalism in the Major years, underpinning the narrative framework of decay and disintegration within which stories about the Conservatives were interpreted after the Black Wednesday crisis of 1992" (2000, p. 53). Major puts it more poetically: "As the mood music to the final act, sleaze chimed with the times" (2000, p. 550).

The narrative of disintegration and decay was expressed in vivid language and striking images by both tabloid and broadsheet press. Mellor had shown "foolishness, disloyalty and insensitivity"; Hamilton was "A liar and a cheat"; MPs "Dishonourable Members"; and all politicians "a sleazy bunch". The endless permutations of the sleaze tale (*The Independent on Sunday* counted a total of 39 in its "Guide to the Scandals of the Major years" published in 1995) played as part of one press-driven narrative. So that, although Major might contend that "many of the offences were, however distasteful, commonplace—of a kind that afflict all governments" (2000, p. 693), their placing in the sleaze narrative gave them a multiplying effect that far outstripped their real importance. Although we might agree—and some of the journalists we interviewed did—that the Mellor story triggered, "one of the silliest sagas in modern British politics: the hunt, using fair means or foul, by the tabloid press for gossip about the private lives of Tory Members of Parliament" on the pretext of exposing the hypocrisy of a government that wanted to go "back to basics" (Major, 2000, p. 552),[6] it is also true that those stories nicely fitted the overarching narrative of moral bankruptcy.

The strength of the narrative was such that the actual gravity of the misdemeanors hardly mattered. And when we look at the British cases, they do not amount to much in the annals of political misconduct: two adulterous ministers, one of whom accepted an undeclared holiday from a family friend; acceptance of payments and gifts in kind from a lobbyist and businessman by two junior ministers; adultery by a Conservative parliamentary candidate; ambivalence about guidelines on equipment exports to Iraq and a subsequent lack of transparency; and "joined-up" government to ensure that injustice was not done to businessmen caught up in the Whitehall snarl-up. The most serious case of all was Jonathan Aitken's attempt to destroy *The Guardian* by lying on oath about who paid his Paris Ritz hotel bill. The actual allegations of receiving payments for arms deals were never proven.

However, scandal outcomes in Britain were significant. The Nolan Report brought about a sea change in the way Parliament regulated itself and in the relationship between parliamentarians and lobbyists. Speaking of *The Guardian*'s role, Preston modestly explained (Preston, personal interview, 2000):

> In a journalistic sense, you didn't set out to get the rules tightened up or pursue a judicial investigation. But when it's all over you'd

probably mildly say, and probably a lot of the members of the Neil Committee [successor to the Nolan Committee] would say, that without that push in 1994, there might not have been a Committee. Things might not have been as tight as they are. So we probably did well.

Journalism about sleaze was more than a kind of tokenism. It did have a long-term impact, and the "sleaze" theme continues to resonate in British politics.[7] As one journalist observed in 1999:

The stories now—types of stories—are dictated by what happened in 1994. It's definitely the case that a sleaze story involving politicians is going to get more airplay than a scandal involving scientific fraud and those stories are there to be got. (Skipworth, personal interview, 1999)

Sleaze coverage opened up virgin territory and created the map, the symbolic environment that orientates both public and elite. Harold Evans, *Sunday Times* editor at the time of the exposure of the thalidomide drug scandal, gave this assessment of the press' power:

The press is a frail vessel for the hopes it is meant to bear. The best that it can do can never be quite good enough to illuminate what Walter Lippmann called the "invisible environment," the complexity of forces and agencies we cannot monitor for ourselves, but which affect all our lives. (1994, p. 460)

In fact, we would argue that this is too modest. The press' power also lies in its ability to create or work within cultural forms that resonate with more ancient forms of storytelling. In this view of media power, "the greatest media effects may not be measurable influences on attitudes or beliefs produced by the media slant but the range of information the media make available to individual human minds, the range of connections they bring to light, the particular social practices and collective rituals by which they organize our days and ways" (Schudson, 1996b, pp. 24-25).

Legalistic Journalism

Spanish journalists relied to an overwhelming extent on legalistic discourse for their scandal tales. The language used was usually dry "courtroom speak", freighted with all manner of technical legal terminology.

Part of the explanation for this was the nature of the scandals themselves, which did become matters for the judges. It might also be hypothesized that the adoption of legalistic language bestowed a legitimacy on the journalists' work, piggybacking onto the prestige won by the judges who had shown great independence in pursuing scandal cases. One of them, Baltasar Garzón was even co-opted into the Socialist government before he left to pursue cases against former colleagues with renewed vigor (Castells, 1998, p. 375).

The Spanish scandal tales lacked the vivacity and compelling character of their British counterparts despite their more serious nature, something that the journalists themselves admitted, as we saw in Chapter 4. The one exception to this was the tale of Roldán's escape. In placing it within the Spanish picaresque tradition, the press paradoxically won a certain amused sympathy for the very dishonest head of the Civil Guard.

The judicial investigations that dominated the development of the Spanish scandals contributed to marking a different narrative rhythm in the press, one less agile than that of the British scandal stories. Narrative tension was lost and public interest dissipated as court proceedings took their slow, measured course. Thus, for example, press coverage of the verdicts in the *Lasa and Zabala* case in 2000 bore no comparison to that of the exposure of the story in 1995.

Part of the difficulty, too, for Spanish journalists was that much of their work was interpreted through an ideological prism and seen as serving partisan political and economic interests. Their narratives became caught up in stories about conspiracies and plots. This was certainly the view of González himself. "Everyone here knows," he claimed in an interview, "that there are certain groups who have tried in a coordinated way to carry out an operation of harassment and defeat of the government. . . . They're known as the 'crime syndicate' . . . obviously as a kind of joke, but it also describes a reality of co-ordinated actions and efforts with a political purpose which is not naturally the function of the media but of the people's representatives" (González, cited in Prego, 2000, pp. 293-294).

The Socialist Party was undoubtedly tarnished by the scandals (graffiti began to appear in which the Spanish acronym for the Socialist Party—PSOE— was altered to read "Corrupsoe", thus uniting the Socialists to corruption). The public registered their deep concern about corruption in surveys in 1995 and 1996 (CIRES, 1997, p. 709), reserving their greatest disquiet for the allegations of state terrorism.[8] Nevertheless, the loss of the elections was not a disaster. PSOE not only did not lose votes, it increased them on the 1993 results. In González's view: "Those who wanted me to lose the elections got what they wanted. But they didn't get exactly what they aimed at, because they wanted me either to lose catastrophically or that I be wiped off the political map" (González, cited in Prego, 2000, pp. 293-294).

MORALITY TALES

The scandal tales told by the Spanish and British press shared to a lesser or greater extent an underlying assumption about the news they relayed. This assumption can perhaps best be expressed as a moral engagement with the material being transmuted into scandal stories, the production of a kind of morality tale about contemporaneous political events. As *Sunday Times* journalist Mark Skipworth said about the Aitken case (1999):

> It's not a sleaze story any more. Aitken's is truly one of the great stories of the nineties. It's the kind of story you'll tell your children: always tell the truth; you don't want to end up like Jonathan Aitken.

What are morality tales? They existed in the European medieval tradition as:

> (a) A literary work or artistic representation inculcating a moral lesson; a moralizing commentary; a moral allegory; and
>
> (b) A drama of a kind (popular in the sixteenth century) intended to inculcate a moral or spiritual lesson, the chief characteristics being personifications of abstract qualities. (*New Shorter Oxford English Dictionary*, 1993, p. 1827)

The equivalent Spanish term, "moraleja", is defined as "a lesson or teaching which can be deduced from a story, fable, example, anecdote, etc." (*Dictionary of the Spanish Language*, 2001, p. 1,400).

In general terms, "[t]he difference between the biblical tradition in medieval drama and the morality tradition is the difference between commemorative reconstruction and hortatory exposition" (Jones, 1996, p. 215).

Of course, modern scandal stories always involve commemorative reconstruction, but perhaps the key to their memorability, and why the British scandal stories seemed to leave a greater popular impress, is their ability to inculcate moral lessons through vivid personifications of abstract principles. This happens at two levels: the creation of news icons and the repertoire of frames used by the press. It could be argued that the news icon—the vivid image or phrase that comes to summarize a whole range of incidents—is a faint trace of what the ancients used in the art of memory, through which "the artificial memory is established from places and images" (Yates, 1994, p. 22). Recommendations from the author of *Ad Herennium* on the formation of images for "things" [*res*] written circa 86-82 B.C. would be readily understood by a journalist on *The Sun*:

> When we see in every day life things that are petty, ordinary and banal, we generally fail to remember them, because the mind is not being stirred by anything novel or marvellous. But if we see or hear something exceptionally base, dishonourable, unusual, great, unbelievable, or ridiculous, that we are likely to remember for a long time. . . . Thus nature shows that she is not aroused by the common ordinary event, but is moved by a new or striking occurrence. Let art, then, imitate nature. We ought, then, to set up images of a kind that can adhere longest in memory. And we shall do so if we establish similitudes as striking as possible; if we set up images that are not many or vague but active [*imagines agentes*]. (cited in Yates, 1994, p. 25)

As we saw in Chapter 7, news icons are symbolic devices that vividly encapsulate an entire story and come to dominate the original narrative. Invoked as a phrase or image, the news icon emerges to stand alone as an emblematic, evocative device that can be used by reporters in the narrative frame of other types of stories and is capable of shifting the framing of other news stories (see Bennett & Lawrence, 1995, p. 26).

We saw in the previous chapter how news icons can both evoke larger cultural themes and allow more autonomy in news reporting. We see now how they can also become the vehicles for social memory, and social memory of a particular kind.[9] The mere mention of "Watergate", for example, can conjure up a world of "Tricky Dickie" politics and Woodward and Bernstein "Deep Throat" reporting. In Britain, "sleaze" will be forever associated with the decaying Conservative government of the 1990s. No such compelling news icon emerged in Spanish reporting, but the words "Roldán" and "GAL" are likely to resonate in the country's social memory for sometime yet.

This brings us to a key characteristic of scandal tales; namely, that whatever else they do, they always point out a moral. Scandal journalism mediates values through the exposition of wrongdoing and its consequences. Like morality plays, scandal stories implicitly "recommend certain patterns of choice and action to members of the audience" (Jones,

1996, p. 215). Journalists acknowledge this in half-embarrassed fashion, as we saw in Chapter 4. When asked whether he thought journalism has a moral function, Peter Preston (Preston, personal interview, 2000) replied, "Yes, I do. But when you're quoted you sound like a religious zealot."

David Hencke said about his coverage of the *Cash for Questions* story, (Hencke, personal interview, 2001):

> I really did think there was a moral imperative. And one of the pleasing things was the setting up of the Nolan Committee and the fact that I don't think many people would dare to take such a risk now. It really stopped people in their tracks from thinking that they could make a fast buck out of being a democratically elected person and I think this is really important for democracy. I sound terribly moral but I actually do feel that.

Just like Everyman in the eponymous morality play (cited in Jones, 1996, p. 217), who tells his audience to mark well the moral of the story, so do journalists conjure up the morality tales of our time.

NOTES

1. Major's statement was made in his autobiography (2000, p. 552). Gonzalez' s comment is cited in Prego (2000, p. 273).
2. This question is also explored in Waisbord's excellent study (2000) of watchdog journalism and political scandal in South America and his two edited volumes with Tumber (2004) of democracies and political scandals.
3. A more weighty impact cannot be discounted even though there is no direct evidence for its existence. It is possible that the Conservative Government's decision in 1995 not to uphold the Calcutt Committee's recommendation to establish a statutory body to oversee the press may have been influenced by a wish not to alienate the press still further in the runup to an election. With hindsight it is hard to see that the press could have been much more hostile to the Conservatives than it consequently proved to be.
4. Although the scandals occurred in the first half of the 1990s, sentencing only took place in 2000 and 2001.
5. Another example is some of the outcomes of the Scott Inquiry. Tomkins' (1998) excellent survey on the impact of the Scott Report on the British constitution provides detailed information on the changes that occurred as a result of Scott. He concludes, however, that Scott's main impact was an "unprecedented contribution to constitutional understanding in modern Britain. The secretive practices of central government which Scott was uniquely able to unwrap have been subjected to the public gaze as never before. In many areas, despite the report's lack of immediate political bite,

the Scott inquiry has resulted in significant and welcome reforms. But its most important constitutional lesson is that there can be no substitute for enhanced parliamentary accountability" (p. 275).

6. See Chapter 2.

7. In March 2001, the Labour apologist, Siôn Simon, was still writing about sleaze in the wake of Peter Mandelson's second resignation, referring to a forgotten telephone call on behalf of passport applications and accusations that the Foreign Secretary had lied to Parliament two years before. Simon's verdict: "It would be wrong to take the current sleaze-mania seriously. This is a particularly un-sleazy government of the world's most un-sleazy country" (12 March 2001, p. 21).

8. In a national survey carried out by the *Centro de Investigaciones Sociológicas*, when asked which news they found most worrying, 31.6% of the public mentioned the GAL case; only 4.6% mentioned the Roldán case, and 1% the Rubio case; other subjects such as the economy, terrorism, and unemployment were mentioned by less than 2% (*El Mundo*, February 12, 1995).

9. The notion of social or collective memory was first explored by Maurice Halbwachs. See *Les cadres sociaux de la mémoire* (1925/1975) and *La mémoire collective* (1950/1992). It became a "hot" topic for scholarly interest in the 1980s and 1990s, particularly in connection with historical and sociological explorations of the making of collective identities (see Hobsbawm & Ranger, 1984; Anderson, 1983; Nora, 1984-1993). The exploration of the media's role as bearer and sustainer of social memory has been examined by Schlesinger (1991), Dayan and Katz (1992), and Morley and Robins (1995), among others.

9

Scandals and
Political Culture

Scandals are usually highly contextual, localized incidents. With few exceptions there is nothing more boring than reading about the details of another country's scandals. And yet, in a national context scandals can be the most gripping stories the media cover (which is, of course, one of the reasons why they do). They can engage the imagination in a way other, more serious issues fail to do. This feature of political scandals underlines their character as cultural events, their rootedness in a particular set of economic, political, and historical conditions.

In Chapters 2 and 3 we saw how the development of mediated politics in liberal democracies has increased the significance of managed visibility in the communication of politics. Trust and credibility are ever more precious commodities where they can be so easily undermined by the media. Of course, trust has always been necessary for good governance. In her 2002 Reith lectures, the philosopher Onora O'Neil cited Confucius's advice to his disciple Tze-kung that three things are needed for government: weapons, food, and trust. If a ruler can't hold on to all three, he should give up the weapons first and the food next. Trust should be guarded to the end, for "without trust we cannot stand." O'Neil goes on to note what she regards as the contemporary role of the media, and in Britain especially that of the press, in spreading a culture of suspicion (2002). The manufacture of distrust and cynicism about public life is one of the most difficult issues facing modern democracy.

Chapters 4 to 7 examined the construction and narration of political scandal stories in Britain and Spain, noting differences and similarities between them that are in part a function of the communication and political environments within which politicians, media officers, and journalists operate. We have seen that scandal narratives do not simply reflect political scandals. They in part construct them and, as we saw in Chapter 8, contribute to their potency. This goes some way to answering the question outlined in Chapter 1, which asked whether, by understanding the role of the press in political scandal coverage, political scandals can show us anything about the nature of press power.

The chief focus of this chapter will be the second of our original questions; namely, whether we can gain understanding of a country's political culture by understanding the media's role in political scandals. We will first explore Thompson's discussion (2000) of the "political cultures" of scandal in relation to the politics of trust and the public sphere. Our study of the coverage of political scandals in Britain and Spain leads us to suggest that the notion of 'media culture' should be brought into the explanatory frame. We then discuss what light our study sheds on Tomlinson's (1997) view that scandals are generators of moral discourse of a certain kind, examining how political scandals as told by the media can act as ethical narratives which fix social meaning.

POLITICAL CULTURE AND TRUST

In Chapter 1 we discussed how political scandals might be taken as entry points for understanding aspects of political culture. To what extent does our study allow us to make such a claim?

Thompson's study (2000) takes up this theme. He focuses first on five significant changes that have contributed to the greater prevalence of political scandal in the modern era: (a) the increased visibility of political leaders; b) developments in communication technology; (c) the growing legal regulation of political life; (d) changes in journalistic culture; and (e) changes in political culture (p. 108).

What does he mean by "changes in political culture"? Here Thompson points to the long-term trend in liberal democracies for politics to be less and less about ideology or class-based party politics. Where this is the case, structural or institutional guarantees of a politician's credibility are undermined. The politics of party are replaced by the politics of trust. Of course, as we noted earlier, politics is always about trust. But in changed social and political circumstances, trust becomes a more fragile commodity. It can no longer be won solely on the basis of party or ideological affiliation. Trust must be earned and, with the increased difficulty of establishing clear blue ideological water between politicians, character not policy comes to play an ever greater part in winning the support of the electorate.

Thompson's understanding of political culture here is as a "broad and rather diffuse cluster of rules, conventions, attitudes and expectations which underpin the conduct of political life and shape the forms of interaction and communication that take place in the political field" (p. 116). His contention is that a subset of these conventions and expectations has coalesced around the phenomenon of political scandal to create a political culture of scandal. By this he appears to mean that there is a common dynamic at work ensuring that political scandal has become "an endemic feature of our contemporary political culture" (p. 116).

Certainly this appears to hold true for a number of liberal democracies, including Britain and Spain. But, as we know well, political cultures are not monolithic. If we can accept that political scandal has become endemic, we may still want to say more about the structure and impact of scandal in different political cultures.

POLITICAL CULTURES OF SCANDAL

Thompson does in fact recognize the considerable variation in dynamics and structure of political scandals from one national context to another. He thus refers to: ". . . a plurality of political cultures of scandal, each characterized by its own distinctive traditions, its own constantly changingly changing cluster of conventions and expectations" (p. 116).

Without claiming that the list is definitive or that each category is sharply demarcated from the next, Thompson identifies three ideal types of political scandal (pp. 120-124):

1. Political sex scandals: These involve the disclosure of allegations concerning the private life of public figures that appear to transgress accepted, although not always legally binding or even generally observed codes about the conduct of sexual relations;

2. Political financial scandals: These concern the disclosure of allegations concerning the misuse of economic resources by public figures in ways that often but not always transgress legal norms;

3. Political power scandals: These involve the disclosure of allegations concerning the improper use of power by public figures in ways that either transgress the norms and conventions of the power game or, we would add, break the law.

Table 9.1 shows how Thompson's template for types of scandal applies to Britain and Spain in the 1990s. Tony Blair's Labour administration from 1997 to May 2001 and José María Aznar's conservative People's Party government from 1996 until March 2000 have also experienced a number of political scandals. These have included for the United Kingdom, scandals about party donations to buy influence, sex (homosexual relations of married minister), and improper use of public office. In Spain, the main cases include allegations of improper financial gain in the sale of a company (no criminal intent was alleged), "fat-cat" earnings (by a privatized company); illegal sale of a company (in which PP counselors were convicted); and accusations that public officials from the Finance Ministry had placed money in tax havens.[1]

TABLE 9.1 Scandal Type (Thompson's Template)

	SEXUAL	FINANCIAL	POWER
Britain	Mellor Yeo Merchant	Cash for Questions	Arms to Iraq
Spain	None	Rubio Roldán	GAL-Lasa and Zabala GAL-Cesid

"No Sex Please. We're Spanish"

The first most striking fact, and one we have discussed in different terms in earlier chapters, is the total lack of sexual political scandals in Spain compared to their abundance and continuity in Britain.

Sex is undoubtedly a major ingredient of British and, indeed, American political scandal. Its absence from continental Europe has often been noted but rarely explained (see Sanders & Canel, 2004). Uniquely prurient Brits seems an unlikely explanation. The worldwide interest in the Clinton/Lewinsky scandal and the marital infidelities of the Prince and Princess of Wales shows that prurience is not the preserve of the Anglo-Saxons. Are the British and the Americans more censorious than their continental counterparts? Again, disapproving voices are to be found in most countries. And if polls on this matter are to be believed, the majority of Americans in fact disapprove of the media attention paid to extramarital affairs and are relatively forgiving of sexual misdemeanors in political life.[2]

Thompson's analysis of the political culture of sex scandals in Britain looks to the fact that there is a "long and venerable tradition of sexual-political scandals in Britain, a tradition which has been nurtured and sustained by the press and which forms part of the political culture" (p. 130). This does, however, rather beg the question and ignores the fact that the "venerable tradition" tended to turn a blind eye to politicians' sexual misdemeanors. One journalist speaking about a Conservative MP's longstanding affair with former prime minister Harold Macmillan's wife, said:

> The situation was fairly well known to a lot of people in politics and journalism, but nobody would think of breaking that story, not simply because of the personal tragedies involved but because you would be offending a certain unwritten ethical code. There was a consensus among journalists as well as politicians that there were certain things that you didn't do. (Goodman in Baston, 2000, p. 42)

Thompson is on stronger ground when he notes the differences in legal restrictions on the press not to report the private lives of individuals that apply in many other European countries but not in the same way in Britain.[3]

However, missing from this analysis is the role of media culture. The development of an irreverent populist press in Britain that considers the private lives of power holders to be a legitimate target of media interest is absent from many parts of continental Europe. In other words, the existence of a political culture of sex scandals is inextricably bound up with that of a certain kind of media. The lack of sex scandals in Spain is not because their politicians lead chaste and blameless lives or because the Spanish are any less prurient. Their heavy consumption of gossip and celebrity-driven magazines such as *Interviú* and *Gente* shows that this is not so. The cultural producers of the continent, those who arbitrate and frame the scandal subjects set before the public, for the moment have ruled "political" sex out of bounds.

In Spain's case, as we noted in Chapter 2, its elite press sets the tone for the serious and somewhat ponderous coverage of politics. However, even the more lively political coverage on the radio, which "goes well beyond the bounds of what would be tolerated in the print media" (Gunther, Montero, & Wert, 2000, p. 69), leaves sex well alone. The debate about whether private morality has a bearing on public morality is simply nonexistent. The question posed about David Mellor (If he lied to his wife, would he lie to the country?) has never been asked by the Spanish media of its politicians. And it is not that the kind of intrusive reporting that sexual scandal implies is rendered impossible by the country's privacy legislation. *El Mundo's* editor was himself the target of extremely intrusive reporting when a video was released allegedly showing him with a prostitute.

The absence of political sex scandals in Spain indicates, then, the importance of taking into account both the norms and values of journalists and the media culture that they inhabit, itself a product of those norms and values, as well as the historical and economic factors that have shaped the contemporary Spanish media industry. The existence or not of political sex scandals would seem to have more to do with prevailing media cultures than political ones.

Pork Barrel Politics

Thompson's analysis of political financial scandals is more satisfying than his examination of sex scandals. The former covers a multitude of sins including bribery, conflict of interests, fraud, and deception. They are most commonly associated with the phenomenon of corruption, although this term, as we saw in Chapter 2, denotes something quite distinct from scandal.

Noting the considerable variation of political financial scandal from one national context to another, Thompson points in explanation to four factors: (a) historical and institutional differences in the systems of political power and the relationship between political and economic power; (b) differences in law and the informal and formal codes of practice governing the activities of civil servants and politicians; (c) the differences in the extent to which journalists investigate and report these kinds of misdemeanors; and (d) the differences in the degree to which publicly disclosed misdemeanors are regarded as politically and morally unacceptable (p. 161).

It can be agreed that these factors bear upon the prevalence of financial political scandal. But the devil is in the detail and we would argue that our study shows the importance of avoiding broad-brush comparative accounts of scandal. Take as an example of this genre a report entitled "Europe's Dirty Secret" in the magazine *Newsweek* (Theil & Dickey, April 29, 2002, pp. 12-15). It claims that: "Across the Continent, corruption is a way of life," it is the political glue that "binds parties, interest groups and national leaders." And it is allowed to prosper because of the combination of an absence of institutional checks and balances; a cowed judiciary; a social acceptance of corruption; a European press that is "hardly the watchdog Americans expect of their fourth estate" and that is "passive towards friends and polemical towards enemies"; increased opportunities for graft; and the growing costs of the "Americanization" of politics in which personality replaces policy.

Allowing for journalistic hyperbole, is *Newsweek*'s sweeping indictment of continental Europe's culture of financial political scandal fairly made?[4] Our study of Spanish and British scandals of this kind shows that in part it certainly is not. Spain has had anything but a subservient judiciary and it is clear, too, that Spanish journalists have been courageous and assiduous in digging out the facts about political corruption. Indeed, it is difficult to see how, if they had not been bravely persistent in their work, some of the stories would have come to light.

On the other hand, our study of the framing of scandal partly bears out the observation that the European press tends to be indulgent to friends and overly hostile to its enemies. Reporting the scandal stories as though they were conspiracies got up by Gonzalez's opponents, which a sector of the press did, could only trivialize their very real importance for the conduct of Spanish politics.

In Britain, as we saw, there was greater journalistic consensus that there was something rotten in a political culture that allowed politicians to act as paid advocates. In other words, it wasn't so much changes to the political culture—the norms, rules, codes, attitudes, and conventions surrounding the practice of politics—as changes in journalistic attitudes to it that precipitated and shaped the reporting of financial political scandal in the United Kingdom.

The Power and the Glory

Power scandals in the political realm involve revelations about the misuse or abuse of power. They are about activities in which the rules, norms, procedures, or laws governing the exercise of power are bent or broken. Often the illicit or illegal use of political power is aimed at covering up corrupt or illegal behavior. Watergate provides the paradigm case of this kind of scandal. Scandals can also erupt in areas where invisible, unaccountable power is allowed to develop, frequently on the grounds of protecting national security.

Once again Thompson points to institutional, legal, and cultural factors as affecting the nature and extent of power scandals (p. 199). In
Britain, for example, he regards the prevalence of power scandals involving the security agencies and what he calls the "blurred boundaries
between the political and military domains" (p. 229) as owing much to
"Britain's long tradition of secrecy in politics" (p. 227). Certainly, as we
saw in earlier chapters, "Whitehall's culture of secrecy" was how much
of the U.K. press chose to frame and attribute blame in the *Arms to Iraq*
scandal, the principal power scandal of British politics in the 1990s.

But what about Spain? Its press did not allege a culture of secrecy in
explaining the much more serious abuses of power by the security agencies and services in the *GAL* case, nor did the scandal provoke a debate
about government secrecy. In both Britain and Spain power was exercised in an unaccountable, arrogant, and opaque manner. But it is only
in Britain that the totem of a culture of secrecy is invoked as the explanatory variable for the scandal.

This might suggest, then, that accounting for the prevalence of kinds
of political scandal on the basis of a combination of institutional, legal,
and political cultural explanations is insufficient. They of course play
their part, but political scandal is also about media culture. "Whitehall
secrecy", whatever its basis in fact, served nicely to explain and tell a
complex story in the *Arms to Iraq* case.[5] If we think about what could
have served as an equivalent for Spanish journalists, we can see the
importance of this point. The Spanish equivalent of Whitehall may be no
less transparent, but the relative youth of the country's democratic institutions left reporters with few useful reference points to tell their story
about GAL. In other words, an alleged culture of secrecy may account in
part for power scandals in Spain, as it seems to in Britain. However,
without the right repertoire of cultural themes and stories in the writing
locker, journalists find it more difficult to tell the story in that way.

We conclude from this that analyzing political scandal and its
impact as a means to understanding political culture has limited heuris-
tic value without taking into account media culture. More than political
cultures of scandal, we should perhaps speak of ecologies of political
scandal in which media culture is given a central place in understanding
the kinds of wrongdoing that become political scandals, the way in
which those scandals are reported and the impact they come to have.

ECOLOGIES OF POLITICAL SCANDAL

In his political culture study *Making Democracy Work* (1993), Robert
Putnam aims to contribute to the understanding of what makes govern-

ments work well. He explores how formal institutions influence the practice of government and politics and asks what are the conditions for creating strong, responsive, effective representative institutions.

His study of Italian local government leads him to conclude that: "Social context and history profoundly condition the effectiveness of institutions" (p. 182). Put simply, institutions shape politics. Their rules and standard operating procedures leave their imprint on political outcomes by structuring political behavior. Outcomes are not simply reducible to the billiard-ball interaction of individuals nor to the intersection of broad social forces. Institutions influence outcomes because they shape actors' identities, power, and strategies.

On the other hand, institutions themselves are shaped by history. They embody historical trajectories and turning points. Counterfactual history shows us how the history we have matters. Therefore, individuals may choose institutions, but they do not choose them under circumstances of their own making (pp. 8-9). Institutions are, then, both an independent variable, whereby change in them affects political actors, and a dependent variable, whereby institutional performance is affected by history.

Putnam's account usefully illuminates the matrix of variables that bear on the specific issue of institutional performance. It also underlines one of the principal reasons for the continuing appeal of the notion of political culture, as Welch (1993) suggests, for it recognizes the insufficiency of accounts of politics that leave out issues of meanings and culture and the paucity of accounts of culture that neglect politics and power (p. 165). And this is precisely why understanding media culture's role is so important. Journalists aren't just the messengers. They are also in part the architects of political meaning from the institutions they inhabit and the traditions they inherit and renegotiate at each given moment. We will take a look now at the notion of media culture.

Media Culture

In his useful overview of research into the sociology of news production, Schudson (2000) examines three main traditions of work. The political economy perspective examines news production, relating the outcome of the news process primarily to economic structures. The second perspective centers on the social organization of news and takes journalists' organizational and occupational routines as the central problem for understanding journalism in liberal democratic societies. The third perspective is what, as we saw in Chapter 3, Schudson describes as the "cultural" approach that, while taking into account structures of ownership and patterns of work relations, examines the given symbolic systems within which both journalists and officials operate. He argues, however, that all three of them, even taken together, "have fallen short of providing adequate comparative and historical perspectives on news production" (p. 177).

Thinking about what Richard Hoggart calls the "cultural air" in which news is produced, Schudson describes the specific style that characterizes journalistic practices. That cultural air, he says, has a form apart from a content. The form consists of assumptions about narrative, storytelling, human interest, and the conventions of photographic and linguistic presentation that shape the presentation of all the news the media produce. In examining the production of news from this cultural approach, news is regarded as a form of literature; the journalist is seen as a storyteller, embedded in a cultural tradition of storytelling, with a number of tacit core assumptions about the world where, as we discussed in Chapter 3, journalists' routines are both social and literary (see Schudson, 2000, p. 193). Their work draws on shared cultural traditions that will mark distinct reporting trajectories in different cultural contexts. As seen in Chapter 3, Zelizer (1992) has made suggestions along similar lines, writing of a view of journalism that looks at journalists as an authoritative interpretative community.

We think this attention to the cultural dimension is important in understanding news content, because it brings into view factors that seem not to be included in certain models for the analysis of influences on media content. For instance, Shoemaker and Reese (1996) propose a helpful model of five levels of influence on media content (the individual level, media routines, the organizational level, the extramedia level, and the ideological level). The cultural approach, however, speaks for certain classes of often tacit cultural traditions taken to be instinctive or acquired only by long experience in the field, "which are the literary, intellectual and cultural scaffolding on which the news is hung" (Schudson, 1995a, p. 84). Thus, for example, much British newspaper reporting of the European Union is framed by a distinct historical and cultural experience. Images of a baroque, corrupt European Commission or headlines such as "Foxtrot Oscar" are taken from shared cultural frames that are as significant as any occupational routines or questions of political economy in shaping our news (Anderson & Weymouth, 1999).[6]

Of course, it would be wrong to reintroduce a Tylorian holistic account of culture as an all-encompassing context in which people are considered to be inevitably embedded.[7] It would also be wrong to present a monolithic view of culture. Media cultures have subnational as well as national components. However, thinking about news production from a cultural perspective allows us to draw attention to aspects of meaning production that are not wholly explicable from an economic or sociological perspective.

In understanding the media's role in political scandal we would extend the explanatory range of the notion of media culture to include not only the sphere of news production but also:

1. The organizational/institutional context. The kind of organization in which journalists work favors certain formats and styles. Facile narratives are greatly prized by tabloid newspapers. On mass-market papers "editors are determined to have stories of certain types—light, frothy ones or breathless, dramatic ones" (Randall, 2000, p. 18).
2. Journalists' professional attitudes and values. Journalistic traditions, practices and principles show some variation from country to country (see Weaver, 1998). As we saw in Chapter 4 there was some variation and considerable similarity between the journalists interviewed in Britain and Spain about their roles in scandal coverage, even if survey evidence would have led us to think otherwise (Canel, Rodríguez Andrés & Sánchez Aranda, 2000; Patterson, 1998).

In other words, media culture is constituted by the organizational, production, and professional assumptions, traditions, and values within and by which, in part, news is produced. Understanding media culture(s) is a necessary first step in understanding the kinds of political scandals that can emerge. In turn it may be claimed that scandals themselves can provide a yardstick for the openness and accessibility of a specific political culture or, on the contrary, destroy the foundations of rational conversation about politics, turning us into the disillusioned spectators of a freak show. We will consider these views next.

Political Scandals and the Public Sphere

The mediatization of politics in liberal democracies suggests that political meanings—including political scandals—will be increasingly permeated by the prevailing media culture(s). If this is the case, understanding, for example, prevailing journalistic attitudes and values (if a journalist considers him/herself neutral or advocate, passive or active in Patterson's typology [1998]), or, say, dominant organizational contexts may help us understand the kind of political culture that is likely to exist. Where there is active, adversarial journalism in tabloid formats, it might be possible to point to a more cynical public and a media-obsessed political class.

Some scholars have suggested that certain kinds of political scandal can be used as a measure of the health of the body politic. McNair (2000), for example, argues that political scandal shows us that those who rule are ordinary mortals like us and that it is "an index of the openness and accessibility of late twentieth-century political culture" (p. 56). Freedland (1998) agrees, claiming that "the advantage of a political culture which can debate matters of national import through the medium of celebrity scandal is that everyone can take part" (p. 61).

On the other hand, a number of scholars have considered that certain kinds of political scandal coverage are having a deleterious effect on the public sphere. Reporting that examines every nook and cranny of a politician's private life can, in the words of some American critics of the phenomenon, turn democracy into a kind of "peepshow or soap opera" (Sabato, Stencel, & Lichter, 2001, p. 1).

In the previous chapter we explored the impact of political scandal and the difficulties in identifying a billiard ball–like interaction between the reporting of political scandal and increasing public disengagement from politics. In a similar way, discussion of political scandals and their relationship to a healthy or ailing public sphere meet similar difficulties. Understood as "any and all locations, physical and virtual, where ideas and feelings relevant to politics are transmitted or exchanged openly" (Bennett & Entman, 2001, pp. 2-3), the public sphere is almost certainly energized by the reporting of political scandal. However, it may be thought more doubtful that Habermas' (1989) ideal public sphere as the orientative place of unfettered, public rational discourse will be assisted by a constant diet of sexual scandal reporting.

Our study of the reporting of scandal does not allow us to come to any clear conclusion. But in a certain respect, in its dramatization of politics we would argue that scandal reporting performs the valuable function of making politics entertaining. We are amused, outraged, engaged by the stories told and sufficiently sophisticated not to be always taken in by the media's own framing of them. In Tomlinson's words (1997):

> The active, interpretive nature of media audiences is now so well demonstrated as to make a strong ideological manipulation thesis difficult to sustain. . . . But apart from this, it seems clear that . . . a critical awareness of the media's role in the framing of scandals is now part and parcel of the way people actually respond to scandals—an aspect of the routine cultural accomplishments of moral agents in mediated modern cultures. (p. 70)

This is not to discount the impact of media framing of scandal. But we conjecture that this impact will be in relation to the extent that the media culture draws effectively upon the wider stock of themes available to it. Edelman (1988), in explaining the dramatic nature of politics, points to this:

> The models, scenarios, narratives, and images into which audiences for political news translate that news are social capital, not individual inventions. They come from works of art in all genres: novels, paintings, stories, films, dramas, television sitcoms, striking rumors, even memorable jokes. For each type of news report there is likely to be a small set of striking images that are influential with large numbers of people . . . (p. 1)

Journalists tap these cultural resources, and our study would seem to indicate that the less well they do this—the case of Spain—the less likely is it that the public sphere will be the space of discourse and debate that scholars hope it will be. The quality of that debate is a different matter.

POLITICAL SCANDALS AS MORAL STORIES

In Chapter 8 we saw how political scandals could be considered as morality tales for modern times. Now we want to consider whether our study can shed light on the cultural contingencies of scandals understood as generators of moral discourse. We will conclude by drawing together some of the threads of this book, thinking about the reporting of political scandal as ethical narrative that provides sentimental education and entertainment about transgressive behavior by public officials, occasionally in ways that can consolidate and transmit social memory.

The Contingency of Political Scandal

"The Cancer of Corruption" was the front-page headline of *Time* magazine's cover story on the global costs of corruption (22 June 1998). The report focused on the narrow subject of bribery, and from Britain and Spain only the *Roldán* case made it into the "megascandals" league. Nevertheless, the story showed that the effects of certain kinds of scandal had come to be seen as a global issue.

Although scandal may be a matter of global concern, it is not, in Tomlinson's view (1997), a *globalized* phenomenon. Tomlinson considers scandals to be *"essentially local affairs"*, examples of a specific type of "cultural-moral event" (p. 67; italics in original), firmly embedded in a local milieu and going against the grain of contemporary processes of cultural globalization.

The same year as the *Time* corruption report, a scandal occurred that managed to transcend the ordinary national limits of such events. The Clinton/Lewinsky saga showed, as Watergate and the Iran-Contra scandals had before, that political scandals can become global affairs and even the defining event of a presidency. Bill Clinton's second presidential term is likely to be forever framed by the words "Monica Lewinsky."

Political scandals—scandals in general—rarely achieve the status of a global event. Examining the spatio-temporal rootedness of scandals provides a useful starting point for an understanding of scandals as cultural events. Tomlinson's argument that there are no global scandals, just re-embedded local ones (1997, p. 81), is based on an interpretation of scandals as generators of moral discourse of a certain kind that impacts on "our sense of our cultural identity—our distinctive understanding of 'how we live here'" (p. 69). He considers that scandals deal with "middle-order moral events" where the center of gravity "is somewhere between the fairly trivial and the extremely serious" (p. 68). Wars and poverty, high-order moral issues, may be scandalous but are not scandals.

In this view the extraordinary ordinariness that scandals capture, their airing of moral dilemmas in personalized, compelling narratives, make them into particularly engaging events but, for these reasons too, especially localized affairs. As they cross cultures, scandals lose "immediacy" or interest for different cultural contexts. Secondly, and more significantly in Tomlinson's view, we "engage with scandals insofar as they are relevant to our ongoing, lived experience" (p. 73). Using Thompson's reworking of the notion of the "relevance structure" of experience (1995), Tomlinson states that "those experiences that penetrate deepest into our lifeworld are the ones that can be imaginatively incorporated into this ongoing narrative of self-identity" (p. 73). Generally local, immediate experiences take precedence over mediated ones. However, mediated experiences that are closest to our lived experience will be given highest priority, and for this to happen their immediacy and relevance structure are key. For Tomlinson, then, scandals are first about middle order moral issues; second, essentially local affairs; and third, cultural-moral events.

This discussion raises a number of interesting issues relevant to our study of political scandals and their connections to political culture.

Let's take first the understanding of scandals as raising middle-order moral issues. Political scientist Anthony King's description of scandals occupying "a sort of middle-ground of impropriety" (1986, p. 176) signals where the problem lies. It has a particularly British flavor: the crimes committed to fund and maintain the GAL death squads could hardly be described as occupying the middle ground of impropriety. And even apparently minor aberrations—Aitken's lie, Mellor's infidelity—can raise great moral questions that are by no means middle-order in their import. Jane Austen's novels may use a smaller canvas than Tolstoy's, but also deal in the great moral themes that have haunted human beings down the ages. Exploring political scandal in different national contexts allows us to throw off the interpretative straitjacket that can all too easily result from looking at and generalizing from one cultural context, which Tomlinson and others appear to have done.

And yet Tomlinson is surely right to emphasize that it is the immediacy and relevance structure of scandals that usually makes them local or, at the most, national affairs. The United States' and hence Clinton's unique economic, political, and cultural pre-eminence might ensure that the Lewinsky scandal would have global interest. But most other political scandals resonate only at most on a national stage.

Ethical Narratives

Political scandals are, then, embedded in specific cultures at certain times and places. However, they are all in some way ethical narratives or contain "moral challenges within narratives that catch people's attention and imagination. . . . When we respond to a scandal we do not just absorb the details, but inevitably engage in moral reflection" (Tomlinson, 1997, p. 69).

Mediated political scandals provide some knowledge of facts. Crucially, they enact the drama of moral agency. I know that charity money was stolen by the head of the Spanish civil guard. I know that Mellor had an adulterous affair. These facts become potent when aligned to provide knowledge of what it is appropriate to do, to say, or to feel. The *Guardian*'s headline "A Liar and a Cheat" tells me that I should feel outrage at Neil Hamilton's actions. In fashioning such narratives newspapers provide a kind of sentimental and consequently moral education.

Education of our emotions is not, of course, the monopoly of the media, nor are we close to having a clear understanding of precisely how the media do educate our emotions. As we noted earlier, despite the considerable outrage of the American media about Clinton's behavior, the American public remained resolutely unfazed. We should not, then, on current evidence, overstate the media's role in our sentimental education. Nevertheless, that they do offer an ethical vision, that they tell us what to feel and how we should judge can hardly be doubted.

They do this partly in narrative. Narration, as we saw in Chapter 3, occupies a central place in ways of understanding and knowing the world. In part experienced reality is created, sustained, and mediated by narratives (see Mechling, 1991, p. 43). Scandal narratives deal with questions of right and wrong. When they are about politics, they raise issues about the appropriate exercise of power, the relationship between private and public morality and the role of money and gain in political life. They are narratives about ethics, about conflicting values, choices, and principles. They are also narratives about journalism and about politics.

As we saw in earlier chapters, newspapers in both Britain and Spain took up positions about their own roles in telling scandal stories. In Britain journalists were far more assured about their role as the moral guardians of the political class, even if there was initial broadsheet queasiness about issues related to private morality. Greater ambivalence was apparent in Spain. Some journalists feared that journalists and editors were being used as pawns in a bigger political game, never a British fear. Despite the marked political partisanship of the U.K. press, there was never a suggestion that journalists were beholden to politicians in the same way as was suggested in Spain. Ferreting out information that someone somewhere does not want published was more straightforwardly seen in Britain as just what reporters do. Being approached by sources, publishing leaked information were—subject to the normal checks for credibility and reliability—considered to be part and parcel of the reporter's craft.

British scandal narratives told a story about journalism in which journalists were depicted as the people's tribunes. In Spain this connection was never made. Journalists were either lone rangers, doing the judges' work, or lackeys of the shadowy political or business figures who really pulled the strings. In this view, journalism was seen as waging politics by other means.

And what about politics itself? In earlier chapters we discussed the debates, generalizations, and identity associations that the scandal stories generated. All of these told a story of what politics is about in each country,—its standards, capacity for reform, its weaknesses. Many of the British stories depicted political "sleaze" as a fall from grace, an unpleasant by-product of the greedy Thatcherite 1980s, in no way comparable to the corruption of other countries yet worryingly corrosive of public trust in the political class. Sleaze also made politics diverting and politicians figures of fun, converting news into entertainment. Sleaze journalism was personalized, name-calling journalism in which politics became a spectator sport for an amused, if not at times bemused public.

Spanish journalism told a more serious story. Apart from the flashes of color provided by the events concerning Roldán, the reporting of scandal consisted of a bewildering account of legal complexity, suspicions of plots and conspiracies, impugned motives, and quite terrible crimes. At times it was as though the reporting of the legal and political twists and turns of Spanish political scandal rendered reporters and the public incapable of seeing the wood for the trees. At one moment the entire political system was considered to be in crisis; at others just the survival of the Socialist Party in government was in question. Ultimately the scandal reporting appeared to engender a weariness of scandal itself (the last acts of the scandals of the 1990s provoked little public interest) and a disillusionment with the Socialist Party and the kind of charismatic politics represented by Felipe González.

Social Memory

We mentioned earlier that political scandal news coverage could be considered as ethical narrative that provides sentimental education and entertainment in ways that can consolidate and transmit social memory. In the British context, the reporting of political scandals has been seen as emblematic of a shift towards the blurring of the division between news and entertainment (McNair, 2000). In Hallin's words (2000, p. 229): "The best journalists have always been good story-tellers. Story-telling is essential to journalism because it generates popular interest."

Furthermore, news isn't just about providing information; it is also, Hallin continues, "a contribution to dialogue about values and collective identity, and that kind of dialogue is carried on largely through narration" (p. 229). The media contribute to the constitution of community The British chief rabbi, Jonathan Sacks (2001), has explained how this works:

> At the heart of any culture is the process by which we bring successive generations into a narrative, the story of which we are a part. There is, of course, not one story but many, but storytelling is the place where identity is found, it is the vehicle of continuity. (Sacks, 2001, p. 143)

In former times this was the role of the elders, the priests, the bards, and the poets. Now it is increasingly the role of the media. And storytelling is immensely important for the values of a community:

> Stories tell us who we are, where we came from and what we might
> aspire to be. A culture is defined by its narratives. If they make
> strenuous demands on the mind and spirit, then a culture has the
> most precious legacy of all. That is why the great dramatists, poets
> and novelists have an influence deeper and more enduring than
> politicians or military leaders. If the great stories are lost, forgotten
> or ignored, then a culture has begun its decline. (p. 143)

Collective identity, self-reflective identity of any kind, is unthinkable
without memory. Writing at the beginning of the twentieth century,
Maurice Halbwachs was the first social theorist to consider in a systematic way the subject of social memory and how it is constructed. His
great insight was that through the membership of social groups, individuals are able to acquire, localize, and recollect memories. As Schwartz
(1991) explains: "'Collective memory' is a metaphor that formulates society's retention and loss of information about its past in the familiar
terms of individual remembering and forgetting" (p. 302).

Social memory is about the possibility of remembering in common
and, as Silverstone has pointed out (1999, pp. 125-133), the media now
have a central place here. The stories of Mellor and Hamilton, Roldán
and Lasa and Zabala, as told by the media, become the stuff of social
memory. And as these smaller stories meld into the larger ones of, in
Spain, *CORRUPSOE*, and, in Britain, *Sleaze*, episodes are brought together that become emblematic of a decade, as well as of a political party in
Spain's case, and of both a political party and politics in general in
Britain's.

In our view, then, discussions of the media's power should address
the mechanisms by which the media furnish the context and content of
social memory and the ways in which this is being eroded in a new
media environment.

Conclusion

Exploring the coverage of political scandal has allowed us to examine
various aspects of media culture in two national contexts. Like other
phenomena of the contemporary era, political scandals are textured and
shaped by the media. And yet they are not some kind of new "media
event" (Dayan & Katz, 1994); the media do not entirely constitute the
scandal; nor do the media, in our view, *simply* provide the battlefield in
which the weapon of scandal politics is wielded to fight the real political
wars (Castells, 1998). However, we would agree, as Garment has pointed out, that scandal is used as a weapon in the political armory (1992, p.
75).

In Chapter 4 we saw that there were considerable similarities both in the process of producing the scandal story and the values and attitudes of the journalists involved. British and Spanish journalists engaged in scandal coverage shared many similar assumptions about the rationale for their work and the procedures to be followed. As we relate in Chapter 5, government attempts to manage and respond to scandal coverage differed considerably and suggest that media management strategies can have unexpected and paradoxical outcomes, despite some of the more ambitious claims—not least by journalists (Jones, 2001)—made about the effectiveness of professional media management.

Examining the frames generated by political scandal coverage in Chapters 6 and 7 illustrated most fully the political and media contingencies that constitute political scandals. British coverage connected to larger themes of the country's political culture and system in a way in which Spanish coverage never did. Instead, the latter became embroiled in and constitutive of a more fractious and faction-ridden politics.

In Chapter 8 we attempted to delineate the power of the media in the telling of political scandal—a theme revisited in this chapter—and sought to locate this power precisely in the *telling* of scandal and in the creation of news icons that can act as vehicles of social memory.

Finally, our study indicates that political scandals are more than economic or ideological epiphenomena (which is, of course, not the same as saying that they are not put to economic and/or ideological use) in that they arise in and out of specific cultural contexts that are extremely influential in shaping the precise features of political scandal in different times and places. Political scandals are, then, examples of global phenomena that are at the same time highly local.

This last point is crucial. As Carey has pointed out, genres of news should be studied against "the cultural tradition in which they are embedded and that they continually express and transform" (1988, p. 16). This underlines the fact that we should resist the search for overly general patterns in understanding the coverage, types, and impact of political scandal and look to the discovery of contingent and no less interesting truths about the relationship between politics and journalism in *national* contexts, showing the continuing salience of the national even in these globalized times.

NOTES

1. Full details of the British scandals can be found in Rawnsley's excellent account of Blair's first period in government (2001).
2. Almost 80% of respondents to a *Washington Post*-ABC News national survey conducted in December 1998 during President Clinton's impeachment

debate said they disapproved of the attention paid to extramarital affairs (Sabato, Stencel, & Lichter, 2001, p. xv).

3. This is now changing in Britain after the incorporation of the European Convention on Human Rights into English law in November 1999.

4. *Newsweek* reproduces a selection of countries from the survey conducted by corruption watchdog, Transparency International, which annually rates nations on a scale of ten (the higher the number, the cleaner the country). The report's American bias is shown by the fact that, despite its talk of "the corrupt air of the continent" and "that graft and political corruption are as close to the heart of Europe's vision of itself as its rosy dreams for the future," the scores of the "corrupt" European states are a little below that given for the United States (the latter scores 7.6, Germany 7.4, Spain 7, and France 6.7).

5. In his memoirs John Major (2000) claims that it was his government's very openness that allowed *Arms to Iraq* to become a scandal: "The very existence of the [Scott] inquiry I myself set up encouraged talk of Whitehall's supposed 'culture of secrecy'; (. . .). Had I let slumbering dogs lie when questions had first been asked, there might have been no scandal, but government would have been less open" (pp. 557-558).

6. "Foxtrot Oscar" is typical of the richly loaded, punning headlines used by Britain's tabloids. The first letters of each word were highlighted in black bold type to give added impact. "Oscar" is Oscar Lafontaine who was Germany's Finance Minister in the 1990s. He had proposed tax harmonization across the European Union, a measure bitterly opposed by the U.K.'s Euro-sceptics. "Foxtrot Oscar" is a Second World War airforce code and the highlighted letters—"FO"—are a reference to an expletive telling Lafontaine to f*** off.

7. E.B. Tylor's classic definition of culture in 1871 was "that complex whole which includes knowledge, belief, art, law, morals, custom, and any other capabilities acquired by man as a member of society" (cited in Kroeber & Kluckhohn (n.d., p. 81). In this work (originally published by Harvard in 1952), they compiled 162 definitions of "culture."

Appendix 1

Scandal News Code Book

CODING FRAME

The Coding Frame was completed for every article and cartoon (see 4 below). The information collected for each unit of analysis included general information including the newspaper title, date, page number, length, section, and genre. Each unit of analysis was assigned an article number to allow easy location using the Statistics Package for Social Scientists (SPSS).

The coding frame also recorded content information including mentions of media organizations, the use of words such "corruption," "scandal" and "sleaze."

CODE BOOK

1. Newspaper Title – Record newspaper title.
2. Date – Date of newspaper to be entered; for example, 030498 (3 April 1998).

3. Page Number – Page number on which article begins.
4. Article Number – The unit of analysis is an article—i.e., a written piece that is separated from others with some kind of graphic device and adds a new angle or covers a different subject. Cartoons should also be coded for categories 1.1 - 1.5, 1.7, 1.8, and 1.13.
5. Length – Length should be calculated according to amount of space occupied by text and any accompanying graphics and photographs (i.e., on the front page, for example, banner headlines and newspaper title occupy space. However, if an article with a photo or other graphic occupies rest of page, this should be coded "4 complete pages"). Adverts do not count in this sense—i.e., ads are considered equivalent to text and length should be calculated according to the total page of possible text.

   Where articles run over on to different pages, the different segments should be added together to give a total figure.
6. Section – This category refers to the labeled section in the newspaper in which an article appears. Not all newspapers divide their paper into sections and where this is the case the article should be coded as "10 No specified section." Where an article appears in a section not listed in the coding categories, it should be coded as "9 Other." Coding label "11 Separate section" should be used for sections enumerated separately from the main body of the newspaper—e.g. the *Sunday Times* section 2. Label "8 special section" should be used to code articles that appear in a section specially created by the newspaper for the particular scandal case.
7. Case – This category refers to a specific political scandal made up of a series of events reported by the press as the constituent elements of the scandal.

   (1) *Arms to Iraq* This label refers to all coverage of events and issues connected to what became know as the "*Arms to Iraq*" case. This covers the events that began with the "Supergun" affair leading to allegations against and prosecutions of various British companies (Sheffield Forgemasters, Matrix Churchill), statements and discussions in Parliament or elsewhere by Ministers and MPs about arms exportation to Iraq, the collapse of the Matrix Churchill trail, the setting up and deliberations of the Scott Committee, and the publication of the Scott report with its surrounding controversy.

   (2) *Cash for Questions* This label refers to all coverage of allegations, disclosures, and parliamentary discussions of the issues and events surrounding MP's receiving cash for asking parliamentary questions. It refers to the subse-

quent controversies surrounding Neil Hamilton and the reports of Nolan and Downey, as well as other associated controversies.

(3) *Sexual Misdemeanors* This label refers to all coverage of allegations, disclosures, and subsequent controversies surrounding sexual misdemeanors of a sample of Conservative MPs and candidates. "Sexual Misdemeanors" is understood to refer to any behavior in private relationships considered improper, inappropriate, and/or immoral.

(4) *Roldán* This label refers to the revelation of the illegally obtained patrimony of the director of the Civil Guard and its consequences (his escape, capture, establishment of a committee of inquiry and trial)

(5) *Cesid* This refers to the CESID documents associated with the foundation of GAL, brought to light by the media, and their subsequent declassification.

(6) *Rubio* This refers to the involvement of the governor of the Bank of Spain in illegal financial operations related to Ibercorp.

(7) *Lasa and Zabala* This refers to the discovery and identification of the bodies of Lasa and Zabala as having been murdered and tortured by members of GAL.

8. Genre — refers to the genre of an article.

(0) *Other* To be used for articles to that none of the genres identified in the following list apply.

(1) *Editorial* To be used for articles that are "as from the editor."

(2) *News* To be used for articles that are reporting something new or adding a new angle to a story. This includes vox pop reports.

(3) *Features* To be used for articles that provide background (history, profiles, procedural accounts) and color (in the sense of ironic/amusing companion pieces) to the story without adding any news dimension to the story.

(4) *Column* (signed opinion—home) To be used for articles that are signed by newspapers' own columnists.

(5) *Column* (signed opinion—guest) To be used for articles that are signed by a guest columnist.

(6) *Diary* To be used for pieces that appear in a diarist's column (a gossip, society, and celebrity column) or diary section.

(7) *Cartoon* To be used for drawn cartoons with caption. Cartoons should not be coded as graphics.

(8) *Interview* To be used for articles that are substantially based on interviews by journalists with someone else.

It is not always entirely clear to which articles photos or graphics should be assigned. This should be determined by examining the headline and opening paragraph of the article and assigning the photograph to the article whose theme it seems most closely related.

For the Spanish code book the following category was added:

(9) *Profile* The biographical description of someone.

9. Photos – This category refers to a photograph that is untreated—i.e., not used as part of graphic or as an emblematic device.

10. Graphics – This category refers to graphic devices, which can include photos, relating to the case. Where these are used as part of a banner headline they should be assigned to the article closest to news.

11. Original document – This refers to facsimiles of, for example, bank statements, faxes, bills, etc., pertinent to the case. It does not include documents concocted by the newspapers, which should be coded as graphics. Documents should be examined closely to determine to which category they belong.

12. Corruption mention – This should be coded as "yes" if an article mentions either in its headlines or text the word "corruption" or any of its cognate forms—e.g., "corrupt," "corrupting," "corrupted," etc., or in a compound form.

13. Sleaze mention – This should be coded as "yes" if an article mentions either in its headlines or text the word "sleaze" or any of its cognate forms—e.g. sleazy—or in a compound form—e.g. "sleaze-ridden." This category was not used in the Spanish code book.

14. Scandal mention – This should be coded as "yes" if an article mentions either in its headlines or text the word "scandal" or any of its cognate forms—e.g., scandalous—or in a compound form—e.g., scandal-free.

15. Media organization mention – This should be coded as "yes" where a media organization other than that of the newspaper being coded or where a program is mentioned—e.g., the *Today* program, *Newsnight*, the *Daily Mail*, News International.

16. Source Identification – A source is understood as that which provides new information in an article. An article will use more than one source in an article. Here the first three identified sources were used, beginning with the headline to establish first source use.

(0) *Cannot be coded* Where the type of source cannot be classified.

(1) *Prime Minister* Where the source is the prime minister. Please note that "Downing St sources" or Moncloa sources should be coded as "26 PM press secretary."

(2) *Member of the government* Where the source is a minister. Please note that "Cabinet sources" should be coded as "2."

(3) *Member of the govt party but not of the govt/government party* Where the source is either identified as an MP, group of MPs, Party officials, Party spokespeople, etc., from the government Party but not belonging to the executive. Please note that "Senior Tory sources" should be coded as "3."

(4) *Leader of the opposition* Where the source is identified as leader of one of the opposition parties.

(5) *Member of an opposition party/opposition party* Where the source is either identified as an MP, group of MPs, Party officials, Party spokespeople, etc., from an opposition Party.

(6) *Member of civil service* Where source is identified as from Whitehall or a home ministry. However, ministry spokespersons should be coded as "24." Please note this coding label should be used for customs officials, director-general of Civil Guard, etc.

(7) *Member of the judiciary* To be used for inquiry heads, lawyers, judges, solicitors, etc.

(8) *Member of the security forces* To be used for police, secret services, and armed forces.

(9) *Financial institutions* To be used for institutions such as the Bank of England, the Bank of Spain, the Stock Exchange, etc.

(10) *Businesspeople/companies* To be used for any private business person or company or for spokespeople speaking on their behalf.

(11) *Family, friends, lovers* To be used for any source of a private connection.

(12) *Other news organization* To be used for any news or media organization or program used, including the same newspaper in which article is published.

(13) *Public opinion poll* To be used where a public opinion company or its data is used as source.

(14) *Public relations companies* To be used where a PR company, when not acting as a spokesperson, is the source.

(15) *Published documents* For any published document (report, letter, etc.).

(16) *Leaked documents* For any document not in the public domain.

(17) *Former MPs* For former Members of Parliament

(18) *Not applicable*

(19) *Other trades/jobs* Where the source is a person with a trade or job—e.g. taxi driver, plumber. Please note that "members of public" and "vox pop" should be coded as "30."

(20) *Experts* Any specified or nonspecified expert, excluding those from the ministry.

(21) *Others* Any source that is identified but fits none of the descriptions listed—e.g., campaign organizer.

(22) *Foreign officials* Any official of an overseas country—e.g., customs official, lawyer, etc.

(23) *Foreign politicians/government* Any representative, leader of an overseas government

(24) *Ministry spokespeople* Any officially designated spokesperson of a home ministry or department.

(25) *Unions* Any representative of the trade unions.

(26) *PM press secretary* The spokesperson of the prime minister, also identified as Downing St or Moncloa sources.

(27) *Lords* Any member of the House of Lords

(28) *Newspaper editor* Any newspaper editor

(29) *Speaker of the House of Commons*

(30) *Members of public/vox pop*

Appendix 2

Interviewees

NAME	POSITION	DATE
	SPAIN	

	NAME	POSITION	DATE
Government and Party Officials	Angeles Puerta	Party Press Secretary (PSOE)	16 March 1998
	Julián Santamaría	Head of ELDECO, the Socialist Party Electoral Department	15 March 1998
	Enrique Guerrero	Secretary of State for Relations with Parliament (Ministry of the Presidency)	25 June 1998
	Alfredo Pérez Rubalcaba	Ministry of the Presidency, Government spokesman	16 March 1998
	Fernando López Agundín	Press Secretary to the Home Office	24 June 1998
Journalists	Pedro J. Ramírez	Editor of El *Mundo*	April 1996
	José María Irujo	Reporter for *Roldán*	18 June 2001
	Melchor Miralles	Reporter for GAL	16 January 2001
	Fernando Garea	Reporter for *GAL-Lasa* and *Zabala*	26 June 1998

	Casimiro García Abadillo	Reporter for *Rubio*	18 March 2002
	Antonio Rubio and Manuel Cerdán	Reporters for *GAL-Cesid*	24 June 1998

UNITED KINGDOM

Government and Party Officials	Sheila Gunn	Press Officer to John Major	25 February 1998
	Howell James	Political Secretary to John Major	18 March 1998
	Charles Lewington	Director of Communications, Conservative Central Office	13 March 1998
	Ann Widdecombe	Government minister and member of Interests and Privileges Committee	25 February 1998
Journalists	Jonathan Foster	Independent reporter for *Arms to Iraq*	19 November 2002
	Bill Hagerty	Editor of the Sunday People for the Mellor case	1 July 2000
	David Hencke	Guardian reporter for *Cash for Questions*	23 January 2001
	George Jones	Political editor of *Daily Telegraph*	14 March 1998
	Nicholas Jones	Political correspondent of the BBC during scandal years	13 March 1998
	David Leigh	Guardian reporter for *Cash for Questions*	22 March 1999
	Richard Norton-Taylor	Guardian reporter for *Arms to Iraq*	30 June 2000
	Peter Preston	Editor of the *Guardian* during *Cash for Questions*	14 June 2000
	Mark Skipworth	Reporter for Sunday Times' Insight team during *Cash for Questions*	16 March 1999
	Lance Price	Political correspondent of the BBC during scandal years	20 February 1998

References

Abbott, Andrew. (1990). Conceptions of time and events in social science methods: Causal and narrative approaches. *Historical Methods, 23,* 140-150.

Actas del Congreso de los Diputados. (1994, June 23). *Debate sobre el dictamen de la Comisión del Investigación sobre la gestión de los fondos presupuestarios asignados a la Dirección General de la Guardia Civil* [Debate about the verdict of the Commission of Investigation into the management of funds assigned to the Directorate of the Civil Guard], No. 83.

Adonis, Andrew. (1997). The UK: Civic virtue put to the test. In Donatella Della Porta & Yves Mény (Eds.), *Democracy and corruption in Europe* (pp. 103-117). London: Pinter.

AEPI (Asociación Española de Periodistas Independientes). (1996). *Contra el poder* [Against power]. Madrid: Temas de Hoy.

Alatas, Syed Hussein. (1990). *Corruption: Its nature, causes and consequences.* Aldershot: Avebury.

Alborg, Juan Luis. (1966). *Historia de la literatura española. Edad media y renacimiento.* [History of Spanish literature. Middle Ages and Renaissance]. Madrid: Editorial Gredos.

Alexander, Jeffrey C. (1988). Culture and political crisis: 'Watergate' and Durkheimian sociology. In Jeffrey C. Alexander (Ed.), *Durkheimian sociology: Cultural studies* (pp. 187-224). Cambridge: Cambridge University Press.

Almond, Gabriel A., & Bingham Powell, G. (1966). *Comparative politics: A developmental approach.* Boston and Toronto: Little Brown and Company.

Almond, Gabriel A., & Verba, Sydney. (1963). *The civic culture: Political attitudes and democracy in five nations.* Princeton, NJ: Princeton University Press (abridged ed. 1965, Boston: Little Brown; repr. 1989, Newbury Park, CA and London: Sage).

Almond, Gabriel A., & Verba, Sydney. (Eds.) (1989). *The civic culture revisited.* Newbury Park, CA, and London, New Delhi: Sage.

Amadeo, Belén. (1999). *La aplicación de la teoría del framing a la cobertura de la corrupción política en Argentina* [The application of framing theory to political corruption in Argentina]. Unpublished doctoral dissertation, University of Navarra, Spain.

Anderson, A. (1997). *Media, culture and the environment.* London: University College London Press.

Anderson, B. (1983). *Imagined communities.* London: Verso.

Anderson, Peter J., & Weymouth, Anthony. (1999). *Insulting the public? The British press and the European union.* London and New York: Addison Wesley Longman.

Anuario El Mundo. (1998). Madrid: Unidad Editorial, S.A.

Anuario El País. (1998). Madrid: Prisa.

Arceo, José Luis. (1982). *Cómo ganar unas elecciones. Tratamiento teórico y práctico de la imagen de los políticos* [How to win an election campaign. Theoretical and practical treatment of politicians' image]. Madrid: Fomento de bibliotecas.

Arendt, Hannah. (1958). *The human condition.* Chicago: The University of Chicago Press.

Arqués, Ricardo, & Irujo, José María. (1993). *ETA, la derrota de las armas* [ETA, the defeat of arms]. Madrid: Plaza y Janés.

Arroyo Martínez, Luis. (1997). Fábulas y fabuladores. El escándalo político como fenómeno de los medios de comunicación.[Fables and fabulists. Political scandal as a phenomenon of mass media]. In Francisco J. Laporta & Silvina Alvarez (Eds.), *La corrupción política* [Political corruption] (pp. 335-358). Madrid: Alianza Editorial.

Audit Bureau of Circulation. http://www.abc.co.uk

Bale, Tim, & Sanders, Karen. (2001). 'Playing by the book': Success and failure in John Major's approach to prime ministerial media management. *Contemporary British History, 4, 15,* 93-110.

Barnett, Steven, & Gaber, Ivor. (Eds.) (2001). *Westminster tales: The twenty-first century crisis in British political journalism.* London/New York: Continuum.

Barnhurst, Kevin G. (2000, Spring). Political engagement and the audience for news: Lessons from Spain. *Journalism Communication Monographs, 2.*

Baston, Lewis. (2000). *Sleaze. The state of Britain.* London: Channel 4 Books.

Bateson, G. (1972). *Steps to an ecology of mind: Collected essays in anthropology, psychiatry, evolution, and epistemology.* New York: Ballantine.

Benavides, Juan, & Palacio, Manuel. (1994). La imagen del Congreso de los Diputados en la Televisión [The image of the Congress of Deputies on television]. In Fernando Huertas (Ed.), *Televisión y política* [Television and politics] (pp. 133-154). Madrid: Editorial Complutense.

Bennett, W. Lance. (1990). Toward a theory of press-state relations. *Journal of Communication, 40(2)*, 103-125.

Bennett, W. Lance. (1996). An introduction to journalism norms and representations of politics. *Political Communication, 13(4)*, 373-384.

Bennett, W. Lance, & Entman, Robert M. (2001). Mediated politics: An introduction. In W. Lance Bennett & Robert M. Entman (Eds.), *Mediated politics. Communication in the future of democracy* (pp. 1-29). Cambridge and New York: Cambridge University Press.

Bennett, W. Lance, & Lawrence, Regina G. (1995). News icons and the mainstreaming of social change. *Journal of Communication, 45(3)*, 20-39.

Bezunartea, Ofa. (1995). *Noticias e ideología profesional. La prensa vasca en la transición política* [News and professional ideology. The Basque press during the political transition]. Bilbao: Deusto.

Bird, Elizabeth S. (1997). What a story! Understanding the audience for scandal. In James Lull & Stephen Hinerman (Eds.), *Media scandals* (pp. 99-121). London: Polity Press.

Bird, Elizabeth S., & Dardenne, R. W. (1988). Myth, chronicle and story: Exploring the narrative qualities of news. In James W. Carey (Ed.,) *Media, myths and narratives* (pp. 67-87). Newbury Park, CA: Sage.

Blumenthal, S. (1980). *The permanent campaign*. New York: Simon and Schuster.

Blumler, Jay G. (1997). Origins of the crisis of communication for citizenship. *Political Communication, 14(4)*, 395-404.

Blumler, Jay G. (1999). Political communication systems all change. A response to Kees Brants. *European Journal of Communication, 14(2)*, 241-249.

Blumler, Jay G., & Gurevitch, Michael. (1995). *The crisis of public communication.* London: Routledge.

Blumler, Jay G., McLeod, J., & Rosengren, Karl E. (Eds). (1992). *Comparatively speaking: Communication and culture across space and time.* Newbury Park, CA: Sage.

Bognador, Vernon. (1997). *The monarchy and the constitution.* Oxford: Oxford University Press.

Bourdieu, Pierre. (1991). *Language and symbolic power.* Cambridge: Polity Press.

Boyd Hunt, Jonathan. (1998). *Trial by conspiracy. The lies, cover-ups and injustices behind the Neil Hamilton affair*, Auckland, and London: Greenzone.

Brants, Kees. (1998). Who's afraid of infotainment? *European Journal of Communication, 13(3)*, 315-335.

Budge, I., Newton, K. et al. (1997). *The politics of the new Europe: Atlantic to Urals.* London: AWL.

Butler, David, & Kavanagh, Dennis. (1997). *The 1997 British general election.* Basingstoke: Macmillan.

Calcutt, David. (1993). *Review of press self-regulation: Presented to Parliament by the Secretary.* London: HMSO.

Campbell, Karlyn Kohrs, & Jamieson, Kathleen. (1990). *Deeds done in words: Presidential rhetoric and the genres of governance.* Chicago: University of Chicago Press.

Canel, María José. (1994). Local government in the Spanish autonomic state. *Studies on Local Government, 20(1)*, 44-59.

Canel, María José. (1998). Los efectos de las campañas electorales [Effects of election campaigns]. *Comunicación y Sociedad, 11*(1), 47-67.

Canel, María José. (1999). *Comunicación política. Técnicas y estrategias para la sociedad de la información* [Political communication. Techniques and strategies for the information society]. Madrid: Tecnos.

Canel, María José, & Innerarity, Carmen. (2000). Elecciones europeas y medios de comunicación [European elections and the media]. In Antonia Martínez & Mónica Méndez (Eds.), *Elecciones europeas en España 1999* [European elections in Spain] (pp. 133-148). Valencia: Tirant lo Blanch.

Canel, María José, & Piqué, Antoni M. (1998). Journalists for emerging democracies. The case of Spain. In David Weaver (Ed.), *The global journalist* (pp. 299-319). Cresskill, NJ: Hampton Press.

Canel, María José, Rodríguez Andrés, Roberto, & Sánchez Aranda, José Javier. (2000). *Periodistas al descubierto. Retrato de los profesionales de la información* [Journalists revealed: A portrait of news professionals]. Madrid: Centro de Investigaciones Sociológicas.

Canel, María José, & Sádaba, Teresa. (1999). La investigación académica sobre las actitudes profesionales de los periodistas. Una descripción del estado de la cuestión [Research on journalists' professional attitudes. A description of the state of the question]. *Comunicación y Sociedad, 12*(2), 9-32.

Canel, María José, & Sánchez-Aranda, José Javier. (1999). La influencia de las actitudes profesionales del periodista español en las noticias [The influence of Spanish journalists' professional attitudes on news]. *Análisi, 23*, 89-108.

Cappella, Joseph, & Jamieson, Kathleen H. (1997). *Spiral of cynicism*. New York: Oxford.

Cappella, Joseph, & Jamieson, Kathleen H. (1996). News frames, political cynicism, and media cynicism. *The Annals of the American Academy, 546*, 70-84.

Carey, James W. (Ed.). (1988). *Media, myths and narratives*. Newbury Park, CA: Sage.

Castells, Manuel. (1998). La política informacional y la crisis de la democracia. [Informational politics and the crisis of democracy]. In *La Era de la Informacion. Economia, sociedad y cultura. Vol. 2: El poder de la identidad* (pp. 341-391). [The information age. Economy, society and culture: Volume 2: The power of identity]. Madrid: Alianza Editorial.

Central Media. (1996). *Informe anual del estado de los medios de comunicación*. Madrid: MRC.

Centro de Investigaciones Sociológicas. Barómetros 1996/1997.

Chippindale, Peter, & Horrie, Chris. (1999). *Stick it up your punter! The uncut story of the Sun newspaper*. London: Simon & Schuster.

CIRES. (1997). *La realidad social en España, 1996-1997* [Spanish social reality, 1996-1997]. Madrid: CIRES.

Cockerell, Michael. (1984). *Sources close to the prime minister: Inside the hidden world of the news*. London: Macmillan.

Cockerell, Michael. (1988). *Live from Number Ten: The inside story of prime ministers and television*. London: Faber and Faber.

Cook, Timothy E. (1996). Political values and production values. *Political Communication, 13*(4), 469-481

Cook, Timothy E. (1998). *Governing with the news. The news media as a political institution*. Chicago: The University of Chicago Press.

Cornwell, Elmer E. (1966). *Presidential leadership of public opinion*. Bloomington: Indiana University Press.

Cotarelo, Ramón. (1996). *El alarido ronco del ganador. Las elecciones de 1996, los medios de comunicación y el porvenir de España*. [The hoarse scream of the winner. The 1996 elections, the media and the future of Spain]. Barcelona: Grijalbo.

Cowley, Chris. (1992). *Guns, lies and spies: How we armed Iraq*. London: Hamish Hamilton.

Dader, José Luis. (1992). *El periodista en el espacio público* [The journalist in the public space]. Barcelona: Ariel.

Dahl, Megan K., & Bennett, Lance W. (1996). Media agency and the use of icons in the agenda-setting process. News representations of George Bush's trade mission to Japan. *Press and Politics, 1*(3), 41-59.

Davis, Aeron. (2000). Public relations, news production and changing patterns of source access in the British national media. *Media, Culture and Society, 22*(1), 39-59.

Davis, Aeron. (2002). *Public relations democracy. Public relations, politics and the mass media in Britain*. Manchester: Manchester University Press.

Dayan, Daniel, & Katz, Elihu. (1994). *Media events. The live broadcasting of history*. Cambridge, MA: Harvard University Press.

De Burgh, Hugo. (Ed.) (2000). *Investigative journalism. Context and practice*. London and New York: Routledge.

De Vreese, Claes H. (1999). *News and European integration: News content and effects in cross-national comparative perspective*. Research Report. Amsterdam School of Communications Research, University of Amsterdam.

De Vreese, Claes H., Peter, Jochen, & Semetko, Holli. (2001). Framing politics at the launch of the Euro: A cross-national comparative study of frames in the news. *Political Communication, 18*, 107-122.

Deacon, David, & Golding, Peter. (1994). *Taxation and representation: The media, political communication and the poll tax*. London: John Libbey.

Deacon, David, Pickering, Michael, Golding, Peter, & Murdock, Graham. (1999). *Researching communication. A practical guide to methods in media and cultural analysis*. London: Arnold.

Del Rey, Javier. (1989). *Comunicación política* [Political communication]. Madrid: Eudema Universidad.

Del Río, Pablo. (1996). *Psicología de los medios de comunicación* [The psychology of the communication media] Madrid: Síntesis.

Della Porta, Donatella, & Mény, Yves. (Eds.). (1997). *Democracy and corruption in Europe*. London and Washington: Pinter.

Denton, Robert E., & Hahn, Dan F. (1986). *Presidential communication. Description and analysis*. New York: Praeger.

Denton, Robert E., & Holloway, Rachel L. (1996). Clinton and the town hall meetings: Mediated conversation and the risk of being "in touch." In Robert E. Denton & Rachel L. Holloway. (Eds.), *The Clinton presidency. Images, issues and communication strategies* (pp. 17-41). Westport, CT: Praeger.

Denzin, Norman K., & Lincoln, Yvonne. (1998). *Collecting and interpreting qualitative materials*. Thousand Oaks, CA and London: Sage.

Dictionary of the Spanish language. Real Academia Española. (2001). *Diccionario de la Real Academia de la Lengua Española*. Madrid: Espasa Calpe.

Díez Nicolás, Juan, & Semetko, Holli A. (1995). La televisión y las elecciones de 1993 [Television and the 1993 elections]. In Alejandro Muñoz-Alonso & Juan Rospir (Eds.), *Comunicación política* [Political communication] (pp. 133-153). Madrid: Universitas.

Diezhandino, Pilar, Coca, César, & Bezunartea, Ofa. (1994). *La élite de los periodistas* [The journalistic elite]. Bilbao: Universidad del País Vasco.

Dijk, Teun A. van (1998). Opinions and ideologies in the press. In Allen Bell & Peter Garrett (Eds.), *Approaches to media discourse* (pp. 21-63). Oxford: Blackwell.

Doig, Alan. (1996). Politics and public sector ethics: The impact of change in the United Kingdom. In Walter Little & Eduardo Posada-Carbó (Eds.), *Political corruption in Europe and Latin America* (pp. 173-192). Basingstoke and London: Macmillan.

Dunleavy, Patrick, & Weir, Stuart. (1995). Media, opinion and the constitution. In F.F. Ridley & Alan Doig (Eds.), *Sleaze: Politicians, private interests and public reaction* (pp. 54-68). Oxford: Oxford University Press.

Edelman, Murray. (1988). *Constructing the political spectacle*. Chicago: University of Chicago Press.

Edwards, G. C. (1983). *The public presidency: The pursuit of popular support*. New York: St Martin's.

Entman, Robert M. (1991). Framing U.S. coverage of international news: Contrasts in narratives of the KAL and Iran air incidents. *Journal of Communication, 41*(4), 6-27.

Entman, Robert M. (1993). Framing: Toward clarification of a fractured paradigm. *Journal of Communication, 43*(4), 51-58.

Ericson, R.V., Baranek, P.M., & Chan J.B. (1989). *Negotiating control: A study of news sources*. Milton Keynes: Open University Press.

Esser, Frank. (1999). 'Tabloidization' of news. A comparative analysis of Anglo-American and German press journalism. *European Journal of Communication, 14*(3), 291-324.

Esser, Frank, & Hartung, Uwe. (2004). Nazis, pollution and no sex. *American Behavioral Scientist, 47*(8), 1040-1071.

Esser, Frank, & Pfetsch, Barbara. (Eds.). (2004). *Comparing political communication. Theories, cases and challenges*. Cambridge: Cambridge University Press.

Esteban, Esther. (1995). *El tercer hombre. P.J. la pesadilla de F.G.* [The third man. Pedro J., Felipe González's nightmare]. Madrid: Espasa Hoy.

Ettema, James S., & Glasser, Theodore L. (1998). *Custodians of conscience: Investigative journalism and public virtue*. New York: Columbia University Press.

European Commission. (2001). *Eurobarometer*, N. 56, Brussels.

Evans, Harold. (1994). *Good times, bad times* (3rd ed.). London: Phoenix.

Fairclough, Norman. (1995). *Media discourse*. New York: Arnold.

Farrell, Nicholas. (2000, February 5). Madeline Albright and the Italians have joined a crusade-against the corrupt *Inglesi*. *The Spectator*, p. 10.

Foot, Paul. (1999). The slow death of investigative journalism. In Stephen Glover (Ed.), *Secrets of the press. Journalists on journalism* (pp. 79-89). London: Allen Lane.

Fowler, Roger. (1991). *Language in the news.* London: Routledge.

Franklin, Bob. (1997). *Newszak and news media.* London: Arnold.

Franklin, Bob. (2004). *Packaging politics: Political communications in Britain's media democracy* (2nd ed.). London: Edward Arnold.

Freedland, Jonathan. (1998). *Bring home the revolution. The case for a British republic.* London: Fourth Estate.

Friedman, A. (1993). *Spider's web: Bush, Saddam, Thatcher and the decade of deceit.* London: Faber.

Fundación Encuentro. (1995). *España 1994. Una interpretación de su realidad social* [Spain 1994. An interpretation of its social reality]. Madrid: Fundación Encuentro.

Gallagher, Michael, Laver, Michael, & Mair, Peter. (1995). *Representative government in modern Europe.* New Cork and London: McGraw Hill.

Gamson, William A. (1989). News as framing: Comments on Graber. *American Behavioral Scientist, 33*(2), 157-161.

Gamson, William A., & Modigliani, Andre. (1987). The changing culture of affirmative action. In R. Braungart & M.M. Braungart (Eds.), *Research in political sociology* (Vol. 3, pp. 137-177). Greenwich, CT: JAI Press.

Gamson, William A., & Modigliani, Andre. (1989). Media discourses and public opinion on nuclear power: A constructionist approach. *American Journal of Sociology, 95*(1), 1-37.

Gandy, O.H. (1982). *Beyond agenda setting: Information subsidies and public policy.* Norwood, NJ: Ablex.

Gans, Herbert. (1979). *Deciding what's news.* New York: Pantheon Books.

García Abadillo, Casimiro, & Cacho, Jesús. (1992). *La estafa Ibercorp* [The Ibercorp swindle]. Barcelona: Temas de Hoy.

Garment, Suzanne. (1991). *Scandal: The crisis of mistrust in American politics.* New York: Times Books.

Garzón Valdés, Ernesto. (1997). Acerca del concepto de la corrupción [On the concept of corruption]. In Francisco J. Laporta & Silvina Alvarez (Eds.), *La corrupción política* [Political corruption] (pp.39-69). Madrid: Alianza Editorial.

Gauthier, Gilles, Gosselin, André, & Mouchon, Jean (comps.) (1998). *Comunicación y política* [Communication and politics]. Barcelona: Gedisa.

Geertz, Clifford. (1973/1993). *The interpretation of cultures: Selected essays.* London: Fontana Press.

Ghanem, Salma. (1997). Filling in the tapestry: The second level of agenda-setting. In Maxwell McCombs, Donald Shaw, & David Weaver (Eds.), *Communication and democracy. Exploring the international frontiers in agenda-setting theory* (pp. 3-14). Hillsdale, NJ: Erlbaum.

Giddens, Anthony. (1991). *Modernity and self-identity: Self and society in the late modern age.* Cambridge: Polity Press.

Giddens, Anthony. (1999). *The BBC Reith lectures*. http://www.bbc.co.uk/radio4/reith1999/lecture1-5_text.shtml.

Gitlin, Todd. (1980). *The whole world is watching*. Berkeley: University of California Press.

Goffman, Erving (1969). *The presentation of self in everyday life*. Harmondsworth: Penguin Books.

Goffman, Erving. (1986). [1974] *Frame analysis. An essay on the organization of experience*. Boston: Northeastern University Press.

Goldenberg, E. (1975). *Making the papers: The access of resource poor groups to the metropolitan press*. Lexington, MA: Lexington Books.

Greer, Ian. (1997). *One man's word. The untold story of the cash-for-questions affair*. London: André Deutsch.

Griffin, Larry J. (1992). Temporality, events, and explanations in historical sociology: An introduction. *Sociological Research and Methods, 20*, 403-427.

Griffin, Larry J. (1993). Narrative, event-structure analysis, and causal interpretation in historical sociology. *American Journal of Sociology, 98(5)*, 1094-1133.

Grossman, Michael B., & Kumar, Martha J. (1981). *Portraying the President. The White House and the news media*. Baltimore: John Hopkins University.

Guardian, The. (1997, July 4). The final, unequivocal and damning verdict: Guilty, as charged, p. 1.

Guerrero, Enrique. (2000). *Crisis y cambios en las relaciones parlamento-globierno (1993-1996)*. [Crisis and changes in parliament-government relations]. Madrid: Tecnos.

Gunther, Richard., Montero, José Ramón, & Wert, José Ignacio. (2000). The media and politics in Spain: From dictatorship to democracy. In Richard Gunther and Anthony Mughan (Eds.), *Democracy and the media. A comparative perspective*. Cambridge: Cambridge University Press.

Gunther, Richard, & Mughan, Anthony. (Eds.). (2000). *Democracy and the media. A comparative perspective*. Cambridge: Cambridge University Press.

Gutiérrez, José Luis. (1996). El periodismo de investigación [Investigative journalism]. In AEPI, *Contra el poder* [Against power] (pp. 57-69). Madrid: Temas de Hoy.

Habermas, Jürgen. (1989). *The structural transformation of the public sphere*. Cambridge: Polity Press.

Hall, Stuart, Clarke, J., Critcher, C., & Roberts, B. (1978). *Policing the crisis: Mugging, the state and law and order*. London: Macmillan.

Hallin, Daniel C. (2000). Commercialism and professionalism in the American news media. In James Curran & Michael Gurevitch (Eds.), *Mass media and society* (3rd ed., pp. 218-237). London: Arnold.

Hallin, Daniel C., & Mancini, Paolo. (Eds.). (2004). *Comparing media systems: Three models of media and politics*. Cambridge: Cambridge University Press.

Harris, R. (1990). *Good and faithful servant: The unauthorized biography of Bernard Ingham*. London: Faber and Faber.

Heidenheimer, Arnold J., Johnston, Michael, & LeVine, Victor T. (Eds.). (1997). *Political corruption. A handbook*. New Brunswick, NJ: Transaction Publishers.

Henderson, Paul. (1993). *The unlikely spy*. London: Bloomsbury.

Hennessy, Peter. (1995). *The hidden wiring: Unearthing the British constitution.* London: Gollancz.

Hennessy, Peter. (2000). *The prime minister. The office and its holders since 1945.* London: Allen Lane.

Henningham, John, & Delano, Anthony. (1998). British journalists. In David Weaver (Ed.), *The global journalist* (pp. 143-160). Cresskill, NJ: Hampton Press.

Heras, Raúl. (1990). *La historia secreta de la beautiful people* [The secret history of the *beautiful people*]. Madrid: Temas de Hoy.

Hermann, E.S., & Chomsky, N. (1988). *Manufacturing consent*. New York: Pantheon Books.

Heywood, Paul. (1995a). *The government and politics of Spain*. London and Basingstoke: Macmillan.

Heywood, Paul. (1995b). Spain. In F.F. Ridley & Alan Doig (Eds.), *Sleaze: Politicians, private interests and public reactions* (pp. 178-189). Oxford: Oxford University Press.

Heywood, Paul. (1996). Continuity and change: Analysing political corruption in Modern Spain. In Walter Little & Eduardo Posada-Carbó (Eds.), *Political corruption in Europe and Latin America* (pp. 115-136). Basingstoke and London: Macmillan.

Heywood, Paul. (Ed.) (1997). *Political corruption*. Oxford: Blackwell.

Hobsbawm, Eric, & Ranger, Terence. (Eds.). (1995). *The invention of tradition.* New York: Cambridge University Press.

Hogg, Sarah, & Hill, Jonathan. (1995). *Too close to call. Power and politics—John Major in No. 10*. London: Little, Brown and Company.

Huertas, Fernando. (1994). El hemiciclo como realidad conformada o imagen virtual [The congress chamber as a constituted reality or virtual image]. In Fernando Huertas (Ed.), *Televisión y política* [Television and politics] (pp. 155-170). Madrid: Editorial Complutense.

Ingham, Bernard. (2003). *The wages of spin*. London: John Murray.

Inglehart, Ronald. (1990). *Culture shift in advanced industrial society*. Princeton, NJ: Princeton University Press.

Innerarity, Carmen, & Canel, María José. (2000). El Parlamento en los medios, terreno de juego [Parliament in the media, a playground]. In Antonia Martín (Ed.), *El Congreso de los Diputados en España* [The Congress of Deputies in Spain] (pp. 343-391). Madrid: Tecnos.

Irujo, José María, & Mendoza, Jesús. (1994). *Roldán, un botín a la sombra del tricornio* [Roldán, booty in the shadow of the "three-cornered hat"]. Madrid: Temas de Hoy.

Irujo, José María, & Mendoza, Jesús. (1996). *Comisión Ilegal* [Illegal payments]. Madrid: Temas de Hoy.

Iyengar, Shanto. (1987). *News that matters*. Chicago: University of Chicago Press.

Iyengar, Shanto. (1992). *Is anyone responsible?* Chicago: University of Chicago Press.

Iyengar, Shanto, & Reeves, Richard. (1997). The effects of news on the audience: Minimal or maximal consequences? In Shanto Iyengar and Richard Reeves, (Eds.), *Do media govern? Politicians, voters and reporters in America* (pp. 211-315). Newbury Park, CA: Sage.

Jasperson, A.E., Shah, D.V., Watts, M., Faber, R.J., & Fan, D.P. (1998). Framing the public agenda: Media effects on the importance of the federal budget deficit. *Political Communication, 15,* 205-224.

Jiménez Sánchez, Fernando. (1995). *Detrás del escándalo político. Opinión Pública, dinero y poder en la España del siglo XX* [Behind political scandal. Public opinion and power in the Spain of the 20th century]. Barcelona: Tusquets.

Jíménz Sánchez, Fernando. (1997). Posibilidades y límites del escándalo político como una forma de control social [Possibilities and limits of political scandal as a form of social control]. In Francisco J. Laporta & Silvina Alvarez (Eds.), *La corrupción política* [Political corruption] (pp. 293-334). Madrid: Alianza Editorial.

Jiménez, Fernando. (2004). The politics of scandal in Spain: Morality plays, social trust, and the battle for public opinion. *American Behavioral Scientist, 47*(8), 1099-1121.

Jones, Marion. (1983; rep. 1996). Early moral plays and the earliest secular drama. Introduction. In A.C. Cawley, Marion Jones, Peter F. McDonald and David Mills, *The revels history of drama in English. Volume 1: Medieval drama* (pp. 213-224). London: Routledge.

Jones, Nicholas. (1995). *Soundbites and spindoctors.* London: Cassell.

Jones, Nicholas. (1997). *Campaign 97.* London: Indigo.

Jones, Nicholas. (2001). *The control freaks: How New Labour gets its own way.* London: Politico's.

Kahneman, D., & Tversky, A. (1984). Choices, values and frames. *American Psychologist, 39,* 341-350.

Kavanagh, Dennis, & Seldon, Anthony. (2000). *The powers behind the prime minister. The hidden influence of Number Ten.* London: Harper Collins.

Kernell, Samuel. (1986) [1993]. *Going public: New strategies of presidential leadership* (2nd ed.). Washington, DC: Congressional Quarterly.

Kernell, Samuel. (1997). The theory and practice of going public. In Shanto Iyengar & Richard Reeves (Eds.), *Do media govern? Politicians, voters and reporters in America* (pp. 323-333). Newbury Park, CA: Sage.

King, Anthony. (1986). Sex, money and power. In Richard Hodder-Williams & James Caeser (Eds.), *Politics in Britain and the United States: Comparative perspectives.* Durham, NC: Duke University Press.

Kroeber, A.L., & Kluckhohn, Clyde. (n.d.). *Culture: A critical review of concepts and definitions.* New York: Vintage Books.

Kuhn, Raymond, & Neveu, Eric. (Eds.). (2002). *Political journalism: New challenges, new practices.* London: Routledge.

Kurtz, Howard. (1998). *Spin cycle. Inside the Clinton propaganda machine.* New York: The Free Press.

Laitin, David. (1995). The civic culture. *American Political Science Review, 89*(1), 168-173.

Lang, Gladys, & Lang, K. (1983). *The battle for public opinion: The President, the press and the polls during Watergate.* New York: Columbia University Press.

Lang, Ian. (2002). *Blue remembered hills: A political memoir.* London: Politico's.

Laporta, Francisco J., & Alvarez, Silvina. (Eds.). (1997) *La corrupción política* [Political corruption]. Madrid: Alianza Editorial.

Leigh, David. (1993). *Betrayed. The real story of the Matrix Churchill trial*. London: Bloomsbury.

Leigh, David, & Vulliamy, Ed. (1997). *Sleaze. The corruption of Parliament*. London: Fourth Estate.

Levi, M., & Nelken, D. (Eds.). (1996). *The corruption of politics and the politics of corruption*. Oxford: Blackwell.

Little, Walter, & Posada-Carbó, Eduardo. (Eds.). (1996). *Political corruption in Europe and Latin America*. Basingstoke and London: Macmillan.

López Agudín, Fernando. (1996). *En el laberinto: Diario de interior (1994-1996)* [In the labyrinth: A diary from inside (1994-1996)]. Barcelona: Plaza & Janés.

Lowi, Theodore. (1985). *The personal President: Power invested, promise unfulfilled*. New York: Cornell University Press.

Lull, James, & Hinerman, Stephen. (1997). The search for scandal. In James Lull & Stephen Hinerman (Eds.), *Media scandals. Morality and desire in the popular culture marketplace* (pp. 1-33). London: Polity Press.

McCombs, Maxwell, & Evatt, Dixie. (1995). Los temas y los aspectos: Explorando una nueva dimensión de la agenda setting [Themes and aspects: Exploring a new dimension of agenda setting]. *Comunicación y Sociedad, 8*, 7-32.

McCombs, Maxwell, & Ghanem, Salma. (2001). The convergence of agenda setting and framing. In Stephen D. Reese, Oscar H. Gandy, Jr. & Auguste E. Grant (Eds.), *Framing public life. Perspectives on media and our understanding of the social world* (pp. 67-81). Hillside, NJ: Erlbaum.

McCullagh, C. (1978). Colligation and classification in history. *History and Theory, 13*, 267-284.

McNair, Brian. (2000). *Journalism and democracy. An evaluation of the political public sphere*. London: Routledge.

Maher, Mike. (2001). Framing: An emerging paradigm or a phase of agenda setting? In Stephen D. Reese, Oscar H. Gandy, Jr., & Auguste E. Grant (Eds.), *Framing public life. Perspectives on media and our understanding of the social world* (pp. 83-94). Hillsdale, NJ: Erlbaum.

Major, John. (2000). *John Major. The autobiography*. London: HarperCollins.

Maltese, John A. (1994). *Spin control. The White House office of communications and the management of presidential news*. Chapel Hill: The University of North Carolina Press.

Mancini, Paolo. (1993). Beyond trust and suspicion: How political journalists solve the dilemma. *European Journal of Communication, 8*(1), 33-51.

Manning, Paul. (2001) *News and news sources: A critical introduction*. London: Sage.

Markovits, Andrei S., & Silverstein, Mark. (Eds.). (1988). *The politics of scandal: power and process in liberal democracies*. New York: Holmes and Meier.

Marr, Andrew. (1996). *Ruling Britannia: The failure and future of British democracy*. Harmondsworth: Penguin.

Martin, Manuel. (1992, October). La objetividad en los periodistas españoles [Objectivity in Spanish journals]. *Nuestro Tiempo*, 116-125.

Mechling, Jay (1991). *Homo narrans*: Across the disciplines. *Western Folklore, 50*, 41-51.

Mendelson, M. (1993). Television's frames in the 1988 Canadian election. *Canadian Journal of Communication, 18*, 149-171.

Meyer, D. (1995). Framing national security: Elite public discourse on nuclear weapons during the Cold War. *Political Communication, 12*, 173-192.

Miles, Matthew B. (1984). *Qualitative data analysis: A sourcebook of new methods.* Beverly Hills and London: Sage.

Miralles, Melchor & Arqués, Ricardo. (1998). *Amedo. El Estado contra ETA* [Amedo. The State against ETA]. Barcelona: Plaza & Janés.

Monzón, Cándido. (1996). *Opinión pública, comunicación y política. La formación del espacio público* [Public opinion, communication and politics. The formation of the public space]. Madrid: Tecnos.

MORI. (2000). www.mori.com/polls/2000/bma2000.shtml.

Morley, David, & Robins, Kevin. (1995). *Spaces of identity.* London: Routledge.

Mortimore, Roger. (1995). Politics and public perceptions. In F.F. Ridley & Alan Doig (Eds.), *Sleaze: Politicians, private interests and public reactions* (pp. 31-41). Oxford: Oxford University Press.

Mount, Ferdinand. (2001, February 2) A golden age of privacy? *Times Literary Review*, p. 11.

Muñoz Alonso, Alejandro, & Rospir, Juan. (Eds.) *Comunicación política* [Political communication]. Madrid: Editorial Universitas.

Murphy, David. (1991). *The Stalker affair and the press.* London: Unwin Hyman.

Negrine, Ralph. (1996a). The inquiry's media coverage. In Brian Thompson & F.F. Ridley (Eds.), *Under the Scott light: British government seen through the Scott report* (pp. 27-40). Oxford: Oxford University Press.

Negrine, Ralph. (1996b). *The communication of politics.* London: Sage.

Neustadt, Richard E. (1960). *Presidential power. The politics of leadership with reflections on Johnson and Nixon.* Cambridge, MA: Harvard University.

New Shorter Oxford English Dictionary. (1993). Volume 1. Oxford: Clarendon Press.

Nieto, Alejandro. (1997). *Corrupción de la España democrática* [The corruption of democratic Spain]. Barcelona: Ariel.

Nimmo, Dan, & Sanders, K. R. (Eds.). (1981). *Handbook of political communication.* Beverly Hills, CA: Sage.

Nimmo, Dan, & Swanson, David. (1990). The field of political communication: Beyond the voter persuasion paradigm. In Dan Nimmo & David Swanson, (Eds.), *New directions in political communication* (pp. 7-47). Newbury Park, CA: Sage.

Nolan Committee. (1995). *First report of the committee on standards in public life* (Cm. 2850). London: HMSO.

Nora, Pierre. (1984-1993). *Lieux de mémoires.* Paris: Gallimard.

Norris, Pippa. (Ed.) (1999). *Critical citizens: Global support for democratic governance.* Oxford: Oxford University Press.

Norris, Pippa. (2000). *A virtuous circle. Political communications in postindustrial societies.* Cambridge: Cambridge University Press.

Norton-Taylor, Richard, & Lloyd, Mark. (1995). *Truth is a difficult concept: Inside the Scott inquiry.* London: 4th Estate.

Norton-Taylor, Richard, Lloyd, Mark, & Cook, Stephen. (1996). *Knee deep in dishonour: The Scott report and its aftermath.* London: Victor Gollancz.

O'Neil, Onora. (2002). *The BBC Reith Lectures.* http://www.bbc.co.ukradio4 /reith2002/lecture1-5_text.shtml.

Oficina de Justificación de la Difusión (1997). http://www.ojd.es

Ortega, Felix, & Humanes, María Luisa. (2000). *Algo más que periodistas. Sociología de una profesión.* [Something more than journalists. Sociology of a profession]. Barcelona: Ariel.

Oxford English dictionary. (1999). (10th ed.). Oxford: Oxford University Press.

Paletz, David L. (1997). *Political communication research: Approaches, studies and assessments.* Norwood, NJ: Ablex.

Paletz, David L., & Lipinski, Daniel. (1994). *Political culture and political communication* (Working paper no. 92). Barcelona: Institut de Ciències Polítiques Socials.

Palmer, Jerry. (2000). *Spinning into control. News values and source strategies.* London and New York: Leicester University Press.

Pan, Zhongdang, & Kosicki, Gerald M. (1993). Framing analysis: An approach to news discourse. *Political Communication, 10,* 55-75.

Paniagua-Soto, J.L. (1997). Spain: A fledgling parliament. *Parliamentary Affairs, 50*(3), 410-422.

Parris, Matthew. (1996). *Great parliamentary scandals: Four centuries of calumny, smear and innuendo.* London: Robson.

Patterson, Thomas E. (1998). Political roles of the journalist. In Doris Graber, Dennis McQuail, & Pippa Norris (Eds.), *The politics of news. The news of politics* (pp. 17-32). Washington DC: CQ Press.

Prego, Victoria. (2000). *Presidentes. Veinticinco años de historia narrada por los cuatro jefes de gobierno de la democracia* [Presidents. Twenty five years of history told by four heads of government of the democratic era]. Barcelona: Plaza & Janés.

Press Complaints Commission. (1991). Report No. 1. London: PCC.

Press Complaints Commission. (1994). Report No. 25. London: PCC.

Protess, David L., Cook, Fay Lomax, Doppelt, Jack C., Ettema, James S., Gordon, Margaret T., Leff, Donna R., & Miller, Peter. (1991) *The journalism of outrage. Investigative reporting and agenda building in America.* New York: Guilford Press.

Putnam, Robert. (1993). *Making democracy work: Civic trends in modern Italy.* Princeton, NJ: Princeton University Press.

Rachlin, A. (1988). *News as hegemonic reality. American political culture and the framing of news accounts.* New York: Praeger.

Ramírez, Pedro J. (2000). *Amarga victoria. La crónica oculta del histórico triunfo de Aznar sobre González* [Bitter victory. The hidden story of Aznar's historic triumph over González]. Madrid: Planeta.

Randall, David. (2000). *The universal journalist* (2nd ed.). London: Pluto Press.

Rawnsley, Andrew. (2001). *Servants of the people. The inside story of New Labour.* London: Penguin.

Reese, Stephen D. (2001). Prologue—Framing public life: A bridging model for media research. In Stephen D. Reese, Oscar H. Gandy, Jr., & August E. Grant (Eds.), *Framing public life. Perspectives on media and our understanding of the social world* (pp. 7-31). Hillsdale, NJ: Erlbaum.

Rhodes, R.A.W., & Dunleavy, Patrick. (Eds.). (1995). *Prime Minister, cabinet and core executive*. Basingstoke: Macmillan.

Ridley, F.F., & Doig, Alan. (Eds.) (1995). *Sleaze: Politicians, private interests and public reactions*. Oxford: Oxford University Press.

Rivasés, Jesús. (1991). *Los secretos del Banco de España*. [Secrets of the Bank of Spain]. Madrid: Temas de Hoy.

Roeh, Itzahak. (1989). Journalism as storytelling, coverage as narrative. *American Behavioral Scientist, 33*(2), 162-168.

Roncarolo, Franca. (1994). *Controllare I media. Il Presidente americano e gli apparati nelle campagne di comunicazione permanente*. [The American President and the apparatus of the permanent communication campaign]. Milan: Franco Angeli.

Rose-Ackerman, Susan. (1999). *Corruption and government. Causes, consequences and reform*. Cambridge: Cambridge University Press.

Rospir, Juan I. (1996). Political communication and electoral campaigns in the young Spanish democracy. In David L. Swanson & Paolo Mancini (Eds.), *Politics, media and modern democracy*. New York: Praeger.

Rubio, Antonio, & Cerdán, Manuel. (1995). *El 'caso Interior'. GAL, Roldán y fondos reservados: El triángulo negro de un ministerio* [The 'Interior case'. GAL, Roldán and reserved funds: The black triangle of a ministry]. Madrid: Temas de Hoy.

Rubio, Antonio, & Cerdán, Manuel. (1997). *El origen del GAL* [The origin of GAL]. Madrid: Temas de Hoy.

Sabato, Larry. (1993). *Feeding frenzy: How attack journalism has transformed American politics*. New York: Free Press.

Sabato, Larry, Stencel, Mark, & Lichter, Robert. (2001). *Peep show. Media and politics in an age of scandal*. Lanham, Boulder, New York and Oxford: Rowman & Littlefield Publishers.

Sacks, Jonathan. (2001). Television, narrative and conversation. In Simon Higdon (Ed.), *Culture and communications. Perspectives on broadcasting and the information society* (pp.142-145). London: ITC.

Sádaba, Teresa. (2000). *La teoría del encuadre (Framing) desde una perspectiva símbolica. Una propuesta de estudio para los medios de comunicación* [Framing theory from a symbolic perspective. A study proposal for the communication media]. Unpublished doctoral thesis, University of Navarra, Pamplona.

Sanders, Karen. (1997). *Nación y tradición. Cinco discursos en torno a la nación peruana 1880-1930*. [Nation and tradition. Five discourses on the Peruvian nation 1880-1930]. Lima: Fondo de Cultura Económica / Universidad Católica.

Sanders, Karen. (2003). *Ethics and journalism*. London: Sage.

Sanders, Karen, Bale, Timothy, & Canel, María José. (1999, December). Managing sleaze. Prime ministers and news management in conservative Great Britain and socialist Spain. *European Journal of Communication, 14*(4), 461-486.

Sanders, Karen, & Harrison, Jackie. (2001). *The press and the people's princess: An analysis of the British press coverage of the death and funeral of Diana, Princess of Wales*. CD of the Proceedings of the 6th ISSEI Conference, International Society for the Study of European Ideas, Israel.

Sanders, Karen with Canel, María José. (2004). Spanish politicians and the media: Controlled visibility and soap opera politics. *Parliamentary Affairs, 57*(1), 196–208.

Scammell, Margaret. (1995). *Designer politics.* London: Macmillan.

Schlesinger, Philip. (1991). *Media, state and nation.* London: Sage.

Schlesinger, Philip, & Tumber, Howard. (1994). *Reporting crime. The media politics of criminal justice.* Oxford: Oxford University Press.

Schudson, Michael. (1992). *Watergate in American memory: How we remember, forget and reconstuct the past.* New York: Basic Books.

Schudson, Michael. (1995a). How news becomes news. *Media Critic, 2*(4), 76-85.

Schudson, Michael. (1995b). *The power of news.* Cambridge, MA, and London: Harvard University Press.

Schudson, Michael. (2000). The sociology of news production revisited (again). In James Curran & Michael Gurevitch (Eds.), *Mass media and society* (3rd ed., pp. 175-200). London: Arnold.

Schultz, Julianne. (1998). *Reviving a fourth estate: Democracy, accountability and media.* Cambridge: Cambridge University Press.

Schwartz, Barry. (1991). Iconography and collective memory: Lincoln's image in the American mind. *Sociological Quarterly, 32*, 301-319.

Scott, Sir Richard. (1996). *Report of the inquiry into the export of defence equipment and dual-use goods to Iraq and related prosecutions,* chaired by Rt. Hon. Sir Richard Scott, 1995-96.

Seldon, Anthony. (1997). *Major. A political life.* London: Weidenfeld and Nicolson.

Semetko, Holli A., Blumler, Jay G., Gurevitch, Michael, & Weaver, David H. (1991). *The formation of campaign agendas: A comparative analysis of party and media roles in recent American and British elections,* Hillsdale, NJ: Erlbaum.

Semetko, Holli A., & Canel, María José. (1997). Agenda-senders versus agenda-setters: Television in Spain's 1996 election campaign. *Political Communication, 14*(4), 457-479.

Seymor-Ure, Colin. (1974). *The political impact of the mass media.* London: Cole.

Seymor-Ure, Colin. (1982). *The American president: Power and communication.* London: Macmillan.

Seymour-Ure, Colin. (1996). *The British press and broadcasting since 1945* (2nd ed). Oxford: Blackwell.

Seymour-Ure, Colin. (1998, March). *Why study Prime Ministers' and Presidents' news operations?* Unpublished paper presented at the European Consortium for Political Research Joint Sessions, Warwick, United Kingdom.

Seymour-Ure, Colin. (2000). Prime Ministers and Presidents' News Operations. What effects on the job? In Howard Tumber (Ed.), *Media, power, professionals, and policies* (pp. 151–166). London: Routledge.

Shannon, Richard. (2001). *A press free and responsible. Self-regulation and the press complaints commission 1991-2001.* London: John Murray.

Sherman, Lawrence W. (1978). The mobilization of scandal. In Lawrence Sherman (Ed.), *Scandal and reform: Controlling police corruption.* Berkeley: University of California Press.

Shoemaker, Pamela J., & Reese, Stephen. (1996). *Mediating the message. Theories of influences on mass media content.* New York: Longman.

Sigal, L.V. (1973). *Reporters and officials*. Lexington, MA: D.C. Heath.

Silverstone, Roger. (1999). *Why study the media?* London: Sage.

Simon, Siôn. (2001, March 12). Labour's not as sleazy as it seems, believe me. *Daily Telegraph*, p. 21.

Smith, Craig Allen. (1983). The audiences of the 'rhetorical presidency': An analysis of presidential-constituent interactions, 1963-1981. *Presidential Studies Quarterly, 13*, 613-622.

Smith, Craig Allen. (1996). Rough stretches and honest disagreements: Is Bill Clinton redefining the rhetorical presidency? In Robert E. Denton & Rachel L. Halloway (Eds.), *The Clinton presidency. Images, issues and communication strategies*. Westport, CT: Praeger.

Smith, Craig Allen, & Smith, Kathy B. (1985). Presidential values and public priorities: Recurrent patterns in addresses to the nation, 1963-1984. *Presidential Studies Quarterly, 15*, 743-753.

Smith, Craig Allen, & Smith, Kathy, B. (1994). *The White House speaks: Presidential leadership as persuasion*. Westport, CT: Praeger.

Smith, Stephen A. (Ed.). (1994). *Clinton on stump, state and stage: The rhetorical road to the White House*. Fayetteville: University of Arkansas Press.

Smith, Trevor. (1995). Causes, concerns and cures. In F.F. Ridley & Alan Doig (Eds.), *Sleaze: Politicians, private interests and public reactions* (pp. 3-13). Oxford: Oxford University Press.

Snow, Jon. (1997, January 27). More bad news. *The Guardian*.

Soukop, Paul A. (1997). Church, media, and scandal. In James Lull & Stephen Hinerman (Eds.), *Media scandals. Morality and desire in the popular culture marketplace* (pp. 222–239). Cambridge: Polity Press.

Sparks, Colin, & Tulloch, J. (Eds.). (2000). *Tabloid tales: Global debates over media standards*. London, Boulder, New York, Oxford, MD: Rowman & Littlefield.

Stanyer, James, & Wring, Dominic. (Eds.). (2004). Public images, private lives: The mediation of politicians around the globe. *Parliamentary Affairs, 57*.

Stephenson, Hugh, & Bromley, Michael. (Eds.). (1998). *Sex, lies and democracy. The press and the public*. London and New York: Longman.

Stone, Lawrence. (1979). The revival of narrative: Reflections on a new old history. *Past and Present, 85*, 3-24.

Sweeney, J. (1993). *Trading with the enemy: Britain's arming of Iraq*. London: Pan.

Takeshita, Toshio. (1997). Exploring the media's role in defining reality: From issue-agenda setting to attribute-agenda setting. In Maxwell McCombs, Donald L. Shaw, & David Weaver (Eds.), *Communication and democracy. Exploring the intellectual frontiers in agenda-setting theory* (pp. 15-27). Hillsdale, NJ: Erlbaum.

Tankard, James et al. (1991). *Media frames: Approaches to conceptualization and measurement*. Unpublished paper presented to the Association for Education in Journalism and Mass Communication, Boston.

Tarrow, Sidney. (1997). *El poder en movimiento. Los movimientos sociales, la acción colectiva y la política* [Power in movement. Social movements, collective action and politics]. Madrid: Alianza Universal.

Taylor, Charles. (1971). Interpretation and the sciences of man. *Review of Metaphysics, 25*, 3-51.

Theil, Stefan, & Dickey, Christopher. (2002, 29 April). Europe's dirty secret. *Newsweek*, pp. 12-15.

Thompson, John B. (1995). *Media and modernity. A social theory of the media.* Stanford, CA: Stanford University Press.

Thompson, John B. (1997). Scandal and social theory. In James Lull & Stephen Hinerman (Eds.), *Media scandals. Morality and desire in the popular culture marketplace* (pp. 34-64). Cambridge: Polity Press.

Thompson, John B. (2000). *Political scandal. Power and visibility in the media age.* Cambridge: Polity.

Tiffen, R. (1989). *News and power.* Sydney: Allen & Unwin.

Time Magazine (1998, 22 June). The cancer of corruption.

Tomkins, Adam. (1998). *The constitution after Scott. Government unwrapped.* Oxford: Clarendon Press.

Tomlinson, John. (1997). "And besides, the wench is dead": Media scandals and the globalization of communication. In James Lull & Stephen Hinerman (Eds.), *Media scandals. Morality and desire in the popular culture marketplace* (pp. 65-84). Cambridge: Polity Press.

Tortosa, Jose María. (1995). *Corrupción* [Corruption]. Barcelona: Icaria.

Tulis, Jeffrey. (1987). *The rhetorical presidency.* Princeton, NJ: Princeton University Press.

Tumber, Howard, & Waisbord, Silvio R. (Eds.). (2004). Political scandal, and media across democracies. Vols. I and II. *American Behavioral Scientist, 47*(8).

Tunstall, Jeremy. (1971). *Journalists at work: Specialist correspondents, their news organizations, news sources, and competitor-colleagues.* London: Constable.

Tunstall, Jeremy. (1996). *Newspaper power. The new national press in Britain.* Oxford: Clarendon Press.

Tversky, A., & Kahneman, D. (1990). Rational choice and the framing of decisions. In K. S. Cool & M. Levi (Eds.), *The limits of rationality* (pp. 60-89). Chicago: University of Chicago Press.

Urbano, Pilar. (2000). *Garzón. El hombre que veía amanecer* [Garzón. The man who saw the dawn]. Barcelona: Plaza & Janés.

Waisbord, Silvio. (2000). *Watchdog journalism in South America: News, accountability and democracy.* New York: Columbia University Press.

Weaver. David H. (Ed.). (1998). *The global journalist: News people around the world.* Cresskill, NJ: Hampton Press.

Welch, Stephen. (1993). *The concept of political culture.* Basingstoke, Hampshire: The Macmillan Press.

White, Hayden. (1984). The question of narrative in contemporary historical theory. *History and Theory, 23,* 1-33.

Wimmer, Roger D., & Dominick, Joseph R. (2000). *Mass media research: An introduction* (6th ed.). Belmont, CA and London: Wadsworth.

Yates, Frances A. (1994). *The art of memory.* London: Pimlico.

Zald, Mayer N. (1999). Cultura, ideología y creación de marcos estratégicos [Culture, ideology and the creation of strategic frames]. In Doug McAdam, John D. McCarthy, & Mayer N. Zald (Eds.), *Movimientos sociales: Perspectivas comparadas* [Social movements: Comparative perspectives] (pp. 369-388). Madrid: Istmo.

Zelizer, Barbie. (1992). *Covering the body. The Kennedy assassination, the media, and the shaping of collective memory.* Chicago: University of Chicago Press.

Author Index

Subject Index

Printed in the United States
42002LVS00002B/207

ALIEN CAPITAL

ALIEN CAPITAL

ASIAN RACIALIZATION AND THE LOGIC
OF SETTLER COLONIAL CAPITALISM

IYKO DAY

Duke University Press | Durham and London | 2016

Designed by Heather Hensley
Typeset in Whitman by Tseng Information Systems, Inc.

Library of Congress Cataloging-in-Publication Data
Day, Iyko, [date] author.
Alien capital : Asian racialization and the logic of settler
colonial capitalism / Iyko Day.
pages cm
Includes bibliographical references and index.
ISBN 978-0-8223-6079-7 (hardcover : alk. paper)
ISBN 978-0-8223-6093-3 (pbk. : alk. paper)
ISBN 978-0-8223-7452-7 (e-book)
1. Capitalism — Social aspects — North America — History.
2. Asians — Race identity — North America. 3. Asians — North
America — Public opinion. 4. Stereotypes (Social psychology) —
North America. 5. North America — Race relations —
Economic aspects. I. Title.
HC95.D35 2016
305.895′07309034 — dc23   2015034387

Cover art: Tommy Ting, *Workers Posing as Workers*
(Chinese Workers for the Great Northern Railway), 2013,
inkjet print, recycled wood, 167 × 298 cm.

Duke University Press gratefully acknowledges Mount Holyoke
College, Dean of the Faculty's Office, which provided funds
toward the publication of this book.

For
DAVID
and
TEI

CONTENTS

ACKNOWLEDGMENTS

It is a welcome pleasure to reflect on entirely different forms of debt and exchange value than those covered in this book. In another world I would send each friend I've neglected to mention here a nice box of chocolates. Words aren't enough, but for now they are a taste of my sincere gratitude to those who helped see me through this project.

This book was inspired and nurtured by great conversations with very smart people, generous readers, and an abundance of external sources of optimism and humor. For many years I have been blessed with the brilliant likes of David Hernández and Jodi Kim; these two have always been my first line of intellectual support, reading numerous drafts, answering a thousand questions, and hearing out all of the turns in my thinking. In Sylvia Chan-Malik and Wes Yu I could not have asked for smarter interlocutors or more sustaining friendships. This work also benefited from the inspiration and wisdom of longtime friends and coconspirators Dory Nason, Danika Medak-Saltzman, and Ofelia Cuevas. Years have passed since my days as a graduate student, but I remain indebted to my professors at UC Berkeley. I continue to be in awe of the brilliance and grace of my dissertation adviser, Sau-ling Wong; the instincts and generosity of Elaine Kim; and the friendship and steadfast support of Michael Omi. And a long-overdue thanks must go to Chris Nealon, not least for encouraging me to read Moishe Postone's *Time, Labor, and Social Domination*, which became an indispensable anchor for this book.

Networks across the United States and Canada were crucial for providing intellectual spaces for the development of my ideas. Mount Holyoke College has been an incredibly generative place to carry out this work, and I'm grateful to my wonderful colleagues in the English department for their supportive engagement over the years. I owe a special debt to Nigel Alderman, Don Weber, Amy Martin, and Elizabeth Young for all of their wise counsel in both research and teaching. Likewise, I am grateful for my colleagues in the Five College Asian/Pacific/American Studies Program for all of the intellectual sustenance they provided. The Connecticut Valley has been an unexpectedly vibrant cultural space, and it has been my pure fortune to have had the opportunity to cross paths with Asha Nadkarni, Diana Yoon, Manu Vimalassery, Jane Degenhardt, Sujani Reddy, Ronaldo Wilson, Tony Tiongson, Siraj Ahmed, Floyd Cheung, and Cathy Schlund-Vials. In Southern California I have cherished the limitless generosity, wisdom, and friendship of Mariam Lam, Setsu Shigematsu, Keith Camacho, and Dylan Rodríguez. Beyond nation-state lines, I am grateful for my fellow Asian Canadianists Chris Lee, Rob Ho, Marie Lo, Henry Yu, Thy Phu, Lily Cho, Guy Beauregard, and Andy Yan. I don't see them enough, but our conversations over the years have taught me so much about the country that Richard Rodriguez once referred to as "the largest country that doesn't exist." Extra-special thanks goes to my editor Courtney Berger for her openness, encouragement, and amazing professional acumen. She is simply the best. I am similarly indebted to the anonymous reviewers for their indispensable editorial advice on the manuscript, as well as to the peer reviewers of an earlier version of the second chapter, which appeared as "Tseng Kwong Chi and the Eugenic Landscape" in *American Quarterly* 65.1 (2013).

I close with thanks to my dear family. I am ever amazed by my talented mother, Yumie Kono; I'm grateful to her for infusing my life with beauty and art. My father, George Day, has continually uplifted me with his humor, optimism, and generosity. Heartfelt appreciation goes to Jack Day, Wendy Lynwood, Donna Day, and the rest of the Day, Kono, and Hernández clans for their love and support. Finally, I am grateful to David Hernández and our daughter, Tei, for a home life that is equal parts love and pure fun. This book is for them.

THE NEW JEWS

Settler Colonialism and the
Personification of Capitalism

No Jew can smell out with keener instinct an opportunity
where money can be made to grow than can a Chinaman.
—*Atlantic Monthly*, 1900

Racial Capital

In August 2012, Bank of Canada governor Mark Carney issued a public apology for purging an image of a female Asian scientist from the newly designed one-hundred-dollar polymer banknote. She was replaced by a "Caucasian-looking woman"[1] who is seen peering through a microscope (figure I.1). In the foreground appears a bottle of insulin that symbolizes nationalist ingenuity through medical innovation. Based on internal reports obtained by the Canadian Press, the decision to remove the Asian scientist came in response to focus groups who previewed the design in Montreal and Charlottetown and felt that her Asian appearance "did not represent Canada"[2] and was "exclusionary . . . since the banknote didn't represent other ethnicities."[3] Although the bank declined requests to release the initial design to the public, a bank spokesperson indicated that the image of a "Caucasian-looking woman" was substituted to "restore neutral ethnicity."[4] News of the bank's decision met sharp criticism from Asian advocacy groups, particularly the Chinese Canadian National Coun-

FIGURE I.1   One-hundred-dollar Canadian bill, Bank of Canada.

cil, who criticized the bank and urged it to stop "'erasing' visible minorities from Canada's money."[5]

This controversy highlights this book's central focus on the interplay of Asian racialization, capitalism, and settler colonialism that, as I will develop below, reveals an economic modality that links constructions of the Asian and the Jew. At first glance, the controversy sheds light on the ever-simmering tension between race and national culture in Canada. In particular, the bank's equation of a "Caucasian-looking woman" with race "neutrality" exposes the normativity of whiteness in an officially multicultural nation. That an erased woman of color's body serves as the battleground for adjudicating cultural legitimacy participates in a long-standing objectification of nonwhite female bodies as litmus tests of racial, gender, sexual, and here *national* normativity and deviance.[6] The Chinese Canadian National Council's admonishment attempts to bare these contradictions but ultimately endorses the superimposing of multicultural iconography onto capital. Even US-based blogger Phil "Angry Asian Man" Yu weighed in on the politics of representation, calling the controversy "racebending on a banknote."[7] In response to focus group members who objected to the Asian scientist for being too stereotypical, Yu remarks, "Sure there is a stereotype of Asians excelling in math or science. But let's be real. The reason why people didn't want an Asian-looking woman on the $100 bill is because an Asian-looking woman couldn't possibly represent a face of Canada. Thus, the rush to redesign her with more Caucasian features."[8] For the Chinese Canadian National Council, "Angry Asian Man," and countless other bloggers and YouTube vloggers, the controversy's significance turns on the variable race of the scientist against the assumed stability of the money form of capital as a representation of nation. To restore the "Asian-looking" characteristics to the scientist would, by extension, restore equilibrium between race and nation. But what seems to be missing from this discussion is the peculiar intersection of race and money—of race as a form of money, or vice versa. How do we understand the variability of money as capitalist (rather than solely nationalist) fetish and its own racialized personas?

For the purposes of this book, the controversy dramatizes ways that Asian North Americans are uncomfortably associated with capital. More benign expressions of this association arise out of recognition of the upward economic mobility of Asians in North America over the twentieth century, which, at least temporarily, secured Asian Canadian representation on the Canadian one-hundred-dollar bill and have earned Asian Americans the title of the "new Jews."[9] Both expressions refer to the increasing affluence and assimilation of a historically excluded minority. In the case of the Asian-Jewish analogy, Matthew Frye Jacobson's discussion of the evolution of Jewish American immigrant identity from a non-Anglo-Saxon to a Caucasian social position in the nineteenth to mid-twentieth centuries emphasizes the progressive and linear orientation of the analogy.[10] This progressive emphasis is amplified in the 2012 Pew Research Center study "The Rise of Asian America," which reported that Asians were the highest-income (earning 33 percent more than median-income households), best-educated, and fastest-growing racial group in the United States.[11] Despite numerous scholarly objections to the Pew Research Center's failure to identify the extended configuration of most Asian households, the high-cost urban residential concentration of those families, and the pronounced income disparities between Asian ethnicities,[12] these facts have had little countervailing influence on the mainstream perception that Asians are more hurt than helped by affirmative action policies. Moreover, from Thomas Friedman's recommendation that US children adopt the competitive traits of their Chinese and Indian counterparts[13] to Québec politician François Legault's declaration that "kids in Québec should work harder, like Asians,"[14] the attributes of Asians in Asia and North America are to be ignored at one's economic peril.

Coupled with the benign recognition of Asian North American educational and economic achievement are more unsettling aspects of the Asian-Jewish analogy. For instance, *Los Angeles Times* reporter Gregory Rodriguez emphasizes how "the Jewish comparison has a dark side."[15] According to Rodriguez, the victorious narrative of the civil rights movement has contributed to the misguided belief that "economic status rises as prejudice decreases, and vice versa . . . [and] that bias is always targeted downward at the weakest and the most vulnerable in society."[16] In other words, the Asian-Jewish analogy should not be read as an indication of what Susan Koshy refers to as a "morphing of race into ethnicity,"[17] a theory stating that Asians in North America have evolved from discriminated racial minority to assimilated ethnic group over the twentieth century. Rather, according to Rodriguez, the Asian-Jewish analogy compels recognition of the *economic* contexts of modern anti-Semitism, which he characterizes as "distrust or disdain of Jews [which] can sometimes be motivated by envy or resentment of an identifiably separate group that's significantly wealthier than the population at large."[18] The economic conflation of Asians and Jews has a long history, explains Jonathan Freedman, who notes that "like Jews, Chinese merchants were traditionally active throughout East and South Asia and faced—again like Jews—resentment, discrimination, and even the occasional pogrom as a result."[19] Intersecting expressions of industriousness, greed, and evil have been infused in popular culture representations of both groups in Europe and North America, from novelist George Du Maurier's 1895 creation of the Jewish-descended Svengali to novelist Sax Rohmer's 1921 invention of Fu Manchu.[20] Both characters are perverse, evil geniuses who aspire to world domination.

Turning back to the controversy over the one-hundred-dollar bill, the bank's initial effort to present an image that promotes Canadian medical innovation through the figure of the Asian Canadian scientist aligns Asian subjects with capital in more abstract, nonhuman ways. In particular, the characteristics of the model minority stereotype—educated, disciplined, obedient—embodied by the Asian Canadian scientist increasingly emphasize economic over human attributes. As Helen Jun explains, the model minority represents the ideal neoliberal subject who manifests the qualities she refers to as "human capital," a term coined by economist Gary Becker in the 1960s to emphasize the role that education plays in adding value to labor.[21] As human capital, the individual is regarded as an "enterprise" driven by market values who embodies an "infinite capacity for 'self-development.'"[22] Jun draws the connection between neoliberal capital and the racialization of Asian Americans in ways that can be extended to the Canadian context:

> We can see that the neoliberal theory of human capital and its notion of individual enterprise and self-regulation are not merely evident in Asian American model minority discourse but are also key tenets by which Asian American racial difference came to be defined in the post-1965 period. The centrality of educational achievement and the importance of family in contemporary discourses of Asian American racial difference are no mere coincidence, as neoliberal theories of human capital championed education and parenting as the most critical investments promising the highest rates of return.[23]

What this passage highlights is how key aspects of model minority discourse are reflected in Asian American racialization as a form of market-driven instrumentality. Further bridging market instrumentality and racial form, the Bank of Canada's "Asian-looking" banknote takes Jun's notion of Asian American human capital to another level by symbolically removing the "human." Projected onto the one-hundred-dollar bill, the Asian Canadian scientist is not merely a form of human capital but a representation of capital itself. Moreover, the eventual jettisoning of her image suggests that she signified an offensive form of capital that had to be "neutralized" by whiteness.

As the personification of bad capital, the rejected "Asian-looking" one-hundred-dollar bill evokes prior economic modalities that have shaped Asian racialization. For instance, Colleen Lye's discussion of pre-1942 expressions of anti-Japanese sentiment in California agriculture demonstrates how economic resentment toward Japanese farmers is represented through the sphere of monopoly capitalism. In the naturalist fiction she examines, Lye notes how the "homogenizing evils of monopoly are entirely displaced onto sinister Japanese characters."[24] It is the "inorganic quality of the Asiatic body"[25] that manifests the "intangibly abstract" threat of finance capital.[26] Reflecting on the role of economic tropes embedded in racist representations of Japanese American success in agriculture in the early twentieth century, a success mirrored by Japanese Canadians in the British Columbia fishing industry, Lye points to what she calls the "economism of Asiatic racial form—a form in which economic interests are not masked but are the primary medium of race's historical expression."[27] The Canadian hundred-dollar-bill controversy is a heightened expression of this economism of racial form insofar as the dehumanized economism of the Asian simultaneously represents the personification of capital.

What precedes the economism of Asian racial form is the similarly destructive economism historically attributed to Jews, highlighting more disturbing implications of the "New Jews" appellation. In his essay "Anti-Semitism and National Socialism," Moishe Postone focuses on the secular elements of anti-Semitism that flourished under National Socialism in Germany, illustrating a historical process by which Jews became associated with the *abstract* evils of capitalism. Because Jews had long been segregated in finance and interest-generating sectors of European society, traditional anti-Semitism identified them as owners of money. Perhaps the most notorious literary example of traditional anti-Semitism is Shakespeare's Shylock, the sinister usurer in *The Merchant of Venice*, whose penalty for late payment is nothing short of a pound of flesh. However, by the nineteenth century, modern anti-Semitism not only identified Jews as the owners of money but "held [them] responsible for economic crises and identified [them] with the range of social restructuring and dislocation resulting from rapid industrialization: explosive urbanization, the decline of traditional social classes and strata, the emergence of a large, increasingly organized industrial proletariat."[28] In short, as Postone explains, "They [Jews] became the *personification* of the intangible, destructive, immensely powerful, and international domination of capital as a social form."[29] Here the attributes of "abstractness, intangibility, universality, mobility"[30] that are associated with Jews are striking in their resonance with characteristic forms of Asian racialization in North America. The racial signifiers of inscrutability, perpetual foreignness, transnational mobility, and flexibility similarly register the abstract features of Asian racialization that this book aligns with the evolution of settler colonial capitalism in North America.

The controversy over the Bank of Canada's initial design of the one-hundred-dollar bill and the "new Jews" analogy may suggest that Asian racialization has entered a new historical phase. Indeed, the model minority stereotype seems far afield from the historical repertoire of yellow perilism denoting disease, vice, and destruction. But rather than expressions associated with two distinct phases, "yellow peril" and the "model minority" stereotype function as complementary aspects of the same form of racialization, in which economic efficiency is the basis for exclusion *or* assimilation. This book therefore engages in the task of demonstrating how the contemporary economism of Asian racial form does not represent a break from the past but rather is part of a continuum of settler colonial capitalism and its racial formations. Building on scholarship that examines the economic modalities of "Asiatic racial form" depicted in the interplay of art and policy by white producers,[31] I focus on contemporary Asian American and Asian Canadian literature and visual culture as a transnational genealogy of settler colonialism's capitalist logics. What Asian North American cultural producers reveal in their rearticulation of settler colonial mythologies is how capitalism operates as a system of representation that is objective but immaterial, immanent but subject to resignification. My methodology is influenced by Marx's dialectical method, which emphasizes dynamic relations rather than causation to illuminate the dualities and contradictions that emerge from capitalism. I am similarly guided by Fredric Jameson's argument that the most important task of cultural interpretation is to reveal a work's "political unconscious."[32] In this spirit, I look to ways that Asian North American cultural production similarly magnifies settler colonial mythologies to reveal a system of representation that reproduces the logic of capitalism. The expansive, transnational scope of the archive also offers a framework for highlighting patterns and convergences across settler colonial borders.

This book's primary thesis is that Asian North American literature and visual culture present a genealogy of settler colonialism that magnifies a key logic of romantic anticapitalism. Romantic anticapitalism is the misperception of the *appearance* of capitalist relations for their essence, a misperception that stems from Marx's notion of the fetish. As Neil Levi points out, what romantic anticapitalism "solves is a problem of representation . . . possess[ing] an intrinsically aesthetic dimension."[33] As an aesthetic dimension, therefore, Asians give human shape to the abstract circuits of capitalism that have "no concrete manifestation, that are quite literally *unrepresentable*."[34] In the manner that Jews came to personify processes internal to finance capital under National Socialism, I argue that the Asian subject in North America personifies abstract processes of value formation anchored by labor. From the economic efficiency associated with Asian racialization, denigrated as "cheap" labor in the nineteenth century and valued as "efficient" in the twenty-first, Asian North American cultural production magnifies the manner through which Asians are aligned with "abstract labor," a concept that anchors Marx's labor theory of value. It is from the vantage of abstract labor, as Dipesh Chakrabarty also notes, that capitalism is both reconstituted and potentially subverted.

Let me elaborate on this connection between race and abstract labor, which I would argue is a key logic of what Cedric Robinson calls "racial capitalism."[35] In particular, by giving material and symbolic weight to the category of abstract labor, my project diverges from the important work of scholars such as Lisa Lowe, David Roediger, and others who have argued that capitalism has profited from labor *not* by rendering it abstract but by *producing* racialized difference. For instance, in Lowe's critique of the labor theory of value, she hones in on Marx's homogenizing definition of "abstract labor 'as the use value which confronts money posited as capital, labour is not this or another labour, but *labour pure and simple*, abstract labour; absolutely indifferent to its particular specificity.'"[36] Her point is to demonstrate that capital has profited from the specifically gendered and racialized character of labor, qualities that are far from indistinguishable or abstract. She presents the notion of abstract labor as the erroneous basis of an equally flawed conception of abstract citizenship in the political sphere:

> Abstract labor, subject to capitalist rationalization and the logic of equivalence through wages, is the adjunct of the formal political equality granted through rights and representation by the state. Yet in the history of the United States, capital has maximized its profits not through rendering labor "abstract" but precisely through the social productions of "difference," of restrictive particularity and illegitimacy marked by race, nation, geographical origins, and gender. The law of value has operated, instead, by creating, preserving, and reproducing the specifically racialized and gendered character of labor power.[37]

In short, she writes, "Asian immigrants and Asian Americans have been neither 'abstract labor' nor 'abstract citizens.'"[38] David Roediger extends this line of argument, asserting that "far from flattening difference by buying undifferentiated units of labor power, US management studiously bought into inequality, preserving and continually recreating race."[39]

While my project is in harmony with the claim that capitalism produces racialized difference, I propose that these differentiating effects are not in contradiction with Marx's formulation of abstract labor. What is missing from Lowe's and Roediger's critiques of abstract labor is a recognition of its dialectical relation to concrete labor. Concrete labor represents the racial, gendered, and qualitatively distinct form of *actual* labor that is rendered abstract as a value expression. Where I locate the principal violence of capitalism is in the very way it abstracts (or renders homogeneous as commensurable units of labor) highly differentiated gendered and racialized labor *in order to create value*. It is therefore the law of value that obscures the racial and gendered character of labor power. For value itself is what necessitates what we could characterize as the metaphoric process of turning particular labor into quantifiable units of abstract labor. So in response to the suggestion that racialized labor is *irreducible* to the conception of abstract labor because of its gendered and racial particularity, no value would be produced if this were the case. Rather, *all* commodity-determined labor plays a socially mediating role that is structured by time. Capital maximizes profit by controlling time: socially necessary labor time. Nothing prevents the exploitation of racial and gendered labor from being a "social necessity" that determines average labor time. Indeed, one core logic of the settler colonial mode of production I explore in this book centers on the systematic exploitation of a racialized, gendered, and sexualized alien labor force. The structuring role of time is precisely the reason that capitalism is an *abstract* form of domination, what Petrus Liu characterizes as "impersonal domination."[40] This doesn't mean that we don't daily bear witness to brutal working conditions or the near enslavement of racialized and gendered labor; rather, the very violence of labor abstraction, what Richard Godden calls "the founding moment of abstraction,"[41] is what subsumes the horrors of highly differentiated labor into an abstracted quantity that is commensurable with all other things. It is the duplicity of value as a social relation that Marx denounces, such that "the various proportions in which different kinds of labour are reduced to simple labour as their unit of measurement are established by a social process that goes on behind the backs of the producers."[42] To put it another way, we don't control the products of our labor; we are controlled *by* the products of our labor. Therefore, while I agree that capitalism produces racialized difference, this book defines social differentiation as a form of destructive abstraction anchored by a settler colonial ideology of romantic anticapitalism.

Romantic Anticapitalism

The historical processes that encode a romanticized distinction between concrete and abstract social relations grow out of Marx's identification of an internalized duality within the commodity. Romantic anticapitalism's confusion over the appearance and essence of the commodity is what Marx refers to as its "fetishism." While a focus on the fetishism of the commodity appears initially removed from the realm of race and social relations, the commodity is foundational to Marx's labor theory of value, which structures social—and hence race, gender, and sexual—relations within a capitalist mode of production. The chief effect of this fetishism is the appearance of capitalist social relations as antinomical: that an antinomy or opposition exists between concrete and abstract realms of society. Under a romantic anticapitalist view, what is real, sensory, or "thingly" is the tree in your backyard, the dusty work boots by the door, the reliable pickup truck in the driveway. These make up the concrete realm. What is unnatural, nonthingly, or intangible is capital accumulation, surplus-value, and money. These form the abstract realm. Therefore, as Levi clarifies, "romantic anticapitalism . . . hypostatizes the concrete, rooted, and organic, and identifies capitalism solely with the abstract dimension of the antinomy."[43] The antinomical view that characterizes romantic anticapitalism *glorifies* the concrete dimension while casting as evil the abstract domination of capitalism. In particular, the specific power attributed to Jews under National Socialism anthropomorphizes the internal workings of the commodity itself. What is remarkable is how the traits of mobility, abstractness, immateriality, and universality that modern anti-Semitism identifies with Jews are the very same characteristics that Marx uses to describe the commodity's value dimension. However, as Postone clarifies, "this [value] dimension—like the supposed power of the Jews—does not appear as such, rather always in the form of a material carrier, such as the commodity. The carrier thus has a 'double character'—value and use-value."[44] In other words, what romantic anticapitalism misunderstands is that value, while seemingly abstract, is nonetheless objectified within the concrete, sensory form of the commodity during the exchange process. Pulling away the veil of the fetish will reveal that commodities are above all the representations (carriers) of social processes that are objectified in things, and as Marx puts it, "its analysis brings out that it is a very strange thing."[45]

The main secret hidden within the commodity is that it comprises a duality of abstract and concrete dimensions. In a section of volume 1 of *Capital* titled "The Dual Character of the Labour Embodied in Commodities," Marx explains that the commodity internalizes two aspects: (a) use-value (a thing of use) and (b) exchange value (the exchangeability of that thing). Here we can observe a distinction between these two characteristics of the commodity; a use-value is concrete in a material sense—a table, for instance—but exchange value is abstract and immaterial in the sense that we can't see or touch it. Dissecting the labor that produces the commodity, Marx continues by saying that "labour, too, has a dual character insofar as [when] it finds its expression in value, it no longer possesses the same characteristics as when it is the creator of use-values."[46] Unpacking this distinction, concrete labor refers to a specific activity—whether hammering or cooking—that produces a use-value. On the other, it is "abstract labor" that objectifies a commodity's value. Before we move on, we can pause to observe a fundamental point about value, which is that it is *immaterial but ob-*

jective:[47] "We may twist and turn a single commodity as we wish; it remains impossible to grasp it as a thing possessing value. . . . Commodities possess an objective character as values *only* in so far as they are all expressions of an identical social substance, human labor."[48] Like gravity, value is invisible but real. What gives objectivity to the value of commodities, Marx asserts, is that they are products of human labor. A commodity's value, therefore, is what Marx defines as "socially necessary labor time." But what determines "social necessity"? This, it turns out, is part of the distinction between abstract and concrete labor.

The main difference between concrete and abstract labor is temporal. The actual time it takes to produce a commodity in the case of concrete labor has no immediate bearing on a particular commodity's value. If it did, a commodity would become more valuable the *slower* a worker labored to produce it, or as Marx puts it, a given product "would be more valuable the more unskillful and lazy the worker who produced it, because he would need more time to complete the article."[49] Concrete labor will only tell us how well made a commodity is; it is the *qualitative* dimension of use-value.[50] On the other hand, abstract labor is a *quantitative* expression of value—it is an unfixed social average of human labor time. As Marx explains, "In the former case [of concrete labor] it was a matter of the 'how' and the 'what' of labour, in the latter [abstract labor] of the 'how much,' of the temporal duration of labor."[51] Time is the ultimate measure of abstract labor and the magnitude of a commodity's value. The quantity of time in abstract labor is not individual or provisional but *socially necessary*. Marx writes, "Socially necessary labour-time is the labour-time required to produce any use-value under the conditions of production normal for a given society and with the average degree of skill and intensity of labour prevalent in that society."[52] From this view of the dual character of labor embodied in the commodity, we see how concrete labor is more directly aligned with the *qualitative* production of use-value, while abstract labor is more directly aligned with the *quantitative* dimension of value. While use-value and value are inseparable, internal features of each and every commodity, they nevertheless *appear* on the surface as discrete.

Money *generalizes* the exchange of commodities and reinforces the fetishistic appearance that use-value and value are oppositional rather than part of the internal duality of the commodity. Marx historicizes money's emergence through his discussion of commodity value. He explains that the only way we can determine the value of a commodity is when it is in motion: through its exchange with a different commodity. In a simple barter situation, I might exchange two forks for your bowl. The magnitude of value — the amount of socially necessary labor time — embedded in my forks and your bowl becomes visible (or objective) only in the exchange process. What we find is that your one bowl holds the equivalent value of my two forks; my two forks express the relative value of your one bowl. Over time certain commodities come to stand as the *universal* equivalent because they offer a stable measure of equivalent value. Historically, gold and other metals have played this role. So, rather than exchanging my two forks for your one bowl, I would give you two forks in exchange for an equivalent value in gold. While gold is useful for expressing equivalent value, carrying it around and circulating it can be cumbersome, which brings us to paper money. Paper money was once the representation of real gold held in a bank, but now it is a representation of floating value contained in a bundled commodity index. As a universal equivalent, the money commodity can be exchanged with any other commodity and express any another commodity's value. Here's the takeaway: after money generalizes the exchange of commodities, money *seems* solely an expression of value rather than of use-value (as a useful piece of colored paper with numbers on it, for example). Marx makes a further observation of the way the commodity's internal duality is expressed externally:

> The internal opposition between use-value and value, hidden within the commodity, is therefore represented on the surface by an external opposition, i.e. by a relation between two commodities such that the one commodity, *whose own* value is supposed to be expressed, counts directly only as a use-value, whereas the other commodity, *in which* that value is to be expressed, counts directly only as exchange-value. Hence, the simple form of value of a commodity is the simple form of the appearance of the opposition between use-value and value which is contained within the commodity.[53]

What this means is that the duality of use-value and value, which are internal characteristics of the commodity, are expressed *externally* as an opposition between commodities and money.

The social consequences of how a binary rather than dialectical view of use-value and value is such that the use-value dimension appears empirically-grounded while the latter, value dimension appears ephemeral or abstract. Specifically, the dialectical tension between value and use-value in the commodity requires that its dual character be materially externalized in the value form, where it appears "doubled" as money (the manifest form of value) and the commodity (the manifest form of use-value). The effect of this externalization, as Postone elaborates, is that "the commodity, although it is a social form expressing both value and use-value, appears to *contain only the latter, i.e., appears as purely material and 'thingly'*; money, on the other hand, then appears to be the *sole repository of value*, i.e., as the manifestation of the purely abstract, rather than as the externalized manifest form of the value dimension of the commodity itself."[54] The point here is that even though a fork and money are both commodities that internalize use-value and value, the fork appears only as a concrete "thingly" use-value and the money as an abstract source of value. This illusory opposition is at the core of the commodity fetish, which disguises the *actual* basis of value, which is "socially necessary labor time." A key aspect of the fetish, then, is the mystification of capitalist social relations that present themselves antinomically, *as the opposition of the abstract and concrete*. Within this antinomy, the social relations specific to capitalism appear as an opposition between the concreteness of labor, commodities, and nature, on one hand, and the abstractness of money and finance, on the other. Moreover, within this fetishistic antinomy, the very origins of value — socially necessary labor time — are completely repressed.

In the nineteenth century, we can see how the social consequences of this antinomical view of capitalist social relations emerge and take on racial significance. As capitalism underwent rapid expansion, the externalization of abstract and concrete forms intrinsic to the commodity fetish became increasingly biologized and racialized in concert with prevailing socio-scientific conceptions of the world. The proliferation of scientific racism with the rise of social Darwinism in the late nineteenth century is an example of how society and historical development were increasingly understood in biological terms, moving from a more mechanical or typological worldview in which events were a reflection of divine power and design to a more secularized, biologized worldview that naturalized an antinomical view of capitalist relations. Enduring features of romanticism, the aesthetic movement that emerged in the nineteenth century, exhibit such a biologized worldview in its human (and often racial and national) identification with the purity of the natural world, portrayed as the valorized antithesis to the negative influences of urbanization and industrialization. From the anti-materialism expressed in Henry David Thoreau's excursion to Walden Pond in the nineteenth century to Christopher McCandless's 1992 divestment of all symbols of material wealth—even setting fire to his remaining cash—for a life in the wilderness,[55] we can discern a romantic attachment to a revitalizing and pure construction of an unchanging nature, in contrast to the alienation attributed to capitalist modernity. Expressing the antinomy of concrete and abstract, nature therefore personifies concrete, perfected human relations against the social degeneration caused by the abstract circuits of capitalism.

This antinomical view of capitalism finds acute biologized expression in the context of anti-Semitism. During Germany's rapid industrialization in the nineteenth century, Jews were perceived as an all-powerful international conspiracy that orchestrated capitalism. Jews not only were identified with money but became a personification of the destructive nature and abstract domination of capital. In other words, the concrete side of this antinomy was naturalized and biologized as real, hardworking Germans. German labor and machines were glorified as concrete "counter principles to the abstract."[56] Alternatively, the manifest abstract dimension of money and finance became biologized as the Jews. As Postone explains, "Jews were not merely identified with money, with the sphere of circulation, but with capitalism itself."[57] Jews came to personify the "intangible, destructive, immensely powerful and international domination of capital as a social form."[58] His insight here is to identify an anticapitalist element of National Socialism that, in *misrecognizing* the role of the antinomy in capitalism, strove to evacuate the world of the abstract dimensions of capitalism, which was seen as the source of all evil and oppression in the world. Jews were identified as controllers of money and thus misidentified as responsible for capitalism's oppression, a misperception based on the erroneous notion that capitalist oppression *was caused by* money—despite the reality that money and commodity forms are relative expressions of value determined by socially necessary labor time.[59] Thus even though Jews were citizens, citizenship was once again deemed politically abstract compared to the more concrete notion of the nation defined by "common language, history, tradition, and religions."[60] As Postone observes, "The only group in Europe which fulfilled the determination of citizenship as a purely political abstraction, were Jews following political emancipation in the nineteenth century. They were German or French citizens, but they were not really Germans or Frenchmen."[61] Instead, they were of the nation only "abstractly, not concretely," which was ultimately a fatal relation to the scourge of "capitalism" and the bourgeois state. Thus anti-Semitism solves a problem of representation by incorporating an aesthetic dimension that gives human form to the abstract circuits of capitalism.[62]

As the controversy over the Canadian one-hundred-dollar bill suggests, Asians too are associated with an abstract dimension of capitalism, but in a different sense. In the case of Jews, their conflation with the abstract domination of capitalism derived from their segregation in financial sectors of the economy. Alternatively, Asians have personified the abstract dimensions of capitalism through *labor time*. In the nineteenth-century context of Chinese railroad building in North America, the subject of chapter 1, the connection between the Chinese and the abstract domination of capitalism evolved through their identification with a mode of efficiency that was aligned with a perverse temporality of domestic and social reproduction. In other words, the Chinese personified the quantitative sphere of abstract labor, which threatened the concrete, qualitative sphere of white labor's social reproduction.

It is from this view of labor's socially mediating role that each chapter explores a different aspect of dominant settler colonial ideology of romantic anticapitalism that triangulates Indigenous, alien, and settler positions. Settler colonialism reinforces this triangulation through a fundamental misperception of capitalism as an opposition between a concrete natural world and a destructively abstract, value-driven one that is personified as Asian. In the sections that follow I clarify the racial interplay of settler colonial exclusion and elimination that frames my analysis of Asian North America and the personification of capitalism.

Settler Colonialism, or Postcolonial Colonialism

In this book I make the claim that the racialization of capitalism emerges from the particular contours of settler colonialism in North America whose conditions are distinct from the geopolitical context out of which modern anti-Semitism arose in Europe. At its core, settler colonialism reflects the common social, cultural, and political racial destiny of a transnational configuration that Marilyn Lake and Henry Reynolds refer to simply as "white men's countries."[63] Beginning in the nineteenth century, the spread of whiteness in nations bordering the Pacific was "a transnational form of racial identification [that was] at once global in its power and personal in its meaning, the basis of geo-political alliance and a subjective sense of self."[64] It was against the backdrop of Indigenous dispossession and the "problem" of Asian migration that settler colonial expansion could be justified through ideologies of liberal democracy. As Adam McKeown notes of the benevolence with which border controls were implemented, "The controls were created by white settler nations around the Pacific that saw themselves as the forefront of the liberal freedoms of the nineteenth century. . . . Modern border controls are not a remnant of an 'illiberal' political tradition, but a product of self-conscious pioneers of political freedoms and self-rule."[65] Thus the patterns of Indigenous decimation and dispossession, racialized labor recruitment and exploitation, immigrant restriction, and internment are evolving elements that tie Canada and the United States to a racial destiny shared by Australia, New Zealand, and South Africa. Indeed, as Lothrop Stoddard, a xenophobic proponent of transnational solidarity among white settler colonies, put it in the 1920s: "Nothing is more striking than the instinctive and instantaneous solidarity which binds together Australians and Afrikanders, Californians and Canadians, into a 'sacred union' at the mere whisper of Asiatic migration."[66] The corresponding features of Asian racialization in settler colonies capture the moving spirit of settler colonialism: a formation that is transnational but distinctively national, similar but definitely not the same, repetitive but without a predictable rhythm, structural but highly susceptible to change, everywhere but hard to isolate. This is what we might call the music of settler colonialism. It is from the past, but never stops playing.

Until recently, white settler colonialism has received far less attention than its "postcolonial" counterpart among the multiplicity of colonial configurations, past and present.[67] On one hand, postcolonialism is the term that has often been applied to franchise colonies—British India or the Dutch East Indies, for instance—regions where economic exploitation occurred *without* large-scale white settlement. While the postcolonial condition remains a nuanced subject of theoretical debate in terms of its history and enduring social, economic, and cultural impact, the formal end of British and Dutch imperial rule and colonial administration in the late

1940s initiated a complex process of decolonization that was encoded into the "post-" of postcolonialism. Settler colonialism, on the other hand, is effectively immune to the process of decolonization. As Ian Tyrell explains, "Settler societies represented a particularly complex and resilient form of European colonial expansion often not recognized as imperial conquest by its own agents precisely because they claimed to do more than extract wealth and then return to the metropolitan space."[68] They are "breakaway" colonies insofar as they transfer the power of the metropolitan center to the periphery, *subverting* a normative logic of colonialism.[69] In the establishing of settler colonies, the primary objective was land acquisition, as Patrick Wolfe points out, rather than the surplus value gained by mixing Native labor with it.[70] Because white settlement was an intentional aspect of colonization in British North America, Australia, New Zealand, and South Africa, neither the revolutionary nor the nonrevolutionary processes of detaching from British imperial rule—becoming "postcolonial," as it were— significantly altered or ended the colonial relationship between settlers and the Indigenous population. In many ways, as Werner Biermann and Reinhart Kössler reflect on the irony of revolutionary settler independence movements like the United States', "settler counter-imperialism cannot, in any sense, be considered of an emancipatory nature, but rather as a defense for atavistic forms of exploitation which by this token take on a politically anachronistic stature as well."[71] Therefore, in settler colonies, the diminishing role of an imperial metropole facilitated successive stages of Indigenous conquest that involved invasion, removal, relocation, reservation, assimilation, termination,[72] co-optation, and self-determination. This renders a paradoxical situation where, as Robert Young describes it, "the postcolonial operates simultaneously as the colonial."[73] In other words, what Taiaiake Alfred calls a "paradigm of post-colonial colonialism"[74] is thus a defining feature of contemporary settler colonialism in North America.

Triangulating Settler Colonialism

While Asians have not held any prominence in popular media projections of settler national culture, which often erases or figuratively disguises Asians as infiltrating replicants or alien invaders,[75] the opposite has been true for Indigenous identities. As Scott Lauria Morgensen explains, the settler colonial imaginary is continually underwritten by Indigenous tropes that convey settler "conquest and incorporation of primitivity."[76] Much like the way the 2011 feature film *Cowboys and Aliens* aligns cowboys and Indians with each other against an invading, technologically superior alien population — read Asian — settler identity is heavily invested in appropriating Indigeneity. This is a mode of white settler identification that Shari Huhndorf calls "going Native,"[77] which functions to cover over colonial invasion and reimagine a natural affiliation to the land. The erasure of the alien and the romantic identification with the Native are two sides of the settler colonial coin.

By mapping out the triangulation of Native, alien, and settler positions, this book moves beyond a binary theory of settler colonialism, which is predominantly structured around an opposition between Indigenous peoples and settlers. While scholarship on the settler-Indigenous dialectic has been tremendously valuable, it often falls short of clarifying the role that nonwhite migration plays within such a framework or how it intersects with other aspects of white supremacy. Reflecting on what she calls the "indigenous-settler binary," Andrea Smith similarly cautions that this "binary certainly exists, [but] our analysis of it is insufficient if not intersected with other logics of white supremacy."[78] In particular, key questions over the status or role that racialized migrants play within white settler colonialism often remain unasked or avoided. In a binary framework of settler colonialism — where one is either a settler or an Indigenous person — are slaves, indentured laborers, or refugees "settlers," despite the involuntary context of their migration to North America? If we observe Jared Sexton's claim that "no amount of tortured logic could permit the analogy to be drawn between a former slave population and an immigrant population, no matter how low-flung the latter group,"[79] do descendants of slaves exceed the conceptualization of migrants more generally? These questions highlight some of the uncertainty that surrounds the nonwhite "alien" and the role of race within settler colonialism. As the cases below signal, slavery and the abject condition of blackness complicate a straightforward approach to settler colonialism organized around a central opposition between settlers and Indigenous peoples. More directly, the "settler" classification collapses important racial distinctions between various contexts of voluntary and forced migration into one homogeneous group of "occupiers."

Recent studies of settler colonialism that have given attention to Asian or other nonwhite, non-Indigenous cultures have often distinguished settler identity by the degree to which migration is intentional. Writing about

Canadian settler imperialism, for example, Adam Barker notes the changing provenance of settlers: "[They are] often people of European descent, but in the contemporary sense Settler increasingly includes peoples from around the globe who intentionally come to live in occupied Indigenous territories to seek enhanced privileges."[80] In essence, settler identity—regardless of race—is predicated on the *intentionality* of migration. For those who may not have intended to migrate, however, Barker is more circumspect: "Attempts to integrate discussions of hybrid identities (such as the descendants of African peoples brought to the Americas against their will, many refugees, or Settler Muslims who are increasingly targeted by the state and other racist Settlers) with Settler and Indigenous identities are complicated and beyond the scope of this inquiry."[81] Complicating Barker's view of voluntarism, Jodi Byrd's theorization of settler colonialism accounts for the involuntary conditions of migration. She offers the term arrivant "to signify those people forced into the Americas through the violence of European and Anglo-American colonialism and imperialism around the globe."[82] For Byrd, structures of coerced migration distinguish the arrivant from the settler.

Alternatively, Patrick Wolfe forcefully opposes voluntaristic approaches that attempt to differentiate the settler from coerced migrant populations such as slaves. He maintains that "the opposition between Native and settler is a structural relationship rather than an effect of the will.... Neither I nor other settlers can will our way out of it, whether we want to or not."[83] In particular, he draws on the Australian context in which unfree white convict labor was imported from Britain in order to pose the rhetorical question, "Does this mean that their descendants are not settlers?"[84] Given that Wolfe concedes that white convicts in Australia did not pass on the condition of their criminality to their offspring, this example fails as a comparative equivalent to a US history of African slavery. The very content of black racialization has been based on the exclusive and transferable condition of racial slavery. Moreover, in claiming that settler identity applies even to "enslaved people [who] *immigrated* against their will," Wolfe implicitly preserves the voluntarism that he otherwise rejects in his construction of the slave as an "immigrant." Such references to immigration project a set of voluntaristic assumptions onto widely divergent conditions of voluntary and forced migration that are central features of the United States' specific configuration as a settler colony. In the contemporary context, the racialized vulnerability to deportation of undocumented, guest-worker, or other pro-visional migrant populations similarly exceed the conceptual boundaries that attend "the immigrant." Our awareness of these distinctions does not absolve any of these groups from being willing or unwitting participants in a settler colonial structure that is driven to eliminate Indigenous people. However, folding them into a generalized settler position through volun-taristic assumptions constrains our ability to understand how their racial-ized vulnerability and disposability supports a settler colonial project.

The most unequivocal work to define Asian migrants as "settlers of color" is the edited volume *Asian Settler Colonialism: From Local Governance to the Habits of Everyday Life in Hawai'i*. Referring specifically to Asian Americans in Hawai'i, editor Candace Fujikane states clearly that "all Asians, including those who don't have political power, are identified in this book as settlers who participate in US settler colonialism."[85] Acknowledging the historical exploitation of Asian plantation labor in Hawai'i, she argues that it is equally important to acknowledge the "ways that they [Asian migrants and their de-scendants] are beneficiaries of US settler colonialism" and how "early Asian settlers were both active agents in the making of their own histories and unwitting recruits swept into the service of empire."[86] In this formulation it is not necessary for migrants of color to migrate "intentionally" to become settlers; rather, settler status is a mixture of both *self-determination and structural contingency*. As Fujikane puts it succinctly, "Colonial intent [does not] define the status of Asians as settlers but rather the historical context of US colonialism for which they unknowingly became a part."[87] Furthermore, she also dispels the notion that Asians represent a "third space" outside the Indigenous-settler dialectic. She admits her previous subscription to this idea, but explains her change of thinking as follows:

> I was attempting to create a "third space" for Asians as another category of the oppressed in Hawai'i. The attempt to ally [Asian] "locals" with "Natives," however, created the illusion of a "shared" struggle without ac-knowledging that Asians have come to constitute the very political system that has taken away from Natives their rights as indigenous peoples.[88]

In this view, given the political power that Asian Americans currently enjoy in Hawai'i, they cannot be said to represent a stable third space that is ex-empted from the settler-Indigenous dialectic or positioned "with" Indige-nous peoples and "against" settlers.

While attributing a settler identity to Asians may be germane in a demographic context such as Hawai'i, it nevertheless remains unclear whether such a settler identity is generalizable to the situation of Asian immigrant formations that exist elsewhere. Even though Fujikane stresses that political and economical subordination does not exempt Asian ethnic groups from participating as settlers in a colonial system—particularly Filipinos[89]—her emphasis on Asian demographic majority, dominant political representation, and economic power in Hawai'i emphasizes how political and economic authority are nonetheless dominant features of settler colonial identity.[90] The importance of economic and political leverage embedded in this characterization of settler identity may explain the absence, for example, of comparable discussions of "black settler colonialism." A case in point is the postemancipation recruitment of black "Buffalo Soldiers" in anti-Indian wars in the western United States and during the Philippine-American War.[91] The Buffalo Soldiers are a clear example of an oppressed group's unwitting (and sometimes unwilling) participation in settler colonialism and imperial invasion, yet the continued economic and political subjugation of African Americans seems to exempt them from most theorizing on settler colonialism, as a "third space" or otherwise. Thus the settler status of racialized migrants to Indigenous lands outside Hawai'i remains undetermined.

In some ways, the conundrum of positioning Asian North Americans within settler states highlights broader inconsistencies that mediate theories of Asian racialization in North America and the role of race in a settler colonial context. Speaking to the racial ambiguity evoked by Asians in the United States, Colleen Lye encapsulates the racial condition of Asian Americans as "racial, racialized, but lacking the certainty of a racial formation."[92] Remarking upon the surfeit of articles and monographs that focus either on Afro-Asian interracial contexts or on how Asian Americans disrupt conceptualizations of race anchored by a foundational opposition between black and white, Lye continues to observe the uncertainty of Asian racialization:

> Asian America's attenuated relation to racial conceptualization can be seen in the extent to which critical focus on the Asian American is so often couched in terms of "needing to move beyond race as a matter of black and white." The Asian American is more easily evoked as a third term to trouble binary habits of racial classification and analysis than to illustrate the genuine multiplicity of racial logics and racisms.[93]

From sophisticated approaches to Asian American racialization such as Claire Jean Kim's theory of Asian America's triangulated relation to black and white, to Susan Koshy's conception of a single hierarchical axis in which Asian Americans have moved progressively away from a racialization associated with blackness toward an ethnicization associated with whiteness, most theories of Asian racialization rely, according to Lye, on the "historical agency of a racism that is foundationally antiblack."[94] However, the problem with this approach is that it constrains our ability to elaborate the specificity of Asian racialization that isn't merely a by-product of a foundational antiblackness. As it stands, what Lye calls an "Asian American analogical dependency" fails to clarify the way contemporary expressions of political liberalism and white supremacy seem to diverge so starkly from those of the late nineteenth century and, importantly, leaves unanswered whether contemporary "Asian American mobility confirms the persistent power of white privilege or whether it represents the detachment of whiteness's symbolic power from material power."[95] The Canadian context only adds to this racial uncertainty, since the absence of a similarly foundational system of racial slavery has not, as "analogical" arguments might suggest, led to divergent forms of anti-Asian racism in Canada. Indeed, the racialization of Asian Americans and Asian Canadians has unfolded as a parallel evolution of yellow peril to model minority—from immigrant restriction and segregation, wartime internment of Japanese civilians, to the 1960s-era liberalization of immigration policy. This mirrored arc of Asian racialization, therefore, cannot be entirely attributable to an inherited legacy or second-order version of antiblack racism given the absence of a similar regime of plantation-based slavery in Canada. This is not to say that structural antiblackness did not play a role in conditioning Canada's entrance into capitalist modernity; rather, the similar pattern of policies directed at Asians in Canada and the United States indicates forces that exceed those that shape the social construction of blackness.[96] To put it another way, a transnational framework contradicts an understanding of anti-Asian racism as solely derivative of a prototypical racialization of blackness. As I will argue, the vicissitudes of racialization are grounded in settler colonial logics.

This book presents a theory of settler colonialism in North America that operates as a triangulation of symbolic positions that include the Native, the alien, and the settler. The distinctions between alien and settler are by no means stable or fixed but are meant to emphasize the role of territorial entitlement that distinguish them. What initially distinguishes the settler from the alien migrant, as Lorenzo Veracini offers, is that "not all migrations are settler migrations."[97] This is both poignantly true and, for African slaves, a profound understatement. As Frank Wilderson describes transatlantic slavery, "From the very beginning, we were meant to be accumulated and die."[98] Alternatively, on the other end of the spectrum, the alien may not only be *complicit* with the settler colonial regime but may eventually inherit its sense of sovereign territorial right, such as Asian settlers in Hawai'i.[99] Acknowledging these inconsistencies, what I demonstrate in this book is that for slaves and racialized migrants, the degree of forced or voluntary migration or level of complicity with the settler state is ultimately secondary to their subordination under a setter colonial mode of production driven by the proprietorial logics of whiteness.

In this light, highly differentiated populations of African slaves and Asian migrants historically represented *alien* rather than settler migrations. This shared status in no way implies an equivalence in the heterogeneous racial experience of African slaves and Asian migrants. Instead, it clarifies their historical relationship to North American land, which was as exclusive and excludable alien labor forces. Their unsovereign alien status was a *precondition* of their exploitation and intersects with the multiple economic logics that require and reproduce alien-ness in settler colonies. While African slaves represented a system of forced migration, unfree alien labor, and property—a form of biopolitical life that was "market alienable"[100]—the later recruitment of indentured and "free" Chinese labor incorporated provisionality, excludability, and deportability into the notion of alien-ness. The heterogeneously racialized alien is a unique innovation of settler colonialism. Race is thus an organizing principle of settler colonialism in North America, a principle that we neglect at the risk of relegating African slaves "to the position of the unthought"[101] and obscuring the persistence and evolution of Marx's notion of primitive accumulation, where "conquest, enslavement, robbery, murder, in short, force, play the greatest part."[102] The governing logic of white supremacy embedded in a settler colonial mode of production relies on and reproduces the exploitability, disposability, and symbolic extraterritoriality of a surplus alien labor force. Therefore, complicating an Indigenous-settler binary, this book's focus on the settler colonial alien follows Byrd's method of "disrupt[ing] the dialectics of settler/native, master/slave, colonizer/colonized."[103] As I attempt to clarify below, what remains fundamental to this triangulated articulation of settler colonialism is how land and labor are constitutive features of heterogeneous processes of settler colonial racialization.

Indigenous Land, Alien Labor

The triangulation of Native, alien, and settler populations comes into view when we examine two subjects who are the most racially antithetical to one another: the African American alien and the Native North American. While some have argued that a race-based framework potentially subsumes the critical importance of Indigenous sovereignty,[104] this exploration highlights the role that land—and land sovereignty—plays in Indigenous racial formation and what Alfred refers to as the "racism that is the foundation and core of all colonial countries."[105] As Patrick Wolfe highlights, the logics of exclusion and elimination have profoundly shaped the distinct racial destinies of colonized groups. In this formulation, the *logic of exclusion* operates as a barrier within national culture to protect and reinforce settlers' social and political control. De jure and de facto practices of segregation, disenfranchisement, exclusion, exploitation, police brutality, detention, and imprisonment are some of the ways that the settler state asserts and maintains control over an internalized alien population. On the other hand, *the logic of elimination* is driven to eradicate an Indigenous population rather than controlling it through various exclusionary measures. Genocide and biological absorption are two contradictory—but complementary—means of extinguishing an Indigenous population: the first attempts to kill the population off, the second assimilates them out of existence.[106] It is worth pausing here to emphasize the dire consequences of assimilation for Indigenous populations, a process that may seem benign or even beneficial to other racialized groups. As Katherine Ellinghaus clarifies, "One of the outcomes of acknowledging the links between miscegenation, assimilation policies, and genocide is . . . an acknowledgment of the underlying biological, physical, bloody aspects of assimilation policies that demonstrate the terrifying resolve of settler governments to rid themselves of the Aboriginal or Indian problem one way or another."[107]

Exclusion and elimination are not discrete logics but operate on a moving spectrum of biopolitical violence. For instance, a logic of exclusion applied to Indigenous peoples, who were conferred US citizenship in 1924 but were still denied the right to vote in many states.[108] In Canada, a logic of exclusion denied the franchise to Indigenous nations until 1958, while a logic of elimination rendered this right of citizenship conditional on the abandonment of "Indian Status" and accompanying right to live on a reservation. In both Canada and the United States, logics of exclusion and elimination inform how Indigenous peoples are incarcerated at higher rates than other groups.[109] While these examples demonstrate how these logics often work in tandem, for Indigenous peoples a logic of exclusion is underscored by an overarching logic of elimination. For aliens, similarly, the eliminatory logics expressed through police-initiated murder or death-penalty sentencing of black men are tactics that simultaneously reinforce the exclusion and exclusivity of blackness.[110] In the following section I clarify how these logics operate when land and labor are at stake in the settler colony. My focus on the comparative racialization of Indigenous peoples and African Americans draws more heavily on the United States than on Canada because the former has a longer national history, and that history presents a foundation that illuminates subsequent racial developments in both countries.

Historically, a distinctive feature of settler colonialism was that the primary objective of settlers was to appropriate land alone rather than appropriate Indigenous labor to expropriate that land's resources. This distinguishes settler colonialism from franchise colonialism — in British India, for example — where Indigenous labor was exploited to produce commodities and extract the land's wealth. Wolfe explains, "Settler colonialism seeks to *replace* the natives on their land rather than extract surplus value by mixing their labor with a colony's natural resources."[111] Therefore the primary logic of settler colonialism is one of elimination, and land establishes the relationship Indigenous peoples have with the colonizer. This is not to say that Indigenous people either never constituted a labor force or have ceased to be one. Rather, while there are numerous historical examples of Indigenous labor in settler colonies, from factory work in canneries in British Columbia to Alaska, Indigenous recruitment into surplus labor (the subject of chapter 3) occurs "*in spite of* rather than as a result of the primary tendency of settler-colonial policy."[112] This logic of elimination helps to contextualize the sequence of actions directed at Indigenous peoples whose primary objective was extermination. A snapshot of these directives in the United States include eastern removal; genocidal actions taken by the US Cavalry; the 1877 Dawes Severalty Act, which turned tribes into individual property owners and resulted in the loss of two-thirds of Indigenous land; assimilationist policies of urban relocation and boarding schools ("residential schools" in Canada); and policy on Indigenous "self-determination." Despite the rhetorical shift in settler discourse that now celebrates Indigenous self-determination as fully incorporated citizens of the settler state through a discourse of reconciliation, this has largely involved implementing federal rather than Indigenous Nation–specific policies. As Glen Coulthard explains, "Although the semantics of the comprehensive claims policy have changed, the legal and political outcomes remain the same."[113] Further, Federal Indian Identification Policy functions as a form of what Annette Jaimes terms "statistical elimination":[114] the effective meaning of the state's definition of "Indian" as a minimum of one-quarter blood quantum is that through intermarriage, Indians will eventually "be defined out of existence."[115] In the Canadian context, Karrmen Crey refers to this form of racial engineering as the "two-generation cutoff."[116] Thus if elimination meant physical relocation and/or death in the period preceding the implementation of the Dawes Act, elimination came to mean absorption in the period following it. While policy history in Canada differs, the spirit of elimination does not.[117] And though the treaty process remains subject to negotiation in Canada while Indigenous nations in the United States have sovereignty, the predictable and ongoing process of treaty revision and violation indicates that treaties function as strategic forms of state accommodation designed to appease rather than to concede blame or to compensate.[118] Despite formal differences, the practice of settler colonial elimination is more consistent in the two nations than not.

If the primary relationship between settler colonizers and Indigenous populations is land, in the case of African slaves transported to the United States it is *labor*. Rather than exhibiting a governing logic of elimination, a logic of racial exclusion clarifies the form of colonial exploitation experienced by African Americans in antebellum and postemancipation contexts. Because the relationship between colonizers and slaves was primarily based on labor, the objective was not to eliminate that population but to *increase* it and, by extension, increase the property value of that exclusive labor force. Consequently, a logic of exclusion applies insofar as slavery was an *inherited* condition, which made blackness equivalent to slavery and racial admixture assignable to it. Distinguishing the logic of elimination and exclusion, Wolfe explains that whereas Indigenous women "became conduits to whiteness . . . black women came to augment white men's property by incubating the additional slaves whom they fathered."[119] While this logic of exclusion functioned to reproduce and grow a discrete population of slaves who became synonymous with the condition of blackness, blackness was not the only condition for enslaveability. For instance, Indigenous peoples were also enslaveable, a lesson that Spanish colonialism in Mexico teaches us. In the most successful regimes of slavery, however, among the most important features that rendered Africans most vulnerable to enslavement was their *alienation*, "not just the natal alienation that Orlando Patterson has made famous, since indigenous societies . . . have also had their children taken away, but the *spatial alienation* that slave transportation effected."[120] The spatial alienation experienced by African slaves made them a more manageable population to control, to thwart insurrection and overthrow, and to prevent from escaping. This form of alienation therefore helps to distinguish, in the case of African Americans, the "alien" position from the Native and settler in a triangular framework. In the United States, African Americans are the original aliens.

In the post–Civil War context, race came into full emergence; it was rooted in slavery but came to life during the shift to black emancipation. Not only did Reconstruction put whiteness into crisis—whiteness was also threatened by non-Anglo-Saxon immigration of Jews and southern and eastern Europeans. Shifting the terms of the logic of exclusion, race reinforced the barrier between whites and blacks that the institution of slavery formerly performed. In other words, race became amplified with the downfall of slavery because racial domination was an implicit feature of slavery. However, in the wake of emancipation and without the barrier of slavery to designate free from unfree labor, race became unambiguously natural, reinforcing an exclusively racial division between black and white populations. By extension, without the barrier that slavery performed, whiteness became the basis of racialized privilege after emancipation. What is significant is that emancipation reproduced for African Americans an anomalous condition that similarly characterized the experience of postfrontier "incorporated" Indigenous Nations. Although freed slaves did not become anomalous as labor—in the South they continued to represent a cheap and hyperexploitable labor force—they became, as Wolfe puts it, "juridically anomalous as equals."[121]

Since the settler colonial solution was to eliminate anomalous postfrontier Indigenous peoples through racial absorption, a key question arises: Why didn't newly freed and anomalous African Americans follow the assimilative racialization of Indigenous peoples and become similarly "eliminated"? Historical attempts to colonize African Americans abroad or assimilate them into the white population point to endeavors to apply a logic of elimination to African Americans. However, given the socially engineered disproportion in the size of the black population vis-à-vis the Indigenous population, neither attempt was practical or, in the case of assimilation, imaginable. Elaborating on the difference between the population of post-emancipated slaves and Indigenous nations, Wolfe highlights the biopolitics of settler colonialism and its "calculated management of life":[122]

> In this case, it represents the difference between one group of people who had survived a centuries-long genocidal catastrophe with correspondingly depleted numbers and another group who, as commodities had been preserved, their reproduction constituting a singularly primitive form of accumulation for their owners.[123]

The hereditary nature of slavery, which fused slavery to blackness, was thus carried over into the postemancipation context to fuse blackness to an "unlimited power to contaminate." Given that emancipated African Americans were neither "immigrants" who could be deported nor a population that could be eliminated through biological absorption, African Americans became an *undisposable* alien labor population, which accounts for the intensity through which subsequent generations of African Americans have been subject to a logic of exclusion where the only means of disposal is death. Furthermore, the force through which blackness was excluded during the Jim Crow era highlights a broader consolidation of whiteness — of Anglo-Saxons and Protestants at first, and eventually extending to other European ethnics[124] — and intensified nation-building in the late nineteenth and early twentieth centuries. In both Canada and the United States, "white nationalism" was the ideological and policy response to nonwhite immigration and black incorporation.

The comparative racialization of Indigenous peoples and African Americans highlights the heterogeneity of race that is anchored by a foundational distinction between land and labor. For Indigenous peoples of North America, race was always subject to dilution and disappearance. In both Canada and the United States, the biological constitution of Indigenous peoples was determined assimilable to whiteness. Describing this evolution in the logic of elimination, Wolfe explains that "mixed-bloodedness became the post-frontier version of the vanishing Indian."[125] For African Americans, on the other hand, the "one-drop rule" relegated to blackness a biological permanence that would survive any amount of interracial mixing. Whereas mixed or light-skinned African Americans who passed as white *frustrated* the settler colonial racial regime, Indigenous people who assimilated to whiteness *upheld* it. Similarly, while Jim Crow and antimiscegenation laws kept the line between blacks and whites from blurring, interracial mixing was not only tolerated among Indigenous people but was often actively encouraged through policy. In the United States, the practice of "checkerboarding" during the administration of the Dawes Act (1887–1934) interpenetrated Indigenous reservations with white allotments to promote intermarriage and decrease eligible heirs to Native Title.[126] In Canada, prior to changes to the Indian Act in 1985, Indigenous women were "rewarded" with the loss of their status as "Registered Indians" for the prize of a white identity, not only if they married non-Native but non-Status men.[127]

As distinct as these black and Native racial formations appear, they were still bound together by an overarching economic rationale of settler colonialism. First, for each group, race became more salient during the rise and development of industrial capitalism. For Indigenous nations, the logic of elimination became aggressively implemented as trading posts were eclipsed by industrial forms of economic production. In Canada, for instance, James Tulley explains that "the end of the British and French wars rendered the military alliances with the First Nations irrelevant. The shift from trade to settled agriculture and manufacture caused the trading treaties to decline . . . undermining Aboriginal economies and forcing Aboriginal peoples into relations of dependency."[128] Being rendered anomalous by industrial modes of production thus signals the full onset of settler colonialism and, with it, a racial logic of elimination. In the case of African American slaves, their emancipation was contextualized by the growing challenges to plantation-based economies and the increasing demand for flexible, free labor for the emerging industrial economy. While plantation capitalism was still highly profitable before the Civil War, Southern plantations were increasingly challenged by their need to expand production into non-slave-holding states.[129] Nevertheless, in the absence of slavery, new demands of the industrial economy rendered postemancipation African Americans anomalous as people and gave rise to an intensified notion of race as a regime of social control. From the view of capitalist expansion that lies at the heart of settler colonialism, the divergent forms of racialization that Indigenous peoples of North America and African Americans have been subject to are entirely reconcilable. As Wolfe puts it unequivocally: "The simple undifferentiated product of the encounter between African labor and Indian law was European property."[130] Mixing alien labor with Indigenous land to expand white property was the basis and objective of settler colonialism.

Disposable/Undisposable Alien Labor and the Heterogeneity of Race

As migrants to North America, Asians' primary relationship to settler colonizers was historically based on labor. Similar to African Americans, Asians represented an alien labor force that mixed with Indigenous land to transform it into white property and capital. What comes to light from this framework is, yet again, the heterogeneity of race under settler colonialism. Rather than presenting a derivative model of Asian racialization that is based on a prototypical antiblackness, the vicissitudes of Asian racialization are primarily shaped by the evolving economic landscape of settler colonialism within a global economy.

While African Americans and Asian North Americans share an alien status in a triangular framework, the divergent historical and economic contexts of Asian and African labor highlight the heterogeneity contained within an alien position. Asian labor migration to North America, as well as elsewhere in the Americas, occurred during the demise of plantation-based slave economies, a decline that began in the 1830s. Given shifting requirements of industrializing economies, which demanded a flexible rather than enslaved labor force, the economic context of Asian labor migration in the nineteenth century inoculated Asians from assuming the status of unfree labor. This distinction renders Asian aliens highly dependent, nevertheless, on the class of settler capitalists. This means, as Biermann and Kössler clarify, that "the migrant workers are not personally free, [although] their illiberty is not in terms of a personal relation of bondage to an individual master."[131] In addition, as Moon-Ho Jung explains, the historical importation of indentured Chinese labors to replace or supplement slave labor in the US

South represented a period of dramatically destabilized labor relations that introduced new and reinvigorated conceptualizations of race and nation.[132] In this tumultuous economic context, Chinese labor migrants would assume none of the hereditary stain of slavery that defined blackness before emancipation or hereditary racialization that determined African American exclusion afterward.

While the presence of African American slave labor was an important context for subsequent Asian-settler labor relations in the United States, the Canadian context demonstrates that parallel expressions of Asian racialization were not wholly contingent on the prior enslavement of black people; rather, they were overwhelmingly conditioned by industrial capitalism. Therefore, in the absence of plantation-based African slavery in Canada, the common denominator of Chinese laborers' analogous experiences of exploitation and exclusion was their alien status rather than their proximity to a racialized notion of blackness. Because the industrial economy that Asian labor served did not require a permanent, reproducible, exclusive, and violently contained population of alien labor, as was the case under US slavery, the exclusionary tactics that Asians were subjected to never approximated those experienced by black slaves.[133] The projection of Asianness as a racial signifier of indelible, exclusively transferable attributes was less necessary as a strategy of containment. Unlike emancipated slaves, Asians *could* be excluded and eliminated from the nation-state.

If the rise of industrial capitalism solidified biological notions of race that subjected Indigenous populations to eliminatory assimilation on the basis of the mutability of their blood, and black populations to Jim Crow exclusion based on the contaminating reach of their blood, the logic of exclusion ascribed alien-ness and spatial vulnerability not simply to Asian blood but to the entire Asian body. Because Asian bodies could be entirely excluded from the nation-state, Asian labor was susceptible to more volatile forms of domestic exclusion than those experienced by African Americans. As a result, the history of domestic segregation and antimiscegenation laws targeting Asians in North America—evoked by racial fears of biological contamination and contagion[134]—was more uneven than its African American counterpart.[135] A much more effective means of exclusion was through immigration control. A form of Jim Crow in a transnational context, immigration policy not only determined entry into the nation but could legally bar an immigrant from naturalizing, voting, owning and transferring property, and working. As Marilyn Lake and Henry Reynolds observe, "In drawing the global colour line, immigration restriction became a version of racial segregation on an international scale."[136]

To the extent that Asians were restricted or excluded from coming to North America until the mid-1960s, and because their deportability constituted a form of what David Hernández calls "lesser citizenship,"[137] the logic of exclusion employed the national border to segregate populations and maintain social control. In a settler colonial context, these variable, exclusionary logics have resulted in the heterogeneous racialization of the alien: the African American, whose *indisposability* in the settler state requires a heightened form of racialized exclusion as a form of domestic social control, and the Asian North American, whose *disposability* from the settler state produces a less fixed and more volatile racialization by virtue of the exclusionary power of immigration restriction. In this framework of abstract labor, Asian North Americans may appear "less racial"—to adapt Lye's language—than African Americans or Indigenous populations, whose racial essences were expressed in the relative power of blood to contaminate or to erase a population, respectively. However, if Asian racialization produced a less blood-defined racial body, it is by virtue of the exclusionary, segregationist logics that were carried out in the extraterritorial arena of immigration control that inhibited Asian exposure to more sustained domestic logics of racial exclusion and elimination. In this context, race is not only a heterogeneous formation; it is also an expression of settler power whose capacity to racialize is not, as Jodi Melamed suggests, "reducible to biology, identity, or ontology."[138] These factors laid the settler colonial groundwork for an understanding of the abstract racialization of the Asian alien that form this book's central concern.

While a logic of elimination functions to increase white property through the decimation of Indigenous populations who stand in the way of territorial expansion, a logic of exclusion serves industrial capitalism by furnishing a vulnerable labor force whose existence could be managed at the border. Bearing some similarity to the spatial segregation of prison inmates from inner cities, the border represents a geographical solution to manage surplus populations.[139] This focus does not discount the many other exercises of racialized domestic social control, which prevented, denied, or rescinded access to naturalization, labor, the franchise, property ownership, and, in the case of Japanese North American citizens interned during World War II, due process or freedom of mobility. My point is that each of these modes of domestic racial control served a broader logic of exclusion that is inherent in immigration restriction: to underscore and preserve Asians' alien status by creating policy that exploited the volatility of an Asian presence. From the perspective of settler colonialism, we can build on this framework by clarifying the importance of spatial alienation (rather than Indigeneity) as a factor in the exploitation of a racialized labor force. In this light, a logic of exclusion is the *prerequisite* for the recruitment of alien labor, functioning either to reproduce an exclusive labor force in the case of African slaves or to render an Asian labor presence highly conditional to the demands of capital. Both are subject to forms of segregation, either on a national or international scale. As each of my chapters argues, this volatility is what makes it possible to view the Asian alien as the embodiment of the abstract evils of capitalism.

By clarifying the evolving triangulation of Native, alien, and settler subject positions, my purpose has been to distinguish both the heterogeneity of race and the heterogeneity of alien racialization. This formation is uniquely tied to settler colonialism, which requires a disposable reserve army labor force. In the chapters that follow, I will situate this heterogeneous racial formation within a settler colonial logic of romantic anticapitalism that hypostatizes whiteness and sublates Asianness into abstract labor and the intangible, destructive dimension of capitalist relations.

Chapter Overview

In order to magnify the capitalist logics of settler colonialism that account for the striking parallels in US and Canadian policy directed at Asian ethnic groups, this book's transnational focus draws on corresponding racial policy making at key turning points since the nineteenth century: Chinese railroad labor in the 1880s and subsequent immigrant restriction laws; the expansion of anti-Asian immigration restrictions in the 1920s; the relocation and internment of Japanese civilians during and after World War II; and the late 1960s neoliberalization of immigration policy. Because one of my goals is to reframe these historical touchstones where Chinese and Japanese populations figured predominantly, the majority of my examples are limited to this East Asian scope. However, because my project is aimed at presenting a theorization of the abstract economism of the Asian alien in a settler colonial framework rather than emphasize the ethnic particularity of any one group, I have strived to construct a flexible rather than ethnically determined model that can be expanded and adapted to accommodate the specific historical circumstances of Asian populations not covered in the book.

In each chapter I explore Asian North American cultural production as a genealogical archive. As such I draw from Michel Foucault's distinction between history and genealogy, one shaped by his principle that "knowledge is not made for understanding; it is made for cutting."[140] Rather than the traditional approach to history as a linear and unified development—"an acquisition, a possession that grows and solidifies"—a genealogy is an "unstable assemblage of faults, fissures, and heterogeneous layers that threaten the fragile inheritor from within or from underneath."[141] As such, genealogy opens up what Foucault calls a countermemory: "a transformation of history into a totally different time."[142] To the three modalities of countermemory that he identifies as parodic, dissociative, and sacrificial reworkings of history, I would like to add a fourth, a "postmemory," in order to call attention to the affective register of racial genealogies. As Marianne Hirsch defines it, postmemory is a "very particular form of memory precisely because its connection to its object or source is mediated not through recollection but through an imaginative investment and creation."[143] She further distinguishes postmemory and memory as follows:

> Postmemory characterizes the experiences of those who grow up dominated by narratives that preceded their birth, whose own belated stories are evacuated by the stories of the previous generation shaped by traumatic events that can be neither understood nor recreated.[144]

Such a conceptualization of postmemory applies to the contemporary Asian North American cultural production I examine in the sense that these works present less of a direct or experiential connection to historical events than a collective consciousness of Asian American and Asian Canadians who have grown up with settler narratives of national identity and belonging that have relegated the Asian as other. I further adapt the notion of postmemory to indicate a form of future memory, a memory yet to come, to capture the simultaneously utopian and apocalyptic capitalist futurity explored in Asian North American reconfigurations of history. Given that my primary focus is on the economic modalities of Asian racialization that are tied to capitalism, my goal is to demonstrate how an Asian North American cultural genealogy of settler colonialism does not simply oppose this economism but, rather, opens it up for further exposure. Laid bare, the symbolic infrastructure of this economism provides a window into what Dipesh Chakrabarty terms History 2, the relations "whose reproduction does not contribute to the reproduction of the logic of capital . . . [even though they] can actually be intimately intertwined with the relations that do."[145] History 2 expresses the potential of countermemory to subvert the social relations embedded in History 1 that reproduce the logic of capital.

Most of the chapters in the book feature a dialogue between literary and visual texts. The multimedia nature of the archive that grounds my analysis of each historical episode aims to meet two objectives. First, a starting point for this book is an understanding that the ideological expression of white settler colonialism and anti-Asian sentiment in North America is a multimedia projection that has glorified whiteness in artistic constructions of landscape and delimited racial belonging in textual definitions of citizenship. Therefore the multimedia archive of Asian North American cultural production in this book is a response to both the literary and visual form of these constructions. Related to this, the visual works I incorporate attempt to address the predominance of mainstream film and television constructions of Asians that evoke untrustworthiness, mystery, or deceitfulness and collectively reinforce the destructive, unrepresentable abstraction attributed to Asian bodies. The mystery and treachery often reinforced through the visuality of Asians in popular media are distinctive because they always point to something invisible and unseen, suggesting that the negative content of Asian racialization is something that we can't see. The visual culture presented in this book thus offers imaginative responses to the challenge of visualizing the unrepresentable.

Each chapter explores how settler colonialism negatively aligns Asians with an abstract dimension of capitalism through an ideology of romantic anticapitalism—that is, through romantic anticapitalism's misperception that social relations are defined either as concrete, natural, visible, and hence noncapitalist *or* abstract, unnatural, invisible, and hence capitalist. Such a misperception of capitalism presents an ideal ideology for rationalizing and forgetting the settler colonial elimination of Native peoples and exploitation of alien labor. Thus what romantic anticapitalism offers is an ideological framework for settler colonialism to respond to economic and technological crises by imagining whiteness through indigenizing tropes of purity and organic connection to land that function to distort and deflect responsibility for capitalist modernity. As such, each chapter examines the expression of white settler romantic anticapitalism both to indigenize whiteness and to align Asians with the threateningly abstract economism of capitalism.

The first chapter, "Sex, Time, and the Transcontinental Railway: Abstract Labor and the Queer Temporalities of History 2," establishes the book's foundational claim that the economism of Asian racialization arises from a temporal alignment of Chinese bodies with abstract labor, which has implications for what constitutes *socially necessary* labor time. This "abstract" racialization is reinforced by romantic anticapitalism, which projects an antinomical character of capitalist social relations expressed as an opposition between concrete and abstract dimensions. I examine how romantic anticapitalism hypostatizes the concrete, pure, and organic dimensions of white labor and leisure time, while identifying capitalism solely with the abstract dimensions of the antinomy, which is personified by Chinese labor. The chapter begins with a reflection on a nineteenth-century sketch of a Chinese laborer's profile surrounded by financial figures drawn by William Van Horne, president of the Canadian Pacific Railroad (CPR). My interpretation of the sketch, whose provocative nature the CPR itself underscored by not granting me permission to reproduce in this book, sets the stage for clarifying the sexualized intersection of race and capitalism. In taking this direction I adapt Postone's theorization of the secular, anticapitalist dimensions of modern anti-Semitism for understanding anti-Asian sentiment. Analyzing Richard Fung's *Dirty Laundry: A History of Heroes* alongside Maxine Hong Kingston's *China Men*, two works about Chinese labor on the transcontinental railroad, I explore the identity—or sameness—relation between Chinese labor, time, and money. Focusing on the range of gender and sexual substitutions represented in these texts, I argue that these works demonstrate how the abstract racialization of Asian alien labor is established through their alignment with a perverse temporality. While Fung's and Kingston's works expose the fungibility of alien labor conditioned by biologized notions of time, they also point to the queer potential of History 2 that resides within abstract labor but does not reproduce the logic of capitalism. Moreover, their contemporary approach to this history highlights the ongoing construction of racialized abstraction in the era of globalization—the new nineteenth century—which is the subject of chapter 4.

The second chapter, "Unnatural Landscapes: Romantic Anticapitalism and Alien Degeneracy," builds on the first chapter's focus on the abstract dimension of capitalist social relations—personified by Chinese labor—by turning its attention to the *concrete* dimension of capitalist social relations personified in artistic depictions of the settler landscape. Turning to the photographs of Tseng Kwong Chi and Jin-me Yoon, I argue that their photographic citations of 1920s- and 1930s-era landscape art parody its romanticization of whiteness-as-nature during a heightened period of Asian immigrant restriction. In particular, Tseng and Yoon respond to themes of regenerative whiteness and autochthonophilia—a term that refers to a settler colonial desire for and identification with Indigeneity—personified in the majestic landscapes by American artists Ansel Adams and Gutzon Borglum and Canadian artists Emily Carr and the Group of Seven. Disidentifying with the romanticization of the concrete, purifying landscape, Tseng's and Yoon's photographs expose the politics of whiteness invested in the identification with nature and Indigeneity. Further developing the theme of perversity associated with abstract labor in chapter 1, Tseng's and Yoon's photographs highlight how Asian bodies evolve to denote a degenerative, antinatural force associated with the abstract dimension of romantic anticapitalism's antinomical social universe.

Chapter 3, "Japanese Internment and the Mutation of Labor," focuses on the consequences of an increasingly unnatural, mechanical abstraction of Asian racialization developed in the previous chapters. To help contextualize the expulsion, internment, and, in the case of Japanese Canadians, postwar relocation east of the Rocky Mountains, I suggest that the modes of abstraction attributed to Japanese agriculture and fishing labor in the United States and Canada contributed to the false impression that Japanese labor held a destructive control over the creation of relative surplus-value. I suggest that Japanese internment is neither reducible to prior modalities of Asian immigrant exclusion nor a rational expression of white accumulation by racial dispossession. Instead, I argue that Japanese internment turns on the association of Japanese labor with the modernizing displacements of technological innovation, which fed a perception that Japanese labor monopolized the creation of relative surplus-value. The chapter probes how the destructive power of Japanese labor was resignified after West Coast expulsion and relocation. Focusing on Joy Kogawa's novel *Obasan* and Rea Tajiri's video-memoir *History and Memory*, I examine how symbolic identifi-

cation with Jewish persecution before the war shifted toward an identification with Native identities after relocation. This cross-racial identification
with Native contexts evokes the neutralization of Japanese labor's association with the production of unnatural value and reconstitution as an ideal
surplus labor force.

The fourth chapter, "The New Nineteenth Century: Neoliberal Borders,
the City, and the Logic of Settler Colonial Capitalism," examines the persistent and evolving economism of Asian racialization in the postexclusion
era, after the United States and Canada removed race-based immigration
criteria in 1965 and 1967, respectively. Turning to Ken Lum's multimedia
works, including his sculpture on the roof of the Vancouver Art Gallery,
Four Boats Stranded: Red and Yellow, Black and White, along with Karen Tei
Yamashita's novel *Tropic of Orange*, I track their works' reconceptualizations
of labor, migration, and political consciousness. Their works point to the
capacity of the neoliberal border to recruit and restrict surplus labor populations from around the world while preserving the racialized abstractions
that surround both high-tech, flexible Asian labor and working-class labor.
As such, free trade becomes a further conduit for the fungibility of bodies
as capital across borders and the continuing perils of abstract labor associated with the "new Jew." Far from symbolizing multicultural inclusion, I
suggest that the border is a central motor for the expanded fulfillment of
a settler colonial mode of production that relies on a disposable migrant
labor system.

The epilogue, "The Revenge of the Iron Chink," offers a meditation on an
exhibition featuring an early twentieth-century fish-gutting machine called
the "Iron Chink" located in my hometown of Victoria, British Columbia,
personifying a racist slur. To explore its contemporary significance I turn
to artist Tommy Ting's reanimation of the Iron Chink in his 2012 sculpture
*Machine (Iron Chink, invented in 1903, found at the Gulf of Georgia Cannery in
Steveston, British Columbia, refabricated in Beijing, China)*. Examining how
Ting's sculpture recontextualizes the original machine, I reflect on aesthetic
and biological dimensions of capitalism that I've tracked through the book.
Probing the question of value in capitalism as the central motor of the metaphoric work of the fetish, I consider what it might mean to imagine human
incommensurability in a world beyond commodity-determined labor.

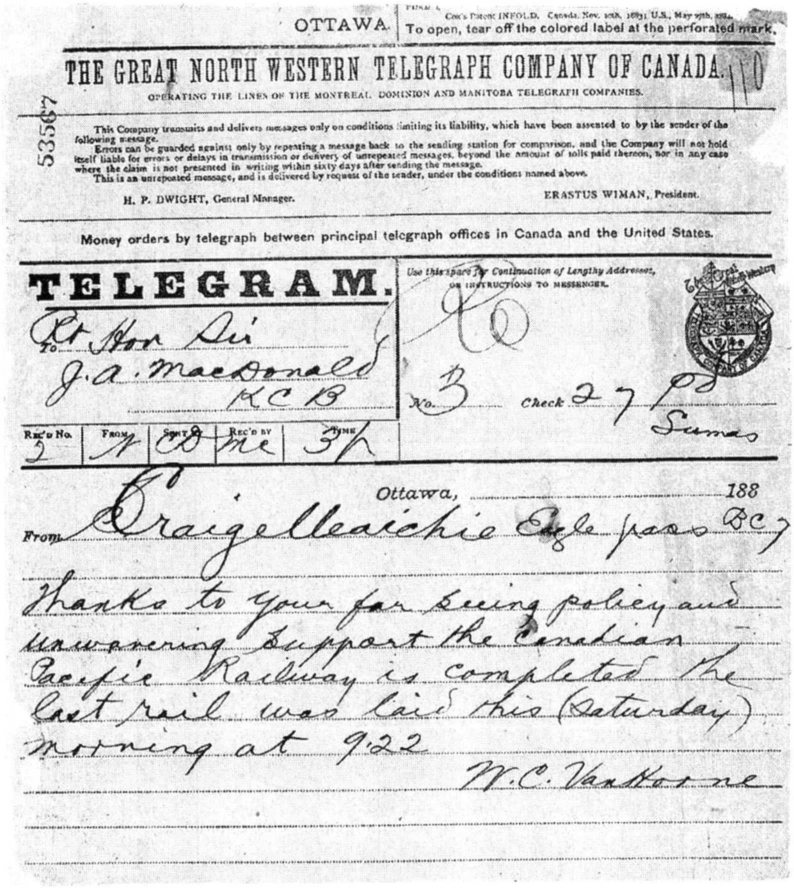

OTTAWA. To open, tear off the colored label at the perforated mark.

Cox's Patent INFOLD. Canada, Nov. 10th, 1883; U.S., May 27th, 1884.

THE GREAT NORTH WESTERN TELEGRAPH COMPANY OF CANADA.

OPERATING THE LINES OF THE MONTREAL, DOMINION AND MANITOBA TELEGRAPH COMPANIES.

This Company transmits and delivers messages only on conditions limiting its liability, which have been assented to by the sender of the following message.

Errors can be guarded against only by repeating a message back to the sending station for comparison, and the Company will not hold itself liable for errors or delays in transmission or delivery of unrepeated messages, beyond the amount of tolls paid thereon, nor in any case where the claim is not presented in writing within sixty days after sending the message.

This is an unrepeated message, and is delivered by request of the sender, under the conditions named above.

H. P. DWIGHT, General Manager. ERASTUS WIMAN, President.

Money orders by telegraph between principal telegraph offices in Canada and the United States.

TELEGRAM.

Use this space for Continuation of Lengthy Addresses, or Instructions to Messenger.

To Rt Hon Sir J.A. Macdonald KCB

No. 3 Check 27 Pd Sumas

Rec'd No. 2 From N Sent CD Rec'd by Mc Time 3½

Ottawa, 188

From Craigellachie Eagle pass BC 7

Thanks to your far seeing policy and unwavering support the Canadian Pacific Railway is completed the last rail was laid this (Saturday) morning at 9.22

W. C. Van Horne

FIGURE 1.1 Telegram from Canadian Pacific Railway president William Van Horne to Prime Minister John A. Macdonald announcing the last spike, November 7, 1885. Library and Archives Canada/Sir John A. Macdonald fonds/e000009485.

CHAPTER 1

SEX, TIME, AND THE TRANSCONTINENTAL RAILROAD

Abstract Labor and the Queer
Temporalities of History 2

We do not ride on the railroad; it rides upon us.
— Henry David Thoreau

Fungibility

Figure 1.1 is the celebrated telegram sent by Canadian Pacific Railway (CPR) president William Van Horne, an American from Chicago tasked with overseeing the construction of the CPR who became, according to Pierre Berton's famous account, "more Canadian than any native."[1] His telegram is addressed to Prime Minister John A. Macdonald and announces the completion of the railroad in Craigellachie, British Columbia, on November 7, 1885. Unlike the well-known photograph of the ceremonial driving of the last spike, the focal point of the telegram is time: it is the hour and minutes — 9:22 A.M. — that precisely mark the consolidation of the settler nation. The telegram, itself a representation of nineteenth-century advances in communications, symbolizes a new national temporality achieved through technological innovation.

Van Horne was known to frequently draw pictures on the reverse side of these kinds of telegrams. On the back side of one of the few that survived is his sketch of a Chinese laborer's facial profile, complete with a long tapered mustache. Surrounding the man's face are a busy series of numerical calculations that seem indicative of Van Horne's financial worries during the railroad's construction. The CPR, now a multi-billion-dollar corporation, objected to the reproduction of the sketch in this book.[2] What's interesting is that the grounds for the CPR's censorship of the image rested on the mere *association* of Van Horne with the Chinese man, suggesting a perverse content attributed to the sketched figure and its capacity to corrupt Van Horne's reputation. This chapter probes exactly what constitutes this unnatural, obscene content and why it is out of sync with the settler temporality glorified on the face of Van Horne's telegram to the prime minister.

Probing the obscene content of Van Horne's sketch of the Chinese man further, the juxtaposition of the human profile and numerical sums evokes the economic connection between Chinese railroad labor and their low wages. Drawing out the financial significance of the image, Margot Francis explains that Chinese labor was "indispensable to the CPR's early financial viability as their 'cheap wages' saved Andrew Onderdonk, the contractor for the western section of the line, between $3 and $5 million and allowed him to escape bankruptcy."[3] The Chinese whom Onderdonk contracted to work the western section were recruited from San Francisco. Many of them had worked on the US transcontinental railroad, which had been completed over a decade earlier, in 1869.[4] Although Chinese labor in North America was vital to the completion of the transcontinental railroads, its profound irony, as Henry Yu observes, is "that the very railroads that Chinese laborers built made it easier and cheaper to transport the settlers who arrived afterwards and demanded that 'the Chinese must go.'"[5] Although railroads were symbols of consolidation for the white nation, they were lines to exclusion for the Chinese laborers who helped build them. In 1885, the same year the CPR was completed, Canada passed its first immigration restriction policy through the Chinese Head Tax, designed to deter laboring classes. Originally set at $50, the tax rose prohibitively, to $100 by 1900 and $500 by 1903. Following completion of the US transcontinental railroad in 1869, the 1875 Page Act was the first federal immigration policy designed to deny entry to prostitutes, overwhelmingly targeting Chinese women on the basis of presumed sexual immorality. The passage of the Chinese Exclusion Act in 1882 dramatically expanded this scope by restricting entry to all skilled and unskilled Chinese labor. The outcome of these immigration controls on both sides of the Canada-US border was the formation of "bachelor" communities that, as homosocial, nonreproductive spaces, reinforced fears of contagion and perversion associated with Chinese men. The reproductive restrictions imposed on the bachelor community was, in Foucault's terms, part of the biopolitics of settler colonialism through its "calculated management of life."[6]

The very existence of Van Horne's sketch of the Chinese man also offers a stark contrast to the traditional iconography associated with the building of the transcontinental railroads in Canada and the United States. The now-famous photographs taken at Promontory, Utah, and Craigellachie, British Columbia, respectively, commemorate the technological feat of white labor, erasing the thousands of Chinese men who worked and died building the western sections of these railroads. As David Eng notes, "While more than ten thousand Chinese American male laborers were exploited for the building of the western portion of Central Pacific track, no one appears in the photograph commemorating its completion."[7] Neither are any of the seventeen thousand Chinese laborers who worked the western section of the Canadian Pacific railroad identified in what Berton calls "the most famous photograph ever taken in Canada," celebrating the union of eastern and western tracks in Canada.[8] Therefore, in the sense that Van Horne's illustration retrieves a repressed aspect of Chinese labor in Canada, it offers us an alternative visual example that Francis suggests "troubles the narratives that posit that only white men were sufficiently enterprising to construct the rail that connected the nation."[9] For the purposes of this chapter, what the missing sketch also brings to the fore is a relationship between the signifiers of race and capital that overshadowed railroad construction. The tension between these signifiers gave rise to the association of Chinese labor efficiency with social perversion and fed into romantic anticapitalism's dehumanization of Chinese workers as abstract labor.

Probing this visual interplay of race and capital, a less linear vision of Chinese labor emerges from Van Horne's sketch. In addition to the *causal* significance of the Chinese face and calculations, insofar as Chinese labor was instrumental for securing the financial viability of the CPR, the juxtaposition of the Chinese profile and numerical figures also projects the sameness of an *identity* relation. In particular, the vertical lines of the Chinese man's mustache in the sketch repeat the tally lines surrounding him, accentuating their symbolic resemblance and projecting a quality of mutability and interchangeability. This visual assonance evokes the peculiar fungibility of the Asian alien, a figure whose interchangeability as a value expression dramatizes the properties of money itself, Marx's "universal equivalent," against which everything is commensurable and exchangeable. Does such a resemblance between alien labor and the universal equivalence of money suggest that racialized labor takes on the abstract qualities of capital? In light of the 2012 controversy over the Asian scientist on the Canadian hundred-dollar bill discussed in the introductory chapter, Van Horne's doodle achieves prototypical significance.

By surrounding the Chinese man's face with a series of financial calculations, what Van Horne's sketch prompts is a reconsideration of the relation between the concrete and the abstract, the concrete specificity of racialized labor and the abstract, universal equivalence of money, which Marx describes as "a radical leveler [that] extinguishes all distinctions."[10] Money "extinguishes all distinctions" because it is universally exchangeable with all other commodities, and "all other commodities make [money] the material embodiment of their uniform and universal form of value."[11] Money is the conduit and expression of commensurability. However, Van Horne's sketch opens a view of racialized labor *as* money. Rather than an exchange relation—of labor for money—his sketch evokes a substitution relation. Such a relation suggests a process whereby *heterogeneous* (i.e., racialized) labor takes on the appearance of something entirely different: the *homogeneous* substance of money, whose qualities are universally commensurable. Unequal labor takes on the appearance of symbolic equivalence. This chapter explores the implications of such a symbolic substitution, particularly in terms of how racialized labor becomes progressively abstract, moving from concrete reality to the spectral domain of capital. Of course, capitalism's key operational logic is one of abstraction, dissolving difference into homogeneous, equivalent forms so they are commensurable—exchangeable. As Dipesh Chakrabarty summarizes, "The logic of capital sublates into itself the differences of history."[12] The question, therefore, is why the concrete particularity of Chinese labor comes to express itself *culturally* as "abstract labor." Does the cultural abstraction of Chinese labor offer new ways of understanding what Yu calls the "irony" of Chinese labor restrictions introduced after the completion of the transcontinental railroads? In particular, if value is based on "socially necessary" labor time, what factors constitute social necessity?

This chapter draws on two Asian North American texts that shed light on social necessity through gendered and sexual temporalities of race, labor, and capitalism in the construction of the transcontinental railroads in Canada and the United States. Addressing themes of labor exploitation and gendered and sexualized exclusion, Maxine Hong Kingston's "The Grandfather of the Sierra Nevada Mountains," from her experimental memoir *China Men*, and Richard Fung's experimental video documentary *Dirty Laundry: A History of Heroes* offer imaginative responses to Van Horne's symbolic provocation of the identity relation between Chinese labor and money. Magnifying a converging theme of gender and sexual resignification and substitution in their texts, Kingston and Fung demonstrate, to quote Elizabeth Freeman, how "time has, indeed *is*, a body."[13] Specifically, in their framing of racialized labor through the interplay of sexuality and temporality, I argue that Kingston and Fung queer the disembodying effects of an accelerating temporal logic of equivalence that constitutes abstract labor. What unites their distinct texts is a recurring theme of substitutions—of ventriloquism for "real" speech, of masturbation for "real" sex, of gay sex for straight sex, of Chinese alien labor for white labor, of maternalism for paternalism, and so on—which function collectively to expose how racial, sexual, and gender difference operates as a degraded substitute within the capitalist logics of white settler colonialism. These substitutions interrupt the accelerating capitalist temporality of railroad labor, which reorganizes the social necessity of a linear, rational, normative time of family, nation, and capital. If time is a body, it is a body subject to relentless disembodiment under capitalism. Yet, for these cultural producers, disembodiment provides an opening for queer resignification that reveals the destabilizing potential of abstract labor. They draw out the potential of Queer Marxism by exposing the tension between concrete labor and abstract labor time, what Petrus Liu identifies as the "incommensurability between the value of a human being and its formal exchangeability."[14]

As alien substitutes for "real labor," I suggest that Kingston's and Fung's texts allegorize a process whereby alien labor is symbolically aligned with the fluctuating *duration* embedded in abstract labor, which establishes value, rather than the here-and-now world of concrete labor. As I elaborated in the introductory chapter, abstract labor represents a social average of labor time to produce a commodity in order to express its quantitative value during exchange, whereas concrete labor refers to the actual time and place of a specific laboring activity that expresses its qualitative use-value.

Chakrabarty offers a useful clarification of abstract labor as a "performative, practical category."[15] He explains that "abstract labor gave Marx a way of explaining how the capitalist mode of production managed to extract, out of peoples and histories that were all different, a homogenous and common unit for measuring human activity."[16] Abstract labor is therefore an objective force made up of what Marx describes as a spectral, phantomlike substance:

> Let us now look at the residue of the products of labour. There is nothing left of them in each case but the same *phantom-like objectivity*; there are merely congealed quantities of homogenous human labour, i.e. of human labour-power expended without regard to the form of its expenditure. All these things now tell us is that human labour-power has been expended to produce them, human labour is accumulated in them. As crystals of this social substance, which is common to them all, they are values — commodity values.[17]

By aligning Chinese bodies with abstract labor, their labor represents human labor *in the abstract*. It is this phantomlike objectivity of alien labor that establishes a commodity's value. White bodies, on the other hand, are symbolically associated with concrete labor, which establishes a commodity's quality.

Such a racial bifurcation of abstract and concrete labor is the work of the commodity fetish, which disguises the social relations behind the products of human labor. In terms of this book's overarching claim, I argue that a key anchor of North American settler colonialism is an ideology of romantic anticapitalism that reifies a distinction between concrete and abstract social relations out of a misunderstanding of the dialectical nature of capitalism. Romantic anticapitalism hypostatizes the concrete, rooted, and pure, on one hand, and identifies capitalism solely with the abstract dimension of social relations, on the other. It glorifies what it sees as the concrete realm of social relations: white labor, the family, and the train itself — a machine whose concreteness is biologized as the "iron horse." Alternatively, Chinese bodies are in nearly exclusive alignment with quasi-mechanized labor temporality, excluded from normative social and domestic temporalities. Once Chinese labor is no longer needed, romantic anticapitalism performs an aesthetic function by giving Chinese shape to the unrepresentable: giving bodily form to the abstract, temporal domination of capitalism.

In this sense, Chinese labor allegorizes the commensurating function of abstract labor that propels capitalism forward. However, as Chakrabarty notes, for Marx the universal category of abstract labor serves two functions: "It is both a description and a critique of capital."[18] Following a Queer Marxist approach, this chapter will explore how abstract labor can pose such a critique.

The focus on temporality in Kingston's and Fung's work also serves to dramatize the impact of industrial technology on conceptions of time in the nineteenth century. In particular, railroad construction was intimately linked to the speed-up and internationalization of uniform time through technological innovation, time-space compression, and the standardization of Greenwich Mean Time. Completing a process of temporal secularization that began in the Middle Ages, time's progressive detachment from the cosmos and human events was achieved in this period of national expansion and consolidation by rail. No longer did biblical events structure and determine time, as they once did within traditional Jewish and Christian conceptions of history; rather, time became increasingly continuous, homogeneous, and independent of events.[19] Postone refers to this secularized temporality as "abstract time," "an independent framework within which motion, events, and action occur . . . divisible into equal, constant, nonqualitative units."[20] Indeed, the progress of abstract time as a dominant form of time parallels the development of capitalism as a socially metabolic totality. In the context of this shift to a more totalizing capitalist temporality, what Kingston's and Fung's texts illuminate is how conceptions of time were racialized and sexualized. Indeed, as Petrus Liu specifies, it is a mistake to view socially necessary labor time as solely the mean labor time associated with technological developments but also in terms of its moral dimensions. He clarifies that "the value of a commodity is the amount of human labor embodied in it, but the value of the commodity of human labor is determined by *moral and discursive operations* outside the capitalist reproduction scheme."[21] Therefore, on one hand, white labor productivity and its heteronormative reproduction become qualitative expressions of morality and rationality associated with time discipline. As Michael O'Malley explains, there was a need "to protect time's virtue," its chastity tied to "scientific discipline requiring years of patient courting to master."[22] On the other, as I suggest in this chapter, Chinese labor becomes associated with the abstract, quantitative domination of labor time. This is what Postone describes as the "temporal dimension of the abstract domination that characterizes the structures of alienated social relations in capitalism."[23] Exposing the racialized temporalities of the labor process under capitalism, Kingston and Fung return with queer temporal revisions of labor and reproduction.

Time Travel

Midway through Richard Fung's video *Dirty Laundry: A History of Heroes*, the camera draws in on a Chinese Canadian train steward scanning a magazine article titled "Canada's Railway: A Symbol under Threat." Several scenes later, the steward is engaged in a passionate kiss with Roger Kwong, a Chinese Canadian journalist for the magazine. After a slow-motion montage of hands caressing undressed bodies, the scene of the two men's sexual encounter gives way to metaphorical expression through a cut to archival film footage taken from the Canadian Pacific Railway (CPR); the grainy black-and-white film transports the viewer around a bend and into a dark tunnel. Besides the discontinuous temporality staged by the juxtaposition of these two scenes—one fictional and contemporary, the other culled from a historical archive—their temporal dissonance is further accentuated by their distinct cinematic *tempos*. The sex scene is slow and methodical, while the train hurtles forward on a predetermined path. The possibility of the gay encounter, Fung suggests, is contingent on but temporally dislocated from the predictable linearity of CPR time. The video pushes temporality and sexuality together in a way that simultaneously emphasizes the temporality of racialized sexuality and the sexuality of time on the transcontinental railway.

Sex on trains is certainly not isolated to experimental Asian Canadian documentaries such as Fung's. Perhaps more obviously, the rapid sequence of the scenes above presents a queer citation to a film such as Alfred Hitchcock's *North by Northwest* (1959), in which the train similarly serves as a symbolic phallus. In Hitchcock's version, the train that disappears into a tunnel also—and comically—references sex between Cary Grant's and Eva Marie Saint's characters. This kind of sexual symbolism has a long history in the popular culture of the railway. Since the nineteenth century, popular film and visual art representations have commonly depicted the sexuality of trains, which, as Lynne Kirby describes, is "most often as a double for male sexuality."[24] As a mirrored projection of male virility over a fertile, feminine body, the train symbolizes either (and often both) the aggressively violent or consummating romance of territorial penetration and domestication. Inside the train, the compression of time and space have disorienting effects, such that chance and illicit encounters are not only possible but probable. Therefore, the railway's temporal duality of social unpredictability and technological predictability nonetheless converge under a dominant symbolism of heterosexual consummation between technology and nature. In other words, the surprise or taboo sexual encounters between passengers who feel out of time and space are not anomalous to the predetermined, linear path of the railway because, as Hitchcock's film demonstrates, the two lovers ultimately mirror the overarching theme of spatial consummation with their bodies—white heterosexual bodies are always in sync with the temporality of the railroad. But when we loop back to Fung's CPR, the two strangers are Asian, and gay sex replaces heterosexual white consummation. Through this substitution, the video suggests that disrupting the train's symbolism with an Asian "anal" tunnel is one reason that the Canadian railway may be "a symbol under threat."

Fung's documentary diverges from the traditional "romance of the rails" by presenting a montage of narrative layers where, as Lisa Lowe observes, "the journey across geography spatializes a temporal exploration of an unknown past."[25] Interwoven through the documentary are interviews, archival film and photographic images, dramatized historical scenes, and a fictional travelogue that follows Roger Kwong's journey from Toronto to Vancouver aboard a CPR train. The documentary does not privilege any one narrative or temporal standpoint, emphasizing instead the interplay of power and narrativity—particularly the racial power embedded in the assembly of historical archives. As Margot Francis observes of the video's back-and-forth movement between historical analysis and fictional travelogue, "The director suggests that he didn't want viewers of the tape to feel too secure with either fiction or history."[26] In its approach to race and sexuality, Fung adapts Michel Foucault's argument in *History of Sexuality* that the late nineteenth century did not so much *repress* sexuality as give rise to a cultural "incitement to speak" about it, leading to a proliferation of discourses and disciplinary apparatuses.[27] Subtitled *A History of Heroes*, the video examines how it was anti-Chinese sentiment in the nineteenth century that was historically linked to the proliferation of discourses about sexual perversion—at the same time that whiteness was coalescing as a normative category of national citizenship. In Foucauldian fashion, Fung demonstrates how conceptions of racial and sexual normativity were *secondary* to and relied on racial and sexual otherness for definition. Rather than indict the conflation of racial otherness with sexual perversion, the video's ironic treatment of perversity is exemplified in its title, *Dirty Laundry*: it seeks to rework the symbolic interplay of racialized sexuality and labor. Through Roger's discovery of his great-grandfather's ambiguous sexuality, the video clears a space outside the temporal frame of official history to identify with sexual fluidity. Moreover, Fung's video playfully channels the eroticism of dirty laundry, which comes into play when an accidental spill initiates the sexual encounter between Roger and the railway steward. The combination of overlapping temporalities, self-conscious narration, and dramatic reversals and substitutions bring to light the queer modalities of racialized labor history.

If we move south to the transcontinental railroad of Maxine Hong Kingston's "The Grandfather of the Sierra Nevada Mountains" in *China Men*, another Chinese railroad worker performs a different kind of queer identity forged out of temporal dislocation. Whether Ah Goong is wandering alone through the Sierra woods or sitting with his family at the dinner table, he has no qualms about baring his penis and subjecting it to worldly questioning. Contrary to the steel certainty of the train's anthropomorphized virility, he continually wonders "what it was that it was for, what a man was for, what he had to have a penis for."[28] Scrutinizing the function and reproductive capacity of his body, Ah Goong presents a warped mirror of the train's phallic symbolism. Far from the pleasures of queer sexuality that Fung's steward enjoys, Ah Goong's inward chastisement outwardly questions the relation between male sexuality and gender. His gender and sexual dislocations are reflected in the acute *temporal* dissonance he experiences as a laboring body. As he works, Ah Goong continually grasps for temporal anchoring while his observations become increasingly unhinged. After he spends three years tunneling through granite with a pickaxe, time becomes a tangible, animate form divorced from a coherent sense of reality:

> When he stumbled out, he tried to talk about time. "I felt time," he said. "I saw time. I saw world." He tried again, "I saw what's real. I saw time, and it doesn't move. If we break through the mountain, hollow it, time won't have moved anyway. You translators ought to tell the foreigners that."[29]

The temporality of granite is dissociated from reality and takes on a materiality that Ah Goong feels and sees. The linear, unidirectional pressures of Ah Goong's labor time confront the seeming immobility of nature, because "it doesn't move." Labor time and natural time are presented as frustratingly out of sync with each other, and even if they "break through the mountain, hollow it, time won't have moved anyway." These temporal disjunctures have alienating gendered and sexual effects on Ah Goong.

The temporal alienation Ah Goong experiences during labor is reinforced by the waning influence of a cosmic temporality. For instance, his ritual observance of the summer reunion of the Spinning Girl and the Cowboy—the Altair and Vega star constellations—becomes increasingly irrelevant to him in the face of a new labor temporality. Looking up at the night sky, Ah Goong "saw the order in the stars,"[30] an astrological system that brings comfort because he recognizes them from China. He recounts the story of the Spinning Girl and Cowboy, in which two lovers are so enchanted with one another, "too happy," that they neglect their work and are punished by the Queen of the Sky. She separates the lovers, "scratch[ing] a river between them." Taking pity on them, the King of the Sky allows them a reunion once a year: "On the seventh day of the seventh month . . . magpies form a bridge for them to cross to each other."[31] The discovery of the stars gives Ah Goong something to look forward to: "Every night he located Altair and Vega and gauged how much closer they had come since the night before."[32] But after the first summer, astrological time seems increasingly disconnected from his own temporal existence. Ah Goong "felt less nostalgia at the Spinning Girl and the Cowboy. . . . The Cowboy's one year away from his lady was no time at all."[33] For Ah Goong, cosmic time is progressively divorced from the demands of earth-bound labor time, which, he observes, has kept some Chinese men working in the country for decades.

Dispensing with his yearly celebration of the Spinning Girl and Cowboy's reunion and, later, casting aside the temptations of a pitiful sex worker brought into the camp, Ah Goong's gender and sexuality become progressively estranged from the consummating imperatives of the railway. He begins to masturbate on the job while lowered in a basket filled with gunpowder and fuses, declaring, "I am fucking the world!"[34] Later, after the railway is complete, he is filled with longing for his own child, a daughter: "He wished for a happy daughter. . . . She would sing for him and listen to him sing."[35] He is deemed insane by his family, and is eventually lost after the 1906 San Francisco earthquake and fire. His consciousness is shaped by an indefinite temporality, and as I develop further in this chapter, it stands in sharp contrast to the gender and sexual imperatives of a consolidating capitalist temporality of the nineteenth century.

Departing from an ordered, sequential, and linear vision of time, Fung and Kingston employ forms of substitution as openings for processes of resignification that reimagine time's relation to race, sexuality, and labor. It is from the dislocated position of abject substitution that time's normalizing function is exposed. Elizabeth Freeman notes how "one of the most obvious ways that sex meets temporality is in the persistent description of queers as temporally backward, though paradoxically dislocated from any specific historical moment."[36] From the displaced vantage of the historically dislocated position of Chinese labor, therefore, Kingston and Fung's texts denaturalize capitalist temporality while reimagining "how time makes bodies and subjects."[37] As capitalism expands and increasingly regulates all aspects of labor and social life in the nineteenth century, we can discern how the morality and character-building activity of concrete labor both structures and reinforces the social and cultural structures of family and leisure. The temporality of the home, which schedules gendered activity, moral education, heterosexual reproduction, progress, and futurity, is thus a crucial regulator of the labor process. As Kingston's and Fung's texts elucidate, the temporality of work and family become embodied by whiteness, a category imbued with morality, belonging, and social necessity. In contrast, the Chinese are identified with a perverse domesticity whose homosociality forecloses any sense of reproductive futurity. Excluded from the moral category of concrete labor, Chinese labor is instead associated with processes of valorization associated with productivity and time, an abstract force that injects temporal volatility into the concrete labor process. Personifying the capitalist adage "Time is money," therefore, the substitutions present in Kingston and Fung's texts expose the aesthetic function of romantic anticapitalism. That white labor appears more "concrete" than Chinese labor is one of the fetishized tropes of capitalism that, as Marx writes, "conceals the social character of private labour and the social relations between the individual workers, by making those relations appear as relations between material objects, instead of revealing them plainly."[38] In the following two sections I explore the way Fung and Kingston respond to the capitalist imperatives of temporal consolidation, one which aligns Chinese labor with the temporal domination of capitalism while simultaneously subverting it.

As personifications of the "phantom-like objectivity"[39] of abstract labor, the Chinese laborers of Kingston's and Fung's texts stage alternative temporalities, inserting a queer temporal vitality that animates Chakrabarty's conception of History 2, a historical formation that he describes as the "excess that capital . . . always needs but can never quite control or domesticate."[40] These are the vital forces that form a constant resistance to capital: "the abstract living labor—a sum of muscles, nerves, and consciousness/will— that, according to Marx, capital posits as its contradictory starting point all the time."[41]

Alien Labor as Dangerous Supplement

During the three years that Ah Goong tunnels through granite mountain in *China Men*, he undergoes profound psychological disembodiment insofar as he becomes progressively unable to distinguish the tangible from the abstract. As he tunnels, his sensory ability becomes estranged, and his perception of the material world reflects his temporal imprisonment in labor, where "a mountain is the same as permanence and time":[42]

> His eyes couldn't see, his nose couldn't smell; and now his ears were filled with the noise of hammering. This rock is what is real, he thought. This rock is what real is, not clouds or mist, which make mysterious promises, and when you go through them are nothing.[43]

Ah Goong's experience of temporal suspension against the impenetrability of rock bankrupts the hope or mystery suggested by "clouds or mist." History is reduced to rock. Later, after the bosses replace pickaxes with dynamite, which "added more accidents and ways of dying,"[44] he is further disoriented in time. After blasting through a tunnel in winter, he begins to think that "it was the task of the human race to quicken the world, blast the freeze, fire it, redden it with blood."[45] Experiencing the shift to the quickening pace of industrial time, Ah Goong tries to counteract the disjuncture of labor speed and the delay of the natural world:

> He had to change the stupid slowness of one sunrise and one sunset per day. He had to enliven the silent world with sound. "The rock," he tried to tell the others. "The ice." "Time."[46]

Responding to the asynchrony of labor time and natural time, Ah Goong attempts to resignify the natural world using the sound of words, which fail to signify new meaning. As natural time cleaves from the laboring body, the Chinese laborers who die from explosions become increasingly disembodied forms, "like puppets [who] made Ah Goong laugh crazily as if the arms and legs would come together again." When he is suspended in his dynamite-lined basket, Ah Goong renders human life abstract: "Godlike, he watched men whose faces he could not see and whose screams he did not hear roll and bounce and slide like a handful of sprinkled gravel."[47] From puppets to sprinkled gravel, human life is progressively stripped of vitality.

As both witness to and subject of the disembodying effects of abstract time, Ah Goong articulates both the inadequacy and potential of the living body. As he lifts his hammer, he tells the men working beside him that "a man ought to be made of tougher material than flesh. . . . Skin is too soft."[48] The impenetrability of the wall further underscores his corporeal lack: "Nothing happened to that gray wall. . . . It had no softer or weaker spots anywhere, the same hard gray."[49] He remarks to his friends, "Our bones ought to be filled with iron."[50] Ah Goong's recognition of the dehumanizing demands of abstract labor time emphasizes a central contradiction of a capitalist mode of production. Within capitalism's drive to accumulate by speeding up time and compressing space, its tendency is to replace human labor with machines, or "bones . . . filled with iron." As Chakrabarty notes, "Capital is thus faced with its own contradiction: it needs abstract and living labor as the starting point in its cycle of self-reproduction, but it also wants to reduce to a minimum the quantum of living labor it needs."[51] Thus, connecting this contradiction to History 2, we find that the crucial variable embedded within abstract labor—a variable that capitalism requires but continuously tries to eliminate—is human life itself, an innately conscious and willing indeterminate force. It is the capacity of being "living" that makes labor a potential source of resistance to capitalist abstraction. The resistance of vitalism, as Chakrabarty elucidates, is such that "life, in Marx's analysis of capital, is . . . in a 'standing fight' against the process of abstraction that is constitutive of the category labor."[52]

Expressing a queer vitalism that upsets the reproduction of a capitalist temporality, Ah Goong's performance of racialized labor as a sexual act queers the value-generating temporality of abstract labor. In the much-discussed scene of Ah Goong's compulsion to masturbate while lowered in a basket filled with dynamite and declaring, "I am fucking the world," he taps into the vital excess of abstract labor. In debates over the political registers of the scene, critics identify these acts as expressions of either sexual frustration or resistance. For Donald Goellnicht, his masturbation signals the "loss and frustration caused by emasculation"[53] in the face of sexual deprivations in the railroad labor camps, suggesting that his sexuality is a belated formation, foreclosed until an unknown future. On the other hand, as David Eng suggests, his autoerotic behavior can be interpreted as staging an act of resistance, "us[ing] his penis to make a statement of racial protest . . . to his devalued racial position in America."[54] Tomo Hattori extends the resistant registers of masturbation, not as a "pathetic substitution for and failure to engage in 'real' sex,"[55] but as an expression of Ah Goong's "critique of the heterosexual and masculinist pretensions of his masters."[56] In this case, his masturbation represents a suspended challenge to the linear, reproductive frame of heterosexual consummation. Extending these analyses of his act's resistant potential, I call attention to the notion of masturbation as dangerous supplement. In Jacques Derrida's deconstruction of Jean-Jacques Rousseau's privileging of speech over writing, nature over culture, and presence over absence, he pays special attention to Rousseau's discussion of masturbation. In *The Confessions*, Rousseau expresses guilt over frequently succumbing to the compulsion to masturbate in the absence of his lover, Therese. He calls masturbation a "dangerous supplement,"[57] regarding the act as a secondary, subordinate addition to the primary and original act of sexual intercourse. But Derrida points to the double meaning of the supplement, as both supplying something that is missing and supplying something additional. Derrida's insight is that the supplement is what sets the terms that make possible the privileged status of the first entity. Supplementarity is the manifestation of the deferral that deconstructs the integrity of the sexual act, which is assumed to be perfect and complete.

Applying this notion of supplementarity to Ah Goong's masturbatory "fucking" of the world, we can examine how his act ventriloquizes the dynamite's literal "fucking" of the world. As a mode of writing, Ah Goong's masturbation gives him discursive presence and embodiment that corrupts the logic of equivalence that capitalism extracts as abstract labor. Moreover, Ah Goong's masturbation blurs the hierarchical distinction between work and play. Masturbation becomes an expression of queer vitalism that frustrates the homogeneity of abstract labor. Simultaneously, the queer vitalism he stages frustrates the capitalist logics of heterosexual reproduction. In his examination of nationalism and sexuality in the nineteenth century,

George Mosse notes that masturbation was likened to "throwing money out the window,"[58] causing impotence and threatening depopulation. And given that masturbation activates, as Tomo Hattori explains, an "autoerotic *homosexuality* . . . [because] the onanist, as both the subject and object of erotic action, is the same gender as itself,"[59] Ah Goong's sexual difference defies the logic of equivalence embedded in abstract labor while disidentifying with the capitalist project of national consummation.

The queer vitalism of Ah Goong's masturbation may also leverage a more dangerous supplementarity to the temporal domination of abstract labor than the labor strike he participates in. Animating the dehumanization of technological speed-up — whereby technology expands the exploitation of human labor — the Chinese workers are presented with a "four-dollar raise per month" that comes with the "'opportunity to put in more time' . . . 'Two more hours per shift.' Ten-hour shifts inside the tunnels."[60] The "railroad demons" reason that "'now that you have dynamite, the work isn't so hard.'"[61] In response, the Chinese laborers recognize the temporal domination of abstract labor through the inhuman push to mechanize their bodies: "'A human body can't work like that.' 'The demons don't believe this is a human body. This is a chinaman's body.'"[62] Here the racialization of labor translates into a temporal embodiment of abstract labor.

When the Chinese workers decide to resist by going on strike, the strike serves to halt the capitalist temporality of labor and becomes a supplementary form of leisure time. On strike, the men emerge as nonequivalents:

> The ones who were sleeping slept on and rose as late as they pleased. They bathed in streams and shaved their moustaches and wild bears. Some went fishing and hunting. The violinists tuned and played their instruments. The drummers beat theirs at the punchlines of jokes. The gamblers shuffled and played their cards and tiles. The smokers passed their pipes, and the drinkers bet for drinks by making figures with their hands. The cooks made party food.[63]

However, rather than a dangerous supplement that destroys the coherent division of work and labor, the strike also serves as a kind of "obscene supplement," which Slavoj Žižek defines as less a *subversion* of capitalism than "an obstacle which is simultaneously the 'condition of possibility' of the exercise of Power."[64] The strike operates as an obscene supplement in the sense that the China Men's victory is a qualified one. The foremen eventually grant a four-dollar raise without lengthening the working day, but this is far less than the fourteen-dollar increase the Chinese laborers demanded. Because the Irish workers refused to join the strike, rejecting their invitation by calling the Chinese strikers "Cheap John Chinaman,"[65] Chinese labor remains aligned with the temporal domination of abstract labor. The strike ultimately serves to uphold rather than undermine capitalism by safeguarding the vital human limits of abstract labor time. Thus when the strike is over, there is no celebration. The China Men merely resume their work within a capitalist temporality. Kingston writes, "The China Men went back to work quietly. No use singing and shouting over a compromise and losing nine days' work."[66] In this case, abstract labor functions less as History 2 than as History 1, which Chakrabarty defines as "the past 'established' by capital because History 1 lends itself to the reproduction of capitalist relationships."[67]

Ultimately, Kingston presents the irony of capitalism's demand for equivalence and substitution performed by fungible alien labor. When the railroad is complete, race complicates the logic of endless substitution — of alien supplementarity — by projecting the concreteness of white railroad laborers through photographs and commemorative celebration at Promontory, Utah, in 1869. The white workers declare that "only Americans could have done it."[68] Chinese labor remains abstract and, as such, invisible: "Ah Goong does not appear in railroad photographs."[69] As Eng clarifies, here "*American* emphatically does not include *Chinese*, as the China Men are driven out and their racialized labor is transformed into an abstracted whiteness."[70] Kingston emphasizes these processes of abstraction and performative substitution at the completion ceremony when a Chinese worker becomes what Eng calls a "body double"[71] for the white man who drives in the commemorative last spike: "A white demon in a top hat tap-tapped on the gold spike, and pulled it back out. Then one China Man held the real spike, the steel one, and another hammered it in."[72] In this scene Kingston reverses the projections of abstraction and concreteness. Here we see that the steel, as an inferior supplement to gold, is what constitutes the "real." The Chinese man who hammers it in is as concrete as the steel that consummates the nation, while the golden spike and the white man remain abstract, fetishized symbols of value. As Eng explains, the scene "underscores the splitting of the real from representation, of reality from the ways it is reconfigured in the laminating photograph that memorializes the event."[73]

By dramatizing the role of representation in romanticized projections of concrete white labor, Kingston allegorizes the way racial difference can be sublated into an abstract supplement of white labor while also serving an aesthetic function by giving Chinese form to the abstract domination of a capitalist temporality that is otherwise unrepresentable.

Unlike Kingston's text, *Dirty Laundry*'s focus is less on the actual labor process entailed in railroad construction in Canada from 1881 to 1885 than its aftermath. In particular, Fung's video provides a complementary view of the ideological forces behind Ah Goong's experience of "The Driving Out"[74] that follows the completion ceremony at Promontory. When Chinese labor is no longer indispensable, Ah Goong realizes, "It was dangerous to stay."[75] What Fung's video explores is how abstract labor becomes aligned with racialized perversity and vice that fuels the ideological basis for expulsion, making it "dangerous to stay." Incorporating themes of substitution, *Dirty Laundry* further reinforces the concrete attributes of white labor and abstract qualities of Chinese labor. In the video's dramatization of sections of the 1885 *Report of the Royal Commission on Chinese Immigration*, we see how concrete white labor is associated with a normativity defined by temporal discipline that sets the parameters of work, leisure, and reproduction. At the same time, Chinese exclusion from normative temporalities of domestic life become manifestations of the destructive attributes of abstract labor. Personifying the abstract domination of a capitalist temporality, the *Report of the Royal Commission on Chinese Immigration* casts Chinese men as a destructive, perverse force that threatens the social order. As historian Dora Nipp, one of the video's interviewees, explains, the railroad became a historical marker that separated abstract Chinese labor from perverse labor: "Initially when Chinese labor was needed for the labor, nothing bad was said about them. Once their labor was no longer welcome, then you hear about vices; you hear about prostitution, leprosy, all kinds of illnesses. . . . [Writers] dwelled on the exotic, the exaggerated, the evil." The range of racial, gender, and sexual substitutions that Fung's video explores offers a different view of the perversity that becomes associated with the abstract qualities of Chinese labor.

Substitution, as repetition with a difference, becomes a visual theme that anchors the video's fictional, archival, and documentary fragments. In particular, the visual refrain that interposes the entire video begins with a Chinese couple: the woman sitting behind her husband braiding his queue before he departs for Canada. The audio that accompanies the scene is of a woman's voice that asks, "Who will braid your hair? Who will cook your rice? Who will wash your clothes? Who will warm your bed?" This scene undergoes multiple substitutions throughout the course of the video, establishing a core thematic refrain that frames the video's other substitutions. In the first metamorphosis, the wife is replaced by a man, and it is a male voice that asks the series of questions that ends with "Who will warm your bed?" And when we fast-forward to the video's conclusion, the scene depicts a contemporary lesbian couple without audio to accompany the scene. In light of the fungibility of abstract labor, one significance of these substitutions is that they redefine substitution not as interchangeability but as repetition with difference. Rather than the undifferentiated assemblage of muscles and nerves that constitute abstract labor—what Marx describes as "human labour-power in its fluid state"[76]—these substitutions highlight gender and sexual difference. Further, that the scene's visual refrain occurs in an intimate domestic space where one lover is braiding the other's hair reinforces the affective dimensions of abstract labor. The repetition of this scene of domesticity counteracts the perverse domesticity to which Chinese labor is consigned. Moreover, working against the fetishism that misrepresents the dual character of commodity-determined labor, one that constitutes a social universe characterized by concrete and abstract dimensions, the substitutions keep the viewer alert to the normative cues and expectations that buffer and conceal the truth of social relations. As I explore below, Fung's substitutions present an allegory of racial fetishism that emerges around abstract alien labor.

Employing different forms of substitution that emphasize the defensive attributes of whiteness, Fung's video makes explicit connections between abstract labor and vice by drawing from the *Royal Commission Report on Chinese Immigration*. This was a report compiled in 1884 to study "objections to the influx of the Chinese People into Canada," which, as Fung's video notes, "leads to a Head Tax in 1885, the year the Canadian Pacific Railway is completed and Chinese labor is no longer needed." The study's primary methodology is to examine the Chinese restrictions in place in sister settler colonies, the United States and Australia, gathering "evidence" in Queensland and San Francisco by interviewing diverse classes of white male "witnesses" to testify on the subject of Chinese immigration. Among the array of subjects, Fung focuses on testimony that addresses Chinese labor and

FIGURE 1.2 Miner (video still). From *Dirty Laundry: A History of Heroes* by Richard Fung. Courtesy of the artist.

"sodomy," a subject heading that appears in the actual report. Unlike the forms of substitution in Kingston's *China Men* that align Chinese labor with the technological speed-up of abstract labor, Fung's video uses substitution ironically to examine the fungibility of whiteness. It is from the position of generic whiteness that negative, perverse content is cast onto the Chinese embodiment of abstract labor.

A scene depicting a white miner's metamorphosis into a senator dramatizes the class convergence of whiteness, which Francis describes as a performance of "authorial transvestism," observing how the "the senator's ventriloquism (transgressing the boundaries of class) functions in the interests of white racial dominance."[77] The white miner (figure 1.2), clad in a dusty work shirt and suspenders, begins the monologue discussing his heteronormative duties and domestic comforts, which become grounds for him to question the moral citizenship of Chinese men. He explains that in terms of labor, all is equivalent, but the costs of reproducing their respective labors puts the white miner at a distinct disadvantage. By the conclusion of his speech, the white miner has undergone metamorphosis into Senator Jones

FIGURE 1.3 Senator (video still). From *Dirty Laundry: A History of Heroes* by Richard Fung. Courtesy of the artist.

of Nevada, dressed in a black suit and bowtie (figure 1.3). The content of the testimony reveals the immorality and degraded nature of abstract labor when transposed to the temporal sanctity of the domestic realm:

> I have hopes to bring up my daughters to be good wives and faithful mothers, and offer my son better opportunities than I had myself. I cheerfully contribute to the support of schools, churches, charitable institutions, and other objects that enter into our daily life. But after I've maintained my family and performed these duties, not much is left of my wages when the week is ended. How is it with the Chinese? The Chinaman can do as much work underground as I can. He has no wife and family. He performs none of these duties. Forty or fifty of his kind can live in a house no larger than mine. He craves no variety of food. He has inherited no taste for comfort or for social enjoyment. Conditions that satisfy him and make him contented would make my life not worth living.

The white miner and senator align the Chinese body exclusively with a homogenized labor disposition. A Chinese body does not have the capacity for domestic enjoyment, community engagement, or social reproduction, which threatens the temporal stability of "socially necessary labor time." He continues to exaggerate the subhuman conditions of Chinese existence by commenting on the cramped living conditions, lack of enjoyable food, and lack of social taste, conditions that "would make my life not worth living." It is precisely the deprivations of Chinese domesticity and civic life that render Chinese labor nonhuman and therefore unfair competition. When the miner transforms into Senator Jones of Nevada, the politician's more confident voice and political status lend further legitimacy to the miner's complaint. Adding an air of authority to the miner's lamentations, Senator Jones makes a strong appeal against the Chinese: "The Chinaman comes in taking advantage of our skill, of our toil, and of our struggles, driving us from fields of industry which we have created and which our race alone can create." Conveying the unity of whiteness through the substitution of the senator for the miner, their casting of Chinese men as a destructive labor form emphasizes the parasitic effects of abstract labor on a concrete white labor host. What is also significant in the testimony is the senator's clear glorification of industrialization—the "fields of industry we have created and which our race alone can create"—emphasizes the concrete value of white labor's "skill . . . toil . . . struggles." This view of the white industrial laborer becomes the romantic anticapitalist counterpoint to the abstract status of Chinese labor who has no social value except to "take advantage." Both the miner and the senator thus attribute a destructive power to the Chinese, one that is constituted by his nonsocial, parasitic, and abstract qualities.

Fung's subsequent dramatizations of testimony from the Royal Commission report incorporate experimental forms of bodily and textual substitution that emphasize processes of signification and resignification. As Roger thumbs through the section on sodomy, the testimonies of a detective, a San Francisco merchant, and a former resident of China come to life to reinforce the perversity attached to Chinese bodies, whose temporal otherness is constituted through figurative alignment with labor duration and social nonreproduction. Their testimony on sodomy is presented in a continuous sequence:

Detective C. C. Cox: Cases of the most revolting crime came before them, for instance of which all details could if necessary be supplied with that of a man who cut out the penis of another who refused to submit to his degrading desires.

San Francisco Merchant Thomas H. King: Sodomy is a habit. Sometimes thirty or forty boys leaving Hong Kong in apparently good health before arriving here will be found to be afflicted about the anus with venereal diseases. And on questioning the Chinese doctors, they admitted that it was a common practice among them.

Six Years Resident of China John T. Tobin: I've never seen sodomy committed between men and men but I have seen it with beasts and detected them in the act with hogs, dogs, and ducks. But not in a great number of cases.

The cumulative effect of these testimonies is to attach bestial perversity to the disembodied form of the Chinese male body. No longer simply the socially abstract and destructive figure that the miner and senator argue "takes advantage" of hardworking, civic-minded white men of industry, perversity becomes the manifest *social* attribute of the abstract power of the Chinese laborer, a perversity that John T. Tobin links to animals. As queer countermemory, the video offers a parody of this "revolting" trajectory of Chinese disembodiment that coalesces around a severed penis, an infected anus, and—more humorously—a duck's rear accompanied by an audible "quack."

A later scene depicting a doctor's defense of Chinese sexual morality captures the relation of substitution as signification at stake in the Royal Commission testimonies. The scene opens to Roger, who appears in the role of a nineteenth-century Chinese laborer. He is bare-chested and moves slowly into a darkened room. As he moves across the screen, the text of the Royal Commission is projected onto his body, while the edge of the screen is illuminated to showcase the testimony of Mr. E. Stevenson, MD, of Victoria, British Columbia. As Mr. Stevenson speaks, his words are projected onto Roger's body. Mr. Stevenson offers an impassioned defense of the Chinese on the subject of their sexual morality:

Gentlemen, you have heard several witnesses testify unfavorably on this Chinese question and they have said they infer so-and-so. And from the fact that so many Chinese males are here and so few Chinese females, it has been inferred by certain people that, I hesitate to say it, that sodomy was by them practiced. I stamp it a damnable slander. A man who so acts bears the mark of Cain not only on his forehead but all over him.

The visual effect of character substitution, of redeploying Roger into the role of Chinese laborer, is to clarify Roger's contemporary relationship to the past, to his sexually ambiguous great-grandfather who worked on the CPR, and to the nation's history of sexuality. Substitution thus becomes a supplementary modality for Roger's countermemorial connection to history and sexual identity—bringing forth Derrida's notion of supplementarity as something that both replaces and adds to. On one level, Stevenson's testimony defends the honor of the Chinese and draws not on myth but on the demographic realities of the tremendous disparity in the population ratio of Chinese men to Chinese women, which fostered the development of segregated "bachelor" communities in North America. However, on another level, Stevenson's testimony remains tied to the earlier white witnesses' condemnation of Chinese perversity in asserting his symbolic power over the sign of race. Whether for or against Chinese immigration, the Chinese body remains an abstract object onto which racial and sexual discourse are literally and figuratively projected. The pages from the Royal Commission report that are projected onto Roger's body become the textual representation of the Chinese body. He becomes an abstract screen for the projection of textual content. Moreover, Stevenson's reference to the mark of Cain adds another layer of irony to the system of signification. When he notes how the mark of Cain appears "not only on his forehead but all over him," Stevenson amplifies the racial meaning of the mark, connecting sexual perversion to racial embodiment. As he speaks, Roger's body moves slowly out of the darkness; he pauses to highlight Stevenson's words "mark of . . . ," which remain projected on his chest until the words disappear as he exits into partial lightness toward Stevenson (figure 1.4). As Roger's character comes face to face with Stevenson, it becomes clear that Stevenson himself is a holographic projection, underscoring their divergent temporalities. He falls short of reaching Stevenson before becoming shrouded again by dark shadows. The ambiguity surrounding Roger's disappearance back into darkness is such that it is unclear whether the darkness that envelops his body is itself the "mark of Cain" or is, instead, a form of representative absence—a moment of unsignification. In either case, as the personification of abstract labor, the sexualization of the Chinese racial body is the discursively constituted and ideological effect of the disciplinary apparatus of an intensifying capitalist temporality. Moreover, rather than sanitize the "dirty laundry" of Chinese labor, Fung undercuts the heteronormative recuperation of Chinese sexual otherness by highlighting instead the discursive constitution of racialized sexual perversion and its ideological effects.

Fung is careful to contextualize the range of substitutions and modes of

FIGURE 1.4 Mark of Cain (video still). From *Dirty Laundry: A History of Heroes* by Richard Fung. Courtesy of the artist.

signification that emerge from these testimonies in a broader international context. Interspersed throughout the Royal Commission testimonies are frames of onscreen text. One indicates that "in 1885, the year Canada institutes the Head Tax, Britain criminalizes all sexual activity between men as 'gross indecency.'" Several frames later, additional onscreen text reads, "In Germany in 1892, the word homosexuality is first used in public," which is quickly followed by "Heterosexuality is coined later." By presenting a larger international frame for the projection of perversity onto the Chinese in Canada, Fung highlights the historical intersection of industrial capitalism and the desire to sexualize labor difference. What the video suggests is that the Royal Commission report represents less a narrative of testimony than a genealogy of settler crisis that turns on shifting social relations brought on by the new temporalities of industrial capitalism.

Queer Temporalities of History 2

In contrast to the jubilant embodiment and incorporation contained in the white settler mythology of the transcontinental railway, *China Men* and *Dirty*

Laundry incorporate temporal symbols of disembodied abstraction and social exclusion. In particular, the temporality of linear progress associated
with railroad technology is suspended, fractured, and defamiliarized. These
texts "see" and "feel" time, as Ah Goong proclaims. But though they exemplify the dehumanizing forces of capitalism's abstraction of labor time,
Kingston's and Fung's texts nevertheless reject the disciplinary temporality
of normative kinship, linear progress, and reproduction. If "time is a body,"
their bodies gesture to a temporal embodiment whose relations and modes
of belonging unfold as History 2. As Chakrabarty states, "In the reproduction of its own life-process, capital encounters relationships that present it
with double possibilities. . . . History 2's are thus not pasts separate from
capital; they are pasts that inhere in capital and yet interrupt and punctuate
the run of capital's own logic."[78] Imagining relations that do not contribute
to capital's self-reproduction, Kingston and Fung present the queer temporalities of History 2.

For Ah Goong, the embodiment of a queer temporality is anchored by
maternal longing and matrilineality. In his repeated, self-directed questioning of the meaning or purpose of a man's life, the literal and symbolic value
of his penis leads him to gender resignification. During the Chinese railroad
strike, Ah Goong wanders the forests pondering the value of masculinity
symbolized by his penis: he "just looked at it, wondering what it was for,
what a man was for, what he had to have a penis for."[79] Within the evolution of his gender resignification, Ah Goong questions not only the norms
associated with masculine power but also the symbolic burdens he's forced
to contend with. His thoughts turn to the "rumor of an Injun woman called
Woman Chief, who led a nomadic fighting tribe from the eastern plains as
far as these mountains. She was so powerful that she had four wives and
many horses."[80] The juxtaposition of these seemingly unrelated reflections
present to Ah Goong the quandary of settler colonialism. While Ah Goong
never sees Woman Chief, the rumor of her existence displaces the gender,
sexual, and spatial norms he associates with masculinity. Instead of expressing paternalistic control over a virginal, "empty" landscape, the Woman
Chief's defense of her land becomes an embodiment of matrilineal power.

Having experienced the disembodied passages of alien labor time, Ah
Goong's disillusionment leads him to express a distinctly maternal and
matrilineal reproductive desire that reverses the normative paternalism
and reproductive logic of white settler colonialism. During the "driving

out" of Chinese labor after the completion of the transcontinental railroad, Ah Goong's matrilineal desire conveys itself through an actively resignified gender lens. As he passes a farm, he finds an "imp child"; he stops and the baby crawls into his lap. He tells the child, "I wish you were my baby. . . . 'My daughter,' he said. 'My son.' He couldn't tell whether it was a boy or a girl."[81] Here Ah Goong's reproductive desire follows a matrilineal arc because it operates outside the norms of blood lineage and paternal inheritance in which strict gender codes are embedded. Not knowing whether the child is a boy or a girl, Ah Goong displaces gender codes altogether. The disembodying temporality of railroad labor here productively disorients the iterative temporality on which gender construction relies.

Ah Goong's matrilineal desire comes into fullest relief after his return to China, when he attempts to substitute the fourth of his four sons with an unwanted baby girl born to neighbors down the road. Disappointed that he has only sons and jealous of his neighbors' daughter, Ah Goong is considered insane, a "man who did not know the value of what he had"[82] with four sons. After secretly trading his son for the daughter, he feels that "with his soul he adopted her, full diaper and all."[83] Later, when he is forced to return the girl, "Ah Goong clung to his baby as if she were holding him up."[84] Without hope of realizing his reproductive desires, he rejects all sense of masculine propriety. It is this reproductive failure that causes him to begin "taking his penis out at the dinner table, worrying it, wondering at it, asking why it had given him four sons and no daughter, chastising it, asking it whether it were yet capable of producing the daughter of his dreams."[85] He becomes a figure of parodic masculinity, whose frequent exhibitionism — "yank[ing] open that greatcoat — no pants"[86] — underscores the phallic unfulfillment of normative paternalistic kinship.

But Ah Goong's story doesn't end with the pessimism of alien temporality; rather, it emphasizes its continual deferral of linear time. After his return to China, he embarks yet again for Gold Mountain and arrives in San Francisco. But here the linear trajectory of his narrative unravels, divorcing space from temporality. Kingston offers multiple narrative possibilities. In the first, Ah Goong is in an underground arsenal under Chinatown, "inside the earth,"[87] and is presumed to have died during the San Francisco earthquake and fire of 1906: "Some say he died falling into the cracking earth."[88] In another version he is brought back to China because "he was not making money; he was a homeless wanderer, a shiftless, dirty, jobless man with matted hair, ragged clothes, and fleas all over his body. He ate out of garbage cans. He was a louse eaten by lice. A fleaman."[89] The narrator offers a final possibility: "Maybe he hadn't died in San Francisco, it was just his papers that burned."[90] In this version he emerges from the "miraculous earthquake and fire,"[91] which burned down the Hall of Records so that "every China Man was reborn out of that fire a citizen."[92] Ah Goong's rebirth is accompanied by another birth: "He had been seen carrying a child out of the fire, a child of his own in spite of the laws against marrying."[93] Each of these versions capture elements of Ah Goong's temporal and spatial estrangement as an undisciplined subject of capitalist social relations: living underground, as a "homeless wanderer," and finally as a father. This reorganization of time, space, and identity is further accentuated by the earthquake, a crisis event that will interfere with the discursive constitution of Chinese bodies as "aliens ineligible for citizenship." In the final version, where Ah Goong emerges phoenixlike from the fire, he becomes an agent of resignification. As Eng notes, "Like the elimination of a single term in a sign chain, the burning of the Hall of Records — the literal destruction of these particular documents — demands a subsequent shift in meaning, a shift in the relational terms that attempt to shore up the historical ruins of the archive."[94] The narrator surmises, "He had built a railroad out of sweat, why not have an American child out of longing?"[95] However, the fulfillment of his "longing" for kinship does not reproduce the temporal discipline of heteronormative reproduction; rather, it expresses a mode of belonging that symbolically fulfills his matrilineal desire. Ah Goong occupies a queer temporality in which alien survival and reproduction arise outside of the temporal discipline of settler capitalism. Countering the symbolic role of the child to reproduce normative logics and values of white life, what Lee Edelman refers to as the "absolute value of reproductive futurism," Ah Goong's "child out of longing" represents the potentiality of matrilineal desire and, against settler biopower, expresses an alien mode of survival. In the aftermath of the earthquake and fire, many of those kin relations will be impurely, discursively constituted as "paper sons." As such, the alien child does not represent the guaranteed futurity of white settler colonialism but a potential deferral of patrilineal reproduction while promoting the fictive, queer kinship of alien longing as one temporality of History 2.

The politics of embodiment are thus expressed in *China Men* through Ah Goong's gender resignification, which rejects the paternalistic codes of setter territorialization and temporal discipline. At the same time, by foregrounding a matrilineal identity that values daughters and empowers women, Ah Goong expresses various desires that intersect with transgender embodiment. Expressing gender and sexual difference as modes of embodiment, he interrupts the stability of gender and its assumed correspondence to biological sex. As an articulation of transgender identifications, Ah Goong disrupts what Susan Stryker identifies as the presumed "'wholeness' of the body and 'sameness' of its sex . . . [as] socially constructed."[96] Desiring a daughter, "fucking the world," and berating his penis, Ah Goong confounds the equivalence of sex and gender, highlighting instead how "'sex' is a mash-up, a story we mix about *how* the body means, which parts matter most, and how they register in our consciousness or field of vision."[97] In the context of nineteenth-century labor, Ah Goong's transgender expression is significant in its disidentification with a notion of equivalence. In other words, his identity is not an expression of an abstract equivalence that can be substituted under the homogenizing process of labor under capitalism, where equality is an enforced condition of alienation.[98] Indeed, as David Harvey puts it: "There is nothing more unequal than the equal treatment of unequals; how the equality presupposed in the market exchange of things deludes us into a belief in the equality of persons."[99] In Ah Goong's performance of gender and sexual difference, he attaches the logic of equivalence that abstracts labor into homogeneous temporal units of human labor to a profoundly masculine logic. Moreover, in his rejection of the terms of equivalence that counteract the reproduction of capitalist logic, he embodies the potential of History 2.

In *Dirty Laundry* the themes of embodiment, retrieval, and difference are captured in the idea of "family resemblance" that becomes part of the narrative frame for the video's historical and fictional sections. The fictional travelogue centered on Roger brings together ideas of queer temporality in order to reanimate and embody Chinese Canadian history. What's at stake in this history is presented as a mystery surrounding the sexual identity of his great-grandfather, whose framed picture Roger's father has insisted he take along with him on his business trip. When he accidentally breaks the frame to reveal a hidden photographic portrait of his grandfather touching hands with another man, he is unsure how to interpret the photograph. The broken picture frame becomes a visual metaphor for what Lowe calls an "alternative mode of inquiry" that allows us to move beyond "the singular history that frames a particular image of Chinese immigrant labour . . . that memorializes the static, single artifact."[100] But in the context of figurative and thematic substitutions that the video foregrounds, the hidden photograph presents a queer opening that works against the fetish to reveal rather than conceal the features of an alien labor temporality.

The analysis of the mysterious photograph expands rather than contracts the range of historical possibilities that relate to Chinese sexuality and assumed perversion. Although Roger admits to the train steward that he doesn't "know how to read" the revealed photograph, the Chinese steward responds, "This is normal in China. . . . Men hold hands." As Francis observes, the steward's reply raises the "question of how the 'normal' is constituted in different cultural contexts and historical eras."[101] After they have sex, Roger asks the steward, "You know what you were saying about men holding hands. What does it mean?" The steward replies, "That they like each other, they're brothers. . . . It's a smart thing. If they're lovers, no one asks any questions." This "smart thing" is the illegibility of queer historiography. The video does not impose a teleology of queer becoming. In many ways, the linear direction of identity formation in the traditional bildungsroman is frustrated here. It is the unresolved, illegible queer history that animates Roger's quest to engage in genealogy. The ambiguity of the great-grandfather's sexuality is what is given ontological priority in the video as an expression of pre-Stonewall conceptions of sexual difference. As Nayan Shah underscores in one of the video's interviews, "The whole notion that sexual identity is your identity, that somehow who you desire and who you sleep with and who you have sexual pleasures with somehow says something very revealing about you, is a completely new notion." Just as Ah Goong's gender resignification takes on a "perverse" relation to masculinist norms, the ambiguity of Roger's great-grandfather's sexual identity frustrates the growing "incitement to speak" that Foucault attributes to the rise of liberal individualism in the late nineteenth century. The point is, his great-grandfather's sexual ambiguity, its deferral of concrete meaning, stands as the content of his difference. Here again, the emphasis on sexual difference frustrates a logic of equivalence that capitalism abstracts out of human labor. In the video's final frame, the photograph comes to life as the great-grandfather and friend/lover walk out of the frame, away from the photographer's studio backdrop. That the photographic subjects are roles played by Roger and the steward creates a correspondence between historical and contemporary notions of same-sex affiliation without collapsing contemporary sexual identities with what Francis describes as the "homo-social ambiguities of history."[102] Rather, the substitution of Roger and the steward for their historical predecessors highlights the role of sexuality for reanimating abstract conceptions of labor and history. In its focus on family genealogy, the video offers a narrative of literal and figurative family resemblances that traces alternative modes of affiliation and belonging that do not reproduce capitalism's disciplinary temporalities. As countermemory, *Dirty Laundry* rejects the iconicity of both the lonely Chinese bachelor and the sexually perverse Chinese body and replaces them with an empty stage that frustrates the reproductive, linear trajectory of History 1.

My argument in this chapter has focused on the way Kingston's and Fung's texts illuminate how the fusion of temporal otherness and sexual vice converge into a biological expression of abstract alien labor. Their experimental forms offer a new context for understanding why the first immigration laws in Canada and the United States were passed in the aftermath of railroad construction to prevent the infiltration and proliferation of abstract alien labor. Although a comparatively smaller population, the fact that Chinese students, diplomats, and merchants were exempted from immigration restriction laws in the United States and Canada exemplifies the way perversity was identified with the particular features of industrial labor within a capitalist mode of production.

I have situated Kingston's and Fung's texts as responses to the celebrated temporality of the telegram that began this chapter that exposes the censored content of Van Horne's sketch of the Chinese laborer. This is the literal and figurative backside of the normative settler temporality celebrated on the face of the telegram. Against the homogenizing logic of racial equivalence, Kingston and Fung present queer recuperations of the "perverse" temporalities of alien labor within the consolidating logic of settler colonial capitalism. In their countermemories of the history of settler national unification by rail, their texts expose the logics of racialized alignment between alien bodies and abstract labor. Exploring queer temporalities of History 2, they counteract the logics of substitution *as* equivalence that reproduce a capitalist labor temporality of expanding the working day and speed-up. In the next chapter, I turn to the other side of the antinomical view of capitalist relations: romantic anticapitalism's hypostatizing of the concrete, natural, thingly side of the antinomy. Drawing on the 1920s and 1930s as the apex of anti-Asian animosity and exclusionary immigration policy in both Canada and the United States, I explore the development of romantic anticapitalism, which expresses its racial animus toward the abstract Asian alien through an identification with the natural landscape and Indigeneity. Within a capitalist logic of settler colonialism, the Native and the land become biologized expressions of the concrete dimension of the social world.

CHAPTER 2

UNNATURAL LANDSCAPES

Romantic Anticapitalism and Alien Degeneracy

[Landscape] is like money: good for nothing in itself, but
expressive of a potentially limitless reserve of value.
—W. J. T. Mitchell, "Imperial Landscape"

Undoing Landscape

I begin this chapter with an unnatural scene: an old photograph of
a tree surrounded by a crowd of onlookers (figure 2.1). It is night-
time. White men under gleaming hats stand with their hands in their
pockets. On the left appear the blurred faces of a couple, walking
arm in arm toward the camera. They are dressed as if they are on a
date at the movies. Some of the bystanders look ahead, away from the
camera, while others look back, impervious to the glare of the flash.
There seems to be nothing aesthetically remarkable about the tree
in the background except its sturdiness, emphasized by its proportional dominance, and its three solid branches jutting out like tines
on a pitchfork. It turns out that the photograph is lying. What we do
not see is that the occasion for the social gathering is the body of a
lynched man who hangs from one of the tree's branches. The photograph belongs to a series by artist Ken Gonzales-Day entitled *Erased
Lynching*, in which he digitally removes the victim from the lynching
scene. These are scenes that were captured and circulated on post-

FIGURE 2.1 Ken Gonzales-Day, *Erased Lynching*, 2006. Courtesy of the artist.

cards in western states from 1850 to the 1930s, and most of the victims were not black. As Gonzales-Day explains, "Native Americans, Chinese, and Latinos of Mexican and Latin American descent were lynched in California . . . guided by anti-immigration sentiments, the fear of miscegenation, a deep frustration with the judicial system, or in combination with white supremacy."[1] The vast majority of lynching victims he uncovered were of Latino descent.

Gonzales-Day's manipulation of lynching scenes is remarkable for the way it produces visibility out of erasure, inverting the power of the visual field. By shifting the spectacular nature of the lynched body onto the spectators, *Erased Lynching* moves the viewer's attention to the visuality of lynching itself. Not only does it draw our attention to the expressions of the spectators, but we are also confronted by the cultural apparatus and circulation of lynching images, what Gonzales-Day refers to as the "aesthetics of the event, from the physical act to the creation of the lynching photograph and its progeny, the souvenir card, view card, and postcard."[2] It also draws our attention back to the tree, whose former innocence is replaced by purposeful attributes of branch height and species — primarily native oak species[3] — that facilitated the mechanics of lynching. In addition, the large, life-size scale of Gonzales-Day's photographic rendering serves to insert the contemporary viewer into the lynching scene, implicating us as consumers of the spectacle of racial violence and participants in their circulation.

For the purposes of this chapter, Gonzales-Day's photograph is significant not only for the way it counteracts the spectacle of the lynched racial body, but also for how it reverses the normative power we associate with landscape. The anchoring tree, as the primary subject of the viewing public, is stripped of the romanticism we attach to "scenery." As a photograph rather than a painting, it communicates less the *spiritual* aesthetic of landscape than what Gonzales-Day describes as an artifact that "remains trapped somewhere between memento and evidence."[4] In its inversion of the visual content of the image — rendering the white spectators, rather than the lynched body, *as* racial spectacle — Gonzales-Day exposes the power of perspective and subjective identification, elements that are intrinsic to the aesthetic technology of landscape. In manipulating viewers' capacity to identify with the scene, *Erased Lynching* activates the notion of landscape as a medium rather than strictly a genre of art. This follows W. J. T. Mitchell's insistence that we examine "not just what landscape 'is' or 'means' but what it *does*, how it works as a cultural practice."[5] In this case, the landscape functions as both a witness and accomplice to racial violence.

Following the last chapter's focus on the racialization of Chinese workers as abstract labor, an economism that aligned Chinese labor with the temporal domination of capitalism, this chapter probes how settler colonial constructions of the landscape express the other side of the antinomy: the concrete, thingly, natural dimension Postone describes as that which "appears as the variegated surface of immediate sensuous experience."[6] While Asian labor personifies the abstract circuits of capitalism, settler colonial constructions of landscape express the opposite: the concrete, pure, and authentic noncapitalist dimension of nature. That the social world *appears* antinomical—that is, characterized by concrete and abstract dimensions—is a function of the fetish, which conceals the social relations behind products of human labor, repressing the duality of commodity-determined labor. As Kingston's and Fung's texts illuminated in the last chapter, Chinese labor was associated with a perverse temporality, one that rendered Chinese bodies fungible (like currency) and a signifier of moral corruption. As such, Chinese bodies occupied the abstract dimension of the antinomy, as subjects "abstracted from all particularity"[7] insofar as Chinese bodies are interchangeable with other Chinese bodies. White labor, on the other hand, was individual, tangible, concrete, and of social value. Postone describes this structure of social relations as a "quasi-natural opposition" of two objective worlds: "The relation of these two worlds of objectivity can then be construed as that of essence and appearance, or as that of an opposition (as has been expressed historically, for example, in the opposition between romantic and positive-rational modes of thought)."[8] Postone's emphasis on the opposition between romantic and positive-rational modes of thought is particularly germane for our consideration of landscape, which is associated with both western romanticism and an imperialist aesthetic. As Mitchell observes, the Chinese antecedents of western landscape "flourished most notably at the height of Chinese imperial power and began to decline in the eighteenth century as China itself became an object of English fascination and appropriation at the moment England was beginning to experience itself as an imperial power."[9] From this view, landscape can be seen to function as a fetish itself, "symptom[atic] of the rise and development of capitalism; the 'harmony' sought in landscape [can be] read as a compensation for and screening off of the actual violence perpetrated there."[10]

It is precisely because landscape *appears* real, natural, and thingly, rather than a way of seeing and a culturally mediated representation of nature, that it seems antithetical to the very circuits of capitalism and imperialism that Mitchell identifies with it. Here, as Postone clarifies, "the opposition of its abstract and concrete dimensions allows capitalism to be perceived and understood in terms of its abstract dimension alone; its concrete dimension can thereby be apprehended as noncapitalist."[11] In other words, capitalism is understood in terms of its abstract dimension, noncapitalism (and anticapitalism) with its concrete dimension. Thus, building on the last chapter's examination of settler exclusion of abstract alien labor because of its "perverse" alignment with capital, this chapter examines the settler identification with the western landscape and idealization of Native peoples as a further expression of the romantic anticapitalism of anti-Asian sentiment and the indigenizing project of settler colonialism. We will see how settler colonialism constructs a landscape that is simultaneously a site of Native erasure and a site of indigenizing purity and authenticity.

In order to excavate the racial logics of landscape in a manner that foregrounds, as Gonzales-Day's photograph does, the interplay of racial violence, settler identification, and landscape, I look to the landscape photography of Vancouver-based artist Jin-me Yoon and the late New York–based photographer Tseng Kwong Chi. As photographic countermemory, their reenvisioning of western landscapes in Canada and the United States identifies romantic anticapitalism as a key ideology of settler colonialism. Their respective photographs of Mount Rushmore, the Canadian Rockies, and the Pacific coast parody the conventions of landscape art of the 1920s and 1930s that were established by artists such as Ansel Adams, Gutzon Borglum, the Canadian Group of Seven, and Emily Carr. In doing so, Tseng and Yoon expose how romantic anticapitalism flourished during the height of anti-Asian immigration restriction to project a settler identification with a personified, Indigenous landscape. The way early twentieth-century artists anchored white settler identity in the landscape reflects contradictory identifications with the "Native" that effectively erased the history of conquest and dispossession while expressing nostalgia for a time before capitalist modernity. This romantic idealization of nature and the "noble savage" captures the settler valorization of the concrete realm of social relations under capitalism, particularly under conditions of rapid industrialization and economic flux leading up to and following the stock market crash of 1929. Within the romantic anticapitalist logics of settler colonialism, the valorization of the concrete over the abstract realms misconstrues the *appearance* of capitalist relations for their reality. As Neil Levi puts it, "Romantic anticapitalism . . . hypostatizes the concrete, rooted, and organic, and identifies capitalism solely with the abstract dimension of capitalist social relations."[12] In this chapter I look at the way works by Tseng and Yoon emphasize how the eugenicism embedded in an expanding conception of whiteness increasingly appropriates Indigeneity as a mode of biologizing the landscape.

I situate Tseng's and Yoon's parodic strategies of countermemory within the theoretical framework of disidentification articulated by José Esteban Muñoz. For Muñoz, disidentification works alternatively as an artistic process, a mode of performance, and a critical hermeneutic. It is a mode of "shuffling back and forth between reception and production."[13] By highlighting disidentification as a frame for Tseng's and Yoon's artistic process and performance, I read their engagement with landscape neither as assimilative identification nor as a wholesale rejection of it. Neither is it, as Muñoz clarifies, an "apolitical middle ground."[14] Rather, disidentification operates as a third mode of dealing with dominant ideology that emerges from the recognition that the subject is constituted *inside* ideology—that there is no privileged position outside ideology from which the subject can oppose its own formation—and that resistance can occur through "negotiations between desire, identification, and ideology."[15] Disidentification, therefore, is about "*recycling* or reforming an object that has already been invested with powerful energy."[16] Tseng's and Yoon's projections of their alien excess against a landscape of normative racial, cultural, and aesthetic values captures the political potential that Judith Butler further ascribes to the disidentificatory encounter, "this uneasy sense of standing under a sign to which one does and does not belong."[17] By analyzing their engagement with the cultural values it activates, I propose that Tseng's *Expeditionary Series* and Yoon's *Group of Sixty-Seven* enact modes of parody that both *recycle* the dominant codes associated with the landscape and *transform* them with their racial excess. Their encounters perform a repetition with a racial difference.

As British settler nations whose colonial objective was primarily land appropriation rather than the exploitation of Indigenous labor,[18] national identity in Canada and the United States has often been defined as a product of the landscape. As Angela Miller explains of the US context, the nineteenth-century landscape encapsulated "the nationalist myth—that the physical environment itself produced national character."[19] Similarly, in the early twentieth century in Canada, as Erin Manning suggests, the "quest for national identity [was sought] through the image of the landscape . . . where the unity of states and citizens [was] constructed on the putative ethnic or racial identity of a nation, which, in turn, is anchored to the representation of landscape."[20] As a vital source for the expression of national identity in both nations, the continuing appeal of landscape art into the early twentieth century was often coupled with disdain for the rise of modernism. In a revealing glimpse of such antimodernist sentiment, when the Group of Seven traveled to New York State in 1913, it was not to attend the influential exhibition of international modern art at the Armory Show but to attend an exhibition of traditional Scandinavian art.[21] Within the diverse media that form the landscapes by Adams, Borglum, the Group of Seven, and Carr, none ironize or subvert—as modernist art often does—nationalist subject matter or the hierarchy of high and popular cultural forms. Instead, their works contain a romantic reverence for and spiritual identification to land as a symbolic anchor for their aestheticized "defense" of national identity.

Uncovering the eugenic and Indigenizing subtexts of romantic anticapitalism that are embedded in the settler landscape, I turn first to Tseng's *Expeditionary Series* to explore its citations to US photographer Ansel Adams, the Group of Seven, and Mount Rushmore sculptor and architect Gutzon Borglum. I demonstrate how his photographs prompt a recognition of landscape as both a biopolitical expression of white supremacy and a personification of white male dominion. Such a personification of the land is precisely a form of what Postone refers to as the biologization of the concrete that constitutes "*expressions* of that antinomic fetish, which gives rise to the notion that the concrete is 'natural,' and which increasingly presents the socially 'natural' in such a way that it is perceived in biological terms."[22] The final section of this chapter turns to Yoon's photographic collage *Group of Sixty-Seven*, whose title makes reference both to the Group of Seven painters and to 1967, the year Canada removed racial barriers to immigration. This legislation was the Canadian corollary to the Hart-Celler Immigration Reform Act of 1965 in the United States, which similarly removed race-based immigration criteria. Building on Tseng's parody of the eugenic whiteness of the landscape, Yoon's project highlights the fusion of the Group of Seven's eugenic ideology with Emily Carr's own autochthonophilia and her intense desire to "go native."[23] Thus, *Group of Sixty-Seven* exposes the eugenic ideology at the core of romantic anticapitalism and the contradictory logics of exclusion and elimination that condition the triangulation of Native, alien, and settler positions within settler colonialism in North America.

Eugenic Landscapes

In 1978 the artist Tseng Kwong Chi transformed himself from an invisible minority to a visible alien. His metamorphosis came about after an experience he had on a family lunch outing at a high-end New York restaurant. Respecting the restaurant's dress code, Tseng arrived wearing the only suit he owned: a Chinese uniform he had purchased at a Montreal thrift store. To his amusement he was greeted by the restaurant's staff and patrons as a Chinese Communist dignitary, much to the displeasure of his parents, who years earlier had escaped from Communist China. His sister, Muna Tseng, recalls the royal treatment her brother received at the restaurant, recounting, "When we arrived . . . the maître d' took one look at [Tseng] and treated him like a V.I.P., a gentleman from the East, an emissary from Cathay. My parents were not amused."[24] The attention he attracted at the restaurant nevertheless produced an artistic breakthrough that led Tseng to undergo a process of orientalization, beginning with his name, which went from Joseph Tseng to Tseng Kwong Chi. Completing his wardrobe with mirrored glasses and a clip-on "Slut for Art" ID badge, Tseng reinvented himself in the stereotypical role of the inscrutable and perpetually foreign Asian. It was an identity that his friend the choreographer Bill T. Jones described as "Chinese drag."[25] Henceforth, in Chinese drag, he took to the streets of New York, gaining unparalleled access to exclusive social events, most famously in 1980 when he crashed the opening night of the Ch'ing dynasty costume exhibition at the Metropolitan Museum. There he mingled with the rich and famous, including Henry Kissinger, William F. Buckley Jr., and Yves Saint Laurent, who, as the art critic Grady Turner relates, "commended Tseng for his fluency in French and asked if he had served in the Chinese embassy in Paris."[26] What Tseng realized during these experiences was the vastness of Westerners' ignorance of Asians. Therefore, drawing on a persona that simultaneously evoked foreigner, visitor, tourist, alien, and imposter, he exploited that ignorance in his photographs, which offered surprising reconfigurations of clichéd tourist scenes in North America and around the world.

FIGURE 2.2 *Seven Peaks, Alberta, Canada, 1986.* Photograph by Tseng Kwong Chi, *East Meets West*, a.k.a. *The Expeditionary Self-Portrait Series 1979–1989.* © Muna Tseng Dance Projects, Inc., New York. www.tsengkwongchi.com.

In the diverse fields in which Tseng's photographs have been analyzed, from performance studies to Asian American studies, the majority of critical attention has focused on the photographs from the earlier period of his *East Meets West* series, for their clever juxtaposition of caricatured foreignness and touristy familiarity of Western monuments and icons, such as the Statue of Liberty, Disneyland, and the Hollywood sign. Reflecting the historical moment, the series title aptly parodied the anticommunist sentiment being reignited in 1979, on the eve of the Reagan Revolution. What many critics found remarkable about his photographs, as Margo Machida explains, is that they "counter[ed] a long history of Orientalist painting and photography by explicitly re-representing the West as if seen through a possessive 'Occidentalist' gaze."[27] In contrast to this reception, however,

Tseng's later photographs featured in the same series, renamed *Expeditionary Series*, have garnered less attention, perhaps because they appear attenuated from the overt culture clash staged in his earlier work. For instance, Tseng's photographs of majestic US and Canadian landscapes, such as the Grand Canyon, Monument Valley, and the Rocky Mountains, have been described as offering more solitary explorations of the individual's relation to nature, which his sister describes as "recalling Chinese landscape paintings of man balanced between sky and earth."[28] Turner further marks the shift toward natural landscapes in Tseng's series as evidence of a romantic turn in his oeuvre:

> [He] put aside the confrontational implications of the earlier title to concentrate on [his] own transformation from alien tourist to American explorer. . . . The Mao suit has become irrelevant. . . . He offers us brief glimpses of a Romantic figure, an artist who has put aside his disguise to revel in the sheer power of nature.[29]

This chapter reconsiders this assessment by asking whether the concerns of the latter phase of his series are absent of "confrontational implications." Rather than a romantic homage to nature's sublimity, I interpret Tseng's *Expeditionary Series* as a queer parody of the Western conventions associated with Canadian and American landscape art of the early twentieth century. Given that landscape art of this period was broadly concerned with honoring nature's vitality and universalizing power, the intrusion of Tseng's alien body is a sign not of life-affirming incorporation but of extravagant degeneration. Reading the managed interplay of life, degeneration, and death as a central feature of settler colonialism and projected onto nature, I argue that Tseng's photographs animate the biopolitics of the settler landscape in Canada and the United States.

In consideration of the vexed modalities of racial impersonation that Tseng's work elicits in Chinese drag, Butler's discussion of gender and drag performance is useful for highlighting the ambivalent agency of parodic recycling that surrounds his work. When Butler evaluates the subversive potential of drag to expose gender constructions through imitation, she locates gender transgression less in the volitional agency of the drag queen than with the drag performance itself: "[Drag] serves a subversive function to the extent that it reflects the mundane impersonations by which heterosexual ideal genders are performed and naturalized and undermines their power by effecting that exposure."[30] In other words, drag *allegorizes* the imitative structure of gender, as a recycled copy that has no original. Butler's theorization of gender and drag presents an opening for considering race through the terms of drag performance, without collapsing the distinctions between the processes of gendering and racialization — or disregarding their intersection.[31] In particular, both racialization and gendering are processes that are historically constituted through a racist and heterosexist system that reproduces itself through its iteration in bodies, institutions, and law. It is a system that both "precedes and exceeds" the *intentions* of the racialized and gendered subject.[32] In the case of Tseng's photographs, although he taps into the symbolic construction of the Asian alien through his performance, Tseng does not invent or choose the terms of his own racialization. Thus, by engaging a disidentificatory hermeneutic, my reading of Tseng's photographs harnesses the *ambivalence* of queer of color parody as an opportunity to further demystify and denaturalize what Muñoz calls the "universalizing ruse of dominant culture."[33] At one level, this mode of reading registers Tseng's deliberate efforts to choreograph the visual dissonance in the juxtaposition of two figurative constructions: the Chinese as alien and the settler nation as landscape. At another, my analysis also mines the *unintentional gaps* between parodic repetition and difference that magnify how, as a queer man of color in racial drag, he epitomizes what Chandan Reddy refers to as a "material nonequivalence" to the settler landscape as an alien abstraction against a concrete expression of nature.[34] It is in this spirit of disidentification that I draw on the way Tseng's photographs evoke the conventions of landscape art produced in the 1920s by the Canadian Group of Seven painters, the American sculptor Gutzon Borglum, and the American photographer Ansel Adams.

Comprising a significant portion of the 150 black-and-white photographs Tseng took from 1979 to 1989, the *Expeditionary Series* captures the variation and range of landscapes he photographed in North America and around the world. A Hong Kong–born Canadian immigrant who attended art school in Paris and lived his adult years in New York among a vibrant set of artists until his death from AIDS in 1990,[35] Tseng's perception of the landscape in North America and elsewhere was undoubtedly informed by his transnational movements. Excavating the historical context surrounding his photographic references to North American landscapes of the 1920s, a generative period of landscape art in Canada and the United States, I focus on Tseng's

Seven Peaks Snowfield and *Lake Moraine*, both located in Banff National Park in Alberta, Canada, and *Mount Rushmore* in the Black Hills of South Dakota.

As "natural wonders" of the West, Banff National Park and Mount Rushmore are two sites firmly positioned in settler colonial mythologies of the North American landscape. Banff owes much of this popular mythology to the Group of Seven landscape painters who made Canada's Western landscape a central subject of many of their paintings. In the United States this mythology is indebted to Gutzon Borglum, the architect behind the colossal sculpture of the four presidents' faces at Mount Rushmore. With respect to the highly aestheticized quality of Tseng's dramatic black-and-white photographs, they also recall the visually operatic Yosemite photographs of Ansel Adams. However, unlike Adams, Tseng disrupts the sublime tranquility of the natural landscape by inserting his caricatured body into the frame. Tseng engages with the mythic landscape as an artistic subject that was foundational for the legacy of the Group of Seven and Adams, as well as in terms of the way space and scale are crucial components of the visual impact of Mount Rushmore. Confronting the tangled strands of national history, artistic convention, and regenerative racial power that are projected onto these diverse landscapes, Tseng's photographs capture what Mitchell calls the "dreamwork" of settler colonialism.[36]

By putting his alien excess into racial tension with the landscape, Tseng's parody of early twentieth-century landscape art brings to light a romantic idealization of nature that, in the context of North America, is infused with eugenic ideologies of white racial regeneration. Evolving out of social Darwinist theory, eugenics emerged in the late nineteenth century and grew in the early decades of the twentieth century with the support of both conservatives and progressives. As Daniel Kevles explains, "The progressives and the conservatives found common ground in attributing phenomena such as crime, slums, prostitution, and alcoholism primarily to biology and in believing that biology might be used to eliminate these discordances of modern, urban, industrial society."[37] According to Kevles, racial thinking "played a major part in American and Canadian versions of this [eugenic] creed,"[38] based on fears raised from the influx of non–Anglo Saxon immigrants and the social degeneracy those groups were associated with. The 1920s and early 1930s represented the apex in the eugenics movement, with the passage of numerous eugenics sterilization laws—particularly in California, British Columbia, and Alberta—which inordinately targeted racial minorities and immigrants.[39] While the scientific justification for eugenics had waned slightly after World War I, eugenics nevertheless persisted in institutionalized forms.

Knowledge of eugenics' false claims did not, as Mary Coutts and Pat McCarrick explain, "decrease the pressure for legislation, judicial action, or immigration controls."[40] Indeed, immigration restrictions directed at Chinese migrants to the United States and Canada coincided with the intensification of eugenic ideology from the nineteenth century into the twentieth. After passage of the 1875 Page Act, which effectively restricted the entry of Chinese women for their presumed sexual immorality, the United States passed its first race-based federal immigration restriction through the Chinese Exclusion Act, which was in effect from 1882 to 1943. In 1885 the Canadian government passed its own race-based immigration restriction through the Chinese Head Tax, a tax designed to deter Chinese migrants from entering Canada. By the mid-1920s, both Canada and the United States had intensified and expanded earlier restrictions on Chinese migrants. In Canada these measures extended restrictions to other Asian migrants and further deterred Chinese immigration through the passage of the Chinese Immigration Act of 1923, which excluded most classes of Chinese migrants until 1947. The United States, having also broadened restrictions to encompass other Asian migrants, passed the Immigration Act of 1924, which intensified previous race-based restrictions through its exclusion of most Asian ethnic groups and foreigners who were deemed "biologically inferior."[41] The persistence and growth of anti-Asian policy from the 1880s to the 1940s reflects what Erika Lee refers to as the "hemispheric Orientalism" that took hold along the West Coast of North America.[42] Despite their nationalist pretensions, Canada and the United States were bound by a shared commitment to preserving the transnational power and normativity of whiteness. As Marilyn Lake and Henry Reynolds put it, the "project of whiteness was a paradoxical politics, at once transnational in its inspiration and identifications but nationalist in its method and goals."[43]

Fears over the degeneration of Anglo-Saxon stock were present in the art world as well. The Canadian Group of Seven painters reflected these anxieties over the diminishing strength of the white Nordic race in their painting, believing that the Canadian landscape held "replenishing power" that could disinfect what one member called a "low receptive reservoir into which pours the chaos of ages, the mixed concord and discord of many varied peoples."[44] Employing tropes associated with hygiene and mental health, they put forward a mission to "clean this reservoir . . . or we will remain a confused people."[45] In the US context, Deborah Bright draws out the anticapitalist basis of Ansel Adams's romanticism, noting that his early twentieth-century photographs represented a "mixture of Progressive Era phobias about industrialization and encroaching alien populations with an equally conservative nostalgia for the myth of preindustrial organic society."[46] Fears of white race suicide also informed Gutzon Borglum's vision of Mount Rushmore, a colossal-scale sculptural project that he began in 1924 and did not live to see completed seventeen years later. Expressing his fears of miscegenation, he once wrote, "Here we have in the filtering of Asiatic and North African blood [into Europe] the complete vitiating of the vigor and intellect of the civilization existing in these once pure European peoples."[47] Thus romantic, regenerative, and preservationist motifs were infused in North American landscape art of the period and reflected deep anxieties over the racial "health" of the industrializing settler nation. And despite the absence of human or nonwhite representation in many of these works, my analysis of these landscapes heeds Martin Berger's assessment that in North American art since the nineteenth century, "a decidedly racialized perspective animated even those cultural products most removed from racial concerns."[48]

The hyperbolic orientalism of Tseng's persona in the *Expeditionary Series* confronts these defensive logics embedded in the romanticized colonial landscape in ways that denaturalize the abstract, universalizing, and absorptive power of its conventions. As such, Tseng's photographs tap into the historicism of parody, which Linda Hutcheon defines as "an inscription of the past in the present [that] embod[ies] and bring[s] to life actual historical tensions."[49] In Chinese drag, Tseng's exaggerated performance "mimes and renders hyperbolic" a host of normative race, gendered, and sexual conventions that are literally and figuratively naturalized in the landscape.[50] As the alien, the dissonance between his body and the landscape delineates the racialized abstraction of Asians and their symbolic excess to national culture. The Chinese male body in North America was historically constituted as nonreproductive, perverse, and feminized, which was reinforced through legal and extralegal restrictions on interracial intimacies, restrictions on the immigration of Chinese women, and aggressive enclosure in the domestic labor market. Thus the alien sexuality Tseng elicits can also be seen as the product of a biopolitical landscape whose regenerative energy is directed at the degeneration and exclusion of alien bodies. Moreover, as a queer artist who referred to himself as a "snow queen" because of his preference for white men,[51] Tseng's queer white desire—a desire for incorporation into a white landscape of artists and gay culture—creates a productive tension with the gender and sexual objectification of the Asian body. The conflicted relations and identifications that Tseng's photography stages capture a mode of disidentification that negotiates "between desire, identification, and ideology."[52] Disrupting an exceptionalist imagining of Canada or the United States as a concrete, pristine wilderness, Tseng's photographs reframe the settler colonial landscape as a racial borderland of symbolic violence.

With the exception of a handful of photographs taken in British Columbia, the main focus of Tseng's Canadian landscapes is the Rocky Mountains of Banff National Park in Alberta. Established in 1885 as Canada's first national park and modeled after Yellowstone National Park in Wyoming, Banff National Park is one of the most iconic wilderness symbols of Canadian national identity. In Rob Shields's analysis of Banff's nationalist symbolism, he suggests that "Banff can serve as a metaphor for the Canadian condition: the peremptory Canadian self of the present clings to an image of a European past (or an ideal future) and refuses to confront the violence and paradox of its own making."[53] In short, Banff reflects the worldview of European settlers who modeled the area after nineteenth-century European spas and tourist retreats. The city itself is named for a country seat on the northeast coast of Scotland between Aberdeen and Inverness, a name indicative of the vast colonial respatialization of Native territory. Resignified and repackaged in an endless series of tourist photographs and postcards, Banff conveys the purity of nature that contrasts with the impurities associated with the urban environment. What is evacuated from Banff's symbolic repository is the displacement of First Nations peoples as the region's original inhabitants. Native voices have largely been silenced, while their identities have been appropriated as tourist commodities that serve to authenticate the "naturalness" of the environment.

The birth of Canada's first national park in 1885 also coincides with the completion of the Canadian Pacific Railway, the transcontinental railroad responsible for the park's creation.[54] As discussed in the last chapter, construction of the railroad employed thousands of Chinese railroad workers recruited from the United States, who tunneled through the most treacherous sections of British Columbia's Fraser Canyon. Only after the Canadian Pacific Railway was completed did a Royal Commission on Chinese Immigration persuade the Canadian government to take measures to restrict the entry of Chinese migrants. As noted earlier, the government responded by enacting its first race-based immigration restriction, the Chinese Head Tax, which required that Chinese migrants pay $50 to disembark in Canada. By 1903 this sum had climbed to $500. Hence the very conditions of possibility for Banff's pristine environment depended on appropriating and eliminating Indigenous peoples and exploiting and excluding aliens. Here, as in other settler states, elimination and exclusion are two ways that settler colonialism cuts both ways.[55]

Despite the fact that Banff National Park is located in the *valley* of the Bow River in the southern part of Alberta, Banff's snowy alpine landscape nevertheless evokes Canada's nationalist identification with the North. Shelagh Grant explains that conceptualizations of the Canadian North have been informed by both British and American romantic idealizations of nature in the nineteenth century: "British aesthetic myth blended with American wilderness myth to reinforce a Romantic image of north."[56] An integral feature of Canada's national identity—showcased no less in the first verse of the national anthem, "O Canada, our true *North* strong and free"—the North is nonetheless a moving construction that is articulated through representations ranging from the Canadian arctic to Banff's alpine elevation. The unfixed character of the North is what Sherrill E. Grace calls "magnetic north," a "north whose parameters seem always to be shifting."[57] The development of Canada's northern identity is often attributed to the landscape paintings of the Group of Seven artists. An artist collective that rose to national fame in the 1920s and was credited with producing the first "national" art, their landscapes set out to reflect what they saw as an authentic Canadian spirit that was not derivative of European or American art traditions. Manning explains that "while the landscape paintings of the Group of Seven do not create the type of nationalism that is based on an ideology of the land, they do play a role in supporting the myth of the 'great white north.'"[58] Drawing on tropes of purity, rugged masculine strength, and individualism, Group of Seven founder and spokesperson Lawren Harris saw the North as a spiritual realm untouched by history, humanity, or capitalist modernity. Harris writes in "The Story of the Group of Seven" that "what I was groping toward [was] Canada painted in her own spirit,"[59] and he elaborates the connections between race, nation, and northernness in his essay "Revelation of Art in Canada":

> We are in the fringe of the great North and its living whiteness, its loneliness and replenishment, its resignations and release, its call and answer — its cleansing rhythms. It seems that the top of the continent is the spiritual flow that will ever shed clarity into the growing race of America, and we Canadians being closest to this source seem destined to produce an art somewhat different from our Southern fellows — an art more spacious, of a greater living quiet, perhaps of a more certain conviction of eternal values.[60]

Harris's conceptualization of a North equipped with the spiritual powers that could "cleanse" the nation through an interplay of "living whiteness" and "loneliness and replenishment" is indicative of his racial anxieties of immigrants who contributed to "the growing race of America." Moreover, crafting an exceptionalist narrative around Canada as the most northerly nation in the Americas, Harris attributes to Canada a primary role as spiritual compass and regenerative source for the continent.

Tseng's Rocky Mountain landscapes contain sly allusions to a romantic conceptualization of wilderness as a purifying and regenerative national symbol that the Group of Seven idealized. For instance, Tseng's *Seven Peaks, Alberta, Canada, 1986* (figure 2.2) references the phallic majesty of mountains, trees, and icebergs that dominate the Group's paintings.[61] Commenting on the Group's authority over the Canadian landscape, Manning remarks that "for many years the quintessential Canadian landscape painting was an image of an unpopulated wilderness, with Tom Thomson's ancient pine tree or Lawren Harris's icebergs at the forefront."[62] The Group's tendency to position these natural subjects — mountains, trees, and icebergs — as visual anchors in their paintings has been well documented as reflecting heavily gendered ideas of nature. Towering mountains and trees were associated with a heroic masculinity that exercised their superiority over the changing, ephemeral, and feminized qualities of water and wind. A case in point is Harris's renowned painting *Mt. Lefroy*, which depicts a large snowcapped mountain that evokes qualities of nobility, imperviousness to change, and purity and expresses, Berger states, "a distinctly masculine aesthetic."[63] In particular, *Mt. Lefroy*'s peak seems to almost puncture the overhead clouds, while light ripples away from the site of entry—as if to illuminate the nobility of the peak's act of penetration. The connotations of forced sexual penetration and feminized submission are intentional, Joan Murray explains, given that Harris "believed in expressing sexuality in symbolic terms, and in his Lake Superior and Rockies subjects, the use of such semi-symbolic sexual imagery (penal [sic] mountains and vaginal clouds) [is] overt."[64] In *Mt. Lefroy*, masculine virility constitutes the power of the mountain and its domination of the feminine ephemera that lie below and hover overhead. These anthropomorphic motifs are consistent with the Group of Seven's broader symbolic language, in which mountains and trees represent white, heterosexual, and paternal resistance to what Robert Linsley calls "inundation from below, and submission to the powers above . . . like a spike that is meant to pin together a stable identity out of spiritual, social, and sexual experiences that are all by nature transitory."[65] The sturdy tree or towering mountain therefore celebrates a virile masculine individualism that is in constant tension with threatening lower elements that allegorized the Group's fears, widespread in the 1920s and 1930s, about racial and ethnic mixing and the corresponding degeneration of a white, Nordic race.[66]

Some of the racial implications of the Group's landscapes come into further relief in the way Tseng's photographs echo Adams's environmentalist photography. Originating in the late nineteenth century, the American environmentalist movement regained momentum after World War I and bore the imprint of escalating eugenicist thought. In particular, eugenic ideology fused wilderness protection with white racial preservation through analogies that linked the degradation of the natural environment with the degeneration of the white race through miscegenation and rising nonwhite populations. Alexandra Minna Stern explains that during the 1920s, efforts to save redwood trees in California served as a "metaphor for defending race purity and ensuring the survival of white America."[67] Inspired by Sierra Club founder John Muir, Bright explains, Adams "se[t] out to produce a photographic version of the nature publicist's writings" and played an immense role in constructing an environmentally focused vision of the American landscape.[68] Despite the progressive agenda attributed to Adams's landscapes, Bright points out that "the rugged western wilderness [was] a locus for the sentiments of white, middle-class Americans around nationalistic and ethnocentric ideals [that] cannot be overlooked in any discussion of the development of environmentally concerned photography."[69] As such, the grandeur of Adams's landscapes, analogous to the Group of Seven's, could provide spiritual reassurance of the durability of the white race, its ability to persevere in the face of lower castes.

Stern explains that eugenicists "profoundly shaped California's landscapes" and subscribed to the belief—reflected in Adams' and the Group of Seven's regenerative narratives about nature—that "exposure to nature" was a "method of containing the worst and actualizing the best of human's evolutionary and hereditary predispositions."[70] Exemplified in *Monolith* (figure 2.3), the mountains and trees featured in Adams's photography stood for what many conservationists viewed as the "stateliness, grandeur, and perseverance—represent[ing] the 'great race.'"[71] Discussing the way conservationists collapsed distinctions between the redwood and white America, Stern writes: "Like Anglo-Saxon America, which was being engulfed by hordes of defectives and mongrels and menaced by the excessive breeding of undesirables, the redwood was imperiled by 'race suicide' from rampant logging, urban encroachment, and human ignorance."[72] While mobilizing against the expropriation and destruction of natural resources was certainly a worthwhile cause, romantic anticapitalism framed the struggle in racial terms. For both the Group of Seven and Adams, racial ideologies could be invisibly projected onto the impermeable mountains in Banff and at Yosemite. As a cultural practice, then, the landscape aestheticized defensive racial ideologies of white supremacy.

Tseng's *Seven Peaks* also plays with what Linsley describes as the "great freeze out of Canadian painting" in the 1920s,[73] referring to the Group of Seven's emphasis on snow and ice, and exhibits an attention to lighting that recalls Adams's compositional details. However, the inclusion of Tseng's body displaces the anchoring image of Harris's and Adams's trees and mountains. If these anchoring images symbolically project the white masculine mastery over inferior forces, Tseng's body fails to convey a sense of stability, permanence, or purity associated with the landscape. Unlike the imposing and phallic tree or mountain peak, Tseng neither dominates the surrounding landscape nor stands, to quote Linsley's assessment of Harris's natural imagery, as "a spike meant to pin together a stable identity."[74] Contrasting the whiteness of his snow-filled environment, Tseng's body highlights his dissonance with the landscape. His isolation does not suggest a rugged individualism in symbolic struggle with the surrounding elements; rather,

FIGURE 2.3 *Monolith*, 1927. Photograph by Ansel Adams. © 2014 The Ansel Adams Publishing Rights Trust.

it evokes the incongruity of his alien body against the overwhelming whiteness of the natural background. As an evolving sign of yellow peril, moreover, Tseng's body exposes the eugenic logics of purity present in the early twentieth-century landscapes he references. As an index of the abstract, degenerative value of nonreproductive, alien sexualities, he highlights the eugenic spirit of white racial reproduction and regeneration projected onto the landscape. Finally, dwarfed by the massive mountain peaks in the background, Tseng animates the desire for what Albert Boime calls a commanding "magisterial gaze" over the landscape, "the perspective of the [North] American on the heights searching for new worlds to conquer."[75] Although the tradition of North American landscape art promotes what Berger identifies as a "natural affirmation of white culture" through a decidedly white male gaze,[76] Tseng's gaze is largely unreadable behind his mirrored glasses. The direction of his gaze only points back to the camera and ultimately to the viewer. In this reversal, Tseng's photographs highlight the racial limits of the landscape's regenerative symbolism in its reflection of white settler identification with an uncorrupted nature that exists outside the circuits of capitalism.

Tseng's photograph of Moraine Lake (figure 2.4) also makes references to the intersecting discourses of northernness and tourism that produce Alberta's national parks. His deliberate or unintentional misidentification of Lake Moraine's location in the Northwest Territories—way, way up north—humorously underscores the northness of its more southern location in Banff National Park. Commodified by Rocky Mountain tourists who frequent the lake and rent canoes, the most literal commodification of the lake occurred when the Bank of Canada issued twenty-dollar bills featuring the lake on the reverse side of the 1969 and 1978 bills (figure 2.5). The scene on the bill that Tseng perfectly captures is known as the "Twenty-Dollar View."

Tseng's recreation scene flaunts the irony at the core of the Group of Seven's conceptualization of nature. His photograph demonstrates that, far from a space untouched by modernity where a pure white wilderness exists as a refuge from corrupting human influences, Moraine Lake represents instead the capitalist conversion of Indigenous territory into tourist sites. The high aestheticism of the mundane tourist snapshot also amplifies what Jody Berland refers to as a form of "staged authenticity," a concept derived from Dean MacCannell's work on the western tourist to "describe the ways in which diverse regional cultures produce themselves as touristic objects."[77] Berland goes on to explain that "because tourists seek new experience through interaction with the *other* . . . they place themselves in contact with personalities and spaces that seem to represent the inside of another culture but which in fact are carefully staged to represent that in-

FIGURE 2.4 *Lake Moraine, Alberta, Canada, 1986.* Tseng Kwong Chi, *East Meets West,* a.k.a. *The Expeditionary Self-Portrait Series 1979–1989.* © Muna Tseng Dance Projects, Inc., New York. www.tsengkwongchi.com.

side to outsiders."[78] Tseng adds another parodic layer to the notion of staged authenticity insofar as his photograph confuses the relation between tourist and other. He is both tourist *and* other. Playing with the various codes of "authenticity" that produce the tourist site, the tourist, and the alien other, he reduces the scene's commodified grandeur to a stage that dramatizes the fetishization of the imagined colonial encounter.

On a more humorous note, Tseng's pose, with oar raised in midstroke, also evokes the figure of the wilderness sportsman. The sportsman movement began in Canada in the late nineteenth century and promoted an ideology of the wilderness that, analogous to the burgeoning conservation movement, represented a domain of white masculine regeneration.

FIGURE 2.5 Twenty-dollar Canadian bill, 1969–1979 Series, *Scenes of Canada*. Bank of Canada.

As Lynda Jessup explains, nineteenth-century landscape paintings that depicted sportsmen coincided with the rise of sportsman clubs that aimed to "revitaliz[e] manhood" against what they perceived were the "degenerative, emasculating, effects of capitalist modernity."[79] The sportsman was thus the antithesis of the Chinese "bachelor" of the exclusion period, who exemplified respective racial and sexual threats to white labor and white female bourgeois respectability. Pictured as an unlikely sportsman, Tseng further underscores his exclusion from the regenerative scripts associated with this wilderness genre of masculinity. In stark contrast to the leisure associated with the sportsman's wilderness enterprise, labor defined the lives of early twentieth-century Chinese male immigrants. As discussed in the first chapter, the colonial management of Asian reproduction was largely accomplished through immigration restriction, antimiscegenation law, and segregation practices that produced "bachelor societies" in Canada and the United States. The constraints on Chinese masculinity amounted to what David Eng calls "racial castration," the "psychic and the material limits circumscribing Asian American male subjectivity."[80] However, in Tseng's adaptation of the iconic nationalist scene, his parody highlights foremost the commodification of nature while prompting recognition of the white racial investment in regenerative narratives embedded in its mythology.

As a multisensory medium that expresses cultural values, the landscape can be "found" in Banff National Park and Yosemite or, as Mitchell outlines, "*put* there by the physical transformation of a place."[81] Examining the latter, I turn to one of Tseng's US landscapes, *Mount Rushmore, South Dakota, 1986*

FIGURE 2.6 *Mount Rushmore, South Dakota, 1986.* Tseng Kwong Chi, *East Meets West,* a.k.a. *The Expeditionary Self-Portrait Series 1979–1989.* © Muna Tseng Dance Projects, Inc., New York. www.tsengkwongchi.com.

(figure 2.6), to demonstrate how Tseng's intrusion onto the patently manu-factured natural landscape also prompts an excavation of the racial logics embedded in the "shrine of democracy." *Mount Rushmore, South Dakota* is in many ways exemplary of the *Expeditionary Series* title in its engagement with the heroic forefathers of the nation and the monument's fearless creator, Gutzon Borglum. Four presidents—George Washington, Thomas Jeffer-son, Abraham Lincoln, and Theodore Roosevelt—were carved into stone in a project that took seventeen years from inception to completion. As the presidents set their gaze on the westward frontier, Tseng's body faces the presidents. What does he see?

Since its completion in 1941, Mount Rushmore has become such an embedded symbol of US nationalism that Cher once admitted to believing that the monument was a naturally occurring rock formation.[82] Even for those who recognize the transparent constructedness of the rock landscape, the monument nevertheless appeals to similar ideals of authenticity and purity present in the Group of Seven's landscape paintings. Fears over the potential degeneration of a superior "Nordic" race that were projected onto the landscape reflected the transnational currency of alarmist race theories in white settler nations. Similar to the Group of Seven, whose trees and icy mountains can be interpreted as personified symbols of white paternalistic dominion over the Canadian nation, Mount Rushmore's granite rock face brings this symbolism to a literal realm in its depiction of the nation's heroic "forefathers." Borglum's rock, a medium that expresses both impermeability and permanence, shares with the Group's paintings a reverence for nature's strength, stability, and resistance to change. As Borglum wrote of his intentions for the memorial, "The purpose of the memorial is to communicate the founding, expansion, preservation, and unification of the United States."[83] Interestingly, although the Group's landscapes and Borglum's mountain sculpture represent spaces of spiritual relief and separation from alienating bureaucratic structures and the economic determinism associated with the city, their artistic undertakings would have been impossible without substantial government funding. And, similar to the Group's romantic pursuit of the true North, Borglum fashioned himself as a rugged explorer who "discovered" the site in the Black Hills. During the memorial's formal dedication ceremony in 1925, he climbed the vertical face of the mountain and planted a flag on its peak. Boime explains that in this feat "Borglum was emulating [John C.] Frémont's dramatic unfurling of the flag on the summit of the Rockies."[84] Thus Borglum and his monument provided for Tseng a rich corpus of heroic, white, masculine, and colonial associations to emulate in his own *Expeditionary Series*.

If the effect of the Group of Seven's paintings was to naturalize conquest by erasing human involvement in the landscape, Borglum's Mount Rushmore was an even more explicit homage to the ideology of Manifest Destiny. Boime observes that the monument "allegorizes the idea of Manifest Destiny" in that all four presidents had a role in the myth of divine territorial intervention.[85] These included Washington's extensive surveying of the frontier; Jefferson's Louisiana Purchase; Lincoln's transcontinental railroad; and Roosevelt's role in the conquest of New Spain and construction of the Panama Canal, which provided an expedient water route to Pacific markets. In short, the monument exemplifies Mitchell's suggestion that the "rise of landscape" is intimately connected with imperial expansion.[86]

Similar to his parodic engagement with the Group of Seven, Tseng's pose and manipulation of scale recalls a romantic tradition of landscape art that privileges a single perspective. Mount Rushmore's participation in this tradition is rendered to the point of exaggeration, captured in the monument's grandiose point of view. This perspective epitomizes what Boime refers to as a "magisterial aesthetics," one that reinforces an "imperial point of view that is often expressed in American landscape painting of the nineteenth century and that remains deeply embedded in the national consciousness."[87] In *Mount Rushmore, South Dakota*, the elevated perspective of the gigantic presidents' faces symbolizes their authority over the land they govern, which is contrasted with Tseng's subordinated and ambiguous perspective. Reversing the direction of their magisterial gaze, Tseng's body is turned away from the viewer, and his concealed face points upward toward the four presidents. And unlike in the earlier *East Meets West* phase of Tseng's series, where he often blew up the scale of his body to give the impression he was a Godzilla-esque figure threatening the various national icons he stood beside — such as the Statue of the Liberty or the Empire State Building — here Tseng's body is dwarfed in the presence of Borglum's homage to the nation's forefathers.

The pose Tseng adopts in this photograph brings to mind the Byronic hero, the lone romantic figure cast in relief against the natural landscape. A well-known example of these "magisterial aesthetics" is captured in a nineteenth-century piece called *The Wanderer above the Sea of Fog* (1818) by the German painter Caspar David Friedrich. Contained in Friedrich's painting (figure 2.7) are the frequently recycled tropes of romanticism. For instance, the clouds and mountaintops intermingle in the painting to emphasize the inseparability of nature from the heavens above. At the center is the solitary traveler, who has climbed to a dangerous vantage point, his back turned to us so that the viewer can share his point of view and spiritual identification with the purity of nature. The mountains in this painting similarly evoke permanence and steadfastness. Joining earth and heaven, the intermingling craggy rocks and clouds convey both endurance and immortality. The anticapitalist subtext of this romantic vision is underscored by the wanderer's traditional folk attire, which valorizes the cultural purity of folk life over the abstract degradations of capitalist modernity.

FIGURE 2.7 Caspar David Friedrich, *The Wanderer above the Sea of Fog*, ca. 1817. Oil on canvas, 94.8 × 74.8 cm. Inv.: 5161. On permanent loan from the Foundation for the Promotion of the Hamburg Art Collections. Photo Credit: bpk, Berlin / Hamburger Kunsthalle Museum / Elke Walford / Art Resource, NY.

Like Friedrich's wanderer, Tseng stands with his back to the viewer. However, he is standing so close that the monument loses its illusions of grandeur. Boime suggests that Mount Rushmore, "like the statue of liberty, . . . succeeds [only] through the impact of scale rather than aesthetic quality."[88] From where Tseng stands, unable to appreciate the impact of scale, the monument cannot succeed. Using his body to emphasize distinctions of scale, Tseng also evokes Chinese landscape paintings of the Song and Yuan dynasties.[89] The small scale of the human figures depicted in the paintings of these periods emphasizes the sanctuary offered by nature and the relative insignificance of human beings against an overpowering natural environment. Maxwell Hearn explains that the disintegration of the Tang dynasty was the main catalyst for the Romantic antidynastic retreat into nature: "Faced with the failure of the human order, learned men sought permanence within the natural world, retreating into the mountains to find a sanctuary from the chaos of dynastic collapse."[90] Whether deliberate or not, the allusion to Chinese landscape painting in Tseng's photograph is amusingly out of place at Mount Rushmore because it subverts, as Mitchell explains, "any claims for the uniquely modern or Western lineage of landscape."[91] In particular, in the context of Mount Rushmore's celebration of Manifest Destiny, the photograph's connection to Chinese landscape painting further underscores the circuits of dynastic power and capital that give rise to imperial dimensions of landscape art. Through the parodic gaps between repetition and difference, Tseng's photography brings to view the imperial dimensions of landscape art that are conditioned by the violent elimination of Indigenous peoples and expropriation of land resources.

Toying with these elements of scale, Tseng dramatizes his insignificance in the face of these forefathers in a parody of heroic frontier masculinity. This parody underscores the cultural importance of frontier masculinity as a constitutive element of US national identity while emphasizing how Asian men literally fall short of its larger-than-life romanticization. As a queer Asian man, moreover, Tseng and his near invisibility underscore the multiple registers of his alienation: from constructions of white masculinity, from the whiteness of US gay male identity, and from patriarchal Asian American cultural nationalisms that reinforce a staunchly heterosexist "heroic" masculinity to combat anti-Asian racism. For instance, according to Frank Chin, Jeffery Paul Chan, Lawson Fusao Inada, and Shawn Hsu Wong of the *Aiiieeeee!* Collective, Asian American cultural politics must challenge the social and cultural emasculation of Asian American men by subverting stereotypes of the "good Chinese man . . . [as] the fulfillment of white male homosexual fantasy, literally kissing white ass."[92] While Tseng assumes the guise of the explorer, however parodic, his contemplation of the four presidents might very well be read as "kissing white ass." Thus, in

Tseng's disruption of cultural nationalist prescriptions, his physical incon-sequentiality may suggest that a masculinist and heterosexist Asian Ameri-can cultural nationalism falls short precisely because it further entrenches a cultural standard of white masculinity. At the same time, Tseng's diminu-tiveness can also be read as a tacit acknowledgment of what Malini Johar Schueller calls "the gendered imperatives of Western imperialism and ori-entalism that have produced the stereotype of the effeminate Asian male."[93] Refusing to adopt the "magisterial gaze" of the four presidents, Tseng turns his attention to the gaze itself and its presumed authority. He faces east rather than west, reversing the westward direction of the frontier that the presidents seem to be surveying. His eastward gaze counters the normative conventions of landscape that, as Patricia Nelson Limerick observes, "ran on an east-to-west track, following the physical and mental migrations of white English-speaking men."[94] Most importantly, his eastward gaze dem-onstrates the fact that the westward movement of white settlers was only one small part of the process of "discovery." A disoriented explorer, Tseng evokes the historical fact that for nonwhite immigrants, as they moved along the west–east axis of labor, internment, and other displacements, the landscape was not the simple, pure, virgin wilderness of the settler colonial imagination. Indeed, Chinese labor in North America offers a salient illus-tration of Raymond Williams's remark that "a working country is hardly ever a landscape."[95]

The subtle lighting in the black-and-white photograph also has the effect of nearly disappearing Tseng. On the one hand, his invisibility underscores the illegibility of his queer Asian difference within the regenerative myths and expansionist ideologies that Mount Rushmore stands for. On the other hand, his disappearance allegorizes the repressed histories that are not etched in stone, most notably the history of the Sioux Nation: the Sioux campaigned vigorously against the monument, which was built on stolen land and commemorated the murder and dispossession of Indigenous peoples. As Boime points out, "Consistent with the pattern of destruction characteristic of national exploration and empire building, the creation and the dedication of the Mount Rushmore monument was one more symbol of the white man's racist and intolerant Indian policy."[96] The site of Mount Rushmore is between what is now Harney National Forest and Custer State Park, what Boime refers to as the "two most hated names in the Sioux lexi-con" because of William S. Harney's and George Armstrong Custer's massacres of Sioux populations that led to illegal gold mining in the Black Hills.[97] The Black Hills, where Mount Rushmore is situated, houses the sacred site of Paha Sapa and is designated by the Sioux as a ceremonial place of prayer and meditation. The memorial was built despite the Fort Laramie Treaty of 1868, which gave Dakota Indians exclusive rights to the Black Hills. Predictably, as soon as gold was discovered, white miners swiftly breached the treaty agreement to begin the illegal expropriation of natural resources and, in the case of Borglum, to blast 450,000 tons of granite from the face of the sacred Black Hills. This history underscores the contradictory logics of settler colonialism, which engages in the violent elimination and dispossession of Indigenous peoples and simultaneously expresses a desire to become Indigenous to the landscape, to naturalize settler colonialism through symbolic projection.

Another history not etched into stone includes the many Chinese who worked in the Black Hills in what Liping Zhu calls the "largest Chinatown east of San Francisco from 1876 to 1910."[98] Only since 2001, when extensive archaeological excavations of Deadwood's Chinatown began, have widespread signs of Chinese life been revealed for examination. As Zhu notes, the gold rush brought thousands of Chinese miners to the western states, including South Dakota—although the population did not surpass 250 residents. Zhu explains that "as soon as the news spread of Lieutenant Colonel George A. Custer's expedition finding gold in the mountains of western Dakota Territory, Chinese immigrants joined the last major gold rush in the nineteenth century, arriving in the Black Hills by the winter of 1875–1876."[99] They were subject to labor exploitation and racial violence. Only recently have the Chinese, who played such an important role in this South Dakota borderland, emerged from historical repression into partial visibility, giving new meaning to the hazy outline of Tseng's body at Mount Rushmore. But as Tseng's suit nearly blends into the rock—suggesting that he is part of the rock—the Chinese of the Black Hills are also embedded in this borderland of invasion, dispossession, and ongoing political struggle.

Like the Group of Seven, Borglum's nationalist project was shaped by his own reactionary beliefs. Despite the rhetoric of democracy he invoked to characterize Mount Rushmore's commemorative spirit, he was unambiguous about the perils of miscegenation. In particular, in addition to expansions in anti-immigration law, the period saw the rise in white supremacist organizations such as the Ku Klux Klan (KKK), an organization that had earlier commissioned Borglum to create a Confederate monument at Stone Mountain near Atlanta, Georgia. His ties to the KKK were not insignificant. Borglum was an impassioned reader of Madison Grant's *Passing of the Great Race*, a scaremongering, pseudoscientific treatise that "became a sacred text for eugenicists, the Klan, and proto-Nazis everywhere."[100] Influenced by Grant's treatise, Borglum also took to the page. In a 1923 letter to prominent Indianapolis Klansman David C. Stephenson, Borglum boasted, "I wrote 2500 to 3000 words on the evils of the alien races."[101] In other letters to Stephenson in the early 1920s he also expressed a profound anti-Semitism in his fears of hypodescent through miscegenation, writing as follows:

> If you cross a thorough-bred with a jackass you get a mule. . . . The lowest race in civilization is the strongest physically and breeding (crossed) is always down. A Negro and a Jew will produce Negro, but Hindu and Jew—Jew; Chinese and Jew, offspring Jew; Italian and Jew, offspring Jew; and European race and Jew, offspring Jew.[102]

As John Taliaferro notes, "He labeled immigrants 'slippered assassins,' . . . [and] warned that America was becoming an alien 'scrap heap.'"[103] Even though Borglum opposed slavery, he blamed African slaves for the degeneration of the white race, writing that "it has been the character of the cargo that has eaten into the very moral fiber of our race character, rather than the moral depravity of Anglo-Saxon traders."[104] His eugenic vision was also explicitly gendered. Boime explains that Borglum's admiration of Benito Mussolini's virile masculinity was in direct contrast to the effeminacy and weakness he associated with Jews. For these reasons he attempted to disassociate himself from stereotypes of the effete artist by engaging in rigorous physical activities such as rock climbing, boxing, and wrestling and crafting an aesthetic vision based on colossal forms. In this light, Tseng's presence on the face of Mount Rushmore stages a confrontation with the manifest masculinity embedded in the shrine of democracy, a confrontation captured in his eastward gaze and richly evocative of the earlier title of the series, *East Meets West*. In sum, the degenerative excess signaled by Tseng's abstract alien body powerfully underscores the romantic anticapitalism embedded in the settler colonial personification of the landscape as a concrete, racially pure, and masculine expression of a noncapitalist universe.

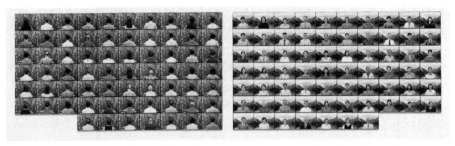

FIGURE 2.8 Jin-me Yoon, *Group of Sixty-Seven*, 1996, 134 chromogenic prints, dimensions variable. Collection of the Vancouver Art Gallery, Acquisition Fund. Photo: Trevor Mills, Vancouver Art Gallery.

Our Home and Native Landscape

To conclude this chapter I turn to Jin-me Yoon's 1996 photographic work *Group of Sixty-Seven*, which usefully complements Tseng's parodic exposure of romantic anticapitalist ideology projected onto the nationalist landscape. *Group of Sixty-Seven* extends the focus on racial constructions of national landscape that first appeared in her 1991 *Souvenirs of the Self* postcard series, in which Yoon poses, much like Tseng, in front of familiar tourist sites in Banff National Park. Continuing her exploration of the interplay of race and landscape, *Group of Sixty-Seven* connects romantic anticapitalism with the fetishization of Indigenous identity and racializes Asians as a negative abstraction. Here Yoon incorporates the paintings of two iconic Canadian painters, Lawren Harris of the Group of Seven and Emily Carr, an artist deeply inspired by the Group of Seven's nationalist vision who became renowned for her artistic interaction with Native populations in British Columbia. From the view of settler colonialism's triangulation of settler, Native, and alien identities, Yoon's work exemplifies how the Native and the Asian personify opposite sides of an antinomical view of capitalist relations, in which the concrete, noncapitalist dimension is Indigenous and the abstract representation of capitalist modernity is Asian.

Group of Sixty-Seven (figure 2.8) consists of two gridlike panels, each panel containing sixty-seven photographs of Korean Canadians from Vancouver, British Columbia. On the left panel, they face away from us (figure 2.9), and on the right, they face us (figure 2.10). We can first observe the various layers of national citation in this piece. The title, *Group of Sixty-Seven*, makes an overt reference to the Group of Seven. The number "sixty-seven" in the

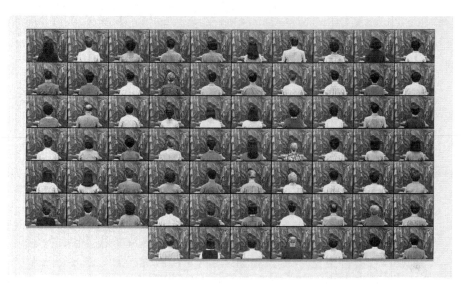

FIGURE 2.9 Jin-me Yoon, *Group of Sixty-Seven* (detail), 1996, 134 chromogenic prints, dimensions variable. Collection of the Vancouver Art Gallery, Acquisition Fund. Photo: Trevor Mills, Vancouver Art Gallery.

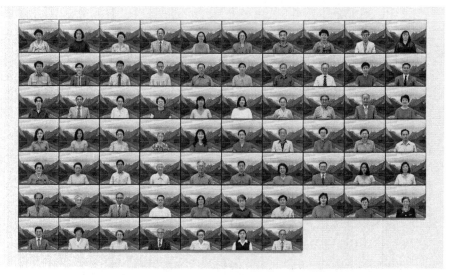

FIGURE 2.10 Jin-me Yoon, *Group of Sixty-Seven* (detail), 1996, 134 chromogenic prints, dimensions variable. Collection of the Vancouver Art Gallery, Acquisition Fund. Photo: Trevor Mills, Vancouver Art Gallery.

title also cites Canadian confederation in 1867 and the elimination of national origins immigration quotas a hundred years later, in 1967—the crucial legal prerequisite for the appearance of many of the sixty-seven Korean Canadian faces featured in the piece. Adding another layer of citation to the Group of Seven artists, we note that behind the heads on the right panel is Lawren Harris's Rocky Mountain painting *Maligne Lake, Jasper Park*. Building on Tseng's references to the Group of Seven painters and their association of white male nationhood with landscape, Yoon's work highlights the commodification of landscape in her use of repetition, recalling the seriality of Andy Warhol's pop art.

Like Warhol's Campbell's soup cans or Marilyn Monroe portraits, Yoon's piece similarly inverts high and low aestheticism and the values associated with originality and duplication. Her postmodern play of surface and depth presents a dramatic recontextualization of Harris's *Maligne Lake*, which was considered the most influential painting in Toronto from the time it was painted in 1924 to 1930.[105] As one of the most celebrated nationalist works of art in Canada, art historian Dennis Reid describes Harris's painting as a "tribute to the spiritualizing force of the country, an incentive to the spiritual capacity in us all."[106] In keeping with his romantic views of a nation united under a spiritual conception of the North, *Maligne Lake* expresses a sense of control and order that defended against the turbulent social realities of the 1920s. This was a period of increasing industrialization, urbanization, and class struggle that fomented increasing antipathy toward racialized aliens, particularly Chinese labor migrants, who were subject to the Chinese Head Tax and would face exclusion through passage of the 1923 Chinese Immigration Act. Thus the "rise of landscape"[107] and escape into a primordial, frozen wilderness in this context can be attributed to an increasing sense of chaos spurred by modernity. By invoking Harris and the Group of Seven so explicitly in this piece, Yoon invites the viewer to explore the intersection of race and romantic anticapitalism in the Group of Seven's artwork, particularly in the racial and spatial depiction of Canada's national identity constructed around the idea of the "Great White North." More confrontationally, Yoon prompts the viewer to consider the relationship between these Korean faces and the essence of Nordic purity celebrated in the Group's depiction of the landscape.

By photographing sixty-seven Korean faces in front of Harris's painted landscape, Yoon imposes what Hutcheon calls "an external order upon a work that is presumed to be original."[108] However, Yoon manipulates the line between the authenticity of the original by repeating Harris's landscape sixty-seven times. In terms of the dissonant media presented in the work, Yoon emphasizes the modernity of the Korean faces through her use of photography—a medium whose infinite capacity for reproduction represents an antithesis to notions of artistic originality contained in Harris's piece. In doing so, Yoon allegorizes the way Korean Canadian bodies become racial signifiers of the abstract dimension of capitalist modernity and, alternatively, how the painted landscape becomes a signifier of the concrete dimension of nature, purity, and originality. But Yoon ultimately frustrates a view of the abstract homogeneity associated with Asians by emphasizing the gender and generational diversity of her Korean Canadian subjects against a *Maligne Lake* that is here reduced to "background," its unoriginality reinforced again by Yoon's repetition of the image. In a twist on the visual codes of the tourist snapshot, what is "real" about the photograph are the Korean faces, emphasizing both the commodification of landscape as tourist scene and its artificiality.

The jarring superimposition of Asian faces onto the constructed landscape also serves as an invitation to consider why Asians have or have not been incorporated into the dominant social and cultural landscape in Canada. While *Maligne Lake* is celebrated as a timeless and noncontradictory representation of Canadian nationalism, it is interesting to note that it was completed one year after the passage of the 1923 Chinese Immigration Act, in a period that saw the rise in organized anti-Asian labor agitation and the continual revision of anti-Asian legislation. What Yoon's piece suggests, then, is that romantic expressions of Canadian nationalism that are conveyed as pastoral retreat must be read as inseparable from a history of yellow peril and anti-immigrant sentiment. If we shift to a more contemporary context, Yoon's faces comment on the xenophobic responses to ways recent Asian immigration has redrawn the racial landscape in large urban cities such as Vancouver. Indeed, the public outcry against Hong Kong immigrant "monster houses" in Vancouver's historically white Shaughnessy and Kerrisdale neighborhoods is one example of how the influx of Asian residential settlement outside the spatial and class confines of segregated Chinatowns reflects, as geographer Katharyne Mitchell observes, "anxiety about the loss of both economic and symbolic control over the defining and marking of place."[109] Thus the images of these unsmiling faces blocking our

FIGURE 2.11 Emily Carr, *Old Time, Coast Village*, 1929–1930. Oil on canvas, 91.3 × 128.7 cm. Collection of the Vancouver Art Gallery, Emily Carr Trust. Photo: Trevor Mills, Vancouver Art Gallery.

view of the aestheticized landscape suggest that these faces are always in excess of nationalist constructions of landscape. By superimposing these faces onto Harris's painting in a gridlike parody of Canada's so-called multicultural "mosaic," Yoon suggests that we can draw no unifying, ideological comfort from the retreat into landscape.

The left panel of Yoon's *Group of Sixty-Seven* offers a related parody of the national landscape by emphasizing the romanticization of Indigenous themes. This panel draws on a painting titled *Old Time, Coast Village* (figure 2.11) by British Columbia painter Emily Carr—an iconic figure in her own right. Emily Carr's association with the Group of Seven was established in 1927 when she was invited by the National Gallery of Canada in Ottawa to participate in an exhibition of West Coast painting. There she met Lawren Harris, whose praise for the Native themes in her art and subsequent years of encouragement became a key motivator for the artistic and literary projects she undertook, including her Governor General award-winning autobiography, *Klee Wyck*, recounting her experiences with Pacific Coast First Nations communities. The book's title is based on the nickname given to her by the Tlingit Nation—an Indigenous people she strongly identified with—which translates to "the laughing one."[110] In a revealing journal entry about the 1927 exhibition, Carr notes proudly, "I felt my work looked dead and dull, but they [Group of Seven] all say I have more of the spirit of the Indian than the others."[111] Not only for Carr, who identified with the First Nations to the point that she imagined herself an Indian, the merit of her own work was judged on its capacity to reflect Native spirituality and cultural vision.

Because she was a female artist and assumed to be lesbian, the First Nations themes Carr drew out in her work, which included reproducing their art forms in her own art practice, are often lauded as exemplary of her anticonformism, which challenged patriarchal and heteronormative gender scripts. Carr traveled alone to Native communities in British Columbia, such as the coastal Haida, Tsmishian, and Tlingit Nations, and began to feature their totem poles in her paintings. In her pursuit of a Native vision, Carr exemplified the role of the romantic hero—but as a woman. Her attraction to First Nations cultures was clearly based on romanticized notions of the "noble savage," who she believed existed in a vanishing state of purity in nature. Art historian Dorothy Shadbolt attests to this belief, explaining that Carr "intuitively grasped the sense in which Indian art was an expression of the native's relation to the natural and supernatural world as he understood it."[112] In figure 2.9 we can observe the proximity Carr observed in the relation between First Nations and "real" nature. In particular, the light-colored totem poles at the center of the piece echo the brown trees in the background, suggesting the indistinguishable features of First Nations culture and nature. From an antinomical view of capitalist social relations, First Nations culture comes to express concrete nature, purity, and originality against the abstract, antinatural oppressions of capitalist modernity. But what complicates Carr's romanticization of First Nations culture here is the overwhelming foliage that drapes the village in a heavy, molten green and serves as protective cover. The trees in the foreground appear human in form, leaning toward the village in cautious observance. Recalling Alexandra Minna Stern's examination of the racial undertones of early twentieth-century conservationism and wilderness protection, Carr's painting betrays not only an ideology of romantic anticapitalism at the core of the settler colonial retreat into nature, but also a suffocating management and control of First Nations cultures. Thus her desire to "go Native" was ultimately more revealing of a defensive investment in whiteness than a respect for Indigenous sovereignty and land claims.

More extreme than the Group of Seven's northern retreat from social and political upheavals of the 1920s that marked life in urban centers, Carr's psychological withdrawal from urbanization manifested itself in illnesses, to the extent that it appeared she was allergic to the city—an ailment Reid refers to as the "'city disease' that was to attack [Carr] whenever she settled in a metropolis."[113] Her loathing of the city, coupled with her idealization of and identification with First Nations culture and appropriation of their art, exemplifies Shari Huhndorf's description of "going Native" as an appropriation of the identity, images, culture, or practices of Indigenous peoples. A settler colonial logic that finds equal expression in Canada as in the United States, she explains that going Native "reinforces the racial hierarchies it claims to destabilize":[114]

> Over the last century, going native has become a cherished American tradition, an important—even necessary—means of defining European American identities and histories. In its various forms, going native articulates and attempts to resolve widespread ambivalence about modernity as well as anxieties about the terrible violence marking the nation's origins.[115]

From this perspective we can reread Carr's gender transgressions as symptomatic of her own white colonial identity crisis, one she attempted to resolve by appropriating and identifying herself with a First Nations identity.

While Carr may have viewed going Native as simultaneously anticapitalist in shunning modernity's spoils and ruins alike, antiracial in her idealization of the coastal First Nations communities onto which she imposed herself, and gender-bending in her adoption of the persona of the lonely romantic genius, she actually reinforced rather than dismantled these structures. In particular, rather than challenging capitalism, Carr's journey to remove herself from the toxic industrial and immigrant-filled environment of the city to find personal and artistic inspiration in Native cultures reinforces capitalism's main values. As Huhndorf explains, "The fixation on self-discovery and self-healing articulate the very Western ideologies of bourgeois individualism."[116] Because her oeuvre relied on the appropriation of First Nations art practice, her relationship with First Nations cultures was largely economic insofar as she profited immensely from appropriating their cultural practices. Finally, Carr's idealization of the naturalness of the "noble savages" of the Pacific coast was contradicted by her antipathy toward the large urban population of Songhees who lived in her hometown of Victoria. As Janice Stewart explains, Carr's view of the Songhees was in keeping with prevailing ideas at the time: they were seen as "'lazy, gambling, drunks' who were 'a nuisance and trouble to the authorities' as 'individuals warranting charity.'"[117] The practice of either idealizing Native peoples as noble savages or denigrating them as inferior and requiring colonial management ultimately performs the same ideological work. On one hand, the romanticization of Native cultures functions to distance North Americans from their European settler roots, thereby displacing responsibility for the conquest and dispossession of the First Nations.[118] It also reinforces racial hierarchies when settlers identify and imagine themselves as "super-Indian" and therefore the rightful inheritors of the land and its resources. On the other, the denigration of Native communities naturalizes European dominance and its ideologies of western progress. It rationalizes the colonization of Indigenous peoples and expropriation of their resources through suggestions that Natives cannot "accept" modernity and civilization. Last but not least, while Carr's adoption of the Tlingit name Klee Wyck can be read as a rejection of Victorian notions of womanhood and the rigid organization of her father's house; as Stewart observes, "For most of her life, Carr turned to masculine authorities . . . for final judgment of her work rather than to her circle of reading ladies or other women artists."[119] As an artist who rose to iconic fame in the 1930s, after the Group of Seven disbanded, by extending their project of defining a distinctively Canadian art, Carr's persona reveals a problematic desire to escape from a social world marked by social upheavals, anti-immigrant sentiment, and industrialization, and a colonial desire to possess First Nations culture to promote the authenticity of her "Canadian" art. If spiritual replenishment for the nation did not spring from the "true North strong and free," as the Group believed, then according to Carr, "our home and Native land"[120] became a national symbol of cultural purity and wholeness.

Yoon's engagement with Carr in the left panel must therefore be read as an engagement with Carr's autochthonophilia and appropriation of First Nations cultural identity. The way Yoon's work performs a disidentification of Carr's painting is registered on multiple levels. If we focus on the way the Korean Canadian heads are turned away from the viewer, we can interpret this "faceless" gesture as a disidentification with the ethnographic gaze embedded in Carr's painting, a gaze that appropriates the Native other for artistic legitimacy and produces art that becomes a romantic index to a defensive settler colonial identity. But at another level, they stage a disidentificatory encounter for the settler looking in. Given that these Korean heads block the view of the village, they foreclose a settler desire to identify with the Native landscape, whose commodification is reinforced through the repetition of Carr's painting. A further irony embedded in this panel is that not only do Yoon's Korean Canadian subjects block an identification with the landscape, but the blackness of the back-turned heads also allegorize the inability of settler culture to "identify" Asians as anything but abstractly homogeneous—as unidentifiable as the black hair in each frame. Adding, then, to the degenerative excess that Tseng's body performs in the romanticized landscape, here Yoon suggests that Asian bodies are an alien antithesis of settler colonialism's indigenizing desire. In short, by viewing capitalism as an antinomy of abstract and concrete dimensions, Asians are as unnatural to the landscape as Indigenous peoples are natural. This is the double edge of settler colonialism.

Conclusion

In Tseng's and Yoon's disidentification with iconic landscapes of North America, their photographs present, to quote Hutcheon again, "inscription[s] of the past in the present [that] embody and bring to life actual historical tensions" and prompt us to delve into the genealogy of landscape art of the early twentieth century.[121] Disidentifying with a shifting set of clichés and stereotypes associated with Asian North Americans and the landscape while preserving the aesthetic beauty of the latter tradition, their photographs use landscape "as raw material for representing a disempowered politics or positionality that has been rendered unthinkable by the dominant culture."[122] Indeed, the alien presence of Asian bodies set against these landscapes foregrounds messy intersections of race science, white nativism, and settler nationalism projected onto the landscape. For Tseng, his parodic repetition of early twentieth-century landscape conventions associated with the Group of Seven's, Adams's, and Borglum's landscapes brings forth the eugenic ideology that conveyed a white, masculine, and paternalistic identification with mountains and trees. Despite conservationists' progressive environmental agenda, their efforts were often intertwined with a eu-genic agenda that opposed the degeneration of the white race by alien races. Juxtaposed with Tseng's alien excess, their projection of virility and obsti-nate resistance to change onto a mountainous and tree-filled landscape ex-presses the contradictory way that racist ideology formed a key subtext of so-called progressive, anticapitalist visions of national unity, conservation, and democracy. In a complementary manner, Yoon draws out the indigeniz-ing dimension of romantic anticapitalism that collapse Native cultures into an unchanging natural purity and authenticity. She also builds on Tseng's evocation of the degenerative excess signified by Asian bodies to exemplify the abstractness and unnaturalness of the Asian body against the landscape. From the period of railroad labor discussed in the last chapter to Asian im-migrant exclusion in this chapter, the perverse abstraction associated with Chinese labor had by the 1920s and 1930s been supplanted by the settler retreat into the aestheticized landscape, whose unnatural antithesis is the Asian alien.

Despite the romantic tribute to national culture embedded in landscape art of the early twentieth century, Tseng's and Yoon's photographic counter-memories suggest that such a "progressive" vision of national culture was "born in the apprehension of imminent loss," as Lake and Reynolds indicate, and part of the anxious growth of "whiteness as a transnational mode of racial identification in settler societies."[123] In the late nineteenth and early twentieth centuries, territorial symbols of regenerative whiteness expressed the proprietorial dimension of British settler colonialism and became, over time, synonymous with whiteness. As W. E. B. Du Bois observed succinctly on the whiteness of territorial expansion, "Whiteness is the ownership of the earth forever and ever, Amen."[124]

Finally, in the spirit of Kingston's and Fung's reimagining of abstract labor as History 2, the potential of Tseng's and Yoon's parody is not in ar-ticulating a more ideal landscape of normative inclusion to symbolize the self-identity of the settler nation. Rather, by queering the aestheticized landscape, Tseng's alien difference animates the contradictions, exclusions, and violent eliminations of settler colonialism that the landscape, as aes-thetic object, fetishizes and naturalizes. Similarly, Yoon's iteration of the interrupted landscape lays bare the fetishized commodity function of the landscape. It is from the ambivalence of the parodic gaps between Tseng's and Yoon's difference to the landscape that their photographs allegorize a state of nonequivalence. Nonequivalence, as Chandan Reddy explains, represents subjects "who are not 'unified' by a prior identity."[125] Disidentifying with the white regenerative ideal projected onto the romantic landscape, Tseng's and Yoon's photographs interrupt and denaturalize the mundane iteration of its symbolic violence.

Following from the first chapter's examination of the perverse temporality of abstract labor and this chapter's focus on antinatural landscapes during a converging period of anti-Asian immigration restriction in North America, the next chapter moves forward to the internment of Japanese North Americans. If Asian North American cultural producers have thus far exposed and recircuited the abstract and unnatural signifiers attached to Asian bodies, what might a transnational approach to Japanese internment narratives expose as internment's governing logics? Continuing my exploration of Asian racialization as a fetishistic alignment with the abstract dimension of capitalist social relations, I track the evolution of romantic anticapitalism and its antinomical view of concrete and abstract dimensions of capitalism. Probing Asian North American representations of labor and landscape in chapter 3, I demonstrate how Joy Kogawa's *Obasan* and Rea Tajiri's *History and Memory* reflect how the perverse abstraction of Asian labor takes on mechanical, nonhuman representation that must be eradicated from West Coast agriculture and fishing industries. However, through the process of labor resignification established through symbolic proximity with Indigeneity, Japanese North Americans emerge renaturalized and recorporealized as surplus labor.

CHAPTER 3

JAPANESE INTERNMENT AND THE MUTATION OF LABOR

> The only tree here is dead.
> —Joy Kogawa, *Obasan*

Underworlds

Paradox defined the late Ruth Asawa in life and art. Born into a poor Japanese farming family in Norwalk, California, in 1926, relocated in February 1942 to Santa Anita Racetrack and later interned at Rohwer Relocation Center, she was by 1946 an unlikely art student at Black Mountain College in North Carolina. When she emerged on the art scene in the mid-1950s, Asawa and her art were, perhaps inevitably, viewed through the prism of race and gender stereotypes. Critics were intent on either casting her sculptures as typically "Oriental" or dismissing them as decorative, feminine craft rather than modernist sculpture.[1] Because of their lack of grandiosity (in stark contrast to Gutzon Borglum's colossal sculpture examined in the last chapter), Asawa's sculptures were interpreted as insubstantial and thus feminine. Unlike the scale and orientation of Mount Rushmore, most of her sculptures are hanging or lie on the floor. In a telling review of her work in 1956, art critic Eleanor Munro contrasts her sculptures to the monumental and masculine qualities we could easily associate with Borglum:

FIGURE 3.1 Ruth Asawa, *Untitled*, ca. 1960–1965. Fine Arts Museums of San Francisco. © Ruth Asawa.

These are "domestic" sculptures in a feminine, handiwork mode — small and light and unobtrusive for home decoration, not meant, as is much contemporary sculpture, to be hoisted by cranes, carted by vans and installed on mountainsides.[2]

At a time when modernist aesthetics were defined through heroic, masculine traits, such as welding and cutting iron,[3] her innovative technique of weaving and tying industrial wire into shapes required viewers to engage with contradictory modalities of hardness and softness, heaviness and weightlessness, and movement and suspension. Asawa would eventually gain recognition for expanding the boundaries of sculpture by bringing visibility to the power of what she referred to as "negative space,"[4] the tension produced by the space inside and surrounding the materiality of the sculpture. In Asawa's work, this negative space functions as an invisible force field that defines and directs the flow of energy.

For the purposes of this chapter, Asawa's work offers a visual metaphor for the negative space within and surrounding Japanese internment in North America. In particular, her tied-wire sculptures (figure 3.1) present a contextual frame for this chapter's continuing focus on romantic anticapitalism. In her art practice Asawa was intent on exploring the limits of duality, making a "shape that was inside and outside at the same time . . . [something] that continually reverses itself."[5] Her tied-wire sculptures' continual inversions and reversals offer a visual motif of *dialectical* process — in stark contrast to romantic anticapitalism's antinomical view of capitalist social relations as an opposition between concrete and abstract dimensions, between universalism and particularism. As I will develop in this chapter, this antinomical view led to an association of Japanese labor with the creation of unnatural value. Fusing the natural and the unnatural, Asawa's sculptures hang from the ceiling as clusters of branches, bringing to mind a tree growing downward. As John Yau observes, "There is the forceful suggestion of an *inverted world*, reinforced by the downward pointing branching shadows cast on the wall."[6] Reversing the properties of the trees depicted in the last chapter — the sturdy hang tree of Gonzales-Day's photograph or anchoring trees of the Group of Seven's paintings — this tree's branches grow ever thinner and more delicate into fine needles. The fragility of the needles is paradoxically suggestive of both regeneration and evanescence. Yau points out the haunting effect of the shadows cast by the sculpture against the gallery wall: "The shadows branch down the nearby walls, conveying a ghostly domain in which everything is in reverse."[7] Gravity, too, whose invisible, abstract force compels her forest of tied-wire trees upside-down, captures the downward pull of mortality. The sculpture ultimately suspends the duality of the material and immaterial worlds, showcasing the interplay of wire, space, and shadow—whose impact is achieved by what is concretely visible and invisible, abstract. Encapsulating the human activity of tying wire with the abstract representation of natural forms, Asawa transcends personal biography while evoking those "things that your body doesn't allow you to leave behind." As such, her work offers an allegory of the dialectics of Japanese internment expressed in forms that are both figurative and nonfigurative.

If Asawa's inverted forest suggests an underworld where the immaterial but objective laws of gravity collapse into the concrete materiality of form, the works by Joy Kogawa and Rea Tajiri that I examine in this chapter extend this vision into both the concrete and affective dimensions of Japanese internment. Unlike the romantic landscapes of the last chapter, onto which a eugenic "natural" white settler identity could be projected, this chapter focuses on its unnatural, negatively abstract counterpart. In this sense, Asawa's art's abstract qualities also serve to capture aspects of Japanese internment in North America that defy concrete representational form, elements that contribute to the way Japanese internment can never be fully compartmentalized in the past. If Asawa's upside-down tree serves as an unnatural marker of those "things your body doesn't allow you to leave behind," its gravitational pull also suggests the weight of psychic excess. For Kogawa and Tajiri, the nightmares, visions, and complex identifications similarly constitute the haunting excess of Japanese internment, of a world mysteriously turned over.

Attending to the competing theories that attribute Japanese internment to economic and/or racial causes, I probe the affective registers of Japanese internment—its negative space—whose insights exceed the empiricism of national historiography. In my reading of Kogawa's and Tajiri's shifting modes of cross-racial identification, first with Jewish and then Native intersections, I suggest that the wartime relocation of Japanese Americans and Japanese Canadians to internment sites was motivated by a perception of the excessive industry of Japanese labor. This excessive efficiency was associated with having control over *relative surplus-value*, the value produced above and beyond surplus-value. Both texts offer a complementary view of this racialization expressed through modes of identification with Jewish peoples under Nazi persecution, animating a corresponding condition of destructive economic abstraction. After West Coast expulsion and relocation, however, Japanese labor's association with the production of unnatural value is neutralized as both texts turn to Japanese-Native intersections. Unlike the destructive economism associated with Jewishness, Indigeneity represents the romantic anticapitalist ideal of organic purity and concrete nature external to economic modernity. Thus Kogawa's and Tajiri's texts' evoke how the brutality of relocation, internment, and labor exploitation function paradoxically to indigenize Japanese North Americans as surplus labor through an ideology of romantic anticapitalism. My reading focuses on how Kogawa and Tajiri evoke this transformation in the way they denaturalize the settler landscape in relation to labor.

Japanese Internment as Irrationality and Postmemory

In both Canada and the United States, the motivation and objective of expulsion have never been completely clear. Historians agree that Japanese expulsion from the West Coast was not, contrary to the rationale given in 1942, due to military necessity—or, by extension, Pearl Harbor. In Canada, Army and Navy leaders, in addition to the Royal Canadian Mounted Police, opposed mass expulsion.[8] Although US Navy chiefs were hostile to Japanese Americans, the army's General Staff opposed wholesale removal and argued that the chances of Japanese invasion were negligible. Moreover, the army's intelligence unit and the FBI concurred that there had been no Japanese American sabotage during or after the Pearl Harbor attack.[9] The fact that most Japanese civilians in Hawaii were not interned speaks to the lack of credible threat posed by Japanese Americans. Ultimately, as Greg Robinson observes, "the 'security' sought by the West Coast could not be resolved by ordinary means because it did not depend on meeting and neutralizing actual threats."[10] If not a military threat, whatever security these governments pursued meant that the label of "enemy alien" would be applied to small children, including those removed from orphanages, and, in the United States, individuals with one-sixteenth Japanese blood. What, then, was the threatening content of Japaneseness that would necessitate such an expansive and meticulous removal project?

Beyond the Pearl Harbor thesis, Japanese internment has also been viewed as a continuation of exclusionary anti-Asian racism that began in the nineteenth century, first targeting Chinese migrants through immigration laws and then extended to other Asian ethnic groups. However, this explanation does not identify what elements of immigrant restriction functioned as antecedents to the qualitative specificity of dispossession, relocation, and confinement that are particular to the Japanese experience on the West Coast of North America. As a result, Colleen Lye points out, "the reliance on racism to explain a historical causation often leads to a dehistorization of racism."[11] In other words, while we are aware of racial dynamics that are clearly in play, it is unclear how anti-Japaneseness extends or exceeds the logics of prior anti-Asian racism. Lye describes this as a failure to grasp "both the racial logic of internment *and* its historical specificity."[12] It remains ambiguous what kind of racial animus was mobilized leading up to such catastrophic policy decisions of 1942, which have retrospectively been viewed as an aberration of western democratic principles.

Economic theories of Japanese internment, in contrast, stress its rationality from the standpoint of white capitalists who stood to benefit from Japanese dispossession. Here Japanese internment is thought to have been engineered by influential economic stakeholders who stood to gain from the elimination of competition from Japanese labor and businesses. According to Gary Okihiro and David Drummond's materialist theory of anti–Japanese American exploitation, immigration restriction was a precursor to Japanese internment. They argue that the anti-Asian racism from 1900 to the Immigration Act of 1924—which introduced a national origins quota system and effectively halted all Asian immigration—was based on the extraction of surplus-value from migrant labor exploitation. This was followed by a second period from 1924 to 1942, characterized by a model of internal colonialism in which value was extracted from racial rent premiums.[13] These premiums were tied to the passage of the Alien Land Law in California in 1913, which restricted property ownership and transfer to "citizens," thus barring the Issei, who were "aliens ineligible for citizenship." Okihiro and Drummond argue that "the alien land laws served to maintain Japanese tenancy and thus their economic dependence."[14] They suggest that the crisis presented by Pearl Harbor enabled a "return to exclusionism and offered an opportunity for immediate profit and the expulsion of the Japanese from the level of farm operators."[15] What remains unclear from Okihiro and Drummond's periodization of anti-Asian racism is why one mode of economic exploitation was supplanted by the other. As Lye asks, "If mass removal and internal colonialism both share the principal aim of economic gain, what explains the priority of 'quick profits' over the long-term attractions of systemic dependency at one moment compared to another?"[16] Because the long-term profitability of rent premiums would greatly exceed the returns on mass removal, the economic motivation for Japanese internment becomes less clear. Further distorting the economic rationale of the Alien Land Laws, these laws led not to the contraction but to the *expansion* of Japanese farm acreage, which doubled between 1910 and 1920.[17] This blurs the precise objective of the Alien Land Laws, though the looming intersection of racialized dispossession and white property is undeniable.

Revising Okihiro and Drummond's theory, I argue that it is racism's economic *irrationality* rather than rationality that forms the central medium of anti-Japanese feeling. This economic irrationality is crucially tied to the fundamental misreading of capitalism that I've been tracking in this book, one that nevertheless projects the economic benefit of racist policy without being actualized. From an expanded North American perspective, the economic irrationality of anti-Japanese sentiment was also visible in the 1920s in Canada, particularly in the fishing industry.[18] As Ken Adachi explains, in the 1920s the Department of Marine Fisheries attempted to take measures to eliminate Japanese Canadian competition in the British Columbia fishing industry, "gradually eliminat[ing] Orientals from the fishery" by reducing the number of licenses issued to them.[19] The denial of fishing licenses to Japanese Canadians was, analogous to US Alien Land Laws, not necessarily effective, and the negative effects stemming from the loss of Japanese canners and fishermen from the industry once again complicate a clear profit motivation.[20] As Masako Fukawa notes, "When rigidly enforced, the license reductions had a negative impact on the existing fishing industry" because there were not enough white fishermen to take the place of Japanese fishermen.[21] The reductions also created hardships for white fishermen who profited from Japanese launching and tugging services. Moreover, the Japanese who were pushed out of fishing were able to successfully adapt to other industries, such as small-scale berry farming and forestry. Thus, as an editor of the *Vancouver Province* noted of the Japanese in 1930, "We have hunted the Orientals out of the fishing industry and they have gone to the woods and they have gone to the farms. . . . We haven't diminished their numbers; we have simply pushed them about."[22] While the economic benefits for whites of Japanese exclusion from agriculture and fishing before Pearl Harbor were not always straightforward, the economic opportunities Japanese internment produced for whites in both farming and fishing industries was more transparent. When used to view the forced sale of Japanese Canadians private property, David Harvey's translation of Marx's concept of primitive accumulation as "accumulation by dispossession" seems particularly apt. Indeed, for sympathetic whites who protested the forced sales, such property dispossession recalled the Nazi's confiscation of Jewish property under the Nuremberg Laws.[23] What this economic history shows, however, is how anti-Japanese agitation both subverted and supported white labor interests. Building on arguments in previous chapters, the mixed economic legacy of Japanese expulsion from the West Coast is shaped by the interplay of settler colonial romantic anticapitalism and the destructive abstraction embodied by Japanese labor. From the fundamental misperception at the heart of romantic anticapitalism, ridding the West of Japanese labor was necessary to *prevent economic destruction* rather than to profit from their disappearance.

Within this book's larger argument that the abstract forces within capitalism are biologized *as Asian*, this chapter probes how the destructively abstract content of Japaneseness mutates after the mass expulsion of Japanese civilians from the West Coast. Following the previous chapters' focus on Asian labor as perverse and antinatural signifiers of abstract labor, I focus on the way Japanese labor transforms in this period from a dehumanizing symbol of modernization into an ideal surplus labor force. This mutation in the meaning of Japanese labor was shaped by the upheavals caused by technological modernization. From the Great Depression through the post–World War II era, modernization had profound effects on labor, urbanization, and domesticity. Since the 1920s, agriculture and fishing industries where Japanese labor was concentrated were transformed by new technologies, such as gas-powered plows and early sonar,[24] innovations that were accompanied by these industries' steady consolidation into corporate monopolies.[25] Population booms in California and Vancouver led to rapid urbanization and suburbanization, giving the West Coast a distinctly "modern" identity. "Midcentury modernism" was the retrospective name given to the aesthetic, architectural, and cultural revolution that accompanied these rapid changes, reflecting a movement away from ornate traditional styles and toward the heightened rationalism of clean lines, functionality, and simplicity. As Andrew Shanken observes, technology was seen a "civilizing force" whereby "better living" became synonymous with modern homes equipped with lighting, electric appliances, and other efficiencies.[26] But the dark side of the fetishization of technological convenience, speed, and mobility was the reconstitution of labor power, environmental change, and a recalibration of the social order. And embedded in this culture of rapid modernization were deeply felt anxieties about social and economic displacement, a breeding ground for romantic anticapitalism.[27]

In this state of anxiety and unpredictability comes renewed attention on the evils of abstraction and the glory of nature, purity, and the concrete. Counterintuitively, the machine—the key agent of modernization—was often anthropomorphized and fetishized as "anticapitalist." As Postone explains, the "positive emphasis on 'nature,' on blood, the soil, concrete labor, and *Gemeinschaft*, can easily go hand in hand with a glorification of technology and industrial capital."[28] Therefore, it was not simply the identification of Japanese labor with mechanization that becomes the target of romantic anticapitalism but, as I will develop later, an association of Japanese labor efficiency with the creation of *unnatural value* that is symptomatic of the destructive consequences of modernization. Evolving from a prior racialization as perverse and unnatural signs of abstract labor in the period leading up to mass removal, Japaneseness became the specter of dehumanization against a world of "better living."

However, in the war's aftermath, Japanese labor was increasingly praised, helping to give rise to the model minority myth. This suggests a profound *resignification* of Asian labor during Japanese relocation and internment, from being associated with a dangerous efficiency before the war to a commendable productivity after it. As my reading of Kogawa's and Tajiri's texts demonstrates, this resignification turns on the symbolic alignment of Japaneseness with the destructive economism of Jewishness before the war, transforming into an association with a romanticized *noneconomism* of Indigeneity after relocation and internment. Unlike the negative economic abstraction associated with Jewishness, Indigeneity represents a sphere external to capitalism, symbolizing romantic anticapitalism's ideal of concrete nature and purity.

Within this complex imaginary of Japanese internment, through which Japaneseness undergoes a shift from a symbolic alignment with the Jew to the figure of the Native, I situate Kogawa's and Tajiri's texts in the frame of postmemory.[29] Marianne Hirsch describes postmemory as an affective connection to traumatic experiences that precedes a generation's birth. For Hirsch it is a way of contextualizing the memories of the children of Holocaust survivors, whose experiences were nevertheless shaped by "cultural or collective traumatic events . . . distinguished from memory by generational distance and from history by deep personal connection."[30] She explains further that "postmemory is a powerful and very particular form of memory precisely because its connection to its object or source is mediated not through recollection but through an imaginative investment and creation."[31] Rea Tajiri's experimental film memoir, *History and Memory*, offers a powerful evocation of Hirsch's description of postmemory in the personal narration she weaves through the film. In the melancholic tone of her voice-over she explains the quandary of having memories disconnected from experience. As a Sansei born over a decade after the release of Japanese American internees from camps, she is haunted by recurring memories — memories of events she never experienced directly — that confuse her sense of identity. Her film becomes an archive of her efforts to probe the emotional residue of Japanese internment that has been implanted into her own subjective experience:

> I began searching for a history, my own history. Because I had known all along the stories I'd heard were not true and parts had been left out. I remember having this feeling when I was growing up that I was haunted by something, that I was living within a family of ghosts. There was this place they knew about. I had never been there, yet I had a memory for it.

Adding to the surreal nature of her connection to a foreign history is her mother's *inability* to remember her own experience of wartime relocation to a camp in Poston, Arizona. In the film, her mother's soft, barely audible voice is heard explaining, "There are so many things I've forgotten." Accompanying her voice is scrolling text that reads:

> She tells the story of
> what she doesn't
> remember
> But remembers one
> thing:
> Why she forgot to
> remember.

Thus Tajiri's film explores the paradoxical interplay of history and memory, capturing an irony that David Eng describes where "the mother has history but no memory, while the daughter has memory but no history.[32] This forms the central irony of postmemory, in which traumatic memories and feelings of loss are unconsciously passed from one generation to the next. Its haunting effects manifest in unrelieved sadness, akin to the experience that Grace Cho describes as transgenerational haunting, "a repetition of trauma that resists all attempts to erase it from personal and public memory."[33] Eng situates Tajiri's postmemory in the domain of melancholia, identifying how "the most difficult losses suffered in melancholia are unconscious ones, psychic forfeitures that cannot be properly grieved."[34] Working through the melancholic layers of postmemory, the film gives visual representation to the negative space of Japanese internment.

I expand on the "post-" of postmemory in my reading of Joy Kogawa's *Obasan*, referring not only to the memory that exists "after," as in the case of Tajiri's film, but also "beyond." Here I am referring to the unconscious, psychic world of attachments that both draw on and exceed memory. Because she is a reserved person, much of the protagonist Naomi Nakane's emotional complexity is conveyed through her graphic, often violent nightmares and daydreams — the negative space of her conscious, rational mind. Her dreams often take place in a wilderness landscape, peopled by relatives, bayonet-wielding soldiers, prosthetic-limbed women, and deceptively "real"-looking robots. Like Asawa's inverted tree, these gothic landscapes convey the unconscious attachments and fears tied to the crisis of relocation, which, in the case of Naomi, is coupled with the disappearance of her mother. In addition, another sense of how the post of postmemory goes "beyond" memory in the novel is in the expression of dialectical consciousness. Although Kogawa experienced Japanese internment in Canada as a child, her novel's blend of autobiographical elements, government documents, and archival sources accentuates the contested nature of personal memory and official history. If the "truth" exists, it exists somewhere between and beyond the text's multiple authorial voices.[35] Similar to Tajiri's mother, as an adult Naomi has repressed her internment experience: of relocation to a ghost town in the interior of British Columbia and postwar dispersal to a beet farm in Granton, Alberta. The terrain of memory that Naomi uncovers is neither linear, individual, nor finite. Mona Oikawa describes Naomi's complex reckoning with the past this way: "As [she] struggles to remember and to know, she confronts the complex ways in which memory is revelatory, both through remembering and forgetting."[36] Thus the post of postmemory also refers to the memory of willful forgetting.

The Jewish Question

In *Obasan* and *History and Memory*, the economic modality of anti-Japanese sentiment is rendered through moments of cross-racial identification and, as I argue in the following section, through the postmemory of landscape. First, in indirect and overt examples, the persecution of Jews under the Nazi regime and the colonial dispossession of Indigenous peoples serve as analogical frames for each text's reckoning with the meaning of Japanese internment. In *Obasan*, general observations of economic jealousy subtly refract the financial modality of anti-Semitism. As Naomi sorts through old letters in the aftermath of her uncle's death, she comes across one of the many unopened letters her Aunt Emily wrote to her sister, Naomi's mother, who was unable to return home from a visit to Japan after the bombing of Pearl Harbor. In the letter, written before the family's expulsion from Vancouver, Aunt Emily reveals an awareness of economic resentment of Japanese Canadian prosperity, noting that "when gas rationing starts [Dad] won't be able to use the car much. It's so sleek it's an affront to everyone he passes. I wish he'd bought something more modest, but you know Dad."[37] Presumably the car is also an affront to less affluent Japanese Canadians, but its acquisition also symbolizes Japanese mobility and access to liberal individualism, a status historically aligned with and guarded by whites. Later in the letter, after enumerating the way Japanese Canadians have become the enemy, Aunt Emily makes a more pointed connection between the effects of war on Jews and Japanese Canadians:

> The things that go on in wartime! Think of Hitler shiploading people into Poland or Germany proper to work for nothing in fields and factories far from home and children — stealing food from conquered people — captive labor. . . . War breeds utter insanity. Here at home there's mass hatred of us simply because we're of Japanese origin.[38]

In this passage, Aunt Emily's observations of Nazi tactics serve as an eerie premonition of what will ensue for Japanese Canadians, as Naomi's father will be sent to labor on a road camp, while the remaining family will be twice relocated before settling as exploited labor on a beet farm in Alberta. Decades after the war, Aunt Emily becomes more direct in her allusions to Nazism as a cultural force. In answer to her rhetorical question "Why in a time of war with Germany and Japan would our government seize the property and homes of Canadian-born Canadians but not the homes of German-born Germans?" she replies to herself, "Racism. . . . The Nazis are everywhere."[39] Thus from prewar to postwar reflections on Japanese internment, anti-Japanese sentiment is expressed through the economic and racial prism of anti-Semitism.

Rea Tajiri's film-memoir also makes reference to the specter of anti-Semitism, but as a threatening identification that is actively suppressed. Without sound, she incorporates scrolling text to highlight the way Japanese internment continues to be sanitized of any connotations of Nazi Germany:

NEW YORK TIMES
AUGUST 28, 1990
ASSEMBLYMAN GIL
FERGUSON, REPUBLICAN
ORANGE COUNTY, CALIF.,
SEEKS TO HAVE CHILDREN
TAUGHT THAT JAPANESE
AMERICANS WERE NOT
INTERNED IN
"CONCENTRATION CAMPS,"
BUT RATHER WERE HELD
IN "RELOCATION CENTERS"
JUSTIFIED BY MILITARY
NECESSITY.

Tajiri's inclusion of this text indicates that in 1990, forty-five years after the end of World War II, two years after the successful redress campaign, and following exhaustive debunking of theories of "military necessity," the primary meaning of Japanese internment remains subject to ongoing deferral.[40] In light of wartime atrocities committed by the Nazis, Roosevelt's initial references to Japanese "concentration camps" were actively redacted. As a result, Japanese internment could only be described through euphemism and negation, as *not* a concentration camp. *Obasan's* Aunt Emily shares a similar reaction to the discursive construction of internment camps as "Interior Housing Projects." She observes, "With language like that you can disguise any crime."[41] Tajiri's silent, scrolling text thus captures the discursive predicament that Japanese internment poses, while emphasizing the ongoing threat of identifying Japanese internment with the symbolism of the Nazi regime.

If we pursue the vexed intersection of Japanese internment and anti-Semitism raised in these texts, we find similar deferrals of meaning that attend the Holocaust. Moishe Postone's reflection on West Germany's emotional response to the late 1970s American television miniseries *Holocaust* illuminates some of the interpretive impasse that, in analogous fashion, surrounds Japanese internment in North America. In pursuing this intersection, my intention is not to conflate the stark disparity of outcomes of "concentration camps" in Europe and North America; rather, it is to further uncover an intersecting economism of anti-Semitic and anti-Japanese racialization. Observing the tendency in postwar Germany of Germans to deny having knowledge of the wartime existence of extermination camps, Postone reflects on the underlying sentiment masked by appeals to ignorance: "'We didn't know' should be understood as 'we *still* don't want to know.'"[42] What *Holocaust* ultimately exposed about the public horrors against Jews, Russians, and Poles that occurred *outside* the camps "undermined the fiction that Nazi genocide was the affair of a small handful of people operating within a context hermetically sealed off from most of the soldiers as well as the rest of the German population."[43] Similar to the ostensibly arbitrary but coordinated will of multiple governments to expel, confine, and/or deport Japanese civilians in the aftermath of Pearl Harbor, the precise motivation within National Socialism for exterminating Jews continues to evolve in the postwar era. Postone troubles theories of fascism and racial prejudice because neither can sufficiently account for what he calls the "qualitative specificity"[44] of the extermination of European Jews. This specificity, he observes, will "remain inexplicable so long as anti-Semitism is treated as a specific example of prejudice, xenophobia and racism in general, as an example of a scapegoat strategy whose victims could very well have been members of any other group."[45] Within this qualitative specificity, neither fascism nor racism *in general* can explain why, during the German army's defeat by the Red Army, they allocated a significant number of vehicles to transport Jews to gas chambers rather than for military reinforcements.[46] This reveals a biopolitics in which the extermination of Jews served a greater purpose than the preservation of German soldiers' lives. Rather than profiting from the elimination of Jews, their extermination was itself a mode of German self-preservation against the evils of capitalism that Jews represented.

What Japanese internment and the Holocaust share is a romantic anticapitalist logic. The transnational frame magnifies how Japanese North Americans were not interned to protect the coast, to rob them of their property (although white citizens certainly profited from their dispossession), to protect them, or to test their loyalty. Neither was the Holocaust motivated by profit or wartime security interests: "They were not exterminated for military reasons, or in order to violently acquire land (as was the case with American Indians and the Tasmanians), or in order to wipe out those segments of the population around whom resistance could most easily crystallize."[47] Rather, in the case of Jews, the qualitative specificity was due to the kind of secular power attributed to them. This power was defined not as the resistance of an oppressed underclass but, rather, as the potentially greater force of a super-race — an overclass — whose power was "mysteriously intangible, abstract and universal."[48] Given that romantic anticapitalism hypostatizes and glorifies the concrete dimensions of capitalist social relations, the abstract dimension "must find a concrete vessel, a carrier, a mode of expression."[49] This biological carrier came in the form of the Jew:

> Because this power is not bound concretely, is not "rooted," it is of staggering immensity and is extremely difficult to check. It stands behind phenomena, but is not identical with them. Its source is therefore hidden — conspiratorial. The Jews represent an immensely powerful, intangible, international conspiracy.[50]

Within this romantic anticapitalist system of representation, Jews represented an immensely powerful conspiratorial force that contributed to the decline of traditional social formations, values, and institutions. Thus the eradication of Jews under National Socialism was a mode of preservation from the abstract evils of capitalism.

If mass removal and internment of Japanese civilians in Canada and the United States was a protective measure, it was for the similarly mysterious and immense power attributed to them. This power, like that represented by European Jews, was defined not by the resistant power of the racialized poor, like that of African American or First Nations communities, but as a destructive economic conspiracy. The dangerous content of the power attributed to Japanese communities along the West Coast was alien, intangible, conspiratorial, and international. In contrast to European Jews' segregation in financial sectors of the labor market—an alignment that was strongly associated with the abstract dimension of capitalism within the binarized social universe of romantic anticapitalism—Japanese communities were associated with farming, fishing, and retail labor. How did their labor come to represent such a negative power?

In order to appreciate how the Japanese became "a concrete vessel, a carrier, a mode of expression" for the abstract dimension of capitalist social relations, we can track the continuity in the evolution of racialized characterizations of "cheap" Chinese labor to the "excessive efficiency" of Japanese labor. As we saw in chapter 1, Chinese associations with the temporal domination of abstract time rendered them a perverse, abstract counterpart to white "concrete" labor. In the rapidly industrializing context of nineteenth-century railroad building and mining, the laboring Chinese body came to signify the consolidation of abstract, homogeneous time that threatened normative social reproduction. Within this regime of intensified labor time, therefore, the Chinese body stood for the *devaluation* of white labor. In chapter 2 I explored how, when Asian immigration came largely to a halt in the 1920s in the United States and Canada, a settler colonial ideology of romantic anticapitalism was expressed in the masculinist personification of nature. As an embodiment of the temporal domination of abstract labor, which is fundamental to the determination of the value of labor-power, Asian aliens represented an antinatural force of value formation—the abstract antithesis of a concrete, pure, and Indigenous natural world. During the global Great Depression and in its aftermath, liberal protections in Canada and the United States intervened in determining the value of labor power to stabilize capitalism, with strategies that included minimum wage standards in British Columbia and Roosevelt's New Deal labor safeguards in the 1930s. These worker protections may have subdued the perception that Asian bodies represented an abstract, alien force that devalued concrete white labor power.[51] However, as Japanese labor and ownership of boats, land, and equipment expanded alongside developments in industrial modernization, the abstract power embodied by Asian labor no longer represented the devaluation of white labor; rather, it represented the creation of *unnatural value*. The excessive industry associated with Japanese labor was threatening precisely because it fed a perception that they had control over *relative surplus-value*, the value produced above and beyond surplus-value.

The form of relative surplus-value associated with the excessive industry of Japanese labor is transient. In "The Concept of Relative Surplus Value" in *Capital*, Marx asks why individual capitalists are driven to innovate, especially because their innovations are beneficial to the entire capitalist class. Specifically, efficiency measures reduce the value of labor power, increase the rate of exploitation, and generate more surplus-value.[52] Are innovators selfless individuals motivated to bolster the capitalist class? Marx says no: individual capitalists are driven to innovate not out of class interests but out of *individual* interests. When a capitalist innovates to produce a commodity more efficiently, the value of his or her product temporarily falls below its social value, which means "they have cost less labour-time than the great bulk of the same article produced under the average social conditions."[53] As discussed in previous chapters, the immaterial but objective source of value is socially necessary labor time: "The real value of a commodity is not its individual, but its social value; that is to say, its value is not measured by the labour-time that the article costs the producer in each individual case, but the labour-time *socially required* for its production."[54] The crucial gap between the *actual time* it takes to produce a product after innovations have been introduced and the *socially necessary labor time* is what yields a surplus on surplus-value. This extra profit—the *relative surplus-value*— is precisely what motivates the individual capitalist to innovate. However, this extra profit is only temporary. Once other capitalists adopt the same labor-saving innovation, the socially necessary labor time will adjust accordingly. As Marx explains, "This extra surplus-value vanishes as soon as the new method of production is generalized, for then the difference between the individual value of the cheapened commodity and its social value vanishes."[55] Because of the coercive nature of competition, the capitalist interest to profit from the temporal gap between a product's individual and social value—the gap that constitutes relative surplus-value—is implicit within capitalism. What this means is that technical innovation or technological modernization does not occur solely as a result of someone's creative genius; rather, as Marx emphasizes, "capital . . . has an immanent drive, and a constant tendency, towards increasing the productivity of labour, in order to cheapen commodities and, by cheapening commodities, to cheapen the worker himself."[56] Innovation is part of capitalism's "immanent drive" to devalue labor. Within this book's larger claim that the abstract forces within capitalism are personified as Asian, the harmful content of Japanese labor thus appears as a negative symptom of modernizing innovation, whose destructive power catalyzes the unnatural creation of relative surplus-value. Evolving from an unnatural sign of abstraction, the Asian becomes a specter of destructive innovation in a landscape of ceaseless modernization.

Born-Again Native

Paradoxically, the *obverse* of the destructive economism traditionally associated with Jews occurs in a second mode of cross-racial identification depicted in Kogawa's and Tajiri's texts: symbolic attachments to and reflections on Indigenous peoples. In this case, I suggest that Japanese identification with Native peoples both replicates and exceeds the settler colonial romantic attachment to the Native in ways that reveal a transformation in the way Asians constitute abstract labor. As I discuss below, their identification with Native peoples is further shaped by the settler colonial conflation of Japanese enemy aliens with Native peoples. Japanese relocation, dispossession, and confinement thus emerge within a dual identificatory framework of anti-Semitic and settler colonial regimes.

In *Obasan*, Naomi repeatedly aligns herself and members of her Japanese Canadian family with First Nations' identities. At the onset of the novel, she accompanies her uncle to the ravine and imagines him as an American Indian warrior hero:

> Uncle could be Chief Sitting Bull squatting here. He has the same prairie-baked skin, the deep brown furrows like dry riverbeds creasing his cheeks. All he needs is a feather headdress, and he would be perfect for a picture postcard — "Indian Chief from Canadian Prairie" — souvenir of Alberta, made in Japan.[57]

Here the optics of Japanese Canadian racial form are staged in *correspondence* to Native identity. The narrator's depiction functions as an attempt to indigenize Uncle on two levels: first, his Indigeneity stems from a phenotypical convergence with Chief Sitting Bull that results in their same "prairie-baked skin," and second, Uncle's Indigeneity is established through his figurative embodiment of landscape, with "dry riverbeds creasing his cheeks." Although this portrayal clearly intends to *naturalize* Japanese Canadians to the landscape, it also acknowledges the iterative circuits of dispossession and commodification that make it possible for a Japanese import to offer a "picture postcard" vision of Indigeneity. Naomi projects a similar analogy between Obasan, her aunt, and an Indigenous fighter. Gauging her aunt's inability to integrate into a community of elderly white Canadians, she concludes that Obasan would be as "welcome as a Zulu warrior."[58] Later, describing her moribund life as a schoolteacher, Naomi once again pauses to reflect on a shared Japanese and Native disposition.[59] She observes that "some of the Native children I've had in my classes over the years could almost pass for Japanese, and vice versa. There's something in the animal-like shyness I recognize in the dark eyes. A quickness to look away."[60]

The implications of these figurative projections of cross-racial identification are justifiably vexed. On one hand, as Marie Lo explains, these identifications "blur the boundaries of what is Native and what is Japanese," placing Japanese Canadians on a broader colonial continuum that begins with dispossession of Indigenous people.[61] On the other, as Lo also points out, these modes of Native identification participate in a long-standing Canadian settler nationalism that has sought to "elaborate a national and autochthonous claim to the land"[62] through white identifications with the figure of the Native. That the novel similarly attempts to *naturalize* Japanese Canadians is reflected no less problematically in Aunt Emily's continual refrain "This is my own, my *native* land."[63] However, as I suggest below, the precondition for this problematic identification with the Native is the dehumanizing effects of their transformation into surplus labor. Relocated to work a beet farm under postwar dispersal orders, the combined sterility of the landscape and tropes of human degeneracy expose the eliminatory logic of settler colonial romantic anticapitalism.

Tajiri's film contains more subtle reflections on Japanese and Native American crossings, less through the mode of identification than spatial intersection. After her family was removed to the Salinas Rodeo Grounds barracks, Tajiri explains how they were relocated again by train to Poston, Arizona, "to live in part of an Indian reservation converted into a concentration camp." The camp was built on a section of the Colorado River Tribal Indian Reservation. Tajiri's film delicately probes the intersection of Japanese internees and Native residents by foregrounding the ironies of colonial dispossession. When she travels to Poston, a resident explains how "the government came in and overnight took over a section of the reservation and started to build the camps." Tajiri emphasizes the poor quality of the barracks, which were made "of this really cheap unseasoned pine and finished [off] with this tar paper." Later, she explains, "they tried to offer the barracks *back* to the Native Americans as compensation for the use of the land." From this vantage point, Poston becomes a space where the dispossessed and the recipients of government "welfare" confront each other as exchangeable figures of colonial management. A single group photograph of Native mothers and children, titled *1942, Native American Residents, Poston*, further accentuates how the internment camp was a space that, as Jodi Byrd points out, spatializes a "recursive colonialism that, during World War II, served to enjamb Japanese American detainees within the histories of containment and expropriation that strip lands and nations from American Indians."[64]

The intersection of Indigenous colonization and Japanese internment in the historical record further exemplifies the conflating tendency of this "recursive colonialism." In particular, the bureaucratic structure governing the incarceration of 113,000 Japanese Americans in ten remote concentration camps was modeled on existing colonial operations. From 1942 to 1946, the US War Relocation Authority (WRA) was largely staffed by personnel from the Bureau of Indian Affairs (BIA). Exemplifying the BIA-WRA connection was Dillon Myers, a ten-year veteran of the Indian Service, who was made director of the WRA for four years at Gila, Arizona, before assuming leadership of the BIA in 1950.[65] The similarities between the way the US government handled American Indians and Japanese internees often stemmed from Myers's conflation of Japanese and Indigenous bodies. A colleague once assessed Myers's tendency to collapse the two racial groups, remarking, "Like all of those guys [in the Indian Service] he feels that there are only two kinds of Indians—gooduns and baduns—and feels that Japs are Indians."[66] Behind the barbed wire, Japanese internees at Poston, Arizona, drew similar comparisons in their inquiries about whether "they would be 'kept' the rest of their lives on reservations like Indians."[67] Indeed, one of Eleanor Roosevelt's chief objections to Japanese internment camps was that it risked producing a culture of dependency: "If we don't look out we will create another Indian problem."[68] Once Japanese Americans were interned, the economic threat associated with them was resignified as the economic burden of social welfare.

In Canada, the government's instinct was similarly to conflate Japanese internees and First Nations peoples. When the federal government was devising plans for the expulsion of twenty-two thousand Japanese Canadians from the hundred-mile "protected area" on the coast of British Columbia, officials explored the possibility of using First Nations residential schools as sites for their internment. Although this plan was never executed, bureaucratic discourse functioned to fuse Japanese Canadians and First Nations as similarly alien to a white Canada and to promote Indigenous colonization as a useful template for Japanese internment. Mona Oikawa explains that one officer reporting to the British Columbia Security Commission stated, "We are hoping that mutually satisfactory arrangements can be made with your Commission so that the present staff could look after the Japanese on the basis somewhat similar to that applying in the case of the Indians."[69] Thus, in stark contrast to conspiratorial and destructive associations of economic power, Japanese internees are here aligned with colonial subjects, who, as the last chapter demonstrated, have been romanticized as existing *outside* of time and money.

One reading suggested by these seemingly incompatible identifications, from the abstract economism of the Jewish analogy to the concrete non-economism of the Native analogy, is that Japanese internment and dispersal *renovated* the connotation of Japanese labor from that of unnatural, excessive industry to some other, more benevolent expression of labor symbolically aligned with Native peoples. Jodi Kim refers to this transformation as a process of "gendered racial rehabilitation," in which Japanese American and Japanese Canadian subjects are transformed into a "model minority."[70] Building on this approach, I turn now to the way Kogawa and Tajiri unpack the question of labor resignification and consider its implications for our understanding of the relationship between settler colonialism and romantic anticapitalism.

Going Native as Surplus Labor

Drawing on the way settler nationalism informs the use of Native figures in contemporary Anglophone Canadian literature, Marie Lo argues that *Obasan*'s representation of Native figures "can be seen as a variant on mainstream nationalism, whereby authors who are marginalized and prevented from identifying with dominant Anglo-Canadian culture can find in Native culture 'a prior superior culture with which to identify.'"[71] My own analysis examines the material preconditions for the novel's alignment with Native identities. This effort is intended to serve a broader objective: to mine the transnationality of Japanese internment in North America through the figurative and spatial alignment with Indigenous peoples that is present in both Kogawa's and Tajiri's texts. If the figure of the Native functions as a settler colonial trope intended to naturalize Japanese Canadians, my analysis excavates the conditions of possibility that make such a trope accessible and legible within the imaginary of Japanese internment. In the case of *Obasan*, it is largely in the aftermath of the family's double removal that an identification with Native peoples is most explicit. Specifically, Naomi's descriptions of Uncle as Sitting Bull and Obasan as a Zulu warrior occur after decades living in Granton, Alberta. I argue that two elements condition this identification: first, that the figurative identification with Native identities relies on the symbolic transformation of labor from excessive efficiency to commendable productivity; and second, that this transformation is expressed as a process of devitalization, of both the land and the laborers themselves. What the novel exposes, therefore, is that the dehumanization of surplus labor reflects the eliminatory core of settler colonialism's romantic fantasy of the Native and reveals the necropolitical interplay of settler colonialism's relation to land and labor.

Although the subject of labor has not been a central literary concern in *Obasan* criticism, it is essential to the historical context that Kogawa's novel excavates.[72] As part of the West Coast removal process, the government created road labor camps for all able-bodied Japanese Canadian men to make badly needed improvements on neglected roadways in the hinterlands of British Columbia.[73] Sugar beet farmers who were desperate for wartime labor also capitalized on the removal orders by petitioning the government for Japanese Canadian laborers.[74] At the war's end, when Japanese Canadians were forced to choose between deportation or "Eastern Placement"—relocation east of the Rockies—the Labour Department was responsible for expanding its network of placement offices. Having enjoyed the economic boom that Japanese labor brought to the beet-farming industry in Alberta, industry leaders benefited further from the continued West Coast exclusion orders. It was not until April 1, 1949, that federal restrictions were lifted, allowing Japanese civilians to return to the hundred-mile British Columbia coastal area.[75]

This labor history figures in the material and speculative worlds of the *Obasan*. These policies had a direct impact on the reconfiguration of Naomi's family, given that her uncle and father are among the men dispatched to remote road labor camps. Like many married men, Uncle is eventually permitted to rejoin the family in Slocan, the ghost town where they are interned. For reasons never made clear, Naomi's father Tadashi is not reunited with the family until the war's end. The family's existence becomes increasingly abject after the war, when they are relocated again as part of the dispersal policy. Perhaps due to his frailty, the Department of Labor deems Tadashi "unsuitable for Eastern Placement,"[76] which results in his continued separation from the family and eventual death. The family is relocated to Granton, Alberta, where they endure the misery of being labor hands on the Barker beet farm, their home a converted chicken coop. For Naomi, it is the beet farm that becomes a central source of her trauma, the living nightmare of double relocation: "I cannot bear the memory. There are some nightmares from which there is no waking, only deeper and deeper sleep."[77] Transforming reality into the language of dreams, these years on the Barker farm are what she refers to as the "sleepwalk years."[78]

The novel's retrospective view of Japanese Canadian relocation emphasizes the mechanical degeneration of organic purity, of life reduced to deathly abjection. In Naomi's dream-memories, the Japanese are progressively deanimated in a lifeless landscape. After Uncle dies, Naomi is pulled back to her postwar home in Granton, Alberta, to come to the side of her aging Obasan, her aunt and primary caregiver through and after the war years. She returns to find the house and her aunt in a parallel state of somnambulance, the house a living appendage of Obasan's frail body, "where memories and dreams seep and mingle through cracks, settling on furniture and into upholstery."[79] In Naomi's first dream in the aftermath of her uncle's death, its nightmarish quality turns on mechanical deception in nature. In the dream Naomi descends into what seems a prelapsarian Eden, but a heavy mist coats the landscape and at turns, transforms its human subjects. As the dream progresses, what comes into foggy relief is how nature meets the mechanical in a field of labor.

In Naomi's dream, the degeneration of human labor is figured as a process of prostheticization that highlights the dissonant intersection of Indigenous nature and mechanized efficiency. Accompanied by a nameless man, Naomi's dream avatar descends on a mountainside forest to encounter another man and woman. For a fleeting moment, she catches a glimpse of the woman's beauty, appearing "as she once was, naked, youthful, voluptuous."[80] In this instant, the woman is Eve—pure, fertile, and without shame. But the vision quickly changes to reveal the woman in her current, fallen state. The dream's imagery underscores the mechanistic degeneration of the human body. Her seductive curves have been transformed into sharp angles: "Her face is now harsh again and angular as quartz. . . . Her body, a matching squareness, is dense as earth."[81] The vitality of the woman Naomi first encounters morphs into harsh quartz angularity. Her squareness suggests a uniformity and steel symmetry; she has more in common with metal than with flesh. The reference to her square body, as "dense as earth," lends an organicism to her embodiment, yet the heaviness of the simile evokes death and entombment. The glimmer of Indigenous, Eve-like purity—"naked, youthful, voluptuous"—is transformed into the organic burden of earth that pulls the body downward so she is capable only of movements that are "slow and heavy as sleep."[82]

Labor enters the dream as an allegory of Naomi's work on the Barker farm. In her dream nature and animate bodies undergo discipline and are transformed into disembodied, devitalized androids. The square woman is engaged in repetitive labor, her back bent over as her "arms sway and swing, front to back, back to front"[83] wielding a sickle, "harvesting the forest's debris, gathering the branches into piles."[84] Alongside her is a man, "taller thinner and precise—a British martinet."[85] Naomi observes that he is in command; equipped with "pruner's shears, he is cutting the trees."[86] With her companion, Naomi is silently entreated into joining the woman and man in labor, threatened by the martinet, whose glance is "a raised baton":[87]

> We move without question or references in an interminable unknowing without rules, without direction. No incident alerts us to an awareness of time. But at some subtle hour, the white mist is known to be gray, and the endlessness of labor has entered our limbs. Weariness.[88]

The man, a vision of patriarchal militaristic authority, enforces the monotonous repetition of their labor, while his pruner's shears cut into and discipline the natural landscape. He is accompanied by a "huge gentle beast—a lion or a dog" whose "obedience is phenomenal."[89] But the beast too, to Naomi's shock, is plastic: "The animal is a robot!"[90] What alerts her is its frozen yawn "when the mechanism that hinges the jaws has proven faulty."[91] By this point, she observes that the laboring woman's arms are now connected by "four hooks locked to make a hinge . . . [which] dangles as she approaches."[92] Therefore, in the process of disciplining the landscape, animate bodies undergo prosthetic degeneration, while deceptively real-looking robots take the place of animals. There is no place here even for language, which devolves in this landscape of mechanized beings. Naomi hears the woman speaking, "but the words are so old they cannot be understood. . . . The language has been forgotten."[93] The destructive rationalism and robotification in the dream allegorize both the progressive dehumanization of labor and the settler colonial disciplining of nature. Moreover, the dream accentuates the dehumanizing condition of surplus labor and the eliminatory spirit of settler colonialism.

The dream's apocalyptic vision of mechanized dehumanization captures the profound abjection of her years working on the devitalized landscape of the Barkers' beet farm.[94] Like the machine people in her dream, the farm landscape is barren and unnatural. As though the land had been subjected to the pruning shears of the British martinet of Naomi's nightmare, "here and there are straight unnatural rows of fierce almost leafless trees pruned like the brooms of a chimney sweep."[95] Even the air is unwelcoming and brutal: "Here, the air is a fist."[96] In this landscape where "plant growth is deliberate and fierce,"[97] both nature and machines are associated with death and confinement. "Round skull-shaped weeds" grow along the miles of "barbed wire fences,"[98] while "skeletons of farm machinery" lie between the shed and the farmhouse "like the remains of dinosaurs in a prehistoric battleground."[99] Naomi's dream refracts the prehistory of this lifeless landscape of coerced, unnatural growth. Succumbing to its deadening effects, Naomi feels like a "scarecrow or a skeleton in the wind."[100] Her brother Stephen, too, is later haunted by monstrous scenes of mechanized nature, once dreaming that "a metallic insect the size of a tractor [was] webbing a grid of iron bars over him."[101] Technological rationalism has turned the natural world upside-down, evoking the nightmarish scenes of her dream's landscape of human degeneration and artifice.

The condition of possibility for the way the novel attempts to indigenize Japanese Canadians through analogies to Native peoples centers on the dehumanization of labor. In this unnatural world, Naomi herself embodies the degeneration of the prosthetic-limbed woman who appears in her dream. Reproducing the metamorphosis of the woman from "youthful" and "voluptuous" into a harsh, square body with a face "angular as quartz,"[102] Naomi, too, "mind[s] growing ugly" in this prisonlike atmosphere where hardships are "so pervasive, so inescapable, so thorough it's a noose around my chest and I cannot move anymore."[103] Like the "endlessness of labor"[104] in the dream, Naomi's work on the beet farm is a nightmare of repetition where she "will never be done thinning and weeding and weeding and weeding," to the point that her body begins to degenerate into an empty shell while her "tear glands burn out."[105] Collectively the family is turned into automatons that switch on or off, "obedient as machines,"[106] through their days filled with the emptiness of labor, seemingly outside of time, space, and sound: "There are no other people in the entire world. We work together all day. At night we eat and sleep. We hardly talk anymore."[107] There is nothing of the symbolic purification in working the land associated with a romantic settler colonial vision of landscape. In this inverted world, both landscape and labor are disciplined and denaturalized into mechanical abstraction, which, as I will discuss further below, exemplifies the racialized condition of surplus labor.

Through this gothic transformation of landscape and labor—and continued exclusion from the West Coast—the dangerous economism of Japanese labor in the prewar period mutates to commendable productivity; the enemy alien morphs into the ideal surplus labor population. As Naomi sifts through Aunt Emily's package of wartime letters and documents, she finds a newspaper clipping filed under "Facts about evacuees in Alberta."[108] A caption that reads "'Grinning and Happy': Find Jap Evacuees Best Beet Workers" accompanies a photograph of a smiling Japanese Canadian family posing by a pile of beets.[109] The article praises the all-time record crop produced by Japanese "evacuee" labor, who worked 65 percent of Alberta's sugar beet acreage: "Generally speaking, Japanese evacuees have developed into most efficient beet workers, *many of them being better than the transient workers* who cared for beets in southern Alberta before Pearl Harbor."[110] This account of the bountiful yields attributed to Japanese labor is striking in its contrast to the dangerous efficiency of prewar Japanese Canadian fishing crews, which previously warranted restrictions on licenses and even the use of gas-powered boats. Thus the symbolic transformation in the postwar era, to be celebrated as commendable productivity, turns on the relocation and resignification of labor. What is especially telling about the article is how Japanese labor is no longer set in relation to white labor. Rather than competing with white labor on the West Coast, the newspaper clipping positions Japanese labor in relation to "transient workers." In short, Japanese Canadian laborers are reconstituted as superior figures of transient labor, which is possible only after their relocation and confinement.

Under these coercive and immobilizing conditions of labor, what enables the mutation of Japanese Canadian labor is their alignment with surplus laboring populations referred to as the "transient workers" in the article. Shedding racialized associations to abstract labor, which is perceived as having a destructive hold on the creation of unnatural, relative surplus-value, Japanese labor is reconstituted into what Marx terms an "industrial reserve army." As a surplus labor population, they regulate—for the benefit of capitalists—the interplay of technological innovation and human labor productivity in the process of capital accumulation. Marx describes the indispensable role played by the surplus population as follows:

> But if a surplus population of workers is a necessary product of accumulation or of the development of wealth on a capitalist basis, this surplus population also becomes, conversely, the lever of capitalist accumulation, indeed it becomes a condition of the existence of the capitalist mode of production. It forms a disposable industrial reserve army, which belongs to capital just as absolutely as if the latter had bred it at its own cost. Independently of the limits of the actual increase of population, it creates a mass of human material always ready for exploitation by capital in the interests of capital's own changing valorization requirements.[111]

Clarifying the expendability at the root of this mode of labor exploitation, Roderick Ferguson explains, "Both superfluous and indispensable, surplus populations fulfill *and* exceed the demands of capital."[112] It is precisely the condition of being disposable that I suggest produces the structural alignment with Native peoples who, as primary subjects of colonial elimination, are also exploited and similarly transformed into latent and then stagnant members of the industrial reserve army.[113] They are wage laborers who are subject to capitalism's need for labor power in uneven quantities and qualities over space and time. Describing the effect of capitalism's ability to "pivot" labor power, Ruth Gilmore explains that as "systemic expansions and contractions produce and throw off workers, those idled must wait, migrate, or languish until—if ever—new opportunities to sell their labor power emerge."[114] This also demonstrates how settler colonial logics of elimination (from land) and exclusion (as exploited alien labor) are not mutually exclusive but dialectically connected. Given that the Native reservation system and urban relocation programs in Canada and the United States functioned to entrench the disposability of Indigenous labor,[115] Native people were especially susceptible to irregular employment. As such, as Marx notes, this surplus labor group "offers capital an inexhaustible reservoir of disposable labour power."[116] Therefore, despite Naomi's anger at the characterization of Japanese beet farm laborers as "Grinning and Happy," it is this, their resignification as surplus labor, that connects Japanese bodies not to racialized value production but to the racialization of surplus labor populations, chief among them First Nations labor.[117] The availability of cross-racial identification in the novel turns on the transformation of Japanese abstract labor into surplus labor, a process of "gendered racial rehabilitation" that renews a white settler colonial hierarchy.[118]

In sum, *Obasan*'s presentation of a landscape of devitalization, a place where "something dead is happening, like the weeds that are left to bleach,"[119] offers several remaining insights. First, in this inverted world, the rehumanization of Japanese Canadians as surplus laborers who are "Grinning and Happy" relies on their dehumanization and dispossession. In other words, this indigenization reveals the dehumanized content at the core of romantic idealization of Native peoples. Second, in Kogawa's identification of Uncle with Chief Sitting Bull and Obasan with a Zulu warrior—non-Canadian Indigenous peoples from the United States and South Africa, respectively—they exemplify a dual condition of alien-ness and Indigeneity that highlights the dialectical interplay of land and labor under settler colonialism that expropriates Indigenous land and exploits racialized labor. That the postwar period saw the coerced recruitment of Native laborers to fill more labor shortages in the southern Alberta sugar beet industry until the 1980s further exemplifies the instrumentality of disposable labor populations, which embodied the condition of hyperexploitability: it was more profitable to consign these laborers to seasonal hand labor than to rely on costlier machines and chemicals. As the central pivot in facilitating the evolution to modern, better living in western Canada, racialized surplus labor bridges the necropolitical dimension of Native elimination to alien exclusion.

In Rea Tajiri's *History and Memory*, the mutation of Japanese labor is similarly expressed in the devitalization associated with the landscape on a Native reservation. Unlike the purely symbolic identification with Native identities in *Obasan*, in Tajiri's film indigenization turns on the relocation and confinement of Japanese internees to the shared colonial site of the Colorado River Indian Reservation in Poston, Arizona. Her film offers an illuminating complement to Kogawa's focus on the degenerative, mechanistic landscape of surplus labor on the beet farm by further probing the dark registers of Japanese internment that are refracted onto the reservation. Contrasting the way the colonial disciplining and rehabilitation of racialized labor are mirrored in the disciplined, unnatural landscape in *Obasan*, the landscape in *History and Memory* also serves as a witness to the modes of erasure enacted upon Japanese labor.

Through a combination of reenacted memories, Hollywood movie reels, text, and voice-overs, Japanese internment is presented as a source of knowledge that can be accessed only indirectly, through these tangled strands of representation. These are the multimedia artifacts of postmemory—memories and visions that are transmitted into Tajiri's consciousness from elsewhere. As David Eng observes of the documentary's experimental aesthetic, "Tajiri presents us with a complex argument concerning the supplemental relationship between political and affective histories of Japanese American internment that cannot be easily reconciled with dominant US or Japanese American accounts of the event."[120] In particular, recurring scenes of water — connected to land irrigation and a water tower — overturn water's associations with vitality and purification. Instead, water imagery serves as a collective trace of devitalization and degeneration. The theme of water is first established through repeated dramatizations of a memory that haunts Tajiri because it is not her own. In the vision her mother crouches at an outdoor tap, filling a canteen. We can identify the vision as postmemory from Tajiri's description:

> I don't know where this came from but I just had this fragment, this picture that's always been in my mind. My mother, she's standing at a faucet and it's really hot outside, and she's filling this canteen. And the water's really cold, and it feels really good. And outside the sun is just so hot, it's just beating down. And there's this dust that gets in everywhere. And they're always sweeping the floors.

The scene is played several times from alternating vantage points, focusing in on the rush of water from the tap, the overflowing canteen, the back of her mother's crouching body, and her mother's face as she splashes water onto it. This visual refrain operates as an abstract contrast to the realism of films that rationalize Japanese internment through numerous Hollywood reenactments of Pearl Harbor and government-sponsored announcements justifying its wartime actions toward Japanese civilians. In the documentary's continual return to the dislocated postmemory of water, Tajiri suggests that the meaning of Japanese internment has been overdetermined by Hollywood's heroic action films and melodrama.

Challenging this representational realism, Tajiri deconstructs the meaning of Japanese internment by presenting indirect channels of meaning that form a nonlinear collage of knowledge that focuses on what water reveals through what it conceals. Alongside the continual return to the scene of her mother at the fountain, a single Hollywood film recurs through the documentary, standing as an exception to normative representations of Japanese internment: *Bad Day at Black Rock*, a 1955 film that, like Tajiri's documentary, deals with Japanese internment indirectly through absence rather than presence.[121] The strength of *Bad Day at Black Rock* for Tajiri is that despite the fact that no Japanese American character ever appears in the film, this absence constitutes a meaningful form of erasure and emptiness, analogous to the visual tension produced by the negative space of Asawa's sculptures. Specifically, it is the disappearance of a man named Komoko in the film that Tajiri uses as a conceptual frame for understanding the Japanese internment experience at Poston. She explains, "Komoko never appears, not even a picture or a photograph." She relates his disappearance to her family's: "Komoko's disappearance from Black Rock was like ours from history. His absence is his presence." Again, the weight of Komoko's absence reinforces Asawa's concept of negative space, as a force that reveals and energizes what exceeds the visual representation and historiography of Japanese internment.

Although Tajiri incorporates only selected clips of *Bad Day at Black Rock*, the entire arc of the film reveals a racialized projection of Japanese labor's excessive efficiency, which generated unnatural value. Part revisionist western, part film noir, the film is saturated with mystery. Spencer Tracy stars as John Macreedy, a one-armed stranger who arrives in Black Rock, a forgotten town where, prior to his arrival, the train had not stopped in four years. Macreedy reveals almost nothing of himself, except that he is a World War II veteran whose purpose is to find a man named Komoko. The lawless townspeople react to his inquiries with intimidation and violence. Although the town's unofficial leader, a man named Smith, claims that Komoko was sent to a Japanese internment camp after Pearl Harbor, Macreedy remains skeptical after finding wildflowers growing outside Komoko's home, a sign that "something's buried up there." He eventually discovers that Ko-moko has been murdered. A rare ally in the town explains the rationale for the mob killing of Komoko one day after Pearl Harbor, which is the result neither of redirected anger for Pearl Harbor nor of any conflation of Japa-nese Americans with Japanese wartime enemies. Instead, it is Komoko's ex-cessive efficiency that has fueled economic resentment and conspiracy. The townsperson tells Macreedy that when the land that Komoko leased—land previously perceived to be too dry and sterile to be productive—yielded growth, they all "figured he must be cheating him . . . [because] you can't grow anything without water." But Komoko does find water by digging a deep well, "climb[ing] down sixty feet," Macreedly learns. This reinforces a larger point in this chapter: that leading up to Japanese internment, Japa-nese labor was associated with the production of unnatural value—an un-natural hold on relative surplus-value. From the perspective of the towns-people in Black Rock, Komoko frustrated natural laws by growing things where there "never was any water." Therefore, through the film's symbolic logic, the discovery of water signifies unnatural growth.

Like the recurrence of water imagery, the symbolism of wildflowers marks decomposition rather than growth and connects *Bad Day at Black Rock* to Japanese internment. Under a scene captioned "Flowers for Ko-moko's Grave" appears Tajiri's mother's flower garden. Rather than serving as sentimental natural imagery, the textual emphasis on Komoko's grave draws out the significance of Macreedy's observation that the wildflowers he identifies in the film are signifiers of death. Having been in Italy during the war, Macreedy has learned that bodies buried in the ground decompose into nutrients that produce wildflowers. Tajiri capitalizes on the dual edge of this natural imagery, as sign of both degeneration and regeneration. In place of her mother's memory, moreover, the wildflowers give materiality to the absence that is also a presence. Here the wildflowers symbolize a landscape that has become witness to events that have been erased or will-fully forgotten. The connection between water, landscape, and labor helps to contextualize the repeated scenes of Tajiri's mother at the water faucet in the larger context of the Poston camp. Tying these scenes into Komoko's ability to bring water to an arid landscape, she notes, "That was the thing about the Japanese. They took barren lands and brought water to it. . . . The irony is that they did it again in Poston: brought water to the land and made things grow." The new context for their labor at Poston enables a transformative regeneration symbolized by Tajiri's mother's flowers, which are simultaneously signifiers of death.

The still photographs of a single water tower, one taken in 1942 and another in 1988, seem to stand as the only evidence of Japanese irrigation labor at Poston, the largest internment camp built in the United States.[122] That Poston was the site of a Native reservation and Japanese internment camp sets in motion what Ruth Okimoto calls "an ironic twist of history," in which "the Japanese detainees at Poston experienced what American Indians did in the nineteenth and early 20th centuries."[123] And it is my argument that this "ironic twist" turns on the mutation of Japanese labor from abstract to surplus labor. It is this spatial context of Japanese confinement on a Native reservation that renovates the prior association of water with unnatural growth in *Bad Day at Black Rock* to sustainability and productivity. As an uncanny precursor to Japanese confinement, Native Americans were similarly relocated to this desolate landscape. As Okimoto explains in her report *Sharing a Desert Home*, "Citing national security and the need to protect white settlers, the US government had similarly herded American Indians onto this desolate, arid, and unproductive stretch of land."[124] Linking the postmemory of water and agriculture woven into Tajiri's film, what Poston exemplifies, therefore, is the spatial paradox of surplus labor. The water tower evokes the way water imagery remains a material trace of an unnatural landscape through the dehumanization of surplus labor.[125] For both the War Relocation Authority, responsible for housing Japanese detainees, and the Office of Indian Affairs, which would manage the subjugation and irrigation projects, the use of Japanese labor represented the high point of settler colonial logics in the managed interplay of land and labor, elimination and exclusion. Not surprisingly, the Colorado River Indian Tribal supported neither the internment camps nor the colonization program.[126] The outcome was clearly advantageous mostly to whites, who benefited from the access to irrigation systems in the desert, in addition to the dispossessed Japanese property on the West Coast. Thus, from the deep well on Komoko's land to the water tower at Poston, water is the conduit for and witness to both unnatural growth and exploited, invisible labor.

To reiterate an earlier point, the mutation of Japanese labor from abstract to surplus labor turned on their conflation with Native populations. Opposing the enthusiasm for efficient Japanese labor, WRA Director Dillon Myers (who became head of the BIA in 1950) became openly concerned that if kept too long in confinement, Japanese internees would become "dependent like Native Americans."[127] In stark contrast to the labor efficiency attributed to Japaneseness, Poston was (like other camps) a space of idled labor, where boredom and inactivity coexisted with coerced labor. This dual condition of coerced and idled labor is the primary condition of a surplus population of reserve labor. Given what Michael McIntyre identifies as "race's long-standing use as a mark of labor,"[128] the prior association of Japaneseness with unnatural "abstract labor" undergoes colonial rehabilitation to the historically racialized category of surplus labor, whose exploitation reinforces whiteness as the basis for property acquisition and expansion. This is the movement from an alien mode of threatening racialized labor to a domesticated form of surplus, racialized labor. A statement by one white farmer plainly reveals the true beneficiaries of using Japanese labor to subjugate Native land: "It will develop a lot of land, bring in irrigation, so white farmers can use it. . . . Couldn't let good land like that go to waste."[129] Tajiri's visual emphasis on the water tower at Poston stands as a remaining artifact of this history, which, like Komoko's body, has been disappeared from the landscape of labor.

For Tajiri it is only a stagnant, unpromising landscape that remains as evidence of the Japanese American internees confined at Poston, whose rehabilitation as surplus labor functioned ironically to indigenize their previously abstract alien labor. The signs that designate Indigenous peoples as surplus populations are continually reinforced through the film's stark panoramas of the overgrown and decrepit state of the Poston barracks. They were turned over to Native American "colonists" after Japanese Americans were released in 1945 and used as classrooms until 1980. With the exception of an alcohol recovery center, the buildings that remain have deteriorated out of neglect. This is the colonial wasteland of surplus, disposed-of populations. The water tower remains, symbolizing the irrigation of Poston land in the Parker Irrigation Project—rearticulated through recurring dramatizations of Tajiri's mother at the desert water faucet—and there are two film stills of palm trees, which text identifies as "Date Palm Grove, Poston, 1988: Planted by internees, 1942." In this landscape of neglect and ruin, the palm trees, like wildflowers, figure as an ambivalent symbol of transformation, of both death and regeneration.

Tajiri concludes the film with similar ambivalence. Ultimately she finds affective reconciliation with her mother, realizing that the recurring image of her mother at the water faucet is rooted in a memory of a rare story her mother once told of her years in camp, and states: "Now I found I could connect the picture to the story. I could forgive my mother her loss of memory." This sentiment is complicated by the final frame of the film, which pans out to a desolate road near the Poston desert, a refusal to find aesthetic resolution in natural vitality. The viewer is left only with a sweep of the empty highway, electrical wires in the distance, and the shrill cry of a hawk. David Eng calls it a "scene of unfolding, a scene of discursive emptiness."[130] It is quite literally a scene of negative space that refuses to animate a central subject. This final vision of landscape is not a romantic symbol of belonging to landscape but, rather, of how the landscape itself is a witness to the necropolitical dimension of the drive to annihilate abstraction within an ideology of settler colonial romantic anticapitalism. As symbols of death's remainder, Komoko's and Tajiri's mother's wildflowers represent the inverted growth of the underworld of Japanese internment, one for which Ruth Asawa's upside-down tree similarly evokes "those things your body doesn't allow you to leave behind."

Conclusion

This chapter explores how Japanese internment was less a final episode in a record of anti-Asian exclusion that began in the nineteenth century than a *turning point* that created conditions for the resignification of Japanese labor as efficient and tractable—the core tenets of the model minority myth—only after being reconstituted as a dependent, surplus labor population. As a result, our understanding of the outcome of Japanese internment in North America shifts the foundational distinction of land and labor that Patrick Wolfe identifies for delineating the interplay of elimination and exclusion that Indigenous peoples and African Americans have been subject to, respectively. In the case of Native North Americans, elimination was achieved through a spectrum of tactics that included genocidal campaigns and the move toward the "statistical elimination" of Indigenous peoples through the strategic dilution of blood-quantum. Exclusion, on the other hand, represents the undissolvable blackness as a transferable category of a racial underclass. Thus the example of Japanese land dispossession and coerced labor within the project of Japanese internment adds a new dimension to this theorization of settler colonialism. In particular, the relocation, dispossession, and dispersal of Japanese North Americans follow a trajectory of colonial elimination through assimilation. In the process, Japanese North Americans underwent resignification: they started out embodying the threat of yellow peril and emerged as a dependent surplus labor force who exemplified liberal individualism rather than a collective, unnatural menace.

In Canada, the elimination of Japanese Canadians from the West Coast was achieved through the postwar dispersal program, which scattered Japanese Canadians across the prairies. In the United States, similarly, officials such as Dillon Myers at Poston worked to implement policies that would enable the disappearance of Japanese Americans. As Okimoto recounts, Myers's belief was that Japanese Americans should "melt or boil away."[131] In 1943, Myers's relocation program — an assimilation program — was designed to relocate and disperse Japanese Americans east of the western states. On their release, only half of former West Coast residents returned; the rest relocated to Chicago, Cleveland, Detroit, Philadelphia, Denver, and New York.[132] Turning the revolving door of colonial history, when Myers became commissioner of the Bureau of Indian Affairs (formerly the OIA) in 1950, he reimplemented the relocation policy for Native nations. Okimoto explains that "under this policy, Indians were convinced to move out of reservations and into cities, where they were told jobs and a better life awaited them."[133] Such relocation policies were instituted as pathways to "termination," a policy exemplified in Canada's failed 1969 White Paper, which sought to terminate First Nations special status, turning them into "equal" citizens with alienable property. Thus Japanese and Native bodies stood in as surplus populations against which conceptions of liberal individualism and property ownership were reconfigured and entrenched. Dispossession, relocation, and labor thus become the eliminatory conduits to "better, modern living."

The next chapter examines the brave new world of racial equivalents, where liberal individualism, corporate personhood, and market freedom reigns. In it I explore how the economic modality of Asian racialization becomes bifurcated and further entrenches the association of Asians with destructive abstraction. Specifically, I look at the significance of the post-1960s neoliberalization of immigration borders to reinforce the abstract racialization of Asians as both poor migrant labor and wealthy, flexible citizens.

FIGURE 4.1 Ken Lum, *Entertainment for Surrey*, 1978 (video still), single-channel video with sound. Collection of the Vancouver Art Gallery, Acquisition Fund.

CHAPTER 4

THE NEW NINETEENTH CENTURY

*Neoliberal Borders, the City, and the Logic of
Settler Colonial Capitalism*

Art Imitates Art

Between 6 and 8 A.M. on four consecutive mornings in July 1978, multimedia artist Ken Lum stood on the east bank of the 152nd Street overpass leading rush-hour commuters into Vancouver from Surrey. *Entertainment for Surrey*, the grainy black-and-white video-recording of this performance, depicts Lum in jeans and a sweatshirt facing oncoming traffic, standing on a strip of grass on the side of the highway (figure 4.1). Recounting his experience, Lum observed, "The first day there was some reaction, the second day there was much more, but on the third day people ignored me."[1] On the fourth day, many commuters had grown accustomed to him, honking and waving as their cars disappeared under the overpass. On the fifth and final morning of the performance, Lum replaced his body with a large white cardboard cutout of himself, a representation of the "living statue" he had become.[2] Lum explained that "people quickly came to expect me on the same spot. I became a sign."[3] The humor in Lum's comment is its double edge: he literally turned his body into a cardboard sign while, at the level of postmodern signification, his body became a referential sign. Turning the highway overpass into a performance art space and the Asian male body into a sign of repetition, *Entertainment for Surrey* collapses the boundary between literal and figurative representation. Even more dramatically, his performance probes the spatial absurdity of the individual—of individualism itself—in an urban environment designed to facilitate the movement of labor, goods, and capital. As Jeff Derksen observes, "The tension between mobility and fixity is often heightened by [Lum's] grinding of the scales between the urban and the global and between capitalism and the subject."[4] Only by recognizing his apparent lack of function or purpose could otherwise baffled commuters have been alerted to the artistic registers of his performance. For the purposes of this chapter, the way Lum stages a visual interruption in the flow of capitalist circulation offers new avenues for mining the abstractions signaled by the Asian body after the neoliberal turn.

In the parallel urban literary world of Karen Tei Yamashita's *Tropic of Orange*, another artist ascends the freeway overpass to deliver daily performances. Enter Manzanar Murasaki, the homeless Sansei who stands atop the Los Angeles Harbor Freeway at the downtown interchange to conduct an orchestra that he alone hears. For this grizzled, white-haired artist, it is "the complexity of human adventure over lines of transit" that fascinate him, and he is grateful for the opportunity to use his silver baton to direct the sounds of traffic, which amount to "nothing less than the greatest orchestra on Earth."[5] Is he crazy? We learn that Manzanar was not always a conductor. He was once a skilled surgeon who abruptly left his profession, family, and friends to become a "missing person."[6] He decided one day to exit the world he knew, "followed an ancient tortoise out into a deep place in his brain and stayed there year after year."[7] Using the alias "Manzanar," he references his birthplace at Manzanar Concentration Camp in the Owens Valley, where he was the first Sansei born into captivity during World War II. We learn that he could easily have applied his artistic talents to becoming "a sculptor in clay, wood, or even marble—any sort of inanimate substance"; however, "strangely, it was the abstraction of music that engulfed his being."[8] Los Angeles commuters rarely take notice of him, though, thinking themselves "disconnected from a sooty homeless man on an overpass."[9] Nevertheless, he had become a "fixture on the freeway overpass much like a mural or a traffic information sign or a tagger's mark."[10] Like Ken Lum in *Entertainment for Surrey*, Manzanar became a sign.

Both Lum and Manzanar bear an uncanny resemblance to David Caspar Friedrich's *Wanderer above the Sea of Fog* discussed in chapter 2, the iconic embodiment of the Byronic hero surveying the vast, mountainous landscape before him. Even Buzzworm, the African American street philanthropist of *Tropic of Orange*, calls Manzanar the "ultimate romantic."[11] However, while Lum and Manzanar evoke the individualism of the romantic figure, they do not adopt Albert Boime's notion of a "magisterial gaze,"[12] given the total absence of control they exert over the oncoming traffic. Observing the way Manzanar responds to the dizzying urban flows of capitalist production with a "quintessentially nineteenth-century aesthetic practice [of] conducting," Mark Chiang highlights the irony that Manzanar "does not control anything. . . . His conducting is an effort to grasp the conceptual order underlying the seemingly chaotic processes of the global system."[13] Thus it is a kind of purposeful purposelessness that binds Lum and Manzanar, two Asian North Americans who abandoned their real and fictional lives as model minorities—Lum's as a scientist and Manzanar's as a surgeon—to yield to an artistic vision that would compel them to their respective freeway overpasses. Against the rational landscape of the freeway and the temporal organization of the workweek, both artists suspend and denaturalize the relation between the body and sign, embodying a postromantic subjectivity whose exaggerated nonproductivity constitutes a strange other of capitalism. Evoking forms of undisciplined labor power, Lum and Manzanar index a sphere of *disability*, a nonrehabilitative population that remains distinct from the exploitable population of racialized and gendered surplus labor. David T. Mitchell and Sharon Snyder designate nonproductive bodies as those "inhabitants of the planet who, largely by virtue of biological (in)capacity, aesthetic non-conformity, and/or non-normative labor patterns . . . [are] not merely excluded from—but also resistant to standardized labor demands of human value."[14] They point to Antonio Negri's term "living labor" to "suggest forms of creativity that cannot be reduced to an economic value."[15] In this sense, both Lum and Manzanar stage a confrontation of capitalism's naturalized modes of consumption, circulation, and social organization—using and misusing the freeway as motif of urban modernity. Most important for this chapter is how their bodies-as-sign animate new relations between labor and the Asian body against the flows of global capital.

A utopian ideal of functional disruption captured by Lum's and Manzanar's performances guides this chapter's focus on the ongoing racial abstractions assigned to the Asian body in an apocalyptic phase of contemporary capitalism. Describing the "catastrophic character of the current phase shift that global capital is undergoing," Chris Nealon labels it a "late late capitalism."[16] The previous chapters in this book have examined capitalism as a representational regime whose fetishism mystifies the social relations embedded in commodity production. Within its social distortion, I explored how alien Asian labor has since the nineteenth century functioned as biological signifier of the destructively abstract dimension of an *antinomical* view of capitalist relations. Moishe Postone ties the origins of this antinomy to the commodity form itself, wherein each commodity's expression of use-value and exchange value is *misperceived* as an antinomical (rather than dialectical) relation of concrete and abstract dimensions. From this view, which I've described as a form of romantic anticapitalism, use-value appears concrete, "as objective in the sense of being objectlike, 'material' or 'thingly,'" while exchange-value appears abstract," as "general, homogenous, and abstracted from all particularity."[17] In other words, even though a commodity such as a chair contains both use-value as something to sit on and exchange-value as a quantitative dimension that enables the chair to be bought and sold, romantic anticapitalism perceives these two characteristics as so completely disconnected they are oppositional — antinomical — rather than dialectically related. As a key ideological anchor of white settler colonialism, romantic anticapitalism always *favors* the qualitative over the quantitative. It prefers the concrete dimension for being natural, material, tactile, and thus closer to earthly origins in an increasingly artificial world. For the romantic anticapitalist, capitalism is identified solely with the abstract exchange dimension of the antinomy, while the concrete dimension is perceived as essentially noncapitalist.

This book interprets anti-Asian racism as a fetishized, one-sided form of settler colonial romantic anticapitalism, an ideology that anthropomorphizes capitalism's abstract dimension as alien Asian labor. As such, my first two chapters explored how Asian North American literature and visual culture exposes and disidentifies with the late nineteenth- and early twentieth-century association of Asian labor with an abstractly perverse, unnatural, and destructive economism that threatened the normative social reproduction of white concrete labor. In the third chapter, on postmemory narratives of Japanese internment in North America, I probed the extent of the destructiveness associated with Japanese labor, whose excessive efficiency and perceived control over the creation of relative surplus-value were key elements in the decision to relocate and confine Japanese civilians. Then, by connecting the relocation of Japanese North American labor to the settler colonial precedent of Native North American relocation evoked by these narratives, I argued that the exploitation of relocated Japanese labor contributed to the resignification of Japanese bodies as an ideal "surplus" labor force, dispossessed of any control over the creation of relative surplus-value. This facilitated a symbolic process that Jodi Kim calls "gendered racial rehabilitation,"[18] which enabled Japanese civilians to be aligned with the ameliorated status of model minority in the midst of civil rights activism in the United States during the Cold War. However, as this chapter will explore further, the neoliberal reconstitution of immigration laws in Canada and the United States in the latter twentieth century has reinforced the destructive abstraction associated with Asian alien surplus labor, an abstraction that comes into heightened relief in Vancouver and Los Angeles, two cities that refract urbanism, immigration, and trans-Pacific economic flows of labor, goods, and capital.

Examining Karen Tei Yamashita's Los Angeles as imagined in her 1997 novel *Tropic of Orange* alongside Ken Lum's Vancouver through his multimedia works—concluding with a reading of his sculpture *Four Boats Stranded: Red and Yellow, Black and White* (1999)—my central argument in this chapter is that these artists bring into focus the border as a key apparatus of neoliberal multiculturalism that facilitates the fulfillment of settler colonial capitalism through the migrant labor system. I demonstrate how the neoliberalization of the border substitutes economic class for race, resulting in a bifurcated economism of Asian racialization. As John Park outlines, the unprecedented rise of skilled and affluent migrants from Asia has been coupled with the similar explosion in undocumented aliens; Park observes that in the United States "up to one million undocumented aliens are now from Asian countries. . . . Their numbers multiplied four or five times over the past 25 years."[19] Immigration policy increasingly privileges flexible Asian citizens with foreign capital, expanding and entrenching the alignment of Asians with an abstract dimension of destructively alien capital. Vancouver's identity as an Asian metropolis and "Pacific gateway" has coincided with widespread resentment of wealthy Chinese investor-migrants, who are blamed for the city's skyrocketing property prices.[20] At the same time, poor Asian migrants situated at the margins of legality represent a perennial threat to the social order and remain indebted to the precarious structure of settler colonial hospitality. In this neoliberal scenario, settler colonial romantic anticapitalism targets *both* the population of highly skilled, capitalized migrants that L. Ling-chi Wang calls "high-tech coolies"[21] *and* the population of poor migrants — we might call them "retro" coolies — who have always been the subject of labor exploitation guaranteed by class-based structures of immigrant exclusion that have been in place in North America since the nineteenth century. We should recall that the 1882 Chinese Exclusion Act in the United States specifically barred laborers and exempted merchant classes, while Canada's 1885 Chinese Head Tax (and later 1923 Chinese Immigration Act) similarly aimed to deter poor Chinese migrants through financial hardship. In a contemporary climate that looks like a neoliberal nineteenth century, therefore, the economic logic of the border reinforces the alignment of Asians with the abstract threat of foreign investment, whose incursion into North America represent an oppressive "takeover" of traditional values and social order. At the same time, the population of undesirables (and provisional desirables, in the case of certain refugees) remains an alien labor threat to the security of citizen wages and normative social reproduction. While Ken Lum's multimedia works evoke the superficiality of neoliberal multiculturalist aesthetics, Yamashita's novel provides a complementary view of alien labor subjectivity conditioned by globalization. I conclude with a reading of the inverted ecology of the border represented in Yamashita's novel and Lum's sculpture *Four Boats Stranded: Red and Yellow, Black and White*, which sits on top of the Vancouver Art Gallery. At stake in Yamashita's and Lum's aesthetic reconfigurations of the border is the value of human labor in late late capitalism.

Lum's Multicultural Discontents

In order to contextualize my reading of Lum's *Four Boats Stranded*, one of his most direct responses to the issue of immigration in Canada, this section establishes his conceptual ties to pop art and minimalism and the way his art probes themes of social exclusion, multiculturalism, and labor. His work powerfully reconsiders the interplay of multicultural citizenship, labor alienation, and stranger hospitality that shapes the landscape of urban racialization.

Since the late 1970s, Lum's work has achieved international renown and acclaim. Through the decades his work has consistently examined the tense boundary between mobility and stasis (as in *Entertainment for Surrey*),

FIGURE 4.2 Ken Lum, *Sculpture for Dream Home*, 1980.

public and private space, access and exclusion, image and text, reflection
and projection. The spatial boundaries Lum erects are often uncomfortably
fraught with race, gender, and class implications. Beginning in the 1980s,
he gained visibility for his furniture sculptures, such as *Sculpture for Dream
Home* (1980), *Red Circle* (1986), and *Corner Bed* (1990). Each of these sculptures engages the spatial politics of domesticity and hospitality, whose symbolism encompasses the personal as much as the national. For example, in
Sculpture for Dream Home (figure 4.2), four identical contemporary sofas
with side tables and lamps are wedged together into a perfect square. At
first glance, the uniformity of the arrangement recalls the impersonal but
functional aesthetic of a hotel lobby. But the viewer quickly realizes that the
sofas are so tightly interlocked there's no way to actually sit down on any of
them. The functionality of the sofas is entirely displaced, and the viewer is
literally marginalized by the sculpture, blocked from accessing its interior,
core space. They evoke Derrida's notion that the "law of hospitality . . . appears as a paradoxical law, pervertible or perverting":[22]

> This right to hospitality offered to a foreigner "as a family," represented
> and protected by his name or her family name, is at once what makes
> hospitality possible, or the hospitable relationship to the foreigner pos-

FIGURE 4.3 Ken Lum, *Red Circle*, 1986. Fabric, wood, 300 cm diameter. Collection of the Vancouver Art Gallery, Acquisition Fund. Photo: Trevor Mills, Vancouver Art Gallery.

sible, but by the same token what limits and prohibits it. Because hospitality, in this situation, is not offered to an anonymous new arrival and someone who has neither name, nor patronym, nor family, nor social status, and who is therefore treated not as a foreigner but as another barbarian.[23]

In other words, *Sculpture for Dream Home* captures the contradictions of hospitality that must distinguish between the foreigner and absolute other, whose provisional guarantee of welcome simultaneously expresses its opposite: rejection. The sculpture thus resignifies the stage of mundane domesticity into one of inhospitality, a hostile expression of isolation that calls into question the spatial boundaries that configure social belonging and exclusion.

Continuing these themes more dramatically is *Red Circle* (1986), which consists of a plump fire-engine-red sofa in the shape of a circle (figure 4.3). Like *Sculpture for Dream Home*, the sofa violates its own function. Despite its inviting, cushiony enclosure, there is no way to actually sit on this sofa. Its sexually inviting minimalist aesthetic, conveyed through its seductive color and symmetrical vertical lines, adds to the sense of calculated exclusion and thwarted intimacy. A modernist ethos of form over function seems responsible for accentuating the viewer's dislocation and nonbelonging. Observing the manner through which these sculptures harness the viewer's sense of exclusion, Okwui Enwezor identifies Lum's furniture works as "social sculptures" in the sense that they invite a social reading of minimalism: "Where minimalism abjured the presence of the subject in order to prioritize the presence of the object, social and relational sculpture reasserted the primacy of the subject."[24] In this view, these sculptures register a critique of minimalism's abstractions and evacuation of historical and social context. Connecting minimalism's focus on pure form and capitalism, Scott Watson calls attention to the way minimalist works such as Donald Judd's boxes or Carl Andre's bricks seem to replicate disturbing transformations in the built urban landscape: "Regularity, logic and order in the art work were suddenly implicated in the conformist tendencies of society; the abstractions of pure form became ciphers from the abstractions of capital itself."[25] That is, the desire for disinterested, abstract, pure form was a reflection of the conformist, homogenizing spirit of capitalism. Moreover, Lum's reconfiguration of the use-value of the sofas as art seems to satirize the modernist ideal of "better living" achieved through the fusion of art and design. Here that view is collapsed into a scene of insecure, empty living.

Among the last of these furniture works, *Corner Bed* (1990) adds a further layer of dysfunction to the social space of the domestic "living" room. The sculpture consists of two unfolded sofa beds that face a corner (figure 4.4). Like *Sculpture for Dream Home* and *Red Circle*, the sofa beds cannot be accessed; the viewer can neither sit nor lie on either sofa bed. What's distinct about *Corner Bed* is how it registers the theme of inhospitality more intensely by evoking an excluded visitor. As sofa beds are mostly used for temporary guests rather than permanent residents, *Corner Bed* suggests an aggressive exclusion of visitors and strangers. Putting the sculpture into the sustained geographical emphasis on the city of Vancouver in Lum's work, the piece also alludes to the city's historical hostility toward Asian migrants who have sought and continue to seek entry to Canada via Vancouver. As Enwezor reflects, the work "propos[es] an analysis of spatial politics that is all too familiar within regimes of border control."[26] Here we see the suggestive refraction of private living space into the social domain of national exclusion. But what complicates a straightforward reading of racial exclusion is the pathetic, half-hearted display of hospitality (the sofa beds are

FIGURE 4.4 Ken Lum, *Corner Bed*, 1990. Two sofa beds, dimensions variable. Courtesy of the artist.

unfolded, for instance) that Lum cuts into these furniture sculptures. The ambivalent message of the furniture's arrangement reinforces the paradox of Derrida's elaboration of hospitality while evoking both an invitation and an expectation of strangers.

The dark humor of Lum's sculptures also marks his photographic works, which probe the unvarnished materiality of urban life in Vancouver. In his portrait-text works, Lum opts for scenes that do not recycle mythologized panoramas of the Lion's Gate Bridge or the sunset over English Bay that project the city's beauty and cosmopolitanism. Rather, Lum's Vancouver often reflects his own background in the working-class and often invisible east side of Vancouver. His grandfather arrived as an immigrant before the Chinese Exclusion Act in 1923 and found work on the Canada Pacific Railway. When Lum was growing up, his mother worked in sweatshops and his father held menial jobs. As a result, the Vancouver Lum projects highlights the decidedly unglamorous side of urban existence: the minimalls, parking lots, and sidewalks populated by immigrants, workers, and people who often seem down and out. These are the characters and locales Lum connects to his own childhood in East Vancouver:

> There were all those families whose fathers worked as dishwashers with the mothers sewing in sweatshops; that's basically my family roots. Then

there are the very desperate, itinerant families at the bottom. East Vancouver is also an area with many immigrants, so there is always a kind of confusion in reference to how people relate to one another.[27]

But as his furniture works suggest, Lum is far from sentimental in his approach to East Vancouver and its inhabitants. Rather, Lum's firsthand experience compels him to weave a dark humor into his portrayal of Vancouver, with an eye to how the global economy shapes urban existence as well as our perception of it. The neoliberal turn in economic commonsense has resulted in increasing production and movement of goods and people, widening the gap between rich and poor, expanding the gendered and racialized global wage-labor force, and swelling the proportions of that global population who live in the city. As Derksen observes, these are dynamics of the global-urban nexus, in which "the city—under its many designations of 'megacity,' 'world city,' 'cosmopolis,' or 'metapolis'—has become a condenser of global forces and an amplifier of global effects."[28] Engaging with capitalism and its racialized tropes, Lum's photographic works explore the dissonance of race, class, and gender between image and text. It is here that the Asian subject of work—of labor—comes to the fore, presenting with barbed humor the relationship between Asians and work, capital, and value production.

Among his large-scale photographic series titled *Portrait Attributes*, Lum pairs a subject's portrait alongside text that we would normally associate with billboard advertising. The portraits are unusual for the way they capture ordinary people in what Kitty Scott describes as the "micro-moments of life."[29] In these works Lum makes central the complex, affective dimension of those often racialized and gendered subjects who are rarely the focus of pictorial representation. In *Melly Shum Hates Her Job* (1989) (figure 4.5),[30] Lum intensifies the boundary between racial theater and social documentary. In this portrait-text work, the subject Melly Shum is sitting at her desk in the midst of accounting work. Her surroundings are lackluster, suggestive of a governmental branch office. The fact that she is crunching numbers on a clunky industrial adding machine suggests her low-level position; she is not a CEO overseeing million-dollar transactions on a computer screen. It appears she is pausing briefly to smile at the camera before returning to her accounting task. Accompanying her portrait is a panel of large, capitalized text that reads, from top to bottom: "MELLY SHUM HATES HER JOB." The vertical orientation of the text accentuates the work's use of billboard

FIGURE 4.5 Ken Lum, *Melly Shum Hates Her Job*, 1989. Chromogenic print, lacquer, enamel on aluminum, Sintra, 182 × 243.8 cm. Courtesy of the artist.

conventions and heightens the emotional impact of the words. The word "HATES" is enlarged and in vivid color, distinguishing it from the more neutral blue font of the other words. The rippled contours of red, yellow, and black typeface make the word "HATES" look sizzling or electrified. This loud advertising typography is totally contradicted by Melly Shum's smiling face. Although there is humorous relief in Melly's sentiments about work in general, that humor has a dark side. In particular, what is disturbing about the relationship between text and image is the way it violates the privacy of the photographic subject. Like many of Lum's subjects, Melly Shum is not a glamorous or heroic worker; rather, she appears as a beleaguered civil servant who, in spite of her gloom, is compelled to smile for the camera. More intrusively, her private thoughts have been broadcast in corporatist type by an omniscient narrator—the artist—onto a public billboard. In a form of ethnographic violence, an exclusive form of dialogue is enabled between the artist and the viewer that excludes Melly Shum altogether. As Kitty Scott remarks, this "doubling of voice and intimate knowledge about a stranger induces a sense of dis-ease in the viewer."[31] What Lum achieves in this photograph is a refusal of what Roland Barthes calls the "good" picture, one in which the "*object speaks* [and] induces us, vaguely, to think."[32] Instead, Melly Shum "'sp[eaks] too much' . . . suggest[ing] a meaning—a different meaning from the literal one"[33] and thus dislocating the photograph's intention.

In the sense that misery becomes an object of artistic consumption—a kind of working-class spectacle—Lum's photographic works approach the threshold of cynicism. Scott Watson observes a long tradition of artistic depictions of the working poor that Lum taps into, particularly eighteenth-century genre paintings of the poor, which were consumed by the aristocratic classes:

> At that time, and throughout the following century, paintings of the poor, especially those who worked the land, identified the poor with all those stable values—family, faith and soil—that capital was eroding. The bourgeoisie took comfort in this illusion because it so blithely ignored class antagonisms.[34]

Later, in the 1930s, we could turn to Dorothea Lange's photographs for the Farm Security Administration, which increased the pathos surrounding the working, rural poor. Absent of illusions of family stability in poverty, Lange's photographs are intended to draw sympathy from the viewer over the plight of displaced laborers. For example, in *Dust Bowl Texas, American Exodus, A.C. Woman* (1938) (figure 4.6), we see the figure of a woman whose world-weariness is captured in the way her hands are clasped onto her forehead and neck. While her ragged shift dress and sun-scorched face testify to her hardship, Lange's effort to dignify her portrait verges on heroism. The fact that the woman stands against an expansive sky, whose low horizon dips below the woman's waist, has the effect of making her appear monumental. The aestheticism of the photograph ultimately carries a romantic undercurrent that attributes a morality to her endurance.

By contrast, in Lum's image-text works, the viewer cannot take comfort in such a sentimental illusion about the poor or working class. Melly Shum evokes neither stable, "natural" values of "family, faith, and soil" nor the pathos of heroic endurance suggested by Lange's work. Rather, there is a sense of irreconcilability evoked by the public nature of her image and sentiments. The unsentimental and unnatural elements of the scene ultimately

FIGURE 4.6 Dorothea Lange, *Dust Bowl Texas, American Exodus, A.C. Woman*, 1938. A67.137.38258.1. © The Dorothea Lange Collection, the Oakland Museum of California, City of Oakland. Gift of Paul S. Taylor.

seem conditioned by social relations that exist outside the work, highlighting a banality of social responses to visions of alienated labor.

Tying this photo-work to the larger questions about Asian racialization as biological signifier of capitalism, *Melly Shum Hates Her Job* presents a stunning antithesis to the model minority scientist who was erased from the redesigned Canadian hundred-dollar bill, a subject I began this book with. In the case of the Asian woman scientist, her erasure signaled the status of Asians as a biological signifier of *bad* capital. She became a metaphor for a destructive logic of equivalence that reduces individual attributes

...phew...

...I'm tired...

..Oh, man...

...man...

...phew...

...tired

FIGURE 4.7 Ken Lum, *Phew, I'm Tired*, 1994. Chromogenic print, lacquer, enamel on aluminum, Sintra, 182 × 243.8 cm. Collection of the Vancouver Art Gallery, Acquisition Fund.

into commensurable, exchangeable forms that Helen Jun calls "human capital." From the view of romantic anticapitalism, the Asian signals the overthrow of traditional, pure, concrete conceptions of labor for an era that reduces human individuality to an abstract form of repetition and equivalence. Melly Shum, however, does not offer us a vision of such racialized abstraction or a picture of sentimentalized, concrete labor. It is unclear how or whether we viewers are to identify with her. It is this sense of nonequivalence that creates what Watson calls a "discomfort zone." Melly Shum refuses to accommodate either an idealized vision of labor or an aestheticized image of multicultural diversity that resolves the material and geographical contradictions of the global economy.

Further reinforcing this sense of discomfort around race and labor is Lum's *Phew, I'm Tired* (1994) (figure 4.7). The portrait features a South Asian man at work in a metal-galvanizing factory. Unlike Melly Shum, the unnamed subject of the photograph is not smiling; rather, he appears to be in distress. On the right half of the work, against a bright orange background, appears light-blue text that reads: " . . . phew . . . / . . . I'm tired . . . /. .Oh, man . . . / . . . man . . . / . . . phew . . . / . . . tired." The words and phrases surrounded by ellipses cascade down the panel in a zigzag formation, an arrangement suggesting a downward spiral that accentuates the weariness of the worker in the photograph. At the same time, the words themselves seem unable to capture the man's pained expression. There is an unsettling tension between the jaunty quality of the corporate typeface and the anguish evoked by the man's face. At the level of linguistic representation, the repetition of the words accentuates the limits language reaches in narrating the conditions of labor. Not only do the repeated words, such as "phew" and "man," seem to comically undermine his situation, but the sounds associated with them also have a comic book quality.

Further displacing the social documentary signifiers of the work, these comic strip elements reference pop art such as Roy Lichtenstein's large reproductions of advertising and comic strip images in a piece such as *Drowning Girl* (figure 4.8). Just as pop artists' use of popular culture and commercial iconography intensified the artwork's *artifice* to challenge the spiritual ambitions and moral seriousness of art conventions (particularly of abstract expressionism), *Phew, I'm Tired* seems to reject the moralism inspired by Dorothea Lange's photographic subjects. Ultimately, as Derksen points out, "the didacticism of the image-text format is made unstable by the oscillation between the representational photos and the ambivalent relationship of text to image."[35] Unlike Lange's documentary camera, Lum's choreographed images intensify their own artifice and theatricality, projecting a sense of indifference that distances the viewer. In its refusal to supply the viewer with a moral standpoint from which to engage with the work, to reconcile image and text, or to join form and content, Lum's work evokes the purposeful purposelessness of nonequivalence. By displacing the photographic subject's racial heroism or pathos through manufactured indifference, the work interrupts a neoliberal logic of racial equivalence that folds race into culture and antiracism into multiculturalism. Instead, the viewer is left only with the irreducibility of form to affect, a state of nonequivalence that interrupts the belief in the equality of persons that is presupposed by free-market exchange and the drive to make unequal forms of human activity commensurable and exchangeable into values.[36] In his representation of racial nonequivalence, Lum therefore interrupts the logic of value production premised on the commensurating function of abstract labor.

FIGURE 4.8 Roy Lichtenstein, *Drowning Girl*. © Estate of Roy Lichtenstein, 1963.
Oil and synthetic polymer paint on canvas, 67⅝ × 66¾ feet. Philip Johnson Fund
(by exchange) and gift of Mr. and Mrs. Bagley Wright. The Museum of Modern Art.
Digital Image © The Museum of Modern Art / Licensed by Scala / Art Resource, NY.

Lum extends this state of nonequivalence to challenge what Jodi
Melamed calls neoliberal multiculturalism, capitalism's new logic of inclusion. Replacing the ideological primacy of white supremacy and colonial
capitalism, she explains that multiculturalism "portrays neoliberal policy as
the key to a postracist world of freedom and opportunity."[37] In other words,
multiculturalism operates as an economic and racial logic that responds to
economic imperatives by celebrating cultural diversity and border-crossing
to facilitate foreign investment and trade. This signals not the end of race
but, rather, its rebranding. Melamed observes, "As historical articulations
of race and capitalism have shifted—with white supremacy and colonial

capitalism giving way to racial liberalism and transnational capitalism and, eventually, to neoliberal multiculturalism and globalization — race remains a procedure that justifies the nongeneralizability of capitalist wealth."[38] This absorption of antiracism into an ideology of multiculturalism has been especially pervasive in Canada, which in 1988 became the first nation to enact multiculturalism as law.[39] As global capitalism's "silent partner,"[40] former prime minister Brian Mulroney could not have made their connection more plain in a speech he delivered at a conference titled "Multiculturalism Means Business,"[41] where he invoked the marketing advantages of multiculturalism: "To cement our prosperity with trade and investment links the world over and with a renewed entrepreneurial spirit at home. . . . Our multicultural nature gives us an edge in selling to that [competitive] world."[42] Adding to the "mixed legacy" that Cheryl Harris attributes to the overturning of legalized segregation in the United States, which defined racial oppression solely through the terms of racial *separation* rather than the domination associated with institutionalized white wealth and power,[43] Canadian multiculturalism sidetracks race and class for a celebration of cultural difference. The result in Canada, as Smaro Kamboureli observes, is a "sedative politics" that manages racial and ethnic difference by making it a universal condition of Canadian culture, repackaging systemic racism as merely a flawed attitude that can be corrected through cultural appreciation.[44] Lum's engagement with images of cultural diversity seems to mock the simplification of such racial and ethnic codes.

In *Nancy Nishi and Joe Ping Chau, Real Estate* (1990) (figure 4.9), Lum offers an alternative view of Asian racialization against a more familiar scene of Vancouver's cosmopolitanism. The high-rise apartments that populate the photograph's backdrop are a signifier of the city's alias as "Hongcouver." This name — used in both pejorative and celebratory contexts — stems from the significant Chinese population in Vancouver, as well as the city's purported architectural, cultural, and economic resemblance to Hong Kong.

Redirecting a pop emphasis on exaggerated artifice, in *Nancy Nishi and Joe Ping Chau, Real Estate*, Lum's advertising motif actually verges on verisimilitude. The top half of the image-text presents a portrait of Nancy Nishi and Joe Ping Chau. They are standing on the balcony of a high-rise apartment, similar to those that appear in the background. Below their portrait in the bottom half of the piece appear their names; their last names, Nishi

FIGURE 4.9 Ken Lum, *Nancy Nishi and Joe Ping Chau,
Real Estate*, 1990. Chromogenic print, lacquer, enamel
on aluminum, Sintra, 182 × 243.8 cm. Courtesy of the
artist.

and Chau, are enlarged and capitalized. Removed from an art gallery context, the only element of the piece that alerts us to its status as art is the car-
toonish 3-D font of the words "REAL ESTATE," which imitates stone carving.
In what Derksen identifies as their "*Flintstones* quality,"[45] the unrealistic
veneer of the lettering humorously undermines the realness of "real" estate.
In addition, in the contrasting relation between image and text—between
the concrete buildings in the background in the photograph and the abstract, textual representation of buildings as real estate commodities—we
can make out a subtle reference to the antinomy of concrete and abstract
dimensions that Moishe Postone associates with capitalism's social uni-

verse. As Derksen observes of the transformation of the concrete into the abstract, "urban materiality is turned into immaterial commodity speculation."[46] Here the abstract representation of "concrete" real estate is reduced to a comically inadequate imitation of actual concrete buildings.

Yet at another level, the portrait of Nancy Nishi and Joe Ping Chau adds to the more racially ominous registers of the friction between image and text. Their relation to the *Flintstones* "real estate" logo adds an air of illegitimacy and artifice to the earnest expressions they bring to their professional endeavor. On one hand, this sense of illegitimacy broadcasts their artificial relation to property; their belonging is rendered a mere abstract signifier against a more concrete sense of citizenship. On the other hand, the artificial concreteness of their profession as realtors also allegorizes an anti-Asian animosity stemming from the perception that Vancouver has been overrun by Hong Kong real estate investors. For example, Katharyne Mitchell notes that in Vancouver, Hong Kong Chinese "are perceived as responsible for house price escalation as a result of using homes for profit through the practice of speculation, rather than as places to live."[47] Much of this anti–Hong Kong Chinese sentiment came to the surface in 1988, when 216 luxury condominiums in the False Creek area were sold exclusively to Hong Kong buyers.[48] The sales took all of three hours and circumvented the Canadian market, leading to charges that Hong Kong investors were taking over the city. Although the roots of the city's demographic shifts and spatial reconfigurations are the result of state-led efforts to expedite Vancouver's integration into the global economy, the racial outcome of these processes has effectively reinforced the perception that Asians represent pure market rationality—their desires represent the psychology of capitalist expansion. Asian investors and business immigrants have only economic rather than "human" motivations. By contrast, for white Vancouver residents, as Mitchell points out, purchasing homes "secures profit yet *does not have to be pursued as profit*."[49] Only white residents have the concrete, "natural" humanity that allows them to "profess ignorance and innocence of any cynical or mercenary motives such as profit, yet establishes their fundamental connection to the underlying systems that generate it."[50] The biologization of capitalism thus renders Asians less human, removed from the concrete associations that align whiteness with property and belonging. As such, *Nancy Nishi and Joe Ping Chau, Real Estate* evoke the form of racial anxiety associated with Asians that we saw in the hundred-dollar-bill controversy: they register a kind of bad capital associated with the abstract sphere of foreign investment and real estate speculation.

Despite the postinternment rehabilitation of Japanese as indigenized surplus labor and the effects of transnational capital, free trade, and the neoliberalization of the immigrant border, Asian North America's association with a destructive capitalism has become even further entrenched. In his discussion of *Mimic* (1982), a photograph by Lum's mentor Jeff Wall, Walter Benn Michaels too probes the signifiers of globalization that attend Wall's presentation of anti-Asian racism in Vancouver in the 1980s:

> Following in the footsteps of the United States Immigration and Nationality Act of 1965, the new Canadian policy *substituted economic desirability for racial desirability.* And this neoliberalization of immigration policy has the same effect in Canada that it did in the United States: a rapid increase in Asian immigration.[51]

In this light, the celebratory discourse of legislated multiculturalism functions as a screen hiding the fact that the infusion of Asian foreign investment and rise of Asian migration into North America project a heightened expression of abstract economic rationality that is mapped onto the Asian body. In what Michaels describes as the substitution of "economic desirability for racial desirability" in immigration reform, we can see how the Asian embodiment of economic abstraction once again threatens the *concrete* human values invested in traditional rather than flexible citizenship. In response, Lum's work exposes the contradictions of multicultural belonging by disidentifying with the visual tropes of multicultural inclusion and, through his image-text works, the sense of nonequivalence evoked by depictions of Asian working-class and professional labor.

Postmodern Coolies and the Political Unconscious in *Tropic of Orange*

Bringing together the aesthetic structure of stranger inhospitality, the tragicomedy of working-class Asian labor, and bad Asian capital explored in Lum's work as conceptual anchors for my focus on Yamashita's novel, my overarching argument is that neoliberal multiculturalism reinforces the abstraction of both wealthy and poor Asian North Americans. In the aftermath of immigration reforms that increasingly privilege wealthy Asian migrants and exclude poor Asian migrants,[52] romantic anticapitalism rejects the former for being agents of an economic takeover *and* the latter for draining economic resources and "stealing jobs," once again bearing out the contradictory promise of settler colonial hospitality. Thoroughly denaturalizing the role of the border as barrier and conduit for flows of labor and capital, Lum's and Yamashita's works highlight the devaluation of human labor as the racial and economic fulfillment of settler colonial capitalism. What *Tropic of Orange* brings to this argument is a view into the dehumanization and subjective experience of both retro and high-tech coolies. Complementing each other's vision of the intersection of race and urban labor, Lum's and Yamashita's works together refract the effects of the neoliberalization of immigration policy and its perversion of race discourse through multicultural rhetoric. Representing an expansion rather than a break from a prior abstract racialization, in the contemporary context of global capitalism, migration, and neoliberal ideology, Asians are both the primary racial *subject* of neoliberal multiculturalism and the ongoing racial *target* of romantic anticapitalism.

As the brief glimpse of freeway conductor Manzanar Murakami that opened this chapter intimates, Yamashita's *Tropic of Orange* is a novel that, like Lum's sculptures and photographs, reworks the Real into a narrative whose fantastical elements are not pure fantasy; neither is its blunt realism an earnest display of social documentary. The novel, whose many moving parts make it difficult to summarize, might best be described as a postmodern bible of neoliberal capitalism: it is temporally organized over seven days that build toward apocalyptic catastrophe. As such it is both a quintessentially LA disaster novel[53] and an allegory of capitalist ruin, combining all the elements of what Žižek describes as "an apocalyptic end point: ecological breakdown, the biogenic reduction of humans to manipulable machines, and total digital control over our lives."[54] The narrative consists of three seemingly disparate plotlines that eventually converge to connect the novel's seven principal characters.

The intersection of these characters from varying racial, economic, and citizenship classes — in addition to the merging of social, spatial, and technological geographies — reveals capitalism as a dynamic ecology. Each strand of connection between these human, technological, and spatial dimensions of the text amplifies the social, mental, and environmental relations that capitalism produces. Marx too refers to capitalism as a quasi-Darwinian organism, not reducible to or fully determined by any one relation (against the claim of economic determinism). Marx asks: "Does not the history of the productive organs of man in society, of organs that are the material basis of every particular organization of society, deserve equal attention [as Darwin pays to the formation of organs of plants and animals]?"[55] His own response might serve as the materialist provocation for the literal and metaphoric strands that Yamashita weaves through her novel:

> Technology reveals the active relation of man to nature, the direct process of the production of his life, and thereby it also lays bare the process of the production of the social relations of his life, and of the mental conceptions that flow from those relations.[56]

Connecting technology, social relations, and mental conceptions, this network of relations is literally and symbolically mobilized in *Tropic of Orange* by a hemispheric thread being dragged from Mexico to Los Angeles by a mysterious, rogue orange. The Southern Hemisphere is pulled into the North, bringing with it histories of colonialism, labor exploitation, trade imbalances, monetary devaluation, and the cross-border "movement of free capital — 45 billion — carried by hidden and cheap labor."[57] Accompanying this thread is Arcangel, a poet and performance artist whose mission exhumes Benjamin's "Angel of History,"[58] to give voice to five hundred years of history and resistance in the Americas and to perform the role of El Gran Mojado (The Great Wetback) in an epic wrestling match against the formidable opponent SUPERNAFTA. The second overlapping plotline concerns a massive traffic accident on LA's Harbor Freeway, which causes explosions and forces drivers to flee while the homeless set up camp in the deserted vehicles. The unyielding traffic jam that ensues over multiple days is, as Jinqi Ling observes, "tantamount to a collapse of capitalist operation in the city of Los Angeles."[59] Finally, in a third interwoven plotline, we meet Bobby Ngu, who is "Chinese from Singapore with a Vietnam name speaking like a Mexican living in Koreatown."[60] A hardworking self-employed night janitor, he works during the day in the mailroom of the *Los Angeles Times*. Abandoned by his Mexican immigrant wife and labor activist, Rafaela, with their young son Sol, he is called by smugglers to pay for safe passage and release of a

Chinese cousin in Tijuana. Thrown into these plotlines are lethal oranges, transnational infant organ trafficking, and a lot of television.

Building on the significant body of insightful scholarship on the novel's critique of free trade, its figurative representation of globalization, its hemispheric and transnational geographic scope, and its parody of multicultural universalism,[61] my reading of *Tropic of Orange* focuses primarily on its three main Asian characters: Bobby, Emi, and Manzanar. This focus aims to illuminate the interplay of labor, immigration status, and capitalism in the neoliberal racialization of Asians that I've tracked throughout this book. In particular, I explore the bifurcation of Asian racialization into the "retro" and the "high-tech" classes of what I'm calling postmodern coolie labor. As a hardworking immigrant janitor, Bobby fulfills the "retro coolie" end of the spectrum, while Emi, an Internet addict and the Japanese American television producer for *NewsNow*, indexes the latter, "high-tech coolie." In my reading of Manzanar, the homeless Japanese American freeway conductor who exemplifies Marx's idea of human freedom, I argue that he stands as a figurative embodiment of the text's political unconscious. Drawing on Fredric Jameson's hermeneutic approach to excavating literature's political unconscious, we can see that within the struggle to "wrest a realm of Freedom from a realm of Necessity,"[62] Manzanar restores "to the surface of the text the repressed and buried reality of this fundamental history [of class struggle]." In many ways he is the essential hermeneutic reader of capitalism, whose primary task, as Chiang notes, "is sheer comprehension, and his conducting is an effort to grasp the conceptual order underlying the seemingly chaotic processes of the global system."[63] Throughout the novel, Bobby's and Emi's struggle to come to terms and act with political agency is symbolically fulfilled by Manzanar.

Although the two characters never come into contact in the novel, Manzanar's and Bobby's connection rests in their unusual relation to what Mimi Nguyen calls "the refugee condition."[64] As a refugee of Japanese American internment, Manzanar is a bodily sign of its unresolved historical excess. Gayle K. Sato observes that Manzanar "embodies and acts out the psychic reality of the inadequacy of the 1988 Civil Liberties Act in itself to enable a Japanese American to be at home in the United States."[65] On the other hand, Bobby, whose US citizenship is the result of his entry as a refugee, is not strictly speaking a refugee at all. From a family rendered destitute after a multinational American bicycle company drove his father's bicycle store out of business in Singapore, Bobby and his younger brother infiltrate a Vietnamese refugee camp and are eventually "Saved by the Americans"[66] and transported to the United States. Passing as so-called legitimate refugees, their claims to refugee status could also be based on how transnational American capital destroyed their chances of economic survival. In spite of Bobby's success, an overwhelming sense of literal and symbolic homelessness haunts him and disconnects him from others. His wife Rafaela sees Bobby's homelessness through his pervasive insecurity: "This fear of losing what you love, of not feeling trust, this fear of being someplace unsafe but pretending for the sake of others that everything was okay."[67] Manzanar has managed, however, to convert his postinternment homelessness into an entirely different plane of consciousness about labor. And while Bobby justifies his nonstop work through profligate, empty spending, Manzanar has interrupted the cycle of labor and consumption by relinquishing material comforts to become homeless, with few possessions. Therefore, as two characters who are subject to US hospitality through redress and refugee protections, they magnify the interplay of alien labor productivity, the ethics of consumption, and the contradictions of legal citizenship.

Manzanar also animates the active repression of his granddaughter Emi's historical and political unconscious. On the surface, his homeless asceticism and "quintessentially nineteenth-century aesthetic practice [of] conducting"[68] dramatically contrasts with his granddaughter's postmodern exuberance for digital media and technological gadgetry. As a TV producer for *NewsNow* and avid consumer of the Internet, Emi's personal disposition reflects the speed-up and commodification of time, where seconds are packaged and sold to commercial sponsors. Despite these differences, Emi's political unconscious is made visible through this very vexed affiliation to Manzanar. While Manzanar's homelessness expresses a selective repression of his former identity and history, Emi's recognition of him exposes her own cultural amnesia and historical dislocation. Notwithstanding the confidence exhibited by her "padded shoulders"[69] and uninhibited personality, "it was questionable if she even had an identity."[70] Responding to her mother's accusation that her attitude and behavior are un-Japanese, she retorts: "Maybe I'm not Japanese American. Maybe I got switched in the hospital."[71] Furthermore, her sense of racial and corporeal displacement is revealed when she confesses to her boyfriend Gabriel, the Chicano reporter, that she had sex with someone else "over the net"[72] but is not sure whether it "counts" as sex. In sum, as the other Japanese American in the novel, Manzanar throws into relief the multicultural aphasia and apathy that thwart Emi's semi-conscious political will.

Bringing the context of migration more explicitly into conversation with the theme of settler colonial inhospitality evoked by Lum's furniture sculptures, Bobby Ngu's character exemplifies the sense of homelessness that results from his indebtedness to the promise of the American Dream. He is described as "always working. Hustling. Moving."[73] Although he owns his home and business, it isn't enough: "Can't explain. Happier he is, harder he works. Can't stop. Gotta make money. Provide for his family. Gotta buy his wife nice clothes. Gotta buy his kid the best. Bobby's kid's gonna know the good life. That's how Bobby sees it." His blind faith in the American Dream is the reason he doesn't understand his wife Rafaela's labor activism. He cannot understand why she joined Justice for Janitors or why she's complaining. His attitude illustrates the paradox of Mimi Nguyen's description of the "refugee condition," as a figure who is both "a target and also an instrument for the gift of freedom"[74] and embodies an "existential condition of suspension or surrender."[75] He suspends thinking and surrenders to work:

> Always working. Washing dishes. Chopping vegetables. Cleaning floors. Cooking hamburgers. Painting walls. Laying brick. Cutting hedges. Mowing lawn. Digging ditches. Sweeping trash. Fixing pipes. Pumping toilets. Scrubbing urinals. Washing clothes. Pressing clothes. Sewing clothes. Planting trees. Changing tires. Changing oil and filters. Stocking shelves. Lifting sacks. Loading trucks. Smashing trash. Recycling plastic. Recycling aluminum. Recycling cans and glass. Drilling asphalt. Pouring cement. Building up. Tearing down. Fixing up. Cleaning up. Keeping up.[76]

But as Nguyen powerfully exposes, the "gift of freedom" is itself bound up in power through the ways "liberal empire marshals its forces for and against others and elsewhere."[77] In Bobby's case, it is a looming sense of unrepayable debt that defines American citizenship and freedom: "Gotta be happy he's alive in America. Saved by the Americans. New country. New life. Working hard to make it. American through and through. . . . Doing

America a favor. Doing his duty."[78] Demonstrating the inseparability of debt from the gift of freedom that Bobby expresses through his endless workdays, Nguyen writes, "The gift of freedom emerges as a site at which modern governmentality and its politics of life (and death) unfolds as a universal history of the human, and the figuration of debt surfaces as those imperial remains that preclude the subject of freedom from being able to escape a colonial order of things."[79] It is out of racial debt that he cannot stop consuming, stop working, stop moving.

His debt-bound life takes its toll on his closest relationships. His wife, Rafaela, whom he helped smuggle across the border from Mexico, shares no such sense of indebtedness that Bobby does. Getting her degree at Los Angeles Community College, she becomes a labor activist to unionize janitorial workers. As a sign of her rejection of his consumer lifestyle, when she leaves him she takes none of the material goods from their house, which is secured by double locks and a security door:

> She left the cherry-red Camaro Z28 with the car seat and The Club. She left the house and the 32" Sony KV32V25 stereo TV with picture-in-picture and the Panasonic PUS4670 Super-VHS VCR, the Sony Super-ESP CD player, the AT&T 9011 cordless phone, the furniture, the clothing, the two-door Frigidaire with the icemaker, the Maytag super-capacity washer and gas dryer, the Sharp Carousel R1471 microwave, everything. . . . Didn't even lock the security door.[80]

The nonsensical series of numbers and letters that accompany each commodity satirizes the meaningless abstractions of commodity culture and the value Bobby sees reflected in them. But the many locks, the security door, and the Club Bobby installs to defend his home and car emphasize the intrinsic insecurity and fear that are the basis of his homelessness. His relationship to his younger brother also suffers. Although he sends money, pays college tuition, and pays for books, "when they get together, there's nothing to say. Bobby's too busy working."[81] He realizes after Rafaela leaves him that she and his younger brother "wanted something more."[82]

After he is called by a snakehead to pay for the release of a Chinese cousin being held in Mexico, Bobby begins to see new relations between debt, consumption, and retro coolie labor that he and his wife perform. His first step is to extricate himself from the spiral of work and consumption: like his smoking habit, it's an addiction that is difficult to quit but will eventually kill him if he doesn't. Rafaela left because "[she] didn't want to watch him die."[83] He begins to reflect on what he had previously refused to hear from Rafaela about their existence as cheap labor, that "we're not wanted here. Nobody respects our work. Say we cost money. Live on welfare."[84] He begins to see that by immersing himself in work he has failed to recognize how devalued his life and work are in the United States. His second step is to take a crash course in global capitalism by reading Rafaela's papers about NAFTA:

> Titles like *Maquiladoras & Migrants. Undocumented, Illegal & Alien: Immigrants vs. Immigration.* Talks about *globalization of capital. Capitalization of poverty. Internationalization of the labor force. Exploitation and political expediency. Devaluation of currency and foreign economic policy. Economic intervention.*[85]

Reading them he realizes, "Maybe he's been too busy. Maybe. But it's not like he don't understand."[86] He begins to see how the circuit of migrant debt and provisional freedom is orchestrated by settler colonial capitalism. The way Rafaela's papers conceptualize the exploitation of free trade resonates powerfully with the novel's poet-prophet, Arcangel, who also understands the flows of migrant labor back and forth across the "New World Border":

> *the deportation of 400,000 Mexican*
> *citizens in 1923*
> *coaxing back of 2.2 million*
> *braceros in 1942*
> *only to exile the same 2.2 million*
> *wetbacks in 1953.*[87]

Here the border extends an invitation or expedites removal, exemplifying the contradictions of hospitality evoked earlier in Lum's furniture sculptures. Alien laborers like him, Bobby realizes, are among the many "gifts from NAFTA," the "oranges, bananas, corn, lettuce, guarachis, women's apparel, tennis shoes, radios, electrodomestics, live-in domestics, living domestics, gardeners, dishwashers, waiters, masons, ditch diggers, migrants, pickers, packers, braceros, refugees, centroamericanos, wetbacks, wops, undocumenteds, illegals, aliens."[88] Here gifts and debt are one and the same: the gift of migrant labor is multiplied in their ongoing debt to settler colonial capitalism.

Bobby's growing awareness of the exigencies of migration born out of the "*capitalization of poverty*" and "*globalization of capital*" is enhanced by the situation of his teenage cousin Xiayue, who is being held by smugglers in Tijuana. Although he is skeptical of their relation, he is compelled to help her when he hears she is from Fujian, the same village his mother came from.[89] Fujian, in particular, has a long history of out-migration, more recently due to economic pressures resulting from the Chinese government's market reforms catering to North American consumer markets. These areas are often classified as Special Economic Zones, which have few labor laws, prohibit trade unions, and slash import and export taxes in order to increase trade. In China, as Peter Kwong remarks, market reforms "have practically eliminated all labor laws, labor benefits and protections. In the 'free enterprise zones' workers live virtually on the factory floor, laboring fourteen hours a day for a mere two dollars—that is, about 20 cents an hour."[90] In the novel, because both of her parents are dead, Xiayue and her older brother knew that they "would have to come [to the United States] sooner or later."[91] His own mother dead too, Bobby identifies with the girl, thinking, "It's like it's maybe twenty years ago. Like it's him and his kid brother,"[92] except her situation is far more dire. Her arrival has none of the protections of being a refugee. Bobby contemplates the fate of her brother, who, if he's alive, will enter an America that hasn't changed since the nineteenth century: "The brother's gonna work. Work like all the celestials before him. Put down rail ties. Pick oranges. Wash shirts. Sew garments. Stir-fry chop suey."[93] The sister's fate is less clear. Passing her off as his daughter, just as he himself passed as a refugee, Bobby gets Xiayue across the border as effortlessly as swiping his credit card: "Drag themselves through the slit jus' like any Americanos. Just like Visa cards."[94] The "collapsing of visas and Visa cards," as Molly Wallace observes, depicts the United States as a "landscape thoroughly mortgaged to global capital. . . . Consumerism, in *Tropic of Orange*, replaces nationalism."[95] But within the Visa's symbolism of debt accumulation, in this case it is poor Third World migrants who must assume that debt. By accompanying Xiayue across the US-Mexico border, Bobby witnesses the transparent economic logic of immigration policy. Just as business immigrants can pay their way into North American citizenship, the poor can purchase entrance, yet the poor must pay off this lifelong debt with insecure citizenship.[96] Through her depiction of US-Mexico border crossing, Yamashita eviscerates the moral standing of the refugee (as the target for the "gift of freedom") and the immoral standing of the undocumented Asian migrant (as unworthy subject of hospitality) to emphasize the shared conditions of economic exploitation that align poor migrants across free trade zones. Their insecurity is captured when Bobby has no response for Xiayue's repeated question "What is social security?"[97]

In the way that Lum's photo-text works *Melly Shum Hates Her Job* and *Phew, I'm Tired* present a visual challenge to the aesthetics of neoliberal multiculturalism by depicting racial and gendered labor ironically, as a kind of sentimental pop art, Emi's character in *Tropic of Orange* also frustrates its homogenizing logics. Unlike Melly Shum's, however, her private thoughts are not betrayed by the artist but, rather, willingly expressed by her character.

Despite Emi's clear disconnect from her Japanese American cultural heritage and racial politics—her idea of real "struggle" is when her parents force her to make "payments on [her] Civic"[98]—her insights about the contradictory interplay of Asian racialization and neoliberal multiculturalism reveal a surfacing political consciousness. With blithe unsentimentality, Emi recognizes the dehumanized mechanical abstraction that the Asian body signifies. Ridiculing the romantic anticapitalist sentiments of her boyfriend Gabriel's desire to reject "all this [materialism]" and commune with nature by "mak[ing] something I can actually touch and eat," she tells him, "I read somewhere that these days, if you are making a product you can actually touch *and* . . . [are] making a comfortable living at it, you are either an Asian or a machine."[99] Her point is that Gabriel's valorization of productive over financial labor, signaled by "planting a tree," is a false one—that there is no nature external to capitalism. Moreover, with deindustrialization and US outsourcing of manufacturing labor, the level of exploitation experienced by Third World Asian laborers reduces them to dehumanized machines. Such a vexed conflation of Asians and machines—as high-tech coolies—is also one of the reasons she admits that "there are producers who would kill me if they knew who I was."[100] However, Emi's own obsession with technological gadgetry and immersion into the ephemeral world of cyber-sex suggest her own resigned participation in the increasing digital abstraction of social lives, as she remarks, "Who needs a reality check?"[101]

Despite Emi's cynical disdain for politics, she is able to see past the multiculturalist veneer of capitalist determinism. At a sushi restaurant she informs Gabriel that money drives everything, that social change has nothing to do with justice or humanity:

It's just about money. It's not about good honest people like you or about whether us Chicanos or Asians get a bum rap or whether third world countries deserve dictators or whether we should make the world safe for democracy. It's about selling things: Reebok, Pepsi, Chevrolet, All-State, Pampers, Pollo Loco, Levis, Fritos, Larry Parker Esq., Tide, Raid, the Pillsbury Doughboy, and Famous Amos. Them that's smart took away the pretense and do the home shopping thing, twenty-four hours. Hey, we're all on board to buy.[102]

In Emi's economic determinist rendition, social justice is just a "pretense"—a fetish of capitalist ideology. But in her view one may as well embrace this reality because there is no ethical outside: "We're all on board to buy." Her pragmatism leads her to take on a particular disdain for the pretext of multicultural ethics, to the extent that she enjoys being as "antimulticultural"[103] as possible. As a favorite pastime, she and Gabriel devise fictional stories about the "multicultural mosaic"[104] of characters while they are eating lunch in the sushi restaurant, including the "Caucasian Japanophiles who talk real Japanese with the sushi man."[105] Predictably, an eavesdropping white woman takes offense to Emi's pronouncements that "cultural diversity is bullshit. . . . It's a white guy wearing a Nirvana T-shirt and dreds. That's cultural diversity."[106] In defense of multiculturalism and cultural diversity, the woman—wearing two "ornately-lacquered chopsticks" in her hair—retorts, "I love living in L.A. because I can find anything in the world to eat, right here. . . . A true celebration of the international world. It just makes me sick to hear people speak so cynically about something so positive and to make assumptions about people based on their color."[107] The woman's morally superior rationale highlights the evacuated antiracist politics that Žižek ascribes to "multiculturalism, or the cultural logic of multinational capitalism," in which "liberal 'tolerance' condones the folklorist Other deprived of its substance—like the multitude of 'ethnic cuisines' in a contemporary megalopolis."[108] In short, the woman's expression of neoliberal moralism converts racial politics into a celebratory form of white cultural consumption, flattening racial difference into a commodified feature of the global city. For this reason we hear an echo of *Melly Shum Hates Her Job* in Emi's retort: "I hate being multicultural."[109] Both Melly Shum and Emi recognize that for the racialized worker operating within a capitalist logic of multicultural equivalence, "you're invisible, I'm invisible. We're all invisible. It's just tea, ginger, raw fish, and a credit card."[110]

At another level, Emi's exchange with the white woman recalls the postmodern racism evoked by Lum's photograph *Nancy Nishi and Joe Ping Chau, Real Estate*: Nancy and Joe can be viewed as the inviolable poster children of multiculturalism, a shield of cultural diversity to deflect criticism of the dramatic escalation of real estate values in Vancouver that is often blamed on wealthy Asian investors. In *Tropic of Orange*, the woman's implication that Emi is being racist by "mak[ing] assumptions about people based on their color" parallels the way that, in the similar urban context of Vancouver, where neoliberalism has reformed immigration policy and expanded the flow of capital across international borders, it has become *racist* to call into question the logic of capitalism. In a perversion of racial politics, open challenges such as Emi's to the multicultural logic of capitalism have been *conflated* with racist and anti-immigrant voices. As Jodi Melamed points out, neoliberal multiculturalism "disconnects antiracism and economic justice, denying race as a structure of capitalist organization" that would reveal "continuities between prewar colonial capitalism and postwar US global ascendancy and expanding transnational capitalism."[111] Moreover, when the white woman accuses Emi of racial intolerance, we see how her neoliberal expression of cultural appreciation obfuscates the profound continuity between racial divisions produced historically—through structures of colonialism and slavery—and the contemporary expropriation of surplus-value from racialized and gendered Third World labor working in free-trade zones. Such an ideology simultaneously *naturalizes* economic disparity by deflecting criticism through moralizing slogans of cultural diversity and racial equivalence. Ultimately, Emi prevails in revealing the superficiality of the woman's moral high ground when she ridicules her self-serving multiculturalist aestheticism, asking her whether she would "consider using these [two forks] in your hair? Or would you consider that . . . unsanitary?"[112] The woman's expression is appropriately "blanched" in response.

After Los Angeles authorities wage a full-scale military assault on the homeless occupants of abandoned cars on the jammed freeway while Emi is tanning on top of the *NewsNow* van, her death by the first bullet evokes the doubleness signaled by the Asian body's economism, an inherently racial ambiguity that positions her both as retro coolie underclass and high-tech coolie/robot overclass. Her last words, "Abort. Retry. Ignore. Fail,"[113] seem to recall the death of a replicant in Ridley Scott's *Blade Runner* and is similarly mired in racial signifiers of mechanical and technological domination.

Following David Palumbo-Liu's reading of the film's representation of the human/nonhuman divide as a racialized phenomenon that "serves to maintain the essential inhuman character of the replicant against that of the human,"[114] the replicants too evoke a doubleness in the sense that they are simultaneously the slaves and potential oppressors of white humans. Blurring the line between human victim and cyborg oppressor, Emi offers a renewed representation of Lye's observation of the conspiratorial economism invested in the Asian figure: "When we are looking at Japanese, we can never be sure whether we are seeing businessmen or coolies."[115] As a conflation of both, she epitomizes a *Homo sacer*, she who "*may be killed and yet not sacrificed*"[116] in the free-fire zone of the homeless-occupied freeway.

Within the logic of Yamashita's narrative, Emi's doubleness is also linked to her political and cultural alienation in the face of her estranged grandfather, Manzanar. The paralysis she experiences is symbolic of her inability to engage with her family history and Japanese American history more broadly. After initially recognizing her grandfather on the overpass and "star[ing] at him in disbelief,"[117] she can only watch him from afar cursing to herself—"Damn that old deadbeat on the overpass"[118]—and never finds "the courage to march up there to meet the man."[119] After Buzzworm repeatedly urges her to meet him, she shrugs him off, asking, "What's the point?"[120] Her death soon after this exchange suggests that it is this sense of apathy that is partially responsible for her untimely death. Even though she begins to absorb Manzanar's consciousness through the music he conducts—"a melody she could not place but knew. Electronic tones representing numerical information, i.e., music"[121]—she shuns her genetic connection to the old man: "Wasn't everything from Alzheimer's to schizophrenia genetic? Damn."[122] After she is shot, Emi dreams that she will be buried in the La Brea Tar Pits and later become "La Brea Woman . . . bones and a holographic image of me."[123] Her identification with the ancient Indigenous woman buried in the tar pits suggests, perhaps, her own regret that she too will become some mysterious, decomposed hieroglyph of history.

Even though her death might stem from political paralysis, her slaying catapults her to the status of Christ-like martyrdom whose endlessly repeated televised death signals the onset of urban war, particularly for Manzanar. The moment she is shot, he can no longer go on conducting the swelling sounds of revolution below him as he awakens to his own anger and pain: "The sound of the shot penetrated Manzanar's very being with a vengeance he did not understand. The moment repeated itself again and again; he clothed it in desperation each time with pain and more pain."[124] Coming back to the surface, his memories return in a flood, triggered by the sight of an infant's heart that has been harvested and trafficked from south of US-Mexico border. In this moment, instead of joining sounds of the freeway into "an entire civilization of sound,"[125] he connects his own history: his wartime confinement in a Japanese American internment camp, his surgical practice of "careful incisions . . . inserting implants, facilitating transplants,"[126] and his life on the societal margins as a homeless freeway conductor. Although he is no longer a surgeon, which, as Ling observes, registers "his refusal to participate in the perpetuation of human tragedy in the name of human need" by "using organs obtained from questionable sources,"[127] the visions of premature death reanimate his connection to the world he left behind. In the profound sensory universe from which Manzanar hails, his "surfacing" is enacted through visual rather than aural stimuli: the sight of the infant heart and of his fatally wounded granddaughter. But his reconnection to the surface world of sight and sound ultimately overloads him: "He had seen enough. And he had heard everything."[128] Our last glimpse of Manzanar is on a gurney hanging from a helicopter holding his granddaughter's hand, witnessing from above a vision of atomic annihilation stopped short:

> Peering cautiously from his higher perch, saw bird's-eye the inflation of thousands upon thousands of automotive airbags, bursting simultaneously everywhere from their pouches in steering wheels and glove compartments like white poppies in sudden bloom. All the airbags in L.A. ruptured forth, unfurled their white powdered wings against the barrage of bullets, and stunned the war to a dead stop. *But Manzanar heard nothing.*[129]

Here the simultaneous bursting of thousands of airbags, like "white poppies in sudden bloom," eerily evoke the mushroom clouds over Hiroshima and Nagasaki. But in this case it is the supernatural force of the airbags' automatic deployment that stops the war. Regardless, Manzanar hears nothing. Manzanar's deafness at this apocalyptic scene exceeds what Ling identifies as the "cognitive plenitude"[130] he performs as a freeway conductor, where his brain is comfortably submerged under an ocean of "foam and floating kelp."[131] Without the orchestral language of his political consciousness, in his confrontation with the sensory overload of capitalist urbanity he "dissolves," as Ling contends, "into the novel's imagined urban tide of carnival revolts."[132] Manzanar's sensory collapse suggests the difficult unity of political consciousness and the materiality of racialized vulnerability to death.

Although the novel ends without a clear sense of Manzanar's fate, his ascent from the overpass onto a gurney flying across LA while "the entire city [had] sprouted grassroots conductors of every sort"[133] presents a tilted ecology of capitalist relations where Manzanar's urban literacy has been disseminated to a next generation of conductors. Like Manzanar, whose romantic detachment as freeway conductor dissolves the moment Emi is shot, Emi and Bobby also undergo metamorphosis. Emi's cultural alienation and immersion into digital technology ultimately leads to high-tech failure as she dies. Bobby, whose working life has turned him into a labor automaton, stops working. Reversing the inhuman tropes of Asians as "killer robots" or "Asian 'dragon' gangs" depicted in narratives that participate in what Mike Davis calls the "literary destruction of LA,"[134] Yamashita's Asian characters collectively register sensory disability (Manzanar), nonproductivity (Bobby), and technological failure (Emi). This generalized sphere of nonproductivity gestures toward what Mitchell and Snyder recognize as "*forms of incapacity* as the new galvanizing agent of post-modern resistance."[135] But we are left with a far-from-sanguine vision of LA: homeless junkies feasting on trafficked infant organs "toasted like marshmallows"[136] and the mutual destruction of SUPERNAFTA and Arcangel in the wrestling match "sponsored by a generous grant from the Ministry of Multicultures [and hosted by] the CIA, the PRI, the DEA, and the INS";[137] "profits from the ticket sales were being divided"[138] after the match. It is a world in suspension, "unplugged and timeless,"[139] on the verge of collapse.

To amplify the political stakes of narrative suspension that concludes Yamashita's novel, I want to bring this chapter to a close by returning to Ken Lum's artwork to tie the themes of labor and neoliberal immigration together with the strands of Asian racialization and romantic anticapitalism I have explored through this book. In particular, like the tilted capitalist ecology presented in Yamashita's novel, Lum's sculpture *Four Boats Stranded: Red and Yellow, Black and White* (figure 4.10) offers a similarly "unnatural" presentation of global movement shaped by settler colonial capitalism. The sculpture

FIGURE 4.10 Ken Lum, *Four Boats Stranded: Red and Yellow, Black and White*, 2000.
Sculpture installation on the roof of the Vancouver Art Gallery, dimensions variable.
Collection of the Vancouver Art Gallery, Vancouver Art Gallery Major Purchase
Fund, The Canadian Millennium Partnership Program of the Millennium Bureau of
Canada and the British Columbia 2000 Community Spirit Fund. Photo: Trevor Mills,
Vancouver Art Gallery.

is the result of a commission Lum won in 1999 that was part of Vancouver's
Millennial Public Art Project, "On Location." The work, located on top of
the Vancouver Art Gallery, cannot be viewed in its entirety from any one
side of the building. It consists of four boats, each placed on a corner of the
gallery roof that faces east, west, north, or south.

The different primary colors chosen for each boat suggest racial typolo-
gies: yellow for Chinese, red for First Nations, white for Europeans, and
black for Indians. The design of each boat also evokes more concrete historical periods and episodes. For instance, the red boat is a representation of a
First Nations longboat used by Coast Salish communities located along the
Pacific coast of British Columbia, Washington, and Oregon. The white boat
depicts the HMS *Discovery*, the Royal Navy ship that led George Vancouver's
exploration of the West Coast of North America between 1791 and 1795. The
black boat in Lum's sculpture is a replica of the *Komagata Maru*, a Japanese

boat chartered by an Indian businessman in the early twentieth century. In 1914, 376 British Indian residents of Hong Kong, China, and Japan who were onboard the *Komagata Maru* were detained for two months in Vancouver Harbor before being turned away. Even though the boat had fulfilled the requirements of a "continuous journey" law, specifically designed to bar entry of Indian immigrants unless they arrived "by a continuous journey on through tickets purchased before leaving the country,"[140] their legal exclusion was ultimately based on their presumed unassimilability in a white Canada. The fourth, yellow boat in Lum's sculpture is a representation of one of the four Fujianese migrant ships that, reprising the *Komagata Maru* incident eighty-five years later, were detained off the coast of Vancouver in 1999 for nearly two months. On board were 599 undocumented migrants from the Fujian province of China, who—unlike Bobby's niece Xiayue— were detained and eventually deported. The title of Lum's sculpture, *Four Boats Stranded*, is a specific reference to the media's characterization of the four Fujianese boats. For the most part, the media coverage exploited their criminality through images of barbed wire, shackles, guard dogs, orange prison uniforms, and guards. As Anna Pratt remarks, this event demonstrated the "slippage between categories of refugees, frauds, and criminals . . . [and] spectacle in the application of sovereign power."[141] Lum's sculpture's subtitle, *Red and Yellow, Black and White*, evokes an American abolitionist context. According to Carla Benzan, the phrase refers to a Civil War–era Sunday school song whose verse goes: "Jesus loves the little children, all the children of the world; red and yellow, black and white."[142] By drawing on dissonant tropes of settler colonialism, Asian exclusion, and racial equivalence, the sculpture's response to the migrant crisis is largely an invocation of immigration history: a history of boat people.

If we consider this sculpture against the aesthetic disorientations of Lum's furniture sculptures and image-text works discussed earlier, *Four Boats Stranded*'s invocation of immigration history is similarly irreverent. For one, despite being a public art commission, the sculpture is located on the roof of the downtown gallery and thus is largely inaccessible to the public audience. Here the work ironically inverts the duality of disinterested high art and low "popular" art in its placement above the gallery, so that it is literally "high" art. In keeping with pop art's challenge of the exclusivity and cultural orthodoxy of the art gallery space, Lum's bright, toylike depiction of the boats similarly evokes the staged pathos of narratives that erase

Native peoples to remind us that we are "a nation of immigrants." Given the themes of commodified repetition in pop art such as Andy Warhol's Campbell's soup cans or Marilyn Monroes, this pop-art rendering of the boats also suggests a banality and reproducibility as subjects of mass consumption. As such, they subvert the association of art as the original product of artistic invention and leave the viewer without a straightforward idea of the sculpture's relation toward the historical and political content it clearly alludes to.

By taking boats out of water and putting them into the air, I suggest, Lum aims here, as in his other works, to offer a decontextualized aesthetics of the border and thereby denaturalize its racial logics. From this view, the placement of the sculpture on the gallery roof connects to Yamashita's novel in terms of the inverted, suspended ecology it similarly evokes. While the landscape of *Tropic of Orange* is transformed by a thread pulling the Southern Hemisphere into the North, Lum's sculpture reconfigures the spatial properties of land, water, and air with boats that apparently fly. The very inaccessibility of these boats also highlights the work of a metaphoric and invisible border that has "stranded" these four boats high in the air. Decontextualizing the North–South border as a thread and the East–West border as air, Yamashita's and Lum's works suggest connection and absence, respectively. For Yamashita, that connection is first rendered ambiguous as Bobby, in the novel's final scene, grasps the thread, asking himself, "What are these goddamn lines anyway? What do they connect? What do they divide?"[143] His decision to let go and rejoin his family suggests that the thread is no longer a border to cross; it is now a line to release. In Lum's sculpture, the apparatus of the border is reconfigured as an art domain, a space of figuration that deconstructs a pop veneer of multicultural equivalence contained in the rhetoric of a "nation of immigrants." Reframing the nation as a field of racial incommensurability, Lum's boats stage a narrative of white settler colonial invasion: the conversion of Indigenous land into sovereign property with the power to *exclude* based on race, in the case of the *Komagata Maru*, followed by the neoliberal power to *include* on the basis of economic class, in the case of the exclusion of poor Fujianese migrants. Adopting a pop aesthetic, Lum's sculpture undermines the rhetoric of the border as a moralizing tool of neoliberal multiculturalism whose hospitality is reserved for flexible citizens and high-tech coolies while exploiting the vulnerability of Fujianese retro coolies and other undocumented arrivals. From a more dystopic perspective, moreover, the suspended boats parody the dream of totally boundless free trade and mobility, what Postone describes as "a fantasy of freedom as the complete liberation from matter, from nature . . . a 'dream of capital' [that] is becoming the nightmare of that from which it strives to free itself—the planet and its inhabitants."[144] Denaturalizing nature itself, Lum and Yamashita redirect the target of romantic anticapitalism toward the field of representation that obfuscates the dehumanizing dialectic of capitalist value.

By animating the border against its North–South and East–West hemispheric histories, Yamashita and Lum accentuate its prominence in the fulfillment of settler colonial capitalism through the migrant labor system. According to Werner Biermann and Reinhart Kössler, "the settler mode of production" relies on a developed capitalist world market and exploitation of the migrant labor system, a system that has advantages over slave holding because it helps to paralyze the resistance potential of domestic labor. They explain that "from purely economic considerations, migrant labour seems more efficient in terms of absolute surplus-value formation and the minimization of the social costs of reproduction."[145] Contrary to the notion that migrant labor is an economic burden, migrant labor often assumes the total costs of its social reproduction. Moreover, the United States' long-standing interventionist mode has transformed economies and governments south of the border and across the Pacific and has contributed to the internationalization and expansion of the surplus labor force from which North America can draw. Settler colonial capitalism continually reinvents the levels of unfreedom through the creation of the debt-bound migrant. As Bierrman and Kössler explain, "Settler capitalism differs from slave-holding in the important respect that here the class of migrant workers as a whole is, in true capitalist fashion, dependent on the class of settler capitalists as a whole. Although the migrant workers are not personally free, their illiberty is not in terms of a personal relation of bondage to an individual master."[146] In Yamashita's and Lum's respective evocations of the suspended function that interrupts the productive flow of migrant labor and capital, they emphasize the destructive interplay of human labor and value production that is objectified at the border.

FIGURE E.1 Iron Chink salmon-gutting machine exhibit. Catalogue number 965.681.1. Image courtesy of the Royal BC Museum, BC Archives.

THE REVENGE OF THE IRON CHINK

> Capital is not a thing, but a social relation between
> persons which is mediated through things.
> — Karl Marx, *Capital*

Figure E.1 is a fish-butchering machine that is on permanent display at the Royal British Columbia Museum, located in my hometown of Victoria, British Columbia. On the other side of the machine, not visible here, its name appears in large, capital letters: "IRON CHINK." The machine was built by the Victoria Machinery Depot in 1909 and replaced a crew of thirty butchers. As indicated on the information placard at the exhibit, "it processed about 60 fish per minute, removing tail and fins, slicing open the belly and scraping out the guts."[1] It was named the Iron Chink for the Chinese butchery crews it replaced in salmon canneries along the Pacific coast, a machine capable of gutting salmon at a rate of sixty to seventy-five fish per minute with a crew of only three laborers. As Geoff Meggs explains, "Before 1900, twenty-five men could handle only 1,500 to 2,000 fish in a ten-hour day. Now a single iron butcher could keep two canning lines amply supplied with a fraction of the labour."[2] Today the Iron Chink resides in the museum as a relic of early industrial innovation and accompanying racial attitudes.

I offer this concluding example of the Iron Chink because it serves as an unusual corollary to the example of the 2012 controversy over the erased Asian scientist from the Canadian hundred-dollar-bill that began this book. In that example, I argued that the controversy animated the negative association of Asians with money, an association that adapts a form of modern anti-Semitism which sees Jews as the architects of a destructive capitalism. The origins of such a racialized alignment of Jews with capitalism stemmed from their historical segregation in financial sectors of the economy. Such interest-generating sectors—that is, financial institutions that make money out of money—have historically been taboo and aligned with moral and sexual impurity and corruption. For example, condemnations of usury are present across Christian, Islamic, Judaic, and Buddhist religious texts. Today Islamic law outlaws charging interest, and until the mid-nineteenth century, the Catholic Church similarly barred the charging of interest.[3] As David Harvey elaborates, "Conservative Catholics often compared investment houses to bordellos and viewed financial operations as a form of prostitution."[4] Images from the period satirized this connection, and Harvey points to one cartoon that depicts a young woman trying to entice a horrified man into an investment house, telling him, "My rate of return is good for whatever amount you wish to invest. I'll treat you very gently."[5] Although investing in interest-generating financial products is the norm today and is no longer compared to hiring a prostitute, the connotations of race, gender, and sexual immorality are not entirely absent. One can point to *Forbes* magazine's review of the 2013 feature film *The Wolf of Wall Street*: according to *Forbes*, the film "proves that Hollywood sees finance as drugs, sex and rock and roll."[6] This is certainly not the first time Wall Street has been portrayed as a perverse universe of greed and sexual vice that corrupts individuals.[7]

This book has explored Asians' negative alignment with a destructive capitalism that is derived from value's origins in labor, specifically abstract labor. The controversy over the one-hundred-dollar bill sheds light on how, as a negative personification of capital, Asians, unlike Jews, symbolize a destructive dimension of value based on what Marx calls "socially necessary labor time." In a settler colonial context that relies on alien labor, Asian labor has had a precarious relation to the racial, gendered, and sexual constitution of "social necessity." If the one-hundred-dollar bill illustrates the abstraction of Asians as money, the Iron Chink highlights the abstraction of Asians as machines. Because value is based on socially necessary *human* labor time, machines are not a source of value—only a source of temporary relative surplus value. What the case of the Iron Chink evokes is the way Asian labor is symbolically transposed onto a machine designed to cut human labor time, the true source of value, in exchange for the more temporary and volatile production of relative surplus-value.[8] Here the dehumanized labor efficiency evoked by the "Chink" suggests both a perverse excess and unnatural form of labor. The link between the one-hundred-dollar bill (as money commodity) and the Iron Chink (as machine commodity) is how racial signifiers animate the work of the fetish to misrepresent the relations between people as the relations between things. As money or machine, the Asian is aligned with the destructive value dimension of capitalism.

Staying at the level of metaphor, it is also interesting that in personifying capital, the erased Asian scientist and the Iron Chink bear a metaphorical trace of the duplicitous role of capitalist value that emanates from the commodity form, whose "mysterious character . . . reflects the social characteristics of men's own labour as objective characteristics of the products of labour themselves, as the socio-natural properties of these things."[9] By projecting racial personifications of quantifiable and qualitative dimensions of labor onto money and machine commodities, both examples offer a similar metaphorical trace of "the social relation of the producers to the sum total of labour as a social relation between objects," insofar as the social relations of race are abstracted onto the commodities themselves "apart from and outside the producers."[10] In this light, the fetishism of commodities is essentially a *figurative operation*, "a substitution [whereby] the products of labour become commodities, sensuous things which are at the same time suprasensible or social."[11] This reinforces one of this book's main points: that capitalism is a representational (and misrepresentational) regime where the metaphoric activity of the fetish "conceals the social character of private labour and the social relations between the individual workers."[12]

The fetish conceals as it substitutes, rendering unequal elements the same by turning them into values. Richard Godden describes this as the "metaphoric moment of the fetish": even though "A is not B any more than a person is a thing or money a person," the metaphoric work of the fetish forces them into a nonidentical unity.[13] We can go a step further and identify the value dimension of commodities as the central engine for this metaphoric work because the only way that commodities can assert their value is through the relative exchange of equivalent units of abstract labor, or socially necessary labor time. Value is thus a "metaphor in hiding" that conceals its own metaphoricity—one that is "structurally essential to capitalist reality, yet one whose advocates disavow its internal contradictions."[14] So whether we're talking about the Iron Chink, the Canadian one-hundred-dollar polymer bill, financial derivatives, debt, and so on, at their core as commodities they retain a dual character that I've tracked through this book: that of concrete labor (qualitatively diverse labor) and abstract labor (commensurate units of labor time). Even though financial products appear to be in a world of their own and seem, as some have suggested, to "have nothing to do with national production or the labor of any nation's citizen subjects,"[15] we should understand this false assessment as a consequence of the fetish. As I've tried to emphasize in this book, neoliberal regimes that deregulate flows of capital are concomitant with the global expansion of exploited surplus labor forces. As Godden puts it, "Given the 'two-fold nature' of financial value, labor, however peripheral to thought and geography, however seemingly disposable, retains its place at value's core."[16] It is precisely this mystified connection between labor and value that must be exposed to even contemplate a world where people control the products of their labor rather than being controlled by them.

Let me clarify this point. I do not mean to suggest that in a postcapitalist world people would control the products of their labor through the ideal of collective ownership of the means of production, an underlying principle that has structured communist and socialist states past and present. By extension, so-called socialist state practices that redistribute wealth and resources, solve problems of overproduction and effective demand (Keynesianism), eliminate private property, support trade unions, or reduce the hours in the workweek will never eliminate capitalism. They accommodate capitalism by making it more bearable, which is certainly not a bad thing. Rather, what I am suggesting is that what underlies the massive racialized and gendered disparities in wealth on a global scale is embedded in the labor process itself, in labor whose sole purpose is to create more and more value. The relation between labor and value is the motor of capitalism's immanent drive to accumulate, and it is this relationship that plays a socially mediating role in humanity's relation to technology, nature, the modes of production, social relations, the reproduction of daily life, and mental conceptions of the world.[17] As I have argued throughout this book, social relations produced out of commodity production are antinomical, externalizing its concrete and abstract dimensions. Here again we discern the metaphoric role of the fetish, which extends its substitutions into the social world. Not only does the dual character of labor as concrete and abstract constitute the very basis of capitalism; this duality also frames the contradictions of social life. Marx's nineteenth-century assessment seems particularly apt for our current situation:

> Everything seems pregnant with its contrary. Machinery gifted with the wonderful power of shortening and fructifying human labour, we behold starving and overworking it. The new-fangled sources of wealth, by some weird spell, are turned into sources of want. . . . This antagonism between modern industry and science on the one hand, modern misery and dissolution on the other hand . . . is a fact, palpable, overwhelming, and not to be controverted.[18]

If we anchor these contradictions in the very duality that structures social relations, we may reconsider cultural and ideological contradictions of race, gender, and sexuality as extensions of the contradictions between abstract universality (of humanity) and concrete particularity of race, gender, and sexual identities. As Postone proposes, "Such an approach can address the constitution of values and worldviews in terms of specific, contradictory social forms, rather than in terms of the cognitive and moral progress of the human species [by grasping] the two-sided character of capitalist development in cultural and ideological terms as well."[19] This proposes that the founding, metaphorical duplicity at the heart of capitalist value, the metaphoric movement of concrete labor into abstract labor, creates tensions that become manifest in social life.

But let us return to the Iron Chink. As a personification of the simultaneous efficiency and disposability of the Chinese laborer, the Iron Chink articulates the contradictions of settler colonial capitalism that expose the inhumanity of commodity-determined labor. Connecting its symbolism to our contemporary moment, artist Tommy Ting's 2012 sculpture *Machine (Iron Chink, invented in 1903, found at the Gulf of Georgia Cannery in Steveston, British Columbia, refabricated in Beijing, China)* resurrects the Iron Chink, giving it a new look and perhaps a new voice. Extending the symbolic presence of Black Frankenstein in American literature and visual culture, the resurrection of the Iron Chink similarly employs a gothic humor, "laughing back as well as haunting back."[20] In this frame we can consider how the monstrously reanimated Asian Frankenstein returns to British Columbia to rebel against its original creators.

The first thing we notice about Ting's *Machine* (figure E.2) is its sly engagement with the original. Eliminating the iron, Ting instead uses PVC, painted "China Red" and manufactured in a modeling factory in China. By adapting pop art strategies, Ting has thus recontextualized the salmon-gutting machine as sculpture, transforming low to high. The bright, gleaming red of the sculpture evokes a sexiness we are more likely to associate with a race car than an early twentieth-century industrial machine. At the level of satire, this projection of sensuality seems to poke fun at the romantic glorification of machine technology. In particular, the presence of the shipping crate undercuts a monumental reading of technological glory. The shipping crate, which itself has undergone transformation into sculptural object, emphasizes the sculpture's status as an import, a migrant machine. This emphasis speaks to our contemporary reality, in which China is the manufacturing source of many of the products we consume in the west—and apparently China is a place where we can even outsource our racial stereotypes. Moreover, as a vessel that carries the personification of a racial metaphor, the shipping crate presents a sardonic comment on the imprisoning, dehumanized conditions of global labor migration.

Part of the dark comedy in Ting's piece lies in how it perfectly embodies the dehumanized abstraction that I've tied to Asian racialization throughout this book. In its shiny new modern form, *Machine* not only evokes the continuing metaphorization of Asian labor but also dramatizes its ongoing allure through its vibrant China Red color. In its seductive appeal, *Machine* hyperbolizes the sexualization of the Chinese female migrant, who was subject to the 1875 Page Law, the United States' first federal immigration law designed to bar entry to Chinese women based on their presumed sexual immorality. In this light, as a feminized Asian Frankenstein, *Machine* stands as an ironic invocation of the sexualized and racialized migrant system so central to the settler colonial mode of capitalist reproduction. But equally, *Machine*'s China Red paint clearly evokes the color of communism, giving rise to both positive and negative connotations. On one hand, the China Red color cheerfully promotes the communist ideal of collective ownership of the means of production. On the other, the color alludes to communism's association with the mechanization of human labor. But the reality is that *Machine* remains, at the end of the day, a commodity whose value is commensurable and thus exchangeable with all other commodities. As the monstrous personification of dehumanized equivalence, Asian Franken-

FIGURE E.2 Tommy Ting, *Machine (Iron Chink, invented in 1903, found at the Gulf of Georgia Cannery in Steveston, British Columbia, refabricated in Beijing, China)*, 2012. Courtesy of the artist.

stein expresses the contradiction between the value of human beings and their exchangeability as equivalents.

Marx refers to value as a "veil" that transforms labor power into a form of equivalence, one that will not be "removed from the countenance of the social life-process . . . until it becomes production by freely associated men, and stands under their conscious and planned control."[21] To remove value's veil of equivalence suggests a world of radical transparency and symbolic control. If we are to imagine a world beyond capitalism, it will require re-constituting commodity-determined labor and its mediation of social and cultural temporality. Only then will it be possible to abolish capitalist value, a form of metaphoric power that obfuscates its own metaphoricity. Only then will labor time cease to play a socially mediating role that is exter-nal to the human beings performing the labor. A world beyond capitalist value means a new set of social relations between people and nature, tech-nology, and mental conceptions but also, and perhaps most importantly, the recognition of the radical incommensurability of humanity as the basis of emancipation.

NOTES

INTRODUCTION

1. Dean Beeby, "Canada $100 Bill Controversy: Mark Carney, Bank of Canada Governor, Issues Apology," *Canadian Press*, August 20, 2012, http://www .huffingtonpost.ca/2012/08/20/asian-100-bill-carney_n_1810925.html.
2. Ibid.
3. Grant Robertson, "Carney Moves to Stamp Out Fire over 'Asian' $100 Bill," *Globe and Mail* (Toronto), August 20, 2012, http://license.icopyright.net/user /viewFreeUse.act?fuid=MTY4MTgxMjQ%3D.
4. Beeby, "Canada $100 Bill Controversy."
5. Ibid.
6. See Somerville, *Queering the Color Line*, and Luibhéid, *Entry Denied*. In her discussion of sexology, Somerville explores the influential role that women of color's bodies had on establishing and adjudicating racial, gender, and sexual normativity. She explains that "comparative anatomy located the boundaries of race through the sexual and reproductive anatomy of the African female body, ignoring altogether the problematic absence of male bodies from these studies" (*Queering the Color Line*, 25). In *Entry Denied*, Luibhéid demonstrates how non-white women served to rationalize restrictions based on psychological and moral "deviance."
7. "'Asian-Looking' Woman Removed from Canada's $100 Bill," *Angry Asian Man* (blog), August 17, 2012, http://blog.angryasianman.com/2012/08/asian-looking -woman-removed-from.html.
8. Ibid.
9. This term gained popularity in the United States after the 1998 publication of

Eric Liu's memoir *The Accidental Asian*, which contains a chapter entitled "New Jews." For a related examination of Asian Americans and Jewish Americans as parallel ethnic formations, see Schlund-Vials, *Modeling Citizenship*, and Freedman, *Klezmer America*. Examples of the Asian-Jewish analogy in Canada are less prominent but have surfaced in relation to high concentrations of Asian students at elite Canadian universities. See Jeet Heer, "Maclean's Article on Asians Familiar to Anti-Semites of Old," *National Post*, November 15, 2010, http://fullcomment.nationalpost.com/2010/11/15/jeet-heer—macleans-article-on-asians-familiar-to-anti-semites-of-old/.

10. Jacobson, *Whiteness of a Different Color*, 126.

11. Pew Research Center, "The Rise of Asian Americans," June 19, 2012, http://www.pewsocialtrends.org/2012/06/19/the-rise-of-asian-americans/.

12. Asian American Pacific Islander Policy and Research Consortium, "Statement by the Asian American Pacific Islander Policy and Research Consortium (AAPIPRC) on the Pew Report," UCLA Asian American Studies Center, June 22, 2012, www.aasc.ucla.edu/archives/pewreport2012.asp.

13. See Jun's discussion of Thomas Friedman's *The World Is Flat* in *Race for Citizenship*, 131–132.

14. "CAQ's Legault: Kids in Quebec Should Work Harder, Like Asians," *Globe and Mail* (Toronto), August 14, 2012, http://www.theglobeandmail.com/news/politics/elections/caqs-legault-kids-in-quebec-should-work-harder-like-asians/article4480487/.

15. Gregory Rodriguez, "New Wave of Immigrants—a New Target Too," *Los Angeles Times*, June 25, 2012, http://articles.latimes.com/print/2012/jun/25/opinion/la-oe-0625-rodriguez-pew-asians—20120625.

16. Ibid.

17. Koshy, "Morphing Race into Ethnicity."

18. Rodriguez, "New Wave of Immigrants—a New Target Too."

19. Freedman, *Klezmer America*, 265.

20. Ibid.

21. Becker, *Human Capital*. Becker's theory of human capital has antecedents in the work of Adam Smith and others whom Marx referred to as "apologetic economists." Like Becker, they attempt to claim that the worker's labor power exists as a form of capital, proving that the worker is also a capitalist "because he always has a 'commodity' (himself) for sale." If this were the case, Marx rejoins, "Even a slave would be a capitalist, even though he is sold once and for all as a commodity by a third person." He clarifies that the worker's labor power is her *capacity* rather than *capital*: "It is the only commodity that he can constantly sell, and he has to sell it in order to live, but it operates as capital . . . only in the hands of the buyer, the capitalist." It is only the capitalist who profits from the laborer's skills. Marx, *Capital*, 2:516.

22. Jun, *Race for Citizenship*, 130.

23. Ibid., 131–132.

24. Lye, *America's Asia*, 122.

25. Ibid., 130.

26. Ibid., 124.

27. Ibid., 102.

28. Postone, "Anti-Semitism and National Socialism," 107.

29. Ibid., 112.

30. Ibid., 108.

31. See Lye, *America's Asia*.

32. Jameson, *The Political Unconscious*.

33. Levi, "'See That Straw? That's a Straw,'" 376.

34. Ibid.

35. Cedric Robinson, *Black Marxism*, 3.

36. Lowe, *Immigrant Acts*, 27.

37. Ibid., 27–28.

38. Ibid., 28.

39. Roediger, *How Race Survived U.S. History*, 69.

40. Petrus Liu, "Queer Marxism in Taiwan," 525.

41. Godden, "Labor, Language, and Finance Capital," 419.

42. Marx, *Capital*, 1:135.

43. Ibid., 1:376.

44. Postone, "Anti-Semitism and National Socialism," 108.

45. Marx, *Capital*, 1:163.

46. Ibid., 1:132.

47. Harvey emphasizes this point in his discussion of commodities and exchange in *A Companion to Marx's "Capital,"* 33.

48. Marx, *Capital*, 1:138, my italics.

49. Ibid., 1:129.

50. Concrete labor does not necessarily lead to the production of commodities.

51. Marx, *Capital*, 1:136.

52. Ibid., 1:129.

53. Ibid., 1:153.

54. Postone, "Anti-Semitism and National Socialism," 109, my italics.

55. Christopher McCandless's 1992 pursuit of a life in the Alaskan wilderness without material comforts is chronicled in Jon Krakauer's *Into the Wild*, later adapted into a feature film.

56. Postone, "Anti-Semitism and National Socialism," 110.

57. Ibid., 112.

58. Ibid.

59. Postone gives an example of Proudhon as a forefather of modern anti-Semitism for espousing the belief that abolishing money would abolish capitalist relations: "He did not realize that capitalism is characterized by mediated social relations, objectified in the categorical forms, one of whose *expressions*, not *causes*, is money. Proudhon, in other words, mistook a form of appearance — money as the objectification of the abstract — for the essence of capitalism." See Postone, "Anti-Semitism and National Socialism," 109, footnote 14.

60. Ibid., 113.

61. Ibid.

62. For a discussion of the complex implications of Marx's own personification of capitalism through Jewish figures and attributes (such as circumcision), see Jay Geller's chapter "From Rags to Risches: On Marx's Other Jewish Question," in *The Other Jewish Question*, 169–211.

63. Lake and Reynolds, *Drawing the Global Colour Line*.

64. Ibid., 3.

65. McKeown, *Melancholy Order*, 7.

66. Stoddard, *The Rising Tide of Color*, 315.

67. Young notes the surprisingly long list of present-day (non-post)colonies; dependent, trust, and unincorporated territories; overseas departments; and "other such names signifying colonial status," including British Gibraltar, the Falklands/Malvinas; Danish Greenland; Dutch Antilles; French Guiana, Martinique, Réunion, St. Pierre, and Miquelon; US Puerto Rico, Samoa, and Virgin Islands; and Spanish Ceuta, Melilla, and the Canary Islands. See Robert J. C. Young, *Postcolonialism*, 3.

68. Tyrell, "Beyond the View from Euro-America," 170, cited in Goldstein, "Where the Nation Takes Place," 835.

69. McClintock, "The Angel of Progress," 84–98.

70. Wolfe, "Land, Labor, and Difference," 868.

71. Biermann and Kössler, "The Settler Mode of Production," 115.

72. Termination was implemented by the Hoover administration in 1954 and represented a series of policies designed to dismantle the reservation system, disband tribal nations, and distribute their assets among tribal members—with or without the consent of tribal nations. Although no termination policies took effect in Canada, Prime Minister Pierre Trudeau's failed 1969 white paper was designed to divest all such nations of special status. Franks writes that "the white paper proposed a drastic shift to liberal individualism and a denial of group rights in some ways even more extreme than the failed termination policy in the United States." See Franks, "Indian Policy," 243.

73. Robert J. C. Young, *Postcolonialism*, 20.

74. Alfred, *Wasáse*, 152.

75. See David Palumbo-Liu's discussion of *Blade Runner* in *Asian/American*, 326–333.

76. Morgensen, "Settler Homonationalism," 118.

77. Huhndorf, *Going Native*.

78. Smith, "Indigeneity, Settler Colonialism, White Supremacy."

79. Sexton, "The Social Life of Social Death," 18.

80. Barker, "The Contemporary Reality of Canadian Imperialism," 329.

81. Ibid.

82. Byrd, *Transit of Empire*, xix.

83. Wolfe, "Recuperating Binarism," 263.

84. Ibid.

85. Fujikane, "Introduction," 6.

86. Ibid., 7.

87. Ibid., 20.

88. Ibid., 29.

89. Ibid., 9.

90. Ibid., 23.

91. Roediger, *How Race Survived U.S. History*, 130, 135.

92. Lye, "The Afro-Asian Analogy," 1733.

93. Ibid.

94. Ibid.

95. Ibid., 1734.

96. See Clarke, "Must All Blackness Be American?," 56–71, and Winks, *The Blacks in Canada*.

97. Veracini, *Settler Colonialism*, 3. Veracini emphasizes how settlers not only move "home," but can also "return," in the case of Jewish peoples to a "homeland" in Israel. See Obenzinger's "Naturalizing Cultural Pluralism, Americanizing Zionism" for a comparative analysis of "Promised Lands." He examines the role that religious justification played in settler colonial settlement in the United States and Israel.

98. Wilderson, "Gramsci's Black Marx," 238.

99. The distinctions between Native and settler have the potential to be blurred as well. Grant Farred has introduced the concept of the postcolonial "unsettler" in the Sudan, where the Arab paramilitary majority functions as a more brutal colonialist extension of the settler, "exceed[ing] the worst excesses of colonial violence" in "evacuat[ing] the land entirely of the native." See Farred, "The Unsettler," 807, 794.

100. Cheryl Harris, "Whiteness as Property," 1733.

101. Hartman and Wilderson, "The Position of the Unthought."

102. Marx, *Capital*, 1: 874.

103. Byrd, *Transit of Empire*, xxxvii.

104. See Lawrence and Dua, "Decolonizing Antiracism," 120–143.

105. Alfred, *Wasáse*, 153.

106. See also Limerick, *The Legacy of Conquest*, and Ellinghaus, "Biological Absorption and Genocide."

107. Ellinghaus, "Biological Absorption and Genocide," 73.

108. See McCool, Olson, and Robinson, *Native Vote*.

109. Franks, "Indian Policy," 226. See also Ross, *Inventing the Savage*, 1998.

110. The critical theory of Afro-pessimism elaborates extensively on this exclusivity. See Sexton, "The Social Life of Social Death" and "People-of-Color-Blindness," and Wilderson, "Gramsci's Black Marx."

111. Wolfe, "Land, Labor, and Difference," 868, my italics. While earlier fur-trading posts in North America allowed for settlers and Indigenous people to coexist, the shift from mercantile (trade-centered) to industrial (land-centered) forms of capitalism marks the shift to settler colonialism.

112. Ibid., 881, footnote 53, my italics.

113. Coulthard, *Red Skin, White Masks*, 123.

114. Jaimes, "Federal Indian Identification Policy," 137, cited in Wolfe, "Land, Labor, and Difference," 889.

115. Limerick, *The Legacy of Conquest*, 338.

116. Karrmen Crey, excerpt from the University of British Columbia First Nation's Studies website: http://indigenousfoundations.arts.ubc.ca/home/identity /aboriginal-identity-the-classroom.html?type=123&filename=Aboriginal%20 Identity%20&%20the%20Classroom.pdf=. Accessed July 28, 2015.

117. For instance, despite the absence of a similar Dawes Act allotment policy in Canada, the government took steps to alienate Indigenous peoples from their lands. However, because reserves in Canada were relatively smaller than those in the US West, only 10 percent of those lands were alienated—compared to the loss of two-thirds in the United States. See Franks, "Indian Policy," 235. Historically, assimilation policies were much more aggressive in Canada, and strategies to divest Indigenous peoples of "Indian status" have been much more extensive.

118. See Coulthard, *Red Skin, White Masks*.

119. Ibid., 878.

120. Ibid., my italics.

121. Ibid., 881.

122. Foucault, *The History of Sexuality*, 140.

123. Wolfe, "Land, Labor, and Difference," 881.

124. See Jacobson, *Whiteness of a Different Color*.

125. Wolfe, "Land, Labor, and Difference," 887.

126. Ibid., 888.

127. Lawrence, "Gender, Race, and the Regulation of Native Identity in Canada and the US." "Status" and "non-Status" denote the federal status of an Indigenous person in Canada. In order to have status, one must be recognized as a "Registered Indian" as defined by the Indian Act.

128. Tulley, "A Just Relationship between Aboriginal and Non-Aboriginal Peoples of Canada," 42.

129. Roediger, *How Race Survived U.S. History*, 70–72. Roediger notes that slaves themselves were among the most profitable US-produced commodities, while cotton accounted for 57 percent of the total value of US exports before the Civil War. It is also a mistake to suggest that Northern industrial capitalists were responsible for pressuring Southern plantation owners to abolish slavery, given that "multiple economic, cultural, and political ties bound Northern capital to Southern slavery." The point is that industrial capitalism was not responsible for ending slavery; rather, it shifted the terms of race, labor, and inequality. Indeed, the expansion of capitalism in the United States was rooted in slavery.

130. Wolfe, "Land, Labor, and Difference," 894.

131. Biermann and Kössler, "The Settler Mode of Production," 112.

132. Jung, *Coolies and Cane*.

133. Not all slave societies reproduced their slave populations in corresponding ways. While the United States reproduced its enslaved population through reproduction, Brazil reproduced it by replenishing the supply of slaves through continual shipments of African slaves. Thus unlike in the United States, the hereditary fact of slavery and its fusion with blackness, which became wholly racialized after emancipation, did not produce a similar racial conception of blackness. Rather, they produced those of caste and color. See Wolfe, "Land, Labor, and Difference," 904.

134. Canadian antimiscegenation policy was even less consistent than in the United States, but various policies such as "Girls and Women's Protection Act" prevented Chinese men from being employed in establishments that also employed white women or girls.

135. See Bow, *Partly Colored*.

136. Lake and Reynolds, *Drawing the Global Colour Line*, 5.

137. Hernández, *Undue Process*.

138. Melamed, "The Spirit of Neoliberalism," 20.

139. See Gilmore, *Golden Gulag*. Gilmore analyzes California prisons as a geographical solution for managing concentrated populations of the racialized poor in urban centers. For a discussion of the dramatic rise in deportation cases involving poor, refugee, and undocumented classes of Southeast Asian migrants in the United States, see Park, "Emergent Divides."

140. Foucault, "Nietzsche, Genealogy, History," 360.

141. Ibid., 356.

142. Ibid., 365.

143. Hirsch, *Family Frames*, 22.

144. Ibid.

145. Chakrabarty, "Universalism and Belonging," 669.

1. SEX, TIME, AND THE TRANSCONTINENTAL RAILROAD

1. Berton, *The Last Spike*, 1.

2. In declining my request to reproduce Van Horne's sketch, which also appears in Margot Francis's *Creative Subversions*, the CPR's manager of corporate communications indicated that the history of Chinese railroad labor would compromise Van Horne's reputation: "My concern is not your work, but is based on the history of the construction period of the CPR. The image is speaks [*sic*] to a larger issue of sensitivities around how the CPR was built, the conditions and the realities of the 1880s. The other consideration is that is a drawing done by the President of the CPR; not some anonymous business figure. My decision on this is final."

3. Francis, *Creative Subversions*, 77.

4. As Richard White notes, neither railroad was, by definition, transcontinental, "for the transcontinentals did not really span the continent." See White, *Railroaded*, xxi.

5. Yu, "Toward a Pacific History of the Americas," xvi.

6. Foucault, *The History of Sexuality*, 140.

7. Eng, *Racial Castration*, 36.

8. Berton, *The Last Spike*, 2.

9. Francis, *Creative Subversions*, 77.

10. Marx, *Capital*, 1:229.

11. Ibid., 1:160.

12. Chakrabarty, "Universalism and Belonging," 655.

13. Freeman, "Introduction, Special Issue on Queer Temporality," 159.

14. Petrus Liu, "Queer Marxism in Taiwan," 526.

15. Chakrabarty, "Universalism and Belonging," 658.

16. Ibid., 655.

17. Marx, *Capital*, 1:128, my italics.

18. Chakrabarty, "Universalism and Belonging," 662.

19. Postone, *Time, Labor, and Social Domination*, 201.

20. Ibid., 202.

21. Petrus Liu, "Queer Marxism in Taiwan," 533, my italics.

22. O'Malley, *Keeping Watch*, 59, 60.

23. Postone, *Time, Labor, and Social Domination*, 191.

24. Kirby, "Steamy Scenes and Dream Machines," 25. For a more extensive discussion of the railroad's cultural significance, see Kirby, *Parallel Tracks*.

25. Lowe, "Break the Frame," 78.

26. Francis, *Creative Subversions*, 80.

27. Foucault, *The History of Sexuality*.

28. Kingston, *China Men*, 144.

29. Ibid., 135.

30. Ibid., 129.

31. Ibid., 130

32. Ibid.

33. Ibid., 135.

34. Ibid., 133.

35. Ibid., 18.

36. Freeman, "Introduction, Special Issue on Queer Temporality," 162.

37. Ibid., 160.

38. Marx, *Capital*, 1:168–169.

39. Ibid., 1:128.

40. Chakrabarty, "Universalism and Belonging," 665.

41. Ibid., 665.

42. Kingston, *China Men*, 135.

43. Ibid., 134.

44. Ibid., 136.

45. Ibid., 137.

46. Ibid.

47. Ibid., 132.

48. Ibid., 134.

49. Ibid.

50. Ibid.

51. Chakrabarty, "Universalism and Belonging," 666.

52. Ibid., 665.

53. Goellnicht, "Tang Ao in America," 204.

54. Eng, *Racial Castration*, 100.

55. Hattori, "China Man Autoeroticism," 230.

56. Ibid., 233.

57. Derrida, *Of Grammatology*.

58. Mosse, "Nationalism and Respectability," 227.

59. Hattori, "China Man Autoeroticism," 232, my italics.

60. Kingston, *China Men*, 139.

61. Ibid., 139–140.

62. Ibid., 140.

63. Ibid., 141.

64. Žižek, *The Plague of Fantasies*, 73.

65. Kingston, *China Men*, 141.

66. Ibid., 144.

67. Chakrabarty, "Universalism and Belonging," 669.

68. Kingston, *China Men*, 145.

69. Ibid.

70. Eng, *Racial Castration*, 65.

71. Ibid.

72. Kingston, *China Men*, 145.

73. Eng, *Racial Castration*, 65.

74. Kingston, *China Men*, 145.

75. Ibid.

76. Marx, *Capital*, 1:142.

77. Francis, *Creative Subversions*, 86.

78. Chakrabarty, "Universalism and Belonging," 670.

79. Kingston, *China Men*, 144.

80. Ibid.

81. Ibid., 147.

82. Ibid., 19.

83. Ibid., 20.

84. Ibid., 21.

85. Ibid.

86. Ibid., 127.

87. Ibid., 150

88. Ibid.

89. Ibid., 151.

90. Ibid.

91. Ibid., 150.

92. Ibid.

93. Ibid., 151.

94. Eng, *Racial Castration*, 67.

95. Kingston, *China Men*, 151.

96. Stryker, "(De)Subjugated Knowledges," 9.

97. Ibid.

98. Postone, *Time, Labor, and Social Domination*, 163.

99. Harvey, *A Companion to Marx's "Capital,"* 305.

100. Lowe, "Break the Frame," 78.

101. Francis, *Creative Subversions*, 88.

102. Ibid., 89.

2. UNNATURAL LANDSCAPES

1. Gonzales-Day, *Lynching in the West*, 3.

2. Ibid., 5.

3. Ibid., 15.

4. Ibid., 5.

5. W. J. T. Mitchell, "Imperial Landscape," 1.

6. Postone, *Time, Labor, and Social Domination*, 174.

7. Ibid.

8. Ibid.

9. W. J. T. Mitchell, "Imperial Landscape," 9.

10. Ibid., 7.

11. Postone, *Time, Labor, and Social Domination*, 174, footnote 115.

12. Levi, "'See That Straw? That's a Straw,'" 376.

13. Muñoz, *Disidentifications*, 25.

14. Ibid., 18.

15. Ibid., 15.

16. Ibid., 39.

17. Butler, *Bodies That Matter*, 219.

18. Wolfe, "Land, Labor, and Difference," 868.

19. Miller, *Empire of the Eye*, 109.

20. Manning, *Ephemeral Territories*, 7.

21. Linsley, "Landscapes in Motion," 81.

22. Postone, "Anti-Semitism and National Socialism," 111.

23. Huhndorf, *Going Native*.

24. Tseng, "Tseng Kwong Chi," 12.

25. Habib, "A Life in 'Chinese Drag,'" 72.

26. Turner, "The Accidental Ambassador," 82.

27. Machida, "Out of Asia," 96.

28. Tseng, "Tseng Kwong Chi," 13.

29. Turner, "The Accidental Ambassador," 83.

30. Butler, *Bodies That Matter*, 231.

31. Unlike normative white gendered identities, racialized genders often experience their difference as a modality of class disparity. As Evelyn Nakano Glenn

clarifies, the "situation of white women has depended on the situation of women of color." See Glenn, "Racial Ethnic Women's Labor," 105.

32. Butler, *Bodies That Matter*, 226.
33. Muñoz, *Disidentifications*, 26.
34. Reddy, "Home, Houses, Nonidentity," 355.
35. Tseng's friends included Keith Haring, Kenny Sharpe, David Wojnarowicz, John Sex, Samantha McEwan, Carmel Johnson, Charles Ludlam, Tereza Goncalves, and Robert Mapplethorpe.
36. W. J. T. Mitchell, "Imperial Landscape," 10.
37. Kevles, "Eugenics and Human Rights," 436.
38. Ibid.
39. Ibid.
40. Coutts and McCarrick, "Eugenics," 163.
41. Ibid.
42. Erica Lee, "Hemispheric Orientalism."
43. Lake and Reynolds, *Drawing the Global Colour Line*, 4.
44. Lawren Harris, "Revelation of Art in Canada," 87.
45. Linsley, "Landscapes in Motion," 85.
46. Bright, "The Machine in the Garden Revisited," 64.
47. Quoted in Larner, *Mount Rushmore*, 219.
48. Berger, *Sight Unseen*, 2.
49. Hutcheon, *A Theory of Parody*, xii.
50. Butler, *Bodies That Matter*, 232.
51. Tseng and Chong, "SlutForArt," 119.
52. Muñoz, *Disidentifications*, 15.
53. Shields, "Imaginary Sites," 26.
54. The park gave exclusive rights for development of the area to the Canadian Pacific Railway.
55. Wolfe, "Land, Labor, and Difference," 868, 875.
56. Grant, "Myths of the North in the Canadian Ethos," 37.
57. Grace, *Canada and the Idea of the North*, 51.
58. Manning, *Ephemeral Territories*, 8–9.
59. Lawren Harris, "The Story of the Group of Seven," 26.
60. Lawren Harris, "Revelation of Art in Canada," 85–86.
61. Deliberately or by honest error, Tseng misnamed these mountains "Seven Peaks," which do not appear on any map of Alberta. I suspect the photograph was taken in the Valley of the Ten Peaks in Banff National Park, which is visible in the backdrop of his photograph of Moraine Lake.
62. Manning, *Ephemeral Territories*, 10–11.
63. Berger, *Sight Unseen*, 67.
64. Murray, *The Best of the Group of Seven*, 21.
65. Linsley, "Landscapes in Motion," 89.
66. For an extended discussion of the Group of Seven's fears of miscegenation, see Linsley, "Landscapes in Motion."

67. Stern, *Eugenic Nation*, 124.

68. Bright, "The Machine in the Garden Revisited," 62.

69. Ibid.

70. Stern, *Eugenic Nation*, 118, 119.

71. Ibid., 124.

72. Ibid.

73. Linsley, "Landscapes in Motion," 90.

74. Ibid., 89.

75. Boime, *The Magisterial Gaze*, 20–21.

76. Berger, *Sight Unseen*, 77.

77. Berland, "Fire and Flame, Lightning and Landscape," 15.

78. Ibid., 16.

79. Jessup, "Landscapes of Sport, Landscapes of Exclusion," 94.

80. Eng, *Racial Castration*, 4.

81. W. J. T. Mitchell, "Imperial Landscape," 14.

82. Taliaferro, *Great White Fathers*, 2.

83. "Mount Rushmore National Memorial: History and Culture," National Park Service, US Department of the Interior, www.nps.gov/moru/historyculture/index .htm.

84. Boime, "Patriarchy Fixed in Stone," 155.

85. Ibid., 150.

86. W. J. T. Mitchell, "Imperial Landscape," 6.

87. Boime, "Patriarchy Fixed in Stone," 144.

88. Ibid., 149.

89. Tseng, "Tseng Kwong Chi," 12. Tseng was very familiar with the tradition of Chinese landscape painting. Muna Tseng explains that in his youth Tseng was a "child prodigy in Chinese brush and ink paintings and calligraphy, brilliantly imitating the old masters."

90. Hearn, *Cultivated Landscapes*, 5.

91. W. J. T. Mitchell, "Imperial Landscape," 9.

92. Chin et al., *The Big Aiiieeeee!*, xiii.

93. Schueller, "Claiming Postcolonial America," 178.

94. Limerick, "Disorientation and Reorientation," 1022.

95. Williams, *The Country and the City*, 120.

96. Boime, "Patriarchy Fixed in Stone," 156.

97. Ibid.

98. Zhu, "Ethnic Oasis," 5.

99. Ibid., 3.

100. Taliaferro, *Great White Fathers*, 192.

101. Quoted in Taliaferro, *Great White Fathers*, 192.

102. Ibid.

103. Ibid.

104. Ibid.

105. Reid, *A Concise History of Canadian Painting*, 152.

106. Ibid.

107. W. J. T. Mitchell, "Imperial Landscape," 6.

108. Hutcheon, *A Theory of Parody*, 4.

109. Katharyne Mitchell, "In Whose Interest?," 230.

110. Stewart, "Cultural Appropriations," 60.

111. Quoted in ibid., 63.

112. Shadbolt, *Emily Carr*, 137.

113. Reid, *A Concise History of Canadian Painting*, 157.

114. Huhndorf, *Going Native*, 3.

115. Ibid., 2.

116. Ibid., 163.

117. Stewart, "Cultural Appropriations," 62.

118. Huhndorf, *Going Native*, 3.

119. Stewart, "Cultural Appropriations," 62.

120. "True north strong and free" and "our home and Native land" are verses of Canada's national anthem.

121. Hutcheon, *A Theory of Parody*, xii.

122. Muñoz, *Disidentifications*, 31.

123. Lake and Reynolds, *Drawing the Global Colour Line*, 2.

124. Quoted in ibid., 2.

125. Reddy, "Home, Houses, Nonidentity," 372.

3. JAPANESE INTERNMENT AND THE MUTATION OF LABOR

1. See Yau, "Ruth Asawa."

2. Quoted in ibid., 12.

3. See Yau's discussion of David Smith's *Australia* (1951) in "Ruth Asawa," 15.

4. Mary Emma Harris, "Black Mountain College," 66.

5. Higa, "Inside and Outside at the Same Time," 30.

6. Yau, "Ruth Asawa," 18, my italics.

7. Ibid., 18.

8. Gregory Robinson, *A Tragedy of Democracy*, 101.

9. Ibid., 116.

10. Ibid., 102.

11. Lye, *America's Asia*, 98.

12. Ibid.

13. Okihiro and Drummond, "The Concentration Camps," 169.

14. Ibid., 174.

15. Ibid.

16. Lye, *America's Asia*, 102.

17. Ibid., 111.

18. See Kelley and Trebilock, *The Making of the Mosaic*, and Roy, *The Oriental Question*, 3. They explain that Japanese naturalization waned after 1923. US-style alien land laws were contemplated when Japanese farmers gained success in the berry industry.

19. Adachi, *The Enemy That Never Was*, 106.

20. Fukawa, *Spirit of the Nikkei Fleet*, 114.

21. Ibid.

22. Quoted in Fukawa, *Spirit of the Nikkei Fleet*, 113.

23. Gregory Robinson, *A Tragedy of Democracy*, 178.

24. Meggs, *Salmon*, 152.

25. Ibid.; Lye, *America's Asia*, 9.

26. Shanken, "Better Living," 494.

27. See McAtee, "Taking Comfort in the Age of Anxiety," 3–25.

28. Postone, "Anti-Semitism and National Socialism," 110–111.

29. Other texts that could fit into the frame of postmemory include Julie Otsuka's *When the Emperor Was Divine*, Cynthia Kadohata's *The Floating World*, and Emiko Omori's *Rabbit in the Moon*.

30. Hirsch, *Family Frames*, 22.

31. Ibid.

32. Eng, *The Feeling of Kinship*, 166–167.

33. Cho, *Haunting in the Korean Diaspora*, 50.

34. Eng, *The Feeling of Kinship*, 167.

35. See Donald Goellnicht's insightful reading of *Obasan* as a postmodern rejection of official history in "Minority History as Metafiction," 287–306.

36. Oikawa, *Cartographies of Violence*, 59.

37. Kogawa, *Obasan*, 99.

38. Ibid., 100.

39. Ibid., 45.

40. See Gregory Robinson, *A Tragedy of Democracy*, and Victor Bascara, "Cultural Politics of Redress." Of all the nations that participated in the removal of ethnic Japanese, only those in the United States and Canada received an apology and compensation for financial losses incurred during wartime confinement. In August 1988, President Reagan signed the Civil Rights Restoration Act, H.R. 442, which enabled each Japanese American affected by Executive Order 9066 to receive a tax-free payment of $20,000. Because Latin American internees in Texas were not covered by Executive Order 9066, they were not eligible for a redress payment. In September 1988, six weeks after redress was granted in the United States, Prime Minister Brian Mulroney signed the redress settlement for Japanese Canadians, which provided $21,000 to the Issei and Nisei who were incarcerated during the war. Although redress was a hard-won and overdue victory for Japanese North American activists, it had the effect of recasting the legacy of Japanese internment as a triumph of democracy over an aberrant, isolated event that occurred in the distant past. But even before redress was won, perhaps the largest irony of Japanese internment in North America was that Japanese civilians were confined as the yellow peril, only to emerge in its aftermath as the model minority.

41. Kogawa, *Obasan*, 41.

42. Postone, "Anti-Semitism and National Socialism," 99.

43. Ibid.

44. Ibid., 105.

45. Ibid.

46. Ibid.

47. Ibid.

48. Ibid., 106.

49. Ibid.

50. Ibid.

51. Roy, *The Oriental Question*, 131.

52. Marx determines the rate of exploitation as the ratio of surplus-value to the variable capital spent on labor.

53. Marx, *Capital*, 1:434.

54. Ibid., my italics.

55. Ibid., 1:436.

56. Ibid., 1:436–437.

57. Kogawa, *Obasan*, 3.

58. Ibid., 169.

59. Ibid., 9.

60. Ibid., 3.

61. Lo, "Passing Recognition," 320, 318.

62. Ibid., 325.

63. Kogawa, *Obasan*, 48.

64. Byrd, *The Transit of Empire*, 187.

65. Ishizuka, *Lost and Found*, 147.

66. Ibid., 148.

67. Ibid.

68. Gregory Robinson, *A Tragedy of Democracy*, 184.

69. Oikawa, "Connecting the Internment of Japanese Canadians," 21.

70. Kim, *Ends of Empire*, 99.

71. Lo, "Passing Recognition," 325.

72. See Cheung, *Articulate Silences*; Goellnicht, "Minority History as Metafiction"; Kanefsky, "Debunking a Postmodern Conception of History"; Miki, *Broken Entries*; McFarlane, "Covering *Obasan* and the Narrative of Internment"; Kamboureli, *Scandalous Bodies*; and Hattori, "Psycholinguistic Orientalism in Criticism of *The Woman Warrior* and *Obasan*." The large body of scholarship devoted to it testifies to the novel's acclaim in both Canadian and US contexts. Passages from the novel were read aloud in the House of Commons during the government's announcement of the Japanese Canadian Redress settlement in 1988, adding to its national significance in Canada. While early criticism was largely concerned with formalist issues or universal themes of overcoming suffering, later criticism engaged in debates over its mainstream reception and probed the implications of the novel's treatment of history, racism, and racial and gendered subjectivity. Among this scholarship, Donald Goellnicht examined the novel's combining of documentary history, archival sources, and fiction as a

postmodern deconstruction of absolute truths. Others, such as Roy Miki and Scott Toguri McFarlane, challenged critical approaches that celebrated the novel's "resolutionary" (rather than revolutionary) ending, which functioned to appease white guilt for historical injuries. Given Naomi's complex psychology, scholars such as Smaro Kamboureli and Tomo Hattori examined the novel through the lens of psychoanalysis, while King-Kok Cheung focused on how the novel balances Western and Asian conceptions of speech and silence.

73. Gregory Robinson, *A Tragedy of Democracy*, 134.

74. During the war, nearly four thousand West Coast Japanese left to work on sugar beet farms in Alberta, Manitoba, and southwestern Ontario. The Issei and Nisei would remain in the three provinces as an exploited source of labor, subject to long hours of hard labor and substandard living conditions. The transparency of the government's economic rather than security priorities came into full relief when the British Columbia Security Commission was dissolved in 1943 and transferred to the control of the Department of Labour. The Labour Department was then given full authority over the movement and resettlement of Japanese Canadians. Under its leadership, coercive measures were instituted to conscript able-bodied Nisei men to labor camps in rural parts of Ontario that were in need of workers. See Gregory Robinson, *A Tragedy of Democracy*.

75. See Gregory Robinson, *A Tragedy of Democracy*. Compared to the Japanese American experience, Japanese Canadians suffered larger financial losses and were barred from the West Coast for longer. Although 75 percent of Japanese Americans lost all their property as a result of their wartime expulsion and confinement, they did not suffer the total liquidation of their property to pay for their incarceration as their Japanese Canadian counterparts did. By 1946, half of the former population of Japanese Americans returned to the coast, while Japanese Canadians remained barred until 1949, by which time few would return. Canada, already at war with Germany, was brought into the Pacific theater with Japan's simultaneous attacks on Pearl Harbor and Hong Kong. The government's immediate actions involved detaining suspected Japanese terrorists, closing Japanese language schools and presses, and impounding twelve hundred fishing boats. On February 24, 1942, on the heels of the US initiative, Prime Minister Mackenzie King's government issued Order in Council P.C. 1486, mandating that the Japanese race be expelled from a one-hundred-mile "protected area" on the coast of British Columbia, where more than 95 percent of the Japanese Canadian population resided. After being held in an assembly center in Vancouver — which, similar to those in the United States, consisted of hastily converted horse stables — twenty-two thousand Japanese civilians, of whom 75 percent were citizens, were confined in deserted mining camps in the British Columbia interior and to labor camps and "self-support" sites in eastern British Columbia. The government subsequently formed the Japanese Fishing Vessel Disposal Committee charged with supervising the forced sale of Japanese boats. In the fall of 1942 the government passed the Veterans Land Act, which gave the Director of Soldier Settlement the right to sell 939 deliberately under-

valued Japanese farms without consulting the owners. On January 23, 1943, the Custodian of Alien Property was authorized to liquidate all remaining Japanese property at rock-bottom prices. All proceeds from liquidation sales as well as the wages of Japanese men forced to work on road projects were used to subsidize the internment — only after their own board expenses and, for a time, unemployment insurance were deducted. After the war, internees were forced to choose either repatriation to Japan or resettlement outside of the West, which led to the deportation of nearly four thousand inmates. It was not until April 1, 1949, that federal restrictions were lifted, allowing Japanese civilians to return to the one-hundred-mile British Columbia coastal area. In large part, Japanese American families remained intact during their confinement, while able-bodied Japanese Canadian men were taken to road camps and separated from their families. Unlike the US government, which paid for the transportation, food, and the lodging of Japanese Americans, the Canadian government supplied only fuel, bunk beds, mail, and medical services. No food was provided, nor were cultivators paid for their labor. It is estimated that the Canadian government spent a third of the US government's total expenditures. The War Relocation Authority's budget was $162 million for housing and the US Army's $75 million for rounding up and transporting Japanese Americans.

76. Kogawa, *Obasan*, 206.
77. Ibid., 232.
78. Ibid., 238.
79. Ibid., 30.
80. Ibid., 34.
81. Ibid.
82. Ibid.
83. Ibid.
84. Ibid.
85. Ibid.
86. Ibid.
87. Ibid.
88. Ibid.
89. Ibid., 35.
90. Ibid.
91. Ibid.
92. Ibid.
93. Ibid.
94. For a discussion of the novel's citation of Revelations, see Gottlieb, "The Riddle of Concentric Worlds in *Obasan*," 44.
95. Kogawa, *Obasan*, 228.
96. Ibid., 229.
97. Ibid., 230.
98. Ibid., 229.
99. Ibid.

100. Ibid., 228.

101. Ibid., 264.

102. Ibid., 34.

103. Ibid., 232.

104. Ibid., 35.

105. Ibid., 235.

106. Ibid., 236.

107. Ibid., 235.

108. Ibid., 231.

109. Ibid.

110. Ibid., 232, my italics.

111. Marx, *Capital*, 1:784.

112. Ferguson, *Aberrations in Black*, 15.

113. Marx defines three tiers of relative surplus populations: floating, latent, and stagnant.

114. Gilmore, *Golden Gulag*, 71.

115. Nichols, *Indians in the United States and Canada*, 294.

116. Marx, *Capital*, 1:796.

117. See Laliberté and Satezwich, "Native Migrant Labour in the Southern Alberta Sugar Beet Industry." After the war, Native workers filled much of the labor demand in the southern Alberta sugar beet industry. They were recruited primarily from northern Saskatchewan.

118. Kim, *Ends of Empire*.

119. Kogawa, *Obasan*, 240.

120. Eng, *The Feeling of Kinship*, 179.

121. The film is critically acclaimed and won numerous awards, including Academy Awards for Best Actor (Spencer Tracy), Best Director (John Sturges), and Best Writing for a Screenplay (Millard Kaufman) in 1956.

122. Gregory Robinson, *A Tragedy of Democracy*, 154.

123. Okimoto, *Sharing a Desert Home*, 5.

124. Ibid.

125. Japanese American families were directed to irrigate the land in order to develop the local economy. Promoting this plan was John Collier, famed for ending the pattern of dispossession enabled by the 1887 Dawes Act and clearing a pathway for the Indian Reorganization Act of 1934. He wanted to seize the opportunity to exploit detained Japanese labor to subjugate the land by digging irrigation ditches, building canals, leveling land, and preparing the land for water. As the reservation had previously been mired in a water rights battle, Collier saw Japanese internment at Poston as a golden opportunity to turn the reservations' undeveloped land into a source of economic sustenance. Linked to this project was a "colonization" program, in which neighboring Native nations living on other reservations that were deprived of water would move to Poston. See Okimoto, *Sharing a Desert Home*, 5.

126. Ibid., 9.

127. Gregory Robinson, *A Tragedy of Democracy*, 155.

128. McIntyre, "Race, Surplus Population and the Marxist Theory of Imperialism," 1506.

129. Okimoto, *Sharing a Desert Home*, 9.

130. Eng, *The Feeling of Kinship*, 195.

131. Okimoto, *Sharing a Desert Home*, 14.

132. Gregory Robinson, *A Tragedy of Democracy*, 225.

133. Okimoto, *Sharing a Desert Home*, 13.

4. THE NEW NINETEETH CENTURY

1. Quoted in Scott, "Ken Lum Works with Photography," 20.

2. "Living Statue Tries Experiment," *Surrey Leader*, July 5, 1978, 12.

3. Scott, "Ken Lum Works with Photography," 20.

4. Derksen, "Fixed City and Mobile Globe," 36.

5. Yamashita, *Tropic of Orange*, 37.

6. Ibid., 56.

7. Ibid., 255.

8. Ibid., 56.

9. Ibid., 34.

10. Ibid., 36.

11. Ibid., 235.

12. Boime, *The Magisterial Gaze*, 20–21.

13. Chiang, "Capitalizing Form," 842–843.

14. Mitchell and Snyder, "Disability as Multitude," 184.

15. Ibid., 183.

16. Nealon, *The Matter of Capital*, 33.

17. Postone, *Time, Labor, and Social Domination*, 174.

18. Kim, *Ends of Empire*.

19. Park, "Emergent Divides," 62. His article discusses how immigration policy in the United States has shifted away from "family reunification" toward employment.

20. Ayesha Bhatta, "Canada Prepares for an Asian Future," BBC News, May 25, 2012, http://www.bbc.com/news/world-radio-and-tv-18149316.

21. Wang, "Model Minority, High-Tech Coolies, and Foreign Spies."

22. Derrida, *Of Hospitality*, 25.

23. Ibid., 24–25.

24. Enwezor, "Social Mirrors," 65.

25. Watson, "The Discomfort Zone," 35.

26. Enwezor, "Social Mirrors," 67.

27. Quoted in Scott, "Ken Lum Works with Photography," 18.

28. Derksen, "Fixed City and Mobile Globe," 32–33.

29. Scott, "Ken Lum Works with Photography," 24.

30. A version of this work is permanently installed outside the Witte de With art space in Rotterdam.

31. Scott, "Ken Lum Works with Photography," 25.

32. Barthes, *Camera Lucida*, 38.

33. Ibid.

34. Watson, "The Discomfort Zone," 34–35.

35. Derksen, "Fixed City and Mobile Globe," 37–38.

36. Harvey, *A Companion to Marx's "Capital,"* 305.

37. Melamed, "The Spirit of Neoliberalism," 1.

38. Ibid., 2.

39. Multiculturalism was first framed as a bicultural French/English government policy in 1971. In 1982 it was incorporated into the Charter of Rights and Freedoms within the Canadian Constitution.

40. Rieff, "Multiculturalism's Silent Partner," 62.

41. Katharyne Mitchell, "In Whose Interest?," 239.

42. Quoted in ibid., 239.

43. Cheryl Harris, "Whiteness as Property," 1857.

44. Kamboureli, *Scandalous Bodies*, 81.

45. Derksen, "Fixed City and Mobile Globe," 37.

46. Ibid.

47. Katharyne Mitchell, "In Whose Interest?," 232. See also Katharyne Mitchell, *Crossing the Neoliberal Line*.

48. Ibid., 222.

49. Ibid., 232, italics in original.

50. Ibid.

51. Michaels, "The Politics of a Good Picture," 178, my italics.

52. See Park, "Emergent Divides," 57–72. Poor migrants' access to alternative legal channels such as family reunification also function to reinforce the heteronormative structure of immigration law. See Reddy, "Asian Diasporas, Neoliberalism, and Family."

53. Davis, *Ecology of Fear*.

54. Žižek, *First as Tragedy*, 92.

55. Marx, *Capital*, 1:493–494, footnote 4.

56. Ibid.

57. Yamashita, *Tropic of Orange*, 200.

58. See Gier and Tejeda, "An Interview with Karen Tei Yamashita." Yamashita states in this interview that she based Arcangel on the performance artist Guillermo Gomez-Peña and the poetry of Pablo Neruda: "Arcangel is a literary interpretation of Peña. Arcangel's performance is grotesque, freakish, yet Christ-like, accounting for 500 years of history in the Americas. He's also like Neruda, who, through his great poem, *Canto General*, expresses all of Latin America."

59. Ling, *Across Meridians*, 131.

60. Yamashita, *Tropic of Orange*, 15.

61. See in particular Wallace, "Tropics of Globalization"; Sue-Im Lee, "'We Are Not the World'"; Sze, "'Not by Politics Alone'"; Palumbo-Liu, "Introduction"; and Chiang, "Capitalizing Form."

62. Jameson, *The Political Unconscious*, 19.

63. Chiang, "Capitalizing Form," 842.

64. Nguyen, *The Gift of Freedom*, 33.

65. Sato, "Manzanar Murakami and Phantom Memory," 128.

66. Yamashita, *Tropic of Orange*, 159.

67. Ibid., 149.

68. Chiang, "Capitalizing Form," 842.

69. Yamashita, *Tropic of Orange*, 19.

70. Ibid.

71. Ibid., 21.

72. Ibid., 180.

73. Ibid., 16.

74. Nguyen, *The Gift of Freedom*, 24.

75. Ibid., 25.

76. Yamashita, *Tropic of Orange*, 79.

77. Nguyen, *The Gift of Freedom*, 4.

78. Yamashita, *Tropic of Orange*, 159.

79. Nguyen, *The Gift of Freedom*, 5.

80. Yamashita, *Tropic of Orange*, 80.

81. Ibid.

82. Ibid.

83. Ibid., 203.

84. Ibid., 80.

85. Ibid., 161.

86. Ibid.

87. Ibid., 198.

88. Ibid., 161–162.

89. Ibid., 76.

90. Kwong, *Forbidden Workers*, 136.

91. Yamashita, *Tropic of Orange*, 203.

92. Ibid., 162.

93. Ibid., 203.

94. Ibid., 204.

95. Wallace, "Tropics of Globalization," 155.

96. See Kelley and Trebilock, *The Making of the Mosaic*, and Park, "Emergent Divides."

97. Yamashita, *Tropic of Orange*, 228, 231.

98. Ibid., 22.

99. Ibid., 23.

100. Ibid., 126.

101. Ibid.

102. Ibid.

103. Ibid., 21.

104. Ibid., 127.

105. Ibid.

106. Ibid., 128.

107. Ibid., 129.

108. Žižek, "Multiculturalism, or The Cultural Logic of Multinational Capitalism," 37.

109. Yamashita, *Tropic of Orange*, 128.

110. Ibid.

111. Melamed, "The Spirit of Neoliberalism," 13.

112. Yamashita, *Tropic of Orange*, 129.

113. Ibid., 252.

114. Palumbo-Liu, *Asian/American*, 327.

115. Lye, *America's Asia*, 129.

116. Agamben, *Homo Sacer*, 8.

117. Yamashita, *Tropic of Orange*, 167.

118. Ibid., 176.

119. Ibid., 235.

120. Ibid., 236.

121. Ibid., 176.

122. Ibid.

123. Ibid., 250.

124. Ibid., 239.

125. Ibid., 35.

126. Ibid., 56.

127. Ling, *Across Meridians*, 127.

128. Yamashita, *Tropic of Orange*, 255.

129. Ibid., 256, my italics.

130. Ling, *Across Meridians*, 129.

131. Yamashita, *Tropic of Orange*, 255.

132. Ling, *Across Meridians*, 133.

133. Yamashita, *Tropic of Orange*, 254.

134. Davis, *Ecology of Fear*, 338.

135. Mitchell and Snyder, "Disability as Multitude," 186.

136. Yamashita, *Tropic of Orange*, 264.

137. Ibid., 256.

138. Ibid., 263.

139. Ibid., 265.

140. Kelley and Trebilock, *The Making of the Mosaic*, 150.

141. Pratt, *Securing Borders*, 14.

142. Benzan, "Going Nowhere Fast," 56–57.

143. Yamashita, *Tropic of Orange*, 268.

144. Postone, *Time, Labor, and Social Domination*, 383.

145. Biermann and Kössler, "The Settler Mode of Production," 112.

146. Ibid.

EPILOGUE

1. Royal British Columbia Museum exhibition placard.
2. Meggs, *Salmon*, 73.
3. Although the line between them is blurry, interest — associated with the credit system — and usury are distinct practices. Marx discusses credit as a *reaction* and corrective to usury, which is perceived as negative because it operates outside a capitalist mode of production. *Capital*, 3: 735. See also Harris Irfan's history and growth of modern Islamic finance that creatively circumvents prohibitions on interest in *Heaven's Bankers*.
4. Harvey, *A Companion to Marx's "Capital,"* 96.
5. Harvey, *Paris*, 119.
6. Lenzer, "'The Wolf of Wall Street' Proves Hollywood Sees Finance as Drugs, Sex and Rock and Roll," *Forbes*, December 19, 2013, http://www.forbes.com /sites/robertlenzner/2013/12/19/the-wolf-of-wall-street-proves-hollywood-sees -finance-as-drugs-sex-and-rock-and-roll/.
7. Some well-known examples are *American Psycho*, *Bonfire of the Vanities*, and *Wall Street*.
8. Marx identifies the "moral depreciation" of machinery as an inevitable consequence of technological innovation. See, in particular, *Capital*, 2:250–264.
9. Marx, *Capital*, 1:164–165.
10. Ibid., 1:165.
11. Ibid.
12. Ibid., 1:168–169.
13. Godden, "Labor, Language, and Finance Capital," 418.
14. Ibid.
15. LiPuma and Lee, *Financial Derivatives*, 206, quoted in Godden, "Labor, Language, and Finance Capital," 420.
16. Godden, "Labor, Language, and Finance Capital," 421.
17. Marx, *Capital*, 1:493, footnote 4.
18. Marx, "Speech at the Anniversary of the *People's Paper*," 578.
19. Postone, *Time, Labor, and Social Domination*, 258–259.
20. Elizabeth Young, *Black Frankenstein*, 11.
21. Marx, *Capital*, 1:173.

BIBLIOGRAPHY

Adachi, Ken. *The Enemy That Never Was*. Toronto: McClelland and Stewart, 1976.

Agamben, Giorgio. *Homo Sacer: Sovereign Power and Bare Life*. Translated by Daniel Heller-Roazen. Stanford, CA: Stanford University Press, 1996.

Alfred, Taiaiake. *Wasáse: Indigenous Pathways of Action and Freedom*. Toronto: University of Toronto Press, 2009.

Asian American Pacific Islander Policy and Research Consortium. "Statement by the Asian American Pacific Islander Policy and Research Consortium (AAPIPRC) on the Pew Report." June 22, 2012, UCLA Asian American Studies Center, www.aasc .ucla.edu/archives/pewreport2012.asp.

Augaitis, Diane, and Sylvie Gilbert, eds. *Between Views*. Banff, AB: Walter Phillips Gallery, 1991.

Barker, Adam J. "The Contemporary Reality of Canadian Imperialism: Settler Colonialism and the Hybrid Colonial State." *American Indian Quarterly* 33.3 (2009): 325–351.

Barthes, Roland. *Camera Lucida: Reflections on Photography*. Translated by Richard Howard. New York: Hill and Wang, 1981.

Becker, Gary S. *Human Capital: A Theoretical and Empirical Analysis with Special Reference to Education*. Chicago: University of Chicago Press, 1964.

Bascara, Victor. "Cultural Politics of Redress: Reassessing the Meaning of the Civil Liberties Act of 1988 after 9/11." *Asian American Law Journal* 10.2 (2003): 185–214.

Benzan, Carla. "Going Nowhere Fast: Ken Lum, *Four Boats Stranded*, and the Aporia of 'Public Art.'" WRECK: *Graduate Journal of Art History, Visual Art, and Theory* 2.2 (2008): 53–64.

Berger, Martin A. *Sight Unseen: Whiteness and American Visual Culture*. Berkeley: University of California Press, 2005.

Berland, Jodi. "Fire and Flame, Lightning and Landscape: Tourism and Nature in Banff, Alberta." In Augaitis and Gilbert, *Between Views*, 12–17.

Berton, Pierre. *The Last Spike*. Toronto: Anchor Canada, 1971.

Biermann, Werner, and Reinhart Kössler, "The Settler Mode of Production: The Rhodesian Case." *Review of African Political Economy* 18 (1980): 106–116.

Boime, Albert. *The Magisterial Gaze: Manifest Destiny and American Landscape Painting, c. 1830–1865*. Washington, DC: Smithsonian Institution Press, 1991.

———. "Patriarchy Fixed in Stone: Gutzon Borglum's 'Mount Rushmore.'" *American Art* 5.1–2 (1991): 142–167.

Bow, Leslie. *Partly Colored: Asian Americans and Racial Anomaly in the Segregated South*. New York: New York University Press, 2010.

Bright, Deborah. "The Machine in the Garden Revisited." *Art Journal* 51.2 (1992): 60–71.

Butler, Judith. *Bodies That Matter: On the Discursive Limits of "Sex."* New York: Routledge, 1993.

Byrd, Jodi A. *The Transit of Empire: Indigenous Critiques of Colonialism*. Minneapolis: University of Minnesota Press, 2011.

Chakrabarty, Dipesh. "Universalism and Belonging in the Logic of Capital." *Public Culture* 12.3 (2000): 653–678.

Cheung, King-Kok. *Articulate Silences: Hisaye Yamamoto, Maxine Hong Kingston, Joy Kogawa*. Ithaca, NY: Cornell University Press, 1993.

Chiang, Mark. "Capitalizing Form: The Globalization of the Literary Field: A Response to David Palumbo-Liu." *American Literary History* 20.4 (2008): 836–844.

Chin, Frank, Jeffery Paul Chan, Lawson Fusao Inada, and Shawn Hsu Wong, eds. *The Big Aiiieeeee! An Anthology of Chinese American and Japanese American Literature*. New York: Meridian, 1990.

Cho, Grace. *Haunting in the Korean Diaspora: Shame, Secrecy, and the Forgotten War*. Minneapolis: University of Minnesota Press, 2008.

Clarke, George Elliot. "Must All Blackness Be American? Locating Canada in Borden's 'Tightrope Time,' or Nationalizing Gilroy's *The Black Atlantic*." *Canadian Ethnic Studies* 28.3 (1996): 56–71.

Cook, Curtis, and Juan D. Lindau, eds. *Aboriginal Rights and Self-Government: The Canadian and Mexican Experience in North American Perspective*. Montreal: McGill-Queens University Press, 2000.

Cornell, Daniell, ed. *The Sculpture of Ruth Asawa: Contours in the Air*. Berkeley: University of California Press, 2007. Exhibition catalog.

Coulthard, Glen Sean. *Red Skin, White Masks: Rejecting the Colonial Politics of Recognition*. Minneapolis: University of Minnesota Press, 2014.

Coutts, Mary Carrington, and Pat Milmoe McCarrick. "Eugenics." *Kennedy Institute of Ethics Journal* 5.2 (1995): 163–178.

Davis, Mike. *Ecology of Fear: Los Angeles and the Imagination of Disaster*. New York: Metropolitan Books, 1998.

Derksen, Jeff. "Fixed City and Mobile Globe: Urban Facts & Global Forces in Ken Lum's Art." In Scott and Hanna, *Ken Lum: Works with Photography*, 31–41.

Derrida, Jacques. *Of Grammatology.* Baltimore: Johns Hopkins University Press, 1974.

———. *Of Hospitality: Anne Dufourmantelle Invites Jacques Derrida to Respond.* Stanford, CA: Stanford University Press, 2000.

Ellinghaus, Katherine. "Biological Absorption and Genocide: A Comparison of Indigenous Assimilation in the United States and Australia." *Genocide Studies and Prevention* 4.1 (2009): 59–79.

Eng, David. *The Feeling of Kinship: Queer Liberalism and the Racialization of Intimacy.* Durham, NC: Duke University Press, 2010.

———. *Racial Castration: Managing Masculinity in Asian America.* Durham, NC: Duke University Press, 2002.

Enwezor, Okwui. "Social Mirrors: On the Dialectic of the Abstract and Figural in Ken Lum's Work." In *Ken Lum* (exhibition catalog), edited by Grant Arnold, 61–92. Vancouver: Douglas & McIntyre, 2011.

Farred, Grant. "The Unsettler." *South Atlantic Quarterly* 107.4 (2008): 791–808.

Ferguson, Roderick A. *Aberrations in Black: Toward a Queer of Color Critique.* Minneapolis: University of Minnesota Press, 2003.

Foucault, Michel. *The History of Sexuality.* Vol. 1, *An Introduction.* New York: Random House, 1978.

———. "Nietzsche, Genealogy, History." In *The Essential Foucault*, edited by Paul Rabinow and Nikolas Rose, 451–476. New York: New Press, 1994.

Francis, Margot. *Creative Subversions: Whiteness, Indigeneity, and the National Imaginary.* Vancouver: University of British Columbia Press, 2011.

Franks, C. E. S. "Indian Policy: Canada and the United States Compared." In Cook and Lindau, *Aboriginal Rights and Self-Government*, 221–263.

Freedman, Jonathan. *Klezmer America: Jewishness, Ethnicity, Modernity.* New York: Columbia University Press, 2009.

Freeman, Elizabeth. "Introduction, Special Issue on Queer Temporality." GLQ 13.2–3 (2007): 159–176.

Friedman, Thomas. *The World Is Flat: A Brief History of the Twenty-First Century.* New York: Farrar, Straus & Giroux, 2007.

Fujikane, Candace. "Introduction: Asian Settler Colonialism in the US Colony of Hawai'i." In *Asian Settler Colonialism: From Local Governance to the Habits of Everyday Life in Hawai'i*, edited by Candace Fujikane and Jonathan Y. Okamura, 1–42. Honolulu: University of Hawai'i Press, 2008.

Fukawa Masako with Stanley Fukawa. *Spirit of the Nikkei Fleet: BC's Japanese Canadian Fishermen.* Madeira Park, BC: Harbour, 2009.

"The Future of Chinese People." *Atlantic Monthly* 85 (January 1900): 80.

Geller, Jay. *The Other Jewish Question: Identifying the Jew and Making Sense of Modernity.* New York: Fordham University Press, 2011.

Gier, Jean Vengua, and Carla Alicia Tejeda. "An Interview with Karen Tei Yamashita." *Jouvert* 2.2 (1998), http://english.chass.ncsu.edu/jouvert/v2i2/yamashi.htm (accessed October 14, 2014).

Gilmore, Ruth Wilson. *Golden Gulag: Prisons, Surplus, Crisis, and Opposition in Globalizing California.* Berkeley: University of California Press, 2007.

Glenn, Evelyn Nakano. "Racial Ethnic Women's Labor: The Intersection of Race, Gender, and Class Oppression." *Review of Radical Political Economics* 17.3 (1983): 86–108.

Godden, Richard. "Labor, Language, and Finance Capital." PMLA 126.2 (2011): 412–421.

Goellnicht, Donald. "Minority History as Metafiction: Joy Kogawa's *Obasan*." *Tulsa Studies in Women's Literature* 8 (1989): 287–306.

———. "Tang Ao in America: Male Subject Positions in *China Men*." In *Reading the Literatures of Asian America*, edited by Shirley Goek-Lin Lim and Amy Ling, 191–212. Philadelphia: Temple University Press, 1992.

Goldstein, Alyosha. "Where the Nation Takes Place: Proprietary Regimes, Antistatism, and U.S. Settler Colonialism." *South Atlantic Quarterly* 107.4 (2008): 833–861.

Gonzales-Day, Ken. *Lynching in the West, 1850–1935*. Durham, NC: Duke University Press, 2006.

Gottlieb, Erika. "The Riddle of Concentric Worlds in *Obasan*." *Canadian Literature* 109 (1986): 34–53.

Grace, Sherrill E. *Canada and the Idea of the North*. Montreal: McGill-Queen's University Press, 2001.

Grant, Shelagh. "Myths of the North in the Canadian Ethos." *Northern Review* 3–4 (1989): 37.

Habib, John Philip. "A Life in 'Chinese Drag.'" *Advocate: The National Gay and Lesbian Newsmagazine*, April 2, 1984, 72.

Harris, Cheryl. "Whiteness as Property." *Harvard Law Review* 106.8 (1993): 1707–1791.

Harris, Lawren. "Revelation of Art in Canada." *Canadian Theosophist* 7 (1926): 85–88.

———. "The Story of the Group of Seven." In *The Best of the Group of Seven*, edited by Joan Murray, 26–31. Edmonton: Hurtig, 1984.

Harris, Mary Emma. "Black Mountain College." In Cornell, *The Sculpture of Ruth Asawa*, 42–66.

Hartman, Saidiya, and Frank B. Wilderson, III. "The Position of the Unthought." *Qui Parle* 13.2 (2003): 183–201.

Harvey, David. *A Companion to Marx's "Capital."* London: Verso, 2010.

———. *Paris: Capital of Modernity*. New York: Routledge, 2003.

Hattori, Tomo. "China Man Autoeroticism and the Remains of Asian America." *Novel* 31.2 (1998): 215–236.

———. "Psycholinguistic Orientalism in Criticism of *The Woman Warrior* and *Obasan*." In *Other Sisterhoods: Literary Theory and U.S. Women of Color*, edited by Sandra Kumamoto Stanley, 119–138. Urbana: University of Illinois Press, 1998.

Hearn, Maxwell K. *Cultivated Landscapes: Chinese Painting from the Collection of Marie-Helene and Guy Weill*. New York: Metropolitan Museum of Art, 2002.

Heer, Jeet. "Maclean's Article on Asians Familiar to Anti-Semites of Old." *National Post*, November 15, 2010, http://fullcomment.nationalpost.com/2010/11/15/jeet-heer--macleans-article-on-asians-familiar-to-anti-semites-of-old/ (accessed October 15, 2012).

Hernández, David. *Undue Process: Immigrant Detention and Lesser Citizenship*. Unpublished manuscript.

Higa, Karen. "Inside and Outside at the Same Time." In Cornell, *The Sculpture of Ruth Asawa*, 30–41.

Hirsch, Marianne. *Family Frames: Photography, Narrative, and Postmemory*. Cambridge, MA: Harvard University Press, 1997.

Huhndorf, Shari. *Going Native: Indians in the American Cultural Imagination*. Ithaca, NY: Cornell University Press, 2001.

Hutcheon, Linda. *A Theory of Parody*. Urbana: University of Illinois Press, 2000.

Irfan, Harris. *Heaven's Bankers: Inside the Hidden World of Islamic Finance*. New York: Overlook Press, 2015.

Ishizuka, Karen L. *Lost and Found: Reclaiming the Japanese American Incarceration*. Urbana: University of Illinois Press, 2006.

Jacobson, Matthew Frye. *Whiteness of a Different Color: European Immigrants and the Alchemy of Race*. Cambridge, MA: Harvard University Press, 1998.

Jaimes, Annette. "Federal Indian Identification Policy: A Usurpation of Indigenous Sovereignty in North America." In *The State of Native America: Genocide, Colonization, and Resistance*, edited by Annette Jaimes, 123–138. Boston: South End Press, 1992.

Jameson, Fredric. *The Political Unconscious: Narrative as a Socially Symbolic Act*. Ithaca, NY: Cornell University Press, 1981.

Jessup, Lynda. "Landscapes of Sport, Landscapes of Exclusion: The 'Sportsman's Paradise' in Late-Nineteenth-Century Canadian Painting." *Journal of Canadian Studies* 40.1 (2006): 94.

Jun, Helen. *Race for Citizenship: Black Orientalism and Asian Uplift from Pre-Emancipation to Neoliberal America*. New York: New York University Press, 2011.

Jung, Moon-Ho. *Coolies and Cane: Race, Labor, and Sugar in the Age of Emancipation*. Baltimore: Johns Hopkins University Press, 2006.

Kadohata, Cynthia. *The Floating World*. New York: Ballantine Books, 1993.

Kamboureli, Smaro. *Scandalous Bodies: Diasporic Literature in English Canada*. Oxford: Oxford University Press, 2000.

Kanefsky, Rachel. "Debunking a Postmodern Conception of History: A Defense of Humanist Values in the Novels of Joy Kogawa." *Canadian Literature* 148 (1996): 11–36.

Kelley, Ninette, and Michael Trebilock. *The Making of the Mosaic: A History of Canadian Immigration Policy*. 2nd ed. Toronto: University of Toronto Press, 2010.

Kevles, Daniel J. "Eugenics and Human Rights." *British Medical Journal* 319 (1999): 435–438.

Kim, Jodi. *Ends of Empire: Asian American Critique and the Cold War*. Minneapolis: University of Minnesota Press, 2010.

Kingston, Maxine. *China Men*. New York: Vintage Books, 1977.

Kirby, Lynne. *Parallel Tracks: The Railroad and Silent Cinema*. Durham, NC: Duke University Press, 1997.

———. "Steamy Scenes and Dream Machines." In *Track Records: Trains and Contem-*

porary Photography, edited by Marnie Fleming, 25–27. Oakville: Oakville Galleries and Canadian Museum of Contemporary Photography, 1997.

Kogawa, Joy. *Obasan*. 1981. Reprint, New York: Anchor Books, 1994.

Koshy, Susan. "Morphing Race into Ethnicity: Asian Americans and Critical Transformations of Whiteness." *boundary 2* 28 (2001): 153–194.

Krakauer, Jon. *Into the Wild*. New York: Anchor Books, 1997.

Kwong, Roger. *Forbidden Workers*. New York: New Press, 1997.

Lake, Marilyn, and Henry Reynolds. *Drawing the Global Colour Line: White Men's Countries and the International Challenge of Racial Equality*. Cambridge: Cambridge University Press, 2008.

Laliberté, R., and V. Satezwich. "Native Migrant Labour in the Southern Alberta Sugar Beet Industry: Coercion and Paternalism in the Recruitment of Labor." *Canadian Review of Sociology and Anthropology* 36.1 (1999): 65–85.

Lange, Matthew, James Mahoney, and Matthias vom Hau. "Colonialism and Development: A Comparative Analysis of Spanish and British Colonies." *AJS* 111.5 (2006): 1412–1462.

Larner, Jesse. *Mount Rushmore: An Icon Reconsidered*. New York: Nation Books, 2002.

Lawrence, Bonita. "Gender, Race, and the Regulation of Native Identity in Canada and the US: An Overview." *Hypatia* 18.2 (2003): 3–31.

Lawrence, Bonita, and Enakshi Dua. "Decolonizing Antiracism." *Social Justice* 32.4 (2005): 120–143.

Lee, Erica. "Hemispheric Orientalism and the 1907 Pacific Coast Race Riots." *Amerasia Journal* 33.2 (2007): 19–47.

Lee, Sue-Im. "'We Are Not the World': Global Village, Universalism, and Karen Tei Yamashita's *Tropic of Orange*." *MFS: Modern Fiction Studies* 52.3 (2007): 501–527.

Lenzer, Robert. "'The Wolf of Wall Street' Proves Hollywood Sees Finance as Drugs, Sex and Rock and Roll." *Forbes*, December 19, 2013, http://www.forbes.com/sites /robertlenzner/2013/12/19/the-wolf-of-wall-street-proves-hollywood-sees-finance -as-drugs-sex-and-rock-and-roll/.

Levi, Neil. "'See That Straw? That's a Straw': Anti-Semitism and Narrative Form in *Ulysses*." *Modernism/Modernity* 9.3 (2002): 375–388.

Limerick, Patricia Nelson. "Disorientation and Reorientation: The American Landscape Discovered from the West." *Journal of American History* 79.3 (1992): 1021–1049.

———. *The Legacy of Conquest: The Unbroken Past of the American West*. New York: W. W. Norton, 1987.

Ling, Jinqi. *Across Meridians: History and Figuration in Karen Tei Yamashita's Transnational Novels*. Stanford, CA: Stanford University Press, 2012.

Linsley, Robert. "Landscapes in Motion: Lawren Harris, Emily Carr, and the Heterogeneous Modern Nation." *Oxford Art Journal* 19.1 (1996): 80–95.

LiPuma, Edward, and Benjamin Lee. *Financial Derivatives and the Globalization of Risk*. Durham, NC: Duke University Press, 2004.

Liu, Eric. *The Accidental Asian: Notes of a Native Speaker*. New York: Random House, 1998.

Liu, Petrus. "Queer Marxism in Taiwan." *Inter-Asia Cultural Studies* 8.4 (2007): 517–539.

Lo, Marie. "Passing Recognition: *Obasan* and the Borders of Asian American and Canadian Literary Criticism." *Comparative American Studies* 5.3 (2007): 307–332.

Lowe, Lisa. "Break the Frame." In *Like Mangoes in July: The Work of Richard Fung*, edited by Helen Lee and Kerri Sakamoto, 78–79. Toronto: Insomniac Press, 2002.

———. *Immigrant Acts: On Asian American Cultural Politics*. Durham, NC: Duke University Press, 1996.

Luibhéid, Eithne. *Entry Denied: Controlling Sexuality at the Border*. Minneapolis: University of Minnesota Press, 2002.

Lye, Colleen. "The Afro-Asian Analogy." PMLA 123.5 (2008): 1732–1736.

———. *America's Asia: Racial Form and American Literature, 1893–1945*. Princeton, NJ: Princeton University Press, 2005.

Machida, Margo. "Out of Asia: Negotiating Asian Identities in America." In *Asia/America: Identities in Contemporary Asian American Art*, edited by Margo Machida, 65–110. New York: New Press, 1994.

Manning, Erin. *Ephemeral Territories: Representing Nation, Home, and Identity*. Minneapolis: University of Minnesota Press, 2003.

Marx, Karl. *Capital*. Vol. 1. London: Penguin Books, 1992.

———. *Capital*. Vol. 2. London: Penguin Books, 1993.

———. *Capital*. Vol. 3. London: Penguin Books, 1993.

McAtee, Cammie. "Taking Comfort in the Age of Anxiety: Eero Saarinen's Womb Chair." In *Atomic Dwelling: Anxiety, Domesticity, and Postwar Architecture*, edited by Robin Schuldenfrei, 3–25. New York: Routledge, 2012.

McClintock, Anne. "The Angel of Progress: Pitfalls of the Term 'Post-Colonialism.'" *Social Text* 31–32 (1992): 84–98.

McCool, Daniel, Susan Olson, and Jennifer Robinson. *Native Vote: American Indians, the Voting Rights Act and the Right to Vote*. New York: Cambridge University Press, 2007.

McFarlane, Scott. "Covering *Obasan* and the Narrative of Internment." In *Privileging Positions: The Sites of Asian American Studies*, edited by Gary Y. Okihiro, 401–411. Seattle: Washington State University Press, 1995.

McIntyre, Michael. "Race, Surplus Population and the Marxist Theory of Imperialism." *Antipode* 43.5 (2011): 1489–1515.

McKeown, Adam M. *Melancholy Order: Asian Migration and the Globalization of Borders*. New York: Columbia University Press, 2008.

Meggs, Geoff. *Salmon: The Decline of the B.C. Fishery*. Vancouver: Douglas and McIntyre, 1991.

Melamed, Jodi. "The Spirit of Neoliberalism: From Racial Liberalism to Neoliberal Multiculturalism." *Social Text* 89 24.4 (2006): 1–24.

Michaels, Walter Benn. "The Politics of a Good Picture: Race, Class and Form in Jeff Wall's *Mimic*." PMLA 125.1 (2010): 177–184.

Miki, Roy. *Broken Entries: Race, Subjectivity, Writing*. Toronto: Mercury Press, 1998.

Miller, Angela. *Empire of the Eye*. Ithaca, NY: Cornell University Press, 1993.

Mitchell, David T., and Sharon L. Snyder. "Disability as Multitude: Re-working Non-Productive Labor Power." *Journal of Literary and Cultural Disability Studies* 4.2 (2010): 179–193.

Mitchell, Katharyne. *Crossing the Neoliberal Line: Pacific Rim Migration and the Metropolis*. Philadelphia: Temple University Press, 2004.

———. "In Whose Interest?: Transnational Capital and the Production of Multiculturalism in Canada." In *Global/Local: Cultural Production and the Transnational Imaginary*, edited by Rob Wilson and Wimal Dissanayake, 219–251. Durham, NC: Duke University Press, 1996.

Mitchell, W. J. T. "Imperial Landscape." In *Landscape and Power*, 2nd ed., edited by W. J. T. Mitchell, 1–34. Chicago: University of Chicago Press, 2002.

Morgensen, Scott Lauria. "Settler Homonationalism: Theorizing Settler Colonialism within Queer Modernities." *GLQ* 16:1–2 (2010): 105–131.

Mosse, George. "Nationalism and Respectability: Normal and Abnormal Sexuality in the Nineteenth Century." *Journal of Contemporary History* 17.2 (1982): 221–246.

"Mount Rushmore National Memorial: History and Culture." *National Park Service*, n.d., www.nps.gov/moru/historyculture/index.htm (accessed November 13, 2014).

Muñoz, José Esteban. *Disidentifications: Queers of Color and the Performance of Politics*. Minneapolis: University of Minnesota Press, 1999.

Murray, Joan. *The Best of the Group of Seven*. Edmonton: Hurtig, 1994.

Nealon, Chris. *The Matter of Capital: Poetry and Crisis in the American Century*. Cambridge, MA: Harvard University Press, 2011.

Nguyen, Mimi. *The Gift of Freedom: War, Debt, and Other Refugee Passages*. Durham, NC: Duke University Press, 2012.

Nichols, Roger. *Indians in the United States and Canada: A Comparative History*. Lincoln: University of Nebraska Press, 1998.

Obenzinger, Hilton. "Naturalizing Cultural Pluralism, Americanizing Zionism: The Settler Colonial Basis to Early-Twentieth-Century Progressive Thought." *South Atlantic Quarterly* 107.4 (2008): 651–669.

Oikawa, Mona. *Cartographies of Violence: Japanese Canadian Women, Memory, and the Subjects of the Internment*. Toronto: University of Toronto Press, 2012.

———. "Connecting the Internment of Japanese Canadians to the Colonization of Aboriginal Peoples in Canada." In *Aboriginal Connections to Race, Environment and Traditions*, edited by Rick Riewe and Jill Oakes, 17–26. Winnipeg: University of Manitoba Press, 2006.

Okihiro, Gary, and David Drummond. "The Concentration Camps and Japanese Economic Losses in California Agriculture, 1900–1942." In *Japanese Americans: From Relocation to Redress*, edited by Roger Daniels, Sandra Taylor, and Harry Kitano, 168–175. Salt Lake City: University of Utah Press, 1986.

Okimoto, Ruth. *Sharing a Desert Home: Life on the Colorado River Indian Reservation, Poston, Arizona, 1942–1945, a Special Report of News from Native California*. Berkeley: Heyday Books, 2001.

O'Malley, Michael. *Keeping Watch: A History of American Time.* Washington, DC: Smithsonian, 1996.

Omori, Emiko, dir. and writer. *Rabbit in the Moon: A Documentary/Memoir about the World War II Japanese Internment Camps.* New Day Films, 1999.

Otsuka, Julie. *When the Emperor Was Divine.* New York: Anchor Books, 2002.

Palumbo-Liu, David. *Asian/American: Historical Crossings of a Racial Frontier.* Palo Alto, CA: Stanford University Press, 1999.

———. "Introduction: Unhabituated Habituses." In *Streams of Cultural Capital: Transnational Cultural Studies,* edited by David Palumbo-Liu and Hans Ulrich Gumbrecht, 1–21. Stanford, CA: Stanford University Press, 1997.

Park, John. "Emergent Divides: Class and Position among Asian Americans." CR: *The New Centennial Review* 6.2 (2006): 57–72.

Pew Research Center. "The Rise of Asian Americans." June 19, 2012, http://www.pewsocialtrends.org/2012/06/19/the-rise-of-asian-americans/.

Postone, Moishe. "Anti-Semitism and National Socialism: Notes on the German Reaction to 'Holocaust.'" *New German Critique* 19.1 (1980): 97–115.

———. *Time, Labor, and Social Domination: A Reinterpretation of Marx's Critical Theory.* Cambridge: Cambridge University Press, 1993.

Pratt, Anna. *Securing Borders: Detention and Deportation in Canada.* Vancouver: University of British Columbia Press, 2005.

Pulido, Laura, and David Lloyd. "In the Long Shadow of the Settler: On Israeli and US Colonialisms." *American Quarterly* 62.4 (2010): 795–809.

Reddy, Chandan C. "Asian Diasporas, Neoliberalism, and Family." *Social Text* 84.5 (2005): 101–119.

———. "Home, Houses, Nonidentity." In *Burning Down the House: Recycling Domesticity,* edited by Rosemary Marangoly George, 355–379. Boulder, CO: Westview, 1998.

Reid, Dannis. *A Concise History of Canadian Painting.* Toronto: Oxford University Press, 1988.

Rieff, David. "Multiculturalism's Silent Partner: It's the Newly Globalized Consumer Economy, Stupid." *Harper's* 287.1719 (1993): 62–72.

Robinson, Cedric. *Black Marxism: The Making of the Black Radical Tradition.* 1983. Reprint, Chapel Hill: University of North Carolina Press, 2000.

Robinson, Gregory. *A Tragedy of Democracy: Japanese Confinement in North America.* New York: Columbia University Press, 2009.

Roediger, David R. *How Race Survived U.S. History: From Settlement and Slavery to the Obama Phenomenon.* London: Verso, 2008.

Ross, Luana. *Inventing the Savage: The Social Construction of Native American Criminality.* Austin: University of Texas Press, 1998.

Roy, Patricia. *The Oriental Question: Consolidating a White Man's Province, 1914–41.* Vancouver: University of British Columbia Press, 2003.

Sato, Gayle K. "Manzanar Murakami and Phantom Memory." *Concentric* 39.2 (2013): 119–135.

Schlund-Vials, Cathy. *Modeling Citizenship: Jewish and Asian American Writing*. Philadelphia: Temple University Press, 2011.

Schueller, Malini Johar. "Claiming Postcolonial America: The Hybrid Asian-American Performances of Tseng Kwong Chi." In *Asian North American Identities: Beyond the Hyphen*, edited by Eleanor Ty and Donald Goellnicht, 170–185. Bloomington: Indiana University Press, 2004.

Scott, Kitty. "Ken Lum Works with Photography." In Scott and Hanna, *Ken Lum: Works with Photography*, 11–30.

Scott, Kitty, and Martha Hanna. *Ken Lum: Works with Photography*. Ottawa: Canadian Museum of Contemporary Photography, 2002. Exhibition catalog.

Sexton, Jared. "People-of-Color-Blindness: Notes on the Afterlife of Slavery." *Social Text* 28.2 (2010): 31–56.

———. "The Social Life of Social Death: On Afro-Pessimism and Black Optimism." *InTensions Journal* 5 (2011): 1–47.

Shadbolt, Doris. *Emily Carr*. Seattle: University of Washington Press, 1990.

Shanken, Andrew. "Better Living: Toward a Cultural History of a Business Slogan." *Enterprise and Society* 7.3 (2006): 485–519.

Shields, Rob. "Imaginary Sites." In Augaitis and Gilbert, *Between Views*, 22–26.

Smith, Andrea. "Indigeneity, Settler Colonialism, White Supremacy." *Global Dialogue* 12.2 (2010), http://www.worlddialogue.org/content.php?id=488.

Somerville, Siobhan. *Queering the Color Line: Race and the Invention of Homosexuality in American Culture*. Durham, NC: Duke University Press, 2000.

Stern, Alexandra Minna. *Eugenic Nation: Faults and Frontiers of Better Breeding in Modern America*. Berkeley: University of California Press, 2005.

Stewart, Janice. "Cultural Appropriations and Identificatory Practices in Emily Carr's 'Indian Stories.'" *Frontiers* 26.2 (2005): 59–72.

Stoddard, Lothrop. *The Rising Tide of Color: Against White World Supremacy*. New York: Charles Scribner's Sons, 1923.

Stryker, Susan. "(De)Subjugated Knowledges." In *The Transgender Studies Reader*, edited by Susan Stryker and Stephen White, 1–17. New York: Routledge, 2006.

Sze, Julie. "'Not by Politics Alone': Gender and Environmental Justice in Karen Tei Yamashita's *Tropic of Orange*." *Bucknell Review* 44.1 (2000): 29–42.

Tajiri, Rei, dir. *History and Memory: For Akiko and Takashige*. Women Make Movies, 1991.

Taliaferro, John. *Great White Fathers: The Story of the Obsessive Quest to Create Mount Rushmore*. New York: Public Affairs, 2002.

Thoreau, Henry David. *Walden*. In *The Norton Anthology of American Literature*, vol. B: *1820–1865*, 8th ed., edited by Nina Baym and Robert S. Levine, 981–1155. New York: W. W. Norton, 2012.

Tseng, Muna. "Tseng Kwong Chi: The Pearl in the Oyster." In *Tseng Kwong Chi* (exhibition catalog), 12–13. New York: Paul Kasmin Gallery, 2008.

Tseng, Muna, and Ping Chong. "SlutForArt." *PAJ: A Journal of Performance and Art* 22.1 (2000): 111–128.

Tucker, Robert. *The Marx-Engels Reader*. 2nd ed. New York: W. W. Norton, 1978.

Tulley, James. "A Just Relationship between Aboriginal and Non-Aboriginal Peoples of Canada." In Cook and Lindau, *Aboriginal Rights and Self-Government*, 39–71.

Turner, Grady T. "The Accidental Ambassador." *Art in America*, March 1997, 82.

Tyrell, Ian. "Beyond the View from Euro-America: Environment, Settler Societies, and the Internationalization of American History." In *Rethinking American History in a Global Age*, edited by Thomas Bender, 168–192. Berkeley: University of California Press, 2002.

Veracini, Lorenzo. *Settler Colonialism: A Theoretical Overview*. London: Palgrave Macmillan, 2010.

Wallace, Molly. "Tropics of Globalization: Reading the New North America." *symploke* 9.1–21 (2001): 145–160.

Wang, Ling-chi L. "Model Minority, High-Tech Coolies, and Foreign Spies: Asian Americans in Science and Technology, with Special Reference to the Case of Dr. Wen Ho Lee." *Amerasia Journal* 33.1 (2007): 51–61.

Watson, Scott. "The Discomfort Zone." *Canadian Art* 9.4 (1992): 30–37.

White, Richard. *Railroaded: The Transcontinentals and the Making of Modern America*. New York: W. W. Norton, 2011.

Wilderson, Frank B., III. "Gramsci's Black Marx: Whither the Slave in Civil Society." *Social Identities* 9.2 (2003): 225–240.

Williams, Raymond. *The Country and the City*. New York: Oxford University Press, 1973.

Winks, Robin. *The Blacks in Canada: A History*. Montreal: McGill-Queen's University Press, 2000.

Wolfe, Patrick. "Land, Labor, and Difference: Elementary Structures of Race." *American Historical Review* 106.3 (2001): 866–905.

———. "Recuperating Binarism: A Heretical Introduction." *Settler Colonial Studies* 3.3–4 (2013): 257–279.

Yamashita, Karen Tei. *Tropic of Orange*. Minneapolis: Coffee House Press, 1997.

Yau, John. "Ruth Asawa: Shifting the Terms of Sculpture." In *Ruth Asawa: Objects and Apparitions* (exhibition catalog), edited by Jonathan Laib, Charlotte Perrottey, and Charlie Adamski, 5–21. New York: Christie's, 2013.

Young, Elizabeth. *Black Frankenstein: The Making of an American Metaphor*. New York: New York University Press, 2008.

Young, Robert J. C. *Postcolonialism: An Historical Introduction*. Oxford: Blackwell, 2001.

Yu, Henry. "Toward a Pacific History of the Americas." *Amerasia* 33.2 (2007): xi–xix.

Zhu, Liping. "Ethnic Oasis: Chinese Immigrants in the Frontier Black Hills." In *Ethnic Oasis: The Chinese in the Black Hills*, edited by Liping Zhu and Rose Estep Fosha, 3–43. Pierre: South Dakota State Historical Society Press, 2004.

Žižek, Slavoj. *First as Tragedy, Then as Farce*. New York: Verso, 2009.

———. "Multiculturalism, or the Cultural Logic of Multinational Capitalism." *New Left Review* 225 (1997): 28–51.

———. *The Plague of Fantasies*. New York: Verso, 1997.

INDEX

Numbers in italics refer to illustrations.

Asian North Americans (*continued*)
stereotype, 101; exclusion of, 32, 33,
42–43, 88, 95, 120–22, 141, 148; immigration policies, 32–33; Jews, comparison to, 3–7; model minority stereotype, 5–6, 7, 23, 123, 135, 148, 155,
212n40; racialization of, 3, 5–8, 19, 22,
23, 32; settler colonialism and, 19–23;
whiteness and, 23; yellow peril stereotype, 23, 92, 107, 149, 212n40. *See also*
Chinese North Americans; Japanese
North Americans
Asian Settler Colonialism (Fujikane, ed.), 21
Atlantic Monthly (magazine), 1

bachelor societies, 64, 95
Banff National Park, Alberta, 87–88, 104
Bank of Canada banknote, 1–4, 2, 6, 7, 93,
95, 164, 191–92
Barthes, Roland, 163
Becker, Gary, 5
Benzan, Carla, 187
Berger, Martin, 86, 93
Berland, Jody, 93
BIA. *See* Bureau of Indian Affairs
Biermann, Werner, 18, 189
Black Hills, South Dakota, 84, 97, 101–2.
See also Mount Rushmore monument
blackness: exclusion and, 26, 27–28,
32, 148; one-drop rule, 30; racializa-
tion and, 23; settler colonialism and,
19, 29; slavery and, 20, 27–29, 32,
205n133. *See also* African Americans
Blade Runner (Scott), 182
Boime, Albert, 93, 97, 101–2, 103, 153
borders. *See* immigration policies
Borglum, Gutzon, 77, 79, 83, 84, 86,
96–97, 102–3, 112
Bright, Deborah, 86, 90–91
Buffalo Soldiers, 22
Bureau of Indian Affairs (BIA), 134, 149
Butler, Judith, 78, 82–83
Byrd, Jodi, 20

Canadian North conceptualizations,
88–89
Canadian Pacific Railway (CPR): Chinese

labor on, 41–44, 45, 56–58, 87–88,
160; completion of, 40, 41, 57, 58, 59;
film footage, 48
capitalism: abstract domination of, 10, 16;
biologization of, 170–71; homogeniza-
tion of, 33–34, 159; industrial, 30; late
late, 154, 156; logic and racism, 182;
racial, use of term, 8; racialization of,
3, 16–18, 32; slavery and expansion,
204n129; social degeneration of, 15;
violence of, 9
Carney, Mark, 1
Carr, Emily, 77, 79–80, 104, *108*, 108–11.
See also specific works
Chakrabarty, Dipesh, 8, 44, 46, 47, 53, 54,
57, 66
Chan, Jeffery Paul, 100
Chiang, Mark, 153, 174
Chin, Frank, 100
China Men (Kingston), 45, 50–58
China Red color, 196
Chinese Canadian National Council, 3
Chinese Exclusion Act (1882), 42–43, 85,
156, 160
Chinese Head Tax, 42, 59, 85, 106, 156
Chinese Immigration Act (1923), 85
Chinese North Americans: abstract labor
of, 16, 43, 46–48, 52, 56–62, 130; anti-
Chinese sentiment, 49, 71–72, 77, 170;
exclusion of, 42–43, 88, 95; immigra-
tion policies on, 32–33, 42–43, 59, 85,
88; indentured labor of, 24, 31–32; investors in Vancouver, 155, 170; mining
labor of, 102; postmodern coolie labor
of, 156, 174, 180, 182–83, 188; railroad
labor of, 41–44, 45, 56–58, 87–88;
resistance by, 56–57. *See also* Asian
North Americans
Cho, Grace, 124
citizenship: abstract, 9, 15–16; economic
aspects, 179–80; exclusions, 25–26,
33, 68, 120; multicultural, 156, 171;
whiteness and, 49–50, 60
Civil Liberties Act (1988), 174
Collier, John, 216n125
colonialism. *See* settler colonialism
commodity value: of abstract labor, 11–12,

CREDITS

FIGURE 2.6 *Mount Rushmore, South Dakota, 1986.* Tseng Kwong Chi, *East Meets West,* a.k.a. *The Expeditionary Self-Portrait Series 1979–1989.* © Muna Tseng Dance Projects, Inc., New York. www.tsengkwongchi.com.

FIGURE 2.7 Caspar David Friedrich, *The Wanderer above the Sea of Fog,* ca. 1817. Oil on canvas, 94.8 × 74.8 cm. Inv.: 5161. On permanent loan from the Foundation for the Promotion of the Hamburg Art Collections. Photo Credit: bpk, Berlin / Hamburger Kunsthalle Museum / Elke Walford / Art Resource, NY.

FIGURE 2.8 Jin-me Yoon, *Group of Sixty-Seven,* 1996, 134 chromogenic prints, dimensions variable. Collection of the Vancouver Art Gallery, Acquisition Fund. Photo: Trevor Mills, Vancouver Art Gallery.

FIGURE 2.9 Jin-me Yoon, *Group of Sixty-Seven* (detail), 1996, 134 chromogenic prints, dimensions variable. Collection of the Vancouver Art Gallery, Acquisition Fund. Photo: Trevor Mills, Vancouver Art Gallery.

FIGURE 2.10 Jin-me Yoon, *Group of Sixty-Seven* (detail), 1996, 134 chromogenic prints, dimensions variable. Collection of the Vancouver Art Gallery, Acquisition Fund. Photo: Trevor Mills, Vancouver Art Gallery.

FIGURE 2.11 Emily Carr, *Old Time, Coast Village,* 1929–1930. Oil on canvas, 91.3 × 128.7 cm. Collection of the Vancouver Art Gallery, Emily Carr Trust. Photo: Trevor Mills, Vancouver Art Gallery.

FIGURE 3.1 Ruth Asawa, *Untitled,* ca. 1960–1965. Fine Arts Museums of San Francisco. © Ruth Asawa.

FIGURE 4.1 Ken Lum, *Entertainment for Surrey,* 1978 (video still), single-channel video with sound. Collection of the Vancouver Art Gallery, Acquisition Fund.

FIGURE 4.2 Ken Lum, *Sculpture for Dream Home,* 1980.

FIGURE 4.3 Ken Lum, *Red Circle,* 1986. Fabric, wood, 300 cm diameter. Collection of the Vancouver Art Gallery, Acquisition Fund. Photo: Trevor Mills, Vancouver Art Gallery.

FIGURE 4.4 Ken Lum, *Corner Bed,* 1990. Two sofa beds, dimensions variable. Courtesy of the artist.

FIGURE 4.5 Ken Lum, *Melly Shum Hates Her Job,* 1989. Chromogenic print, lacquer, enamel on aluminum, Sintra, 182 × 243.8 cm. Courtesy of the artist.

FIGURE 4.6 Dorothea Lange, *Dust Bowl Texas, American Exodus, A.C. Woman,* 1938. A67.137.38258.1. © The Dorothea Lange Collection, the Oakland Museum of California, City of Oakland. Gift of Paul S. Taylor.

FIGURE 4.7 Ken Lum, *Phew, I'm Tired,* 1994. Chromogenic print, lacquer, enamel on aluminum, Sintra, 182 × 243.8 cm. Collection of the Vancouver Art Gallery, Acquisition Fund.

FIGURE 4.8 Roy Lichtenstein, *Drowning Girl*. © Estate of Roy Lichtenstein, 1963. Oil and synthetic polymer paint on canvas, 67⅝ × 66¾ feet. Philip Johnson Fund (by exchange) and gift of Mr. and Mrs. Bagley Wright. The Museum of Modern Art. Digital Image © The Museum of Modern Art / Licensed by Scala / Art Resource, NY.

FIGURE 4.9 Ken Lum, *Nancy Nishi and Joe Ping Chau, Real Estate*, 1990. Chromogenic print, lacquer, enamel on aluminum, Sintra, 182 × 243.8 cm. Courtesy of the artist.

FIGURE 4.10 Ken Lum, *Four Boats Stranded: Red and Yellow, Black and White*, 2000. Sculpture installation on the roof of the Vancouver Art Gallery, dimensions variable. Collection of the Vancouver Art Gallery, Vancouver Art Gallery Major Purchase Fund, The Canadian Millennium Partnership Program of the Millennium Bureau of Canada and the British Columbia 2000 Community Spirit Fund. Photo: Trevor Mills, Vancouver Art Gallery.

FIGURE E.1 Iron Chink salmon-gutting machine exhibit. Catalogue number 965.681.1. Image courtesy of the Royal BC Museum, BC Archives.

FIGURE E.2 Tommy Ting, *Machine (Iron Chink, invented in 1903, found at the Gulf of Georgia Cannery in Steveston, British Columbia, refabricated in Beijing, China)*, 2012. Courtesy of the artist.